# COMMUNITY
# PSYCHOLOGY

# COMMUNITY PSYCHOLOGY

## Linking Individuals and Communities

### FOURTH EDITION

BRET KLOOS • JEAN HILL • ELIZABETH THOMAS

ANDREW D. CASE • VICTORIA C. SCOTT • ABRAHAM WANDERSMAN

AMERICAN PSYCHOLOGICAL ASSOCIATION

Published by
American Psychological Association
750 First Street, NE
Washington, DC 20002
https://www.apa.org

Order Department
https://www.apa.org/pubs/books
order@apa.org

In the U.K., Europe, Africa, and the Middle East, copies may be ordered from Eurospan
https://www.eurospanbookstore.com/apa
info@eurospangroup.com

Typeset in Minion Pro and Gotham by TIPS Technical Publishing, Inc., Carrboro, NC

Printer: Sheridan Books, Chelsea, MI
Cover Designer: Anne C. Kerns, Anne Likes Red, Silver Spring, MD

**CIP data is available for this title from the Library of Congress**
Library of Congress Control Number: 202093787

https://doi.org/10.1037/0000207-000

*Printed in the United States of America*

10  9  8  7  6  5  4  3  2  1

# DEDICATIONS

*To Suzanne, Sarah, and Bonnie for their love and support. Your efforts to identify and address injustice are an inspiration to me. Your work to create better communities—one cake, work of art, or powerful argument at a time—gives me hope for the future.*

*—Bret Kloos*

*To Tom, who, although he still believes community psychology is just a form of sociology, has always been an amazing source of support in my work and my life; and to Mikaele, in the hope that her passion for social justice will continue to inform and inspire her life.*

*—Jean Hill*

*To Chris and Bo, whose love and support bring me courage and great joy; and to my parents and sister, with much love and gratitude as well. I am inspired by your wisdom and strength.*

*—Elizabeth Thomas*

*To my wife DeAundra, who without knowing it has taught me the value of community; and to my daughter Harlow, who makes the struggle to create a better world worth it.*

*—Andrew D. Case*

*To J. V., who placed the heartbeat of the community in a yellow thread and led me to the discovery of third-degree love; to my girls, Vienna and Sierra, who lead with joy; and to Max Ehrmann for "Desiderata."*

*—Victoria C. Scott*

*To my wife Lois, whose love and wisdom make me happy and wiser; and to my sons and especially to my grandsons, whose joy and future inspire me even more to work toward contributing to the betterment of communities.*

*—Abe Wandersman*

# BRIEF CONTENTS

# CONTENTS

## VI. Using Community Psychology to Promote Community and Social Change

# PREFACE

Welcome to the fourth edition of *Community Psychology: Linking Individuals and Communities*! In this book, we hope to get students excited about the work of community psychology, including research and social action, and show how the principles of this field are applicable to everyone, including nonpsychologists. We also take a more values-focused approach than in previous editions, one that makes more explicit the importance of social justice, anti-racism initiatives, and creating second-order change at multiple ecological levels.

In this new edition, we remain committed to integrating pedagogy into the text to promote student reflection, insight, application, and action. To accomplish this, we have significantly expanded the book's pedagogical features by including additional examples and exercises that highlight how community psychology is relevant to addressing modern societal issues, along with extensive discussion questions that can help students internalize key concepts and apply them to their own lives. We continue the previous editions' primary focus on advanced undergraduate students. However, through enrichment sections, updates of current research, and online discussion formats, we have developed this book to be a resource for graduate courses as well. Furthermore, with advances noted in this book, it can serve a third function as a record of advances in the field for community psychology professionals.

We recognize that many students using this book in your course will not become community psychologists. We wrote this edition to make ideas from community psychology accessible and helpful for those who will have careers in human services and for all of us who participate in civic life. Community psychology frameworks can assist critical review of social problem definitions and proposed solutions that students will encounter as citizens, community leaders, and professionals. We have colleagues who have used material from the book in social work, counseling, education, urban studies, and public health courses. Finally, we seek to make conceptual contributions to community psychology, posing issues for scholars and activists in our field to consider and adding to the ongoing conversation that allows our field to evolve and grow.

We welcome two new authors to this fourth edition: Andrew D. Case and Victoria C. Scott. They were instrumental in our discussions reflecting on developments of the field since the third edition. We wrote all our chapters after a wide-ranging reading of new developments in the field. This edition benefits from the multiple perspectives and varied experiences of the author team, who used a collaborative writing process to promote continuity between the chapters. We challenged each other's viewpoints and developed a consensus for the revisions. Each chapter has a primary author whose perspective led our revision. Bret Kloos is primary author for Chapters 2 and 14 and took responsibility for coordination of this edition; Jean Hill is primary author for Chapters 1, 6, 10, 11, and 13; and Elizabeth Thomas is primary author for Chapters 3, 4, and 8. Andrew Case collaborated with Elizabeth on Chapter 7 and Bret on Chapters 5 and 9; Victoria Scott and Abe Wandersman collaborated on Chapter 12.

We also want you to know that we donate 10% of our royalties to the Society for Community Research and Action (SCRA), an international body of community psychologists and scholars in related fields devoted to enhancing well-being and promoting social justice. To learn more about SCRA or to become a member, see their website at http://www.scra27.org/.

## Highlights and Changes to the Fourth Edition

Throughout the book, we have included greater consideration of ethics and reflexivity in community psychology practice and research. We incorporated more examples that demonstrate how social justice is an overarching value of the field. For example, we extended discussion of critical perspectives and second-order change across multiple levels of analysis. We added calls to action for the field to incorporate decolonial perspectives as community psychology evolves as a field. We also expanded discussions of minority-related and acculturative stressors, expanded discussion of counterspaces, and introduced the notion of "brave spaces" for engaging tensions and experiencing discomfort as we learn together.

In terms of pedagogy, there are also several new features that are intended to make the content more accessible and engage students in broader discussions of what it means to "change perspective" in psychology and how one could "do psychology" differently. We have continued the Community Psychology in Action features from the third edition and added Changing Perspectives features, both of which include discussion questions to encourage reflection and constructive critique. Each chapter begins with an opening exercise and discussion questions to set the stage for the main themes of the chapter. We include a marginal glossary to introduce key terms with definitions immediately available for students. We have moved chapter summaries to the book's companion website, where student and instructor resources can be accessed at the following link: http://pubs.apa.org/books/supp/kloos4/. Where we had to cut material, we have also moved it to the companion website to be part of the instructor's manual so that it is still available to instructors who would like to continue to feature it in their teaching. Below, we highlight the goals of each chapter as well as key revisions.

## Chapter 1. The Fundamentals of Community Psychology: Promoting Social Change

The main goal of this chapter is to help students negotiate the conceptual shift in how problems are defined and addressed to a community psychology perspective. We developed a new exercise to link values to community research and social change—testing DNA evidence of sexual assault cases that had been warehoused. The chapter has been revised to give greater clarity to why community psychology requires a shift in perspective. We have integrated values of community psychology throughout the chapter, particularly social justice as an overarching value for the field. We provide more examples of the concept of second-order change at multiple ecological levels. Research on youth participatory approaches in community research and intervention is used to illustrate these concepts. The discussion of community psychology values has also been modified and extended to include the concepts of collective wellness and a multilevel, strengths-based perspective.

## Chapter 2. The Development and Practice of Community Psychology

This chapter addresses how you "do psychology" differently if you have a shift in perspective. We build on Chapter 1 by introducing theories and practices that have enabled the new field of community psychology to act upon its shift in perspective. We emphasize the importance of problem definition and responding to social forces in (a) understanding the development and practice of community psychology and (b) encouraging students to examine how community responses to challenges shape the field today. We have further developed discussion of community psychology practice, including ethics and emerging global dialogue about viewpoints and practices across regions. Our view of community psychology's development is written from a North American perspective. However, we note parallels and differences in the practice of community psychology in different countries and regions. We frame the chapter as an account of the ongoing development of community psychology.

## Chapter 3. The Aims of Community Research

Chapter 3 is the first of two chapters dedicated to research. It focuses on the goals and commitments of contextually grounded inquiry, with additional attention in this edition to researcher reflexivity and the ethics of participatory and collaborative strategies. Chapter 3's Community Psychology in Action feature provides an updated account of a longtime partnership between researchers at the University of Illinois at Chicago and El Valor, a community-based organization serving mostly Latinos with developmental disabilities across the life span, as well as their families.

## Chapter 4. Methods of Community Psychology Research

This chapter builds on themes of community collaboration, participatory approaches, and research across levels of analysis, providing illustrations of qualitative, quantitative, and mixed-methods research in community psychology. This edition offers additional examples of inquiry conducted by academic and community researchers outside North America, opening with participatory action research from the Garo Hills region of Northern India. We include a more extended discussion of the value of multiple methods and new examples of mixed-methods research.

## Chapter 5. Understanding Individuals Within Environments

Chapter 5 continues our presentation of fundamental ecological concepts of the field. In this edition, we open with a new discussion of "blue zones" and consider how place and environments are related to health, well-being, and life expectancy. We retained the third edition's review of six approaches to understanding persons in context. In some cases, we tightened the presentation (e.g., Barker's ecological psychology) to allow for expanded discussions of activity spaces and counterspaces. We updated our discussion of creating new spaces when current alternatives are insufficient. We close with the historical example of the Fairweather Lodge and consider current efforts to expand use of this alternative model to mental health services.

## Chapter 6. What Defines a Community?

In this chapter, we invite readers to consider "community" as a transformation from "place" to "space." We have added discussions of alternative settings and counterspaces, the research on the tension between the values of human diversity and community, and the greatly enhanced body of research on sense of community online (including the sometimes harmful effects). We have also extended our discussion of sense of community in spiritual communities to explicitly include concepts of hope and transcendence.

## Chapter 7. Understanding Human Diversity in Context

We open Chapter 7 with an invitation to engage in diversity conversations with courage and humility. We introduce the notion of brave spaces as a holding place for engaging tensions and growing more accustomed to experiencing discomfort as we learn together. The chapter is also framed by an expanded discussion of intersectionality, as well as extensive discussion questions that encourage students to reflect on their own social identities. We illustrate socialization in cultural communities through research on activity settings, including interventions to prevent youth suicides in Alaska Native communities and counterspaces for individuals to challenge deficit-oriented societal narratives concerning their identity. We strengthen the section on oppression and liberation with the call to action that decolonial perspectives offer to our field.

## Chapter 8. Empowerment and Citizen Participation

Chapter 8 (Chapter 11 in the third edition) is now focused on empowerment and citizen participation. We moved this chapter forward to build upon the invitations for engagement and calls to action offered in the diversity chapter and to focus on collective and community responses to challenges. We emphasize how an empowerment perspective changes how we think about problems and solutions and how we work with others. We include a Community Psychology in Action feature that provides an example of empowerment through long-term action by community psychologist Marci Culley and residents of Sugar Creek, Missouri, as they responded to environmental pollution in their community. The theme of citizen participation to address environmental injustice is elaborated in new examples, including the Flint, Michigan, water crisis and long-term activism around nuclear energy. In our discussion of empowering practices and settings, we attend closely to features of relational contexts across multiple levels. Examples include Family Violence Coordinating Councils, the Highlander Research and Education Center, and the Riot Youth LGBTQ+ Theater Group.

## Chapter 9. Understanding Stress and Coping in Context

In Chapter 9 (formerly Chapter 8), we spend more time than in the previous edition developing and explaining risk and protective factors in an ecological model of stress, coping, and change. First, we wanted to make concepts of distal and proximal risk more accessible to students and to make the connections to intervention in other chapters. We have also expanded discussions of minority-related and acculturative stressors, traumatic growth, and the potential for positive growth. After the discussion of the model, we close with three community-based approaches for responding to challenges presented by stressors and consider the potential of these approaches for promoting positive change: social support, mutual help, and spiritual–religious resources.

## Chapter 10. Key Concepts in the Science of Prevention and Promotion

Chapter 10 (formerly Chapter 9) presents students with an introduction to prevention and promotion as alternative ways to address problems. We emphasize the idea that they will all someday be involved in community or organizational prevention programming efforts. The goals of this chapter and Chapter 11 continue to be to generate excitement about the demonstrated potential of prevention and promotion programs and to provide students with the knowledge and skills they need to join in these efforts. In Chapter 10, we have increased our emphasis on wellness promotion and added a new figure and metaphor to illustrate the relationships between risk and protective factors and interventions across multiple ecological levels.

## Chapter 11. Implementing Prevention and Promotion Programs

In Chapter 11 (formerly Chapter 10), we significantly increased our discussion of implementation science, including an extended discussion of the concepts of capacity and readiness. We begin with an example asking students to think about their high school experiences and what challenges they might identify for which a prevention program could be helpful. This provides the backdrop for more explicit discussion of how programs are introduced and adapted. We encourage students to think about which program components, organizational capacities, relationships, resources, and systems need to be in place to promote successful implementation.

## Chapter 12. Program Development, Evaluation, and Improvement

With an emphasis on evaluation, Chapter 12 (previously Chapter 13) links the concepts of program development, evaluation, and improvement. Like the previous edition, it opens with examples of how evaluation and program improvement are pervasive in everyday life. We expanded the description of Figure 12.1 to clarify the link between program development, evaluation, and improvement, and we updated examples throughout the chapter. Additionally, we introduce (a) formative evaluation, a type of evaluation that is increasingly used in community improvement initiatives, and (b) the inquiry–observation–reflection framework, a mixed-methods framework for data collection. We retained two widely used evaluation approaches: Empowerment Evaluation and Getting To Outcomes, revising the examples associated with both approaches to increase accessibility.

## Chapter 13. Improving Society Through Community Action

Chapter 13 (previously Chapter 12) is designed to engage students in a broad view of social change and to help them envision themselves participating in those efforts. We retain our examples from the PICO network as powerful stories of how individuals can become involved in community development initiatives in their communities. The section describing community development practices has been reorganized for greater conceptual clarity. We provide a new example of the relationship between prevention science and crime policy, and we updated and expanded the discussion of the impacts of state and federal policies on poverty.

### Chapter 14. Emerging Challenges and Opportunities: Shifting Perspective to Promote Change

In Chapter 14, we seek to promote students' optimism for their own engagement in community and social change. We consider emerging trends of (a) increasing social-justice–focused social action and (b) responding to challenges of globalization with community building and systematic efforts to decolonize our approaches to research and practice. We have expanded discussion of how students may use concepts and community psychology practice skills as citizens or social service professionals by adapting the points made by J. G. Kelly (1971) and Langhout (2015) about personal qualities that can help them achieve social change in collaboration with community partners. For students interested in obtaining training in community psychology or related fields, we expand our discussion of training, finding jobs, and careers. Consistent with other chapters, we discuss the expanding awareness of critical perspectives in the field. We close by encouraging students to think about how, where, and when they can use ideas from the text to address concerns in their communities.

## Alternative Orderings of Chapters

We recognize that we each have our favorite ways to organize the concepts and themes of the field. We encourage instructors to use chapters in an order that supports your pedagogy. In fact, members of the author team use different orderings in our classes, in part because the settings where we teach vary, as do the backgrounds and interests of our students. We have ordered chapters in this edition to build on the core concepts of the field and foster student recognition of interrelated strands among community psychology concepts. We think of Chapters 1–3 and 5–9 as providing conceptual frameworks that help psychology "shift its perspective." Chapters 4 and 10–13 provide tools for "doing community psychology"; we organized these chapters to begin with more person- or microsystem-focused approaches that then extend to broader community and social change in Chapter 13. Chapter 14 is intended to engage students in thinking about how they can use ideas from the course to work toward community and social change. Some possible chapter orderings follow.

All our suggestions use Chapters 1 and 2 to introduce the field, although some instructors may choose to rely on Chapter 1 alone. After the introductory chapters, you might want to proceed directly to Chapters 5–8 (ecology, community, diversity, and empowerment and citizen participation). To highlight a social change perspective early, you could pair Chapters 8 (empowerment and citizen participation) and 13 (community social change) much sooner than they appear in the book. If your course has many clinically minded students (this includes graduate students in clinical or counseling psychology, but it is also an implicit focus of many undergraduates), enlarging their perspective to think ecologically and preventively may be an important goal. To engage their interest, you might assign Chapter 9 (stress and coping in context) early to highlight the integration of clinical and community concepts to engage them in thinking about shifting perspectives. Alternatively, Chapters 9–11 (coping and prevention/promotion) can form an integrated unit on coping and prevention at some point in the course. Chapter 12 could be added to illustrate how local program evaluation can improve implementation and quality. However, we believe that full coverage of community psychology requires covering Chapters 5–8 and 13 at some point.

For a focus on community-engaged research, you may wish to assign Chapter 12 (program development, implementation, and evaluation) following the research focus of Chapters 3 and 4 to illustrate how the logic of scientific thinking can be adapted to practical community program monitoring and improvement. We have developed these chapters to explicitly link research and action and to challenge the received view that many students have of what constitutes rigorous research. Some instructors assign Chapters 3, 4, and 12 near the end of the course. The emphasis these chapters place on participatory research and cultural anchoring may have deeper meaning for many students after reading about ecology, community, diversity, and empowerment. Of course, these are only some of the possible orderings of chapters in this text. We encourage you to develop your own approach.

## Language and Identity

Respect for human diversity is a core value of community psychology. Language is a key mode of conveying this respect, particularly by referring to individuals and groups using their preferred self-identifying labels. We also recognize that the terms we use for identities are often contested. The terms preferred by individuals and groups can be an index of diversity in communities and familiar examples of how we negotiate inclusion and visibility. In this book, we refer to individuals' and groups' identities based on how they self-identify; where possible, we use language used by community members from the examples we cite. We also try to use inclusive language when referring to groups more broadly. However, language and identity are quickly changing, and once the book is published, it will be outdated. Our understandings of gender and how to adapt gendered language (e.g., pronouns) is quickly evolving. We also realize that different members of the same community may prefer different labels. For example, "Latina," "Latino," "Latinx," "Hispanic," and other terms may be appropriate when referring to some people from Spanish-speaking or Latin American cultural backgrounds in different regions or groups, but those terms may be inappropriate when referring

Photo by David Asiamah. Reprinted with permission.

This community-woven basket represents community psychology's mission to promote well-being, resist oppression, and cultivate a sense of community diversity across ages, genders, ethnicities, and other social and cultural characteristics.

to other groups and individuals from those backgrounds. We sometimes use "Latinx" as a broad, gender-neutral term, but we recognize that using this term can diminish the experiences of Latina women. We have used the term "Black" to be more inclusive as not all persons of African descent identify as African American, but we use the term "African American" when authors or community members have used it.

We encourage you to examine the use of language with your classes and to criticize what we have written where more appropriate language is needed. We are aware of how quickly language and the politics of representation can change; we have painfully reread a few passages in the third edition that are now out of date. In Chapter 1, we include a note to students to think reflexively about how they use language when referring to their own social identities, those of classmates, or of anyone else, whether those identities concern ethnicity, gender, ability/disability status, or any other characteristic that is important to someone.

## Additional Resources

Finally, we want you to know that there are additional resources for the textbook online. For students, these include lecture enrichments, recommendations for further reading, and links to video clips. For instructors, we include materials for lecture enrichments. These include in-class exercises, PowerPoint slides for each chapter, background material on classic studies in community psychology, example assignments, and suggestions for student evaluation. Student and instructor resources can be accessed at the following link: http://pubs.apa.org/books/supp/kloos4/.

## Acknowledgments

This book would not have been conceived or written without the support of many individuals and of the multiple communities in which we live. Jean Ann Linney, Jim Dalton, Maurice Elias, and Abe Wandersman first conceived of writing a new community psychology textbook with an engaging pedagogy and have encouraged us after other commitments precluded them continuing with it. David Becker and Elise Frasier, our editors at APA Books, helped us to navigate the tremendous changes occurring in publication and production of textbooks and to prepare a text that is engaging and is delivered on multiple platforms. We express our appreciation to nine masked peer reviewers for their encouragement and critical comments to improve this edition. Our reviewers' support and critiques were genuinely thoughtful and valuable. We also appreciate the students at Rhodes College, the University of North Carolina at Charlotte, and the University of South Carolina who provided similar constructive criticism.

Our perspectives on community psychology have been strongly influenced by mentors, colleagues, and students. We very much appreciate the examples of our mentors who introduced us to community psychology or shaped the way we think about community psychology: Mark Aber, Nicole Allen, Carla Hunter, Leonard Jason, Thom Moore, and Julian Rappaport. We expect that they will recognize many of their influences in the book. We also thank many colleagues and students who have given us comments and suggestions in class, at conferences, on surveys, and by email. We also acknowledge the value of reading recent community psychology textbooks by other authors, especially those by Manuel Riemer, Stephanie Reich, and Scot Evans; John Moritsugu, Elizabeth Vera, Frank Y. Wong, and Karen Grover Duffy; Leonard A. Jason, Olya Glantsman, Jack F. O'Brien, and Kaitlyn, N. Ramian; Geoff Nelson and Isaac Prilleltensky; Murray Levine, Douglas Perkins, and David Perkins; and Jennifer Rudkin. All these make valuable contributions to the ongoing conversation of our field.

We also need to acknowledge the gifts of vision, confidence, and generosity that Jim Dalton and Maurice Elias gave to us by recruiting us to be stewards for the future development of this textbook as a resource for community psychology. They have consistently been encouraging and helpful. It is a somewhat sobering responsibility to follow their lead, but we will strive to produce a text and supplementary resources that thoughtfully present community psychology in ways that engage students and current social issues.

Bret thanks his community partners in social change efforts and his students for challenging his thinking. He is especially grateful to community partners for demonstrating the value of perseverance and creativity in promoting sustainable social change. Jean thanks Jim, Mo, and Abe for their work on earlier editions of this book and for their amazing generosity in sharing that work with us. She also thanks her students and colleagues who have enthusiastically supported her community work, even when they did not really share her excitement. Elizabeth thanks her community partners at the family center for all that they have taught her about collaboration and building inclusive communities. She thanks her students for the energy and insights they bring to community-based learning and action research efforts. Andrew thanks God for providing the opportunity to help write this edition with such a wonderful group of people. He thanks his mentors—both spiritual and academic—for their gifts of time, understanding, and support. Victoria thanks her doctoral program advisors for welcoming her through the door of community psychology over a decade ago and illuminating the value of linking community research and action in service of social improvement. Abe thanks his students and former students for their valuable contributions to theory, research, and action that make community psychology valuable to our communities. Finally, we deeply thank our families, whose love, patience, and support always nurture and enrich our lives.

Social justice is one of community psychology's core values that guides much of its work in improving communities and society, making sure that all voices are heard.

arindambanerjee/Shutterstock.com

# 1 The Fundamentals of Community Psychology: Promoting Social Change

## Looking Ahead III➡

**After reading this chapter you will be able to answer these questions:**

1. What is the shift in perspective that makes community psychology different from other fields?

2. How does the concept of second-order change relate to that shift in perspective?

3. What are ecological levels of analysis and how do they relate to community psychology theories and practice?

4. Why is community psychology viewed as a values-based field and what are those values?

## Opening Exercise

## Testing Warehoused DNA Evidence

In a city police storage unit in Detroit, over 11,000 sexual assault kits sat ignored and untested, some for over 3 decades. Most, if not all, of the victims who had undergone the invasive physical examinations required to obtain that evidence had no idea that the DNA of their assailants had never been tested. Neither did many members of the Wayne County criminal justice system, including the assistant prosecutor who discovered the kits in 2009.

The prosecutor's office put together a multidisciplinary task force to assess the problem and asked community psychologist

Rebecca Campbell to lead it. The task force was asked to determine how large the problem was and why the kits had never been tested. Additionally, the group was asked to develop a plan for testing the kits and notifying the victims of the results.

The obvious answer to why this immense backlog occurred might be that there was not enough money or resources to test all those kits, and that definitely was a factor. But as Dr. Campbell's research team conducted qualitative analyses of the police records, they discovered that a lack of resources was not the only factor, or even the most powerful

**Testing Warehoused DNA Evidence (continued)**

one. Instead, strong biases against sexual assault victims, particularly young victims and those the officers characterized as sex workers, resulted in many cases literally being warehoused.

The task force had more than 1,500 of the kits tested. The results showed that more than a quarter of the kits resulted in DNA matches in the FBI national database. Of those, 549 were to suspected serial rapists.

Today, police departments around the United States are using the protocols and training developed by the task force headed by Dr. Campbell to ensure that sexual assault kits are tested and that the victims are informed of the results in a supportive and appropriate manner. Even with those efforts, at least 100,000 sexual assault kits are still in warehouses, untested. That number may be much higher; many states do not know how many untested kits they have. For additional information about what your state is doing to end the backlog of sexual assault kit testing, you can visit http://www.endthebacklog.org/.

### What Do You Think?

1. Who would you say was responsible for the 11,000 untested kits found in Detroit?
2. What do you think is best way to solve this problem?
3. The field of community psychology explicitly values and centers social justice in its work. Why would untested sexual assault kits be viewed as a social justice issue?

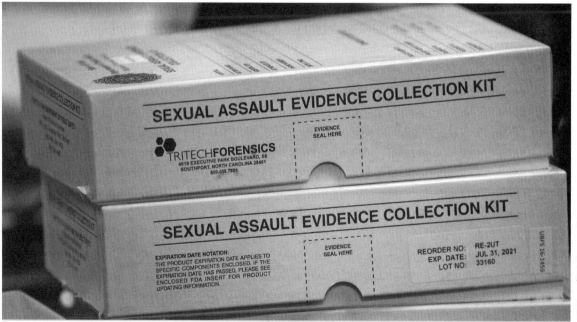

These untested rape kits represent a social justice concern that community psychology is well-equipped to solve for the betterment of individuals, communities, and society as a whole.

# What Is Community Psychology?

**community psychology** concerns the relationships of individuals with communities and societies. By integrating research with action, it seeks to understand and enhance quality of life for individuals, communities, and societies.

Community psychologists work in a multitude of fields, including child development, mental health, criminal justice, education, community health, homelessness, substance abuse, and organizational psychology. What unites us is not the *area* in which we choose to work but rather the *perspective* we bring to that work. Community psychologists seek to understand people within the social contexts of their lives in order to promote a better quality of life for all people. Community psychologists believe that often the best way to alleviate human suffering and advance social justice is through a focus not on changing individuals but rather on changing the relationship between those people and the settings, organizations, and structures in which they live. This viewpoint may be best illustrated by the words of Martin Luther King, Jr., when he addressed the American Psychological Association in 1967. His address was titled "The Role of the Behavioral Scientist in the Civil Rights Movement."

> I am sure that we will recognize that there are some things in our society, some things in our world, to which we should never be adjusted. There are some things concerning which we must always be maladjusted if we are to be people of good will. We must never adjust ourselves to racial discrimination and racial segregation. We must never adjust ourselves to religious bigotry. We must never adjust ourselves to economic conditions that take necessities from the many to give luxuries to the few. We must never adjust ourselves to the madness of militarism, and the self-defeating effects of physical violence.

In that address, Rev. Dr. King called for the creation of a new organization, the International Association for the Advancement of Creative Maladjustment. The field of community psychology arose around the same time as his address, and as a field we embrace the concept of creative maladjustment, not only in relation to the social justice issues he listed but in response to any structural context that impedes optimal human health and well-being.

Keeping in mind the diversity of community psychologists' interests and personal views, we offer this definition of the field: **Community psychology** concerns the relationships of individuals with communities and societies. By integrating research with action, it seeks to understand and enhance quality of life for individuals, communities, and societies.

Let us unpack this definition. Community psychology concerns the multiple relationships between individuals, communities, and societies. We define "community" broadly. An individual lives within many communities and at multiple levels: family, networks of friends, workplace, school, voluntary association, neighborhood, and wider locality—even cultures. All these exist within larger societies and, ultimately, within a global context. The individual must be understood in terms of these relationships, not in isolation.

Community psychology's focus is not on the individual or on the community alone but also on their linkages. The field also studies the influences of social structures on each other (e.g., how citizen organizations influence the wider community). But unlike sociology, community psychology places a greater emphasis on individuals and their complex interactions with the social structure.

Community psychology is also committed to engaging in research and developing valid psychological knowledge in the interest of improving community life. In the community psychology perspective, knowledge is constructed through research and action. The community psychologist's role has often been described as that of a *participant–conceptualizer* (Bennett et al., 1966, pp. 7–8), actively involved in community processes while also attempting to understand and explain them, as aptly summarized in these statements:

> If we are afraid of testing our ideas about society by intervening in it, and if we are always detached observers of society and rarely if ever participants in it, we can only give our students ideas about society, not our experiences in it. We can tell our students about how society ought to be, but not what it is like to try to change the way things are. (Sarason, 1974, p. 266)

Community psychology research is intertwined with efforts to change a community and social action. Findings from research are used to build theory and to guide action. For example, a program developed in a high school setting to prevent youth violence (i.e., action) can generate greater knowledge of the problem, adolescent development, the local school and community, and

---

### Box 1.1    Changing Perspectives: Homelessness

Bessie Mae is 97 years old and homeless. She has her two boys, and that is about all. She and sons Larry, 60, and Charlie, 62, live in a 1973 Chevrolet Suburban they park each night on a busy Venice street. Bessie worked as a packer for the National Biscuit Co. until she was in her 60s. Charlie worked in construction and as a painter before becoming disabled by degenerative arthritis. Larry was a cook before compressed discs in his back and a damaged neck nerve put an end to it. He began working 26 years ago as a full-time caregiver for his mother through the California's In-Home Supportive Services program. That ended about 4 years ago, when the owner of a Palm Springs home where they lived had to sell the place. At the same time, the state dropped Larry and his mother from the support program, he said. The three have tried at various times since to get government-subsidized housing. But they failed, in part because they insist on living together (Pool, 2009). It was not until the publication of Pool's article in the *Los Angeles Times* that Bessie Mae and her sons were able to obtain housing from a nonprofit organization: the Integrated Recovery Network.

Bessie Mae and her sons are not alone. On one specific night in January 2019, an estimated 568,000 people were homeless in the United States (Department of Housing and Urban Development, 2020). Nearly one fifth of those people were children. Only 63% of those who were homeless were staying in shelters or other types of transitional housing. The remaining 37% were living on the street, in their cars, or in other places where people are not meant to live.

**What Do You Think?**

1. Consider the news stories you have heard about the problem of homelessness or perhaps the homeless people you have encountered yourself. Why do you think these people are homeless?

2. Take a minute to list what you think are the top three contributing causes to homelessness.

how to design future prevention programs (i.e., research). Moreover, community psychology research and action are collaborative, based on partnerships with the persons or communities involved.

Community psychology is different from other fields of psychology in two ways. First, community psychology offers a different way of understanding human behavior and how to support individual, family, and community wellness. We focus on the community contexts of behavior. That shift in perspective (which is the first thing we discuss in this chapter) leads to the second difference: an expansion of the definition of appropriate topics for psychological study and intervention. Community psychologists are interested in effective ways to prevent problems rather than treat them after they arise. The field emphasizes promoting healthy functioning for all members of a community rather than intervening when problems develop for a few of those members. And we focus our research on factors at the neighborhood, community, and societal level that support or impede healthy development.

If you are like many people, you listed such things as substance abuse, mental illness, and domestic violence—problems affecting the lives of the people who become homeless. These are indeed contributing factors. But they are not the primary factors. All these variables are more common among persons who do not become homeless than among those who do (Shinn, 2009; Shinn et al., 2001). The most important factor contributing to the problem of homelessness in the United States has nothing to do with the character or personal circumstances of the individuals who become homeless. It is a lack of affordable housing in our communities. The best predictor of the extent of homelessness in a community is the ratio of available affordable housing units to the number of persons and families seeking them (Shinn, 2016; Shinn et al., 2001).

Structural factors are often more influential than individualistic factors when solving societal problems like homelessness. We must address these problems from multiple structural levels, while being respectful of individual differences and empowering those directly affected by these issues. Empirical grounding is also essential because studying and solving these problems, strengthening communities, and achieving social justice for all members of those communities is nearly impossible without a sound scientific basis. These are some of the fundamental values of community psychology, which we explore later in this chapter.

# Individualistic Versus Structural Perspectives

**individualistic perspective**
focuses on the life choices and behaviors of individuals when addressing societal problems.

**structural perspective**
also referred to as an ecological perspective, it examines how systemic factors at various levels impact the lives of individuals, families, and other groups within a community.

As mentioned at the beginning of the chapter, many people tend to focus only on individuals' behaviors or life choices instead of considering structural factors when thinking about the roots of societal problems like homelessness. Listing factors such as substance abuse, mental illness, and domestic violence as the main causes of homelessness represents an **individualistic perspective**, focused on how homeless persons and families are different from those with housing. While this viewpoint is an important one, as individual factors do matter, we are going to ask you to consciously make a perceptual shift and to analyze problems in living through a **structural perspective** as well. Using this perspective requires you to think about how organizations, neighborhoods, communities, and societies are structured as systems and how those systems affect the lives of individuals and families. In community psychology, this is generally presented as taking an *ecological perspective*, and that is how it will be discussed in this book.

This shift in perspective can be made clear by viewing homelessness as a game of musical chairs (McChesney, 1990). In any community, there is a finite number of affordable housing units—just as there is a finite number of chairs in a game of musical chairs. And in both situations, there are more people than there are available chairs (or housing units). While individual variables do influence who becomes chairless (or homeless), these are not the defining factors in the game. These factors determine who gets the available seats and who is left standing *but not how many chairs are available*. The game is structured from the beginning to ensure that someone is left without a chair.

A study of solely individual-level variables in homelessness misses this larger reality. A social program for homelessness that focuses only on such factors as treating individual mental disorders or promoting job-interviewing skills may reshuffle which people become homeless and which do not, but it does nothing to increase the availability of housing. Addressing community or societal problems such as homelessness requires a shift in perspective—from an individualistic perspective to a structural/ecological one. Within this broader perspective, community psychologists have much to contribute (e.g., M. A. Bond et al., 2017). We revisit the issue of homelessness and what can be done about it in Chapter 13.

The shift from an individualistic to a structural/ecological perspective is related to another issue we would like you to consider in this class: problem definition. As we are sure you have learned in other psychology courses, human beings are rarely content to just observe something. We want to understand it, and we will, almost automatically, construct some sort of explanation. These personal explanations then become the basis for how we define social problems. If you view an issue through an individualistic perspective, your definition of the problem will center on individual-level variables. The issue of

Community psychology examines societal issues like homelessness through an ecological lens, addressing systemic causes rather than just individual factors.

problem definition is not an incidental one. How we define a problem shapes the questions we ask, the methods we use to answer those questions, and the way we interpret those answers. And all those things affect the types of interventions we will consider. How we define a problem has such far-reaching effects that social scientists have declared problem definition to be an ethical issue (O'Neill, 2005).

Assumptions we make about a problem determine how we define the problem, which in turn determines the ways we approach and try to solve it. This may be particularly true when we are not consciously aware of the assumptions we are making. Our cultural background, personal experiences, education, and biases (and sometimes the biases that came with our education) help shape those assumptions, which may actually prevent effective responses to the problem. Our assumptions can thus become the real problem. If we ignore how problems are framed—the viewpoint through which we derive our definitions—we will be imprisoned by those frames (E. Seidman & Rappaport, 1986). In this book, we hope to broaden your thinking about framing problems and the process of problem definition. We will encourage you to become participant–conceptualizers for how problems are defined and addressed in your communities. Community psychologists strive to think outside the traditional boxes of psychology to define problems and generate interventions at many levels.

Actually, there are no truly individual problems or interventions. Everything that humans do takes place in social contexts: in a culture, a locality, a setting (e.g., workplace, school, playground, home), and a set of personal relationships. For example, a child matures within many social contexts that shape their development. When a client arrives for a psychotherapy session, they bring a personal set of life experiences (in social contexts), as does the therapist. The two form a relationship that is rooted not only in who they are as persons but also in cultural, gender, social, economic (e.g., who pays for treatment, and how does that affect it?), and other contexts. Even the atmosphere of the waiting room, interpreted in cultural terms, makes a difference.

In this chapter, we first expand our discussion of how community psychology involves a shift of perspective from the viewpoint of most of psychology. We then elaborate on the community psychology perspective by describing some of its basic assumptions about persons, contexts, and two types of change. Next, we discuss two conceptual frameworks central to the field: ecological levels of analysis (multiple layers of social contexts) and eight core values of the field. This chapter is the first of two that introduce and define community psychology in Part I of this book. In Chapter 2, we trace how community psychology developed a different way of "doing" psychology and provide examples of its current practice.

## Community Psychology: A Shift in Perspective

In the previous section, we presented homelessness as an example of how a shift from an individualistic perspective to a structural/ecological perspective changes how we define a problem and what types of interventions we consider. In this book, we discuss a number of approaches to addressing problems from a structural perspective. Here is an overview:

- **Prevention/promotion programs** reduce the future likelihood of problems—for example, by strengthening protective factors and reducing risk factors in individuals, families, schools, organizations, and communities (see Chapters 10 and 11).

- **Consultation** focuses on roles, decision making, communication, and conflict in organizations to promote employee job satisfaction or effectiveness of human services, social change organizations, or schools (see Chapters 12 and 13).

- **Alternative settings** arise when traditional services do not meet the needs of some populations (e.g., women's centers, rape crisis centers, self-help organizations for persons with specific problems—see Chapters 9 and 13).

- **Community organizing** at grassroots levels helps citizens organize to identify local issues and decide how to address them. Community coalitions bring together citizens and community institutions (e.g., religious congregations, schools, police, business, human services, government) to address a community problem together instead of with separate, uncoordinated efforts (see Chapter 13).

- **Participatory research**, in which community researchers and citizens collaborate, provides useful information for action on community issues. Program evaluation helps determine whether community programs effectively attain their goals and how they can be improved (see Chapters 3 and 4).

- **Policy research and advocacy** includes research on community and social issues, efforts to inform decision makers (e.g., government officials, private sector leaders, mass media, the public) about courses for action, and evaluation of the effects of social policies (see Chapter 13). Community psychologists are engaged in advocacy regarding homelessness, peace, drug abuse, positive child and family development, and other issues. One goal of this book is to introduce you to tools for advocacy, as a citizen or professional, at levels from local to international.

Any reader of this book is quite likely to participate in community initiatives such as these in the future, whether as a community psychologist, clinical counseling psychologist, or another health professional, educator, researcher, parent, or citizen. One goal of this book is to give you tools for doing so.

Understanding diverse cultures, including your own, may also require another shift of perspective. Cultural traditions of individuals, families, and communities provide personal strengths and resources for effective action. Community psychology emphasizes understanding each culture's distinctiveness while not losing sight of that culture's core values and shared human experiences. A further goal of this book is to provide you with some tools for learning about and working in diverse cultures (see Chapter 7).

# Persons, Contexts, and Change

The shifts of perspectives that we have described involve underlying assumptions about two questions: How do problems arise? How can change occur? Every day, each of us acts on our own assumed answers to these questions. Next, we describe some assumptions among community psychologists about these questions.

## Persons and Contexts

Some of our most important assumptions about problems concern the importance of persons and contexts. Shinn and Toohey (2003) coined the term

**context**

encapsulates all the structural forces that influence an individual's life, including family and social relationships, neighborhood, school, religious and community organizations, cultural norms, gender roles, and socioeconomic status. Not adequately accounting for these structural forces leads to flawed research and practice, which is called context minimization error.

*context minimization error* to denote ignoring or discounting the importance of contexts in an individual's life. **Context** (a term we use throughout this book) refers to the encapsulating environments within which an individual lives (e.g., family, friendship network, peer group, neighborhood, workplace, school, religious or community organization, locality, cultural heritage and norms, gender roles, social and economic forces). Together, these make up the structural forces that shape the lives of individuals. Context minimization errors, where people focus primarily on an individual's behavior and overlook or discount structural factors, lead to psychological theories and research findings that are flawed or that hold true only in limited circumstances. These errors can also lead to therapy interventions or social programs that fail because they attempt to reform individuals without understanding or altering the contexts within which those individuals live.

A key concept of social psychology is the *fundamental attribution error* (Ross, 1977)—the tendency of observers watching an actor to overestimate the importance of the actor's individual characteristics and underestimate the importance of situational factors. When we see someone trip on a sidewalk, we often think "how awkward" or wonder if the person has been drinking. We seldom look to see if the sidewalk is flawed. Context minimization is similar but refers to contexts and forces that include those beyond the immediate situation. Cultural norms, economic necessities, neighborhood characteristics, and the psychological climate of a workplace are examples. Contexts influence our lives at least as much as individual characteristics do.

Consider the multiple contexts that influence a child in a first-grade public school classroom. The personalities of teacher and students certainly influence the classroom context; the curriculum and routine ways that the teacher engages with students are also important. But also consider the relationships of the school principal, faculty, and staff with the child and their family. The class occurs in a physical room and school in a wider neighborhood and community, which can support or interfere with learning. Relationships between administrators, school board members, and citizens (and taxpayers) certainly influence the classroom environment, as do community, state, and national attitudes and policies about education. These contexts have important influences beyond simple effects of the individuals involved. Actions to improve learning for students in that first-grade classroom will need to change multiple contexts (Weinstein, 2002a).

***Persons and Contexts Influence Each Other.*** Community psychology is about the *relationships* of persons and contexts. These are not one-way streets. Contexts affect personal life, while persons, especially when acting together with others, influence and change contexts. Stephanie Riger (2001) called for community psychology to appreciate how persons respond to contexts and how they can exercise power to change those contexts.

Persons influence context when, for example, citizen efforts in a neighborhood lead to improved safety, neighboring connections among residents, assistance for people affected by domestic violence, affordable housing, or reduced pollution from a neighboring factory. Persons who share a problem or illness can influence contexts of human services or health care when they form a mutual help group to support each other. Community psychology seeks to understand and to improve individual, community, and societal quality of life. One of our goals for this book is to whet your appetite for involvement in community and social action in ways that draw on your personal strengths and community resources.

***Reading This Book "in Context."*** In reading this book, we expect that, at times, you will disagree with or recognize limitations to what we write. Respectful disagreement is important in community psychology. Community psychologist Julian Rappaport (1981) playfully yet seriously proposed Rappaport's rule: "When everyone agrees with you, worry" (p. 3). Diversity of views is a valuable resource for understanding multiple sides of community and social questions.

As you read this book, identify your specific life experiences that lead you to agree or disagree, and identify the social contexts of those experiences. If possible, discuss these with your instructor, with a classmate, or in class as a group. In our experience, many disagreements in communities and societies are based on differing life experiences in different contexts. It is important to discuss those experiences with respect and to understand them. That discussion can deepen your own and others' learning. Sharing your perspectives can help others be better participant–conceptualizers in their communities.

## Structural Perspectives and First-Order and Second-Order Change

Developing a comprehensive understanding of the problem of homelessness introduced earlier in this chapter requires a conceptual shift from an individual-level only perspective to a person-in-context, structural perspective. This perceptual shift may be particularly difficult for those of us who were raised in the American cultural tradition of individualism. This tradition holds that America, from its founding, has offered equal opportunities for all, so what we make of our lives solely depends on individual talent and effort. While we do not discount the importance of individual knowledge, skills, and effort (in fact, community psychologists actively work to develop programs to increase these attributes in individuals, as you will see in Chapters 10 and 11), we believe that the role of structural forces in human behavior has been undervalued in psychology as a whole. One of the major skills we want you to take away from your reading of this book is the ability

**first-order change**
altering, rearranging, or replacing the individual members of a group without addressing the structural issues that are the root cause of the problem.

**second-order change**
resolving a problem by changing relationships within a community, which includes shared goals, roles, rules, and power dynamics. This approach requires more extensive and dynamic efforts but is more likely to result in positive, long-term change.

to look at a problem and ask yourself, "What structural factors influence this problem or behavior? How could those be modified to improve the lives of individuals and families?"

One of the first major studies demonstrating the importance of structural forces was a study of crime and juvenile delinquency in Chicago in the first half of the 20th century. Two sociologists, Clifford Shaw and Henry McKay (1969), looked at official sources of juvenile delinquency rates (e.g., arrests, adjudications) in Chicago neighborhoods during three time periods: 1900–1906, 1917–1923, and 1927–1933. These were periods of rapid change in Chicago: successive waves of immigration by different ethnic groups, increased industrialization, sharp increases in population density, and high levels of mobility. What they found was that, over time, rates of juvenile delinquency remained high in certain neighborhoods, even though almost the entire population of those neighborhoods had changed! Even when the ethnic makeup of a neighborhood completely changed (as existing immigrant groups moved to more desirable neighborhoods and new immigrant groups moved in), the high rates of juvenile delinquency persisted. Shaw and McKay concluded that it was structural factors in the neighborhoods (poverty, overcrowding, and the social disorganization that accompanies rapid change) that were causing the high crime rates, not the characteristics of the individuals who lived there. The theory they developed, social disorganization theory, is still an influential theory in the field of criminology, but the general point about the importance of structural forces has important implications well beyond that field. Their research also illustrates the difference between first-order and second-order change.

Writing of the family as a social system, Watzlawick et al. (1974) distinguished between two kinds of change. **First-order change** alters, rearranges, or replaces the individual members of a group (the neighborhood in C. Shaw and McKay's, 1969, research). This may resolve some aspects of the problem. However, in the long run, the same problems often recur with the new cast of characters, leading to the conclusion that the more things change, the more they remain the same. Attempting to resolve homelessness by counseling homeless individuals without addressing the supply of affordable housing represents first-order change. You may help that individual, but the social problem will persist because you have not addressed all the reasons that homelessness exists.

A group is not just a collection of individuals; it is also a set of relationships among them. Changing those relationships, especially changing shared goals, roles, rules, and power relationships, is **second-order change** (Linney, 1990; E. Seidman, 1988). For example, instead of preserving rigid lines between bosses who make decisions and workers who carry them out, second-order change may involve collaborative decision making, giving workers power to make decisions. Instead of rigid lines of expertise between mental health professionals and patients, it could involve finding ways that persons with disorders may help each other in self-help groups. The point is not that specific interventions need to be used but rather that the analysis of the problem takes into account these sets of relationships, power, and contexts as possible contributing sources of the problems. Second-order change can help transform individuals' lives and the communities where they live.

Try a thought experiment suggested by community psychologist Seymour Sarason (1972) to analyze the educational system. Criticisms of schools, at least in the United States, often focus blame on individuals or collections of individuals: incompetent teachers, unmotivated or unprepared students, or uncaring parents or administrators. Imagine changing every individual in the school—firing all teachers and staff and hiring replacements, obtaining a new student population, and changing every other individual from the school board to the classroom—yet leaving intact the structure of roles, expectations, and policies about how the school is to be run. How long do you think it will be before the same issues and criticisms return? Why? If you answer "not long," you are seeing the limits of first-order change. It is sometimes enough, but often, it is not.

Next, we present two detailed examples of second-order change, one in relation to substance abuse recovery and the other in relation to the role of youth in their communities.

***Oxford House: Second-Order Change in Recovery From Substance Abuse.*** Traditional professional treatments for substance abuse have high recidivism rates. Methods that rely more on persons in recovery helping each other offer promising alternatives. One example is twelve-step groups such as Alcoholics Anonymous. Another is Oxford House, a network of residential settings (Jason, Olson, & Harvey, 2015).

Many recovery homes (halfway houses) are located in areas of higher crime and drug use, have crowded and time-limited accommodations, and impose rules that limit resident initiative and responsibility. Some of these limitations reflect the reluctance of the larger society to support or have day-to-day contact with persons in recovery. In contrast, Oxford Houses offer more spacious dwellings in lower-crime residential neighborhoods. Residents are required to be employed, pay rent, perform chores, and remain drug-free. The resident may choose whether to be involved in professional treatment, mutual help (e.g., twelve-step) groups, or both. Separate Oxford Houses exist for women and men. Each house is governed democratically, with leaders chosen by residents but without professional staff. Current residents vote on applications of prospective residents to join the house; a resident who returns to drug use or who is disruptive can be dismissed by a similar vote. The new resident joins a community in which there is support, shared responsibility, and shared decision making.

Oxford Houses represent second-order change because they alter the usual roles of patient and staff, making persons in recovery more accountable for their own behavior and for each other, in a context of equality, support, and shared community. Evaluations indicate positive outcomes and reduced recidivism.

In many cases, achieving second-order change requires not only a shift in how we think about a problem but also a change in the methods we use to understand and address the problem. Youth inquiry approaches are an example of this.

***Youth Inquiry Approaches: Creating Second-Order Change in the Environments of Children and Adolescents.*** Children and adolescents have been studied intensively in social science research, including in a whole field of study—child development—devoted exclusively to them. But in all that research, youth have been the objects of study, not the creators of research. That distinction illustrates a specific structural understanding of the role of children and adolescents in the research process. Their role is to be studied by adults. Their voices have been silent in deciding what questions should be asked, what methods should be used, what data should be collected, how those data should be understood, and what should be done with the results.

Over the past 2 decades, that structural understanding of the role of youth in the research process has been challenged through the use of youth inquiry approaches (Kennedy et al., 2019; Langhout & Thomas, 2010a). Youth inquiry approaches are research and social change methods that center youth, rather than adults, as the primary knowledge generators and change agents. Adults are involved as collaborators and support providers, not as directors. All these changes in role relationships represent second-order change.

Instituting that second-order change in our structural approach to understanding and improving the environments in which youth live has resulted in measurable changes in those environments. A majority of studies of projects using youth inquiry approaches demonstrate significant environmental outcomes (Kennedy et al., 2019; Langhout & Thomas, 2010a). These include changes in the way youth are perceived and valued by the adults in their schools and communities, changes in peer norms, the development of new programs and improvement of existing ones, and the adoption of new policies.

For example, youth participatory action projects in two urban high schools resulted in more diversity-related discussions between adults and students and in structural changes within the schools through which students could inform and influence hiring decisions, teaching practices, and other policies at the schools (Ozer & Wright, 2012). A youth participatory action program in Minneapolis involved youth investigating and mapping youth-friendly opportunities in their neighborhoods. They then developed innovative ways to bring those opportunities to the attention of other youth and their families. Finally, they worked to educate their communities about unmet needs of youth and barriers to participation in existing opportunities. Safe and reliable transportation to youth programs was identified as one such barrier, and youth in one neighborhood were able to create two new bus routes specifically to transport youth to parks, libraries, and other youth programs (Walker & Saito, 2011).

***Limits of Change in Social Contexts.*** Even second-order change does not "solve" community and social problems. Attempts to resolve community and social issues represent a problem-resolution process rather than problem solving. A series of changes is likely needed to transform the lives of individuals and their communities. Every problem resolution creates new challenges and perhaps new problems: unintended consequences, altered alignments of human or material resources, or new conflicts involving human needs and values. This is not a reason to give up. The change process leads to real improvements if communities and societies carefully study both history and likely future consequences (Sarason, 1978).

## Ecological Levels of Analysis in Community Psychology

As individuals, we live within webs of social relationships. Urie Bronfenbrenner (1979) proposed a levels of analysis framework (describing levels of social contexts) that is influential in developmental psychology and community psychology. Our discussion of ecological levels is partly based on Bronfenbrenner's approach, but our frame of reference is the community, not just the developing individual. Thus, we differ in some details from his approach. Historically, community psychology has used ecological levels as a way of clarifying the different values, goals, and strategies for intervention associated with each level of analysis (Rappaport, 1977a, 1977b; E. Seidman & Rappaport, 1974). In addition, this approach helps us focus on the interactions between systems (see also different concepts of ecological levels in Maton, 2000; Moane, 2003; G. Nelson & Prilleltensky, 2010).

Thinking in terms of ecological levels of analysis helps clarify how a single event or problem has multiple causes. For example, factors that contribute to a child's problems in school may include forces at multiple levels. Powerful adults at school, in the local community, and at national and global levels make policy decisions that affect the resources that determine the quality of education the child receives. Family members, friends, and teachers have a great impact, but even their thinking and values are influenced by the school system; the local community; and cultural, societal, and even global levels.

Thinking in terms of ecological levels of analysis also helps illustrate multiple ways to address an important question for community psychology: What is a community? While originally tied to place or a locality, "community" has come to refer to sets of relationships among persons at many levels—whether tied to place or not (see Chapter 6). Thus, a classroom, sorority, religious congregation, online community, or cultural group (e.g., the Mexican American community) may be considered a community.

Figure 1.1 illustrates our typology of ecological levels of analysis for community psychology. The most proximal systems, closest to the individual and involving the most face-to-face contact, are closer to the center of the diagram. The more distal systems, less immediate to the person yet having broad effects, are toward the outside of the diagram.

As you can see in the diagram, some of these systems overlap; for example, some organizations, such as small businesses or community groups, are so small that they have many of the psychosocial qualities of microsystems. The examples in italics in Figure 1.1 are illustrative and do not represent all groups at each level.

**Figure 1.1** Ecological Levels of Analysis for Community Psychology

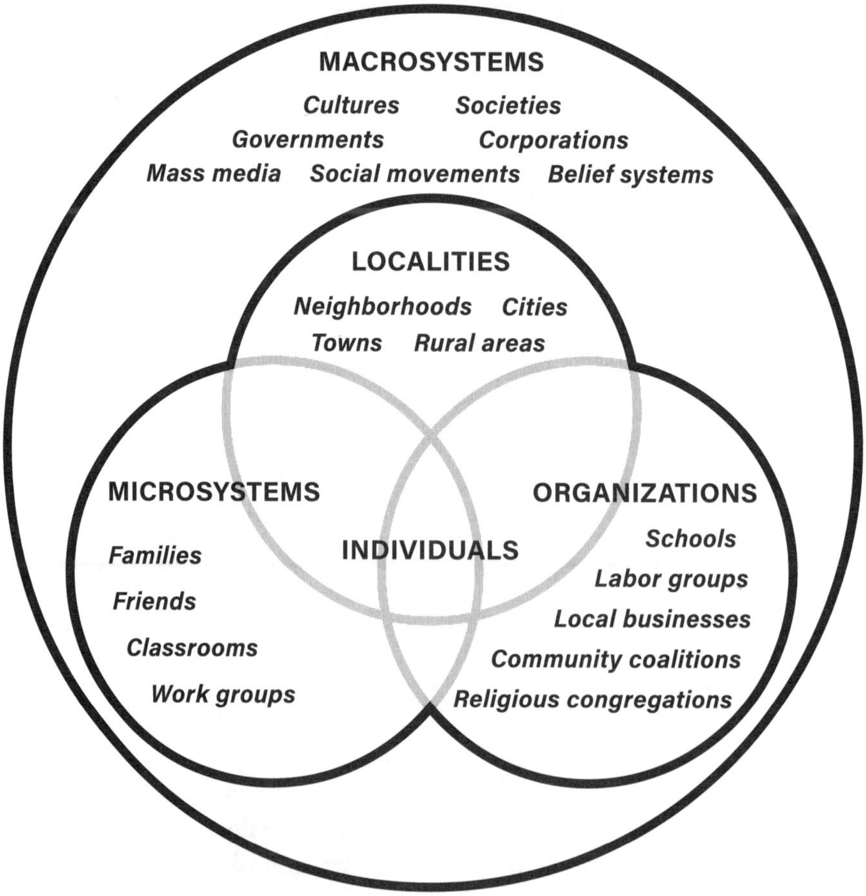

**individual**
the smallest ecological level, it involves total consideration of a person's experiences, memories, thoughts, feelings, relationships, culture, and other defining factors.

**microsystems**
smaller environments or groups within an ecological framework where the individual often communicates or interacts directly with others (e.g., families, classrooms, musical groups, sports teams).

Individuals, societies, and the levels between them are interdependent, and their contributions to behavior and social problems may overlap in different ways. Indeed, community psychology is based on that interdependence of persons in contexts. It is at the point where these systems link that community psychology interventions can often have their greatest impact: the point where community members have identified an issue and where multiple people, groups, and community resources must be brought together in an intentional way to address it. It is for this reason that community psychology is referred to as a linking science (see Chapter 2).

## Individuals

The concept of the **individual** in this model encompasses all of a person's experiences, relationships, thoughts, and feelings. Consider the individual person, nested within the other levels. The person chooses their relationships or environments to some extent and influences them in many ways; likewise, these influence the person. Each person is involved in systems at multiple ecological levels (e.g., family and friends, workplace, neighborhood). Much research in community psychology concerns how individuals are interrelated with social contexts in their lives.

Community psychologists and others in related fields have developed individually oriented preventive interventions to increase personal capacities to address problems in communities. These interventions have been documented to be effective in reducing such problems as difficulties in the social and academic development of children, adolescent behavior problems and juvenile delinquency, adult physical health and depression, HIV/AIDS, difficulties during family transitions such as parenting and divorce, and family violence (we discuss these in detail in Chapters 10 and 11). Many preventive approaches promote social-emotional competence and skills for adapting to challenging contexts or ecological transitions from one context to another, such as entering school or becoming a parent (Weissberg et al., 2003).

## Microsystems

**Microsystems** are environments in which a person repeatedly engages in direct, personal interaction with others (Bronfenbrenner, 1979, p. 22). They include families, classrooms, friendship networks, athletic teams, musical groups, neighborhoods, residence hall wings, and self-help groups. In microsystems, individuals form interpersonal relationships, assume social roles, and share activities (Maton & Salem, 1995).

Microsystems are more than simply the sum of their individual members; they are social units with their own dynamics. For example, family therapists have long focused on how families function as systems beyond their individual members (Watzlawick et al., 1974). Members have roles, differential power in making decisions, reactions to the actions of other members, and so on.

**setting**
an important concept in community psychology that encompasses physical surroundings and relationships among individuals. It can span multiple places and can apply to microsystems and larger organizations.

**organizations**
large ecological systems with solid, clearly defined structures, including titles, missions, rules and policies, schedules, and hierarchies, among other things (e.g., workplaces, religious congregations, neighborhood associations, schools). They often consist of multiple microsystems and can be part of larger social units (e.g., a neighborhood association operates within a city).

**localities**
geographic settings within an ecological framework—such as counties, towns, neighborhoods, or even entire cities—that often contain multiple organizations or microsystems, including governments, economies, media outlets, and educational and health systems.

Microsystems can be important sources of support for their members but also sources of conflict and burdens.

The concept of a **setting** is important in community psychology (see Chapter 5). In this psychological usage of the term, setting is not simply a physical place but an enduring set of relationships among individuals that may be associated with one or several places. A chapter of a self-help group is a setting, even if its meeting place changes. Physical settings such as playgrounds, local parks, bars, or coffee shops may provide meeting places for microsystems. The term "setting" is applied to microsystems and to larger organizations.

## Organizations

**Organizations** are larger than microsystems and have a formal structure: a title, a mission, bylaws or policies, meeting or work times, supervisory relationships, and so on. Organizations studied by community psychologists include human service and health care settings, treatment programs, schools, workplaces, neighborhood associations, cooperative housing units, religious congregations, and community coalitions. These important forms of community affect whom people associate with, what resources are available to them, and how they define and identify themselves. Employed persons often introduce themselves by where they work.

Organizations often consist of sets of smaller microsystems. Classes, activities, departments, staff, administrators, and boards make up a school or college. Departments, shifts, or work teams make up a factory or restaurant. Religious congregations have choirs, religious classes, and prayer groups. Large community organizations usually work through committees. However, organizations are not simply the sum of their parts; the dynamics of the whole organization, such as its organizational hierarchy and its informal culture, are important.

In turn, organizations can be parts of larger social units. A local congregation may be part of a wider religious body, or a retail store part of a chain. A neighborhood association offers a way for citizens to influence city government. The largest organizations (e.g., international corporations, political parties, religious denominations) are macrosystems, which are discussed later.

## Localities

Although the term "community" has meanings at many levels of analysis, one prominent meaning refers to geographic **localities**, including rural counties, small towns, urban neighborhoods, or entire cities. Localities usually have governments; local economies; media; systems of social, educational, and health services; and other institutions that influence individual quality of life.

Localities may be understood as sets of organizations or microsystems. Individuals participate in the life of their shared locality mainly through

**macrosystems**
the largest systems within an ecological framework that form contexts that influence individuals, microsystems, organizations, and localities. These other ecological systems can in turn influence macrosystems through social advocacy or widespread action. Example macrosystems include cultures, political parties, corporations, religions, and governments.

**populations**
a broadly shared characteristic that links people together within a macrosystem. They can form the basis of a community (e.g., the Deaf community),

smaller groups. Even in small towns, individuals seldom influence the wider community unless they work alongside other citizens in an organization or microsystem. An association of neighborhood residents is an organization, while the entire neighborhood is a locality. That neighborhood may also host microsystems of teen friends, adults who meet for coffee, and parents and children who gather at a playground. However, a locality is not simply the sum of its citizens, microsystems, or community organizations. Its history, cultural traditions, and qualities as a whole community surround each of those levels.

An example of the linkage between organizations and localities is the development of community coalitions, composed of representatives of various community groups and organizations and formed to address wider community issues such as drug abuse or health concerns. While community coalitions may be a new concept for many of you, they are important elements of community psychology practice and have been shown to be effective in increasing and mobilizing community resources to achieve community goals (Bess, 2015; C. Harper et al., 2014; Oesterle et al., 2018; V. Shapiro et al., 2015). We discuss community coalitions in detail in Chapters 10, 11, and 13.

## Macrosystems

**Macrosystems** are the largest level of analysis in our system. While Figure 1.1 portrays only one macrosystem, in fact individuals, microsystems, organizations, and localities are all continually influenced by multiple macrosystems. Macrosystems include societies, cultures, political parties, social movements, corporations, international labor unions, multiple levels of government, international institutions, broad economic and social forces, and belief systems. Community psychology's perspective ultimately needs to be global.

Macrosystems exercise influence through policies and specific decisions, such as legislation and court decisions, and through promoting ideologies and social norms. Ideals of individual autonomy greatly influence U.S. culture and the discipline of psychology. Mass media communicate subtle forms of racial stereotyping and cultural expectations for thinness, especially for women. Macrosystems also form contexts within which the other levels function, such as how the economic climate affects businesses. But systems at other levels can influence macrosystems through social advocacy or through actions such as buying locally grown foods.

An important level of analysis that we include under macrosystems is the population. A **population** is defined by a broadly shared characteristic (e.g., gender, race, ethnicity, nationality, income, religion, sexual orientation, ability or disability status). Populations can be the basis of a broad form of community (e.g., the Jewish community, the gay community). However, not all individuals within a population will identify with it as a community.

Many studies in community psychology concern more than one level of analysis. For instance, a study of children in Head Start programs investigated

**mediating structures**

institutions that link individuals to public life, including formal organizations and settings (e.g., schools, churches) and less formal ones (e.g., self-help groups, clubs, organized supporters groups for a favorite sports team). They can act as a buffer in dealing with stressors from larger institutions (e.g., unemployment, discrimination) and can be important intervention points when helping communities.

neighborhood-, family-, and individual-level factors related to educational success. The researchers found that neighborhood-level factors (including the number of families of low or high socioeconomic status and the number of homes in which English was a second language) had significant *direct* effects on the cognition and behavior of children in Head Start (Vanden-Kiernan et al., 2010). These direct neighborhood-level effects were not mediated by such family-level factors as family structure, income, ethnicity, or family processes (e.g., amount of social support available to parents, parents' involvement in their children's education). What this means, for example, is that living in a neighborhood marked by concentrated poverty had a significant negative effect on the cognitive and behavioral development of children, even if those children lived in a two-parent home with high income and parents who were highly involved in their education. The negative neighborhood-level effects were strong enough to overwhelm any positive effects the children received from their parents. We discuss the strong effects of neighborhood context on child development in Chapter 5.

## What Do You Think?

1. What are the most important microsystems, organizations, localities, and macrosystems in your life? How are those settings related to each other?

2. Think about one specific setting in your life. What resources does it provide for you? What challenges or obligations does it present? What are its strengths and weaknesses?

3. Name something that you would like to change about that setting. Why?

4. At what level does that setting exist (microsystem, organization, locality, or macrosystem)? How would changing that setting affect settings at the other levels? How would changes at the other levels affect that setting?

## Levels of Intervention

Ecological levels of analysis are helpful tools in shifting perspective about where to look to improve social outcomes. Systematically examining an issue across levels of analysis can uncover multiple contributing factors to that issue. However, examining social issues across levels of analyses is not sufficient to promote change; that is, understanding where to look is only the first step of the community psychology shift in perspective.

One way in which levels of analysis can help suggest appropriate points of intervention is through the concept of **mediating structures**, "those institutions standing between the individual and his private life and the large institutions of public life" (Berger & Neuhaus, 1977, p. 2). Peter Berger and John

Neuhaus were sociologists who developed a strategy to promote well-being for individuals and communities by developing mediating structures. Central to this theory is that society can exert stressful conditions on individuals, some of whom have difficulty coping with these stressors. However, a strategy of promoting the development of mediating structures focuses on settings that can assist individuals in coping with society's stressors. In our ecological levels of analysis framework, these might be organizations (e.g., schools, mutual help groups, churches) or less formal settings. Community psychologists have been interested in the potential of settings that can serve as mediating structures—many of which are underutilized resources in communities already. In some cases, community psychologists focus on creating new alternative settings that better meet the needs of the individuals affected by the focal concern.

What to change and how to change it are crucial components of any change strategy. In the coming chapters, we elaborate on how and what to change. For this introduction of the community psychology perspective, we emphasize two related points that need to be paired with any consideration of ecological levels of analysis: problem definition and selection of interventions that are linked to ecological levels of analysis.

The focus of any change effort requires a problem definition to organize resources and action. It is critical to examine how a problem is framed and how this dictates interventions. In the example of homelessness presented earlier, if homelessness is defined as a problem with the person only (e.g., addiction, mental health, lack of job skills) or problem of the environment only (e.g., lack of affordable housing), the selected interventions will be quite different (e.g., a treatment for an individual deficit vs. the creation of a program to increase access to affordable housing). By focusing on a single level of analysis (e.g., individual problems), the intervention strategy is constrained to individual change efforts and will be ineffective in addressing homelessness if aspects of the problem at higher levels of analysis are not addressed (e.g., access to safe, affordable housing). Too often, the change strategy ignores or does not match the level of analysis. In North America, many communities have programs to help homeless individuals change but do little to address the lack of affordable housing. From a community psychology perspective, addressing such issues as homelessness or joblessness will require multiple interventions at more than one level of analysis. If interventions are not implemented at multiple levels of analysis, they will likely fail to effectively address the issue.

Furthermore, there are three ways that we may fall short of addressing issues even if we examine multiple levels of analyses. First, it may be that action is necessary but not taken (e.g., additional resources for treatment of homeless persons or affordable housing are not committed). Second, it may be that action is taken where it should not be (e.g., arresting homeless

**errors of logical typing**
taking action at the wrong ecological level (e.g., city ordinances that limit panhandling, which targets individual behaviors resulting from homelessness, not the root causes of homelessness within localities and macrosystems).

persons for sleeping on the street; how does this prevent homelessness?). Third, and perhaps more common, action is taken at the wrong level of analysis (e.g., the only action taken is passing city ordinances to limit panhandling or loitering—observable individual-level behaviors of some homeless persons that are troubling to many community members). In community psychology terms, this is referred to as an **error of logical typing** (Rappaport, 1977b; Watzlawick et al., 1974). While panhandling and loitering can be problematic, focusing change efforts on this individual level of analysis likely will not reduce homelessness. These efforts may also not reduce behaviors perceived to be problematic; rather, these behaviors will likely be moved to different locations as the root causes for homelessness have not been addressed.

How do community psychologists decide how to frame problem definitions? How can you choose which levels of analysis need to be included in an intervention strategy? In the next section, we present core values of community psychology that help guide these decisions.

## Eight Core Values in Community Psychology

**values**
deeply held ideals in individuals and communities about what is considered moral, right, or good. They can influence goals, the means to achieve those goals, or both. Community psychology is guided by eight core values, as shown in Exhibit 1.1.

*Our personal values about relationships, accountability, social change priorities, and our personal political world view all shape our priorities and agenda for community work.*
—M. A. Bond, 1989, p. 356

*Our work always promotes the ends of some interest group, even if we do not recognize that explicitly.*
—Riger, 1989, p. 382

Values play a central role in both research and social action. The decisions about what issues to investigate, how to research them or intervene, and who should be involved in those activities are all formed by the values of the people involved. This is true for all research and action, but for much of history the central role played by values in those activities has been largely ignored. Many of you are likely aware of the Tuskegee syphilis study conducted by the U.S. Public Health Service from 1932 to 1972 (CDC, n.d.). A research program that was intended to provide data supporting more resources for the treatment of syphilis in poor Black communities resulted in hundreds of men being denied effective treatment, even when it became available. There were many systemic failures responsible for this ethical catastrophe, but at the heart of them all were the values of the people designing and running the study. They valued the data they received from the men recruited for the study more than they valued the men themselves.

But what exactly do we mean by "values"? **Values** are deeply held ideals about what is moral, right, or good. They have emotional intensity; they are honored, not lightly held. Values may concern ends (goals), means (how to attain goals), or both. They are social; we develop values through experiences with others. Individuals hold values, but so do families, communities, and cultures. Values may be rooted in spiritual beliefs or practices but can also be secular. Many ethical conflicts involve choices about which of two worthy values is more important in a given situation (R. Campbell & Morris, 2017b; G. Nelson & Prilleltensky, 2010; O'Neill, 2005).

In community psychology, discussions of values are useful for several purposes. First, values help clarify choices for research and action. Even defining a problem is a value-laden choice, strongly influencing subsequent action (E. Seidman & Rappaport, 1986). Public definitions of community and social problems often reflect the worldviews of the powerful and thus help maintain the status quo. Attending to values can lead to questioning those dominant views.

Second, the discussion of values helps identify when actions and espoused values do not match (Rappaport, 1977a). Consider a community leader who helps found a neighborhood social center to empower teens who are gay, lesbian, bisexual, or questioning their sexuality. The leader decides how to renovate the space and plans all the programs, allowing the youth themselves little say. Despite the leader's intent, this actually disempowers the youth (Stanley, 2003). The leader talks the talk but does not walk the walk.

Or consider an alternative high school that seeks to empower students, their families, and teachers (Gruber & Trickett, 1987). But when decisions are to be made, the teachers have sources of day-to-day information and influence that students and parents lack; teachers thus dominate the discussion. Despite the espoused values of all involved, the organizational practices do not empower students and families. The problem is not individual hypocrisy but an organizational discrepancy between ideals and outcomes.

Third, understanding a culture or community involves understanding its distinctive values. For instance, Potts (2003) discussed the importance of Africanist values in a program for middle school African American youth. Native Hawaiian cultural conceptions of health are closely tied to values of *'ohana* and *lokahi* (family and community unity) and of interdependence of the land, water, and human communities. A health promotion program in Native Hawaiian communities needs to be interwoven with these values (Helm, 2003).

Fourth, community psychology has a distinctive spirit (J. G. Kelly, 2002)—a shared sense of purpose and meaning. That spirit is the basis of our commitment and what keeps us going when obstacles arise (J. G. Kelly, 2010). It is thoughtful but also passionate and pragmatic, embodied in research and action.

In our experience, the spirit of community psychology is based on eight core values, listed in Exhibit 1.1. Our discussion of these eight values is influenced

**Exhibit 1.1  Eight Core Values in Community Psychology**

1. **Social justice** is the fair and equitable distribution of resources, opportunities, obligations, and power across communities within a society. All members in a socially just society have the same rights and are subject to the same processes, which are developed collaboratively with input from all members of that society.

2. **Respect for human diversity** acknowledges and honors the variety of communities and social identities based on gender, ethnic or racial identity, nationality, sexual orientation, ability or disability, socioeconomic status, age, religious and spiritual beliefs, and other characteristics. Communities are understood on their own terms, and research, interventions, and other psychological work are tailored based on those terms.

3. **Sense of community** is a feeling of belongingness, interdependence, and mutual commitment that links individuals as a collective. It is integral to community and social action and is a resource for social support and clinical work.

4. **Collective wellness** is an overall sense of contentment within a community that balances the objective and subjective needs of all individuals and groups within that community and resolves conflicting needs for the general good.

5. **Empowerment and citizen participation** are essential components to all work in community psychology, ensuring that community involvement exists at all ecological levels in making decisions and that community members can exert control.

6. **Collaboration** entails an equal relationship between community psychologists and community members. Psychologists lend their expertise but do not assume a position of hierarchical superiority, giving citizens the opportunity to contribute their own knowledge, resources, and strengths.

7. **Empirical grounding** is using empirical research to make community action more effective and using the lessons from that work to make research more valid for understanding communities. Community psychologists also acknowledge that no research is unbiased, so they are open about values and the impact of context in their work.

8. **Multilevel, strengths-based perspective** avoids focusing only on the individual level and addresses all ecological levels of analysis, recognizing and integrating community strengths at these levels in the work of community psychology.

by, yet different from, the discussions of values by Isaac Prilleltensky and Geoffrey Nelson (2002; G. Nelson & Prilleltensky, 2010; Prilleltensky, 1997, 2001, 2012). These eight values are just one way of summarizing the field's values. In addition to these common values, each individual and working group within the field must decide what values will be central to their work. Our discussion here is intended to promote the discussion of these values and the issues they raise for community life. As M. A. Bond (1989) and Riger (1989) asserted in quotations at the beginning of this section, community psychology will be guided by some set of values and serve someone's interests, whether we realize it or not. It is better to discuss and choose our values and how to put them into action.

**distributive justice**
an aspect of social justice that involves the fair and equitable allocation of resources (e.g., money, access to quality education and healthcare) among community members.

**procedural justice**
an aspect of social justice ensuring that everyone within a setting has the same rights and is subject to the same rules and procedures. In law, it is understood as due process, but it applies to other settings as well.

## Social Justice

*Social justice* can be defined as the fair, equitable allocation of resources, opportunities, obligations, and power in society as a whole (Prilleltensky, 2001, p. 754). Social justice has two aspects especially important here. **Distributive justice** concerns the fair and equitable allocation of resources (e.g., money, access to good quality health services or education) among members of a social group. **Procedural justice** ensures that everyone has the same rights and is subject to the same procedures. Procedural justice is often understood in terms of due process in the legal system, but Prilleltensky (2012) argued for an expansion of that concept to include all settings and all relationships. So if two children commit the same transgression, they both receive the same treatment from their parents, and they both understand the basis of that treatment and consider it (reasonably) fair. Or if an organization has a pool of money to use for staff raises, everyone in the organization understands how the raises are distributed and considers that process fair. From a community psychology perspective of social justice, in order for processes to be just, everyone should be involved in their development. Following these definitions, a just setting is one in which every member receives an equitable share of the resources, everyone is involved in the development of the processes that govern the settings, and those processes are applied fairly.

Psychology's record of support for social justice in the United States has been mixed. It has sometimes been at the forefront of social justice struggles, as in the involvement of psychologists Mamie and Kenneth Clark and others in research cited in the 1954 school desegregation case *Brown v. Board of Education*. However, psychological research and practice has also had the effect of supporting sexism, racism, and other injustices, for instance in the area of intelligence testing (Gould, 1981; Prilleltensky & Nelson, 2002). The tradition of liberation psychology, rooted in Latin America, and the related fields of critical psychology and feminist psychology exemplify psychological pursuit of social justice (M. A. Bond et al., 2000a, 2000b; Martin-Baro, 1994; Montero, 1996; Prilleltensky & Nelson, 2002; Watts & Serrano-García, 2003).

## Respect for Human Diversity

This value recognizes and honors the variety of communities and social identities based on gender, ethnic or racial identity, nationality, sexual orientation, ability or disability, socioeconomic status and income, age, religious and spiritual beliefs, or other characteristics. Understanding individuals-in-communities requires understanding human diversity (Gomez & Yoshikawa, 2017; Trickett, 1996). Persons and communities are diverse, defying easy generalizations and demanding that they be understood in their own terms.

This is not a vague respect for diversity as a politically correct attitude. To be effective in community work, community psychologists must understand the traditions and folkways of any culture or distinctive community with whom they work (Gomez & Yoshikawa, 2017; O'Donnell, 2005). That includes appreciating how the culture provides distinctive strengths and resources for living. Researchers also need to adapt research methods and questions to be appropriate to a culture. This is more than simply translating questionnaires; it involves a thorough reexamination of the aims, methods, and expected products of research in terms of the culture to be studied.

Respect for diversity must be balanced with the values of social justice and sense of community—understanding diverse groups and persons while promoting fairness, seeking common ground, and avoiding social fragmentation (Prilleltensky, 2001). To do that, the first step is usually to study diversities in order to understand them. A related step is to respect others as fellow persons, even when you disagree. We explore the value of human diversity in relation to community psychology throughout the book and provide additional conceptual frameworks for understanding diversity in Chapter 7.

## Sense of Community

Sense of community is the center of some definitions of community psychology (Sarason, 1974). It refers to a perception of belongingness, interdependence, and mutual commitment that links individuals in a collective unity (D. McMillan & Chavis, 1986; Sarason, 1974). For example, community psychologists have studied sense of community in neighborhoods, schools and classrooms, mutual help groups, faith communities, workplaces, and internet virtual environments (e.g., Buckingham et al., 2018; Fisher, Sonn, & Bishop, 2002; Newbrough, 1996). Sense of community is a basis for community and social action as well as a resource for social support and clinical work. We discuss psychological sense of community in detail in Chapter 6.

## Collective Wellness

Community psychologist Isaac Prilleltensky (2012) defined wellness as "a positive state of affairs, brought about by the simultaneous and balanced satisfaction of diverse objective and subjective needs of individuals, relationships, organizations, and communities" (p. 2). This definition differs from others in its focus on multiple ecological levels. Prilleltensky believes that the concept of wellness extends beyond the individual. Organizations can experience varying degrees of wellness, as can communities and societies.

This definition also reflects the diversity embodied in those settings. The needs of individuals, families, communities, and societies are multiple, complex, and sometimes in conflict. It is in recognition of these points that we have chosen the term "collective wellness" to describe this value in community psychology. This value as it is reflected in the field of community psychology is further discussed in Chapters 7, 10, 11, and 13.

## Empowerment and Citizen Participation

You are probably familiar with the concept of empowerment viewed through an individualistic perspective—a feeling people experience of being able to exert power over their own lives. Community psychology views empowerment through ecological, collaborative, and structural perspectives; at multiple levels; and as a process rather than a feeling (Christens, 2019). *Empowerment* is the process of enhancing the possibilities for people to control their own lives (Rappaport, 1987). From this perspective, empowerment is an empirical construct. Tangible changes are made in settings that increase the opportunities for members to come together to exert control over how those settings function.

*Citizen participation* can be defined as "a process in which individuals take part in decision making in the institutions, programs and environments that affect them" (Wandersman et al., 1984, p. 339). Increased citizen participation both results from and contributes to increased empowerment. These values will be explored further in Chapter 8.

## Collaboration

Perhaps the most distinctive value of community psychology, long emphasized in the field, involves *relationships* between community psychologists and citizens and the *process* of their work (Case, 2017). Psychologists traditionally assume an "expert" role, which creates a hierarchical, unequal relationship of expert and client—useful in some contexts but often inappropriate for community work. Psychologists also traditionally address deficits in individuals (e.g., diagnosing a mental disorder), while community psychologists search for personal and community strengths that promote change. Community psychologists do have expertise to share with communities. However, they also need to honor the life experiences, wisdom, passionate zeal, social networks, organizations, cultural traditions, and other resources (in short, the community strengths) that already exist in a community. Building on these strengths is often the best pathway to overcoming problems (D. D. Perkins et al., 2004).

Furthermore, community psychologists seek to create a collaborative relationship with citizens so community strengths are available for use. In that relationship, both psychologist and citizens contribute knowledge and resources, and both participate in making decisions (Javdani et al., 2017; Kelly, 1986). For example, community researchers may design a study to meet the needs of citizens, share research findings with citizens in a form that they can use, and help use the findings to advocate for changes by decision makers. Developers of a community program would fully involve citizens in planning and implementing it.

### Empirical Grounding

This value refers to integrating research with community action, basing (grounding) action in empirical research findings whenever possible (Rappaport, 1977a; Tebes, 2017). This uses research to make community action more effective and makes research more valid for understanding communities. Community psychologists are impatient with theory or action that lacks empirical evidence and with research that ignores the context and interests of the community in which it occurred.

Community psychologists believe no research is value-free; it is always influenced by researchers' values and preconceptions and by the context in which the research is conducted. Drawing conclusions from research thus requires attention to values and context, not simply to the data (Tebes, 2017). This does not mean that researchers abandon rigorous research but that values and community issues that affect the research are discussed openly to promote better understanding of findings. We explore how the field of community psychology approaches this integration of research and values in Chapters 3 and 4.

### Multilevel, Strengths-Based Perspective

Earlier in this chapter we introduced the concept of ecological levels of analysis, each of which offers a unique perspective for understanding and defining areas of concern and identifying potential points of intervention. That emphasis on moving beyond an individual level of analysis, and the shift in perspective that requires, is a defining aspect of the field of community psychology.

Along with that focus on context and an imperative to recognize and work in the multiple settings that structure our lives, community psychology shares with other disciplines a strengths-based perspective (Maton, Humphreys, Jason, & Shinn, 2017; Rappaport, 1977a). This is the understanding that all individuals, families, organizations, and societies have significant strengths and that those strengths must be acknowledged, celebrated, and utilized in efforts to enhance collective wellness.

The community psychology value of a multilevel, strengths-based perspective is reflected throughout the field and is specifically addressed in Chapters 5, 10, 11, and 13.

## The Interrelationship of Community Psychology Values

Of course, none of the eight values we have presented can exist in isolation. For example, in Chapters 7, 10, and 11 we discuss how evidence-based prevention and promotion programs (which are empirically grounded) should embody a multilevel, strengths-based perspective; be designed and implemented based on a collaborative, empowering relationship with the community; be adapted

**Box 1.2    Community Psychology in Action: Tom Wolff and Community Coalitions**

Community psychologist Tom Wolff was engaged by a community health coalition to work with local citizens to plan health initiatives. He held an evening meeting open to all citizens. At such a meeting, one might expect to discuss a lack of affordable health care in the community, a need for health promotion and prevention programs, or mutual help groups. Instead, the most important need identified by many citizens was for street signs! Wolff barely contained his amazement. Yet recently in this community, emergency medical care had been delayed several times, with serious consequences, because ambulances could not locate residences.

Wolff duly noted this concern, then sought to turn the conversation to matters fitting his preconceptions. However, the local citizens would not have it; they wanted a plan for action on street signs. When that need had been met, they reasoned, they could trust the health coalition to work with them on other issues. Wolff then shifted to working with the citizens to get the municipality to erect street signs. Instead of pursuing his own agenda, he worked with citizens to accomplish their goals (Wolff & Lee, 1997).

**What Do You Think?**

1. What community psychology values are reflected in Tom Wolff's work?
2. How did recognizing and implementing these values affect his ability to effectively work with the health coalition?
3. Can you imagine yourself being part of a coalition in your community working together to solve a community problem? How might community psychology values affect your approach to that work?

to reflect the diversity, history, and culture(s) of that community; and hopefully result in increased sense of community, increased collective wellness, and, ultimately, increased social justice.

This seems like a lot to expect from what are, in many cases, small interventions, but think back to the discussion of the evidence on youth inquiry approaches earlier in this chapter. There is a growing body of evidence for their efficacy at promoting change at multiple ecological levels, which results in increased collective wellness and a sense of community. They are based on a recognition of the existing strengths of children and adolescents and, often, on an explicit recognition of their diversity. Ultimately, they result in changed roles, increased power and recognition for youth in their communities, and a more equitable distribution of resources, even if only in relatively small ways. Community psychology practitioner Tom Wolff presents an example of small wins from his work in Box 1.2.

Not all interventions are small ones. In Chapter 13, we discuss public policy work, which can produce impacts at local, regional, national, and international levels. But large or small, the goal of community psychology is to promote the vision of Martin Luther King, Jr., and engage in creative maladjustment. The goal is to advance social justice.

## Overview of This Book

In this chapter, we discussed the shift in perspective that is central to community psychology and the values of the field. In Chapter 2, we present how the field developed core methods and concepts or adapted them to act on this shift in perspective. Chapters 3 and 4 deal with the research methods that underlie community research and how those methods derive from the basic values of the field. Chapters 5–9 present some underlying concepts of the field and the theories and research related to them. These chapters present the field's approach to understanding communities. Chapters 10–12 present a major focus of intervention in community psychology: the prevention of disorder; the promotion of wellness for individuals, families, and organizations; and the implementation and evaluation of programs designed to meet those goals. Chapter 13 extends community psychology's approach to change to the community and society levels. In Chapter 14, the final chapter, we talk about some challenges and opportunities facing the field and encourage you to think about how you can use tools of community psychology as citizens, in human services careers, or even as aspiring community psychologists.

At the beginning of each chapter in this book, we present an opening exercise that is designed to help you explore community psychology. The exercise might present an opportunity for a shift in perspective or an expansion of what it means to engage in psychology. In many of the chapters, we also present stories of Community Psychology in Action, focusing on the personal stories of people doing community work. We also present similar Changing Perspectives features with examples that encourage you to look at the world in a different way and perhaps revisit your preconceived notions and biases. Along these lines, we present self-reflection questions that ask you to engage more directly with the material on a more personal and meaningful level.

## Using Respectful Language to Discuss Social Identities

As noted earlier in this chapter, respect for human diversity is a core value of community psychology. Language is a key factor in conveying this respect, particularly by referring to individuals and groups using their preferred self-identifying labels. In this book, we therefore refer to specific individuals and groups based on how they self-identify. We also try to use inclusive language when referring to groups more broadly. However, sometimes different members of the same community prefer different labels. For example, "Latina," "Latino," "Latinx," "Hispanic," and other terms may be appropriate when referring to some people from Spanish-speaking or Latin American cultural backgrounds but also inappropriate when referring to others from those backgrounds. We sometimes use "Latinx" as a broad, gender-neutral term, but using this term can also sometimes diminish the experiences of Latina women. We encourage you to use more appropriate language as needed when referring to your own social identities, those of your classmates, or anyone else, whether those identities concern ethnicity, gender, ability or disability status, or any other characteristic that is important to someone.

## Learning Goals

While we hope that by the end of this book some of you will consider further education in community psychology, we realize that for many of you, this may be your only formal involvement with the field. However, it is our firm belief that all of you will—at various times in your life—be involved in initiatives that will benefit from the theories, research, and skills we present in this book. While the number of people who formally identify themselves as community psychologists may be relatively small, the influence of the field is much larger than those numbers would suggest. Community psychology theories and research are reflected or directly cited in the work of public health experts, social workers, sociologists, public officials, and other psychologists.

We hope that you finish this book with several accomplishments:

- a better understanding of community psychology;

- increased skills for working effectively in diverse contexts and communities;

- a greater appreciation of the intertwining of individual, community, and society;

- a greater awareness of your own values;

- a willingness to explore the many sides of community and social issues; and

- a passionate engagement in changing your communities and society for the better.

We came to community psychology because it engaged our minds, our values, and our lives. We hope this book does that for you.

## For Review

### Discussion Questions

1. Go back to the opening exercise in this chapter about the untested sexual assault kits. How have your answers to those questions changed after reading the chapter?

2. In what ways do your values align with those of community psychology?

3. Think of a current issue you care about in a community of which you are a member. Using the ideas and approaches discussed in this chapter, how might you analyze and define that issue?

4. How might you create an intervention to address that issue?

### Key Terms

community psychology, 3

individualistic perspective, 6

structural perspective, 6

context, 10

first-order change, 12

second-order change, 12

individual, 17

microsystems, 17

setting, 18

organizations, 18

localities, 18

macrosystems, 19

populations, 19

mediating structures, 20

errors of logical typing, 22

values, 22

distributive justice, 25

procedural justice, 25

### Learn More

A detailed summary of the chapter, along with other review materials, is available on the *Community Psychology, Fourth Edition* companion website at http://pubs.apa.org/books/supp/kloos4/.

Rather than providing mental health care in large hospitals, community psychologists like George Fairweather sought to develop new ways of supporting participation in community life for ex-patients.

Steve Heap/Shutterstock.com

# 2 The Development and Practice of Community Psychology

## Looking Ahead

**After reading this chapter you will be able to answer these questions:**

1. Which theories and practices enabled the new field of community psychology to act upon its shift in perspective?
2. How is community psychology a linking science? How is it a linking practice?
3. What are some ways community psychology is practiced around the world?
4. How have social forces shaped the development of community psychology? How do they shape the field today?

## Opening Exercise

## Searching for Different Ways to "Do Psychology"

In 1960, George W. Fairweather accepted an exciting new project in his role as a psychologist at a VA hospital in California. He and his colleagues had the responsibility to design a program to make de-institutionalization of mental hospitals feasible. The conditions of many state mental hospitals had become oppressive, with documented cases of neglect and maltreatment that resulted in court intervention to mandate more humane care (Applebaum, 1999; Chamberlin, 1978). Fairweather and colleagues wanted to help longtime patients move into community settings to live independently rather than staying in hospitals. This was an ambitious goal because most of the mental health care available at the time was designed to be delivered in large institutions removed from society. Many patients had lived at the mental hospital for years. Fairweather and colleagues worked hard to develop a program to train patients in life skills needed to live independently. They taught patients skills related to keeping an apartment and maintaining connections to treatment while they still resided in the hospital, and they encouraged patients to exercise more autonomy in their activities. The psychologists were excited to create a new model of care that would not rely on services within a large institution. In preparing the individuals to move, they focused on developing the abilities of patients who were identified as being ready to leave the hospital. However, despite their efforts to prepare patients for community living, the program did not go as planned. When the patients left the hospital, many became overwhelmed or lost contact with their treatment; many did not do well living on their own and returned for institutional care.

Rather than give up, Fairweather and colleagues realized that they needed to shift their perspective on what was needed to support ex-patients living in the community. Instead of focusing primarily on preparing persons to fit into community settings before leaving the hospital, they reconceptualized their task as being located outside the hospital. They needed to create settings that could support living in community and link ex-patients with resources. That is, rather than focusing on changing individuals, Fairweather and colleagues needed to find ways to support ex-patients that went beyond their standard practice of clinical psychology. Their shift in perspective to support community living for ex-patients required them to find new ways of doing psychology.

Fairweather and colleagues decided that they needed to create a new setting, take on new roles as staff, encourage new roles for ex-patients, and propose new goals for resident success beyond controlling symptoms and staying out of the hospital. They developed a community resource program to encourage independent living. First, they created an alternative setting that they called a "community lodge" where ex-patients could live together with support to take responsibility for operating the residence themselves. It was a radical notion at the time that a group of people with serious psychological disorders— working together and helping each other in their own daily lives—could live together successfully outside the hospital. Next, the psychologists changed their role and activities

to be consultants, supporters, and advocates rather than clinicians. They initially focused on setting up rules and supervising operation of this new setting but progressively transitioned to encouraging resident decision making and operation of activities and, eventually, to resident leadership of the lodge. With support of these psychologist consultants, residents founded a business to provide employment and resident governance of the lodge. The success of the community lodge contradicted many mental health professionals' assumptions about the capabilities of persons with mental disorders. Its success was principally due to the emergence of unrecognized strengths and mutual support among its participants.

An important point in any community partnership comes when citizens assert control. Fairweather later described the poignant moment when the first lodge members thanked him for his efforts but also stated "it's time for you to go." Fairweather termed this a "horrible moment for a professional," yet he understood and accepted their decision. The lodge had become its own community, and the presence of a professional, however well-intentioned and supportive, would hinder its future development. Fairweather shocked mental health professionals when he described the desired outcomes of the community lodge program as being "full citizenship," "meaningful roles in society," and "equal social status" for ex-patients. As we discuss more in Chapter 5, the original lodge and others have enjoyed sustained success (Fairweather, 1994; J. G. Kelly, 2003).

Fairweather's shift in perspective to support community living for ex-patients required him and his colleagues to find new ways of doing psychology. He used the lessons learned from the community lodge effort to help shape the development of community psychology in the United States, in part by founding a graduate training program, the Ecological-Community Psychology Program at Michigan State University.

## What Do You Think?

1. How would you promote full citizenship and equal social status for people who are marginalized and excluded from meaningful roles in society (e.g., those who are homeless)?

2. How does the psychologists' approach in the lodge example compare to your expectations of how psychologists help people?

3. How can the lessons learned from the lodge program be applied to other social issues (e.g., substance abuse, poverty)?

**linking science**
looks for relationships among factors across multiple ecological levels, including individuals, microsystems, localities, and macrosystems. Through this approach, community psychology seeks a comprehensive understanding of what influences the health and well-being of individuals and communities.

In Chapter 1, we introduced community psychology as an alternative framework for how problems might be defined and addressed. These shifts in perspective required community psychology to develop alternative ways of "doing psychology." Like any field, community psychology did not develop in a vacuum. Similar to the Fairweather lodge example, looking for new ways of doing psychology can be a response to limitations of current practice. As we present in this chapter, it can also be a reaction to dissatisfaction with the status quo and looking integrate one's values into practice. Doing psychology also requires us to respond to current events and social forces of the time. We argue that contextual factors challenge the field to develop better ways of understanding challenges and better ways to address challenges. Social forces influenced the foundation of the field and continue to shape its practice today.

The viewpoints we present here are not the only ways to view the development and practice of community psychology. Our goal is to stimulate your critical thinking about psychology as a field and to create dialogue about how we can respond to current social issues as citizens and as professionals. Writing from our experience, we focus the chapter on the development of community psychology in North America while we draw upon the work of colleagues to recognize its international roots and illustrate that community psychology is a global field.

# Community Psychology as a Linking Science and a Linking Practice

How can psychology be done differently? Community psychology aims to be a linking science and linking practice (Stark, 2012). As a **linking science**, community psychology looks for relationships among factors across micro to macro levels of analysis to construct a more comprehensive understanding of what can influence the health and well-being of individuals and communities. Many social and health sciences focus on one level of analysis (e.g.,

**linking practice**
brings together multiple community stakeholders, including members who are often overlooked, to address community issues. Community psychology uses this approach to develop comprehensive, collaborative interventions.

individual, societal). As a **linking practice**, community psychology brings together multiple community stakeholders, some of whom are often overlooked, to address community issues (J. H. Dalton & Wolfe, 2012). For prevention of children's educational and behavioral problems, these stakeholders may include students, parents, teachers, and administrators but also leaders from neighborhoods, civic and religious organizations, businesses, and government agencies. The work of a community psychologist often focuses on bringing people together to address common concerns.

Second, consider how community psychology links how we define problems to how we address them. Community psychology explicitly connects its core values and levels of analysis to defining social problems. For example, consider efforts to promote children's academic achievement and avoid school dropout. A focus on how experiences in a school (i.e., organizational level of analysis) contribute to students' problems would lead to efforts to change classroom practices or policies in school. However, with the same concern, we might ask different questions and take different action if we focused on children's experiences in a neighborhood (i.e., locality level of analysis) or the funding of schools (i.e., policy of a locality) or racism (e.g., societal levels of analysis). The level of analysis that we use to define a problem constricts which interventions are considered to be appropriate. Stated another way, community psychologists might encourage stakeholders to reexamine how problems are defined to change the approaches selected for intervention. Community psychology systematically considers different levels of analysis in analyzing how problems are defined and addressed. Furthermore, community psychology looks to explicitly link its values to its practice. As the core values of collaboration and empowerment presented in Chapter 1 suggest, community psychologists deliberately reach out to work with others to address community-based challenges. The metaphor of linking helps (a) explain the purpose of the field and (b) describe what community psychologists do. This is why we have titled our book *Community Psychology: Linking Individuals and Communities.*

# The Practice of Psychology in the 20th Century

Community psychology in the United States and Canada developed in the historical and cultural context of mid-20th-century society and psychology. Psychology as a field was greatly influenced by the aftermath of two world wars and various social movements around the world. To understand the development of community psychology, we must go back to "before the beginning" (Sarason, 1974) to set the stage. First, we consider two characteristics of U.S. psychology that led psychologists to look for new models to conduct research and interventions: an overly individualistic focus and a limited interest in cultural understandings on human behavior.

## Individualistic Practice

*If [early psychologists] had put not one but two or three animals in a maze, we would have had a more productive conception of human behavior and learning. (Sarason, 2003a, p. 101)*

Psychology, especially in the United States, has traditionally defined itself as the study of the individual organism. Even social psychologists have primarily studied the cognitions and attitudes of individuals. The tradition of behaviorism includes the importance of environment but has seldom studied sociocultural variables. Psychodynamic, humanistic, and cognitive perspectives have primarily focused on individuals rather than their environments. A focus on individuals has had considerable benefits for the development of psychology, but it also has limitations that created the need for alternative viewpoints, including those of community psychology.

Similarly, professional psychological practice focuses primarily on interventions with individuals. The psychometric study of individual differences has long been linked to testing in schools and workplaces. Individuals are measured, sorted, and perhaps changed, but the environments of classroom and worksite seldom receive such scrutiny. In addition, much of Western psychotherapy is based on the assumptions of individual primacy. The client focuses inward to find new ways of living that yield greater personal happiness. Concern for others is assumed to automatically follow from this concern for self (Bellah et al., 1985). This approach is often helpful. However, it overlooks interpersonal, community, and social resources for recovery that can be important for individual, family, and community well-being. In general, an individual focus emphasizes self-fulfillment and says little about commitment to others. In many Western societies, an individualistic perspective frames the ways we view ourselves. This cultural emphasis on an individual perspective has had a powerful influence on how the discipline of psychology conceptualizes helping people and the role of psychologists in our society.

Alternatively, many of us can think of examples of how changes in organizations, communities, or society have affected quality of life for individuals. While individually based research, testing, and psychotherapy have been helpful, psychology is severely limited in how it can understand and help people when it is overly reliant on individualistic methods. To be a robust field, psychology needs a broader range of methods. Community psychology seeks to expand how we do psychology.

Psychology in North America did not have to develop with so much focus on the individual. Two prominent early psychologists, John Dewey and Kurt Lewin, defined psychology as the study of how individuals are related to their sociocultural environment (Sarason, 1974, 2003a). Lightner Witmer opened the Psycho-Educational Clinic in Philadelphia in 1896, the first psychological clinic in the United States. Witmer asserted that every child can learn and sought to change teaching methods to fit the needs of each child. He also worked collaboratively with public schools. About the same time, W. E. B. Du Bois challenged the definition of "the Negro problem" in Philadelphia and its focus on the deficits of Black individuals by conducting one of the first systematic social science surveys. Du Bois documented a diverse community of African Americans living in the city's Seventh Ward that had a range of strengths. He concluded that residents did not face one problem but a range of social problems, including discrimination and unequal opportunity (Sundquist, 1996). In Chicago, Jane Addams and others led the settlement house movement as a community-based response to the needs of newer immigrants. They focused on making social connections and participating in community life as well as addressing individual needs (Addams, 1910). Events in Europe also had an impact on the development of U.S. psychology in studying individuals in relation to their social environments. Kurt Lewin and Marie Jahoda fled Europe during the rise of Nazi Germany. Based on their experiences, they asked new research questions focused on social relations and contextual factors related to health, and they demonstrated how research could be used as an active force to improve the social world. These early developers of psychology and social science laid the groundwork that would later be picked up in forming community psychology. Despite these examples, most psychological practice focused on individual disorders and on professional treatment, primarily with adults.

## Psychology in Cultural Perspective

For most of its history, North American psychology has been primarily conceptualized, researched, and practiced by men of European ancestry. When women were included in research studies, it was often within a theoretical framework based on male experience. It was rare that the experiences of persons of different racial and ethnic backgrounds were the focus of study until recently. Basing our understanding of human experience on a limited sample is a problem if one wants to claim that research findings are largely universal across contexts and people. As more women and persons of color conduct and participate in psychological studies, a broader range of questions are being asked and a deeper understanding of human experience is being constructed. Contemporary discussions of cultural influences on behavior, interdependence in relationships, and the relationships of individuals to communities are important for community psychology, as we discuss in Chapter 7. Consideration of the diversity of human experience continues to be a concern for much of psychology (e.g., Gone et al., 2017; Jagers et al., 2017; Sánchez et al., 2017; Tran & Chan, 2017).

From a cross-cultural perspective, many psychological concepts and ways of intervening would be very different if they were based in cultural understanding (Gone, 2011). High self-esteem, prized in individualistic cultures, could be considered an excessive focus on oneself in cultural contexts that emphasize interdependence among group members (Gergen, 1973). Similarly, seeking to control events and outcomes in one's life might communicate a lack of respect for others in some cultural contexts. Social conformity, something to be resisted in the worldview of Western individualism, could be interpreted as behavior cementing the solidarity of an important group in a collectivist cultural context. This is not to say that individualistic concepts are mistaken, simply that they are not universal.

Power and control are psychological concepts especially influenced by individualistic thinking (Christens, 2019; Gone, 2011; Riger 1993). Psychologists often have focused on whether an autonomous individual can exercise control over their circumstances. The belief that one has such internal control is often associated with measures of psychological adjustment in individualistic contexts (Rotter, 1990). The concept of internal control assumes an independent self with a clear boundary between self and others. While applicable in individualistic contexts, such a view does not hold in contexts where interdependence is prized: in non-Western cultures or in close-knit communities in Western cultures (van Uchelen, 2000). Individuals in more collectivistic contexts assume that to exert control, they must cooperate with others. This weakens the psychological distinction between "internal" and "external" control. Moreover, feminist thinkers (e.g., J. B. Miller, 1976; Riger, 1993) have noted that psychological conceptions of control often equate pursuit of one's goals or interests with dominating others. Yet greater control of one's circumstances often can be pursued through cooperation (D. H. Shapiro et al., 1996; van Uchelen, 2000).

These examples are only a few of the issues for which cultural awareness is needed in psychology. Community psychology aims to study individuals within cultural and social contexts. Yet, as we shall see in this and later chapters, this aim is not always easily put into practice. Community psychology represents both a reaction to the limitations of mainstream psychology and an extension of it. The field developed through this tension and continues to experience it today. To understand further how the field has developed in North America, we briefly consider historical events during the mid-20th century.

# The Formative Contexts of Community Psychology

## The Growth of Psychology After World War II

During the 1930s and 1940s, most countries of the world were confronted with a disastrous economic depression and involvement in World War II, which had wide-ranging effects on social life. While fighting and casualties were limited on U.S. and Canadian territory, the social forces of the depression and war shaped community life in ways that had not been expected. Women entered the paid workforce in unprecedented numbers. Many of them were laid off at the war's end, yet their competence had been established and helped fuel later feminist efforts. Black people and other persons of color served their country and returned home less willing to tolerate racial discrimination. American troops of Japanese ancestry earned recognition for bravery while, at home, persons of Japanese descent in Canada and the United States were incarcerated in detention camps. Anti-Semitism, which had been openly practiced in academia and elsewhere, lost influence in the wake of the Holocaust. Social forces and environmental factors in people's lives were accepted as major influences and, thus, the focus of study and intervention.

Similarly, large-scale interventions were seen to be effective during the 1930s and 1940s. Roosevelt's New Deal created social safety net structures (e.g., Social Security) that continue to this day in the United States. The social policy established by the postwar GI Bill sent large numbers of veterans to college, broadened the focus of universities, and helped spur economic development, although we should note that many veterans of color were excluded. A new postwar government in Canada created universal health care, veterans' pensions, and social welfare for older adults. Government policy was seen as an active force in promoting individual and community well-being. If the government could organize a response to win a world war fought on three different continents, what could it not do? In terms of health care, widespread psychological problems among combat veterans led the U.S. and Canadian governments to fund the expansion of clinical psychology training and helped establish the modern field of clinical psychology. There was a belief that we could improve society with policy and resources. Similarly, countries in Western Europe began exploring ways that they might cooperate economically and politically, resulting in the creation of the European Union and a common currency. Many countries created new initiatives to address human needs and avoid the pain and suffering inflicted by economic crisis and war.

These events set in motion important changes in societies during the 1950s to the 1980s that have led to the emergence of community psychology across the world (Reich et al., 2017). We describe five forces that influenced the emergence of community psychology in the United States and still influence its development. Admittedly, this framework oversimplifies the many factors involved; see M. Levine et al. (2005) for a detailed alternative account of these origins. These forces reflect increasingly community-oriented thinking about personal and social problems:

- interest in preventive perspectives
- reforms in mental health systems
- developments in group dynamics research and action
- movements for social change and liberation
- optimism about social change efforts

Some of these factors have been important for the development of community psychology in other countries, as we discuss later in the chapter. The relative importance of each factor varies based on national and regional contexts. For our discussion, we begin with examples from the United States, where community psychology presents itself as an academic discipline and field of practice.

## Preventive Perspectives on Problems in Living

*No mass disorder afflicting humankind has ever been eliminated or brought under control by attempts at treating the affected individual. (Gordon, quoted by Albee, 1996)*

The first of these forces was the development of a preventive perspective on mental health services. Looking for alternative ways of thinking about mental health, early community psychologists drew on the concept from public health. The field of public health is more concerned with preventing illness than treating it. Prevention may take a variety of forms: sanitation, vaccination, education, early detection and treatment. Moreover, public health takes a population perspective, focusing on control or prevention of disease within a community or society, not merely for an individual. As implied in the quotation above, long-term successes in controlling diseases such as smallpox and polio have come from preventive public health programs, not from treating persons already suffering from the disease. (Treatment is humane but does not lead to wider control of disease.) Responding to a greater need for mental health services after World War II, a few psychiatrists began applying public health perspectives that emphasized environmental factors in mental disorder. They proposed early intervention for psychological problems and community-based services as primary modes of intervention rather than isolation in hospital settings. Furthermore, they wanted to use community strengths to prevent problems in living (G. Caplan, 1961; D. C. Klein & Lindemann, 1961). This new approach emphasized the importance of life crises and transitions as the points of preventive intervention for mental health services. Rather than waiting for full-blown disorders to develop, the mental health clinics could develop education about coping and support for the bereaved to have a preventive effect.

A public health prevention model was also applied to programs that addressed mental health needs of children in schools. In 1953 in St. Louis County, Missouri, psychologist John Glidewell joined Margaret Gildea to establish programs in schools and with parents designed to prevent behavior disorders in children (Glidewell, 1994). In 1958, Emory Cowen and colleagues began the Primary Mental Health Project in the elementary schools of Rochester, New York, seeking to detect early indicators of school maladjustment in students and intervene before full-blown problems appeared (Cowen et al., 1973). Although not within a public health framework, another early program in schools was noteworthy. Seymour Sarason and colleagues at the

Yale Psycho-Educational Clinic began collaborating with schools and other institutions for youth in 1962. (Sarason took the clinic's name from Lightner Witmer's early clinic mentioned above.) Working alongside school staff, the clinic staff sought to understand the culture of the school and to identify and foster contexts of productive learning to promote youth development. The clinic focused on understanding and changing settings, not just individuals, taking an ecological approach that foreshadowed important community psychology themes (Sarason, 1972, 1995a). These innovative programs involved collaboration with community members that helped initiate second-order change. They also evaluated their efforts with empirical research. Thus, they helped forge the community psychology values of wellness, community collaboration, and empirical grounding.

While prevention encountered sharp resistance by advocates of traditional clinical care, prevention perspectives have entered evidence-based psychology and medicine. As discussed in Chapters 10 and 11, prevention collaboration with colleagues in public health has continued (D. D. Perkins & Schensul, 2017).

## Reforms in Mental Health Systems

*They had more patients than beds, more patients than blankets. It was run like a feudal estate that turned money back to the state every year. . . . One of our group documented all these things and brought it to the state legislature, which had a special session and appropriated more money for all the state hospitals. . . . This is an example of how, if you take action, good things can happen. (Edgerton, 2000)*

A second force leading to the emergence of community psychology involved sweeping changes in the mental health care systems in North America. These began with World War II and continued into the 1960s (M. Levine, 1981; Sarason, 1988). After the war, a flood of veterans returned to civilian life traumatized by war. In the United States, the Veterans Administration (VA) was created to care for the unprecedented numbers of veterans with medical problems, including mental disorders. In Canada, the National Health Grants Program and Veterans Affairs Canada were established to address these needs. In addition, the U.S. National Institute of Mental Health (NIMH) was established after World War II to coordinate funding for mental health research and training. These federal initiatives relied heavily on the field of psychology (J. G. Kelly, 2003).

These events led to a rapid expansion of the field of clinical psychology and continue to influence it today. Clinical training became a specialized program within university psychology departments. Clinical skills were primarily learned in medical settings (often VA hospitals, working with adult male veterans). This medical approach to psychology was codified at the Boulder Conference in 1948. Its emphasis on individual psychotherapy was a product of the needs of the VA and the treatment orientation of a medical model. The environmental perspective of Witmer's and other early psychological clinics offered an alternative path for the development of psychology, but it was largely overlooked (Humphreys, 1996; Sarason, 2003a).

A movement for reform in the quality of mental health care also emerged in the postwar society (M. Levine, 1981; Sarason, 1974). This movement called for reducing the reliance on large mental health hospitals to treat individuals' mental health problems. Journalistic accounts and films documented inhumane conditions in psychiatric hospitals, and citizen groups advocated reform. Advances in psychiatric medication made prolonged hospitalization less necessary and strengthened reform efforts. Over the past 50 years, the number of regional mental hospitals has been greatly reduced throughout most industrialized countries; many have been closed and deemed not worth reforming (Kloos, 2010). Between 1972 and 1982, the number of hospitals with over 1,000 psychiatric beds was reduced by 50%–80% in Denmark, England, Ireland, Italy, Spain, and Sweden (Freeman et al., 1985). Similar patterns occurred in North America and Australia (Carling, 1995; Newton et al., 2000). With so many large mental hospitals closing, new models of care were needed.

In the 1960s, systematic studies of the mental health care systems of Canada and the United States recommended changes. The Canadian Mental Health Association's 1963 report *More for the Mind* argued that the mental health care system should be organized in the same professional manner and with similar resources as those for physical illnesses and should provide community-based services (Lurie & Goldbloom, 2016). In the United States, the Joint Commission on Mental Illness and Mental Health (1961) recommended sweeping changes in mental health care. In one of the commission's studies, psychologist George Albee (1959) reviewed research that documented surprisingly high rates of mental disorders, compared these results with the costs of training clinical professionals, and concluded that the nation could never afford to train enough professionals to provide clinical care for all who needed it. Albee and others called for mental health care to create an emphasis on prevention. Psychologist Marie Jahoda headed efforts to broaden thinking about mental illness by defining qualities of positive mental health, a forerunner of current concepts of wellness, resilience, and strengths (see Box 2.1 for a Changing Perspectives feature describing Jahoda's work). Jahoda also advocated for (a) identifying conditions that inhibited personal mental health and (b) working to change those conditions through prevention and social action (Albee, 1996; J. G. Kelly, 2003). However, in their final report, most joint commission members remained committed to individualized professional treatment (M. Levine, 1981).

As a response to these reports, the federal governments of Canada and the United States proposed creating a system of community mental health centers (CMHCs). With the support of President Kennedy, whose sister suffered from a mental disorder, and through timely advocacy by members of Congress, NIMH, and the National Mental Health Association, Congress passed the Community Mental Health Centers Act in 1963. CMHCs were given a different mandate from traditional psychiatric hospitals, including care for persons with mental disorders in the community, crisis intervention and emergency services, consultation with community agencies (e.g., schools, human services, police), and prevention programs (Goldston, 1994; M. Levine, 1981). Indeed, in many countries, CMHCs were founded with the charge of developing care for serious mental health problems within the community contexts where people lived so that they would not have to go to hospitals (Kloos, 2020). The implementation of the CMHC approach also laid the groundwork for the emergence of community psychology.

---

**Box 2.1 Changing Perspectives: Marie Jahoda—A "Foremother" of Community Psychology**

The work of Marie Jahoda, a social psychologist, foreshadowed and influenced today's community psychology. In 1930, Jahoda and her associates formed an interdisciplinary team to research the psychological effects of unemployment (Jahoda et al., 1933/1971). They studied Marienthal, an Austrian village where the principal workplaces closed as worldwide economic depression deepened. Their study was the first to connect unemployment with psychological experiences, which ranged from resignation and despair to practical coping and hardy resilience. The research team focused on studying the community as well as individuals and used documents, questionnaires, interviews, individual and family histories, and participant and nonparticipant observation. They collaborated as partners with community members and found practical ways to serve the community. They sought to understand Marienthal in its own terms, not to test hypotheses for generalization to other locales. Their research has influenced much later work, including community psychology research today (Fryer & Fagan, 2003; J. G. Kelly, 2003). When fascists took power in Austria, Jahoda was jailed for her association with socialist political groups, then allowed to emigrate to Britain; she also lived in the United States (R. Unger, 2001).

Partly because of Jahoda's research on resilience and strengths among Marienthal families, in the 1950s the U.S. Joint Commission on Mental Illness and Mental Health asked her to lead an interdisciplinary committee to define positive mental health, not simply as absence of mental disorder but as the presence of positive qualities. The group's report identified criteria of positive mental health, including a strong personal identity; motivation for psychological growth; pursuit of values; resilience under stress; independent choices and actions; empathy; and adequacy in love, work, play, and interpersonal relations. Jahoda and associates concluded that positive mental health is a value-laden concept influenced by social context. For instance, they argued that autonomy is a key component of positive mental health for Western cultures, whereas it may be less important elsewhere (Jahoda, 1958/1980; Jahoda, in J. G. Kelly, 2003). The report defined qualities of persons, but not of conditions, that might foster mental health. Yet it was an important advance, foreshadowing current concepts of community psychology and positive psychology.

## What Do You Think?

1. How does Marie Jahoda's work represent a shift away from historically individualistic approaches in psychology?
2. How are the values of community psychology reflected in her work?
3. What implications does her work have for how psychology can be practiced?

**action research**
research that informs and contributes to positive social change. Participatory action research in particular is collaborative in nature, empowering community members to be active participants who guide the research process.

**group dynamics**
the study of how groups form, how people interact with each other in groups, and how groups can impact their members attitudes and behaviors.

## Group Dynamics and Action Research

*Kurt Lewin was not concerned with research topics considered "proper" within psychology, but with understanding interesting situations. . . . Lewin was a creative person who liked to have other people create with him. (Zander, 1995)*

A third force influencing the development of community psychology in the United States originated in social psychology: the group dynamics and action research traditions that began with Kurt Lewin (J. G. Kelly, 2003; Marrow, 1969; Zander, 1995).

Lewin spent much of his career demonstrating to laboratory-based psychologists and to citizens that social action and research could be integrated in ways that strengthen both. He is known for asserting "there is nothing so practical as a good theory" (Marrow, 1969). Lewin was a founder of the Society for the Psychological Study of Social Issues (SPSSI), long an important voice in U.S. psychology. During the 1940s, as a Jewish refugee from Nazi Germany, he became interested in how the study of group dynamics could be used to address social and community problems.

The first community problem addressed by the Lewin action research team was not formal mental health issues. The team was asked to help develop methods to reduce anti-Semitism in Connecticut communities and decided to conduct citizen group discussions (Marrow, 1969, pp. 210–211). First proposed by Lewin, **action research** is conducted to inform and contribute to social change. Similar to community psychology values, Lewin linked research and action. In Connecticut, the citizens insisted that they be included when psychologists analyzed these discussions of reducing anti-Semitism. Their insistence and their disagreement with the psychologists' views led Lewin's team to focus on **group dynamics**, that is, the study of how people interact with one another in groups, how groups form, and how they can affect attitudes and behavior. After Lewin's death, his students and others founded the National Training Laboratories (NTL) in Bethel, Maine, a center for professionals and citizens to learn about the dynamics within and between groups in everyday life (Marrow, 1969; Zander, 1995). The NTL workshops (still offered today) focus on the development of skills for working in groups and communities. They are not therapy or support groups and are not clinical in orientation.

Instead, they embody the social-psychological concern with group dynamics. This is another approach that ran counter to the prevailing individualism and laboratory focus of psychology in that it focused on collaborative partnership of professionals and citizens.

Several early community psychologists (Don Klein, Jack Glidewell, and Wil Edgerton) worked with NTL. Through them, group dynamics and action research traditions were linked to prevention and community mental health, leading to new ways of thinking about how to promote well-being and address social problems (Edgerton, 2000; Glidewell, 1994; D. C. Klein, 1995). Lewin's focus on action research, in collaboration with citizens, was a forerunner of community psychology research today. The importance of personal relationships and group processes can be seen in an exemplary early setting in community psychology, profiled in the Changing Perspectives feature in Box 2.2.

---

**Box 2.2   Changing Perspectives: Exemplary Early Setting in Community Psychology**

Community psychology emerged not simply from individuals but from trailblazing *settings*, many of them where psychologists and citizens worked together. We wrote about the community lodge example in the opening exercise. Here we take a closer look at the Yale Psycho-Educational Clinic, founded by Seymour Sarason, and how it involved collaboration with citizens, appreciation of community strengths, and second-order change in role relationships. Those themes appear especially clearly in interviews with many early community psychologists, including Sarason, that were conducted by James Kelly and students (excerpted in J. G. Kelly, 2003).

Sarason described the Yale Psycho-Educational Clinic as having three aims: to understand the "culture of the school" and how that often inhibits productive learning, to gain that understanding experientially through performing services in schools, and to model for university students the everyday practical involvement of their faculty in schools (J. G. Kelly, 2003). These goals indicate a willingness to step outside the usual research methods, to ask open-ended questions and learn from rigorous analysis of personal experience, and to take risks to promote learning.

At the outset, Sarason and his colleagues were not entirely sure what they were looking for or what roles and findings might evolve in their work. Murray Levine described his first job at the clinic as being to "go out to the schools and find a way to be useful." A smiling Sarason later told students how he applied for grants to support the clinic yet was unable to specify exactly what he meant by "culture of the school" or what research methods he would use to study it. His proposals were rejected twice. Yet the clinic's approach eventually led to influential books, papers, and concepts that permeate community psychology today. Clinic staff analyzed their experiences intensively in Friday staff meetings. These involved deep, wide-ranging scrutiny of personal experiences and events at the school, asking tough questions about their meaning (Levine, in J. G. Kelly, 2003; Sarason, 1995b).

The Psycho-Educational Clinic experience was deeply personal for its staff and students. Many influential community psychologists testify to the clinic's importance in their lives. Rhona Weinstein's innovative work in schools began there; Sarason intervened on her behalf when her application was rejected by those at Yale who did not desire to admit women (Weinstein, 2005). Murray Levine still carries his key to the old clinic building, a token of his personal attachment to the people there (Levine, in J. G. Kelly, 2003).

## What Do You Think?

1. How do the three goals of the Yale Psycho-Educational Clinic reflect the general goals of community psychology that are discussed in Chapter 1?

2. Sarason and colleagues did not start with a solid plan for accomplishing the clinic's goals. Why do you think that is? What sorts of challenges do you think they might have encountered early on? How would you have suggested addressing those challenges if you had attended one the clinic's weekly staff meetings?

3. Consider the deep personal connections experienced by the clinic's staff and students. What about the clinic's approach do you think created this sense of community? Now imagine another clinical setting that does not have this same sense of community. What do you think is lacking in this setting, and how could that be changed?

## Movements for Social Change and Liberation

*I'm not going to say that there hasn't been change; I'm saying that it all came as a result of struggle. The power structure doesn't give anybody anything.*
—Modjeska Monteith Simkins (Robbins, 2014, p. 13)

A fourth force influencing the development of community psychology involves movements for social change and liberation. It is a force in the formation and continuing development of the field. For U.S. community psychology in the 1960s, the civil rights and feminist movements most directly influenced psychology, but the peace, antipoverty, environmental, gay rights, and labor movements were also important. These movements are associated with the public concerns of the 1960s, although all had much deeper historical roots. Whenever social justice movements reach a crescendo, such as the 1960s and early 1970s, they change national dialogue, bringing their grievances and ideals to attention. Community psychology and other disciplines are challenged to respond. The activism and disruption in the 2010s and into the 2020s around the world suggest that challenges and calls for change are building again.

The insights of these social movements had several commonalities (J. G. Kelly, 1990; Wilson et al., 2003). One was the need to challenge hierarchical, unequal role relationships: between Whites and people of color, men and women, experts and citizens, straight persons and sexual minorities, and the powerful and the oppressed. Youth often assumed leadership: College students held sit-ins at segregated lunch counters, participated in Freedom Rides through the segregated South, led antiwar protests, and organized the first Earth Day in 1970. Values common to these movements match well with some core values of community psychology: social justice, citizen participation, and respect for diversity (Wilson et al., 2003).

Another commonality of these social justice movements was that they sought to link social action at the local and national levels. Advocates in each movement pursued change in local communities and nationally. "Think globally, act locally" became a familiar motto. The movements advocated changes at each of the ecological levels of analysis that we outlined in Chapter 1. For instance, the National Association for the Advancement of Colored People (NAACP) employed policy research and legal advocacy in the courts for decades. Other organizations used community-mobilizing approaches: time-limited mass demonstrations that attracted media attention (e.g., Freedom Rides, Birmingham and Selma campaigns, the March on Washington). Less recognized local people pursued long-term community organizing for voter registration and other aims, an approach that generated fewer famous names but many enduring community changes (J. Lewis, 1998). Women, including Ella Baker, Septima Clark, Fannie Lou Hamer, and Modjeska Monteith Simkins, often were important leaders whose contributions need to be recognized (Collier-Thomas & Franklin, 2001). This advocacy coincided with the emerging power of national television to portray social conflicts to national audiences. It became more difficult to deny the existence of racism and sexism (Wilson et al., 2003).

***Civil Rights.*** A few psychologists played a policy advocacy role in the civil rights movement. The research of Kenneth and Mamie Clark, African American psychologists, was cited in the 1954 Supreme Court desegregation decision in the case of *Brown v. Board of Education*. The Clarks' research, which originated in Mamie Clark's master's thesis, compared children's reactions to dolls of differing skin colors to measure the self-esteem of African American and European American children. Advocacy and research, including court testimony, by Kenneth Clark and members of SPSSI was important in the NAACP lawsuits against segregated schools (e.g., K. Clark, 1953; K. Clark et al., 1952/2004). However, the reaction of the professional psychological establishment was mixed. Other psychologists testified to defend segregation. Clark later came to believe that the social science advocacy that led to the 1954 court decision had underestimated the depth of racism in the United States (Benjamin & Crouse, 2002).

***Feminism.*** Feminist movements have shared many goals with community psychology and continue to challenge the field (Gridley & Turner, 2010; Riger, 2017). In 1968, psychologist Naomi Weisstein gave an address with the title "Psychology Constructs the Female: Or the Fantasy Life of the Male Psychologist" (Weisstein, 1971/1993). Weisstein's paper has been described as an "earthquake . . . shaking the foundations of psychology" (Riger, in J. G. Kelly, 2003), a formative event for many women in community psychology and women's studies. Weisstein questioned whether psychology at the time

Social change movements of the 1960s and 1970s, including Black civil rights and feminism, have greatly influenced community psychology's goals and values.

knew anything about women at all, after years of research that systematically excluded women or interpreted their responses from men's perspectives. Moreover, she emphasized (a) the importance of social context in shaping choices and acts and (b) the ways in which contexts constrained women's choices. Her critique was based in one of many roots of feminist scholarship that have transformed concepts and methods of inquiry in many disciplines, including community psychology. Weisstein and others in the women's movement were activists in their communities, founding settings to support women's development and advocating for social change (Dan et al., 2003). Although there are substantial common values between feminism and community psychology, there are differences, principally that feminism arose as a social movement willing to take risks (Gridley et al., 2017; Mulvey, 1988), whereas community psychology originated as an academic discipline.

As the social change movements of the 1960s progressed, many psychologists became convinced that citizen and community action was necessary to bring about social change on multiple fronts and that psychology had a role to play (Bennett et al., 1966; J. G. Kelly, 1990; Sarason, 1974; R. Walsh, 1987). In 1967, Martin Luther King, Jr., addressed the APA, calling for psychologists to study and promote youth development, citizen leadership, and social action, especially among African Americans (King, 1968); an excerpt was presented in Chapter 1. Yet the vision of a socially involved psychology was not widely supported in the field. King's speech was arranged by activist psychologists, including Kenneth Clark, over the objections of APA leaders (Pickren & Tomes, 2002).

## Undercurrents of Optimism

*We had just won a huge war, the biggest ever. And we had started from way back—we had been about to get whipped. If we could do this, we could do anything, including solving all the social problems of the U.S.: race relations, poverty. . . . There was a sense of optimism . . . a messianic zeal. . . . We believed that we could change the world, and we felt that we had just done it.*

*Solving social problems is sobering. . . . To win wars, you kill people and destroy things. To solve social problems, you must build things, create things. (Glidewell, 1994)*

Glidewell's (1994) remark illustrates a fifth force that has provided underlying support for each historical force that we have described: an optimism about the ability to find solutions for social problems. Optimism about social change has been described as being part of U.S. progressive social norms (J. G. Kelly, 1990; M. Levine & Levine, 1992; Sarason, 1994), and it supported the emergence of community psychology in the United States. In 1965, President Johnson's administration initiated a collection of federally funded Great Society programs, popularly known as the War on Poverty. These included educational initiatives such as Head Start, job-training and employment programs, and local community-action organizations. Federal funders of these initiatives looked to the social sciences, including psychology, as a source of scientific solutions to social problems. This attitude grew out of a faith in science and technology to solve problems that was based on experiences with World War II, the Cold War, and the space program.

Since the 1970s, different senses about the possibility for social change have prevailed, as has the perceived utility of social science in contributing to change efforts. Prevention is now viewed as a legitimate focus in psychology, although treatment is still more prevalent. Mental health systems are expected to provide a range of services, not just those provided at a state hospital. Inclusion of women and minorities is expected in many organizations, although documented inequities point to work that is still needed. Historical forces continue to shape the development of the field wherever it has been established (e.g., decolonial practices, economic conditions, Me Too movement, Black Lives Matter). As we discuss in later chapters, concerns about social injustice affecting health, well-being, and opportunity suggest the need for renewed social change initiatives. Current efforts to organize for social action and to cultivate contributions of citizens in achieving such change can be seen as a renewed faith in the possibility of change that was portrayed in Glidewell's remarks above.

**What Do You Think?**

1. Which of these social forces are still having an impact on psychology today?

2. How are social forces and current events shaping how we define and address problems today?

3. What are the roles of government and of citizens in shaping how psychology is practiced?

4. How does psychology, including community psychology, need to change to be responsive to the challenges of contemporary life?

# Community Psychology: Developing an Identity

As a new field, community psychology had to distinguish itself from other fields, such as clinical psychology, social psychology, sociology, and community mental health. As an emerging field with a shift in perspective, it needed to develop new conceptual frameworks for linking individual well-being with higher levels of analysis. It needed to propose new ways of conducting research and interventions. A shared focus on social justice and community-level change has helped orient these developments. Thus, community psychology expanded its scope for intervention; individual-level change alone was no longer the sole focus. Poverty, lack of access to resources, and organizational functioning became important targets for intervention. As the field developed its own identity, it proposed new ways of defining problems and new kinds of interventions.

## The Swampscott Conference

In May 1965, 39 psychologists gathered in Swampscott, Massachusetts, to discuss training psychologists for new roles in CMHC system (Bennett et al., 1966). Most of the participants described themselves as atypical psychologists because their involvement in community work had transformed their interests and skills (Bennett et al., 1966). Traditional, individual-oriented interventions were no longer sufficient for what they wanted to do. Many were forging new connections between academic researchers, mental health professionals, and citizens. At Swampscott, they took over a conference called to design a training model for community mental health and made it a founding event for the new, broader field of community psychology in the United States.

The new field would concern "psychological processes that link social systems with individual behavior in complex interaction" (Bennett et al., 1966, p. 7). It would not be limited to mental health issues or settings, and it would be distinct from community mental health, although the two would overlap.

**participant–conceptualizer**
used to describe an important role for a community psychologist, this refers to someone who contributes their expertise in research and/or intervention methods to creating positive social change in collaboration with community members.

Conferees articulated a different way of doing psychology and agreed on the concept of **participant–conceptualizer** to describe the role of a community psychologist. This is someone who acts as a community change agent and a partner with community members in those efforts. A participant–conceptualizer uses their skills as a professional in research or intervention as part of their partnership with community members. Conferees discussed new roles and activities to promote well-being beyond an individual level of analysis: consulting with schools and community agencies, developing prevention programs, advocating for community and social change, and collaborating with citizens. Notice that they proposed these new ways to act as a psychologist to distinguish their activities from those of clinical psychology (e.g., assessment, testing, and therapy). They also called for interdisciplinary collaboration with other social science and health fields to address the multifaceted nature of social issues. Similarly, they recognized the need for humility in community-based partnerships in the face of complex community dynamics involved in social issues (Bennett et al. 1966). Many had felt isolated in traditional academic and clinical settings and rejoiced to find colleagues with similar visions and values. "We found each other!" is a common memory among Swampscott participants and provided energy for the formation of a new field (D. C. Klein, 1995).

## Establishing a Field of Community Psychology

U.S. and Canadian community psychology gradually developed its own distinctive identity and diverged from community mental health. During the 1970s, community psychologists created many conventions necessary for founding and sustaining a new discipline. These included training programs and federal initiatives to fund community psychology research and intervention (Rappaport, 1977a). Many universities were expanding at this time, and community psychology provided an academic discipline that could help address the social issues so prominent in public discourse. Textbooks for the new field had to be written; they helped shape its identity and are still influential (Heller & Monahan, 1977; M. Levine & Perkins, 1987; Rappaport, 1977a). This new field's perspectives on research and intervention were not always well received or well understood in existing academic psychology journals. In 1973, two new journals were founded that continue to serve as records of the development in community psychology research, theory, and action: the *American Journal of Community Psychology* and the *Journal of Community Psychology*.

During this formative period in U.S. community psychology's development, several key conceptual frameworks and clarifications of values were proposed that have become cornerstones of the field. Initially, community psychologists had some difficulty in charting a new path consistent with the vision of their new perspective. Emory Cowen's (1973) *Annual Review of Psychology* article "Social and Community Interventions" (the first devoted to this new field) found that less than 3% of community mental health research articles had a prevention focus. Nonetheless, he called for more emphasis on *prevention*, which had been expected given early adoption of public health perspectives to psychology. Cowen identified a number of interventions, principally dealing with child or youth development, and often focused on disadvantaged populations and collaboration with local citizens, which we discuss in Chapters 10 and 11. Second, James Kelly, Edison Trickett, and others proposed that *ecological* concepts could enhance understanding of how individual coping or adaptation varied in social environments (e.g., schools) with differing psychosocial qualities (J. G. Kelly, 1979; Trickett et al., 1972). This approach suggests that we try to understand how environments and individuals are interrelated and is presented in greater detail in Chapter 5. Third, Seymour Sarason (1974) published another early critique of the field, *The Psychological Sense of Community*. He proposed that community psychology abandon its individualistic focus on mental health services and embrace a broader concern with the "psychological sense of community." As we discuss in Chapter 6, he argued that community psychology should focus broadly on the relationships between individuals and their communities rather than just on the psychological adjustment of individuals.

Fourth, Julian Rappaport (1977a) made persuasive arguments that the field of community psychology needs to focus on its *values to guide research and social action*. In summarizing the first 10 years of the field's development, Rappaport proposed valuing *human diversity, collaboration, strengths* rather than deficits, and *social justice* as unifying concepts that are needed to guide the field's value of *empirical* investigation of social problems. A few years later, Rappaport (1981) extended these ideas to argue that an emphasis on a community's *self-determination* and *empowerment* was as vital to the field of community psychology as *prevention* (see Chapter 8). Finally, Barbara Dohrenwend (1978) in her presidential address to the Society for Community Research and Action proposed an influential framework for an *ecological model of stress and coping* that integrated many of the emerging themes in community psychology and provided a guide for intervention (see Chapter 9 for a discussion). Many of these concepts are now familiar notions but were innovations at the time. These advancements were critical in helping community psychologists define the field and articulate its core values.

## Community Psychology in Shifting Social Contexts

As it has developed a distinctive identity, community psychology has also coped with changing social and political contexts. The contexts and conditions that helped create community psychology in the 1960s and 1970s began to change in the 1980s, requiring community psychologists to examine the relevance of their field as societies changed and to adapt to those changes. Many countries with active fields of community psychology, including Australia, Britain, Canada, Germany, New Zealand, and the United States, became more socially conservative in the 1980s. Over time, countries have elected leaders that are identified as more liberal or conservative, although what is considered liberal or conservative has shifted. In this section, we consider how ongoing economic, political, and social forces have shaped contemporary community psychology.

## Societal Shifts Toward Individual-Level Conceptualization of Social Problems

In the 1980s in the United States, the community-social perspective on defining social issues that had helped create community psychology was supplanted by strongly biomedical views. Influenced by changes in politics, medicine, and science, national discussions changed how problems were defined, which problems were considered important, and which interventions were seen as being worthy of funding. In general, problems were conceived more on an individual level, and individual interventions to these problems were promoted. These critical changes were propelled in part by genuine advances in biomedical research and treatment. However, the pendulum swing was also the result of social forces. As society and government became more conservative, funding agencies called for psychological research on biomedical causes of mental disorders rather than social causes, and researchers' interests followed suit (Humphreys & Rappaport, 1993).

Federal attention also shifted from mental health to substance abuse. Social factors associated with mental health had been a particular emphasis of the 1960s–1970s progressive social era. In the 1980s, President Reagan declared the War on Drugs. It focused on causal factors for drug abuse within the individual, such as genes, illness, and willpower. It also greatly expanded the use of police and prisons while shifting attention and resources away from mental health. The federal prison population doubled during the Reagan administration; most of the increase was due to drug offenders (Humphreys & Rappaport, 1993).

As these forces now defined and prioritized social problems differently, research followed this trend. Psychological journals for the years 1981–1992 contain 170 articles for drug addiction and personality and only 3 references for drug addiction and poverty; similar findings appear if similar index terms are searched. Similarly, primary federal funding for research on homelessness was provided by the Alcohol, Drug Abuse, and Mental Health Administration, not the Department of Housing and Urban Development. Research thus focused on the subgroup of homeless persons with substance abuse and mental disorders rather than on affordable housing and employment, issues that affected all homeless persons (Humphreys & Rappaport, 1993; Shinn, 1992).

After declining during the 1960s and remaining largely steady during the 1970s, the proportion of children living in poverty rose after 1980 to previous levels. Similarly, homelessness became a visible problem in many U.S. cities in the 1980s. The focus of community psychology practice shifted and began to address these issues more than explicit mental health interventions (M. Levine et al., 2005).

In the United States, this generally conservative period has persisted into the 21st century, with some ups and downs in intensity and with either political party in power. Political shifts pose challenges and opportunities for community psychology. Many citizens and opinion leaders fail to recognize the impact of complex social and economic forces on personal life. Faced with many voters who are suspicious of government, elected officials have cut taxes and slashed funding for many community and social programs. Community programs that are growing tend to focus on helping individuals and families change and have emphasized a microsystem level of analysis more than higher levels of analysis. For instance, involvement in self-help groups and spiritual small groups (not dependent on government funding) has grown (Kessler et al., 1997; Wuthnow, 1994) while comprehensive, integrated mental health systems have not (New Freedom Commission on Mental Health, 2003). Problem definitions that are not socially conservative also have difficulty obtaining funding. Community programs involving sexuality (e.g., teen pregnancy, HIV prevention, sexual orientation) have been especially controversial.

## Emergence of Globalization as a Movement

Globalization and its focus on economic trade had been heralded by some as a strategy for increasing quality of life in the early 21st century. In the late 1990s and early 2000s, proponents of globalization focused on making links between countries to promote free trade, based on the premise that freer access to markets would increase the well-being of all involved. Western democracies promoted democratic movements around the world, and several dictators and totalitarian governments lost their power and were replaced by new democratic movements. However, globalization has had negative consequences that have been overlooked or neglected. The 2008 global recession was the largest since the 1930s and affected many countries. The recession and its aftermath of austerity in many countries challenged the adequacy of past solutions to social problems. Many critics in the Global South (e.g., Africa, South America, parts of Asia) pointed out how globalization served the purposes of countries in the industrialized Global North (e.g., Europe, North America, Japan, South Korea) but exploited the people and resources of the Global South. The colonial legacies of government and economic policies limited the development of many countries in the Global South and prompted renewed efforts to decolonize their policies and practices. In the 2010s, increasing awareness of the inequities of globalized wealth and opportunity led to dissatisfaction with the status quo and questions of who benefits from these policies. Perhaps because of these economic changes and increased global connectivity, large movements of people fleeing war, terrorism, or economic deprivation stressed the social safety networks of many countries. Many of the people fleeing oppressive conditions moved to areas where they were racial, ethnic, or cultural minorities. At the same time, changes in traditional media and social media platforms have made acts of discrimination, harassment, police-involved shootings, and sensational crime more visible. Some media have sought to heighten fear and distrust. As the social stresses of migration; social inequities; and racial, ethnic, and gender-based cultural tensions have risen, acts of violence and discrimination have also increased. Community psychologists of the 2010s began to make more explicit efforts to address social inequities (S. D. Evans et al., 2017); promote antiracism initiatives (David et al., 2019); and incorporate decolonial critiques into their teaching, research, and practice (Dutta, 2018; Seedat & Suffla, 2017).

## Defining Social Issues in Progressive and Conservative Eras

The way that we define social problems guides how we address them. Murray Levine and Adeline Levine (1970, 1992), a community psychologist and a sociologist, wrote a classic historical analysis of how social and political forces in the United States have shaped problem definitions, public beliefs about social problems, and the way that helping services are organized. Their historical work concerned services to children and families in the early 20th century, but their analysis also fits several trends in the history of community psychology.

Levine and Levine (1992) proposed a simple hypothesis. In times that are socially and politically more progressive, human problems will be conceptualized in environmental terms (e.g., community or societal). Progressive times are marked by optimism about the potential to address social problems with interventions at locality or societal levels of analysis (e.g., government programs, community organizing). It is important to note that this framework views "progressive" as the way that social challenges are defined and is not necessarily associated with a particular political party. When progressive social forces are dominant, precedence in problem definition is given to social causation of poverty, drug abuse, crime, violence, and other social problems. Intervention efforts at a community or societal level of analysis are seen as appropriate responses. From this perspective, individual and family well-being are best addressed by improving persons' circumstances and access to resources and by providing greater freedom and choice in their lives. Not all political progressives will endorse an environmental view, but when progressive social forces are more dominant in society, citizens of different political parties are more supportive of social intervention programs.

During times when conservative social forces are more influential, the same human problems will be conceptualized in more individualistic terms and emphasize individual level of analysis in causation. From a more conservative framework, problems are located within the biological, psychological, or moral makeup of an individual. Intervention efforts focus on how individual deficits must be remedied by changes in the individuals themselves. Programs are designed to change the individuals (and perhaps families) rather than social factors. Within this framework, it is assumed that persons' improved ability to cope with environmental circumstances will be sufficient to address social problems. As noted earlier, conservative times are tied not necessarily to one political party but to the belief that individual-level changes are more important than wider social change; during conservative eras there is more pessimism about whether social problems can be lessened. Not all social conservatives will endorse an individualistic view of all social problems, of course, but a conservative trend in society overall tends to strengthen it.

Not only do social forces influence how communities define and address social problems; they also define what research is considered worth doing (and worth funding). As we have noted, community psychology in the United States developed in the 1960s, a progressive era that emphasized social and economic root causes of social problems. As we just described, since the 1980s, individualistic thinking has dominated much research funding on topics such as mental health, drug abuse, and homelessness. Changes in laws and organizational practices to address violence against women might suggest more progressive times. Efforts to find genetic vulnerability for interpersonal violence or psychiatric diagnoses might suggest more a conservative era. Psychological research and practice cannot be insulated from such swings in sociopolitical public thinking.

It is important to note that differences between more progressive and more conservative periods, and between individualistic and environmental perspectives, are not absolute (Levine & Levine, 1992). In any historical period, both perspectives are part of the dialogue about how to respond to human problems. Some historical periods are difficult to categorize as one or the other. Moreover, a worldview of individualism, focused on individual happiness and autonomy, often outweighs other American ideals (Bellah et al., 1985). A focus on individuals becomes most dominant in more conservative times yet is still powerful even in progressive times in many cultural contexts.

Both individualistic and environmental perspectives hold some value; neither completely accounts for personal and social difficulties. Thinking about how to link individual and environmental perspectives can be another way that community psychology is trying to do something different. Environments (including macrosystems) and personal factors and choices shape our lives. Yet progressive and conservative advocates articulate very different goals for social policy and community life, and these often reflect differences along the lines we are discussing. As Levine and Levine (1992) documented, the political contexts of the time influence which of those ideas are more widely accepted.

**What Do You Think?**

**1.** Reflecting on recent events and shifting social contexts in your communities, choose a social problem in your community. Which current events and social forces are shaping how people understand the problem(s) where you live?

**2.** Which levels of analysis are emphasized in defining problems?

**3.** What kinds of interventions are deemed appropriate?

# Developing New Conceptual Frameworks to Inform the Practice of Community

**blaming the victim** thinking about societal problems from an individualistic perspective, assuming they are caused by individual deficits and life choices rather than broader macrosystem factors, and focusing on one ecological level rather than looking at factors across multiple levels.

As the field became established, it had to develop not only new ways of doing psychology but also new ways of thinking about its work. In this section, we highlight key developments in conceptual frameworks for community psychologists.

## Addressing Social Issues and Equity

To illustrate the importance of problem definitions and community contexts, we consider two classic examples from community psychology's formation. While the field developed, it examined how social issues are defined and addressed, particularly issues associated with inequality. Community psychologists examine both how people understand social issues and how interventions are carried out. Consider these two examples.

***Blaming the Victim.*** Psychologist William Ryan's 1971 book *Blaming the Victim* provided a classic critique of individualistic thinking about social problems. It had widespread impact and was important in the development of community psychology. When we assume that problems such as poverty, drug abuse, educational failure, crime, or unemployment are caused by deficits within individuals, we ignore larger macrosystem factors such as economic conditions, discrimination, or lack of access to good-quality health care. In terms of our ecological levels of analysis presented in Chapter 1, we focus only on one level and ignore the potential factors at other levels of analysis. Even if we assume that personal deficits are caused by one's family, or by "cultural deprivation," we still locate the deficit within the person and ignore larger factors. Ryan (1971), coining a now-popular term, called this thinking **blaming the victim**.

For instance, in a community with underfunded schools, in neighborhoods where violence is common and where many students do poorly on standardized tests, are we to blame the individual students for the lack of educational attainment? Their parents? Something about their community's culture? (All of these can be ways of blaming victims if you focus on one level and ignore the possibility that broader social issues also may play a role.) Alternatively, we could ask: Why are schools in some communities underfunded? How can the larger society help fund better education for all? What can be done to make all children safe? What community resources could be involved? Are the tests really valid measures of learning, and who decided to use them? These questions address social conditions at multiple ecological levels (see Weinstein, 2002a). The social justice values of community psychology call for us to examine social problems at multiple ecological levels and not expect individuals affected by the problem to be the only ones who need to change to address the problem. Community psychology also places pragmatic value in empirical findings, which leads us to systematically examine multiple ecological levels of analysis to account for what contributes to a situation. It is ineffective to ignore potential reasons why someone may be having a problem. Focusing on only one level of analysis violates both the social justice and empirical values of community psychology. Intervention efforts that consider only one level of analysis will likely be limited in their effectiveness.

Ryan (1971) also questioned whether researchers, policymakers, or others who have never directly experienced a social problem (e.g., poverty) have the best viewpoint for analyzing it. Many community members have a middle-class perspective that is not an accurate understanding of poverty's everyday realities. For someone who grew up with the blessings of family and community advantages, success in school and life may seem largely due to personal characteristics or effort (especially if one does not recognize how important those privileges are). For persons living in poverty and other oppressive conditions, however, success is heavily influenced by social and economic realities; too often their personal efforts are constrained by those factors.

Many of the programs that Ryan criticized were "liberal" social and educational programs focused on individual, family, or "cultural" deficits of program participants. Such social programs become prone to victim blaming when they fail to address economic and sociopolitical roots of social problems. Certainly, it is true that personal effort and responsibility are important in life and are vital to change efforts. And not every person with a problem is necessarily a victim; the term "victim" has been stretched far beyond Ryan's original usage (see Sykes, 1992, for a critique). Yet Ryan drew attention to how social conditions and problem definitions can create or worsen problems that are overly characterized as personal problems. He wanted us to examine how we often are trained to ignore those conditions. For Ryan, improving the quality of community life means addressing social and economic root causes.

***Fair Play and Fair Shares: Contrasting Definitions of Equality and Equity.***
The individualistic and environmental perspectives discussed above also influence how we define fairness. Writing for a U.S.-based readership, Ryan (1981, 1994) argued that there are two different definitions of the cherished

**fair play**
one definition of equality that seeks to ensure fairness in competition for social, educational, or economic advancement. It assumes that everyone starts in the same place and that different results are due to individual merit, talent, or effort.

**fair shares**
another definition of equality that focuses on lessening extreme outcome inequalities while also ensuring that fair procedures are set in place. It looks beyond individual factors and considers broader influences, such as access to resources or opportunities, to ensure equal competition for social, educational, and economic advancement.

American value of equality. The **fair play** definition of equality seeks to ensure rules of fairness in competition for economic, educational, or social advancement. The central metaphor is that of a competitive race, with everyone starting at the same place and rules of the contest treating all individuals similarly. If the rules are fair, then fair players assume that differences in results are caused by individual merit, talent, or effort. Those emphasizing a fair play vision of equality are more likely to accept great differences in the outcomes: "The Fair Player wants an equal opportunity and assurance that the best get the most" (Ryan, 1994, p. 28).

A fair play orientation often leads to agreement with statements such as "The most important American idea is that each individual would have the opportunity to rise as high as his talents and hard work will take him" (Ryan, 1994, p. 29). Examples of fair play social policies include basing educational and employment decisions on test scores and enacting flat rates of taxation (all income groups are taxed the same percentage).

Ryan (1981, 1994) described an alternative perspective of **fair shares**, which is concerned not only with fairness of procedure but also with minimizing extreme inequalities of outcome. It is more concerned about equity. Using the example of a competitive race, a fair shares perspective would use fair play rules but would also go beyond them to consider other factors that can influence preparedness for the race. A fair shares perspective would ask about a person's training and support before they got to the starting line, whether they are using the same equipment, or whether they are even running the same course. If access to these resources or opportunities were not similar, the race would not be considered fair and certainly not an equal competition.

The central metaphor of the fair shares perspective is a community taking care of all its members. Although Ryan did not use the term, he was concerned about equity. For instance, fair sharers would be concerned about access to affordable housing and quality education. A fair shares framework is used in analyzing income inequality and finding ways to increase resources for people so that everyone has a minimal level of economic security. A common way to do this in many Western democracies is to use tax codes to place more burden (i.e., a higher tax rate) on those that can afford it to pay for programs that address basic needs. From a fair shares perspective, it can make sense to limit accumulation of wealth so that everyone has some minimum level of economic security. While achieving absolute equity is unlikely, a fair shares approach seeks to avoid extreme inequalities (Ryan, 1994).

Fair sharers tend to agree with statements such as "For any decent society, the first job is to make sure everyone has enough food, shelter, and health care" and "It simply isn't fair that a small number of people have enormous wealth while millions are so poor they can barely survive" (Ryan, 1994, p. 29). Examples of fair share social policies include universal health care, enriching

**bottom-up approaches**

grassroots strategies for creating social change that come from citizens instead of professionals and powerful stakeholders. They are grounded in the experiences and ideas of the people who are affected the most by community or social issues.

**top-down approaches**

strategies for creating social change that are developed by professionals, leaders, or other elites. Their strategies are rooted in empirical research and often backed by more resources, but they can also reflect biases and interests of the powerful and privileged.

educational opportunities for all students (not just the gifted), and affirmative action in college admissions and employment.

Ryan (1981, 1994) emphasized that although both perspectives have value, fair play thinking dominates American discussions of equality and opportunity. Yet fair play presumes that all participants in the race for economic and social advancement begin at the same starting line and that we only need to make sure the race is conducted fairly. In fact, few citizens really believe that all persons share the same economic or educational resources, the same chances of employment in well-paying jobs, or the same starting line for advancement. In the United States, as in many countries, a very small proportion of the population controls a very large proportion of the wealth. In our view, and in the view of many community psychologists, some methods of strengthening fair shares seem necessary to set up truly fair play.

## Bottom-Up and Top-Down: Contrasting Approaches to Social Change

Whatever our theories about causes of a social problem, we can characterize social change strategies into two broad categories: bottom-up and top-down. Both are important for citizens and community psychologists to understand; both were involved in the social initiatives of the 1960s and both are used today. As we discuss in later chapters, the choice of change strategies will depend on your problem definition, level of analysis, resources, and which community psychology values you emphasize.

**Bottom-up approaches** originate at the "grassroots," among citizens rather than professionals or powerful stakeholders. These change strategies used by ordinary people are efforts to assert control over their everyday lives. They are grounded in the experiences and ideas of people most affected by a community or social problem (Fawcett et al., 1995). In contrast, **top-down approaches** are designed by professionals, community leaders, or similar elites who may have spent years or their whole careers addressing particular social issues. Their work is usually grounded in research findings, yet their approaches tend to reflect the life experiences, worldviews, and interests of the powerful. Even when they are well intentioned, they usually preserve existing power structures while addressing social problems (perhaps with some reform). Furthermore, they often overlook the strengths of a community that could be used as part of social change (Kretzmann & McKnight, 1993).

Professional mental health care represents a top-down approach; self-help groups tend to use a bottom-up approach. Centralizing decisions in city hall offices is a top-down approach; enabling neighborhood associations to make local decisions is a bottom-up approach. Relying only on psychologists or other professionals to design a program to prevent drug abuse is a top-down approach; involving citizens in making decisions about that program is a bottom-up approach.

**divergent reasoning**
an approach to social issues that avoids simplistic, one-sided answers and recognizes that conflicting viewpoints can coexist and lead to more effective solutions. It also involves questioning the status quo or commonly accepted viewpoints and welcoming new perspectives.

Neither approach is always best. Community psychology values of empowerment, citizen participation, collaboration, and community strengths are linked to bottom-up approaches. Values of empiricism, prevention, and promotion are more often linked to top-down approaches. The two approaches can complement each other, as when mental health professionals and mutual help groups collaborate or when psychologists, acting as participant–conceptualizers, and citizens collaborate on research that assists the community. Outside resources (e.g., grant funding) are often easier to acquire with a top-down approach, which also may better apply research findings on effective programs elsewhere. As we discuss in later chapters, the integration of bottom-up and top-down strategies often sets community psychology efforts apart from other academic disciplines.

## Diversity of Viewpoints, Divergent Reasoning, and Dialogue

In most communities, there is a range of opinions on any issue. Often, responses to social issues generate opposing viewpoints. These opposing views can both be true (at least, both can hold some important truth). Can community members talk about their opposing viewpoints and find a way to work together? Already in this book we have discussed several such oppositions in defining and responding to problems: persons and contexts, first-order and second-order change, potential conflicts among community psychology core values, individualistic and environmental perspectives on social issues, and progressive and conservative viewpoints.

Recognizing important truths in opposing perspectives would force us to hold both in mind, thinking in terms of "both/and" rather than "either/or" (Rappaport, 1981). (This thinking has roots in the dialectical philosophies of Hegel and Marx but is not identical to either system.) Rappaport (1981) advocated that community psychologists use **divergent reasoning** as participant–conceptualizers in promoting dialogue about how our communities respond to social issues. First, recognize that conflicting viewpoints may usefully coexist; perhaps a problem may be better addressed by listening to different viewpoints and resisting easy answers that may privilege one viewpoint over others. The best thinking about social issues takes into account multiple perspectives and avoids one-sided answers (Tebes, 2018).

Dialogue that respects both positions, rather than a debate that creates winners and losers, can promote divergent reasoning. A good metaphor for this process, often suggested in feminist theory (L. A. Bond et al., 2000; Reinharz, 1994), is a frank yet respectful conversation among multiple persons. It involves boldly setting out one's views in one's own voice but also carefully listening to others and recognizing that many positions hold some truth. Divergent reasoning recognizes conflict between differing perspectives as a path to knowledge. It is not a search for complete objectivity but a process of learning through dialogue. In community psychology, that conversation is often multisided, not simply two opposing poles.

Divergent reasoning also involves questioning the status quo or commonly accepted view of an issue (Rappaport, 1981). In discussion of a social issue such as poverty, there is often a dominant, widely accepted view and an opposing pole that is largely ignored. The dominant view serves the interests of the powerful by defining the issue and terms of debate. Psychology has often adopted or been co-opted by dominant views rather than questioning them (S. D. Evans et al., 2017; Humphreys & Rappaport, 1993; Langhout, 2016; Ryan, 1971, 1994; Sarason, 1974, 2003b). Often this happens as psychologists and citizens think solely in individual terms, ignoring the importance of context (Shinn & Toohey, 2003). Questioning the status quo often involves listening carefully to the voices of persons who have direct experience with an issue, especially those whose views have been ignored. For instance, research that investigates the experiences and perspectives of persons who have lived in poverty can illuminate their strengths and focus on their rights to make decisions in their own lives as well as support their needs (Rappaport, 1981).

Finally, divergent reasoning requires humility. No matter how strong your commitment to your own point of view, it is likely to be one-sided in some way, and there is likely to be some truth in an opposing view. Remember Rappaport's rule: "When everyone agrees with you, worry."

# What Do Community Psychologists Do?

Community psychology's shift in perspective calls for different ways of educating psychologists and the promotion of competencies different from those of most traditional psychologists. Many of these skills were adopted from other fields. As we discuss in later chapters, many of these skills can also be used by citizens interested in working for social change. First we discuss the training of community psychologists.

## Training for Community Psychology

As the field emerged, the shift in perspective of community psychology required new models of training. One hallmark of an established field is the promotion of training programs at universities (Reich et al., 2017). Creating new programs and courses was some of the first work in establishing community psychology. Master's-level training programs in community, counseling-community, or clinical-community psychology have been established in many nations (e.g., Canada, Egypt, Italy, New Zealand, South Africa, the United Kingdom, the United States), as have doctoral programs in community, interdisciplinary studies, social-community, or clinical-community psychology (e.g., in Australia, Canada, New Zealand, Portugal, Puerto Rico, the United States).

Periodically, community conferences have focused on the development of the field through education and training. Prevention of psychological problems and promotion of social competence, especially in schools, represented one important theme of the first conference on community psychology training held in Austin, Texas, in April 1975 (Iscoe et al., 1977). A second theme concerned social advocacy to address issues such as poverty, racism, and sexism. Austin's conference participants were more diverse than Swampscott's, reflecting a third theme of emerging diversity. Swampscott's participants were all White and included only one woman. While the Austin conference included women and persons of color, whose concerns and perspectives were voiced to a greater degree than before, many of these groups were concentrated among students and junior professionals, not among senior professionals, who were slow to engage these perspectives (Mulvey, 1988). Reports from working groups of Blacks, Latinas, and women challenged prevailing paradigms and called for translating espoused values of the field into tangible changes in training, research, and action (Iscoe et al., 1977; T. Moore, 1977). While community psychology in the United States has become more diverse in terms of membership, inclusion of racial and ethnic minorities continues to be slower than many had hoped, reflecting similar challenges for inclusion in broader society. In 2007, a summit on community psychology practice was held at the conference of the Society for Community Research and Action. The summit was a day-long discussion of how to promote development of community practice skills in graduate training that has generated articulation of community practice competencies and training models (V. C. Scott & Wolfe, 2014). We discuss current training opportunities in greater detail in Chapter 14.

## Community Psychology Practice

Now we consider expanding the traditional roles and skills of psychologists to promote well-being and work for social change (V. C. Scott & Wolfe, 2014). As you might guess, this involves taking active roles in community settings (as opposed to staying in a clinic) and adopting different expectations and wider boundaries for professional relationships. Community psychologists work collaboratively with others to help strengthen systems, challenge systems, increase access to resources, and optimize quality of services for individuals, organizations, and community groups. Community psychologists build on existing strengths of people, organizations, and communities to create sustainable change.

### *What Professional Roles Can Community Psychologists Choose From?*
The potential roles of a community psychologist go well beyond seeing clients in a clinic. They can range from delivering services as a community-based

prevention specialist to serving as a program director or a policy leader. Some roles focus on helping others promote well-being by working as consultants, trainers, and program evaluators. Community psychologists can work in social change efforts as community organizers and policy leaders. Alternatively, community psychologists can choose to focus on community-building and community-development activities. Finally, many community psychologists work as educators and professors, choosing to help develop the capacity of others to work for change (V. C. Scott & Wolfe, 2014).

***Where Do Community Psychologists Work?*** With expanded levels of analysis and expanded roles, community psychologists can work in a variety of settings. These include social service agencies (e.g., health equity advocacy organizations), private policy organizations (e.g., community foundations), and government agencies or institutes (e.g., CDC). These established settings may focus on promoting change in education, health, or legal systems. Alternatively, some community psychologists may choose to create their own settings for work. These include starting their own consulting practice, starting a nonprofit to work on an issue not being adequately addressed by existing agencies (e.g., homeless services for unaccompanied youth), or creating a social change organization. While working at colleges and universities, a large number of community psychologists work with community partners in many of these settings. Many community psychologists have been involved in service learning as one way of linking research, action, and training. Over the course of a career, a community psychologist may work in several different capacities, roles, and settings.

Throughout the book, we highlight the work of community psychologists and others involved in social action in most of our chapters with sidebar features where you can learn about their work. We call this feature "Community Psychology in Action." Box 2.3 presents the experiences of community psychologists in Portugal who have used their academic training to create an alternative setting to promote social change and support for persons with mental illness and their family members. The leaders determined that the rights of persons with mental illness and their access to resources were not sufficiently well addressed by existing settings.

## Community Psychology Practice Skills

Community psychology promotes training in a wide range of practice skills required to promote change across levels of analysis (V. C. Scott & Wolfe, 2014). Each community psychologist develops skills particularly suited to their interests (Stark, 2012). J. H. Dalton and Wolfe (2012) developed a framework for training in community psychology practice competencies. These include four broad domains: (a) program development and management, (b) community and organizational capacity building, (c) community

## Box 2.3   Community Psychology in Action: Social and Political Change in the Mental Health System in Portugal

José Ornelas, Maria Moniz-Vargas, and Teresa Duarte; Associação para o Estudo e Integração Psicossocial (AEIPS; Association for Study and Psychosocial Integration)

The mental health system in Portugal during the 1980s was structured around large psychiatric hospitals or wards integrated into general hospitals as well as institutional facilities managed by religious congregations. In 1987, through a small grant provided by the State Mental Health Department, we began to organize group meetings with people in the community who were discharged to the community of Olivais in Lisboa. Our group created a nongovernmental organization named the Association for Study and Psychosocial Integration (AEIPS) to implement a community-based service system, which has involved over 750 mental health services users to date.

Drawing upon values and concepts from community psychology, we sought to promote opportunities for social integration of people with mental illness, accessibility to individualized housing, mutual support, supported employment, and the same use of social contexts as any other person. We wanted to create settings that would allow people with histories of psychiatric treatment to choose the location where they would live, work, study, or socialize. In the housing area, we have helped create a range of options by providing group or individualized opportunities with tailored professional intervention focused on the maintenance of the housing, even in crisis situations. Currently, one of the most relevant and recognized services provided by our organization is the supported employment program. It is a system to assist people with the experience of mental illness to work in the open labor market. The program promotes opportunities to reach the labor market and actively participate in society, and it emphasizes the diversity of employment options depending on a person's interest, educational background, or specific training. The model is one person working in one company. The supported education program is focused on opportunities to return to school for this group that often has unfinished degrees. In creating opportunities to address the living concerns of persons with mental illness, we seek to support the transformation of individuals' lives that emphasizes processes of building or renewing individual social support systems and participation in community life.

The main lesson that we have learned over the past 40 years is that applying an empowerment paradigm to mental health services requires consistent attention and measurement of processes and results. While this new perspective has helped us see how we needed to create new settings to support persons with mental illness to participate in community life, we realized that we need to collaborate with stakeholders (services, consumers, families, and professionals) at all ecological levels to promote individual, family, and community well-being.

### What Do You Think?

1. How does the AEIPS's approach to treating mental illness differ from more traditional, individualistic approaches?

2. How did AEIPS link individual level of analysis with higher levels of analysis (e.g., microsystem, organization, locality, macrosystem)? What sorts of benefits might one-on-one interventions provide? How can they contribute to a broader, more ecologically focused program like the AEIPS?

3. What challenges do you think the AEIPS may have encountered when working with so many stakeholders? What implications does their approach have for how psychology is practiced?

and social change, and (d) community-based research. We have adapted J. H. Dalton and Wolfe's (2012) descriptions to summarize the skills involved in these competencies. While we present these competencies and associated skills as separate domains, community psychologists often draw upon more than one competency to be effective. In the coming chapters, we will provide examples of how community psychologists do this work.

*Community Program Development and Management.* These skills are often focused on using empirically supported research findings to inform practice and policy. Although not necessarily top-down, many of the efforts bring an initiative to a new community and need to determine how best to introduce and use the program. Community psychologists contribute their expertise in formal intervention efforts to community initiatives.

- **Program Development, Implementation, and Management.** The ability to partner with community stakeholders to plan, develop, implement, and sustain intervention programs in community settings. This competency includes skills in assessing community needs, strengths, and resources. It requires the abilities to formulate program goals, adapt programs to meet the needs and resources of the setting, and measure desired outcomes.

- **Prevention and Health Promotion.** The ability to articulate and implement a prevention perspective and to operate prevention and health promotion community programs. This competency involves working with community partners to develop multilevel prevention programs that link empirically supported prevention initiatives to policy priorities. Sometimes, this will require program development and implementation skills cited above to help settings be effective in their prevention efforts.

*Community and Organizational Capacity Building.* In this competency domain, community psychologists focus on building the capacities of individuals or organizations to address their concerns.

- **Mentoring.** The ability to assist community members to identify personal strengths and social/structural resources that they can develop further and use to enhance empowerment, community engagement, and leadership. This may involve teaching effective methods of connecting with others and practicing critical reflection of one's own work.

- **Resource Development.** The ability to identify, coordinate, and use community assets and social capital to support community initiatives. These include human, informational, and material resources. Community psychologists use their skills and position to link community initiatives to resources (e.g., assisting in grant applications, advocacy) that will help a community organization address its concerns. Resources can be material resources, information, or social networks.

- **Consultation and Organizational Development.** The ability to facilitate growth of an organization's capacity to attain its goals. Community psychology consultation seeks to facilitate organizational learning, problem solving, and decision making. It typically involves collaborative strategic planning of organizational goals, desired outcomes, and action initiatives.

*Community and Social Change.* While the previous competencies might be used most often with small groups or organizations, these next competencies tend to be used at higher levels of analysis (e.g., localities, society).

- **Collaboration and Coalition Development.** The ability to help groups with common interests and goals work together to do what they cannot do apart. Community psychologists seek to facilitate community member efforts to identify community issues, resources, and goals for collective action. This often requires building a network of constructive work partnerships among community stakeholders and including people with representative views from all segments of a community.

- **Community Organizing and Community Advocacy.** The ability to bring together community members to gain the power to improve conditions affecting their community. While these efforts may require collaborative skills and coalition building, they will likely require some level of confrontation and action to address community members' concerns. A community psychologist assists community members in taking sustained collective action to bring about systems change.

- **Public Policy Analysis, Development, and Advocacy.** The ability to communicate research findings and the impact of policy decisions on people's lives to policymakers, elected officials, and community leaders. Community psychologists may translate research findings, present testimony, or consult with agency directors and elected officials. This work includes skills in building and sustaining effective working relationships with policymakers and identifying opportunities to change public policy.

*Community Research.* This competency domain focuses on using research skills to promote action. While all community psychologists seek to link action and research, some may choose to specialize in community research skills.

- **Participatory Community Research.** The ability to work with community partners to plan and conduct research that meets high standards of scientific evidence and is contextually appropriate. It also includes the ability to communicate the research findings in ways that promote community capacity to pursue community goals. Echoing Lewin's focus on action research, community psychologists look for ways that they can work with community members to gather data with rigorous methods and use research-based information to shape programmatic and policy decisions. They work to communicate findings in a way that has utility for community members, practitioners, and stakeholders.

- **Program Evaluation.** The ability to partner with community members and assess whether programs are meeting their goals. Often, community members may develop a program and look for expertise to help them evaluate its effectiveness. Program evaluators can assist with planning for program improvement and create tools for accountability to stakeholders and funders. Community psychologists develop culturally sensitive and responsive program evaluation methods appropriate for each community and program context. They work to integrate evaluation findings into ongoing program development and improvement.

*Developing Competency Across Skills.* While it is unlikely that any one community psychologist would develop competence in all of these skills for practicing community psychology, the framework for community psychology practice competencies provides a guide for deciding which skills can assist community psychologists in achieving their career goals. Many of these skills could also be valuable for their community partners and for building the capacity of their organizations. The competencies framework can also guide students in making decisions about training, degrees, and the kinds of careers they want to pursue in community psychology or in other fields such as public health, social work, community development, urban planning, and several different areas of psychology. Some students may decide to focus on organizational or social change, requiring skills at higher levels of analysis (e.g., community organizing, policy change, social action). Others may focus on change in microsystems or organizations that may require health promotion, program development, or evaluation skills. Community psychology's emphasis on research and action requires that community psychologists develop (a) *design skills* in formulating problem definitions appropriate for social conditions and level of analysis, (b) *action skills* in mobilizing resources to work with others to address the issue, and (c) *relationship skills* that can bring people together and sustain action over time (Stark, 2012).

## Ethics in Community Psychology

With expanded roles, new practice skills, and work in a range of community settings, it is not surprising that frameworks for ethical decision making would also need to expand and require reconsideration. Community psychologists embrace a view of "positive ethics" that can guide decisions for what we want to do, how we want to develop our relationships, and which values we want to promote in our behavior rather than only avoiding problems (R. Campbell, 2016; Knapp & VandeCreek, 2012; Morris, 2015). Ethical decision making is needed to balance our values and social roles with demands of the situation. Community psychologists follow the *Ethical Principles of Psychologists and Code of Conduct* of the American Psychological Association (APA, 2017a). These include orienting principles about avoiding behavior that can harm others and conducting work with integrity as well as standards for professional conduct in regard to resolving conflicts and engaging in work where one has developed competence. One particularly helpful guideline is an expectation that you do not do ethical decision making by yourself. In complex situations, it can be hard to sort out your emotions, self-interest, and responsibilities to others and to the field. Consulting with others can provide feedback, prompt other questions, and avoid blind spots in considering ethical issues. While the APA framework is helpful, it is limited. The demands of community-engaged work require additional consideration. R. Campbell and Morris (2017a) proposed a framework that would expand the APA ethical principles. For example, Principle E:  Respect for People's Rights and Dignity, would need to be expanded beyond concern for individuals to include diverse identities, community partnerships, and populations/cultures. Principle A: Beneficence and Nonmaleficence, involves doing work that can benefit others and avoids doing harm. These principles could be expanded to consider risks and benefits at the group, community, and cultural levels of analysis. Principle D: Justice, would be expanded beyond consideration of fairness, equality, and avoiding bias to promoting empowerment and liberation and avoiding collusion with oppressive systems. In addition, APA's Multicultural Guidelines (2017b) provide additional resources for addressing diversity within relationships and communities. A comprehensive, systematic ethical framework that is codified like APA's Ethics Code is still needed for community psychology. Recent developments may be the beginning of a formal ethical framework for the field (R. Campbell & Morris, 2017b).

# The Global Contexts of Community Psychology

Distances between cultures and communities are shrinking. People can more easily connect through social media, travel, trade, and cultural exchange than ever before. Sadly, exploitation and violence are also becoming global in scope. Community psychologists have also sought greater dialogue to understand shifting contexts and connections globally (Reich et al., 2017). Below, we briefly present how community psychology has developed in different countries to understand how the values, questions, and actions of community psychologists vary across countries and regions. Given the field's emphasis on understanding people in context, it is not surprising that community psychology varies around the world.

## Unique Development in Different Contexts

The 1960s, 1970s, and early 1980s saw the emergence of community psychology across the world. The origins differed somewhat: in South Africa, opposition to apartheid was a unifying force; in Germany, social movements for women and the environment played a role; in Australia, New Zealand, and Canada, disenchantment with purely clinical concepts of human strengths and problems was important. Today, community psychology is a burgeoning international field. Learning from and working with Indigenous peoples is an organizing principle in several countries, for instance, partnering with the Māori in New Zealand, Aboriginal peoples in Australia, and Maya peoples in Guatemala (Glover et al., 2005; Lykes, 2017). Each region has developed its own journals, and online platforms carry articles from an international array of community psychologists. The exchange and critique of ideas have expanded dialogue across regions. Similarly, training programs and practitioners now exist across Latin America, Europe, Japan, New Zealand, Australia, Israel, South Africa, Canada, and the United States. There is not space in this chapter to review community psychology in each country. We have selected a few to give you an idea of community psychology's diversity.

## Community Psychology in North America

Canada has a 5-decade history of community psychology that shares many of the contexts that were formative for the field in the United States but have developed uniquely Canadian features. English-speaking Canada sought to expand on limitations of clinical psychology while French-speaking Canada extended applied social psychology to address inequality and injustice (Reich et al., 2017). Several universities offer undergraduate and graduate training programs in French and English. Conferences and journals are bilingual with presentation in both languages. The University of Ottawa hosted the 2017 conference of the Society for Community Research and Action, a community psychology conference based in North America that draws scholars and activists from around the world. G. Nelson et al. (2007) suggested that there have been six main areas of emphasis that have distinguished community psychology from the broader field of psychology in Canada: values and ethics, health promotion and prevention, social network intervention, promotion of inclusion, and community economic development.

Mexican community psychology dates back more than 40 years at several universities (Montero, 2007). While having some connections to Canada and the United States, Mexican community psychologists have had more

**liberation psychology**
inspired by liberation theology in Latin America, this approach seeks to understand and address the situation of oppressed and impoverished communities by challenging the sociopolitical structure they currently exist in. It emphasizes values like citizen empowerment and social justice and has influenced community psychology's development.

interaction with community psychologists across Latin America. Community psychology in Mexico has blended humanistic psychology, community psychology, and liberation psychology. Community psychology efforts in Mexico are known for developing interventions working with Indigenous communities, documenting cultural traditions, and collaborating to preserve cultural traditions. Addressing poverty and infrastructure needs in rural areas has been a long-term concern. In 2010, Universidad Iboamericana hosted the third International Conference on Community Psychology in Puebla.

## Community Psychology in Latin America

During the 1970s, community psychology developed among psychologists throughout Latin America, largely independent of North American trends (Comas-Díaz et al., 1998; Montero, 1996). Latin American community psychology developed from liberation psychology and social psychology and their involvement in social change movements. In some countries (e.g., Chile, El Salvador, Guatemala), movements were a response to repressive government regimes and armed conflict. These movements were also influenced by liberation theology, which blended many values of progressive Christianity and Latin American liberation struggles. At the community level, liberation theology and psychology emphasized empowerment of citizens, power to contest social inequities and abuses of power, and power to work for justice (Martin-Baro, 1994). Another influence was the approach of Brazilian educator and activist Paulo Freire (1970/1993). He proposed models of raising consciousness about the impact of social conditions on personal and community lives. Dialogues raising consciousness created beginning points for social transformation directed by community members seeking answers for why social inequities were so prevalent. Freire's dialogues often began with practical, local initiatives for social change.

A distinctive Latin American social-community psychology has emerged that is more concerned with social critique and liberation than the early North American community psychology. It emphasizes democratic participation, social justice, concepts of power and ideology, and social change, and it has established a presence in Venezuela, Colombia, Brazil, Argentina, Chile, Cuba, and other countries (Montero & Varas Diaz, 2007). Much of the work in Latin America is not well known in the United States because of language barriers. However, the ideas have been influential, particularly in **liberation psychology**, which aims to actively understand the psychology of oppressed and impoverished communities by conceptually and practically addressing the oppressive sociopolitical structure in which they exist (Montero et al., 2017; Sloan, 2002). In Chapter 8, we discuss liberation and oppression. Developments in Latin American community psychology have encouraged more social justice–focused, critical community psychology in the United States.

Community psychologists from Puerto Rico have been particularly influential in the development of Latin American social-community psychology. At the University of Puerto Rico, Rio Piedras established a master's program in 1975 and a doctoral program in 1986. Puerto Rican community psychologists have developed Spanish-language textbooks, conducted large-scale federally funded research projects, and produced over 100 graduates in the past 3 decades (Montero & Varas Díaz, 2007; Reich et al., 2017; Serrano-García, 1994). Community psychologists have had to defend the viewpoint of the field in contrast to other subfields of psychology in Puerto Rico. They have put particular emphasis on producing psychologists that are "interested and committed to intervention in research, promoting interventions simultaneously with research projects" (Montero & Varas Díaz, 2007, p. 71).

## Community Psychology in Europe, Australia, and New Zealand

Community psychology in Europe, Australia, and New Zealand is quite varied in emphasis. In Portugal and Spain, the field emerged as fascist regimes were pushed out of power in the 1970s. In Northern Europe and Australia, early development of community psychology paralleled developments in the United States and Canada of extending community mental health but soon branched into other areas based on the challenges of each national or regional context (Reich et al., 2017). Within the context of the European Union, community psychologists have promoted new ways of addressing homelessness, international migration, and social exclusion of persons with mental health problems (R. M. Greenwood et al., 2019). In Australia and New Zealand, concerns about social justice and Indigenous rights raised awareness of the need to chart their own development. For community psychologists in New Zealand, collaboration with Māori peoples is a keystone of their work that extends to examining its philosophy of science to its methods for intervention (Robertson & Masters-Awatere, 2007). They are trying to undo understandings of psychology developed during colonial eras along with power differences between Māori and primarily European settlers. In Australia, a conflict model of social change is emphasized to highlight the need for resources and a battle between groups that results in social inequalities (Reich et al., 2017). The development of community psychology in Australia and New Zealand draws upon influences from Europe through their shared cultural histories. However, contemporary expressions of community psychology emphasize the realities of their location in the Asia-Pacific region (e.g., Indigenous rights, environmental justice, migration, racism, rural health).

Italy has a rich history of community psychology research and intervention. The development of community psychology emerged as a new, decentralized model for health services was being implemented. The perspectives of community psychology were helpful in defining new roles for psychologists, promoting self-help groups, and changing the culture of health care. Promoting and measuring sense of community has been a particular concern in Italy, as has working for action that results in a balance of individual efficacy, collective resources, and well-being. Italian community psychologists have been active in promoting European views of community psychology, hosting conferences, and serving as leaders in European professional networks (Franscescato et al., 2007).

Of course, there is not a single European community psychology or New Zealand–Australian community psychology that integrates different emphases of each country. However, community psychologists across these regions are shaping the development of the field. For example, the European Congress on Community Psychology, a professional society, holds regular conferences and exchanges across countries. Community psychologists in Lisbon, Portugal, and Barcelona, Spain, have hosted the International Conference on Community Psychology, and Melbourne, Australia, will host the 2020 international conference.

## Community Psychology in Africa

Community psychology practitioners have been active in Africa for 35 years, but formally organized programs have been founded more recently. In 14 countries across Africa, psychologists have been drawn to perspectives of community psychology to address the shortcomings of traditional psychological approaches (Reich et al., 2017). Community psychology graduate education programs in Egypt and South Africa have worldwide reach. In South Africa, community psychology's focus on liberation and social justice was resisted by psychologists during the apartheid years. There was more interest and support for community psychology in English-speaking universities than those using Afrikaans. While community psychology is still not recognized as its own discipline in South Africa, it has become a valuable resource for clinical psychologists who now have a compulsory community service requirement due to changes in health care laws (Bhana et al., 2007; Reich et al., 2017). Two journals and edited books have been developed to feature community psychology. An interesting discourse for a global community psychology is emerging in South Africa about the need to adapt North American and European conceptualizations of community psychology to be relevant in poor areas of Africa. South African community psychologists have been at the forefront of articulating the limitations of northern hemisphere community psychology and the need for developing community psychology theory and practices that respond to the realities of communities in the southern hemisphere (Suffla & Seedat, 2015). The 2016 International Conference on Community Psychology in Durban, South Africa, focused on decolonialization of community psychology theories and action (Sonn et al., 2017).

Scholars from the Global South have noted that much of how we think about research and helping people derives from what was developed in the Global North and imported to or imposed on their communities (Suffla & Seedat, 2015). For example, theories of self and locus of control may not be as effective in supporting people's efforts to address social issues as understandings of group consciousness and commitment to others. Furthermore, local ways of knowing and addressing concerns were dismissed by Northern colonial administrations across Africa, Asia, and South America. Decolonial theory seeks (a) to move the assumptions about how we do our work away from an automatic placement of traditions from the Global North in the center of how we create knowledge, how we act, and how we relate to each other and (b) to integrate information into many regions in ways that are appropriate for local contexts. For example, seeing a counselor may not be the preferred way for persons to get help with grief. Use of a survey may not be the best way to learn about how elders view changing gender roles. As we discuss more in Chapters 3 and 14, decolonial theory is shaping current development of community psychology in the Global South and across the world.

## Community Psychology in Asia

Community psychology in Asia varies greatly by national context and history. In some countries, community psychologists have established their own professional society and training programs, and in others it is quite new. In Japan, a professional society for community psychology was organized in 1998. Several universities have graduate training programs. A major emphasis in Japan has focused on school settings and promoting adaptation of students. Although early Japanese community psychology paralleled developments in North America, Japanese community psychologists are working to develop cross-cultural models to enhance understanding of community psychology perspectives in Japan (Sasao & Yasuda, 2007). Responses to natural disasters such as the March 2011 Great East Japan Earthquake and the resulting tsunami and nuclear meltdown at the Fukushima Daiichi Nuclear Power Plant have provided new challenges for community psychologists in Japan working to promote community-based and community-building responses to this triple disaster (Reich et al., 2017). In Hong Kong, community psychologists have challenged prevailing approaches to mental health care and have encouraged self-help initiatives. In India, community psychologists have founded their own journal and focused on empowerment and community development. In mainland China, Indonesia, the Philippines, South Korea, and Thailand, community psychologists are adapting ideas of community psychology from other regions in responding to local challenges. They are developing community psychology consistent with their helping traditions and histories of addressing social conflict (Reich et al., 2017; Sasao & Yasuda, 2007).

## Moving Toward Global Dialogues in Community Psychology

Since the last edition of this book, community psychologists in different regions around the world have continued to build connections in efforts to create global understandings of community psychology. Community psychology is now practiced in 37 countries on 6 continents. A review of community psychology trends across the world found that addressing social injustice and unequal power is a primary connecting link of the field (Reich et al., 2017). International dialogues about community psychology are growing. Theories and practices developed in one area can enrich those in other regions, but they must be examined for match to local history and current realities.

The best illustration of the development of global exchanges in community psychology is through its gathering for conferences. In 2006, the first International Conference on Community Psychology was hosted in Puerto Rico. This was an exceptional site for bringing together community psychologists from different traditions and different countries. Puerto Rico's unique

Community psychologists representing different communities from around the world need to learn from each other to advance the field.

history as a leader of community psychology in Latin America and many connections with North American community psychology were instrumental in linking community psychology traditions from different countries. Community psychologists in Lisbon, Portugal, hosted the 2008 conference and have played a similar role linking European community psychology to North America. The international conference has continued every 2 years, demonstrating the vibrancy of community psychology around the world: Puebla, Mexico, in 2010; Barcelona, Spain, in 2012; Fortaleza, Brazil, in 2014; Durban, South Africa, in 2016; and Santiago, Chile, in 2018. International exchanges continue to build on the rich traditions of community psychology in different countries while building new understandings of what a global community psychology might be. The 2020 conference is planned for Melbourne, Australia, where the unique contexts of how Australia has addressed inequalities and social injustice will be the focus of the field. We expect that developments across different regions will enrich community psychology throughout the world as critics of current practice seek to innovate for their communities and cultural contexts.

## Conclusion

*The major job was getting people to understand that they had something within their power that they could use, and it could only be used if they understood what was happening and how group action could counter violence. (Baker, 1970, p. 2)*

*When those of us working in this field in the early 1960s began, we were innocent of the questions as well as of the answers. Now at least we are developing an intellectual framework within which diverse experiences make some sense. We can at least ask questions that are more meaningful than ones we were able to ask. (M. Levine et al., 2005, p. 9)*

Community psychology continues to develop as a field, steering away from North American psychology's historical focus on individualism. Social forces and historical events in the mid-20th century—such as mental health care reform after World War II, the civil rights and feminist movements of the 1960s, and the Swampscott Conference in 1965—were instrumental in the formation of community psychology in different national contexts and are still important for how community psychologists do their work. Key principles that were established in the 1970s continue to affect community psychology's growth, including an ecological perspective, community empowerment and social justice, valuing human diversity, and a focus on prevention. Like pioneering researchers such as Kurt Lewin and Kenneth and Mamie Clark, most community psychologists share a conviction that addressing social conditions and engaging community members as citizens are important aspects of improving individual and community well-being. Ella Baker's quote above helps capture the spirit of the period as she worked with the Southern Christian Leadership Conference and the Student Non-Violent Coordinating Committee. In this chapter, we also discussed community psychology's development of new concepts (e.g., blaming the victim) and promotion of training in specific intervention skills (e.g., prevention, consultation, community organizing) to realize its goal of being a linking science and a linking practice. We also examined the strengths and limitations of top-down and bottom-up approaches for solving social problems, as well as the differences between conservative and progressive perspectives on these solutions.

Community psychologists practice in a wide array of settings and professional roles. They may work in nonprofit organizations, government agencies, or companies; start their own businesses; or work in education. The professional roles include consultants, program developers, policy specialists, community organizers, community developers, evaluation specialists, and more. Consideration of (a) roles for community psychologists and (b) community psychology practice skills can help inform career decisions.

As the Levine et al. (2005) quote illustrates above, community psychology is still maturing as a field. It has made important contributions to understanding and intervening with social issues. However, even the most experienced community psychologist is still a student of relationships between individual and community life at many ecological levels. Every generation of students builds on the experiences of prior generations as it reinvents community psychology in new contexts and continues to challenge the status quo by integrating diverse perspectives from groups whose viewpoints are not normally heard. In North America, these include seeking out international contributions from Latin America, Africa, Asia, and other parts of the world that are essential for developing a global approach to social change, one that recognizes the unique needs and beliefs of Indigenous peoples.

## For Review

## Discussion Questions

**1.** Which social forces supported the goal of doing psychology in a different way in your country? Which forces are shaping the continued development of the field today?

**2.** Which community psychology values from Chapter 1 did you see guiding the development of community psychology?

**3.** How did Ryan's critique of blaming the victim relate to how social problems are defined? Is his critique still relevant today?

**4.** How does Ryan's concept of fair play and fair shares relate to discussions of equality and equity today?

**5.** Which community psychology practice competencies can you envision using to address a concern in your community?

**6.** From a community psychology perspective, why would you expect the practice of community psychology to vary in different countries?

## Key Terms

linking science, 35

linking practice, 36

action research, 45

group dynamics, 45

participant–conceptualizer, 52

blaming the victim, 58

fair play, 60

fair shares, 60

bottom-up approaches, 61

top-down approaches, 61

divergent reasoning, 62

liberation psychology, 72

## Learn More

A detailed summary of the chapter, along with other review materials, is available on the *Community Psychology, Fourth Edition* companion website at http://pubs.apa.org/books/supp/kloos4/.

Action research with community members provides useful knowledge for decision making, planning, and action at multiple levels.

Pichayanon Pairojana/Shutterstock.com

# 3 The Aims of Community Research

## Looking Ahead III➡

After reading this chapter you will be able to answer these questions:

1. Why do community psychologists examine the values and assumptions that they bring to their work as researchers?

2. How do community psychologists promote community participation and collaboration in research decisions?

3. What are key issues in conducting research in different social and cultural contexts?

4. How does an ecological perspective inform community psychology research?

## Opening Exercise

## Reflexivity in Participatory Action Research

Jesica Fernández and Regina Langhout are community psychologists who engage in participatory action research with youth. In a partnership between their university and a local elementary school, they were part of a research team that collaborated with elementary-aged children from working class families, many of Latina/o/x descent (Fernández et al., 2015; Langhout & Fernández, 2014). They facilitated a process in which young people identified a problem in their school, collected and analyzed data to learn more about the problem, and created school-based murals to raise awareness of their concerns. Then, the research team looked back on the challenges they experienced, including tensions in working with school administrators to have a mural design approved and figuring out how to best support the youth through that contentious process (Fernández, 2018b). In looking back at their experiences, they engaged in the practice of reflexivity, examining how their own values, assumptions, and positions influenced their research,

**Reflexivity in Participatory Action Research (continued)**

including their relationships with community partners (Case, 2017). These are a couple of their reflections:

> In community-based research, power, privilege, and oppression require a constant examination of where we position ourselves as researchers, and who we position ourselves with. (Fernández, 2018b, p. 231)

> In terms of my own actions, I am most comfortable engaging in participatory action research [PAR]. Yet, PAR is not the

only way for a community psychologist to be accountable to themselves, the field, and the broader community. There are many ways to be accountable, and this should be negotiated with the relevant stakeholders. In the end, I hope we each take up Sarason's questions: Am I being consistent with what I believe? Am I behaving in ways that are true to my values? Equally engaging the head, hand, and heart through an effective political lens enables me a better vantage point to answer these questions. (Langhout, 2015, p. 277)

## What Do You Think?

1. Why do these researchers think that reflexivity in community-based research is so important?

2. Community-based research includes navigating relationships with partners. What are the values that should guide research relationships?

3. The researcher reflections raise questions about who benefits from research with community partners. Who should benefit from research in communities?

# Action Research in Community Psychology

**reflexivity**
a process through which researchers seek to understand how their values, biases, and positions as experts influence their findings and relationships with community partners.

Community psychologists use action research to pursue answers to questions about how individuals shape ecological contexts and how ecological contexts impact individuals. As we discussed in Chapter 1, community psychologists value empirical answers to our questions; we are impatient with theory or action that lacks evidence based in systematic observation and measurement. We base our action in research findings, and we use research to understand the impact of our actions. Our community research aims to provide useful knowledge for decision making, planning, and action at multiple levels, from local action and community change efforts to state, federal, and international policymaking. And, as described in the opening exercise, community psychologists seek to understand how their values, biases, and positions as experts influence their research through **reflexivity**.

Action research was introduced to many community psychologists in the United States through the work of Kurt Lewin and his colleagues (remember our discussion in Chapter 2). Roots of action research can also be found in the

Highlander Research and Education Center, which we discuss in Chapter 8, and the work of scholar activists in Latin America, including Paulo Freire and Ignacio Martín-Baró (Lykes, 2017; Montero et al., 2017). Action research in communities provides useful knowledge for engagement at multiple levels. Yet it represents a departure from much research in psychology. Take a minute and think about the shift in perspective that community-based research represents for psychology. How do you think research conducted in community settings is different from research conducted in the laboratory? What new challenges might you face conducting research in community settings?

Many psychologists conduct their research in university classrooms and designated lab spaces. Laboratories are, of course, useful settings because they offer the researcher a great deal of control. The laboratory psychologist largely controls the choice of phenomena to study, the perspective from which to study it, methodology, treatment of participants during the procedure, format in which those participants provide data, analysis of data, interpretation of findings, and reporting of results. That control promotes clarity of conclusions and the production of some forms of knowledge. Of course, the researcher must make all these choices within accepted ethical limits. Yet the degree of control granted to the psychological researcher in the laboratory is great.

However, while many individuals (e.g., students in introductory psychology courses) are willing to briefly participate in a laboratory experiment, few citizens are willing to cede control in the settings where they and their families live every day (e.g., school, work, neighborhood). The settings that are most significant for community psychology research are also the most important to the people who work, live, learn, and play in them. We have much to learn from those community members, who are agents and experts in their own lives, rather than simply subjects in our research projects.

In this chapter, we engage the questions raised in the opening quotes as we discuss the values, assumptions, and goals community psychologists bring to research practice. We present a view of control different from the one we might find in the laboratory: *Sharing* control with community members can *enhance* the knowledge gained from community research. Well-designed community research, conducted within empowering and collaborative relationships with community partners, can yield insights not available in the laboratory. Sharing control does not mean giving it up. In a collaborative relationship, both community members and researchers plan and implement research. In this chapter, our goal is for you to better understand and respect the interests of communities as well as the methods for community psychology research.

This chapter is the first of two on community research. In Chapter 4, we describe specific methods for community psychology research. We hope that by reading both chapters, you learn how community research becomes richer by embracing and seeking to understand the complexities of community life.

## Community Research Practice: Shared Commitments in Contextually Grounded Inquiry

Research can support or harm persons in communities, so values are involved in every step of that research. Community psychology is committed to the value of research; along with action, it is central to our identity. All community psychologists are engaged in some form of inquiry whether we identify ourselves primarily as researchers or practitioners. Across a variety of settings and types of engagement, we strive for rigor and excellence, using the very best strategies and methods to answer our research questions. Yet our research questions are grounded in the way that we define problems and priorities for inquiry. Further, each community research project must resolve larger questions about the relative priority of several other values: citizen participation and collaboration, social justice, respect for human diversity, and searching for community strengths. These issues can be summarized in this general question: Who will generate what knowledge, for whom, and for what purposes?

Seymour Sarason (1972), one of the founders of community psychology to whom Regina Langhout refers in the quote at the beginning of the chapter, spoke of the important time *before the beginning* of a community initiative. In that period, the persons involved become aware of a problem or challenge to be addressed, trying to make sense of the problem and determine what to do about it. This concept also fits well with the early stages of a research project, well before a design is chosen and data collected. Important, overarching concerns for community psychology research can be summarized in terms of the following four commitments. After summarizing these grounding commitments below, we will take up each in detail in the rest of the chapter.

***Examining the Values and Assumptions We Bring to Our Work.*** Psychology researchers need to be clear on their fundamental values and their assumptions about research and its relation to community and social action. Basically, researchers need to understand why they are conducting research in the first place. At this fundamental level, researchers are asking two questions: What is the value of empirical research in general? And what can be learned from this research project in particular? Researchers need this clarity before approaching a community to conduct research, although their ideas about these issues will continue to be influenced by their experiences and reflections with community members in the research process.

***Promoting Community Participation and Collaboration in Research.*** The most distinctive quality of community psychology research is its process of conducting research within a participatory, collaborative relationship with citizens and communities. That distinctive approach developed from the practical experiences and careful reflection of community psychologists and action researchers in related fields. They grapple with questions such as these: How, specifically, can researchers and citizens collaborate in planning and conducting research? How can that collaboration be empowering and productive for both? How can respectful relationships between researchers, community members, and research participants best be created and maintained? And what are the ethical challenges in conducting this research?

***Attending to the Cultural and Social Contexts of Research.*** Community research always occurs within a culture, perhaps more than one. Often the cultural assumptions and experiences of researchers differ from those of community members, so an early task is for researchers to deepen their knowledge of the community with whom they seek to work. Community researchers also may seek or need to address questions of human diversity beyond culture (e.g., gender, sexual orientation, ability or disability, social class). A related concern is that the research should take account of strengths of the individuals, communities, and cultures studied.

***Conducting Research With an Ecological Perspective.*** Community researchers make decisions, explicitly or implicitly, about the ecological level(s) of analysis they will focus on. The history and practices of psychology draw attention to individual processes, but community psychology draws our attention to linkages between individuals and contexts as well as larger social systems. Such choices of focus are better made explicitly.

# Examining the Values and Assumptions We Bring to Our Work

Recall the discussion of homelessness in Chapter 1: Unrecognized assumptions about problems often prevent resolution of those problems. Similarly, unrecognized assumptions influence researchers' choices of what to study, what theoretical perspectives to draw from, and what methods to use. Those assumptions can concern one's most basic ideas of what constitutes social-scientific knowledge and how it can best be used. We begin with a contrast between three different views of what constitutes knowledge and how to obtain it.

## Three Philosophies of Science for Community Psychology Research

A philosophy of science refers to one's beliefs about what scientific knowledge is, what methods are appropriate to use in the pursuit of scientific knowledge, and how scientific knowledge is related to social action. You may never have thought of yourself as having a personal philosophy of science, but your ideas about research and how to do it (perhaps as you learned it in prior psychology or other social science courses) reflect a philosophy of science. In this section,

**positivism**
the dominant philosophy of science during psychology's development that emphasizes objectivity, value-free neutrality in research, understanding cause-and-effect relationships through hypothesis testing and controlling external variables, and quantifiable data. It seeks universal laws and findings that apply to multiple contexts.

**postpositivist philosophies of science**
these approaches recognize that no researcher is truly objective yet aim to reduce bias as much as possible. They adapt positivist methods based on the community being studied.

**constructivist philosophies of science**
these approaches openly acknowledge and evaluate researcher biases rather than trying to avoid them. Researchers are considered coproducers of knowledge alongside community members.

we discuss three general philosophies of science for community psychology research—postpositivist, constructivist, and critical approaches—and compare them briefly in Table 3.1. Each is actually a family of related approaches, not a single school of thought, and other branches of philosophy of sciences exist. Riger (1990, 1992), R. Campbell and Wasco (2000), and G. Nelson and Prilleltensky (2010) provide succinct overviews of these three philosophies of science, and our summary here especially relies on these sources.

In the development of the field of psychology, **positivism** was the dominant philosophy of science. Positivism has assumed many forms, but a few common elements important in psychology are these: pursuit of objectivity and value-free neutrality in research, an ultimate goal of understanding cause-and-effect relationships, hypothesis testing with control of extraneous factors to clarify cause and effect, and measurement as the source of data. Positivist science seeks to construct generalized laws, based on research findings, that are applicable to many circumstances. If you have taken prior courses in psychological research methods, what you learned there was influenced by positivism.

This vision of research has come under increasing criticism. No observer is value-free; for example, one is always a member of a culture and influenced by it. Moreover, the particular qualities of cultures, historical circumstances, and settings limit the generalizability of research findings from one context to another (Gergen, 1973, 2001; Tebes, 2017). These and other critiques have led to **postpositivist philosophies of science** that recognize that although no researcher is truly objective, each seeks to reduce biases and build shared understandings as much as possible. Postpositivist approaches in community psychology adapt experimental methods, hypothesis testing, and psychological measurement to community settings. A community psychologist using a postpositivist approach might, for example, compare measures of bullying and social climate in high schools that have created gender and sexuality alliances (GSAs) with those that have not. GSAs, also known as gay–straight alliances, are student-led, school-based clubs that aim to provide a safe environment in schools for LGBTQ students and their allies. The presence of GSAs and participation in GSAs are associated with reduced bullying and enhanced school climates for LGBTQ youth (Marx & Kettrey, 2016).

**Constructivist philosophies of science** take a different approach (R. Campbell & Wasco, 2000; Gergen, 2001; Montero, 2002; G. Nelson & Prilleltensky, 2010; Tebes et al., 2014; Trickett, 2009). Instead of pursuing the ideal of value-free objectivity, constructivists assume that knowing occurs in relationships. The idea is not to eliminate researcher bias, which constructivists consider impossible, but to put the assumptions of the researcher on the table to be discussed and evaluated. This puts responsibility on researchers to make their assumptions explicit and to describe carefully the relationships in which research was conducted.

**critical philosophies of science**
similar but not identical to constructivist philosophies, these approaches assume that knowledge is shaped by power relationships created and maintained by social institutions and belief systems. They encourage researchers to question who holds the power to state what is true, who defines research relationships, and how their background influences the research process. Critical researchers are activists who challenge injustices.

In a constructivist framework, researchers are understood to be coproducers of knowledge with others, often community members, and research is enhanced by distributed thinking and expertise (Tebes, 2017; Tebes et al., 2014). Further, there are always limits and constraints on knowledge; understandings of community issues and social problems will change over time and across contexts. Thus, constructivists examine the social context of research itself, including the perspectives and experiences each person brings to their work as a researcher. This emphasis on knowing through connection, collaboration, and mutual understanding is a particular emphasis of qualitative research and of some feminist researchers (see R. Campbell & Wasco, 2000; Riger, 1992; Stein & Mankowski, 2004), although constructivist approaches may also serve as the foundation for quantitative experimental methodologies (Shinn, 2016; Singh et al., 2018).

Constructivist approaches seek to understand a particular social context and what it means to the people who experience it. Rather than trying to transcend local contexts to achieve universality, they see the study of particular contexts as a legitimate endeavor. Useful knowledge is built by examining processes and relationships within and across contexts. Methodological pluralism is valued, given the constraints of any one way of knowing. For example, a researcher using a constructivist framework to ground a case study of a GSA at a local high school might ask the GSA participants to share their understandings of how the GSA related to their sense of school connectedness and safety at school.

**Critical philosophies of science** take a third position, related to constructivism yet distinct from it (R. Campbell & Wasco, 2000; Dutta, 2016; Eagly & Riger, 2014; G. Nelson & Prilleltensky, 2010). They assume that knowledge is shaped by power relationships created and maintained by social institutions and belief systems. They ask questions about who has the power to state what is true and who gets to define the nature of research relationships. Critical approaches put responsibility on the researcher to recognize and question their own position in social systems and how this affects research. The gender, race, ethnicity, social class, and other social positions of the researcher and research participant strongly influence what they experience in everyday life because these positions reflect greater or lesser degrees of social power. Critical researchers also take an activist stance, conducting research that can lead to challenging injustice. Critical community research may use specific research methods drawn from either postpositivist or constructivist approaches. Some feminist, liberation, and decolonial approaches to community psychology reflect a critical philosophy of science. Of course, an activist stance influences research choices and findings, putting responsibility on the researchers to make their assumptions and viewpoints explicit (as with constructivist approaches). A researcher taking a critical perspective might ask, for example, why so few high schools have GSAs given that research indicates that they have a positive impact on school climate for LGBTQ students. The researcher might use multiple methods to examine barriers to creating and sustaining student-led GSA clubs.

Thus, postpositivist, constructivist, and critical philosophies of science have different aims "before the beginning" of research. They are based in different ideas of the roles of researcher and research participant, different conceptions of how to use research, different ideas about how to deal with researchers' values and assumptions, and even different conceptions of what is "knowledge" (see Table 3.1). Much useful community research has postpositivist features, especially use of measurement and experimentation modified to fit community settings. Constructivist approaches have become increasingly influential in community psychology, especially fitting the field's emphasis on collaborative and participatory approaches. Critical approaches also have become influential, in part because they call attention to integrating research and action and because they note the importance of power dynamics in social systems. All three philosophies of science are useful in community psychology research, and a study may incorporate elements of more than one of these three philosophies.

For example, imagine that you wanted to develop a study that examines the effects of a neighborhood on children's lives (Nicotera, 2007). You might draw on multiple measures, including those developed from each of the three frameworks. The study might measure structural characteristics favored by postpositivists, such as census data that provide demographic information

**Table 3.1** Three Philosophies of Science for Community Psychology Research

| Philosophy of science | Epistemology | Methodology |
| --- | --- | --- |
| Postpositivist | Knowledge is built through shared understanding, using rigorous methods and standards of the scientific community. | Emphasis is placed on understanding cause-and-effect relationships, hypothesis testing, modeling, and experimental methods. |
| Constructivist | Knowledge is created collaboratively in relationships between researchers and participants. | Emphasis is placed on understanding contexts, meanings, and lived experiences of participants; often, qualitative methods are used. |
| Critical | Knowledge is shaped by power relationships and location within social systems. | Emphasis is placed on integrating research and action, attending to unheard voices, and challenging injustice using a variety of methods. |

and reveal the social and economic composition of the neighborhood. Yet you might also be concerned that using census data alone leaves out social process measures of the neighborhood more often brought to the fore by constructivists. These measures would help focus on how the residents of the neighborhood understand the neighborhood. In other words, what is it really like to live there? This might lead you toward residents' perceptions of norms, opportunities, barriers, dangers, and available resources. A critical focus would also be useful, helping you think about power, how different stakeholders might define the neighborhood differently (e.g., what areas are safe, what resources are available), and how children's perceptions should be included as well as adults. Our main point here is not that you should measure everything; instead, it is to show how each perspective guides research questions and strategies. No perfect research design exists; there are always trade-offs in conducting research. Yet we advocate that community researchers make their choices explicit in planning their research.

## Problem Definition in Research

Community researchers must decide how their research will relate to social action. A postpositivist approach to social problems seeks concrete, pragmatic, generalizable answers supported by research findings. It applies (with modifications) the scientific methods and findings of psychology to society in terms often defined by policymakers and funders. Much social science research assumes this stance, which dominated the early development of community psychology.

This approach can be very useful. For instance, how does a nation or a community prevent the spread of AIDS, improve child health, or reduce violence in schools? Community research can identify causes of these problems, develop programs or social policies to address those factors, and evaluate the effectiveness of those programs or policies. The National Academy of Medicine's approach to prevention science involves such a process: conducting research on factors that lead to health or behavior problems, using that knowledge to develop prevention programs, testing the programs' effectiveness in controlled studies, and then disseminating the most effective programs for replication in other settings (Hawkins et al., 2015). We will have the opportunity to discuss the benefits and limits of this prevention science approach further in Chapters 9 and 10.

For now, however, we will point out that the usefulness of such research depends in part on how problems, causes, and appropriate responses are defined (Price, 1989). Consensus around problem definitions and solutions often does not exist. Even with public health problems that are clearly defined and for which causal factors are understood (e.g., the diagnosis and transmission of HIV infection), there is often great controversy about prevention methods (e.g., needle exchanges, education about condoms and condom negotiation).

Conflicts mushroom when citizens cannot even agree on the definition of the problem and its causes, as with many issues of sexuality, child and family problems, and drug use, for example.

Does such conflict mean empirical research on social and community issues is useless? We argue that it is not. Instead of seeking to be value-neutral, researchers can acknowledge that social issues involve multiple positions, each with different value assumptions, different definitions of the problem, different theories about its causes and effects, and different interventions to prevent or treat it. Researchers can point out when the empirical evidence overwhelmingly favors particular problem definitions over others. Marybeth Shinn (2016), for example, has conducted research with colleagues for over 2 decades on the effectiveness of different approaches to reduce homelessness. Experimental evidence shows that strategies providing people more autonomy and resources (i.e., housing-first models) are more effective than approaches that require consumers to engage in multiple forms of treatment before they are eligible for housing (Tsemberis, 2010). The evidence that these researchers have accumulated has been so compelling that it has shifted the way policymakers define the problem of homelessness in the United States and Canada.

Community psychologists have also contributed to changing definitions of intimate partner violence, which at one time was considered by many people and institutions in power to be an acceptable form of social control. Simply recognizing and researching the use of force in relationships *as violence* has resulted in social change (N. E. Allen & Javdani, 2017). Action research around intimate partner violence continues across multiple ecological levels, from individual interventions to community-level coalitions to larger social systems change. In these efforts to understand and reduce interpersonal violence, as in addressing any complex problem, multiple divergent solutions across multiple ecological levels of analysis may be most effective (R. Miller & Shinn, 2005; Rappaport, 1981; Wandersman et al., 2008). In using evidence to improve understanding and contribute to change, researchers must still be intellectually honest, recognize the value of opposing views, use defensible methods, and be willing to present findings that turned out contrary to their assumptions (G. Nelson et al., 2001). Boldly and explicitly stating one's premises and values can actually improve research by clarifying the assumptions on which it is based.

## Attending to Marginalized Voices

We now return to the questions Jesica Fernández poses in the opening quote: Where do we position ourselves as researchers, and whom do we position ourselves with? One's personal values are an important guide. Ongoing reflexive practice in conversation with others is critical as well (Suffla et al., 2015). An additional guideline is to look for whose viewpoints are missing in the

**attending to marginalized voices**
conducting research that draws attention to and incorporates the knowledge and experiences of communities who are overlooked, identifying community strengths and resources.

**voice**
a metaphor drawn from feminist thinking that refers to a person's knowledge, experiences, words, intuitions, and insights.

debate over a social issue (Freire, 1970/1993; Rappaport, 1981; Riger, 1990). Discussion of social issues is often dominated by the powerful, who define the problem and set the terms of debate (N. Caplan & Nelson, 1973). Their ideas become the conventional wisdom about the problem. Thus, an important role of community researchers is to identify a community whose views are being overlooked and to conduct research that helps bring attention to the experiences and views of persons in that community. This provides broader knowledge of the issue, and it also may identify community strengths and resources. This approach can be termed **attending to marginalized voices**.

The metaphor of **voice** comes from feminist thinkers (Belenky et al., 1986; Reinharz, 1994; Riger, 1990). In their view, positivist methods and theories in psychology obscured and distorted women's experiences and knowledge. Women's voices—their words, intuitions, and insights—have not been clearly heard or understood. This obscuring of voices has also happened to other groups not historically well represented among researchers: persons of color, low-income persons, youth, and those with physical or mental disabilities, for example. Students in schools are seldom asked for their experiences and views in research on teaching and learning (Weinstein, 2002a). Reinharz (1994) noted that researchers cannot "give" voice to excluded groups or individuals; voice is something one develops oneself with support from others. Yet researchers can create ways to listen to and learn from voices of diverse persons and help bring their voices into psychology's knowledge base. Additionally, the knowledge base will shift and expand as academic institutions are more intentional about training a diverse group of researchers who bring new questions and concerns to our field (Dutta, 2016).

Attending to marginalized voices involves beginning research from the perspective of the less powerful individuals within social systems—the people who are most affected by the practices of any given social system (e.g., global economy, workplace, mental health services, school system or university) but who have the least control over those practices. Study the issue through their experiences, from their point of view, to understand the multiple social systems that affect them. That knowledge can then be used to advocate for social change to improve their lives and, perhaps, quality of life for the whole community or society. Rappaport (1981) advocated this approach in his early discussions of empowerment. It is especially consistent with critical philosophies of science (G. Nelson & Prilleltensky, 2010).

Many examples of feminist community psychology (e.g., Angelique & Mulvey, 2012; M. A. Bond et al., 2000a, 2000b; Salina et al., 2004) illustrate research that is explicit about values and premises, attends to marginalized voices and identities, and supports an activist approach to social change. They also call attention to how multiple ecological levels are intertwined, examining how macrosystems, organizations, and interpersonal forces are connected to oppression and liberation of women (recall the feminist slogan "The personal is political"). Feminist community researchers often (a) show how their own life experiences influence their perspectives, (b) seek to be explicit about their assumptions, and (c) aim to learn from others' perspectives. Research becomes a process of personal development and interpersonal bonding, not simply an intellectual undertaking—a distinctively feminist theme.

Cris Sullivan and associates collaborated with community women's advocates and survivors of intimate partner violence to develop a program in which paraprofessional advocates worked with women with abusive partners, helping them access resources related to legal assistance, housing, employment, and education. The research was grounded in feminist values and analysis and used randomized experimental designs with representative samples. These studies, which still influence research and practice in the field today, demonstrated that survivors of intimate partner violence who were involved in the advocacy relationship reported less violence, more social support, and better perceived quality of life than those in a control group (Bybee & Sullivan, 2002; Sullivan, 2003).

## What Do You Think?

1. Although the voice metaphor is rooted in feminism, women's voices are not the only ones that have been marginalized. Think of another community whose voice has also been marginalized. How could you attend to this unheard group through research?

2. "Feminism" is a broad term that covers a wide variety of groups and beliefs. Do you think that there are voices within feminism or other movements that have been marginalized and could be empowered?

# Promoting Community Participation and Collaboration in Research Decisions

The quality and usefulness of research data depend on the context in which they are collected and, especially, on the relationship between researcher and research participants.

One metaphor for the researcher–community relationship is that of guest and host (Robinson, 1990). Research is conducted by guests in a host community; among the good manners that might be expected of such guests are fully disclosing their intent and methods, seeking permission for their activities, respecting the host's wishes and views, and giving meaningful thanks for hospitality. Researchers receive the gift of cooperation from the community in providing data; reciprocating that gift involves providing products of that research in a form useful to the community. Another metaphor for this

**heart work**
incorporating values, emotions, and personal relationships into collaborative community research, in addition to expert knowledge.

relationship is a collaborative partnership, with both parties having some degree of choice and control and with open communication, compromise, and respect regarding those choices. Each partner brings unique resources to the shared work.

These metaphors imply a concern for the long-term interests of the community. The partnership metaphor especially involves participation by community members in planning and conducting research. The approaches we discuss below have been termed *participatory community research*, *participatory action research*, *action research*, *collaborative research*, and *community science* (Jason et al., 2004; J. G. Kelly et al., 2000; Reason & Bradbury, 2001; Tolman & Brydon-Miller, 2001; Trickett & Espino, 2004; Wandersman, Kloos, et al., 2005). Many of these are intellectual descendants of Lewin and colleagues' action research efforts in the 1940s.

Many researchers have exploited communities as "pockets of needs, laboratories for experimentation, or passive recipients of expertise" (Bringle & Hatcher, 2002, pp. 503–504). The metaphor of data mining fits the approach of researchers who conduct community research that benefits the researchers but not the community studied. To extend the metaphor of guests and hosts, we might say that researchers have not been particularly good guests. Reciprocity has not been the norm for much research conducted by academic researchers working in community settings. Those communities are understandably reluctant to cooperate with future researchers. As community psychologists, we have to keep this history in mind, making sure that we do not repeat these patterns and do follow through on commitments to create useful research products for our host communities. While collaborative methods are not a panacea, they do address issues of power and control, and they seek to avoid exploitation.

These control-related issues become even more important when the research involves an intervention or action program. The problem to be addressed, the specific objectives of the intervention, and the manner of implementation and evaluation are all issues to be decided. Long-term commitment by researchers is needed if the intervention is to be incorporated into the everyday life of the setting (Primavera, 2004). The practice of conducting collaborative research involves values, emotions, personal relationships, and conflict resolution. Researchers need not only an intellectual understanding of the issues involved but also social-emotional insight and skills. Recall the phrase from the last sentence of Regina Langhout's (2015) quote at the beginning of the chapter, in which she emphasizes **heart work**, drawing not only from her head and hands but also from her embodied emotions and felt political commitments to conduct collaborative research.

Genuinely collaborative research often leads to personal change for both citizens and researchers (Foster-Fishman et al., 2005). Cultural misunderstandings, power differentials, divergent values, and other factors create challenges but also can lead to richer understandings and better research (Jason et al., 2004; Primavera & Brodsky, 2004; Sarason, 2003b). This is a key point. In collaborative research practice, we are often able to gain key insights into community processes and learn things that we would not have otherwise known using more traditional approaches to research (Chirowodza et al., 2009). Some of what we learn is personal and can be uncomfortable as we gain better insight into our hidden values, biases, and assumptions and the places they conflict with our intended goals for research. This too is a part of our reflexive journey (Case, 2017).

In this section, we review specific approaches to facilitating researcher–community partnership and citizen participation in research decision making at each stage of community research:

1. Develop a relationship "before the beginning" with community partners that enables research collaboration.

2. Make research decisions, including how to define the topic of research and how to collect data.

3. Analyze and interpret findings of the research.

4. Report results and evaluate the impact of the research.

At each step, we present approaches that maximize participation by community members. We do not advocate that these methods are useful or appropriate in every context. Community research varies along a spectrum from minimum to maximum community participation, and participation may be understood as a process in which capacity is built over time (Bess et al., 2009). Each community research project requires a different matching of researcher and citizen roles (Pokorny et al., 2004).

## Developing a Relationship "Before the Beginning"

The research partnership may begin with the entry of researchers into a community, as well as identification of researchers already within a community. For example, Elizabeth (one of the authors of this textbook) began a research partnership with a local youth organization in Memphis by attending an orientation for youth fellows, participating in events hosted by the fellows over the course of a school year, and facilitating research training and workshops on participatory action research. She and her undergraduate students developed a relationship over time with staff and a group of 30 youth organizers from across the city who are working to increase youth voice in the political process; create more brave, safe, and educated spaces for LGBTQ+ youth; unite youth activists to end the school-to-prison pipeline; and stop sexual harassment and assault. The research team is now studying intersectional approaches to youth organizing and the role of peer mentoring in sustaining the work.

Initial questions for developing research partnerships include the following: Who are the researchers, what institutions support or fund them, and what are their purposes? Are researchers invited into the organization or community? By whom, and under what terms? Who are the community partners, and which facets of the community do they represent? Who will benefit from research in this organization or community?

The resources of researchers and the host community are both valued. To build true collaboration, both sides will need to devote time and effort and decide how to share control. Not every community needs or wants the same resources from researchers: an economically oppressed community may look for economic resources or greater visibility for their work, while in a more affluent community the need may be for emotional support or respect for persons with chronic illness (G. Nelson et al., 2001). Community members offer many resources, such as practical knowledge of the community and culture, social networks, and access to community settings. The youth Change Fellows with whom Elizabeth works, for example, are experts in their own lived experience, and the knowledge and strategies that emerge from youth–adult partnerships are critical for positive community change.

Partnerships, or the interdependence of researchers and citizens, must be built through interpersonal relationships. That involves plenty of informal face-to-face contact, getting to know each other across contexts. It also involves commitments for a longer period of time than a traditional research or intervention project might require. For community researchers, important interpersonal skills include self-awareness of one's emotions and of how one appears to others; self-disclosure in the process of building trust; and clear communication of aims, viewpoints, and values. Having community members explain their community and culture to researchers in an atmosphere of learning and respect is valuable. Humility and willingness to learn are essential. As in the example above, both volunteer community service and informal socializing with community members can be helpful. It is important for researchers to recognize differences in social status, power, culture, and life opportunities between researchers and community members and to acknowledge how those differences can limit the perspectives of researchers (we will discuss this more in the section on culturally anchored research and return to this in Chapter 7). For example, in Elizabeth's work with the Change Fellows, challenging "adultism" has been useful in thinking through best practices for youth–adult partnerships. This concept refers to the assumption that adults are better than young people and entitled to act upon young people without their agreement (Bell, 1995).

Researchers may need to demystify the images many people hold about research. To promote effective communication within the team, researchers must be willing to find a vocabulary that is commonsensical yet not condescending. Language communicates power, and the use of technical jargon can alienate community partners. Researchers also need to learn from community members' experiential, cultural, "insider" knowledge.

## Research Decisions: Defining the Topic and Collecting Data

In community-based research, decisions need to be made collaboratively. One option for making research decisions is to create a community research panel composed of representatives of community organizations and other citizens, which allows researchers to communicate and negotiate with community members. It also improves the ability of researchers to understand the cultural characteristics of the community and provides a way for the community to hold researchers accountable. Instead of creating a new panel, researchers can establish a formal relationship with an existing body in the community (e.g., a tribal council or neighborhood association).

Another model for research decision making is to include community stakeholders as part of the research team itself. For example, Michelle Fine and her colleagues (2003) worked with incarcerated women to study (a) the impact of college education on women's self-understandings and lives while in prison, (b) the prison environment, and (c) the world outside the prison. A small group of women in prison enrolled in a college-level research methods course and learned to become interviewers and analysts. They joined the research team and shared difficult decisions about the research process as it unfolded. As persons holding insider knowledge and as skilled researchers, they were able to document a process of women's transformation in which "individuals move from being passive objects to active subjects—critical thinkers who actively participate in their lives and social surroundings; who take responsibility for past and future actions; who direct their lives, networks, and social actions in the world" (Fine et al., 2003, p. 186).

In both models—a community research panel working with professional researchers and a research team comprising university–community partners—research is planned in partnership. Some examples of issues to negotiate include whether to use a control group (which does not receive a promising program), whether observers of mutual help group meetings are acceptable, the format and questions for questionnaires, and even where original data will be kept and how its confidentiality can be ensured.

These and similar decisions have trade-offs. For instance, lack of a control group may limit the evaluation of a program's effectiveness. Open-ended interviews fit the norms of many communities better than standardized questionnaires but make it more difficult to develop reliable, valid measurements and use a large sample. Negotiating methodological or practical decisions within a community takes time and involves compromise. Yet the traditional psychological paradigm, in which researchers make these and other choices in the interest of experimental control, is also limited. Many community

**reciprocity**
creating an atmosphere of trust in a relationship between researchers and community members in which the partners focus on outcomes that benefit everyone, rather than focusing solely on one's own interests.

questions simply cannot be studied with traditional methods. Moreover, genuine collaboration with community members can increase the validity of measurement as researchers craft more appropriate methods and research participants take the research more seriously. (Have you ever completed a survey hurriedly because you had no investment in the results?) Studies with mutual help groups that have involved the group as a genuinely collaborative partner have had very high response rates (Isenberg et al., 2004). Creating a positive relationship with a community affords returning there for future studies.

A collaborative, participatory approach with partners can involve experimental methods. The research on advocacy around intimate partner violence conducted by Sullivan (2003) and associates (described earlier in this chapter) involved women's shelters, community advocates, and survivors of violence in decisions about all aspects of the research, including development of assessment questions and measures. The most difficult decision involved whether to use an experimental design, randomly assigning women to the advocacy program or to a control group that received the usual shelter services. The community members were wary of the randomization at first but eventually were convinced of its fairness and of the value of carefully evaluating the actual effects of the program.

### Interpreting Findings

Another step in the community–researcher partnership is interpretation of results. One useful step is to present results to the community research panel or other community members, asking for their interpretations. Researchers and citizens can consider questions such as the following: Are these results surprising? Is further refinement of methods needed? How can these results be useful to the community? How might they harm the community? For example, if a community needs assessment identified high rates of adolescent risk behaviors or substance abuse, how will this be understood? And what will be done with these results? Will they be used to further stigmatize a community or to leverage additional resources?

Interdependent relationships grow from **reciprocity**, in which each partner moves from a focus on satisfaction of one's own interests to a focus on outcomes that benefit both partners over the long term, in an atmosphere of trust (Bringle & Hatcher, 2002). Affirming shared values and long-term aims fosters this development, especially when conflicts arise. That does not mean an end to conflicts, but it does build a climate in which to resolve them. It also is important to share credit for successes and work together to address challenges and conflicts. Important interpersonal skills for making collaborative research decisions include providing interpersonal support, asserting and accepting disagreement, avoiding defensiveness, sharing power, and recognizing and managing conflicts. Close monitoring and discussion of these issues fosters relationship development. Primavera (2004) described the ebb and flow of relationships in a university–community partnership for a family literacy program, concluding that "if there is gold to be found in community research and action, it lies in the *process* of our work" (p. 190). Again, how we make research decisions is just as important as the decisions that we make.

In Chapter 1, we discussed the Oxford House movement, in which persons in recovery from substance abuse live together and promote each other's recovery without professional supervision. This nationwide movement began in a Chicago recovery home without any researcher or professional involvement. Over many years, Oxford House and a research team from DePaul University developed a collaborative partnership that has benefited both. The DePaul team entered the relationship "before the beginning" of the research with an interest in innovative models of recovery and believed that involving Oxford House members in all phases of the research would enhance its validity and practical value. Oxford House members and researchers met weekly for an open exchange of ideas and to monitor ongoing research; these meetings were open to any Oxford House member. Likewise, Oxford House meetings, even when sensitive topics were discussed, were open to researchers. Both partners worked to promote trust in the relationship. The research began with student researchers attending Oxford House activities and conducting interviews with residents to learn about the process of recovery at Oxford House from the residents' perspective. This qualitative research became the basis for later quantitative studies, including a randomized experiment comparing Oxford House to other substance abuse recovery conditions such as outpatient treatment. After 24 months, those in the Oxford House condition had significantly lower substance use, significantly higher monthly income, and significantly lower incarceration rates than those in the usual-care condition (Jason et al., 2006).

Research decisions were made collaboratively. Research design and assessment instruments were discussed thoroughly and approved by Oxford House representatives. In grant-supported studies, the staff who recruited participants and collected data were current or former Oxford House residents, approved by Oxford House representatives and the research team. The partnership has built the capacity of the research team to interpret findings of the research. The team is better able to understand and measure the utility of the Oxford House approach, and Oxford House staff are better able to perform their own ongoing evaluation and program development. Researchers have become advocates for Oxford House and have worked with the movement in establishing new houses for women with children (Suarez-Balcazar et al., 2004).

## Reporting Research and Evaluating Its Impact

Research typically generates scholarly reports in conference presentations, edited volumes, books, and peer-reviewed journal articles. These further the researchers' careers but usually do little for the community.

Important questions concern products of research: Who is actually benefiting from this research? Will researchers share their findings with community members in a form useful to them? Did citizens gain knowledge, skills, funding, or other resources to pursue their own goals? Have the researchers and the community members built an ongoing alliance for future collaborations? Even broader issues arise when macrosystems are also considered: Will the research methods or findings promote social justice? Will research products accurately portray the strengths of the individuals, communities, or cultures studied? How can the research inform future decisions by citizens, communities, organizations, governmental bodies, or other groups? How can the research speak directly to policymakers at local, regional, and national levels? Refer to the Community Psychology in Action feature in Box 3.1 describing a partnership that has focused on research processes and products that benefit all involved.

Examples of additional research products might include reader-friendly newsletters for citizens; opinion essays or letters to the editor in newspapers; articles in popular magazines; interviews on broadcast media; expert testimony in legislative hearings or in court; advocacy reports or visits to policymakers; teaching materials for formal or informal courses; contributions to community art projects; and development of educational videos, role plays, skits, or other performances (Stein & Mankowski, 2004). For example, while conducting interviews on the psychological effects of unemployment, Fryer and Fagan (2003) used a handheld computer to calculate eligibility for government entitlements and programs (for those who were willing to share the financial information needed). This was the first time those benefits had been helpfully explained to many participants.

In the project described at the beginning of the chapter, aimed at understanding and enhancing children's experience of an elementary school, the research team (including community psychologists, university students, and elementary school students) created murals as one of the ways to share their research findings and create change (Langhout, personal communication; see photo on p. 100). The elementary student researchers named one of their murals *We Are Powerful*, and they offered the following inscription: "We hope our mural themes of community, education, and diversity will help all feel like this is a place for them, and will inspire all to see they have the power to change their community." In each of these examples, collaborative research teams moved from simply having good intentions to intentionally trying to make a difference (J. Smith, 2006).

Prilleltensky (2003, 2008) proposed that community psychology research be evaluated not only in terms of methodological (often positivist) forms of validity but also in terms of two other criteria, which are part of his concept of psychopolitical validity. First, does the research account for the influence of

---

**Box 3.1 Community Psychology in Action: Research Collaborations in Which Everyone Wins**

Yolanda Suarez-Balcazar, University of Illinois at Chicago, and Luisa Lopez, El Valor

While we get ready to begin a community-engaged research meeting, the students and I admire the artwork created by El Valor's clients: large, colorful Mexican dolls made of papier-mâché and picture frames decorated with dried flowers are displayed all around the conference room. El Valor is a community-based organization serving mostly Latinos with developmental disabilities across the lifespan and their families. El Valor is located in a working-class Latino neighborhood in Chicago, which is home to a Mexican arts museum and borders the University of Illinois at Chicago (UIC) campus on its south side. El Valor was founded by a Latina immigrant mother with a child with a developmental disability who could not find services for her child at the time. The Spanish word *valor* means "courage," which the founder used to communicate the will and power of Latinos with disabilities and their families that allow them to succeed.

The goals of our collaboration, which has expanded for over 18 years, include to facilitate the empowerment of individuals with disabilities, their families, and the staff members serving them and to foster a positive partnership that benefits El Valor's participants and their families as well as UIC researchers and students.

During years of working together we have been able to foster a strong collaboration in which each partner is willing to work toward benefiting the other. Thus, Yolanda has participated in United Way program reviews and El Valor staff have spoken at classes taught at UIC. We both have supported each other in grant-writing activities and program evaluation. In the last 4 years, we have been working together developing, implementing, and evaluating a community healthy lifestyles program called *Familias Saludables* (Healthy Families) to support the well-being and health of Latino families with youth with disabilities. The mutual collaboration yielded an evidence-based 9-week program that focuses on promoting physical activity (through Zumba dancing), health and nutrition education through hands-on and dynamic activities and snack preparation, family goal setting, and social learning discussions. El Valor staff and local mothers helped design the intervention. With funding from the Chicago Community Trust, the program has been implemented for over 4 years and now El Valor is sustaining it on their own. Staff received capacity training and mothers were empowered to deliver the program. El Valor's staff and participants were very interested in a culturally tailored, language-relevant community intervention that included the whole family, in part because of the high incidence of obesity and the few resources available to them in the community.

### What Do You Think?

1. How does the work of El Valor represent some of community psychology's key values, such as respect for human diversity, sense of community, empowerment and citizen participation, and collaboration?

2. Although El Valor and the *Familias Saludables* program were designed to help community members, how do you think the researchers benefited from this work? How could this affect their findings and benefit future studies and interventions?

3. Think of a community you belong to or that you are interested in studying. Is there a particular issue you would like to address within that community? How could you collaborate with the members of that community to do so?

This mural created by elementary school researchers to share their research findings and create change demonstrates how community psychologists can creatively share knowledge with community members.

macrosystem and other social forces, especially social injustice, on the lives of individuals and communities? Were these forces measured or studied in the research and discussed with community members? Second, does the research promote the capacity of research participants and community members to understand macrosystem forces and to become involved in liberating social change? For instance, did citizens gain skills for understanding injustice, articulating their views, forming alliances, resolving conflicts, gaining power, making decisions, and similar capacities for advocating their community's interests?

Pursuing these aims involves careful thinking not only "before the beginning" but also about what happens "after the ending." Throughout our research, we should be thinking not only about the benefits of our research but also about how our research might be problematic. This reflexive practice helps us attend to possible unintended consequences and *iatrogenic effects*, or harmful effects, of the research. We return to this in our discussion of prevention and promotion programs in Chapter 11.

**research ethics**
a values-focused framework that ensures the well-being of participants—both individuals and groups—during the research process by avoiding paternalistic stances and respecting persons, partnerships, communities, and cultures. It helps researchers bridge the gap between the abstract goals of research and the actual practice of research in a community setting.

## Ethics of Participatory Approaches

Participatory, collaborative research methods can be challenging. As you have probably experienced, working with a diverse team to make decisions and solve problems means that disagreements, tensions, and conflicts are likely. How do we resolve these conflicts and solve problems as they arise? As R. Campbell (2016) suggests, the work can get "sticky," a term that acknowledges the interconnectedness of relationships in participatory research as well as the idea that sometimes we can get stuck and not know what to do. We need an ethical framework to guide how we conduct our research with community partners and to help us when we find ourselves in a sticky situation. In Chapter 1, we introduced community psychology values; here, in our discussion of **research ethics**, we are focusing more on the practice of our values in action research. Ethics help us think about how to navigate the space between *what ought to be* and *what is on the ground* (R. Campbell, 2016).

As you may have learned in other psychology classes, ethical frameworks for research with human subjects have been developed in response to historical research and human rights abuses. Institutional review boards (IRBs) are now in place at universities and research institutes, and IRBs use these ethical frameworks to protect individual human participants in research. Yet these frameworks, focused on individual well-being and safety, do not adequately consider the well-being of groups or communities or the types of relationships and responsibilities found in collaborative research partnerships with communities (Banks et al., 2013).

As Case (2017) argued, we need to expand our consideration of ethics beyond IRB approval. Community psychologists continue to elaborate an ethical framework that incorporates respect for persons and care for their well-being at the individual levels while articulating what it means to respect partnerships, communities, and cultural groups (R. Campbell & Morris, 2017a). And determining respectful partnerships is something that needs to be codefined and constructed with community partners to reflect both what ought to be and what is on the ground.

Through partnerships, community researchers also seek to change oppressive systems. Action research designed to change how organizations and systems operate can create ethical challenges as well. How, for example, does a researcher maintain partnerships with the more powerful people and groups in the system so that they can enact changes, but not participate in collusion with those oppressive systems?

Javdani described her experience as a researcher designing and evaluating an intervention for girls involved in the juvenile justice system (Javdani et al., 2017). She noted the fine line between research that represents collusion with systems of control (i.e., the juvenile justice system) and research that offers a challenge and resistance to that system. Through a reflexive process with others on her team, she came to understand that their research needed to contribute not to further paternalism and punishment but to redistribution of resources and opportunities for girls involved in the system. Their ethical commitments led them to create a youth advisory board made up of girls who had participated in the intervention. They also changed the training for those collecting data from girls and their families to become more culturally competent and to collect data that would not just focus on individual girls' pathology but also assess key aspects of their context.

In this example, ethical practice is built on evolving, inclusive frameworks and ongoing reflexivity in research. For participatory research, particular attention is paid to the ethics of building and maintaining multiple relationships, as well as the possibilities and challenges of engaging communities in the research process (S. E. Collins et al., 2018).

Terms such as "participatory" and "collaborative" have multiple meanings that can be divergent or even contradictory (Trickett & Espino, 2004), and we return to this in Chapter 8. We have emphasized the commonalities of a number of participatory-collaborative approaches, which provide specific ways to enact core community psychology values. They embody the Swampscott ideal of the *participant–conceptualizer*, introduced in Chapter 2, who is actively involved in community processes while attempting to understand and explain them. And they represent a distinctive contribution of community psychology to academic research and to communities.

# Attending to the Cultural and Social Contexts of Research

All research, even a laboratory study, occurs within a culture, perhaps more than one. Understanding diverse cultures, populations, and settings is essential for community psychology (Kral et al., 2011). It is especially important that community researchers study a variety of cultures and communities, especially those that have been ignored by mainstream psychology. Researchers also need to understand how they themselves are affected by culture. In this section, we focus on a few specific cultural issues in conducting research. We leave for Chapter 7 a larger analysis of cultural and related concepts for understanding human diversity.

## Three Methodological Issues Involving Culture

Cultural assumptions influence every research decision. Yet psychologists often fail to consider how these assumptions limit the meaning and interpretation of our research findings (M. A. Bond & Harrell, 2006; Brady et al., 2018). Too often, cultural variables have been included without adequate reflection about what is meant by these constructs, why they may be important for a given study, and how they are to be measured or assessed.

For example, suppose a study finds that Latino/a adolescents are pushed out of high school more often than European American teens, a seemingly simple empirical effect (yet note already what a difference it makes to say "pushed out" instead of "dropped out" of high school; this is another illustration of how problem definition shapes our approaches to research and action). This seemingly obvious difference between groups, however, is useless—even harmful—as a basis for designing social policy or prevention programs unless important conceptual questions are answered. For example, Latino/a adolescents may be labeled as less academically motivated or persistent in school, or they may become the target of an inappropriate intervention. So we need to ask, what is the specific context for this finding? Were confounds such as socioeconomic status, effects of stereotyping and discrimination, access to educational opportunities, and first language (English or Spanish) considered in this study? Is this difference due to factors within "Latino" cultures or to external economic forces or discrimination? Which Latino/a ethnicities (e.g., Mexican American, Puerto Rican, Cuban, Dominican) were represented in the sample? How might these specific ethnic groups differ from each other? How many Latino/a adolescents were recent immigrants or longer term U.S. residents? These questions illustrate the methodological issues we describe next (see Brady et al., 2018; Sperry et al., 2019).

***How Is Cultural, Racial, or Ethnic Identity Assessed?*** These and similar concepts are often assessed with simple "box checking" based on the participant's self-reported choice among a limited set of categories. For instance, on a questionnaire, "Asian American" may be the only available category for Americans of Japanese, Vietnamese, Indian, and other ancestries (the category is even wider if Pacific Islanders are included). Related issues include the following: Is there a coding scheme for multiethnic or biracial responses? Are one's first language, birthplace and parents' birthplaces, and length of residence in the country assessed? What is the extent of one's personal identification with an ethnic or cultural tradition? If researchers rely on simple box checking, even with more specific boxes to check, they assess only the surface of racial, ethnic, or cultural identities, not the deeper reality (Frable, 1997; Schwartz et al., 2014; Trimble et al., 2003). Deeper understanding of identities rather than simple categorization also may be an issue in examining concepts such as sexual orientation, ability or disability, and religion or spirituality. Yet even with problems that accompany box-checking measurement, attending to how researchers categorize social identities at this surface level remains important for action research and social policy. How we count socially defined groups matters because more accurate measurement may contribute to the visibility of groups that have been marginalized or disadvantaged, such as immigrant groups (M. Williams & Husk, 2013).

**assumption
of population
homogeneity**
categorizing all
individuals within a
cultural group as being
alike without properly
acknowledging
differences.

**assumption of
methodological
equivalence**
assuming that research
methods work equally
well in multiple
cultural settings
without modification
and not properly
evaluating how cultural
differences can impact
research findings.
This can occur even if
culture is not the topic
being studied.

*Assumptions of Population Homogeneity.* A related issue concerns accurately understanding the diversity within every culture. An **assumption of population homogeneity** (Sasao & Sue, 1993) categorizes all members of a cultural group as alike and overlooks differences among them. Research in social categorization suggests that this results from the cognitive tendency to think about members of one's cultural in-group in more detail than persons outside it (J. G. Kelly et al., 1994). Thus, people understand members of their own culture in complex ways, as individuals and as members of various groups or categories. People think more simplistically about members of other cultures or communities and tend to categorize them in more general terms. This is ethnocentrism, although it is often inadvertent. It also reflects lack of detailed knowledge and experience with phenomena we wish to understand in the communities where they occur. Forming a collaborative relationship with community members helps counteract assumptions of population homogeneity.

For example, there are important differences between generations of immigrant groups (e.g., first-generation immigrants from Mexico, second- and third-generation Mexican Americans), as well as gender, socioeconomic, or other differences within ethnic or racial categories (Goodkind & Deacon, 2004; Hughes & Seidman, 2002). In studies of alcohol use among Americans of Japanese ancestry, findings from samples in Hawaii differed from those on the mainland (Sasao & Sue, 1993). At the individual level, some members of an ethnic population may consider their ethnicity a very important aspect of their personal identity, while others do not. And characteristics such as gender and gender identity make a great deal of difference in worldview and life experiences in any culture.

*Assumptions of Methodological Equivalence.* A third issue concerns **assumptions of methodological equivalence** across cultures—that is, assuming that research methods will work equally well with multiple cultural groups without modification (Burlew, 2003; Hughes & Seidman, 2002). Such assumptions can occur even when cultural differences are not the topic of research or recognized by researchers. Linguistic equivalence of questionnaires or other measurement instruments is the simplest example. Tanaka-Matsumi and Marsella (cited in Hughes & DuMont, 1993) found that the English clinical term *depression* and the closest Japanese translation *yuutsu* were not equivalent. When asked to define depression, U.S. citizens described internal states such as "sad" and "lonely," whereas Japanese citizens described yuutsu using external states such as "dark" and "rain." Careful checks on translation can reduce but not eliminate such problems. Some measures may simply be inappropriate for some cultural groups. For example, Coppens et al. (2006) described the problem of using self-esteem measures with teens engaged in a Cambodian dance group. The self-esteem measures were based on Western understandings of selfhood and self-esteem as a protective factor in youth development, while both the teens, whose families were recent immigrants to the United States, and the dance group were rooted in an interdependent, non-Western cultural tradition.

Issues of scale equivalence refer to whether choices on questionnaires or other measures mean the same thing across cultures. Hughes and Seidman (2002) cited evidence that African American and Hispanic participants were more likely to use the extremes of Likert scales (e.g., a scale that asks for a rating on a continuum from *strongly disagree* to *strongly agree*), whereas European American respondents were more likely to use the intermediate areas of such scales. More generally, the quantitative approach of Western psychology is unfamiliar in many cultures. Goodkind and Deacon (2004) discussed how they developed qualitative and quantitative methods for research with two groups of refugee women: Hmong women from Laos and Muslim women from the Middle East, Afghanistan, and Africa. Combining qualitative and quantitative approaches proved to be most effective because both approaches had strengths and limitations. Survey methods emphasizing forced choice responses were sometimes experienced as silencing but also allowed for longitudinal analysis over time. Qualitative interviewing required overcoming extensive language and translation barriers but allowed for listening to often unheard voices and rich understanding of refugee women's experiences.

## Conducting Culturally Anchored Research

What can researchers do to recognize issues of culture and respond to them?

We return to these issues in Chapter 7, where we discuss cultural competence and the important role of cultural humility in some detail. For now, note that the first steps begin with oneself. Cultivate an understanding of how your own culture and experiences have shaped your worldview. In addition, adopt a "stance of informed naivete, curiosity, and humility" in learning about another culture: an awareness of your own limited knowledge and a genuine willingness to learn (Mock, 1999, p. 40). Recognize that this learning will be an ongoing process.

This learning cannot be cultivated in isolation. Seek experiences and personal relationships that promote learning about your own culture and the culture in which you seek to do research. Those experiences may include informal socializing or attending community celebrations and events, or more structured interviews with interested community members. *What* you do may be less important than *how* you do it, with respect and willingness to listen.

Create settings for discussion where researchers and citizens can personally explore difficult issues of culture and power: how one's own culture influences and limits one's worldview, strengths of different cultural worldviews and values, personal effects of social injustice and oppression, how to

Respecting human diversity and avoiding cultural assumptions are essential to community psychology research.

plan research to promote empowerment of community members, and access to resources that are wanted by the host community. Examples include the following.

Gary Harper and his research team collaborated with Project VIDA, a community-based organization in Little Village, a Mexican American neighborhood in Chicago (G. W. Harper, Bangi, et al., 2004; G. W. Harper, Lardon, et al., 2004). Project VIDA conducts HIV prevention programs for Latinx LGBTQ+ youth. The researchers were interested in learning about the community's narratives: the shared stories that express important values, historical events, folkways, and emotions. They read Latinx magazines and newspapers, especially those for teens. They visited Little Village repeatedly, learning about cultural murals and the neighborhood's decorative gateway, shopping and eating locally, attending cultural events, and meeting Project VIDA staff and Little Village residents. They sought to learn stories associated with Mexican culture, Little Village, and individuals involved with Project VIDA. Meetings with project staff began with sharing of food and personal stories. The study itself used individual and group interviews to elicit stories from adolescent participants and program staff about culturally based expectations that can promote or hinder HIV prevention among Latinx adolescents.

Gerald Mohatt et al. (2004) also drew on narratives in research on sobriety in Alaska Native communities. They took a strengths perspective by studying personal stories of pathways to sobriety. They developed a collaborative research relationship with a coordinating council composed mostly of Native Alaskans, while negotiating steps of the research with a number of Native Alaskan tribal boards and village councils. Tribal Elders rejected the idea of monetary payment for participation, saying that their participation was not for sale and that many persons would participate to contribute to the community. IRBs required that tapes of interviews be destroyed after the research, but Elders also rejected this notion, pointing out the usefulness of tapes for future prevention activities. The researchers developed procedures for each participant to choose whether to receive payment or donate it to charity and whether to allow retention of tapes with confidentiality ensured. When recruitment of participants greatly outpaced all expectations (152 persons volunteered for an initial study requiring only 36 participants), the Elders insisted that each volunteer be interviewed, to respect their willingness to help. Researchers developed a briefer interview process for this purpose. Researchers also had to forge compromises between federal funders, who desired quantitative methods, and Native preference for qualitative interviews that allowed them to tell their own stories. The patience of Native representatives and the research team was rewarded with a rich archive of interviews that expressed cultural strengths and provided a basis for sobriety promotion in Native communities.

## Conducting Research With an Ecological Perspective

For any study, the researchers need to choose the ecological level(s) of analysis. Recall our discussion of levels of analysis in Chapter 1; we will return to this ecological framework in greater detail in Chapter 5. The challenge for a community psychology researcher is addressing the interrelationships among these different levels of analysis, not just studying one level in isolation (Christens et al., 2014; Fowler & Todd, 2017). For example, in a study of protective factors for adolescent resistance to drug use, variables across multiple levels should be considered. These may include individual needs and strengths, microsystem factors (such as family and peer influences), neighborhood characteristics, cultural values and resources, economic factors, and political influences on drug laws and enforcement.

### An Example of the Importance of Considering Levels of Analysis: Supported Housing Environments

How do we understand the ecology of persons living with, and recovering from, serious mental illness? How do key contexts for living, such as housing, affect well-being? P. Wright and Kloos (2007) addressed these questions, paying particular attention to multiple levels of analysis. They used survey data and observations to examine factors related to well-being for persons living in supported housing (i.e., persons living independently with a housing subsidy and mental health services that they choose to utilize). Researchers looked at the apartment level, the neighborhood level, and the community level, examining residents' perception of their apartment and their neighborhood, qualities of apartments and neighborhoods rated by outside observers, and census-tract data. Neighborhood characteristics, particularly the residents' perceptions of belonging, acceptance, and community tolerance, were most predictive of differences in well-being. Wright and Kloos caution that neighborhood characteristics stood out in part because there was less variability in the quality of the apartments, but their findings show that neighborhood variables were just as important to the residents as the quality of their individual apartments. Many people typically think of the apartment level as the most proximate and most important level for well-being, but it could be that the social qualities of the neighborhood are "closer" in some ways to one's sense of home than the qualities of the apartment itself. The findings point to the importance of social relationships and individuals' overall sense of comfort in their neighborhood. They suggest that supported housing programs focus not just on quality control in terms of the physical conditions of an apartment and its safety but also on increasing acceptance for diversity and disability in neighborhoods, as well as increasing opportunities for social contact between neighbors. Further research indicated the value of including persons living with and recovering from mental illness in the design of neighborhood indicators as well (Townley & Kloos, 2014).

## How Can Ecological Levels Be Studied?

How can researchers study the characteristics of levels of analysis beyond the individual, such as microsystems, organizations, and communities? These cannot solely be studied by administering individual measures familiar to psychologists. Individuals within a classroom, an organization, or even a locality may be interdependent members of a community, which complicates statistical analysis and interpretation (Shinn & Rapkin, 2000). Community psychology seeks to answer questions about the effects of larger ecological units on individual lives.

Increasingly, community psychologists approach complex social settings and contexts as systems (Christens et al., 2014; Shiell & Riley, 2017). Recall, for example, our discussion earlier in this chapter of a hypothetical study that examines the effects of a neighborhood on children's lives. We suggested that multiple measures might be used to understand the neighborhood context, including demographic census data and different stakeholders' perceptions of problems, opportunities, and resources in the neighborhood. We might also think about the neighborhood (and the children in the neighborhood) as part of a system with boundaries, ecological layers, niches, organizations, and actors (Foster-Fishman et al., 2007). We might begin by asking, for example, how to determine the boundaries of the neighborhood. What would children who live in the neighborhood tell us about this (or show us on a guided tour or draw for us on a map)? How would we reconcile the perspectives of children with the perspectives of their caregivers and other stakeholders in the neighborhood, as well as the boundaries created by elementary school catchment areas, service delivery systems, public transportation routes, and census tracts? A focus on ecological systems might not make our jobs as researchers easier, but it may help us focus on dynamic, multilayered contexts and second-order, participatory strategies.

In Chapter 5, we describe in greater detail a number of ecological concepts that community psychologists use to think about these issues (for useful reviews, see also Hawe, 2017; Linney, 2000; Trickett, 2009). Multiple ecological levels are embedded in the name "community psychology." Researchers in the field choose ecological level(s) of analysis for every study, even if only by default. Research is improved by making those choices explicit and by addressing factors at multiple ecological levels.

## Conclusion

This chapter on the aims of community research is organized around four commitments:

- examining the values and assumptions we bring to or work
- promoting community participation and collaboration in research
- attending to the cultural and social contexts of research
- conducting research with an ecological perspective

Our format of four commitments for community research may seem to imply that a research team addresses each of these issues separately. Actually, these choices are interdependent. It is not unusual for an existing partnership with a community organization to influence the researcher's choice of phenomenon, perspective, and level of analysis for a study. Or a researcher may study their own culture or population, often within an existing relationship with a specific community. What is certain is that all four commitments are involved in community research, whether explicitly chosen by the researcher or implicitly assumed without reflection. Community research always occurs within a culture and a community, always concerns levels of analysis, and always studies a phenomenon from a particular framework of values. Our purpose in this chapter has been to help you become more aware of questions that will arise in the research process and thus become more capable of making explicit, reasoned choices in performing community research. In the next chapter, we turn to specific research methods.

## For Review

### Discussion Questions

1. Return to the opening exercise about reflexivity in research. How might your answers to those questions have changed after reading this chapter?

2. If you were to conduct research about a community issue that you care about, which of the three philosophies of science would ground your work? Why would you use that framework?

3. Imagine that you were returning to your high school to develop an action research project with students there. How would you design that project in collaboration with students and other stakeholders? How would you make decisions about how to proceed?

4. Now imagine that you were developing an action research project with students from a high school that you did not attend, in a part of the world that is less familiar to you. How would you design that project in collaboration with students and other stakeholders? How would you make decisions about how to proceed?

### Key Terms

reflexivity, 81

positivism, 85

postpositivist philosophies of science, 85

constructivist philosophies of science, 85

critical philosophies of science, 86

attending to marginalized voices, 90

voice, 90

heart work, 92

reciprocity, 96

research ethics, 101

assumption of population homogeneity, 104

assumption of methodological equivalence, 104

### Learn More

A detailed summary of the chapter, along with other review materials, is available on the *Community Psychology, Fourth Edition* companion website at http://pubs.apa.org/books/supp/kloos4/.

Community psychologists use a variety of collaborative and participatory methods to answer research questions, including qualitative, quantitative, and mixed-methods approaches.

Rawpixel.com/Shutterstock.com

# 4 Methods of Community Psychology Research

## Looking Ahead  ⫸

After reading this chapter you will be able to answer these questions:

1. What are the strengths and limits of qualitative methods for community research?

2. What are the strengths and limits of quantitative methods for community research?

3. How might you utilize mixed-methods research to gain the advantages of both qualitative and quantitative approaches?

## Opening Exercise

## Attending to Marginalized Voices and Building Social Inclusion

Urmitapa Dutta (2017) examined how youth in the Garo Hills region of Northeast India fostered civic engagement and social inclusion in the context of ongoing ethnic conflict in their community. The Garo tribe, of Southeast Asian lineage, is the largest ethnic group in the region. The conflict, rooted in colonial history, has placed the Garo in a long-standing antagonistic relationship with groups characterized as nontribal or non-Garo. Dutta, a nontribal community psychologist born and raised in the region, acted as a *participant–conceptualizer*, collaborating with 10 university students from both Garo and nontribal ethnic groups to create a participatory action research project utilizing

qualitative methods. The team of student researchers named themselves Voices, and they focused on local community problems they identified as a team, including a lack of public accountability and the absence of ordinary citizens' perspectives in policy decisions. The students engaged in research training with Dutta that enabled them to conduct interviews with diverse stakeholders, analyze their data, and present their findings at a widely attended community event.

Following the public presentation and discussion of the research findings, Dutta held focus groups and individual interviews with the university students to better understand their experience as researchers. Initially, they had been afraid to speak out about systemic issues, such as poor-quality education, corruption, and lack of infrastructure. Later in the process, they felt empowered to speak as a research team, representing the views of ordinary citizens that were gathered through a rigorous data-gathering and analysis process. One student said, "People appreciated it because it was about common people but also because everything was presented so systematically. It was a new kind of a thing that we were doing— new methods, new systems."

Youth also developed more inclusive identities as researchers, identities that had previously been marked by their location as actors in long-standing narratives of ethnic division and conflict between Garo and non-Garo groups in the region. Engaging in reflexive practice, they were able to see themselves in relationship with one another and as having common problems, perspectives needed for healing in contexts of protracted conflict. One student shared:

> We came to the meeting and everyone else was Garo so we felt uncomfortable. We felt like they'll be wondering what we're doing here. In our group . . . we had originally decided to remain in the background. But a lot of things changed. At some point, we realized we all care about our place, that is, Garo Hills, and the tribal versus non-tribal distinction became less important.

The student researchers were also able to articulate a sense of possibility and agency, as they saw their perspectives being granted legitimacy by a variety of stakeholders. Two different student researchers reflected:

> When all the important people were sitting in front of us, we were nervous but one thing that strikes me is that I was feeling really good. The local people's opinions— they had conveyed their message to us and we were conveying it to the people sitting there. At that moment I felt like we can really bring change to the society.

> At first, I thought we would have to do research only on politicians' visions. But then, I came to understand that we are also thinking of our vision, and that it is about future development. For example, how can we improve roads and communication? How we can remove corruption? How we can build a bright future? Through our awareness, other people will also become more aware.

Through this study, student researchers examined their own and others' experiences as civic agents working toward social inclusion. In the dissemination of this research, other researchers and citizens gained tools for participatory research and action in their own communities, even as they learned from the meaningful experiences of this particular group of student researchers.

## What Do You Think?

1. How does this study align with your thoughts on what makes for good research? What additional information would you want in order to assess its strengths and limitations?

2. Think about what you have learned about community psychology so far. How do the methods in this study reflect the values and goals of community psychology? How do they contribute knowledge to the field?

3. This study relied primarily on qualitative interviewing methods. What additional methods would you use to investigate problems in your own town or city?

# Answering Research Questions in Community Psychology

**qualitative research**
research methods that seek to understand social, behavioral, and other phenomena in their natural environments, not in a laboratory setting. These methods provide detailed analysis of complex, dynamic, and meaningful life experiences; study phenomena based on the meanings people bring to them; and give voice to perspectives not fully articulated in existing studies.

What research approaches and specific methods do community psychologists use to answer research questions? In this chapter, we discuss research methods used by community psychologists, building on themes highlighted in Chapter 3, including community collaboration and contextually grounded inquiry across levels of analysis. We cover qualitative and quantitative approaches to research, with examples of specific methods and summaries of their strengths and limitations. We also examine how these approaches can be integrated in mixed-methods research to study complex community phenomena (R. Campbell et al., 2017; Creswell & Creswell, 2018). Our overall themes are these:

- Qualitative and quantitative approaches yield complementary forms of useful knowledge.

- Choice of methods must depend on the questions to be answered in the research.

- Both qualitative and quantitative methods can be used in participatory-collaborative community research of the type we discussed in Chapter 3.

- Multiple methods often strengthen a specific study.

- Contextual and longitudinal perspectives often strengthen community research.

- Community psychology is best served by a diversity of forms of knowledge and methods of research.

# Qualitative Methods

The Garo Hills research shows the commitment to collaborative, participatory approaches and contextually grounded inquiry that we emphasized in Chapter 3. With its use of interviewing and its focus on the meanings that participants make of their experience, it also provides a good example of qualitative research methods. **Qualitative research** is a process of naturalistic inquiry that attempts to make sense of phenomena in terms of the meanings that people bring to them (Denzin & Lincoln, 1994). Qualitative approaches are useful for examining situations, processes, and contexts that have not been studied in detail. They give voice to perspectives that have not been fully articulated in existing research. Thus, some community researchers use qualitative approaches in the initial exploration and theory development stages of a project, generating hypotheses that can be tested later in quantitative research. Yet qualitative approaches also stand on their own, providing detailed analysis

**thick description**
an important aspect of qualitative data presented in written form as notes or transcripts, it is a thorough account of the research participants' experiences that is detailed enough to clearly reflect reality, document key information and patterns, and allow for later analysis and interpretation by the original research team and other researchers.

of complex, dynamic, and meaningful lived experiences across a variety of social and cultural contexts (Brodsky et al., 2017; Camic et al., 2003; see also Box 4.1). This detailed analysis of meaningful human experience in particular contexts is essential for advancing scientific knowledge in community psychology (Tebes, 2005). Qualitative research includes a diversity of methods, yet most of them share these common features:

- **Contextual meaning**. The principal aim of qualitative research is to understand the meaning of a phenomenon for persons who experience it, in the contexts of their lives. This involves allowing persons to "speak in their own voices" as much as possible, although interpretation by researchers is also involved. Contextual understanding represents a form of "insider knowledge," although generated in part by discussions and analysis with researchers who have different life experiences.

- **Participant–researcher collaboration.** Contextual meaning is created within relationships that evolve over time between research participants and researchers. These methods thus are especially apt for collaborative research with community members and for understanding diverse social and cultural contexts. Participatory approaches extend modes of collaboration so that participants contribute directly as members of the research team.

- **Purposeful sampling**. The researcher develops a richly layered understanding of a particular community group or setting. The sample of persons included in the research is usually small to facilitate the level of detail needed. Researchers may also rely on their own experiences as sources of information.

- **Listening**. As much as possible, the researcher sets aside preconceptions and attempts to understand the persons or setting on their terms, in their language and context. Attentiveness, open-ended questions, and freedom for interviewees to structure their own responses are preferred over standardized questionnaires (which often reflect researchers' preconceptions or theories).

- **Reflexivity**. Researchers also seek to be reflexive, stating their interests, values, preconceptions, and personal statuses or roles as explicitly as possible, both to the persons studied and in the research report. They also reexamine those assumptions in light of what they learn from the research participants. This makes potential values and assumptions as transparent as possible.

- **Thick description**. Qualitative data in psychology usually are in the form of words. The researcher seeks specific **thick description** of

**coding**
identifying current and repeating themes or categorizing and comparing different sets of data or stages in the research process. Using multiple coders and checking the level of agreement between the coders strengthens the data's reliability.

personal experiences, detailed enough to provide convincing evidence of realism. This also affords later checking for significant details and patterns. Other researchers can also use these detailed notes or transcripts to check the validity of analysis and interpretation.

- **Data analysis and interpretation.** The processes of data collection, data analysis, and interpretation overlap, and the researcher moves back and forth among them. Analysis often consists of identifying (**coding**) repeating themes or separating and comparing distinct categories or stages. Researchers can test the validity of themes or categories by collecting and analyzing more data. Multiple coders and checks on intercoder agreement are used to strengthen reliability.

- **Checking**. After several rounds of refinement through data collection and analysis, the researcher may check themes and interpretations by presenting them to a research collaborator. Collaborators might include community members who offer corrections, clarifications, or additional interpretations. Participatory methods allow community members to critically evaluate themes and challenge interpretations from the beginning of the analysis process.

- **Multiple interpretations**. It is possible to have multiple interpretations or accounts of a topic. Although an account should be internally consistent in terms of its realism and thick description, the tensions and competing perspectives that arise from within a participatory research team can provide compelling evidence as well.

- **Generalization**. Generalization of findings is less important than understanding meaning among the persons sampled. Researchers may generalize findings by identifying converging themes from multiple studies or cases.

As emphasized throughout this section, qualitative approaches are useful for attending to voices of persons from marginalized groups and bringing awareness to power differentials between researcher and participant. They also afford a deeper, contextual understanding of a culture, community, or population.

Researchers draw from a number of different qualitative approaches and research traditions, including participatory action research, phenomenological research, grounded theory, and ethnography (see Creswell & Creswell, 2018, for an extended discussion). Here, we focus on specific research methods that are utilized in several of these approaches. We discuss the strengths and limitations of four types of qualitative methods and approaches: participant observation, qualitative interviews, focus groups, and case studies.

**participant observation**

a qualitative research method that involves interviews and conversations with community members while taking careful, detailed notes and performing conceptual interpretations. The researcher becomes part of the community and participates in community life, allowing the researcher to develop deeper knowledge of the community. Limitations of this method include limited generalizability of findings to other communities and the potential for researcher bias in their observations and interpretations.

## Participant Observation

Many community researchers, especially if they conduct participatory research, perform at least some participant observation. It is a key component of ethnographic research in anthropology and other social sciences, and it is increasingly valued in community psychology for its ability to help us understand culture and context, as well as change over time within communities (Case et al., 2014).

Both words in its title are important. **Participant observation** involves careful, detailed *observation*, with written notes, interviews or conversations with citizens, and conceptual interpretation; it is not just a description or a memoir. It is also *participation*, as the researcher becomes a member of a community or a collaborator in its efforts, an actor in community life. This provides at least some of the experiential insider knowledge of community members, while the researcher also strives to maintain something of the outsider perspective.

***Strengths and Limitations.*** Participant observation is the method of choice for a researcher seeking maximum insider knowledge and depth of experience in a community. The participant observer knows the setting thoroughly and can communicate its essence vividly. This method also maximizes researcher–community relationships and affords thick description of many aspects of community life.

However, that depth of knowledge comes at a price. First, the focus on one setting necessarily means that generalizability to other settings may be limited. This can be reduced by visiting other settings, usually in less depth but long enough to discern the applicability of one's findings.

A second issue concerns whether the researcher's experiences and records are representative of the setting and its dynamics. The participant observer relies at least in part on field notes as data, often supplemented by other methods such as interviews. The researcher's notes, analysis, and interpretation are affected by selective observation, memory, and interpretations. As in any study, findings are also affected by the sample of informants or of situations studied (e.g., observations of formal meetings but not informal caucuses or personal contacts). Researchers need to report explicitly the settings and contexts in which they observed and their value commitments relevant to the study so that readers can judge the effects of these choices on data collection and interpretation. Another concern is that the researcher may influence (at least weakly, but perhaps strongly) the phenomena or community under study just by being in the setting. Related to this concern is the role conflict that may be created by playing both participant and observer roles (Wicker & Sommer, 1993).

Ethical concerns include deciding an appropriate level of engagement in the community setting, negotiating the transition into and out of the setting,

**qualitative interviewing**
a qualitative research method in which the researcher asks open-ended questions about the lived experiences of an individual and the meaning they make from those experiences. The questions and research protocols are established before the interview but are flexible enough to adapt to unanticipated questions that arise. Data collection is more standardized, reducing the potential for researcher bias, but the sample sizes are typically small, which limits generalizability to the wider community.

and figuring out an appropriate representation of a setting and its members (Case et al., 2014). For example, Todd (2012) was a participant observer for 18 months in his research with two religious interfaith organizations, learning about their social networks and pursuit of social justice goals. He realized that one of the interfaith groups would be described by outsiders as evangelical, but insiders avoided this language in their own networks. He noted their discomfort with this label and used language that resonated with the members of the organization (Case et al., 2014). Playing a role that is both an insider and a researcher can be stressful. Striking a balance between these is an important part of gaining entry, forming and attending to relationships, representing a community, and seeking benefits in partnership with the community.

## Qualitative Interviewing

The purpose of **qualitative interviewing** is to ask questions that elicit the lived experience of another person and the meaning they make of that experience (I. Seidman, 2006). Qualitative interviews are often semistructured, meaning that the researcher is well prepared and develops a set of questions, or protocol, before the interview, but also that there is enough flexibility in the context of the interview to pursue a question of interest that emerges during the interview. Researchers ask open-ended questions, which encourages participants to describe their experiences in their own words. Samples are usually small to allow for conducting interviews and analyzing data in depth. The researcher is not necessarily a participant in the community under study but usually does collaborate or maintain extended contact with interviewees.

***Strengths and Limitations.*** Qualitative interviewing allows flexible exploration of the phenomenon of interest and discovery of aspects not anticipated by the researcher. It is based in a strong relational context between researcher and participant. It involves attending to the voices of participants and thick description of their experiences. It can challenge the researcher's preconceptions and affords contextual understanding of a community, culture, or population.

Interviewing has several advantages over participant observation. Data collection can be more standardized, limiting biases of selective perception, memory, and interpretation. Interviews can be recorded and transcripts prepared so that analysis can be based on participants' actual words. Analysis can also be standardized and performed by multiple independent raters, not just the interviewer, which increases reliability and validity. The interviewer can develop a relationship with the setting and participants that is mutual and trusting, yet with less role conflict than participant observation.

These advantages require intensive study of a small sample, which means that generalizability of findings is often limited. Also, the time required for research interviews may subtly exclude participants in marginalized groups or demanding circumstances (Cannon et al., cited in R. Campbell & Wasco,

**focus groups**
a qualitative research method consisting of a discussion with a small group of people who share a characteristic the researcher wants to study. A moderator encourages natural dialogue among the participants with open-ended questions and discussion prompts. Researchers compare and contrast differences between individuals and observe reactions elicited by fellow community members to develop a contextual understanding of their shared experiences. Group sizes are generally small and can limit generalizability.

2000). Differences of interpretation between participants and researchers may create challenges (Stein & Mankowski, 2004). The Dutta (2017) participatory action research project with university students in Northeastern India, described at the beginning of this section, provides an example of a qualitative interviewing study.

## Focus Groups

A **focus group** discussion is an interview with a group of people. It generates thick description and qualitative information in response to questions or discussion topics posed by a moderator. Using focus groups, researchers can assess similarities and differences among individuals and allow participants to elaborate on ideas and themes by reacting to each other, not just to an interviewer.

In focus group research, the group, not the individual, is the unit of analysis: The sample size is one for each group. Individual comments are not independent of other group members; indeed, one of the purposes of the focus group is to elicit discussion. Each group is usually composed of six to 12 participants who share some characteristic that is of interest to the researchers, for example, attending the same high school, working similar occupations, or having the same health problem. This shared experience helps promote free discussion and ability of participants to build upon one another's ideas. Multiple focus groups are often used to provide broader information and to compare populations (first-year students vs. seniors in college, for example). However, as with qualitative interviewing, samples are seldom representative of a large population. The goal is to generate contextual understanding (Hughes & DuMont, 1993).

The moderator's responsibilities include creating an environment conducive to free discussion, speaking in language comfortable to all participants, ensuring that all members participate, eliciting both agreement and disagreement, and balancing between being nondirective and covering all topics of interest to the researchers. The moderator uses a discussion guide that includes topics to be discussed and that moves from general topics to specific phenomena relevant to the research. Analysis of focus group data is similar to the process of analyzing individual qualitative interviews.

Hirokazu Yoshikawa and colleagues (2003) used focus groups to understand the experiences and lessons learned by frontline peer educators in a community agency conducting HIV prevention programs in communities of Asian/Pacific Islanders in New York City. These workers knew their communities and cultures well and were rich resources for understanding effective, culturally anchored techniques for disseminating information and influencing behaviors that often transmit HIV. The researchers convened focus groups for workers with different populations (youth, gay/bisexual/transgender persons, women, heterosexually identified men). Their protocol questions concerned

**case studies**
a qualitative research approach that uses multiple qualitative methods, possibly existing data and quantitative methods as well, to develop a deep understanding of a single person, setting, locality, phenomenon, or system. Case studies are usually longitudinal, lasting for an extended period of time, and can identify complex patterns in natural settings. Multiple case studies can be conducted in one analysis to improve generalizability.

"success stories" of effective outreach and behavior change as well as how the peer educators adapted their techniques to different ethnic groups and in populations of different immigration and socioeconomic statuses. They reviewed the interview transcripts and developed categories of responses, including cultural norms about sexuality, contexts where peer educators focused their outreach, specific strategies used for that outreach, and specific risk and protective behaviors. Then they reached agreement among coders (interrater reliability) about which comments belonged in which categories. The results showed the influence of culture, social oppression, and immigration status on HIV-related behaviors along with effective, culturally appropriate methods of addressing these.

***Strengths and Limitations.*** The strengths and limitations of focus groups are similar to those of qualitative interviewing. However, focus groups have several advantages over other qualitative methods. Researchers can structure discussion and learn about topics of interest and personal experiences of others more easily than with participant observation. Compared to individual interviews, focus groups allow greater access to shared knowledge and mutual discussion. They also allow researchers to observe social interaction among group participants, perhaps revealing patterns unavailable in individual interviews. However, a focus group moderator has less flexibility to ask for elaboration, control changes of topic, or learn about individuals in depth than an interviewer of individuals. Focus groups are not a good approach for understanding an individual's unique experiences and cannot simply be used as a substitute for individual interviewing.

## Case Studies

The **case study** approach uses multiple methods to understand a single phenomenon or bounded system (Stake, 2003). The phenomenon of interest may be an organization, locality, neighborhood, or change process (M. A. Bond & Keys, 1993; S. D. Evans et al., 2007; Mulvey, 2002; Thomas et al., 2015). Community psychologists also can study an individual in relation to the settings in that person's life (Langhout, 2003). They may conduct multiple case studies so that comparisons can be made. For example, Neigher and Fishman (2004) used multiple case studies to describe planned change and evaluation in five different community organizations.

Case studies provide a bridge connecting qualitative and quantitative approaches. A case study may rely on any or all of the qualitative methods we have described. It may also use qualitative archival data (i.e., from archives or records) such as minutes of group meetings, organizational policy manuals, or newspaper stories. Archival data can also be quantitative records such as police statistics, records of attendance at programs, or quantitative evaluations of whether a program attained its goals. Case studies also can use other quantitative measures such as questionnaires. Later in this chapter we will describe case studies using both qualitative and quantitative methods. In Chapter 8, we will return to a community case study of a hazardous waste dispute (Culley & Hughey, 2008).

***Strengths and Limitations.*** Like participant observation, a case study can examine in depth a single person, setting, or locality. Case studies are excellent for understanding the nuances of a particular cultural, social, or community context. They can afford thick description and contextual understanding. By using multiple data sources, researchers can check assumptions. The longitudinal focus of most case studies is also useful. Although case-study researchers cannot study causes and effects with experimental control, they can identify complex patterns of causation in natural settings.

Their focus on a single case is also the principal limitation for case study methods. Generalizability of findings to other settings is uncertain. Researchers can include multiple case studies in one analysis, but that may weaken some of the strengths described above. Sometimes, description and analysis of one case is the goal, not generalization to other cases. Involvement in the setting or locality studied may create insider–outsider role conflicts, as discussed earlier.

The use of archival records presents both advantages and problems. Written records can provide information on meetings or other events not attended by the researcher and remembered imperfectly by interview informants. Archival records also can document events in the history of an organization or community. However, researchers who review archival data may not discover the processes that they are most interested in. For instance, conflict and compromise preceding a group decision are usually omitted or sparingly recorded in meeting minutes.

---

**Box 4.1   Community Psychology in Action: Qualitative Research With Women in Afghanistan (continues)**

Anne Brodsky (2003, 2009; Brodsky et al., 2017) used a variety of qualitative methods to study the Revolutionary Association of the Women of Afghanistan (RAWA). Her book *With All Our Strength* describes the history, philosophy, actions, resilience, and sense of community shared by the members of this remarkable Afghan women's movement. Since 1977, RAWA has advocated forcefully yet nonviolently for women's and human rights and for a democratic, secular government in Afghanistan. Founded in 1977 by a 20-year-old college student, RAWA promotes indigenous feminist values that defy both traditional Afghan patriarchal values and the stereotypes of Afghan women widely held in the outside world. RAWA members (all volunteers, all women) publish advocacy materials and maintain a website, document and publicize abuse and atrocities, aid women suffering from many forms of trauma, distribute humanitarian assistance, conduct literacy and educational classes for women and girls, work with men who share their goals, hold protest rallies in Pakistan, and conduct international outreach (Brodsky, 2003). These activities have generated such fierce opposition that RAWA is a clandestine, underground organization that nonetheless engages in public actions.

**Box 4.1 Community Psychology in Action: Qualitative Research With Women in Afghanistan (continued)**

Brodsky was especially interested in how RAWA acted and sustained itself as a community. She was also interested in their shared resilience in the face of vigorous and violent opposition and many setbacks and losses, including the assassination of Meena, RAWA's founder (Brodsky, 2003). Her use of a research framework and methods based in feminist qualitative research fits well with the feminist philosophy of RAWA, with the need to take Afghan culture and context into account, with the need to attend to emotions in RAWA members and in the researcher, with the fact that RAWA is a clandestine organization and that a participatory-collaborative research relationship was necessary, and with the goal of empowering RAWA and other feminist organizations through the research.

Brodsky (2003, 2009; Brodsky et al., 2017) used multiple qualitative methods. She has been very involved with RAWA's outreach in the United States for several years. For this research, Brodsky visited Pakistan and Afghanistan in 2001 and 2002, beginning before September 11, 2001, and the U.S.-led war in Afghanistan. She interviewed 225 members and supporters of RAWA, women and men, in Afghanistan and Pakistan. Interviews often lasted 2–3 hours, and many persons were interviewed more than once. Brodsky also conducted group interviews and spent many hours in participant observation and informal conversations with RAWA members, visited 35 RAWA projects in 10 localities in Pakistan and Afghanistan, and reviewed archival records and sources. Most of her interviews were conducted in Dari, an Afghan language, with Tahmeena Faryal, a translator, key informant, and collaborator who was a RAWA member. Brodsky knew the language well enough to serve as a check on accuracy of translation but remained in many ways an outsider (see Brodsky & Faryal, 2006, for further discussion of the challenges and rewards of their insider–outsider collaboration).

Brodsky's findings are rich and contextual. She examines the strong sense of community for members and supporters of RAWA in the context of the other Afghan communities to which they also belong, including extended families and villages. She finds in RAWA a positive sense of community that is consistent not only with its feminist ideals and practices but also with the collective orientation of Afghan culture that makes it difficult, if not impossible, for women to choose not to be part of a community. Resilience in the face of trauma and violent opposition is another theme. These themes are expressed in the ongoing commitment of RAWA members to their ideals, and the emotional caring and practical support offered among RAWA members. Two interview excerpts express these themes and illustrate the power of qualitative methods.

From a member who joined RAWA in a refugee camp:

> I found everything; I escaped out of my grief and sadness. There were classes, the handicraft center, and I found these people serving the rest of the people of Afghanistan and going toward the lightness. . . . By lightness I mean education. . . . RAWA giving education, hope and enables us to serve our people. (Brodsky, 2003, p. 245)

From a member who compared the freedoms afforded women inside and outside of RAWA:

> In [RAWA] I have all my rights and what I believe. I have education, go outside . . . talk to anyone I want. I have the same rights as men. But not in my village. My father would say nothing. But I have male cousins that are my age who I can't talk with. Here I talk to men and it is fine. . . . When I go to my village I just stay in the house. And I can't go out without a scarf or talk to boys. They will kill me. I think here if a member really believes in a right she can do it. (Brodsky, 2009, p. 182)

## What Do You Think?

1. How do Brodsky's methods and the quotes from the research participants represent the values of community psychology?

2. Consider what you know about traditional research approaches in the social sciences or in other sciences. How do Brodsky's qualitative methods compare and contrast with these approaches? Can you think of any benefits and limitations to her methods?

Community psychology research can support local community efforts while also expanding the field's knowledge, as shown in Anne Brodsky's work with the Revolutionary Association of the Women of Afghanistan.

## Two Concluding Issues

We conclude this section by discussing two overarching issues for qualitative methods: (a) how they elicit narratives and meaning and (b) how they address the criteria of reliability, validity, and generalizability.

***Narratives in Qualitative Research.*** Qualitative methods often tap narratives. Narratives have a plot, or sequence of events, and meaningful characters and settings. They are individual stories and cultural myths that shape our understandings of ourselves and of one another. They provide insights

**narratives**
shared stories, myths, and traditions that communicate important events, values, and other themes that are important for the community's identity and sustainability.

**personal stories**
similar to narratives, an individual's own unique accounts they create to make sense of their life.

into psychological and cultural themes, and they convey emotions and deeply held values in memorable ways (Rappaport, 1993, 1995, 2000; Thomas & Rappaport, 1996). For instance, the Dutta (2017) action research project in the Garo Hills region of Northeast India was framed in part as a shift from long-standing conflict narratives between ethnic groups to new, more inclusive narratives of shared agency and possibility. In another study, Lehrner and Allen (2008) showed how the narratives of advocates underlie and support different understandings of intimate partner violence. Some advocates' narratives framed intimate partner violence as a problem that must be addressed by social change efforts, while others drew upon a more person-centered frame and suggested individual-level, therapeutic solutions.

Rappaport (2000) defined **narratives** as being shared by members of a group. A community or setting narrative communicates events, values, and other themes important to the identity and sustainability of that group. Cultural myths and traditions are also narratives. **Personal stories** are individuals' unique accounts, created to make sense of their own lives. Personal identity is embedded in a life story. Qualitative research methods can be designed to elicit shared narratives or personal stories or both. Both are studied in anthropology; sociology; and cognitive, personality, and developmental psychology. They can be analyzed for descriptive details and abstract themes. Looking across personal stories and shared narratives is an excellent opportunity to examine persons in context across multiple levels of analysis.

***Reliability, Validity, Generalizability.*** Students educated in the thinking of positivist, quantitative methods may wonder about the reliability, validity, and generalizability of qualitative methods. It is important to remember that the aims of qualitative methods differ from those of much quantitative research. In a qualitative study, sensitivity to participants' interpretations is more important than standardization. Yet many qualitative methods use scientific criteria analogous to the reliability and validity criteria of a more positivist approach (Lincoln & Guba, 1985).

For qualitative methods, reliability is sometimes demonstrated by interrater reliability among multiple readers who are coding or categorizing verbal data. Reliability may also be demonstrated by evidence of the *dependability* of researchers, who have developed a deep understanding of a particular context.

Generalizability of findings to other persons or populations is more limited than with larger studies but is usually not the aim of the qualitative study. However, the thick description generated by qualitative research allows readers to understand more fully the persons and contexts being studied and to compare them with other samples. The reader is then able to decide whether or not the findings have *transferability*, proving useful in other contexts.

Qualitative research addresses validity in part by the use of different methods to understand the same phenomenon. These can be interviews and

**credibility**

how accurate research findings are at presenting individuals, communities, systems, and related phenomena in a realistic manner. This can be enhanced through deep, detailed qualitative research.

**convergence**

using multiple different research methods to study the same individual, group, or phenomenon to determine the credibility of the findings based on how similar the results are across methods.

**verisimilitude**

a common goal of qualitative research, it entails eliciting a powerful, emotional response in a reader that is similar to the response of the research participant being described.

personal observation, use of several informants who can be expected to have different viewpoints, use of multiple interviewers, or use of quantitative measures along with qualitative information. The use of multiple methods can increase the judgment of validity, or **credibility** of research, if very similar results are found across different methods. This is known as **convergence** (Morgan, 2019).

Credibility is also enhanced by the thick, detailed description of experiences in qualitative research; this offers convincing realism, *showing* the story rather than simply *telling* it. Moreover, the connection of researcher and participant in qualitative studies allows clarifying and elaborating of the meaning of participant responses to questions, an issue of validity overlooked in standardized questionnaires.

A common goal of qualitative research is to provide not only intellectual evidence of validity but also **verisimilitude**, eliciting a personal experience in a reader similar to the original experiences of the research participant. For example, recall the quotations earlier in this chapter from the Afghan women of RAWA (Brodsky, 2003). If you experienced the emotional power of their words, that is verisimilitude. Yet, "whether numbers or words, data do not speak for themselves" (Marecek et al., 1997, p. 632).

As this quotation emphasizes, both qualitative and quantitative methods must be interpreted and placed in context. Choices of what to study and how to analyze findings are matters of theory and values, whatever the method. Reflexivity (discussed earlier in this chapter and in Chapter 3), including explicit statements of the researcher's perspective, is useful in any study. Regardless of method, multiple interpretations of complex phenomena will arise because diverse persons and groups have different perspectives. Both qualitative and quantitative methods can illuminate those perspectives.

## Quantitative Methods

We now turn to **quantitative research** methods that emphasize measurement, statistical analysis, and experimental or statistical control. They address different purposes and questions from qualitative methods. Quantitative methods are historically based in a positivist philosophy of science but can be used effectively within contemporary frameworks for scientific practice (Tebes, 2017), including the postpositivist, constructivist, and critical philosophies of science described in Chapter 3. Quantitative methods are particularly useful in helping us describe and model the multileveled influence of environmental factors on individual health and well-being (Fowler & Todd, 2017). While general philosophical differences exist between qualitative and quantitative approaches, they are not a simple dichotomy.

**quantitative research**

methods that seek specific cause-and-effect relationships and emphasize obtaining and analyzing numerical data through standardized measures, statistical analysis, and experimental or statistical controls. They are most useful for studying generalizable conclusions about how environmental factors affect health and well-being across contexts, settings, and communities at various levels.

## Common Features of Quantitative Methods

A great diversity of quantitative methods exists. However, most quantitative methods in community research share some common features. We do not wish to repeat all of what you may have learned in previous methodology courses, so the following list focuses on features that offer clear contrasts with qualitative methods and highlights how quantitative methods can be adapted to community research.

- **Measurement, comparisons.** The principal aim of quantitative methods is to analyze measurable differences among variables and the strength of relationships among those variables. They facilitate understanding variables, predicting outcomes, and understanding causes and effects. Quantitative research can generate "outsider knowledge" that affords comparisons across contexts.

- **Numbers are data.** Although some variables are categorical (e.g., an experimental program compared with a control group), the purpose is almost always to study their relationship to measured variables. While researchers using qualitative methods look for patterns in words and narratives, researchers using quantitative methods seek patterns in numbers.

- **Cause and effect.** One important objective is to understand cause-and-effect relationships. This can then lead to prediction of consequences and can inform social action to promote desirable changes. Experiments and similar methods are often used to evaluate the effects of social innovations, programs, or policies. Even nonexperimental quantitative studies identify empirical relationships that can eventually lead to knowledge of causes and effects and to social innovation.

- **Generalization.** Another important objective is to derive conclusions that can be generalized at least to some extent across contexts, settings, and communities (e.g., empirical findings showing that a prevention program or social policy is effective in many communities).

- **Standardized measures.** Standardized measurement instruments are preferred, to ensure reliable, valid measurement. The flexibility and contextual sensitivity of qualitative methods are lost, but comparability of findings across studies and control of extraneous variables are increased.

Next, we discuss four specific types of quantitative methods in community psychology research: quantitative description, randomized field experiments, nonequivalent comparison group designs, and interrupted time-series designs. These are only some of the available quantitative methods for community research.

## Quantitative Description and Inference

Quantitative description methods include a variety of procedures: for example, surveys, structured interviews, behavioral observations of community settings, epidemiological studies, and use of social indicators (e.g., census data, crime and health statistics). They are quantitative but not experimental: They do not involve manipulation of an independent variable. They can be used for purposes such as the following:

- to compare existing groups (e.g., older and younger adults' perceptions of crime)

- to study associations between survey variables (e.g., correlation of family income with health, changes over time in adolescent sexual attitudes)

- to measure characteristics of community settings (e.g., the frequency of emotional support and advice-giving in mutual help groups)

- to conduct epidemiological studies to identify factors predicting the presence or absence of an illness (e.g., behaviors that increase or decrease risk of HIV infection)

- to study relationships between geographic/spatial and social environments (e.g., correlation between density of liquor stores and crime rates in neighborhoods)

Statistical analyses may include correlation, multiple regression, path analysis and structural modeling, and $t$ tests and analyses of variance to compare naturally occurring groups. These studies may be cross-sectional, sampling only one point in time, or longitudinal, sampling repeatedly over time.

Quantitative description usually samples more individuals than either qualitative studies or experiments. This facilitates statistical analysis and generalizability. To enable a study of this breadth, these methods rely on previous knowledge and/or exploratory research to determine which variables to study, how to measure them, and whom to sample. As we mentioned earlier, qualitative research is very useful for this.

***Correlation and Causation.*** Early undergraduate education in psychology typically contrasts correlation and causation. Just because two factors are associated statistically does not mean that one causes another. The causation could just as easily run in the opposite direction from what you think (B causes A rather than A causing B). Or the causal factor may be a "third variable" that determines both correlated variables (C causes both A and B). For example, the number of churches and liquor stores are highly correlated; can you think of a third variable that contributes to this correlation? One option might be the size of the town or city, but there are other possible variables you might have come up with.

**community surveys**
a quantitative method that uses standardized questionnaires or other measurements to gather quantitative data from community samples that identify defining factors of that group.

**epidemiology**
the study of the frequency and distribution of disorders, as well as related risk and protective factors. It is generally a precursor to experimental studies looking for factors that cause these disorders and is essential in prevention and treatment interventions.

Under some conditions, however, nonexperimental designs can be used to identify causal patterns and test causal hypotheses. The simplest case involves precedence in time: If change in A is correlated with change in B, yet A consistently precedes B, a causal interpretation (A causes B) is more warranted (although a third variable still may be involved). A theoretical model, based on prior knowledge of relationships among A, B, C, and other related variables, strengthens causal inference from nonexperimental data. Such causal inference relies on logic models and/or statistical control of extraneous variables, not experimental control.

**Community surveys** are a method that provides quantitative description. They are gathered from community samples in the field, using standardized questionnaires or other measurements. For example, the Australian Community Capacity Study is a large-scale longitudinal survey of residents conducted in Brisbane, Queensland, the third largest city in Australia. Over 4,000 people were randomly drawn from 148 neighborhoods and took part in the telephone survey, designed to understand the community context of crime. Rebecca Wickes and colleagues (2013) analyzed results from the survey to better understand neighborhood capacity to respond to violence, children's misbehavior, and political/civic problems. They found that neighborhoods with more residential stability had more of a sense of collective efficacy for dealing with community violence, such as breaking up a fight or doing something about a mugging. But they did not have more of a sense that they could do something about children who were spray-painting graffiti or disrespecting adults or about addressing political or civic matters, such as speeding cars or a fire station closing down. The results suggest that certain neighborhoods may differ in their ability to deal with particular tasks and that efforts to build collective efficacy may need to be tailored to particular strengths and needs of neighborhoods and their residents.

Community surveys can also focus on organizations as the unit of analysis. Community coalitions bring together representatives of various segments of a locality to address an issue such as intimate partner violence (N. E. Allen, 2005; N. E. Allen et al., 2008, 2013) or promoting positive youth development (Feinberg et al., 2004). Feinberg et al. (2004) conducted structured interviews with representatives of 21 local Communities That Care coalitions and derived quantitative measurements from them. Results indicated the importance of community readiness, and internal functioning of the coalition as a group, for perceived coalition effectiveness. N. E. Allen (2005) surveyed and interviewed representatives of 43 local domestic violence coalitions, finding that perceived effectiveness was most related to having an inclusive climate of shared decision making and active membership participation.

**Epidemiology** is the study of the frequency and distribution of disorders along with the risk and protective factors for them. Epidemiology is usually a precursor to more experimental studies of causal factors of these disorders

**incidence**

in epidemiology it is the rate of new occurrences of a disorder in a population within a specific time period—usually a year. It is the primary target of prevention efforts in community psychology.

**prevalence**

in epidemiology it is the rate of existing occurrences of a disorder in a population within a time period. It includes new cases and continuing cases that began before the time period being examined and can inform mutual help or mental health services and policy.

**risk factors**

factors that are associated with an increased likelihood of a disorder. These can range from direct causes to correlated factors. Example risk factors include exposure to stressors and limited resources.

**protective factors**

factors that are associated with a lower likelihood of a disorder. They can counteract the effects of a disorder or strengthen resistance to them, or they can be indirect, correlated factors. Social support is an example protective factor in community settings.

and is essential to practical planning of prevention and treatment. It is most often used in the discipline of public health, but it is also used in the social sciences (e.g., Mason et al., 1999). Epidemiology is useful for community research concerned with health and mental health.

Two basic epidemiological concepts are incidence and prevalence. **Incidence** is the rate of *new* occurrences of a disorder in a population within a specific time period (usually a year). It is thus a measure of the frequency of the onset of a disorder. **Prevalence** is the rate of *existing* occurrences of a disorder in a population within a time period. It includes both new cases during the time period studied and continuing cases of the disorder that began before that time period. Both concepts are usually expressed as rates (e.g., the number of cases per thousand persons in the population). The incidence–prevalence distinction is important for community psychology. Prevention is more concerned with incidence, the frequency of new cases. Prevalence, the rate of existing cases, is relevant to mutual help or mental health services policy.

When incidence and prevalence rates have been determined for a population, epidemiological research is focused on identifying risk and protective factors. **Risk factors** are associated with increased likelihood of a disorder. These may be causes of the disorder or simply correlated with it. Exposure to stressors or lack of coping resources are examples of risk factors. **Protective factors** are associated with lesser likelihood of a disorder; they may counteract or buffer the effects of the disorder's causes or simply be correlated with other factors that do so. Personal or cultural strengths and support systems are protective factors. Note that we discuss risk and protective factors more fully in Chapter 10, where we focus on the prevention of disorders and promotion of health.

Consider the following example. Casale et al. (2015) conducted a cross-sectional household survey with over 2,000 pairs of teenagers and their adult caregivers in South Africa's KwaZulu-Natal province. This is a region of South Africa in which many children are greatly affected by poverty and are at risk of being orphaned because of high prevalence rates of HIV in their communities. Zulu fieldworkers conducted the surveys with dyads of teens and caregivers in face-to-face interviews. They found that caregiver social support was a key protective factor for children's positive development and relationships with peers (Casale et al., 2015). Not surprisingly, the survey findings indicated that outcomes for youth were related to the social networks and support systems of their adult caregivers. This makes intuitive sense and aligns with research suggesting that parents with better social support report better well-being and better interactions with their children. Yet the research also found that this relationship could not be understood simply in terms of the quality of parenting provided by the adult caregiver. The community survey showed the critical, direct importance of a larger familial social support network on the health

**geographic information systems (GIS)**
a method of mapping physical and social environments by plotting data on a map that connects physical–spatial aspects of a community with psychosocial qualities.

**decontextualized knowledge**
knowledge provided by quantitative methods that is gathered from individuals but not associated with existing settings, communities, or cultures. It can lead to wider sampling, but it limits knowledge of contextual factors and causal relationships.

and well-being of youth, especially in a context of individual, family, and community stress related to the illness and death of adult caregivers. These findings have led to community-level interventions in the region to increase adolescent social support as they also address large-scale HIV prevention and public health needs (Casale et al., 2015).

*Mapping Physical and Social Environments.* Designed to capture, store, and present data visually, **geographic information systems (GIS)** methods offer a rich resource for studying relationships between physical–spatial aspects of communities and their psychosocial qualities (Chirowodza et al., 2009; Luke, 2005). GIS methods can be used to plot onto a map any data available for spatial locations. Archival data sources can include census information on population density or average household income or social indicators such as neighborhood crime rates or density of fast-food restaurants. Community survey data can also be entered in GIS databases if associated with respondents' residences (Van Egeren et al., 2003). GIS data and resulting maps can be used for quantitative statistical analysis or for visual searching for spatial patterns (a more qualitative approach). For example, Townley and colleagues (2016) used GIS methods to examine the places where youth experiencing homelessness in Portland, Oregon, spent most of their time on a daily basis. Ruiz et al. (2018) mapped 297 Chicago elementary schools to illustrate the relationship between school academic achievement and neighborhood economics and crime statistics. GIS also can be used to track changes in localities over time.

*Strengths and Limitations.* Quantitative description methods have a number of strengths. Standardized measurement affords statistical analysis and large samples that provide greater generalizability. These methods can be used to study variables that cannot be manipulated in an experiment. Epidemiological research can be used to identify risk and protective factors and evaluate the outcome of preventive efforts.

Finally, these studies often identify factors that can be targeted for social or community change, even without experimental knowledge of specific causes and effects. One need not know all the cause-and-effect relationships for youth violence, for instance, in order to identify risk and protective factors and to initiate change efforts.

However, these methods have several limitations. They rely on prior knowledge to select and measure variables and populations. Also, except for GIS approaches, the knowledge provided by these studies is usually **decontextualized knowledge**, gathered from individuals but not associated with existing settings, communities, or cultures. This can increase breadth of sampling but limits knowledge of these contextual factors. Study of causes and effects is limited, as we have discussed.

**randomized field experiments**
a quantitative method used to test the effectiveness of an intervention by randomly assigning individuals or settings to experimental or control groups. The experimental group receives the intervention being studied while the control group does not. Comparisons between the experimental and control groups are conducted before and after testing to identify whether the intervention had any notable effects.

The focus of epidemiological research on disorders also limits its utility for community psychology (Linney & Reppucci, 1982). Community psychology is concerned with overall psychological well-being, including but not limited to disorders. When mental disorders are studied, difficulties of accurate diagnosis and measurement make the related epidemiology more difficult than that of physical disease. Also, while community psychology's focus on promotion of strengths includes identifying protective factors for disorders, it goes beyond that to concern development of positive qualities.

## Randomized Field Experiments

In **randomized field experiments**, participants (individuals or settings) are randomly assigned to experimental or control groups. These are compared at a pretest before the implementation of an intervention, when they are expected to be equal on measures of dependent variables. They are compared again at posttest(s), when they are expected to differ because of the effects of the intervention. Follow-up posttests can continue over several years.

The individuals or settings that experience the intervention represent the experimental condition. The control condition can often be "treatment as usual" under existing policy or practices. For example, in a study foundational to the field of community psychology, men discharged from a psychiatric hospital were assigned either to a Community Lodge program (a shared home that offers independence and support for persons with mental illness) or to the usual treatment and aftercare procedures for the hospital (Fairweather, 1979). Another experimental approach is to compare two different innovations with each other, such as two contrasting prevention programs in a school (Linney, 1989). A third approach is to provide the experimental innovation to members of the control group after the posttest. They first serve as a control group, then receive the innovation, minimizing ethical problems with their not receiving it originally.

A key issue is the method of assignment to experimental and control conditions. If this is random, many confounding variables are controlled. These include individual differences in personality, coping skills, social support networks, and life experiences that may affect participants' responses to the innovation. Confounds also include differences between groups in demographics such as gender, age, race, culture, and family income. In the laboratory, random assignment is taken for granted, but in the community, it must be achieved by collaboration and negotiation with community members (Sullivan, 2003).

***Strengths and Limitations.*** Randomized field experiments are unsurpassed for clarity of cause-and-effect interpretation, for example, for testing effects of a social innovation. With greater control over confounding factors, researchers can make more confident interpretations of its effects. Moreover, if experimental studies demonstrate the effectiveness of a social innovation, advocacy for it can be more effective. For instance, randomized field experiments have helped document the effects of many preventive interventions and increase the credibility of prevention efforts generally (Weissberg et al., 2003).

However, experiments require substantial prior knowledge of the context to propose interventions worth testing and to choose measurements. A useful sequence might be to conduct qualitative studies to understand the context and key variables, then create quantitative descriptions to specify risk and protective factors and refine measurements, then develop an experimental intervention and conduct an experiment to evaluate its effectiveness.

As we noted in Chapter 3, the intrusiveness of experiments also raises issues of control in community settings. Permission is needed to collect quantitative data (often longitudinally in multiple waves), and to randomly assign participants to experimental conditions. Those decisions must be explained and negotiated with community members.

### Evaluating a Crisis Residential Program With a Randomized Field Experiment.

Consumer-managed services, like the crisis residential program studied in this experiment, have a long history that is closely related to the development of community psychology. Remember, for example, the Community Lodge program introduced in Chapter 2, in which male veterans with severe mental disorders lived in a community setting and supported one another with minimal professional supervision. Other forms of consumer-managed services now include advocacy organizations, clubhouses, and mutual help groups (which we discuss in greater detail in Chapter 9). While support for these consumer-managed services is widespread, few resources are dedicated to sustaining them. And there have been few controlled studies that demonstrate the effectiveness of this type of service for those who are in crisis.

Thomas Greenfield and colleagues (2008) used a randomized experimental design to evaluate the effectiveness of a crisis residential program managed by mental health consumers. The program served as a treatment alternative for adults in acute psychiatric crisis.

This experiment compared outcomes for adults with a psychiatric disability who were randomly assigned to either the experimental condition—an unlocked crisis residential program emphasizing client decisions and involvement in recovery—or the usual care condition, a locked inpatient psychiatric facility that was professionally staffed and working from a medical model of treatment. Participants in this study were facing civil commitment in California. They were assessed by a psychiatrist as gravely disabled or a threat to themselves, but they were not considered a threat to others.

The findings indicated that those who were randomly assigned to the unlocked crisis residential program had greater reduction of symptoms, including

**nonequivalent comparison group designs**
a quantitative method that is used when assignment to experimental and control groups cannot be randomized. It relies on existing groups as comparison points, such as different classes within the same school or different schools within the same locality.

psychoticism, depression, and anxiety. Level-of-functioning outcomes, including problematic behavior and living skills, were not significantly different for the two groups, yet participants assigned to the crisis residential program were significantly more satisfied with services, including staff and program, medications and aftercare, day/night availability, and facilities.

Given the lower costs of the crisis residential program ($211 per day, compared with $665 per day for the traditional inpatient treatment) and the outcomes demonstrated in the study, the researchers argued for expansion of these less restrictive, consumer-run services (Greenfield et al., 2008).

## Nonequivalent Comparison Group Designs

For a variety of reasons, many settings simply cannot support random assignment to experimental and control conditions. For instance, seldom can a school randomly assign some children to an innovative classroom and others to a control classroom. Even if it did, the students may mix at lunch or recess so much that the independence of experimental and control conditions would be greatly reduced. Providing an innovative program or curriculum for all students in a grade and comparing their outcomes to another school or to students in a previous year would mean, of course, that assurance of equivalence between groups would be lost. Comparing a sample of schools rather than a sample of individuals (making the unit of analysis the school, not the individual) may be prohibitively expensive. Yet many of the strengths of the experiment can be retained if researchers are creative about working around such obstacles. Using a nonequivalent comparison group is a common approach.

**Nonequivalent comparison group designs** are used whenever assignment to experimental or comparison condition is not random. For instance, different classrooms within a single school or different schools within a region may serve as experimental and comparison conditions. Assignment to classroom or choice of school is not random, but the classes or schools may be similar. The choice of comparison group is critical to generating interpretable results. In schools, student socioeconomic status, race, gender, and age are examples of variables to equate as much as possible between the two groups. Teacher demographics, school size, and curriculum also need to be similar (Linney & Reppucci, 1982).

*Strengths and Limitations.* Using an existing group as a comparison condition is practical and less intrusive than randomized experiments. However, the control of confounding factors is much weaker, and clarity of interpretation and confidence in conclusions is decreased. Researchers in this situation must collect as much data as possible on factors that may confound the comparison. This allows them to document the similarity of the two conditions or to use those variables as statistical controls. For instance, researchers may be able to show that the average family income of the experimental and control conditions was similar or to control effects of family income statistically. The ultimate goal is to weaken or eliminate plausible competing explanations for findings.

### Evaluating School Reforms With a Nonequivalent Comparison Group.

Rhona Weinstein and associates (1991) used qualitative and quantitative methods to study how teacher expectations and school curriculum policies affect student performance. Weinstein described this multiyear program of research in *Reaching Higher* (Weinstein 2002b). The researchers implemented practical reforms to enhance learning for students not considered capable of college preparatory courses in an urban California high school. Our concern here is with the empirical evaluation of that intervention, conducted with a nonequivalent comparison group design. It used both quantitative and qualitative methods.

"Los Robles High School" (a pseudonym), a midsize urban school in an aging, run-down building, drew students from both wealthier and lower income areas. Over two thirds of the students but only one fifth of the teachers were members of ethnic minority groups. School student achievement scores were below the state median, yet the school also ranked high in the number of graduates admitted to the selective University of California system. The school staff culture held a bimodal view of the students: some were very talented and hardworking, others were not, and little could be done to change this. Weinstein and her team discovered that students assigned to a "lower track" curriculum in ninth grade, based on tests that often underestimated their strengths, were assigned to classes that did not prepare them for college. These classes often were taught with uninteresting materials and teacher-centered methods that did not generate discussion. Students in this track were disproportionately African American (68%). Classes for honors students, in contrast, were often discussion oriented and used challenging yet interesting materials. Similar situations are all too common in U.S. schools (Weinstein, 2002b).

Weinstein and her team implemented acn ongoing series of workshops with some teachers (volunteers) of reputedly lower ability ninth-grade classes. Workshops focused on the importance of challenging and motivating students to higher performance, involving all students more actively in classroom learning, involving parents, and using more challenging yet interesting materials (often from the honors curriculum). Teachers met and discussed their efforts to alter teaching strategies and classroom climate. Weinstein's team worked with them to devise responses to obstacles. Although a year of these workshops resulted in positive results, it also showed the need for training more teachers and for curriculum reform and administrative changes. These became the next goals of the project.

A team of school staff and university researchers worked collaboratively to plan the research evaluating project effectiveness. Qualitative analysis

**interrupted time-series designs**
a quantitative method for studying an intervention by repeatedly measuring the same individual, setting, locality, etc. using the same method across a period of time. A baseline measure is taken before implementing the intervention then compared with data collected after the implementation to study the effects of the intervention.

of meeting records indicated positive shifts in teacher expectations, teaching strategies, and curriculum policy. The research also used a quantitative comparison of grades and other records for 158 students involved in classes in the project (the experimental group) and grades and records for a demographically similar group of 154 students from the previous 2 years' classes (the nonequivalent comparison group). Analyses statistically controlled prior differences between students in achievement. Project students attained higher overall grades and had fewer disciplinary referrals than comparison students in the 1st year of the project. They also were less likely to leave the school in subsequent years. The project's effects on grades ebbed after 1 year, suggesting the need for curriculum reform and wider teacher training to spread the positive changes throughout the school.

These outcomes cannot be as confidently attributed to the project as the outcomes of a randomized design experiment could be. Possible confounding differences between the experimental group and comparison group could have included subtle changes in the student body between comparison and experimental years, events during the experimental year that altered student performance, or changes in teacher grading practices (Weinstein et al., 1991). Yet there were many qualitative signs of project effectiveness. For the first time, so-called lower track students were excited about school, despite challenging reading and writing assignments (Weinstein, 2002b).

## Interrupted Time-Series Designs

Another approach is the use of **interrupted time-series designs**. In the simplest case, this involves repeated measurement over time (a time series) of a single case (an individual, organization, locality, or other social unit). In an initial baseline period, the participant or setting is monitored as measurements of dependent variables are collected. This provides the equivalent of a control condition. Then the intervention or policy is introduced, while measurement continues. Data collected in the baseline period are compared to data collected during or after the implementation of the innovation. This is termed an *interrupted* time-series design because the intervention interrupts the series of measurements. This approach combines time-series measurement with an experimental manipulation, providing a useful design for small-scale experimental social innovation when a control group is not available.

***Strengths and Limitations.*** Time-series designs are practical. They also afford understanding of change over time in a specific context, such as one community, while standardizing measurement and minimizing extraneous confounds.

However, a time-series design with one group still is open to a number of external confounds (Linney & Reppucci, 1982). These include seasonal or cyclical fluctuations in the variables measured. An example is that the number

**multiple baseline designs**
a form of interrupted time-series design that involves multiple time-series studies conducted with different communities to compare the effects of an intervention in these communities. Each community is studied at a different time so that external factors that affect all the communities at the same time are not confounded with the effects of the intervention.

of college students who seek counseling rises as final exams approach. If seeking counseling is used as a dependent variable in a time-series study, researchers must take this seasonal rise into account. A further confound concerns historical events that affect the variables measured. An example is negative national publicity about tobacco use at the same time as implementation of a local tobacco-use prevention program for youth. If youth tobacco use drops, the publicity may have been the real cause, not the local prevention program. Finally, findings from a single case or community, even over a long time period, may not generalize to other communities.

A key issue for time-series designs is the number and timing of measurements in the baseline and experimental periods. Interventions or policy changes may have gradual or delayed effects difficult to detect in a short time-series design. Seasonal or cyclical fluctuations (confounds) in the dependent variable may be detected if the time series is long enough.

*Multiple Baseline Designs.* **Multiple baseline designs** are a form of interrupted time-series design that reduces the problems of external confounds and generalizability. Think of this design as a set of time-series studies, each conducted in a different community and compared with each other. The intervention is implemented at a different time in each community so that effects of an external historical factor (happening at the same time for all communities, such as national publicity about tobacco use) will not be confounded with the innovation. If measures of the dependent variable show a change soon after the implementation of the innovation, at a different date in each community, confidence can be stronger that the innovation caused this effect. This also provides some evidence of generalizability. In effect, the design tests whether findings from one community can be replicated in other communities, within a single study (Biglan et al., 1996; Watson-Thompson et al., 2008).

The multiple baseline design combines the strengths of the interrupted time-series and nonequivalent comparison group designs. However, the multiple communities studied are still nonequivalent (assignment of individuals to them is not random), and differences among them still exist that complicate interpretation. However, it is a very useful way to combine repeated measurement, contextual study of a single community, and replication across communities.

*A Community-Level Multiple Baseline Study.* Can a community intervention emphasizing positive reinforcement reduce tobacco sales to youth in multiple communities? Anthony Biglan and colleagues (1996) addressed this question. They studied whole localities, using multiple baseline, time-series methods. They analyzed the antecedents and consequences of illegal sales of tobacco products to youth by retail merchants, devised an intervention, and evaluated its effectiveness in a multiple baseline design in localities in rural Oregon.

**mixed-methods research**

research that combines qualitative and quantitative methods in a single study. Sometimes qualitative methods are used first to identify variables that then inform the design of quantitative approaches. Other times quantitative methods are used first and are followed by qualitative methods that help explain why the research found the quantitative results that they did.

**complementarity**

where quantitative or qualitative methods that complement each other achieve something that the other cannot do. Quantitative methods are more effective at determining cause-and-effect relationships, while qualitative methods provide deeper knowledge about the lived experiences of individuals and communities.

In each town, the research team and local community members organized a proclamation by community leaders opposing tobacco sales to minors. Community members then visited each merchant to remind them of the proclamation and to give the merchant a description of the law and signs about it for posting. A key element was intervention visits to merchants by teen volunteers seeking to purchase tobacco products. If the clerk asked for identification or refused to sell, the volunteer handed the clerk a thank-you letter and a gift certificate donated by a local business (positive reinforcement). If the clerk was willing to sell, the volunteer declined to buy and gave the clerk a reminder statement about the law and proclamation. The researchers periodically provided feedback to merchants about their clerks' behavior in general (but not about individual clerks). In addition, community members publicly praised clerks and stores who had refused to sell, in newspaper articles, ads, and circulars (again providing reinforcement).

Measurement of intervention effectiveness was conducted with assessment visits to stores by teens seeking to purchase tobacco. These measurement visits were separate from the intervention visits and did not provide reinforcement of refusals to sell or reminders of the law. Teens simply asked to buy tobacco, then declined to buy if a clerk was willing to sell. Over 200 volunteer youth, male and female, aged 14 to 17, participated as testers. Attempts to buy were balanced by gender.

Researchers measured effectiveness of the intervention by locality, not by individual store, because they had implemented a community intervention. The dependent variable was the proportion of stores in a community willing to sell tobacco to youth in assessment visits by youth. The researchers studied four small towns; all had fewer than 6,000 residents, mostly European American.

Biglan et al. (1996) collected baseline assessments in each community before implementing the intervention, then compared those data to similar assessments taken during and after the intervention. They conducted up to 16 assessment periods in each town. They used multiple baseline techniques by conducting the intervention at one time in two communities and later in the other two. In two communities, Willamina and Prineville, clerks' willingness to sell during assessment visits clearly decreased following the intervention. These differences were statistically significant. Because the intervention occurred at different times in these two communities, these results indicate that the intervention, not an extraneous factor, caused the reduction. In Sutherlin, a third town, willingness to sell decreased, but not immediately after the intervention began. In Creswell, the fourth town, baseline willingness to sell was somewhat lower than elsewhere, and the intervention did not make a significant difference. Unknown local community factors influenced the intervention's effectiveness.

**divergence**
key differences that emerge between qualitative and quantitative results. These differences can lead to constructive dialogues and a more complete picture of a complex situation than just one method type could.

The generalizability of these findings may be limited because the sample was only a small number of relatively similar localities. In addition, it is not clear which element of the intervention accounted for its success (i.e., community proclamation, reinforcement of clerk refusals to sell, feedback to merchants, or some combination of these). Yet the intervention package, in most communities, was effective in reducing retail clerks' willingness to sell tobacco to youth. Biglan et al. (1996) noted that preventing sales in one community does not necessarily mean youth will not use tobacco, because they may obtain it from adults or in other communities. However, both behavioral analysis and common sense suggest that the more difficult it is to obtain tobacco, the less likely it is that youth will begin to use it.

## What Do You Think?

1. How do the quantitative methods reviewed in the previous section compare with your perceptions of traditional scientific research methods?

2. Think back to the qualitative methods presented earlier in the chapter. What are some of the key differences between these methods and the quantitative methods just discussed?

3. How are the values of community psychology reflected in the quantitative methods reviewed in this chapter? Do you think it might be more difficult for quantitative research to reflect these values than qualitative research? Why or why not?

# Mixed-Methods Research

Qualitative and quantitative methods can be used in a single study to offer the advantages of both perspectives and overcome the limitations of each; this is known as **mixed-methods research** (R. Campbell et al., 2017) and illustrates the principle of **complementarity**, in which each method does something that the other cannot easily do. In some mixed-methods research, qualitative methods are used first in the research design. They serve an *exploratory* role, helping the researcher ask better questions in their quantitative research. In other research designs, qualitative methods come later in the research sequence. They serve an *explanatory* role, helping uncover why the researcher found the quantitative results they did.

Next, we discuss three examples that illustrate the benefits of multiple methods to study communities, interventions, and social change. As the first example demonstrates, we might see not only complementarity but also **divergence**, or key differences, across different qualitative and quantitative results, which can create a generative dialogue around the differences that are found (Morgan, 2019).

## Combining Participatory Methods and GIS Mapping to Understand Community

Researchers combined ethnographic, participatory, and GIS methods as part of a randomized controlled study on the effectiveness of community-based HIV awareness and prevention strategies within 48 communities in Zimbabwe, Tanzania, South Africa, and Thailand (Chirowodza et al., 2009). Before intervention in each of the communities, the multilingual and transnational team of researchers needed to work with members of each of the communities to identify (a) community boundaries, (b) how the community was defined socially and geographically, (c) where to deliver services, and (d) individuals, groups, and community networks with whom to partner in delivering services. GIS technologies were used to generate maps of the geographic area and relevant community sites. Yet, in order to identify and define community resources, ethnographic and participatory methods were needed to complement and extend the GIS technologies.

Participatory mapping and transect walks were used in a rural community in South Africa, for example, so that community members could describe the community as they experienced it. Facilitators worked with community teams to create maps, usually on the ground outdoors with natural materials, such as sticks, leaves, and stones. Community members identified features such as community landmarks, infrastructure, transport routes, places for livelihood and dwelling, and boundaries. Maps were transferred to charts by community members for record keeping. Transect walks were then conducted with community members serving as guides to explore key community networks and resources in greater detail.

The participatory process complemented and challenged quantitative descriptions generated by outsiders. Use of multiple methods illuminated key divergences between the mental maps of communities, maps generated by government surveys, and census data. A multimethod approach more effectively named community boundaries, challenges, strengths, and resources than any one research method alone.

## A Mixed-Methods Evaluation of Peer Support for Early Adolescents

Louise Ellis and colleagues (2009) integrated quantitative and qualitative methods to evaluate a peer support program in Australia for schoolchildren making the transition to adolescence and high school. The peer support program is one that was widely implemented in Australia, with over 1,600 schools adopting the program in New South Wales (including the metropolitan region of Sydney). The program was offered as a set of 12 once-a-week sessions in which high school seniors (who received initial and ongoing training and

Transect walks and participatory mapping can help researchers understand communities, such as in this Malawi village where community members guide researchers interested in studying and improving local sanitation. *Source*: https://creativecommons.org/licenses/by/2.0/

support) worked with small groups of seventh-grade students. The groups discussed and practiced goal setting, decision making, problem solving, and developing support networks.

The quantitative component of the evaluation included a sample of 930 students from three high schools. In the first year of the longitudinal study, all seventh-grade students were assigned to the within-school, baseline control group. Researchers collected data at three points from the beginning to the end of the school year. In the second year, new seventh-grade students from the same three schools participated in the peer support program. As with the control group, data were collected at three points from the beginning to the end of the school year. Surveys measured the students' self-concept (e.g., physical abilities, relationships, academic abilities), personal effectiveness (e.g., self-confidence, leadership), coping, and perceptions of bullying.

Results for the experimental group were compared with those of the control group and with the experimental group's own baseline data. Multilevel path analysis indicated that the program enhanced psychological well-being and adjustment and that some benefits emerged after time elapsed at the end of the program and were stronger over time. Researchers found this sleeper effect surprising, given the steady loss of benefits once many interventions have concluded.

The qualitative component, designed to privilege the personal perspectives of participants, included open-ended questionnaires and focus groups with seventh-grade student and peer support leaders. Content analysis showed themes that were not fully named or examined in the researcher-designed surveys. For example, the strongest finding that emerged was that the program helped strengthen student connectedness and understanding of others. Students also emphasized how the program helped them deal with difficult situations and fostered a sense of possibility for their own futures. Mixed methods strengthened the study, providing complementary evidence and allowing for participants' voices to be included.

## A Mixed-Methods Evaluation of the Sexual Assault Nurse Examiner Program

Rebecca Campbell and colleagues (2011) conducted an evaluation of a community intervention for sexual assault survivors using quantitative and qualitative methods. Too frequently, survivors of rape in the United States are referred to hospital emergency departments for a medical exam that can be retraumatizing and that may not be used in criminal prosecutions. The nursing profession created an alternative model of care in response, the Sexual Assault Nurse Examiner (SANE) program. Nurses work in collaboration with victims and advocates to conduct an exam while striving to preserve victims' dignity and provide physical and emotional support. Nurses also work directly with state crime labs and provide expert witness testimony if the case is prosecuted. Campbell and her colleagues wanted to understand whether SANE programs contributed to increased prosecution rates for sexual assault and, if so, how they did this. Focusing on both *process* and *outcomes*, they first used quantitative data to determine that there were indeed higher rates of prosecution with SANE programs in place, comparing rates several years before and after SANE programs were established in multiple locations. Then they used qualitative data to explain how the programs were successful. They found that the nurses provided police and prosecutors with valuable evidence and helped streamline the investigations. They also found that the nurses focused on the victims' health and recovery and did not emphasize the need to report to police, which enabled survivors to come forward and participate in the difficult process of prosecuting the crime.

# Conclusion

Table 4.1 summarizes the distinctive features, strengths, and limitations of the qualitative and quantitative methods described in this chapter. That summary is simplified to save space, so remember that each set of methods has nuances and can be applied in many ways. There is plenty of room for creative imagination in designing community research.

Six themes run through this chapter:

1. Qualitative and quantitative methods tap different sources of knowledge and complement each other. As you probably noticed, the limitations of one are often the strengths of the other. No single approach provides a royal road to knowledge.

2. Much can be gained by integrating qualitative and quantitative approaches in one study to provide differing perspectives.

3. A longitudinal perspective often enhances community research. Studying changes over time reveals the workings of communities in ways not available in cross-sectional analysis.

4. Both qualitative and quantitative approaches can be used within a participatory-collaborative partnership with community members. Many studies we have described embody this theme.

5. No one method is best for every research question. Community researchers would be wise to respect and know how to use both qualitative and quantitative methods. Ideally, the nature of the research question to be studied would play an important role in choosing methods. Realistically, every community researcher cannot be equally competent with qualitative and quantitative methods; some specialization is to be expected. Yet the student of community psychology needs to be familiar with multiple approaches to knowing.

6. Finally, an overarching theme is that community psychology as a field is best served by a diversity of forms of knowledge and methods of research.

It is important to think of our two research chapters as a unit. Chapter 3 concerns the importance of social values in community research; of participatory, collaborative research in partnership with community members; and of sensitivity to cultural and social contexts and multiple ecological levels. Chapter 4 illustrates specific methods for conducting community research along those lines in order to provide knowledge useful to a community and to the world beyond it.

**Table 4.1** Comparison of Community Research Methods

| Methods | Distinctive features | Strengths | Limitations |
|---|---|---|---|
| **Qualitative methods** | | | |
| **Participant observation** | Researcher "joins" community or setting as a member, records personal experiences and observations | Maximum relationship with community, thick description, contextual understanding | Generalizability limited, sampling and data collection not standardized, researcher influences setting studied, potential role conflict |
| **Qualitative interviewing** | Collaborative approach, open-ended questioning to elicit participant understandings in their own words, intensive study of small sample | Strong relationship with participants, thick description, contextual understanding, flexible exploration of topics, more standardized than participant observation | Generalizability limited, less standardized than quantitative methods, interpretation may create role conflict |
| **Focus groups** | Similar to qualitative interviews, but conducted with a group to elicit shared views | Similar to qualitative interviews, but allows group discussion, especially useful for cultural understanding | Similar to qualitative interviews, except less depth of understanding of individuals |
| **Case studies** | Study of single individual, organization, or community over time (can use qualitative and quantitative methods) | Understanding of setting in depth, understanding of changes over time, thick description, contextual understanding | Generalizability limited, less standardized than quantitative methods, limitations of archival data, interpretation may create role conflict |
| **Quantitative methods** | | | |
| **Quantitative description** | Measurement and statistical analysis of standardized data from large samples, without experimental intervention | Standardized methods, generalizability, study of variables that cannot be experimentally manipulated | Reliance on prior knowledge, often decontextualized, limited understanding of cause and effect, epidemiology focuses on disorder |
| **Randomized field experiments** | Evaluation of social innovation, random assignment to experimental and control conditions | Standardized methods, control of confounding factors, understanding of cause and effect | Reliance on prior knowledge, difficulty in obtaining control groups in community settings, generalizability limited |
| **Nonequivalent comparison group designs** | Similar to field experiments, without random assignment to conditions | Standardized methods, some control of confounds, practicality | Reliance on prior knowledge, less control of confounds than randomized experiments, generalizability limited |
| **Interrupted time-series designs** | Longitudinal measurement of one or more settings before and after intervention, may use multiple baseline design | Measurement in context, practicality, longitudinal perspective | Reliance on prior knowledge, less control of confounds than randomized experiments, generalizability limited (multiple baseline is better) |

## For Review

### Discussion Questions

1. If you wanted to understand whether a community intervention was effective, what methods would provide the strongest evidence? What are some of the challenges you would face in conducting this research?

2. If you wanted to understand *why* a community intervention was effective, what methods would you use? What are some of the challenges you would face in conducting this research?

3. In mixed-methods research, qualitative and quantitative methods may complement one another. One also might see divergence across different methods. Is that a problem? When could that be useful?

### Key Terms

qualitative research, 113
thick description, 114
coding, 115
participant observation, 116
qualitative interviewing, 117
focus groups, 118
case studies, 119
narratives, 123
personal stories, 123
credibility, 124
convergence, 124
verisimilitude, 124

quantitative research, 124
community surveys, 127
epidemiology, 127
incidence, 128
prevalence, 128
risk factors, 128
protective factors, 128
geographic information
    systems (GIS), 129
decontextualized knowledge,
    129

randomized field experiments,
    130
nonequivalent comparison
    group designs, 132
interrupted time-series designs,
    134
multiple baseline designs, 135
mixed-methods research, 137
complementarity, 137
divergence, 137

### Learn More

A detailed summary of the chapter, along with other review materials, is available on the *Community Psychology, Fourth Edition* companion website at http://pubs.apa.org/books/supp/kloos4/.

Community psychologists seek to understand ecological contexts that explain how individuals and groups are impacted by their environments, and vice versa, which is essential for improving community wellbeing.

Rawpixel.com/Shutterstock.com

# 5 Understanding Individuals Within Environments

## Looking Ahead ⏵

**After reading this chapter you will be able to answer these questions:**

**1.** What is an ecological context?

**2.** What are the main frameworks community psychologists use to understand how ecological contexts influence individuals?

**3.** What are ways in which individuals influence their ecological contexts?

## Opening Exercise

## Blue Zones

Imagine the following scenario. Within a country there is a particular city whose residents live longer and happier lives than other citizens. What do you think accounts for the better health and well-being of this city's residents compared with the rest of the population? You might first wonder whether these residents are somehow related and hit the genetic jackpot of longevity and happiness! But let us assume that these residents are no more related than those of nearby cities and towns. At this point, you might begin to wonder how the city itself differs from other cities and towns. Does it have a better health care system? Does it have less pollution or better paying jobs?

In other words, you question whether the environment—the physical, social, economic, and political conditions that surround residents' lives—results in better health and well-being.

Such places exist. Some refer to them as "blue zones," geographic locations where people live longer than average lives. Research is beginning to identify what it is about the environment of blue zones that promotes health and well-being. There have even been efforts to create blue zones through changing aspects of a city's environment such as providing convenient healthy food options in supermarkets and creating public areas for exercise and leisure.

The United States' blue zone is Loma Linda (Spanish for "beautiful hill"), a city of less than 25,000 residents located in San Bernardino County, California. Its residents live, on average, 4–7 years longer than the average American. In addition, the rates of cardiovascular disease, cancer, and other chronic health conditions are lower in this city than in the national population.

What about Loma Linda's environment promotes health and well-being? There are several factors. One is the social-cultural environment, particularly the religious faith of residents. Most are Seventh-day Adventists,

a Protestant Christian denomination whose adherents practice a strict vegetarian diet and abstain from drinking alcohol and smoking. Research has shown that these particular behaviors promote health and prevent disease. Residents also exhibit strong and supportive social bonds, which studies have shown help buffer the effects of stress on health. There are also aspects of the physical and economic environment of Loma Linda that support health. Most restaurants, including fast-food restaurants, feature a vegetarian menu. Also, selling alcohol and smoking are prohibited within city limits.

## What Do You Think?

1. What changes can be made to your neighborhood or school to improve health?
2. Are there other communities you can think of that could benefit from health improvement efforts? What changes could improve health in those communities?
3. How would efforts to change these communities compare with efforts in Loma Linda or in your community?

What we know about Loma Linda and other blue zones prompts important questions about how we study our environment and its influences on our health and well-being. It also helps us think about how we might change environments to promote health and other important outcomes. In this chapter, we focus on the various ways that community psychologists understand, research, and intervene in environments to support favorable environmental conditions.

The study of persons in their environments has been a central theme for community psychology. At the 1965 Swampscott Conference that organized community psychology in the United States, participants identified a central focus for the new field: "the reciprocal relationships between individuals and the social systems" (Bennett et al., 1966, p. 7). That said, an interest in understanding environmental influences on individuals is common among many disciplines: for example, anthropology, public health, social work, and sociology. For over a century, ecological context has been implicitly recognized as important for understanding human behavior. At the turn of the 20th century, Lightner Witmer and the staff of the early child development clinics did their work in the settings where children lived and went to school; they made changes in those settings to help children learn. Following the work of W. E. B. Du Bois, the Chicago school of sociology documented the importance of neighborhood and city environments for personal life (e.g., Park, 1952). Social psychologist Kurt Lewin (1935) argued that behavior is a function of person *and* environment. Theories of personality proposed by Murray (1938), Rotter (1954), and Bandura (1986) emphasized the interaction of person and situation, although applications of their concepts focused on individuals. Even scientists studying genetic contributions to behavior argue that it is important to understand how environments interact with individual factors (Thapar & Rutter, 2019). However, the specific ways in which contexts and individuals interact are not well understood. As discussed in Chapter 2, psychology has primarily focused on individual variables, devoting much less attention to environmental factors. Other disciplines have focused on understanding variables related to the environment but have not understood well how they link to processes that affect individuals. As a linking science, community psychology seeks to understand both the environmental factors and their connections to well-being. For example, community psychologists may focus on linking research across levels of analysis (e.g., examining potential locality and organizational impact on individuals' well-being) or on linking action and research (e.g., learning about effective ways to reduce bullying behavior from efforts to change a school's organizational climate).

As individuals, we are embedded in many contexts. But how do we know where to look to consider which contextual factors may have an impact on our everyday life? In Chapter 1, we present the first tool community psychologists use to consider the potential impact of contextual factors on our well-being, an ecological levels of analysis framework. In the example of school bullying, you might consider how *microsystems* like families could be influential in a child's well-being. At an *organizational* level of analysis, you might consider schools, sports teams, and arts organizations. Alternatively, you might focus on *localities* such as neighborhoods or on *macrosystem*-level contexts like state policies for education funding or community safety. This ecological framework can help you systematically consider potential contextual factors at each level of analysis and then decide which contexts might be most relevant to address.

In this chapter, we add to the conceptual tools for understanding contextual influences on individuals, families, and communities. We examine major approaches used in community psychology for understanding specific ecological contexts. Second, we illustrate how understanding of contexts can inform research and action regarding the interplay of neighborhood, family, and personal life. Finally, we highlight an exemplary community program that changed ecological contexts to improve the well-being of individuals and families.

**interdependence**
mutual reliance and connectivity among systems; alterations to one portion of a system can impact relationships within that system or other systems.

This chapter is the first of four chapters to focus on key concepts in community psychology. All concern understanding the links between contexts and individuals. In this chapter, we cover major ways of understanding environments and individuals' functioning within environments. Chapter 6 covers concepts of community, Chapter 7 discusses ways of understanding human diversity, and Chapter 8 provides an overview of how empowerment and citizen participation frameworks are fundamental to community psychology's shift of perspective.

# Conceptual Models of Ecological Context

To understand interactions between environment and individuals within an ecological level of analysis, community psychologists typically focus on particular contexts where people interact and experience everyday life. In research terms, the unit of analysis is conceptualized as an environmental *setting*. The setting of interest might be physical (e.g., a school) or social (e.g., a team) and is nested within levels of analysis (e.g., microsystem, organizational, or locality). As you read about these six models for understanding ecological contexts and their impacts on individuals, note how they conceptualize environmental settings and keep in mind the levels of analysis that we introduce in Chapter 1. Some of the models can be used at multiple levels; others fit one or two levels best. Key concepts from the six ecological frameworks are listed in Exhibit 5.1.

## Four Ecological Principles

Community psychology's foundational framework for understanding context uses ecological metaphors to examine social environments and their physical settings. Adapting concepts from the biological field of ecology, James G. Kelly (1966, 1979) and Edison Trickett and colleagues (1972, 2000) proposed four key ecological principles in understanding human environments: interdependence, cycling of resources, adaptation, and succession. These principles are about characteristics of settings, not of individuals. Workplaces differ in the extent of interdependence among workers, in what resources are exchanged, and in what processes are needed to adapt to the setting. Of course, these factors can influence people's lives greatly, as well as the functioning of schools, families, workplaces, and other settings. This framework guides where and how to observe within particular environments. Let us look at these principles in greater detail.

*Interdependence.* As with biological ecosystems, any social system has multiple related parts and multiple relationships with other systems. Changes in one of these parts can affect the others; they are **interdependent** (Trickett et al., 1972). For a public school, interdependent components include students, teachers, administrators, secretaries, janitors and other staff, parents, board members, and district taxpayers. Actions or problems of any of these groups can affect everyone else. State and national governments and local and international economies also can affect local schooling.

Consider the ecology of a family as another example. If one family member gets the flu, everyone else is affected in one way or another. If a young child is sick, an older member of the family will likely miss work or school to stay at home with them. Others in the family may also become ill. If the primary caregiver gets the flu, then meal preparation, laundry, transportation,

---

## Exhibit 5.1 Six Key Ecological Frameworks in Community Psychology

1. Kelly: Four Ecological Principles
   - interdependence
   - cycling of resources
   - adaptation
   - succession
2. Moos: Social Climate Dimensions
   - relationship
   - personal development
   - system maintenance and change
3. Seidman: Social Regularities
   - role relationships
   - distribution of resources
   - inclusion and exclusion
   - power and authority
4. Barker: Ecological Psychology
   - behavior setting
   - optimally populated
   - overpopulated settings
   - underpopulated settings
5. O'Donnell et al.: Activity Settings
   - intersubjectivity
   - counterspaces
6. Environmental Psychology
   - environmental stressors
   - environmental design

**cycling of resources** refers to the process of understanding a system by examining how resources are used, allocated, preserved, and transformed.

**personal resources** an individual person's skills, expertise, experiences, strengths, or other attributes that can be used to address challenges.

**social resources** collective beliefs, values, rules and other assets that come from having shared connections and relationships within a community.

**physical resources** the tangible, material features of a location that individuals can utilize, such as specific types of rooms in a building and the objects they contain.

and a host of other daily operations for every other member of the family are affected. The change may be temporary, with the family system returning to its previous state after a few days. Other changes may be longer lasting, such as having an ailing grandparent join the household.

A corollary of the principle of interdependence is that *any change in a system will have multiple consequences*, some of them unanticipated and perhaps unwanted. Similarly, change efforts within a system may be thwarted because concerns of interdependent components of the system were not addressed. For instance, a teacher may introduce cooperative learning techniques in a classroom, only to face resistance from students, the principal, parents, or other teachers if the wider culture strongly endorses individual competition in education.

*Cycling of Resources.* The second ecological principle is closely related to interdependence. **Cycling of resources** specifies that any system can be understood by examining how resources are used, distributed, conserved, and transformed (Trickett et al., 1972). Community psychologists are also interested in how members of settings define and exchange resources. **Personal resources** include individual talents, knowledge, experiences, strengths, or other qualities that can address challenges in a setting. **Social resources** occur in relationships among members of the setting, including shared beliefs, values, formal rules, informal norms, group events, and sense of community. **Physical resources** are the material or tangible characteristics of a setting: a library with rooms for group study, quiet nooks for individual study, and places to take a break. From an ecological perspective, social settings have many more resources than are commonly recognized. Community psychologists can help define and utilize resources that have been overlooked (e.g., students at a school for an antibullying program).

What resources are important for a family? Time, nurturance, attention, emotional support, and money are some examples. By examining the availability and use of resources, one can begin to characterize family priorities and connections. You may not recognize how family members are important until you encounter a stressful life event that they have lived through and can advise you about. A quiet person who understands others well is a valuable resource for a group but may be overlooked among more outspoken members. An implication of James G. Kelly's (1966) approach is to search any environment (e.g., family, organization, neighborhood) for resources (tangible or intangible) that can contribute to individual or system well-being.

Stack's (1974) classic study of a low-income Black community highlighted the importance of understanding patterns of resource sharing. In the Flats (a public housing community with limited financial resources), residents shared furniture, child care, food stamps, and money beyond their own families. For example, a member of the community loaned furniture to a neighbor for an

**adaptation**
focuses on interactions between people and their environments and specifically, how an environment can restrict or form people's behavior, and, conversely, how environments can change because of their members.

**succession**
the understanding that settings and social systems are in an ongoing process of change.

extended period after that neighbor had cared for her child while she was looking for work out of town. To an outsider without an ecological perspective, this exchange of resources may seem risky for families with little money, but it made sense to those within the system. By examining patterns of resource use within this community, Stack recognized that resources were allocated to those who needed them; today's provider may be tomorrow's recipient. Stack's detailed study documented the value of an ecological perspective in recognizing the interdependence of the community members and their cycling of resources.

*Adaptation.* The third ecological principle concerns the transactions between person and environment. **Adaptation** is a two-way process: Individuals cope with the constraints or demands of an environment, and environments adapt to their members (Trickett et al., 1972). Recall how you adapted to the demands of your first job, for instance. To adapt, you probably learned new skills without losing your unique identity. Some jobs require changes in appearance, changes in relating to people, or changes in schedules. Environments also adapt to their members. Think about the changes in a family triggered by events such as the birth of a child, a parent starting a new job, or children moving away from home. At a higher level of analysis, an organization that does not respond to the needs of its members will find it difficult to retain member involvement or attract new members. For individuals and social systems to survive, they need to adapt to each other (J. G. Kelly et al., 2000).

Social settings also adapt to the larger environments in which they are nested (J. G. Kelly et al., 2000). A local school system, for instance, adapts yearly to changes in the requirements and funding of local, state, and national government, as well as changes in the student makeup of the schools. Changes in technology, the economy, and cultural ideas about education also affect local schools.

A further implication of the adaptation principle is that every environment demands different skills. Skills students need are somewhat different from those for factory workers or homemakers or police officers. For example, consider the roles of neighborhood contexts in parenting. Effective parenting in dangerous neighborhoods is necessarily more directive, setting more rules and firmer limits, than effective parenting in safer neighborhoods (Gonzales et al., 1996).

*Succession.* Settings and social systems change over time, according to the principle of **succession**. Interdependence, resource cycling, and adaptation must be understood in that perspective (Trickett et al., 1972). This principle applies to families, organizations, and communities. How many times have you heard that "you have to work at keeping a relationship healthy"? Over time, patterns of partner interdependence; the cycling of resources, such as emotional support; and adaptation of each partner to the other can change without their noticing. The nature of the relationship changes over time. With successful adaptation and cycling of resources, the relationship continues and may deepen. If adaptation is difficult over time or needed resources are not available or utilized, perhaps partners drift apart. You can see succession in these relationship "settings" when there is a divorce, when new relationships start, or when children make decisions about their life commitments based on their parents' experiences.

An implication of understanding succession in settings is that psychologists need to understand a system's history before they plan an intervention in that system. In trying to make a neighborhood a safer place, community psychologists need to ask multiple questions. What have people tried to do in the past? What worked? How did the problems develop? Psychologists also should carefully consider the likely consequences of the intervention, including possible unintended consequences. How can the community continue the intervention after the formal involvement of the psychologist ends? We discuss these considerations more in the prevention and promotion chapters (Chapters 10 and 11).

***Example of the Use of Kelly's Model.*** The rise of mutual help groups (i.e., self-help groups) since the 1970s illustrates these ecological principles. Mutual help has become an important element in mental health care, largely without professional planning or intervention. Mutual help organizations have been recognized for their contributions to addressing violence against women, managing addictions, and coping with chronic illnesses. They can strengthen individual adaptation of their members, challenge the idea that only experts have answers for their members' problems, and create settings where members have their needs met. Interdependence is encouraged, often including individual contacts outside the group meetings. Social support, information, and other resources are exchanged. The members who have gone through the same experiences themselves are resources for each other that are often overlooked by helping professionals. People who often think of themselves as needing resources can have the uplifting experience of providing resources to others. The way that a local self-help group maintains itself, especially after its founders move on, is a matter of succession. We discuss mutual help in greater detail in Chapter 9.

***Contributions of the Four Ecological Principles.*** These four ecological principles provide distinctive, useful concepts for describing the dynamics of social environments. They address aspects not emphasized in other approaches to understanding context (e.g., interdependence, succession) and can be a heuristic guide for thinking about who could be involved in addressing a problem (i.e., a resource) who has been overlooked (Kloos & Shah, 2009; S. D. Tandon et al., 1998). Furthermore, James G. Kelly et al. (2000) argued that ecological concepts can guide the development of preventive interventions in community settings.

**social climate approach**

the method for evaluating perceptions of a social environment that are shared among its members; a key framework for understanding environments that stresses how people experience and comprehend settings.

**social relationships**

the connections that occur between people who interact in a social setting, including mutual social support, involvement, and coordination.

**personal development**

the process of fostering an individual's autonomy, growth, and skills within a social setting.

**system maintenance and change**

involves the preservation of order, relaying rules and expectations and monitoring behavior in a system, as well as the need for adaptation, innovation, and positive change.

## Social Climate Dimensions

A second major framework for understanding environments emphasizes how people experience and understand settings. Rudolf Moos and colleagues argued that many psychological effects of environments are best assessed in terms of persons' *perceptions* of the environment and its meaning (e.g., Moos, 1973, 2003). Moos and colleagues developed a **social climate approach** to assess shared perceptions of a setting among its members and have created several scales to measure social climate in settings (e.g., Moos, 1973, 1994, 2002). Perceptions of social climates can affect social relationships and organizational functioning. Studying social climates of settings has been important for (a) understanding how individuals cope and (b) identifying which aspects of settings can help promote well-being (Kloos & Shah, 2009; Kriegel et al., 2020; Moos & Holahan, 2003). The social climate approach to understanding environments is based on three primary dimensions that can characterize any setting: how they organize social relationships, how they encourage personal development, and how they promote maintenance or change in the setting (Moos, 1994).

*Social Relationships.* The **Social Relationships** dimension of settings concerns mutual supportiveness, involvement, and cohesion of its members (Moos, 2002). The social climate approach looks for evidence of relationship qualities among members in each setting. For example, the Classroom Environment Scale, which measures high school classroom environments, contains subscales on the extent to which students are involved in and participate in class, the extent of affiliation or friendship they report among classmates, and the amount of support they perceive from the teacher (Fike et al., 2019; Moos & Trickett, 1987). These constructs are conceptually related to Kelly's principles of interdependence and cycling of resources just discussed.

*Personal Development.* The **Personal Development** dimension of settings concerns whether individual autonomy, growth, and skill development are fostered in the settings (Moos, 2002). Settings will vary on how much they focus efforts on the improvement of their members. For example, the Ward Assessment Scale (Moos, 1974) includes a subscale about how much a psychiatric treatment environment focuses on helping clients address their particular health needs. The Classroom Environment Scale contains a subscale on competition among students (Moos & Trickett, 1987). These environmental demands are related to Kelly's principle of adaptation.

*System Maintenance and Change.* The **System Maintenance and Change** dimension of settings concerns their emphasis on order, clarity of rules and expectations, and control of behavior (Moos, 2002). Some settings will spend a large amount of time and resources to maintain the rules and organization. The Classroom Environment Scale contains subscales concerning the extent to which class activities are organized and orderly, the clarity of rules, the strictness of the teacher, and the extent to which innovative activities and thinking are welcomed (Moos & Trickett, 1987). Settings may vary on the basis of who has authority to make decisions and who may challenge those decisions. These are conceptually related to adaptation and succession in Kelly's framework.

### Contributions and Limitations of Social Climate in Research and Practice.
The social climate approach assumes that settings will vary on how much they emphasize relationships, personal growth of their members, or maintenance of their practices. Persons in a setting complete social climate surveys to report their perception of these dimensions of that setting. Their responses are aggregated to form a profile of the shared perceptions of the setting's particular environment (Kloos & Shah, 2009; Moos, 2002). Furthermore, patterns of responses across the three dimensions can be compared among setting members and between different settings.

Social climate scales measure important aspects of settings, such as supportiveness, clarity of expectations, and individual growth. Social climates influence the well-being of individuals, microsystems, and organizations. They connect subjective experience with settings in a way that other approaches do not. The conceptual value and ease of use of social climate scales has fostered research and practical applications in a variety of settings, generating a rich literature of empirical findings.

Social climate approaches have been used for research on settings at the microsystem and organizational levels of analysis, including classrooms, workplaces, university residence halls, psychiatric inpatient settings, correctional settings, supported community living facilities, military units, and classrooms (Moos, 2002). Social climate scales are also useful in consultation and program development (Kloos & Shah, 2009; Kriegel et al., 2020; Moos, 1984). A consultant may compare the perceptions of different stakeholders in a setting, such as teachers and students completing the Classroom Environment Scale. Differences in perceptions and common views can be used to start a discussion about how to improve a classroom or school. Similarly, a consultant may have setting members complete two forms of a social climate scale: the *real form* to report current setting functioning and the *ideal form* to report how they desire the setting to be. The consultant then presents the aggregated group scores on both forms, and the group discusses how to change the environment to become more like the shared ideal profile. The social climate approach can be a useful tool in documenting differences in how the settings are experienced and in monitoring efforts to change them.

The chief limitation of the social climate scale approach to understanding environments is that a score for a social climate cannot represent the depth of persons' experiences of the setting, even if it is helpful for comparing experiences. Perceptions of the setting are a combination of setting characteristics

**social regularities**
routine patterns of social interactions among the people within a setting that can affect resource allocation, access to opportunities, and power to impact social issues.

and personal perceptions and not simply a measure of the setting. Individuals or subgroups within the setting will likely see its social climate differently. For instance, Trickett et al. (1982) found differences between students and independent observers in rating the qualities of schools. These discrepancies suggest that social climate measures are influenced by one's personality or social role in the setting, not just by the setting's overall characteristics. The same environment may generate quite different perceptions among women and men, for example. Documenting and comparing perceptions of settings are important and can lead to efforts to address inequities in settings. Thus, social climate scores should be examined carefully for variation among individuals or subgroups in the setting (Moos, 2003; Shinn, 1990).

## Social Regularities

The two previous approaches to understanding environments concentrate on setting resources, how they change, and how members see them. A third approach looks at how settings create predictable relationships among their members and how those qualities persist over time regardless of the individuals involved (E. Seidman & Capella, 2017). Settings can be understood in terms of these **social regularities**, defined as the routine patterns of social relations among the elements (e.g., persons) within a setting (E. Seidman, 1988, pp. 9–10). A social regularities approach focuses not on individual personalities but on patterns of social relationships in communities that can affect distribution of resources, access to opportunities, and authority to address social issues.

Think back over your schooling for a moment. Who asks most of the questions in the school or college classroom? Your answer (e.g., teacher) is a social regularity (Sarason, 1982; E. Seidman & Capella, 2017). Why is this so predictable, despite the diversity of teachers and students and levels of education? Both teachers and students often focus on attributes of persons (e.g., boring teachers, lazy students). Instead, might this regularity be based on our assumptions about the roles and relationship of teacher and students and about how learning takes place—perhaps even about power in the classroom?

To discover social regularities, search for patterns of behavior that reveal roles and power relationships among setting members (e.g., teacher–student, therapist–client, employer–employee, parent–child). Roles are enacted in a specific setting in ways that affect power, decision making, resources, and inequalities (E. Seidman & Capella, 2017).

A historical social regularity in the United States is that schools have been a sorting mechanism for separating students by achievement or test scores, then preparing them for different roles in society. Segregated schools once also sorted students by race. When the courts mandated an end to segregation, communities brought Black and White students into the same schools.

**behavior settings**
a specific place with
recurring patterns of
conduct for specific
times. The patterns
of behavior are
predictable because
of demands of the
setting and time.

Yet both research and commonsense observation reveal that in many schools, a new form of sorting takes place. On the basis of (mainly White) staff perceptions of students' abilities, and on test scores that may not fairly measure those abilities, Black (and often Latinx and Native American) students are assigned disproportionately to classes and curricula that limit their ability to apply for college and their future attainments (Linney, 1986; E. Seidman & Capella, 2017; Weinstein, 2002). By sorting on this basis, school systems have continued (in modified form) the historical U.S. social regularity of racial separation. The new form of sorting may be unintentional rather than accomplished segregation by law. Nonetheless, it has similar effects on students' lives and opportunities.

***Contributions of the Social Regularities Approach.*** The concept of social regularities calls attention to the role of relationships and power in settings. It also offers a way of understanding why it often seems that the more things change in a setting, the more they remain the same. If a setting changes the actors (e.g., new teachers or principal in a school) but not the fundamental social regularities of how it functions and who makes decisions, it will promote only first-order change. Often, attempts to change a setting, such as a school, are undermined by social regularities that are not changed, such as decision-making power and role relationships. It is only when those social regularities are altered that the system itself is changed (E. Seidman & Capella, 2017; Tseng & Seidman, 2007), resulting in second-order change. These aspects of settings and relationships are discussed more in Chapters 7 and 8. Identifying social regularities often requires rich understanding of a setting and prolonged engagement. Methods for doing this include naturalistic observation, case study, and ethnographic approaches. Once regularities are identified, quantitative methods may also be used.

## Ecological Psychology and Behavior Settings

Roger Barker and colleagues developed a comprehensive approach to understanding patterns of behavior in environments rather than focusing on individuals (Barker, 1968; Wicker, 1979). We review the main components of their theory as an example of the power of settings on human behavior. The theory and methodology of Barker's ecological psychology has been important in the formation of environmental psychology and community psychology.

***Behavior Settings.*** Barker (1968) developed this concept as the primary unit of analysis for his theory of ecological psychology. A **behavior setting** is defined by having a place, time, and standing pattern of behavior. Consider the example of a small town or a neighborhood; Barker and colleagues actually spent years living in a small town, observing patterns of behavior in specific settings. For example, the behavior setting of a third-grade class would include meeting weekdays in one classroom at the school, which is predictable teacher and student behavior regardless of which individuals are present. A playground would constitute another setting where the same children would act differently than they do in classrooms but still exhibit predictable behavior patterns for a playground. A drugstore behavior setting would have wider time boundaries and more turnover of "inhabitants" (i.e., customers and staff) but would also occur in a single place and involve standing behavior patterns, again regardless of which individuals were present. Some behavior settings are embedded within larger settings, such as classes within a school. Others stand alone, such as a gas station. Some occur only occasionally, such as a wedding or talent show, whereas others can be daily events. Barker (1968, p. 106) and colleagues identified 884 behavior settings in the town of "Midwest" in 1963–1964; almost all could be grouped into five categories: government, business, educational, religious, and voluntary associations.

A behavior setting is not simply a physical place. While the sanctuary of the Methodist church in Midwest was a physical setting, several behavior settings occurred within it. Each sanctuary-based behavior setting had a time and specific standing behavior pattern: worship services, choir practices, community meetings, funerals, and weddings. In contrast, many small retail shops had only a single behavior setting in their physical place. In Barker's perspective, the same patterns of behavior occur in a behavior setting irrespective of specific individuals in the setting; persons are largely interchangeable when predicting behavior that will happen there.

A baseball game provides an illustration of Barker's approach. The game is a behavior setting, a standing pattern of behavior occurring within a given time and place. The baseball field defines the physical environment but reveals little about the game. Similarly, we would not be able to understand the game or individual players' acts by focusing on each player in isolation. Imagine, for example, a film showing the first baseman alone, without the context of the field or of plays not involving that player. Very little could be learned about what this person is doing and why, and it would be quite difficult to predict their behavior. By observing the context of the entire behavior setting, the program circuits or rules become clearer—so do the relationships among players during the game. Barker (1968) suggested that it is the combination of the physical field, game time, and the standing patterns of behavior among players and fans that constitute the behavior setting of a baseball game.

***Population of Settings and Behavior.*** A second contribution of Barker's ecological approach has been the study of manning theory (now known as staffing theory), which refers to the number of members in a setting relative to the number of roles within a behavior setting (Barker, 1968). Barker and colleagues observed that some settings were very good at getting everyone involved in activities and having most people feel valued, which Schoggen

**optimally populated settings** environments where most people are actively involved and feel appreciated.

**overpopulated settings** environments where too many people are available to fill roles and some people feel marginalized or excluded.

**underpopulated settings** environments where there aren't enough people available to fill roles; if people are committed to maintaining the setting, then members may try to develop these skills personally or teach others these skills; in severely underpopulated settings, members may be too overstretched and the setting may ultimately be abandoned.

(1989) called **optimally populated settings**. Other settings had more competition for roles and left some people out. In a classic study—Big School, Small School—Barker and Gump (1964) compared involvement of students in extracurricular activities (one form of behavior settings) in large and small high schools in Kansas (enrollments ranged from 35 to over 2,000). In the smaller schools, they found greater rates of student involvement in performances and in leadership roles and higher levels of student satisfaction and attachment to school. However, in larger schools, there were only a slightly greater number of opportunities for involvement. Their research found that students in smaller schools were twice as likely to participate in active ways and, on average, participated in a wider variety of activities. Barker and Gump also found that students in smaller schools perceived more responsibility to volunteer for activities. Such students often reported a sense that even if they were not talented in a particular activity, their help was needed. The larger schools had higher rates of uninvolved students and students who felt "marginal" with little sense of commitment to the school or social connection with school peers or staff. The number of people in the settings and how they were organized had an impact on student motivation, achievement, and isolation.

Studies in a variety of settings have established that the critical factor is the ratio of the number of roles available in a behavior setting compared with the number of individuals available to play those roles (Wicker, 1979, 1987). An **overpopulated setting** has many more people than roles to be filled. Settings easily recruit enough members to fill their roles; however, other students are marginalized or left out. Barker (1968, p. 181) theorized that vetoing circuits (behaviors that screen out potential members) would be common in these settings because there are plenty of replacements available. A large school will need to have tryouts for athletic teams, musical groups, dramatic productions, and so on. Often, only the most talented will be able to participate. Barker and Gump (1964) found that larger schools contained more overpopulated settings.

Alternatively, an **underpopulated setting** has more roles than members. That increases members' sense of responsibility for maintaining the setting and offers them the chance to develop skills they otherwise might not have learned. It may also increase the diversity of persons participating in the setting, attracting unused resources. For example, a shy person who otherwise would not try out for a school play is pressed into service, developing social skills or perhaps revealing hidden talents. In addition, members of an underpopulated behavior setting would engage in deviation-countering circuits rather than vetoing circuits. They would invest time and effort in teaching the skills needed for a role in the setting rather than excluding the shy person. This strategy makes sense if members are needed to play roles necessary for maintaining the setting. Barker and Gump (1964) found that smaller schools contained more underpopulated settings. Of course, members in an

**activity settings**
the integration of the physical setting and behavior of the people conducting an activity with their beliefs, participant roles, and the relationships they form and experience over time.

extremely underpopulated setting will burn out; the setting may even be disbanded. Yet moderate understaffing may lead to positive outcomes for individuals (greater skill or personal development) and the setting (greater commitment among members).

*Contributions and Limitations of Behavior Setting Theory.* Ecological psychology has generated an enduring body of concepts and research that has influenced the development of other ecological perspectives in community psychology. Behavior setting methodology has been applied in schools, churches, mutual help groups, and work settings to encourage engagement and support of members (Barker & Gump, 1964; Luke et al., 1991; Maya Jariego, 2016; Oxley & Barrera, 1984). The concepts of behavior setting and underpopulated settings represent two especially important contributions. Many small-group initiatives within large schools or congregations are consistent with ecological psychology's observation about overpopulated and underpopulated settings; creating a network of small groups where people interact and care for each other can build more satisfaction and help a larger organization be more responsive to needs of its members. One limitation is that Barker and associates focused on behavior, largely overlooking cultural meanings and other subjective processes; we address alternatives that include cultural meanings in the next section. A second limitation is that behavior setting theory focuses on how behavior settings perpetuate themselves and mold the behavior of individuals. This is one side of the picture, but it underplays how settings are created and changed, and how individuals influence settings (Maya Jariego, 2016; D. V. Perkins et al., 1988). Having originally been developed in a small-town setting, the theory has an emphasis on stability rather than change that is understandable yet limited in scope.

## Activity Settings

While similar to behavior setting theory in focusing on specific settings, activity setting theory incorporates subjective experiences and cultural understandings to investigate the meaning of behavior in context (O'Donnell et al., 1993; Shin, 2014). O'Donnell and colleagues were influenced by the Russian developmental theorist Vygotsky, by contextualist epistemologies, and by working in Hawaii and Pacific cultural contexts.

An **activity setting** is not simply a physical setting, and not just the behavior of persons who meet there, but also the subjective meanings that develop there among setting participants, especially *intersubjectivities*: beliefs, assumptions, values, and emotional experiences that are shared by setting participants. Key elements of an activity setting include the physical setting, positions (roles), people and the interpersonal relationships they form, time, and symbols that setting members create and use. Intersubjectivity develops over time as persons in the setting communicate, work together, and form

**intersubjectivity**
the process and outcome of sharing experiences, knowledge, understanding, and expectations with others; shared knowledge that is understood among community members but difficult to relay to strangers.

**counterspaces**
alternative activity settings that are developed to provide safety and well-being to individuals who typically face oppression, isolation, and marginalization in existing settings.

**narrative identity work**
the effort of counterspace members to develop positive personal and group identities that work against the internalization of negative stereotypes.

relationships. They develop symbols, chiefly language but also visual or other images, to express what they have in common. This perspective calls attention to cultural practices used in the settings and to the meanings that members attach to them (O'Donnell & Tharp, 2012).

In many spiritual settings, for instance, sacred written works and vocabulary, visual art, and music are important symbols whose meaning is both intensely personal and widely shared. In political rallies, particular colors, music, topics, and stories are used to connect current circumstances to historical precedents. Much of what is important about any culture is **intersubjective**, widely understood within the culture yet difficult to communicate to outsiders. Even within one culture, families and organizations develop intersubjective uses of language and gesture that outsiders cannot understand and that reflect important insider attitudes. Activity settings are often intentionally created to bring people together for a particular purpose, such as making meaning of life events, inspiring others, or navigating difficult circumstances.

*Counterspaces.* **Counterspaces** can be thought of as a type of activity setting that promotes well-being for participants who experience oppression. Counterspaces take a variety of forms, from organizations to friend and peer networks. The concept emerged with critical race theorists as a way to understand how African American college students used their participation in specific campus settings to cope with racism (Solórzano et al., 2000). Building on this initial work, Andrew Case and Carla Hunter (2012) developed a framework that describes how counterspaces promote psychological well-being for individuals who are members of various groups that experience oppression and marginalization (e.g., racial/ethnic, sexual, and religious minorities). In part, these spaces provide a refuge for their members, a space where there are systematic efforts to ensure that the oppression that exists in the larger society is not reproduced within. For instance, in a study conducted by McConnell, Todd, and colleagues (2016) examining the Michigan Womyn's Music Festival as a counterspace for cisgender lesbian feminist women, one participant described that counterspace in these terms:

> The safety that I feel on the Land is something that is hard to describe to people in my life. . . . I've seen women burst into tears when they first feel that. . . . I have learned to always be wary, be careful, you are female, you are in danger, you are fragile, somebody will DO SOMETHING to you. . . . I can walk naked (if I want to) in the dark (no moon) at 3:00 in the morning on that Land, and feel NO fear, NO sense of anything but safety. (p. 479)

At least three social processes are believed to occur within counterspaces that lead to positive psychological outcomes. The first, **narrative identity work**, involves counterspace members fostering positive personal and group identities to counteract the internalization of negative dominant narratives

**acts of resistance**
deliberately behaving in ways that protest oppression or that embrace suppressed cultural behaviors, such as wearing nonmainstream clothes.

**direct relational transactions**
social exchanges between members of a counterspace that create social support by offering guidance, opportunities for emotional release, and encouragement in the face of oppression.

(e.g., stereotypes). For instance, Case and Hunter (2014) found that among African American youth who were labeled "bad" either at school or through their involvement in the juvenile justice system, participation in a leadership development program helped them recast their identities in a positive light—as youth leaders.

Another process, **acts of resistance**, refers to the intentional engagement in behaviors that protest oppressive conditions or that affirm subjugated but culturally congruent behaviors. A counterspace provides individuals a safer avenue to practice these behaviors, which may include speaking in slang or wearing nonmainstream apparel that is associated with one's group. Case (2014) found that among African American college students at a predominantly White institution, membership in a Black cultural center allowed them to tell "whoopin' stories"—accounts of their worst experiences of physical punishment at the hands of parents—without being considered "strange." As a tradition in African American culture, these stories progress in a comedic fashion with each person providing a story to outdo the previous one.

**Direct relational transactions** that foster social support are interpersonal exchanges between members of a counterspace that provide instruction, venting and emotional release, and encouragement in the face of oppressive experiences. Wexler and colleagues (2013), for example, found that Inupiak (an Alaska Native community) youth cultivated relationships as a resilience

michaeljung/Shutterstock.com

Counterspaces are alternative social settings within larger settings that promote the psychological well-being of members of marginalized groups by giving them a safe space to explore their culture.

**environmental psychology**
studies the relationship between physical environments, especially human-constructed environments, and human behavior.

**environmental stressors**
environmental stimuli that negatively impact physical and mental health. Examples include noise, air pollution, hazardous waste, and crowded living spaces.

strategy to counteract culture loss. One of the effects of colonization for Indigenous populations is rapid and often dramatic changes in the ways they live, including language, food production, and schooling. An important consequence of this is the displacement of traditional culture that provides the basis for how people understand and cope with the world and each other. The researchers found that Inupiak youth intentionally forged relationships that would connect them with their traditional culture and provide them with supports and opportunities. Some reported maintaining relationships that helped them stay sober, while others pointed to relationships that enabled them to temporarily leave distressing situations at home to live securely elsewhere. Counterspaces are also discussed in Chapters 6 and 7.

***Contributions of the Activity Setting Approach.*** Activity setting theory offers a broader conception of social settings than ecological psychology. It has been used to study child development, juvenile delinquency, education, and community interventions. It has underscored the importance of subjective meaning in understanding links between individuals and their contexts. It is especially useful in working across cultural boundaries, as O'Donnell and associates have shown in their work in Hawaii, Micronesia, and elsewhere (O'Donnell & Tharp 2012; O'Donnell & Yamauchi, 2005), and in understanding cultural boundaries faced by racial and ethnic minorities within the United States (Case & Hunter, 2012; Shin, 2014).

## Environmental Psychology

**Environmental psychology** examines the influence of physical characteristics of a setting (especially built environments) on behavior (De Groot, 2018; Saegert & Winkel, 1990). Environmental psychology in the United States arose at about the same time as community psychology. Its founders were primarily social psychologists interested in the physical environment and behavior. Yet both fields emphasize a shift of perspective from individual to individual-in-environment, and they overlap in several ways (Shinn, 1996). Both fields emphasize research conducted in field settings and application of their concepts to social action.

***Environmental Stressors.*** A major focus of environmental psychology is the study of the psychological effects of **environmental stressors** that can have negative effects on mental and physical well-being, such as noise, air pollution, hazardous waste, and crowded housing (Mennis et al., 2018; Rich et al., 1995; Saegert & Winkel, 1990). For instance, the psychological effects of two notable incidents from the late 1970s have been researched intensively and longitudinally. At Love Canal, near Niagara Falls, New York, residents discovered in 1977 that they were living above a chemical waste dump when birth defects began appearing. The effects of that disaster, and of citizen activism in response, were studied by Adeline Levine and associates (A. Levine, 1982;

**environmental design**
developing architecture, neighborhood features, and other elements of a constructed setting with consideration for the psychological effects they will have.

Stone & Levine, 1985). The Three Mile Island nuclear plant near Harrisburg, Pennsylvania, had a serious accident in which radiation was released in 1979; the stressful effects of this accident on nearby residents have been studied over time (Baum & Fleming, 1993). In both cases, uncertainty about the levels of actual exposure to radiation or toxic substances and inconsistencies in public statements by industry and government officials exacerbated the stressful effects of the event (see also Wandersman & Hallman, 1993). After the Three Mile Island incident, blood pressure remained elevated, immune system functioning depressed, and symptoms of posttraumatic stress were more common among nearby residents than in comparison samples. A worse nuclear accident in Chernobyl, Ukraine, in 1986 appears to account for poorer subjective well-being and higher rates of depression 20 years after the disaster among those who were not exposed to high levels of radiation but lived in or near the area (Danzer & Danzer, 2016). A growing area of research has looked at how regular engagement in natural environments may act as a buffer or promote health. For example, Mennis et al. (2018) found that regular activity in urban greenspace appears to be associated with lower stress and better attention for African American adolescents who live in stressful neighborhoods.

*Environmental Design.* Environmental psychologists also study the psychological effects of architectural and neighborhood design features, which is called **environmental design**. Examples include studies of enclosed workspaces, windows, and aspects of housing design (De Groot, 2018). For a personal example, consider arrangement of furniture in indoor spaces on your campus or in your workplace. My (Bret Kloos's) psychology department recently remodeled common spaces in the department to make space for faculty to interact socially before and after meetings. We wanted to create more opportunities to build a sense of community. There are rooms for gathering and smaller, undedicated offices to be shared where any faculty member can work for short periods between meetings. Many of the faculty felt disconnected, as we have research labs spread across the campus and usually only come to the department building for meetings before returning back to our labs. For students, there are similar challenges and demands on their time. We created small rooms for study groups and improved the break room near mailboxes and the computer lab. All the renovated space is located near the psychology department's large conference room and administrative offices. This creates a social space to encourage faculty and students to engage each other outside class, as well as space for study and quiet work.

The New Urbanism movement in residential architecture and neighborhood design tries to encourage community experiences. Plas and Lewis (1996) studied Seaside, Florida, a community designed along New Urbanist lines, with building codes that require front porches and low picket fences for each house and town design with walkways to the town center and beach and limited automobile access. Businesses are accessible on foot from anywhere in the community. These features encourage neighboring and are based on the study of older, established towns and neighborhoods with a strong sense of community (e.g., J. Jacobs, 1961). Surveys, interviews, and naturalistic observation in Seaside indicated that these features did encourage neighboring contacts and sense of community (Plas & Lewis, 1996).

However, studies in other locales show that physical design does not always promote sense of community as intended (Hillier, 2002). For instance, in the 1960s, planners of the new town of Columbia, Maryland, put all mailboxes for a block together to encourage neighboring, yet the new residents demanded mailboxes at their houses. In addition, a convenience store was planned within a short walk of every house, yet residents preferred to drive a few minutes to larger stores in the town center, and the convenience stores failed (Wandersman, 1984, p. 341). Part of the problem may have been contextual: The principles used by the Columbia planners are useful in urban neighborhoods and small towns, where walking to corner stores is familiar, but Columbia is a suburb, where residents expect to drive to supermarkets. Citizen participation in planning also is important (J. Jacobs, 1961).

***Contributions and Limitations of Environmental Psychology.*** By emphasizing the importance of the physical environment, environmental psychology complements the more social perspective of the other approaches. Although its focus is different from that of community psychology, there are significant areas of overlap. However, those who implement changes in environments in a top-down manner do not always consider the impact on persons affected. For example, after Hurricane Sandy flooded many communities near New York City in 2012, local governments wanted to buy property that was vulnerable to future storms as a way to manage risk. The buyout program used disaster data and an environmental design approach to policy to recommend how to rebuild the affected areas. However, government officials and the disaster data analysts did not consider the community relationships and quality of life that were major considerations for residents in deciding whether to participate in the buyout (Binder et al., 2015).

## Comparing the Six Perspectives on Ecological Context: An Example

To compare these six perspectives, consider a play to be performed by students in a high school setting. A high school play is a *behavior setting*. It has boundaries of time (for practices and performances) and space (an auditorium or theater). It has a standing pattern of behavior: During performances, the actors, audience, and others behave in predictable ways and locate themselves in predictable places. These behavior patterns indicate the program circuit or agenda: to perform a certain play to entertain an audience.

If the setting is *underpopulated* (i.e., having fewer participants than roles or functions to be filled), the principles of ecological psychology would predict that setting members (i.e., director, cast, and crew) will seek to recruit additional help and be likely to take on extra roles or tasks. A person with no drama experience may be pressed to join the cast or crew, developing new skills or revealing hidden talents. If, in contrast, the setting is *overpopulated*, a member who cannot learn a role or task can be replaced easily. There will be auditions for parts, and only the best actors will be accepted. Other students will become marginalized. If many students seek to be involved in the play, the staff could create the benefits of underpopulated settings by having two casts of different actors perform the play on alternate nights or by staging a second production with different actors (Wicker, 1973).

Performing a play is not just following a literal script; it involves re-creating a world on stage that involves the relationships among actors and seeks to engage the audience. Actors seek an intangible "chemistry" between themselves and with the audience. That *intersubjectivity* is the focus of *activity setting* theory (O'Donnell et al., 1993). Engaging theater communicates intersubjective meanings through words, gestures, set, costumes, lighting, and perhaps music. The bonding that occurs among actors and crew during the long hours and shared work of a production also creates intersubjectivities.

How could the high school play be described in terms of Kelly's ecological principles? By working together, students and faculty build *interdependent* ties. This provides a basis for exchange of resources such as encouragement, instruction (especially from the director), and socialization. In addition, the play has interdependent relationships with other settings within the school. Its existence allows students who are not outstanding in other areas (e.g., academics, athletics) to feel connected with others, to contribute to school life, and perhaps to shine, becoming recognized for their work (Elias, 1987). The play is also a way for the school to connect with and be recognized in the community.

From an ecological perspective, a *cycling of resources* would be expected between those involved in the play and the school as a whole. In a school in which drama is prized, money, facilities, student interest, and overall support will be plentiful; in one that does not prize drama, the play will receive little of these. Availability of resources also depends on the strength of interdependent relationships built between the drama faculty and administration, parents, school board members, and others. In turn, the play may generate a flow of resources from the community to the school. For instance, families, friends, and businesses may contribute resources such as props, costumes, food for intermission, and encouragement.

*Adaptation* for students involved in the play will involve learning skills in performance, set design, lighting, and so on. All members may have to help in publicizing and managing the production. These skills may also have adaptive value in the larger environments of school or community, for instance in future employment. In addition, the play will occur within a pattern of *succession*. It may be the first such production or the latest in a line of successful, well-attended productions; the latter may have more resources available but may also place higher expectations on the cast and crew.

To apply Moos's *social climate dimensions*, members of the production (including director, actors, and crew) could complete questionnaires about their perceptions of the production environment. If they generally agree that play members were actively involved and supported each other well, and they believe the director was supportive, scores will be high on *Relationship* dimension scales. Questions on that dimension might also assess conflict among members. The *Personal Development* dimension would concern whether participating in the play provided them opportunities to develop skills or experience personal growth. *System Maintenance and Change* items would measure their perceptions about how organized the production was, how much control the director exerted, the clarity of expectations for members' performance, and how much creativity was valued.

If different perceptions of the group social climate occur among subgroups (e.g., director, actors, stage crew, men, women), discussion could focus on what events and processes led to those differences. Using both the real and ideal forms of a social climate scale would afford comparisons between the current group functioning and the visions of an ideal group held by all or by subgroups. Conclusions about social climate could be used in planning the next production.

What *social regularities* (E. Seidman, 1988) and role relationships are involved here? One concerns the roles of director and actors. The director, usually a faculty member, will assume a powerful role. Choosing the play, making casting decisions, coaching actors, and assuming responsibility for the quality of performance are all functions that the director may perform. With inexperienced actors, that assumption of power may make sense. However, each of these functions could be shared with experienced actors to promote their skill development and personal growth. Such altering of social regularities could also mobilize resources such as hidden leadership talents among the students. It changes the usual role relationship in schools but promotes the educational and perhaps artistic value of the production. (Indeed, using students as directors and in other authority roles seems more common in drama than in other areas of many schools.) The concept of social regularities calls attention to power and resources predictably invested in social roles in the setting and how these may be changed to promote the development of individuals or settings.

Finally, an environmental psychologist would examine how the *physical environment* could be manipulated to promote the artistic themes of the play. The stage set, lighting, sound, and costumes are not merely backdrops but artistic elements that help create mood and reflect the progress of the plot. Audience participation could be promoted by altering the room or seating. Actors in character could meet patrons at the door and create an atmosphere of immersion in the play. A play involves the creation of a believable world on stage that engages the audience, using artistic elements that parallel the concerns of environmental psychology.

**What Do You Think?**

1. Which of the six approaches to understanding contexts would be most useful for identifying areas to improve at a school?
2. Would you choose a different method if you were focused on students' perspectives, or those of teachers, administrators, or parents?
3. Which approach lends itself to taking action to make improvements?

# The Importance of Understanding Ecological Contexts for Intervention

As you probably gathered from the overview of different approaches to understanding ecological contexts, community psychologists use these frameworks to identify potential areas for intervention. From a community psychology perspective, a better understanding of what contributes to problems forms the basis of choosing where to intervene. If the ecological contexts of social issues are left unexamined, the interventions chosen may overlook particular challenges contributing to a problem, and the intervention effort will likely be limited in its effectiveness. In the remainder of this chapter, we illustrate how ecological thinking influences community research and action.

## Research: Linking Neighborhoods, Families, and Individuals

Neighborhoods provide one example of relationships between ecological contexts and the lives of individuals and families. From an ecological viewpoint, all neighborhoods have their strengths and local resources, as well as problems and limitations. Community psychologists seek to understand the complexity of neighborhoods, how resources are used, and how neighborhoods are related to individual and collective well-being. Some of this research supports what may seem intuitive: Neighborhoods with more problems are stressful and contribute to problems in adaptation for individuals. However, some of the research has demonstrated that much of what we assume about the relationships of neighborhood factors may be wrong or, at least, oversimplified.

For instance, Gonzales et al. (1996) studied predictors of grades in school for a sample of urban African American adolescents. They examined factors about family support for students, family income, parents' past schooling, and neighborhood conditions (e.g., occurrence of crime, gang activity, violence). Somewhat surprisingly, not only were worse neighborhood conditions one of the variables that predicted poorer academic achievement: neighborhood risk was a *stronger predictor of grades than family characteristics* such as parent education, family income, and number of parents living in the home. From the standpoint of interventions, the researchers found that neighborhood risk made a difference in what kind of parenting style was associated with higher grades. In lower risk neighborhoods with better conditions, teens whose parents were *less* restrictive had higher grades; this is consistent with many studies in developmental psychology. But in higher risk neighborhoods, teens whose parents were *more* restrictive had higher grades. A similar pattern of findings was found with children demonstrating more externalizing behaviors at school (e.g., ADHD) in more distressed neighborhoods except when parents were more restrictive (Beyers et al., 2003). Emerging scholarship has looked more closely at which kinds of monitoring could be more effective in neighborhoods with heightened risks for adolescents. Bendezú et al. (2018) suggested that active and involved monitoring by parents through discussion of daily plans may be more effective in reducing delinquency than curfew rules by themselves because those rules do not increase parents' knowledge or communication with the adolescent.

Studies of pregnant mothers provide another example. Women in higher crime Baltimore neighborhoods had a risk of poor pregnancy outcomes (e.g., premature birth, low birth weight) that was 2.5 times higher than those in lower crime areas. Moreover, while providing prenatal care and education about pregnancy reduces the risk of poor pregnancy outcomes, this reduction in risk was much less for women living in neighborhoods with high poverty rates and high unemployment than for women in other neighborhoods (Caughey et al., 1999). This finding indicates that for women in high-poverty neighborhoods, access to prenatal care may not be enough. In Baltimore, the Healthy Start program develops jobs in the community and works to improve housing quality, as well as providing prenatal care (Caughey et al., 1999). These problems are also rooted in macrosystem forces, requiring policy changes by governments and corporations. High poverty in neighborhoods has consistently been shown to affect birth outcomes since these first studies (Cubbin et al., 2020).

***Understanding Neighborhood Research.*** Before describing other research on neighborhood contexts, we must make a few introductory points. There are many challenges in studying neighborhoods. First, there is little consensus on an exact definition of a neighborhood in social sciences; it is larger than

**neighborhood risk processes**
neighborhood practices that increase an individual's risk for mental disorders, behavioral issues, and distress.

**neighborhood protective processes**
strength or resources that provide positive individual outcomes and may guard against the impact of risk processes.

**distal processes**
within an ecological framework, these systems are not as immediate to the individual yet have substantial impacts on their life (e.g., cultures, governments, corporations, ideologies, mass media).

**proximal processes**
within an ecological framework, these are the systems closest to the individual that involve the most face-to-face interactions (e.g., families, neighborhoods, classrooms, religious congregations, workplaces).

an urban block and smaller than a city. Neighborhoods have somewhat fluid boundaries (Shinn & Toohey, 2003). A small town may have the qualities of a single neighborhood. Nevertheless, most of us have a rough, intuitive idea of what a neighborhood is.

Second, there is much diversity in the ecologies of neighborhoods. There can be many differences between neighborhoods in how resources are organized, exchanged, and shared. Generalizations about the effects of neighborhoods on their residents can have many exceptions. Even within a single neighborhood there may be different areas. Within one Baltimore neighborhood, areas varied greatly in income, rates of home ownership, and unemployment: "Blocks of vacant, boarded-up public housing projects are only a few blocks from streets of well-maintained homes with well-manicured lawns and gardens" (Caughey et al., 1999, p. 629).

Third, neighborhoods are dynamic settings that are continually adapting. While a neighborhood may appear stable, in fact it may be in the process of gaining or losing population, jobs, or quality and affordability of housing stock. Its ethnic mix or average income level may be changing. It may be in transition from a neighborhood whose residents live there for decades to a neighborhood with higher resident turnover, or vice versa. Of course, individuals and families also are continually changing as members mature and their actions and attitudes change over time. Thus, while many of the characteristics that we describe next may seem to be stable, they are actually snapshots that capture one point in ongoing change.

In our consideration of how neighborhoods can affect individual functioning, we distinguish between **neighborhood risk processes**, which are statistically correlated with problematic individual outcomes such as personal distress, mental disorders, or behavior problems, and **neighborhood protective processes**, which are strengths or resources associated with positive individual outcomes. Protective processes may offset or buffer the impact of risk processes. Risk and protective processes may be different in different neighborhoods.

We also distinguish between **distal processes**, which are broader in scope and indirectly affect individuals, and **proximal processes**, which affect individuals more directly and immediately. "Proximal" and "distal" are not absolute categories but differ along a continuum. Here we consider structural neighborhood processes (more distal), neighborhood disorder and physical-environmental stressors (both more proximal), and protective processes (proximal and distal). We discuss distal and proximal risk and protective factors in greater detail in Chapters 9 and 10. To understand how neighborhoods may have an impact on individuals, we introduce them here.

***Distal Socioeconomic Risk Processes.*** These involve social and economic or physical characteristics of a neighborhood as a whole that are correlated with individual problems. For example, mental health and behavioral problems, delinquency, cardiovascular disease, and pregnancy problems are, on average, more common in neighborhoods where many residents have low incomes. Another distal social process is residential turnover: In neighborhoods with higher turnover, juvenile delinquency is more common.

Distal socioeconomic processes are not limited to cities. In a study in rural Iowa, community disadvantage (computed from community rates of unemployment, receiving of government assistance, and proportion of population with less than high school education) predicted rates of conduct problems among adolescent boys, while the proportion of single-parent households in the community predicted rates of conduct problems among adolescent girls (Simons et al., 1996).

It is important to note that these neighborhood-level statistics do not mean that low-income or single-parent families themselves are to be blamed for such problems; recall our discussion of blaming the victim in Chapter 2. Economic macrosystem forces (e.g., unemployment) are often the root causes in any community, but this is not the only way to understand those neighborhoods. As we will note shortly, low-income neighborhoods and families also may have protective processes at work.

Risky physical environments like dense, low-income neighborhoods lead to increased health hazards and psychological stress.

Atosan/Shutterstock.com

*Risky Physical Environments.* Socioeconomic root processes also create hazardous physical environments, which have more direct (proximal) effects on individuals and families. Residents of low-income neighborhoods are more likely to breathe polluted air and drink polluted water. They endure higher levels of traffic noise, which has been shown to limit academic learning in children, and higher exposure to lead, which limits cognitive development. Their neighborhoods have more hazardous traffic crossings and higher child pedestrian injury rates. Low-income neighborhoods often lack sources of healthy food: Supermarkets are often hard to find, yet convenience and liquor stores are abundant. Housing is often of lower quality, presenting many health hazards. Overcrowded housing also is associated with psychological distress in children (G. W. Evans, 2004).

*Neighborhood Disorder.* Another more proximal approach focuses on processes of neighborhood violence and incivilities. For instance, about one quarter of U.S. urban youth witness a murder in their lifetime. Exposure to violence is associated with posttraumatic stress disorder; depression; and other distress, aggression, and behavior problems (Hastings & Snowden, 2019; Kwon, 2019; Shinn & Toohey, 2003).

Incivilities are noticeable signs of neighborhood disruption that raise fears of crime. Physical incivilities include abandoned or dilapidated buildings, litter, vandalism, and graffiti. Social incivilities include public drunkenness, gang activities, and drug trade. D. D. Perkins and Taylor (1996) reported that residents of U.S. city blocks with more incivilities (especially physical ones) tended to have greater fears of crime, more depression, and more anxiety than those of neighborhoods with fewer incivilities. Neighborhood disorder also leads to restrictive parenting and even withdrawal from the community by parents concerned for their own and their children's safety (Bendezú et al., 2018).

*Protective Processes.* Not every neighborhood with statistical risk factors has higher levels of individual problems or distress. This observation leads to inquiry about what protective processes neighborhoods may have. Distal protective processes may include having a larger proportion of long-term residents and owner-occupied housing in a neighborhood (Shinn & Toohey, 2003). In addition, more proximal processes can be protective, such as relationships and sense of community among residents. For instance, Gearhart (2019) examined data from a study of Seattle's neighborhoods and found that neighborhoods where residents had a sense of mutual efficacy and social cohesion had more control and less disorder. In Baltimore neighborhoods that had higher levels of community organization (more voters registered, greater participation in community organizations), women had much lower risk of problems with pregnancy than women in neighborhoods with low levels of such organization. Risks were also lower in neighborhoods with more community services, businesses, and health care (Caughey et al., 1999).

## Promoting Neighborhood Quality of Life

These protective processes suggest avenues for community interventions. Community health and prevention programs, and clinical interventions, can link families with community resources such as jobs and child care. Community-level interventions have included working with neighborhood networks to promote social connection, efforts to improve housing quality and affordability, and policy advocacy to address wider social issues (Maton et al., 2004; Rania et al., 2019).

For example, consider this example of how citizen participation and cooperative housing initiatives for low-income residents in New York City addressed residents' concerns about building and neighborhood quality (Saegert & Winkel, 1990, 1996). When the city government seized buildings from absentee landlords for unpaid taxes, it helped finance sale of the buildings to cooperatives of low-income tenants, who then managed the buildings. Cooperative housing was rated higher in management quality, safety, freedom from drug activity, and resident satisfaction than city-owned housing or buildings owned by private landlords (Saegert & Winkel, 1996, p. 520). Effective citizen leaders emerged, particularly among women and elderly residents, who worked to improve conditions (Saegert, 1989).

The Dudley Street Neighborhood Initiative (DSNI) is an example of neighborhood-based community development. DSNI has transformed an inner-city area of Boston into a thriving neighborhood. In 1984 the area was one-third vacant lots, with unauthorized dumping by trash haulers and frequent arson while city government looked the other way. The Dudley Street neighborhood now boasts new parks, businesses, community agricultural gardens, playgrounds, and community centers. Vacant lots have been rehabilitated for homes and community uses, over 400 new homes built, and over 500 housing units rehabbed. Street life is vibrant and safe. All this has been planned and implemented by residents, working through DSNI, which has more than 3,760 members. Outside grants and city collaboration have helped, but DSNI citizens insisted on and won local control. They use local resources and make decisions for the local community, transforming their community "from the inside out." While there is a healthy diversity of opinion on each DSNI project, there also is a real community spirit and tangible evidence of a transformed community that continues to address issues of justice (Dudley Street Neighborhood Initiative, n.d.; R. B. Peterson, 2018; Putnam & Feldstein, 2003).

# Creating and Altering Settings

**alternative settings** new and different initiatives created to address the unmet needs of those who are not helped by existing options.

As discussed earlier, ecological frameworks can be used to improve environmental conditions that affect functioning. However, changing existing settings can be difficult, even when one can identify the contextual variables that need to be addressed. Settings, social systems, and individuals within them generally resist change and try to preserve the status quo. For example, we have had evidence for 40 years that secondhand smoke is bad for health, but it took nearly that long to pass laws that restricted smoking in public buildings. The concepts of interdependence, adaptation, and social regularities suggest some ways in which changing environmental conditions might happen. In the face of such resistance, community activists and community psychologists sometimes take a different approach to improving individual and family well-being. They stop trying to change the existing settings and work to create a new and different setting to address the needs unmet by the status quo. Community psychologists refer to this strategy of change as creating an **alternative setting**. Alternative settings are designed not necessarily to replace current settings but rather to provide conditions and resources that support the functioning of people for whom the current options do not work.

Next, we describe an exemplary environmental intervention that created community settings to promote well-being rather than treat needs. The Community Lodge created alternative places to live and work for persons being discharged after long-term mental health hospitalizations (Fairweather et al., 1969). The existing approaches to address the challenges faced by persons leaving institutional care might have addressed "needs" of ex-patients, but Fairweather and colleagues were seeking a more transformative approach that could promote second-order change in roles and opportunities for participation in community life. Rather than creating new programs to address each need in a treatment plan, the leaders of the interventions decided that a more comprehensive approach was necessary to change the environments and to support the development and functioning of the people they wanted to help. In Chapter 9, we discuss mutual support and self-help groups as examples of social support, but they could also be cited as examples of creating alternative settings.

## The Community Lodge: Creating an Alternative Setting

The Community Lodge (Fairweather, 1979, 1994; Fairweather et al., 1969) is a classic study and was an early influence on community psychology and community mental health (we describe it briefly in Chapter 2). Yet some of its principle elements have never been widely adopted in mental health systems. Those elements happen to be the aspects that continue to pose the most interesting challenges to social regularities of mental health care. Here we revisit the Community Lodge movement because it illustrates the creation of alternative settings to standard mental health care.

The Community Lodge idea began in a Veterans Administration psychiatric hospital in the 1950s. After working in psychiatric hospital care for some time, Fairweather and others recognized that the ecological context of the hospital did not promote independent community living for persons with serious mental illness. In hospital settings, the patient had few opportunities for decision making and autonomy. "Good behavior" usually meant following orders. In contrast, once discharged, an individual would need to take initiative, make independent decisions, and form supportive relationships with others.

Fairweather and colleagues developed inpatient group treatments that promoted the ability of men (veterans) with even the most serious mental disorders to participate in group decisions to prepare for living outside the hospital. However, even those treatments were not enough; those men, once released, still returned to the hospital at too high a rate after too short a period in the community. The problem, Fairweather and associates realized, was that there was no community setting, set of roles, or adequate support following release from the hospital. They recognized that altering the social regularities within the hospital was not enough.

Fairweather and colleagues then created an alternative setting in which patients released from the hospital moved together to a residence in the community (Fairweather, 1979, pp. 316–322, 327–333). An old motel was leased and refurbished for this new setting that they named the Lodge. After visiting the Lodge several times, the members were discharged from the hospital and moved in. After several trial-and-error experiences, Lodge members became self-governing. They developed Lodge rules that, for instance, made it acceptable to discuss symptoms of mental illness with other Lodge members but not with neighbors. The researchers were surprised that some of the previously most seriously impaired persons became active members of the community. With consultation of the staff, Lodge members established a janitorial and gardening business and eventually became economically self-supporting. Finally, the members felt confident enough that they ended their professional relationship with Fairweather, although infrequent social contacts continued (Fairweather, 1994). Fairweather and colleagues conducted rigorous experimental designs to promote the adoption of the Lodge model in community mental health systems (Fairweather, 1994; Hazel & Onaga, 2003). However, as we discuss in Chapter 13, empirical evidence itself is not sufficient to change policy. The data and successful outcomes for Lodge members were compelling scientifically, but Fairweather encountered difficulty in getting other mental health professionals to shift their perspective on how to help those with psychiatric disabilities.

Although this innovation in mental health care has not changed community mental health systems broadly, it has been widely disseminated as an alternative setting. Currently, 16 states in the United States have Community Lodges (Coalition for Community Living, n.d.). The programs actively work together to promote the ideals first demonstrated by Fairweather and the first Lodge members to create alternative supports where the setting is part of the local neighborhood and supports the autonomy and development of the residents (Haertl, 2005, 2016).

Community Lodges have several distinctive features, all involving changed role relationships that are usually found in mental health care. The most important and surprising one is that Lodge residents govern themselves. This is radically different from most mental health settings and an example of second-order change discussed in Chapter 1. Professionals serve only as consultants and have a collaborative role that seeks to maximize members' autonomy (Haertl, 2007). Ideally, the professional role is limited. Lodge members assume responsibility for monitoring each other for taking medication, behaving responsibly within and outside the Lodge, and related issues. Each Lodge decides for itself whether to admit new members or to dismiss members (Fairweather, 1979, 1994).

In controlled studies using volunteers randomly assigned to a Lodge or to ordinary psychiatric aftercare, Fairweather (1979) and Fairweather et al. (1969) demonstrated that Lodge members, although similar to the control group on background variables, relapsed less often, spent fewer days in the hospital when they did, and spent more days employed than the controls. These differences persisted for 5 years of follow-up studies. Moreover, the Community Lodge method was less expensive than traditional community aftercare. Recent studies have documented that Lodge members had a 90% reduction in hospitalization rates over a year compared to their preadmission records (38 days compared to 5 days a year; Haertl, 2007). Furthermore, their annual earned income rose 515% 5 years after completing occupational training compared to their pre-Lodge involvement, although it still represents a limited annual income of $6,708 (Haertl, 2007).

By demonstrating the effectiveness of community-based housing and economic ventures, the Community Lodge studies have demonstrated the possibility of shifting perspectives and expanding mental health care in communities. Yet their key element, self-government by Lodge members, has seldom been adopted (Fairweather, 1979). Perhaps that is because it undermines a social regularity many professionals believe is essential for helping persons with mental illness: professional supervision and control. As Fairweather often has pointed out, the Community Lodge findings indicate otherwise. Proponents of the Fairweather Lodges working to establish a new research base of program fidelity standards include Lodges as an evidence-based practice that is promoted by federal agencies as a viable alternative in mental health systems and policy (Haertl, 2016). For further description of a Lodge, see the following Community Psychology in Action feature in Box 5.1. Chapters 11–13 provide more details about how program implementation research and evaluation can be used to help establish policy.

## Box 5.1   Community Psychology in Action: Embracing the Fairweather Model

Kristine Haertl, PhD, OTR/L

"You aren't lonely here." "We care for each other." "It's like a family." These quotes were all expressed by Lodge members during focus group interviews researching the unique aspects of the Fairweather model.

As I drove up to the duplex in a quiet suburban neighborhood, I noticed two cars and a motorcycle in the driveway. The vehicles were owned by Lodge members, all of whom were able to afford them through productive work at the organization's large corporate janitorial and mail room services. Although the five Lodge members carpooled to work, the vehicles provided autonomy on weekends and during events away from the Lodge. While some use their own vehicles, others use the public transit system. Each Lodge also has a van, and members are given training opportunities in order to serve as drivers.

During my visit, two of the members were making dinner for the group while others planned a shared outing. As we sat down to dinner and began the interview, one of the clients became delusional and agitated, claiming his belt was gone and disappeared forever. Rather than intervene, I sat back and watched as a Lodge peer said, "Don't worry, Jack,* I believe it is on your bed; we can check later." This small insightful response from his peer calmed the member down, and dinner proceeded as planned. This example of mutual peer support is integral to the peer culture that often occurs within the Lodge. Members support each other throughout all phases of health and wellness.

As a former employee and longtime board member of a large mental health Fairweather organization (Tasks Unlimited), I've witnessed the powerful effects of the environment on health, wellness, and recovery. Within Fairweather programs, the Lodge is the central housing model incorporating shared resources, work, chores, and support. The concept of interdependence is integral to the supportive culture offered by the Lodge, and members have extensive decision-making power in house functions. In working with various mental health programs, I've noticed the Fairweather Lodge treats individuals as community participants rather than patients (such as those in medical expert-based models). Often, group-living environments are time limited, and the emphasis is on short-term stays.

In Fairweather programs, individuals can make the Lodge a home for life. For example, Mary, a woman with chronic schizophrenia, had been in and out of state and county hospitals for decades. She entered Tasks Unlimited in her 40s through a Fairweather program offered at the state hospital that eventually transitioned to the community. Mary found that she thrived in the group living environment, enjoyed the work offered by the organization, and later took leadership roles in the Lodge (including maintaining the weekly house budget). With the supportive environment, she developed many friendships, was afforded opportunities for numerous activities and various trips, and remained at the program and out of the state hospital for over 30 years— atypical from most mental health residential houses. She was able to live nearly all of her adult life in a quality environment until her death of natural causes in her mid-70s.

The support and comprehensive services enabled Mary to transition from years in the state hospital to decades out of the hospital and in a nice home with friends, productive work, and numerous recreational opportunities. The affordance of quality peer-based living is an important addition to residential options. Concepts of interdependence and productive meaningful engagement in daily activities are central to the Fairweather model. This holistic approach to developing a peer supportive culture has impressive outcomes in providing long-term quality residential, psychiatric, vocational, and recreational services through Fairweather programs.

* The names and identities of the individuals in the Community Psychology in Action feature have been disguised to maintain confidentiality for all participants.

**What Do You Think?**

1. What are some strengths and limitations of the Fairweather model?
2. Which community psychology values does the Fairweather model exemplify?
3. What factors might help explain why this model has not been adopted more widely?
4. What strategies could be used to address these factors and adopt the Fairweather model in other communities?

# Conclusion: Promise and Challenges of Changing Environments

The Fairweather Lodge example demonstrates the potential of using an ecological perspective to promote the well-being of individual and families. Environments can be sources of problems for individuals but can also offer resources for negotiating challenges in individual and community life. Rudolf Moos (2002, 2003) spent his career developing frameworks and measures for understanding the role that environmental factors can play in well-being. He identified four enduring questions about the relationships between individuals and ecological contexts that summarize the complexity of these relationships. These questions are helpful considerations for anyone interested in changing the environmental conditions of their neighborhoods or community.

## How Are Contexts Both Powerful and Fragile in Their Influences on Individuals?

Neighborhoods, community settings, treatment settings, families, and other contexts can have influences on opportunities and well-being of members. Cohesive settings can exert especially powerful influence on members' attitudes and actions. Yet that power is also risky; for instance, cohesion and loyalty can become paramount over individual well-being. "Any setting that is powerful enough to produce constructive personal change is also powerful enough to elicit self-doubt, distress, even suicidal behavior" (Moos, 2003, p. 8). The risks of promoting cohesion and the power of settings must be understood and considered. Building settings that truly respect diverse members and views is challenging.

Yet the impacts of settings on individual lives also can be fragile, in the sense that when persons leave the setting, its influence can change and may wane. Research amply demonstrates that while treatment settings and prevention programs may have short-term effects on individuals and communities, these changes are difficult to sustain over the long term. It is critical to find ways to create environments that sustain positive changes. Community psychologists can study which aspects of community settings can support individual development and need to be sustained as members leave and new people join settings.

### How Can We Understand Ecological Contexts as Dynamic Systems That Change Over Time?

Communities, settings, and other contexts have their own histories, which must be understood as an ongoing story of changes. Recall the discussion of succession in Kelly's ecological metaphor presented earlier. While the concepts we have presented in this chapter may give the illusion of stability in environments, in fact these contexts are works in progress, changing over time. Families change as their members mature. Neighborhoods change as their social and cultural makeup, economic resources, and institutions evolve. Community organizations often begin in a period of energetic efforts and optimism yet often evolve into predictable, structured forms or disband. We still only partially understand how these changes over time are related to internal forces within the environment and to external influences, such as relations with other settings and macrosystem forces.

### How Can We Clarify the Mutual Relationships Between Individuals and Contexts?

Studying the characteristics of environments is challenging, given that many of their most psychologically important qualities are subjective, as described with the Moos social climate scales. Methods exist for aggregating these into variables describing environments, yet there is still much to be worked out (Fowler & Todd, 2017; Moos, 2003). Moreover, the relationships between environments and individuals are reciprocal. Persons certainly select and influence contexts as well as being influenced by them. Teasing out causal patterns is difficult.

### How Are Ecological Contexts Influenced by Culture, Ethnicity, Gender, and Other Social Processes?

Communities, neighborhoods, settings, and other contexts differ in their cultural, historical, and social characteristics. This is important not only for explaining ecological contexts but also for developing them. For example, to create effective community settings for helping individuals overcome alcohol abuse, the cultural and spiritual resources, ways of involving individuals, and shared ritual practices would be different among European Americans in an East Coast suburb and among Native Alaskans in rural villages (Hazel & Mohatt, 2001; Mohatt et al., 2004). Creating counterspaces to navigate experiences of racism, confront them, and receive support can be critical for minority students on large college campuses (Case & Hunter, 2012).

Understanding ecological context is central to community psychology. In many ways, the entire field is about understanding how contexts and individuals influence each other. The remaining chapters of this text build on this chapter to inform how and when we may promote change.

# For Review

## Discussion Questions

**1.** What are the advantages of focusing on settings to understand behavior and well-being?

**2.** Consider one model of ecological context: the classroom. What are the important features of your classroom environment that influence your behavior while in class?

**3.** Are there other aspects of ecological context that you can think of that are not represented in the discussed models?

**4.** Alternative settings have been created when the resources available did not adequately serve the needs of people. Can you think of alternative settings that might be needed in your community? If so, who would be involved in creating them?

## Key Terms

interdependence, 147
cycling of resources, 149
personal resources, 149
social resources, 149
physical resources, 149
adaptation, 150
succession, 150
social climate approach, 152
social relationships, 152
personal development, 152
system maintenance and change, 152
social regularities, 154

behavior settings, 155
optimally populated settings, 157
overpopulated settings, 157
underpopulated settings, 157
activity settings, 158
intersubjectivity, 159
counterspaces, 159
narrative identity work, 159
acts of resistance, 160
direct relational transactions, 160

environmental psychology, 161
environmental stressors, 161
environmental design, 162
neighborhood risk processes, 168
neighborhood protective processes168
distal processes, 168
proximal processes, 168
alternative settings, 172

## Learn More

A detailed summary of the chapter, along with other review materials, is available on the *Community Psychology, Fourth Edition* companion website at http://pubs.apa.org/books/supp/kloos4/.

Neighbors in Naco, Mexico, and Naco, Arizona, used the fence dividing their community as a volleyball net until a taller fence was installed, an example of how physical environment impacts sense of community.

Jeff Topping

# 6 What Defines Community?

## Looking Ahead  III➡

**After reading this chapter you will be able to answer these questions:**

**1.** How has our understanding of community changed over time?

**2.** What is the psychological sense of community and how can it affect our lives?

**3.** What factors help promote a sense of community?

**4.** What are some of the benefits, and costs, of belonging to a community?

**5.** How can a negative sense of community be adaptive?

## Opening Exercise

## The Experience of Community

In 1979, the small community of Naco started a tradition of an annual volleyball game, held each April. While many communities have similar traditions celebrating their common history, this one is unique. Naco is officially two towns: Naco, Sonora, in Mexico and Naco, Arizona, in the United States. The volleyball was hit not over a net but over the rusted fence that divided the two municipalities and marked an international border.

Sixto de la Peña, who served as town historian for Naco, Sonora, recalled that the neighboring teams had two problems:

The first is that the barbed wire punctured the balls, so we had to learn how to kind of "grab and throw" the punctured balls, although later we decided to simply cover the barbed wire with a rubber tarp. . . . The second was that the team that lost three out of five matches had to host a party for the other team. But the fence was there, so we fixed that by cutting a hole in the fence so that the Mexican side, which always won, could go to the party on the American side. (Gallón, 2017, paras. 4–5)

There had been a fence of some kind dividing the two towns since the early 1900s,

**The Experience of Community (continued)**

put up initially at the request of the Mexican government to help organize traffic between the two countries. But it had not done much to disrupt the sense of shared community. Residents would easily cross the border daily to visit family and friends; to go to school, work, or church; or to shop.

This story is mirrored in communities across the U.S.–Mexican border, including much larger cities such as El Paso/Ciudad Juarez, San Diego/Tijuana, and Nogales, Arizona/Nogales, Sonora (commonly referred to as Ambos Nogales by the residents). But in the last several decades, those daily interactions and shared identities have been curtailed by changes in immigration policy in the United States. In the late 1990s, the wire fence was replaced by one of large, metal beams. At first, the volleyball game just moved out into the desert, where the wire fence still existed—but the party ended. The metal fence eventually outgrew the community completely. The last volleyball game was held in 2007 (Gallón, 2017).

**What Do You Think?**

1. What does the word "community" mean to you?
2. Who gets to define a community?
3. Think of the multiple communities of which you have been a member. How has that membership affected you and your life?
4. Now think about the cross-nation community of Naco. If you lived in this community, on either side of the border, would this change your answers?

Community psychology has a clear focus on communities. Communities are the ecological level at which we conduct the majority of our research and interventions. They are what the field is about. In this chapter, we explore the question of what makes a community. How are they formed? How do they change and evolve? What are the benefits of belonging to a community, and what are the costs?

# An Ecological-Transactional Model of Communities

We invite you to imagine the many times you have walked into a completely new space in your life, one where you had no previous experience. Maybe the space was already filled with people, or maybe you were the first one there. You might have immediately seen familiar faces, or you might have looked and seen no one you knew. You may have been struck by how much you had in common with the people there, or by your differences, or by both at the same time. As you entered those spaces, how did you feel? Did you feel a sense of anticipation, anxiety, or excitement?

**ecological-transactional model of community**
the reciprocal interactions between us and the communities we encounter.

In Chapter 5, we introduced you to the concept of ecological contexts and their impact on the health and well-being of individuals. In this chapter we would like to extend that ecological metaphor to include communities. Throughout our lives we interact with a multiplicity of communities. Those interactions are reciprocal—we are changed by the communities with which we engage, and those communities are changed by us. Together, those ideas of ecological contexts and reciprocal relationships give rise to an **ecological-transactional model of community**. Some of the first ecological-transactional models were developed in the field of child maltreatment, when researchers sought to model the complex, reciprocal relationships between factors associated with low or high rates of child maltreatment, including factors such as the level of violence the community (Cicchetti & Lynch, 1993).

Ecological-transactional models do not just illustrate the reciprocity and interdependence between us and the contexts in which we live our lives; they also highlight the construction of settings and the development of individuals over time. We are constantly modifying the settings in which we live our lives, and at the same time, those settings are changing us.

One way of thinking about those transitions is the transformation from a "space" to a "place." The distinction perhaps first arose in the field of humanistic geography and is meant to distinguish between an abstract space with no meaningful associations attached and a place made rich from a history of experiences. When you enter a new space, you have no associations with that environment, no known constraints, and no history upon which you can build. Anything can happen. When you walk into a place, there is familiarity, history, and expectations. An ecological-transaction model of community is fundamentally about the transition from space to place.

## What Is a Community?

Ferdinand Tönnies was a German sociologist who lived from 1835 to 1936. This was a period of rapid and extensive social change as Western countries became increasingly urban, industrial, and technological. Tönnies was fascinated with the question of how those societal-level changes affected human relationships, particularly at the community level. Tönnies (1887/1988) proposed a famous distinction between Gemeinschaft and Gesellschaft relationships. *Gemeinschaft* is often translated as "community." It refers to relationships that are multidimensional and are valued in their own right, not just as a means to an end. When you do something for someone or spend time with someone solely because you value that person and your relationship with them, that is a Gemeinschaft relationship. Small towns are often described as being dominated by Gemeinschaft relationships. The members of the communities know

**locality-based communities**
the traditional view of community, such as city blocks, neighborhoods, and towns.

**relational communities**
communities that are defined more by shared goals, interests, activities, or social identities than by geographical location or physical proximity. Examples include online discussion groups, religious congregations, workplaces, and political parties.

each other in many different roles and work to maintain those relationships. There is a shared sense of obligation to each other, not for any specific reason but because of the shared relationships.

*Gesellschaft* is often translated as "society" and refers to relationships that are based upon a specific transaction. The relationship is instrumental in the sense that the participants view the relationship fundamentally as a means to an end, not as something that has value in its own right. This is a relationship you engage in solely because you expect to benefit in some way from the interaction, and the same is true for the other person. Thus, your relationships with your family and friends are Gemeinschaft relationships, while your relationship with the guy who runs the register at the grocery store where you shop is a Gesellschaft relationship.

Tönnies recognized that all of our lives involve both types of relationships, but he believed that it is Gemeinschaft relationships that define communities. An amazing number of historians, social scientists, and philosophers have been agreeing with him ever since. Seymour Sarason (1974), a founding member of the field of community psychology, defined a community as "a readily available, mutually supportive network of relationships on which one could depend" (p. 1). Sarason is essentially saying that a community is a setting defined by Gemeinschaft relationships.

We do not mean to imply in this discussion that communities are defined by one variable. We have learned a great deal since Tönnies and realize that communities are complicated entities that we are still beginning to understand. In the rest of this chapter, we explore those complexities.

## Types of Communities

Definitions of community in sociology and in community psychology distinguish between two meanings of the term: community as locality and community as a relational group (e.g., Bernard, 1973; Bess et al., 2002). As you read this section, reflect back on our earlier discussion of space versus place. In that context, "space" can refer to both locality-based and relational communities.

*Locality-Based Community.* The traditional conception of community, **locality-based communities** include city blocks, neighborhoods, small towns, cities, and rural regions. Interpersonal ties exist among community members (residents); they are based on geographic proximity, not necessarily choice. When residents of a locality share a strong sense of community, individuals often identify themselves by their locality, and friends are often neighbors. In many nations, political representation, public school districts, and other forms of social organization are delineated by locality.

*Relational Community.* **Relational communities** are defined by interpersonal relationships and a sense of community but are not limited by geography. Internet discussion groups are communities completely without geographic limits. Mutual help groups, student clubs, and religious congregations are defined by relational bonds.

Although relational communities may be based only on friendships or recreation (e.g., sports leagues), many are organizations bound by a common task or mission. Workplaces, religious congregations, community organizations, chambers of commerce, labor unions, and political parties are examples.

Locality-based and relational communities form a spectrum rather than a dichotomy. Many primarily relational communities are seated in a locality (e.g., universities, religious congregations). An online discussion group where the members have never actually met each other face to face anchors the purely relational pole of the continuum; a town or neighborhood represents the opposite locality-based pole.

## Levels of Communities

A fundamental point of any ecological-transactional model of communities is the fact that communities exist at different ecological levels. As discussed in Chapter 1, these include

- microsystems, such as classrooms and mutual help groups;

- organizations, such as workplaces, religious congregations, and civic groups;

- localities, such as city blocks, neighborhoods, cities, towns, and rural areas; and

- macrosystems, such as the Filipino community, political parties, and nations.

The transactional aspect of the model emphasizes that communities are related across levels. Classrooms exist within a school, which often draws its population from a specific locality. Macrosystem economic and political forces influence workplaces, schools, community programs, and families. These relationships are transactional in that a change in one setting or one ecological level will trigger changes in the other settings. This is an example of the ecological principle of *adaptation*, discussed in Chapter 5. Improving community and individual life often involves interventions that are designed to change one level but result in changes at multiple levels.

If communities exist at different levels, what is the smallest group that can be usefully called a community? Could your immediate family or your network of friends be considered a community? Certainly these have some of the psychological qualities of communities. However, previously we have argued that for conceptual clarity, connections with families and friends should be considered social networks, not communities (Hill, 1996). We defined "community" as a larger grouping of individuals *who may not know* all the other members yet who share a sense of mutual commitment. In this chapter, we exclude immediate families and immediate friendship networks from our discussion of communities, as a way to focus our discussion.

## Who Defines Communities?

The issue of who defines communities is conceptually related to the issue of problem definition introduced in Chapter 1. How a community is defined has far-reaching implications, affecting issues such as the inclusion and exclusion of community members and the political power of the community. The ability of communities to define themselves may require a struggle, and external systems (e.g., government planners, political forces) may be involved.

For instance, Sonn and Fisher (1996) studied the sense of community among "Coloured" South Africans, a racist category created by apartheid laws. Despite this artificial, externally imposed categorization, "Coloured" South Africans managed to build shared ideas and commitments that helped them resist racist oppression and that persisted even among those who emigrated to Australia. In Australia itself, discussion of the Aboriginal "community" has often been in terms defined by European Australians in government and academia. Thus, it is phrased in Western concepts and often fails to recognize diversity among Indigenous Australian peoples (Dudgeon et al., 2002). This also occurs in dominant views of Native Americans and other dispossessed groups. Finally, concepts of what it means to be Australian (or any other national identity) are socially constructed and challenged over time (A. Fisher & Sonn, 2002).

In a 2001 study of neighborhood boundaries for families and children, census tract definitions of neighborhoods in Cleveland, Ohio, often did not match residents' own drawings of neighborhood maps. Measures of social indicators such as rates of crime and teen childbearing differed depending on whether census or resident maps were used. This would greatly affect both community research and community programs that use census data (Coulton et al., 2001). Studies like this have resulted in a move to emphasize member-defined communities in community research. Techniques such as Google Earth, GIS (geographic information systems) software, and photovoice have been used to allow community members to self-identify the geographic and social boundaries of their communities, particularly with marginalized populations such as people who are homeless (Lohmann & McMurran, 2009; Pruitt et al., 2018; Townley et al., 2018; Wise, 2015). The need for these types of participatory methods (see Chapter 4) in all aspects of community definition is fundamental to a membership-based approach to understanding communities. We cannot hope to understand how communities affect the lives of their members unless we start with an understanding of how those members define those communities.

# Sense of Community

Take a look at the following quotes. Try to make some guesses about who these people are and what kinds of settings they are referring to.

> When I was going through a rough time, a rough patch during year 12, in some cases, I could talk to people that I knew . . . they may have gone through the same thing and they could help me. I knew that I could talk to people . . . if I was having trouble at something and just needed to talk.

> People walk through there all the time . . . and I get to know them. I've probably meet hundreds of people who go through there who speak to me every morning and evening, and I've made some quite good friends amongst some on the street.

> We have encountered so many good people and we feel at home here. In the church, too, there are very good people, there is a lot of help given and very good people. . . . They offer us the things we need but treat all of us equal.

> Yeah, like when we were at meetings, they always asked our opinion. That was kind of fun being able to give your opinion when you have only been there a month. I thought that was great.

All of these quotes are from qualitative studies of people's perceptions of community. The first quote is in reference to an online gaming community (O'Connor, Longman, White, & Obst, 2015, p. 469), the second is from a person talking about walking his dog in his town in Western Australia (Bulsara et al., 2007, p. 48), the third quote is from a Latina immigrant in the United States (Bathum & Baumann, 2007, p. 172), and the fourth quote is from a study of adolescents and their involvement in community organizations (S. D. Evans, 2007, p. 699).

## What Do You Think?

1. What do you think these people are talking about?
2. Are they all talking about the same thing?
3. How do the communities discussed in these quotations vary along the relational–locality continuum we discussed earlier?

Community psychologists believe that people have emotional relationships with their communities, and we believe that the quality of those affective relationships has important implications for well-being and happiness. We call that affective relationship *sense of community*.

> I have never met anyone—young or old, rich or poor, black or white, male or female, educated or not—to whom I have had any great difficulty explaining what I meant by the psychological sense of community. (Sarason, 1974, p. 1)

This quote is from the book *The Psychological Sense of Community* by Seymour Sarason. In that book, Sarason set the tone for how community psychologists think about the relationships between individuals and communities. Sarason defined community as "a readily available, mutually supportive network of relationships on which one could depend" (p. 1). Sarason argued that the "absence or dilution of the psychological sense of community is the most destructive dynamic in the lives of people in our society." Its development and maintenance is "the keystone value" for a community psychology (p. x). He applied the term "community" to localities, community institutions, families, street gangs, friends, neighbors, religious and fraternal bodies, and even national professional organizations (pp. 131, 153).

Look back at the quotes at the beginning of this section. Do you think those people all felt a sense of community?

Sarason (1974) defined the psychological sense of community as

> the perception of similarity to others, an acknowledged interdependence with others, a willingness to maintain this interdependence by giving to or doing for others what one expects from them, the feeling that one is part of a larger dependable and stable structure. (p. 157)

David McMillan and David Chavis (1986) reviewed research in sociology and social psychology on sense of community and group cohesion. Their definition of sense of community resembled Sarason's:

> a feeling that members have of belonging, a feeling that members matter to one another and to the group, and a shared faith that members' needs will be met through their commitment to be together. (McMillan & Chavis, 1986, p. 9)

Since Sarason's first discussions of the concept in 1974, psychological sense of community has been embraced by a wide variety of disciplines, including social work (Itzhaky et al., 2015; Ohmer, 2007), sociology (Cope et al., 2016), medicine (S. Anderson et al., 2016; Vora & Kinney, 2014), nursing (Buck, 2017; Laing & Moules, 2014), and many others. While we will discuss several different community-level constructs in this chapter, they all relate to the psychological sense of community.

## Benefits of a Sense of Community

A strong, positive sense of community has been associated with multiple individual-, organizational-, and community-level benefits. Research has demonstrated repeatedly that a positive psychological sense of community is correlated with a number of positive outcomes for individuals. A positive sense of community has been shown to correlate with adolescent identity

Feeling a sense of belonging to a community and being a valued member who shares an emotional connection with other members can greatly benefit both individuals and the group.

formation, individual well-being, life satisfaction, and recovery from substance abuse (e.g., Farrell et al., 2004; Jason et al., 2016; Pretty, 2002; Zhang & Zhang, 2017). Neighboring is also correlated with a positive sense of community (e.g., D. D. Perkins & Long, 2002; Prezza et al., 2001), which we discuss later in the chapter.

Sense of community has also been linked with positive outcomes for communities, such as participation in community coalitions, neighborhood groups, and religious institutions and the development of immigrant communities (e.g., Buckingham et al., 2018; Nowell & Boyd, 2014; Perisho Eccleston & Perkins, 2019; D. D. Perkins & Long, 2002). Finally, some correlates of a positive sense of community have national implications, such as voter participation (Xu et al., 2010).

*Levels of Sense of Community.* Is sense of community simply in the eye of the beholder, the individual perception of the wider community? Or is it a characteristic of a community as a whole? Most studies have measured sense of community with questionnaires for individuals, analyzed at the individual level. However, those measurements from people can be aggregated to indicate an overall sense of community at the community level. Those measures at the community level can have separate and sometimes different outcomes

**membership**
one aspect of sense of community, it is the feeling of being an integral member of one's community. Membership is defined by five attributes: boundaries, common symbols, emotional safety, personal investment, and sense of belonging and identification.

**boundaries**
a set of standards for defining who is member of the community and who is excluded. These can include geographic boundaries in a locality-based community or shared characteristics or goals in a relational community.

**common symbols**
easily identifiable markers that denote membership, including visual elements, like colors and symbols, and audible elements, like slang, jargon, and anthems.

**emotional safety**
this can refer to a sense of security from crime and harm or to a deeper sense of having secure relationships within a community that are created through group acceptance and mutual processes for sharing emotions and concerns.

from those at the individual level. Please remember that analyses always require multiple samples from the ecological level of interest. In other words, if you want to know something about how sense of community has different effects at the community level, you need data from more than one community.

A recent example of this type of analysis comes from a large study of the relationship between school sense of community, teacher support, and students' perception of school safety. At the level of individuals, students who reported lower levels of school sense of community and teacher support reported feeling less safe at school. At the school level, lower average levels of school sense of community were associated with lower average levels of school safety; however, this relationship no longer held true for teacher support. Notably, the relationship between school sense of community and feeling unsafe at school was higher at the school level than at the individual level. In the words of the researchers, "According to our results, for each one-unit increase in school-level sense of community, students were five times less likely to feel unsafe within the school context" (Lenzi et al., 2017, p. 534).

## Four Elements of Sense of Community

It is one thing to give a name to a construct like sense of community, but a name alone does little to give us a theoretical understanding of sense of community, or about the elements and processes that result in that construct. McMillan and Chavis (1986) provided the first theory of sense of community by studying how people understood their own experiences of community. They identified four elements that formed the basis for a sense of community: membership, influence, integration and fulfillment of needs, and shared emotional connection. These elements help translate the overarching theme of a sense of community, which characterizes Sarason's thinking, into a coherent theory, measurable constructs for research, and specific objectives for action. In their formulation, all four elements must be present to define a sense of community. No one element acts in isolation; all strengthen each other. Our description of these elements is based primarily on McMillan and Chavis (1986) and McMillan (1996). The elements are summarized in Exhibit 6.1.

Think of a community to which you belong as you read about these four elements.

*Membership.* **Membership** is the sense among community members of personal investment in the community and of belonging to it (McMillan & Chavis, 1986, p. 9). It has five attributes. The first attribute, **boundaries**, refers to the necessity of defining what includes members and excludes nonmembers. For a locality, this involves geographic boundaries; for a relational community, it may involve personal similarities or shared goals. Boundaries may be clearly or obscurely marked, and they may be rigid or permeable. They are

---

**Exhibit 6.1** Four Elements of Sense of Community

1. Membership
   - Boundaries
   - Common symbols
   - Emotional safety
   - Personal investment
   - Sense of belonging and identification
2. Influence
3. Integration and Fulfillment of Needs
   - Shared values
   - Exchange of resources
4. Shared Emotional Connection

*Note.* Based on McMillan and Chavis (1986) and McMillan (1996).

---

**personal investment**
the level of long-term commitment, effort, and participation one has in a community. Examples include buying a home, joining a club or organization, or volunteering within the community.

**sense of belonging and identification**
feeling accepted by other community members and having one's membership in their community being part of their personal identity.

necessary for the community to define itself. Ingroup–outgroup distinctions are pervasive across cultures (Brewer, 1997).

Boundaries are partly defined through **common symbols**, identifying members or territory. Examples include the use of Greek letters among campus sororities, colors and symbols among youth gangs and sports teams, religious imagery, university decals on automobiles, characteristic slang expressions and jargon, and national flags and anthems (A. Fisher & Sonn, 2002).

In a community with clear boundaries, members may experience an increased sense of **emotional safety**. This can mean a sense of safety from crime in a neighborhood. More deeply, it can mean secure relationships for sharing feelings and concerns. Emotional safety in that sense requires mutual processes of self-disclosure and group acceptance (McMillan, 1996).

A member who feels safe is likely to make a **personal investment** in the community. McMillan (1996) referred to this as "paying dues," although it is often not monetary. Investment indicates long-term commitment to a community, such as home ownership in a neighborhood, membership in a religious congregation, or devotion of time to a nonprofit community organization. It can also involve taking emotional risks for the group.

These acts deepen a member's **sense of belonging and identification** with the community. The individual is accepted by other community members and defines personal identity partly in terms of membership in the community. Individuals may identify with being a resident of a neighborhood, adherent of a religion, member of a profession or trade, student in a university, or member of an ethnic group.

**influence**
an aspect of sense of community that refers to the amount of persuasion a specific individual or group dynamic can have on members of the community. It is a reciprocal relationship in which the individual can influence the community and the community in turn influences the individual.

**integration**
refers to how much relationships within a community contribute to an overall sense of community. It is defined by two elements: shared values and exchange of resources.

**shared values**
goals and ideals that are agreed upon by members and contribute to community involvement.

**exchange of resources**
also referred to as fulfillment of needs, refers to meeting community members' needs and sharing the means to achieve those ends.

**shared emotional connection**
an aspect of sense of community, it is a common bond that unites community members that isn't easily defined but is understood by those who share it. This spiritual bond can be expressed through behavior, speech, or other elements and is developed through shared narrative of the community.

*Influence.* The second element in a sense of community, **influence**, refers both to the power that members exercise over the group and to the reciprocal power that group dynamics exert on members. McMillan and Chavis (1986) based their discussion of influence in part on the group cohesiveness literature in social psychology. Members are more attracted to a group in which they feel influential. The most influential members in the group are often those to whom the needs and values of others matter most. Those who seek to dominate or exercise power too strongly often are isolated. The more cohesive the group, the greater is its pressure for conformity. However, this is rooted in the shared commitments of each individual to the group, not simply imposed on the individual. (It does, however, indicate a disadvantage of a strong positive sense of community that we will discuss later.) Thus, the individual influences the wider group or community, and that community influences the views and actions of the person.

*Integration and Fulfillment of Needs.* **Integration** refers to the extent to which relationships within a community contribute to a sense of community. Integration has two aspects: shared values and exchange of resources. **Shared values** are ideals that can be pursued through community involvement. For instance, improving educational quality may be the shared value of a parent-school group, and ministering to those in need may be a shared value of a religious congregation.

The second aspect, **exchange of resources** (also called fulfillment of needs), refers to satisfying needs and exchanging resources among community members. McMillan (1996) referred to this as a "community economy." Individuals participate in communities in part because their individual needs are met there. Needs may be physical (e.g., for safety) or psychosocial (e.g., for emotional support, socializing, or exercising leadership). Integration is similar to *interdependence* and *cycling of resources* in Kelly's ecological perspective (see Chapter 5).

*Shared Emotional Connection.* Considered the "definitive element for true community" by McMillan and Chavis (1986, p. 14), a **shared emotional connection** involves a "spiritual bond": not necessarily religious-transcendent, and not easily defined, yet recognizable to those who share it. Members of a community may recognize a shared bond through behavior, speech, or other cues. The bond itself is deeper, however, not merely a matter of behavior. Shared emotional connection is strengthened through important community experiences, such as celebrations, shared rituals, honoring members, and shared stories (Berkowitz, 1996; McMillan, 1996; Rappaport, 2000). It is a shared narrative of the community and describes what it means to be a member.

## Questions and Issues for Defining and Measuring Sense of Community

Psychological sense of community has proven to be a valid and important construct in community research. Sense of community has been defined and used in a diversity of ways, raising a number of questions and issues. These illustrate the strengths and limitations of the concept.

***Theories and Measurement of Sense of Community.*** Does the McMillan–Chavis theory provide the best model for understanding the basic elements of sense of community? While empirical research has established the validity and importance of the overall sense of community construct, research supporting the McMillan–Chavis theory, and particularly the four elements, is limited. The most widely used tool for measuring sense of community as specified by McMillan–Chavis is the sense of community index (SCI; D. D. Perkins et al., 1990).

Research designed to validate the SCI, and the model it represents, has been mixed at best, particularly concerning the independence and validity of the four elements (Chipuer & Pretty, 1999; Flaherty et al., 2014; Long & Perkins, 2003; Loomis & Wright, 2018; Obst & White, 2004; N. A. Peterson et al., 2008). While the specific findings from those studies are mixed—some found support for three of the elements, some for a unified, single construct—the body of research expressing lack of support both for the SCI and, consequently, for the model upon which it is based has called for new approaches to the conceptual understanding and measurement of psychological sense of community (Flaherty et al., 2014; Jason, Stevens, & Ram, 2015; Lin & Israel, 2012; Proescholdbell et al., 2006).

Just as communities are contextual, so is sense of community, which varies among different cultures and communities (Bess et al., 2002; Hill, 1996). In this ecological view, the McMillan–Chavis model (or any other single framework) might describe the basic elements in some communities, but other communities would require different conceptualizations. Indeed, that is one way to interpret some of the findings just discussed. For instance, research has found support for a measure of sense of community specifically in LGBT communities (Lin & Israel, 2012; Proescholdbell et al., 2006). New conceptual frameworks may be especially needed in cultures markedly different from Western ones, for instance among Australian Aboriginal groups (Bishop et al., 2002; Dudgeon et al., 2002).

Sense of community is a rich concept. At this point in its development, it is probably best studied in a variety of ways: with the McMillan–Chavis model and other frameworks, at individual and community levels, and with qualitative and quantitative methods, while remaining sensitive to contextual differences.

**neighboring**
personal interactions among neighbors, who are often acquainted but not close friends, that includes informal contacts and assistance. It can refer to a sense of comfort, trust, and shared mutual interests and needs that overlap with sense of community but is distinct.

**social support**
is help provided by others to promote coping with stress.

# Concepts Related to Sense of Community

Sense of community is conceptualized as the affective component of our relationship with our communities. But that affective component is related to, and perhaps built upon, specific behaviors and connections. Some of these concepts include neighboring, place attachment, citizen participation, and social support.

*Neighboring.* D. D. Perkins and Long (2002) defined **neighboring** as informal contacts and assistance among neighbors. In their view, it involves specific behaviors, while sense of community is strongly emotional and cognitive. It also refers to personal interaction among neighbors, not to participation in neighborhood associations. For instance, in a study of neighboring, D. Unger and Wandersman (1983) asked residents of city blocks the following questions.

How many of the people on this block would you

- know by name?

- feel comfortable asking to borrow some food or a tool?

- feel comfortable asking to watch your house while you're away?

- feel comfortable asking for a ride when your car is not working?

Neighboring often occurs between persons who are not close friends but acquainted sufficiently to pass on information and news, recognize mutual interests as neighbors, and provide limited assistance. These contribute to integration and fulfillment of needs. Yet they can occur to some extent even in neighborhoods with little sense of community, and between neighbors who feel little connection to the wider community. Neighboring thus overlaps with sense of community, particularly as it relates to the element of integration and fulfillment of needs, but can be understood as distinct from it (Prezza et al., 2001).

*Citizen Participation.* As we discuss in Chapter 1, citizen participation is having a voice and influence in community decision making, and it is a core value of community psychology. It involves activities such as voting, running for office, signing petitions, attending demonstrations, or contacting public officials to express your opinion, as well as many others. A recent meta-analysis of 34 published studies found a moderate, consistent relationship between sense of community and citizen participation (Talò et al., 2014). These studies were correlational, so no conclusions can be drawn regarding a causal relationship between the two constructs. The researchers also emphasized the context-dependent nature of both constructs, with variations by age, nationality, and other features of the communities involved (Talò et al., 2014). We discuss citizen participation in more detail in Chapters 8 and 13.

*Social Support.* **Social support** is help provided by others to promote coping with stress. Social support and sense of community overlap, but they also

**sense of community responsibility**
"a feeling of personal responsibility for the individual and collective well-being of a community of people not directly rooted in an expectation of personal gain."

differ. Certainly, a group with a strong sense of community will provide social support; this is one aspect of integration and fulfillment of needs. However, the community in which one feels a sense of belongingness may be much larger and less intimate than the immediate network of persons who provide support for coping with a specific stressor. Also, sense of community is not solely a resource for coping but also related to other important processes, including citizen participation. In Chapter 8, we discuss social support in detail.

*Mediating Structures.* Some groups and organizations connect individuals or smaller groups with a larger organization, locality, or society. Joining these groups provides a sense of community for the individual and a practical way to participate in the larger community or society. These intermediate communities link different ecological levels and are called mediating structures (Berger & Neuhaus, 1977). For instance, parent-teacher associations, civic clubs, political advocacy groups, and neighborhood associations all offer ways to become involved in wider communities and can give collective voice to their members' views about community issues. They mediate between individuals and the wider community. In a university, student clubs, residence hall organizations, and student government are mediating structures. Our understanding of mediating structures reinforces the importance of viewing communities through an ecological lens.

*Sense of Community Responsibility.* While much of the research on psychological sense of community views it as a resource for enhancing personal and community wellness, the past decade has seen the emergence of a separate but related construct—a **sense of community responsibility** (Nowell & Boyd, 2010, 2014). Nowell and Boyd (2014) defined sense of community responsibility as "a feeling of personal responsibility for the individual and collective well-being of a community of people not directly rooted in an expectation of personal gain" (p. 231). It is the sense that you have a responsibility to your community, that you should act in ways that promote the welfare of the community.

Researchers have found evidence that sense of community responsibility is related to but distinct from sense of community among members of community collaborations. In their 2014 study, Nowell and Boyd found that sense of community was related to general participation in the collaborative, but sense of community responsibility was related to the amount of time, effort and resources members were willing to devote to the collaborative and whether or not they were viewed as leaders. Research since then has supported these general findings, as well as a scale measuring the construct (Boyd & Nowell, 2017; Boyd et al., 2018; Nowell et al., 2016; Treitler et al., 2018). Research on sense of community responsibility is a promising avenue for increasing our understanding of the ecological relationship between sense of community and community wellness.

# The Complex Realities of Communities

It should be clear by now that the role communities play in our lives is a complex one. We all belong to multiple communities, which exist at different ecological levels and are often nested within each other. These communities are continually changing, as are we, and all of those changes trigger adaptive responses in those communities and in ourselves. It may be tempting to view the concept of community, and in particular sense of community, in a simplistic, romanticized way, but in reality, communities overlap, are sometimes in conflict, and may actually have negative effects for their members and societies. We do not have complete control over the communities we belong to, and in some cases we may be counted as members of communities that may endorse values in conflict with aspects of our identities and beliefs. Viewing communities through an ecological-transactional model emphasizes the fact that communities are continually changing, as are we, and a community that may have been full of positive meaning for us at one point in our lives may evolve into a much more conflicted place. In this section we discuss some of those complex realities.

Strong communities do not come without their costs. If you think back to McMillan and Chavis's four elements of sense of community (see Exhibit 6.1), these costs become obvious. A sense of community involves a personal investment, which almost always involves some kind of obligation. Your communities expect things from you, and those community obligations often "cost" you personal resources, such as your time. Membership in a community means that you are acknowledging that a community can influence your behavior, your beliefs, and even your personal identity. While social scientists may have emphasized the positive aspects of community, these costs have not been ignored. It is understood that communities can sometimes painfully restrict individual development and freedoms. Communities are complex places, and even communities with multiple strengths can present dangers.

Psychological sense of community is negative when a person has strong negative feelings about the wider community (Brodsky et al., 2002). Thus, the person may resist community involvement, concluding that it will be harmful.

The views expressed by the mothers in the Brodsky (1996) study regarding their neighborhood were decidedly negative in general. They drew a strong boundary between family and neighborhood: "And when you come into my house it's totally different. . . . It's my world . . . when you close that door, leave that world out there" (Brodsky, 1996, p. 351).

Physical and emotional safety, a key characteristic of sense of community in the McMillan–Chavis model, seldom existed in their neighborhood. These mothers also shared few values with many others in the neighborhood. The

**Box 6.1    Changing Perspectives: Negative Sense of Community**

The following quote is from a study conducted by Anne Brodsky (1996) with 10 resilient single mothers, all of whom were living and raising daughters in an urban U.S. neighborhood with high rates of crime and violence. These women were nominated as especially resilient, effective mothers by two sources in their daughters' elementary schools. All were parenting at least one child and working full time or part time. Some were also pursuing education or taking care of other family members.

> *I don't go out here. I don't start things with people. I don't bother people. I go home, I close my door, I lock my door, I stay in my house. Don't bother me and I won't bother you. Don't bother my kids, I won't bother you. (Brodsky, 1996, p. 357)*

### What Do You Think?

1. What is this woman talking about? Does it have anything to do with sense of community?

2. So far, we have discussed sense of community in positive terms. But does individual perception of sense of community vary only from neutral to highly positive, or can it be negative? What are some examples of how sense of community can be negative?

neighborhood did have some positive resources for parents, and these women were involved in some of them (e.g., resident council, school), especially where involvement directly benefited their children. Yet this involvement did not alter their views of the neighborhood at large. Their strength as persons and mothers involved resistance to neighborhood forces, not sense of community (Brodsky, 1996).

A study conducted in geographic communities in Italy helped validate the concept of a negative sense of community (Mannarini et al., 2014). The researchers developed a measure of negative sense of community based upon Brodsky's research and the McMillan–Chavis model of sense of community. While well-being, life satisfaction, and community participation were all positively associated with sense of community in the study, the opposite relationship was true for negative sense of community. The purpose of the study was to test a model and measure of negative sense of community—it was not an attempt to determine whether a negative sense of community played an adaptive role in the lives of the respondents. Hopefully future research will address that question.

Research on negative sense of community suggests that sense of community is not a unipolar construct—is not just present or absent. Rather, it should be viewed as a bipolar construct, ranging from positive through neutral to negative (Brodsky et al., 2002; Mannarini et al., 2014). In addition, it is important to remember that individuals are members of multiple communities at any point in time, and the quality of their sense of community may be positive for some, neutral for others, and negative for the rest.

The potential adaptive value of a negative psychological sense of community may lie in its role as a motivating force to seek new communities. Consider, for example, a community with limited acceptance of diversity, where conformity pressures are strong. Persons who are not accepted there may strengthen their well-being by distancing themselves from the community and seeking settings where they are accepted. In some cases, they may actively work to construct those spaces.

## Counterspaces

In Chapter 5, we introduced you to the concept of counterspaces, spaces that promote well-being for people who are experiencing oppression or marginalization in the other settings in their lives. These spaces can take the form of social networks, or they can expand beyond that level and take the form of a community, as that term is used in this chapter. As described in Chapter 5, there are at least three processes thorough which counterspaces promote psychological wellness: fostering positive group and individual identities through narrative identity, providing support and a safe place to engage in acts of resistance, and encouraging direct relational transactions that build social support (Case & Hunter, 2012, 2014).

Those processes may not all need to be active in order for a counterspace to support well-being. For example, in an exploration of the relationship between transgender identity, transgender community belongingness, and well-being, it was found that, while identifying strongly as transgender was positivity related to well-being, that relationship only existed when there was a strong sense of belonging to a transgender community (Barr et al., 2016). This finding suggests that belonging to a transgender counterspace community was key to developing a strong, positive identity as transgender.

Counterspaces are often deliberately constructed spaces—they are specifically created to provide support and community for defined groups who historically lacked such settings. Some counterspaces may have been forced areas of geographic isolation but were transformed by the residents into vibrant communities showcasing the intellectually and artistically rich lives of their members. An example is Harlem, New York, which fostered the Harlem Renaissance in the 1920s and continues to claim the title of "Capital of Black America" today. Other counterspaces served communities so isolated from the majority culture that their very existence was illegal.

Counterspaces play an important role in people's lives, but they are never the only community of importance in an individual's life. Humans always have multiple community settings and multiple identities. These facts are reflected in the idea of intersectionality, which is explored further in Chapter 7.

## Box 6.2   Changing Perspectives: Christopher Street and the Stonewall Inn

Note that the language in this example reflects the gender and sexual orientation identifiers used by those involved at the time and may not reflect currently accepted terminology.

In the early morning of June 28, 1969, police raided the Stonewall Inn, a bar on Christopher Street in the West Village area of Manhattan. This was nothing unusual. Christopher Street was home to a vibrant LGBTQ community that stood out as being welcoming to people who were marginalized even within those groups: homeless youth and street hustlers, gender benders including drag queens, and gays and lesbians of color. For those people, Christopher Street was a very special place.

Antisodomy laws were still on the books in every state except Illinois, even though they were only enforced against gays and lesbians. Many cities, including New York, also had legislation that outlawed cross-dressing. But perhaps the most frequently enforced laws were ones that allowed for the denial or revocation of liquor licenses to businesses that allowed "disorderly conduct." Across the United States, these laws were used to deny liquor licenses to establishments that served sexual minorities. In New York, the Mafia saw this as an opportunity and began opening bars such as the Stonewall Inn that served LGBTQ communities. The Mafia paid the police to ignore the lack of a liquor license and, reportedly, blackmailed the clients of the bars. Police raids occurred regularly just to ensure that the clients knew how vulnerable they were (D. Clark, 2004).

But this raid was different. At first it seemed like any other raid, including one that had occurred at the Stonewall just a few days before. Most of the patrons where lined up at the door, checked for ID, and released. But anyone suspected of cross-dressing was arrested. Normally, those who had been released would have just left, but on this night they stayed in the street outside the Stonewall, waiting for friends who they knew were still inside. The crowd knew that these people were being subjected to physical "searches" supposedly designed to identify their "biological gender" as a basis for arresting them. As the drag queens came out under arrest, they called out and waved to the crowd, who responded with humor.

That humor disappeared quickly. Accounts differ but generally agree that a butch lesbian who had been among those detained inside the Stonewall resisted arrest, escaping from the police several times before being violently thrown into a police wagon (D. Clark, 2004). She yelled at the crowd, "Why don't you guys do something!" The crowd started advancing on the police, and a group of the street youth started throwing pennies. Nickels followed, then quarters, then bricks and cobblestones. An officer was hit in the eye, and the police retreated into the Stonewall and began barricading the doors and windows as they waited for reinforcements (D. Clark, 2004).

It was called a riot, and it continued on and off for 6 days. But many disagreed with that description. As Stormé DeLarverie declared, "It was a rebellion, it was an uprising, it was a civil rights disobedience—it wasn't no damn riot" (itlmedia, 2009, 3:43). By the second night, a crowd had gathered and chants of "Gay power" and "Equality for homosexuals" were soon replaced by more specific demands of "Christopher Street belongs to the queens!" and "Liberate Christopher Street!" (D. Clark, 2004, p. 183).

The Stonewall never fully reopened, even after the rebellion ended. "We'll have to find another place, that's all there is to it," sighed one participant (Lisker, 1969/2016). But while the Stonewall itself never again served as a gathering place for the LGBTQ community, its importance in the struggle for equality cannot be overstated. The Stonewall Inn and Christopher Street Park were designated as the Stonewall National Monument in 2016. It was the first National Monument designated as an LGBT historic site, and perhaps the only nationally recognized counterspace in the United States.

## What Do You Think?

1. Look back at the beginning of this section and review the three processes that are theorized to promote psychological wellness in counterspaces. Do you see any of those processes reflected in Christopher Street?

2. After reading this example, can you think of any places you have been that were serving as counterspaces for a group of people?

3. In the next chapter, we discuss the concept of empowerment, an important value in community psychology. What role do you think empowerment played in the history of Christopher Street and the Stonewall Inn?

Christopher Street and the Stonewall Inn illustrate how counterspaces can help a marginalized community develop a greater sense of community in the face of oppression.

## Multiple Communities in a Person's Life

Individuals belong to many communities. We form multiple identities as members of multiple communities, such as student, employee, family member, and neighbor. Sometimes these multiple commitments compete for our time and energy or conflict in important ways. Our experience in one community affects our experiences in the others, a concept known as *intersectionality*.

Intersectionality is the understanding that everyone has multiple identities and that those identities are never isolated from one another. They intersect, and the result of those intersections is that, for example, the experience of being female is quite different for a person who is heterosexual compared to one who is bisexual. We explore the concept of intersectionality further in the next chapter.

A student may experience a sense of belonging both to the college in which they are enrolled and to their hometown or neighborhood, with friends in both, yet neither of these communities may appreciate the student's loyalty to the other. Individual adult life is often filled with multiple identities in multiple communities and balancing commitments among them. On the other hand, some communities in our lives revitalize us, providing resources and energy for involvement in other communities. Spiritual and mutual help communities can have this effect, but so can an exercise class or musical group. The key to understanding multiple community membership is the role of each community in a person's life. Individuals choose how committed they are to the various communities in their lives (Hunter & Riger, 1986). Community psychology is only beginning to study how these multiple communities interact (Brodsky et al., 2002).

Our membership in communities changes continually over our lives, as does the relative importance of the communities to which we belong. As we grow older, we may see ourselves making more conscious choices about our community connections. For example, we may actively decide to distance ourselves from a community that has been important to us but no longer feels supportive. There may even be times during our lives when we do not feel a need for a sense of community and do not feel particularly engaged with any community, instead focusing on family relationships. These changes in community relationships, and in our need for sense of community, are another area that has not received significant attention in the research to date.

## Conflict and Change Within a Community

*The psychological sense of community has a virtuous sound, stimulating as it does visions of togetherness and cooperation uncluttered by conflict, controversy, and divisiveness. Such visions are hard to resist, but they must be resisted because they are illusory. (Sarason, 1974, p. 11)*

Because members of a community also participate in other communities and have multiple identities, relationships between communities can be complex and interacting. Often, these interacting communities reflect the diversity of the people involved. So you may identify yourself as a member of your college community and also as a member of the community of gay students or biology majors (or both) at your college. This identification as gay or a biologist probably extends beyond your college to include communities in your town

**myth of "we"**
ignoring the differences in a community and focusing solely on what is similar between individuals, idealizing a sense of community while ignoring diversity.

or state, or even national communities. This diversity can be a strength for a community, but only if it is recognized and valued (Trickett, 1996).

An emphasis on the similarities without attending to the differences in a community is what Wiesenfeld (1996) termed the **myth of "we"** in a community. Romanticizing sense of community without recognizing diversity within a community supports the myth of "we."

An example of the myth of "we" occurred among residents of four southeastern U.S. cities in response to Hurricane Hugo (Kaniasty & Norris, 1995). After the hurricane, these communities seemed to unite to help each other. Overall, citizens who had suffered greater loss and personal harm received greater amounts of social support from others. A sense of "we" did exist within these communities. However, some groups received less support, especially if they had suffered greater harm: African Americans, persons with less education, and unmarried persons. In action, the sense of "we" did not include the entire community. Similar patterns have occurred following other disasters in the United States (Kaniasty & Norris, 1995).

Relationships among diverse communities can create conflict. Yet that is where constructive community change often begins (Wiesenfeld, 1996). For instance, the societal transformations of the civil rights movement and the women's movement in the United States began with some communities, especially African Americans and women, attempting to change their local communities and the nation as a whole.

Without attention to these complex interrelationships among communities, and to the conflict and change that can result, sense of community can become a static concept, supporting an unjust status quo instead of showing the way to constructive social change (see A. Fisher & Sonn, 2002). Ignoring conflict, stifling dissent, or excluding specific groups eventually undermines a community, while constructive resolution of conflict can strengthen it.

"A community has changed, is changing, and will change again" (Sarason, 1974, p. 131). Change is inevitable for communities. Sense of community ultimately is a process. The Michigan Womyn's Music Festival, discussed in Chapter 5, is an example of this (McConnell, Odahl-Ruan, et al., 2016). Michfest was founded in 1976 with a policy of being a space for "womyn-born womyn." This policy was first questioned in 1991, when a transgender attendee was asked to leave the festival. The ongoing controversy about the policy was at least partly responsible for the decision to discontinue the festival in 2015.

This should in no way be seen as a failure of Michfest as a counterspace. As shown in the quote in Chapter 5, it served as an incredibly important and affirming community for women for decades. But Michfest existed within the larger context of feminism and specifically lesbian culture in the United States. The transactional nature of that relationship both gave rise to Michfest and presented challenges, eventually resulting in its discontinuation. As one of the founders of the festival wrote in a statement, "We have known in our hearts for some years that the life cycle of the Festival was coming to a time of closure" (Vogel, 2015, para. 4). She also had this to say about the highly contested decision to exclude transgender women:

> There have been struggles; there is no doubt about that. This is part of our truth, but it is not—and never has been—our defining story. The Festival has been the crucible for nearly every critical cultural and political issue the lesbian feminist community has grappled with for four decades. Those struggles have been a beautiful part of our collective strength; they have never been a weakness. (Vogel, 2015, para. 5)

A danger of strengthening sense of community is the potential that it may increase conflict between communities, especially if they encourage prejudice or hostility toward others. Sense of community may be strong, for example, in communities that scapegoat outsiders, in privileged communities that deny problems of poverty and injustice, or in groups whose values are repugnant to many others, such as neo-Nazi or vigilante groups or youth gangs (McMillan & Chavis, 1986, p. 20; Sarason, 1974). Exclusion can be extremely painful when the person involved greatly values the community from which they are excluded.

For a practical example of these issues, imagine that you are approached for help with community development by a neighborhood organization whose members are all European Americans. You soon learn that their underlying aim is to exclude persons of color (especially African Americans and Hispanic Americans) from moving into their neighborhood. Unless those exclusionary aims are changed, strengthening sense of community within the neighborhood would have racist effects (Chavis, personal communication, October 1987). This dilemma reflects a potential conflict between core values of community psychology: sense of community in one neighborhood versus social justice and respect for human diversity (and, ultimately, individual wellness of all). An ethical response would be to decline to work with the organization unless it genuinely renounced its exclusionary aims.

## Respect for Diversity and Sense of Community

Two of the foundational values of community psychology, as discussed in Chapter 1, are respect for human diversity and sense of community. Research has suggested that in some situations these two values could be in conflict, such that high community diversity is related to a lower sense of community, while homogenous communities are more likely to have a strong sense of community (e.g., Townley et al., 2011). For example, people with serious mental illnesses tended to report a stronger sense of community when they were living in neighborhoods populated with other residents who also had serious mental illnesses compared to those living among neighbors who did not have that experience (Townley & Kloos, 2009). This tension was also demonstrated

**social capital**
social capital on a community level refers to features of social life—networks, norms and trust—that enable participants to act together more effectively to pursue shared objectives.

to some extent in two studies using agent-based modeling (Neal & Neal, 2014; Stivala et al., 2016).

This tension is predicted by our theoretical understanding of sense of community. Sarason (1974), in his original writings on sense of community, explicitly stated that sense of community is "the perception of similarity to others" (p. 157). It is also predicted by long-standing research in social networks showing that people tend to demonstrate homophily, the tendency to bond with people who are similar to them (McPherson et al., 2001).

The extent to which this tension is demonstrated in a variety of communities, and its meaning, is still a matter for debate and research (Z. Neal, 2017). But there is agreement that any interventions designed to increase sense of community in a specific setting need to be consciously examined for unintended negative effects in relation to the diversity of the setting and vice versa.

The issues that we have just discussed involve balancing sense of community with other values. Newbrough (1995) argued that traditional concepts of community do not address issues of justice and equality. He proposed a concept of the just community, whose members would seek to balance values of community, individual liberty, and equality (social justice), both within the community and in relations with the wider world. His view raises questions such as the following: How much concern does a community have for other communities and for its own diverse subcommunities and individual members? How is that concern expressed in action?

## The Importance of Community

Why are communities important? Social scientists have long argued that strong communities are essential for well-functioning societies. Durkheim (1893/1933) expressed the dominant view when he stated that it is because of our membership in communities that we adhere to social norms. This is the belief that our conscience lies in our bonds to other people. If community membership means nothing to us, then community norms and sanction have no influence over our behavior.

Earlier in this chapter, we discussed the positive effects of a sense of community at both the individual and community levels. These positive outcomes for communities and societies are often discussed in terms of a concept related to sense of community: social capital.

### Social Capital

*If the crime rate in my neighborhood is lowered by neighbors keeping an eye on one another's homes, I benefit even if I personally spend most of my time on the road and never even nod to another resident on the street. (Putnam, 2000, p. 20)*

In the preceding quote, the political scientist Robert Putnam is referring to the concept of **social capital**. This concept was first developed by the sociologist Pierre Bourdieu, who originally used it to explain class-related differences in children's educational outcomes (Bourdieu, 1972/1977). Bourdieu's point was that children of the upper class in France were not just dependent upon their education to succeed; they also had access, through their parents, to an extended array of powerful social networks. So, for example, when they were looking for a job or starting a business, there was a wide group of people, some of whom they may have never met, who could be counted on to help them. A person may have significant social capital even if they do not personally own a large amount of economic capital (i.e., monetary wealth).

James Coleman took Bourdieu's concept and extended it to include the idea that it was not just the members of the upper class who benefited from social capital (Coleman & Hoffer, 1987; Field, 2003). His research on educational attainment of children living in poverty in 1960s America found that children who attended Catholic schools had better educational outcomes than their counterparts in public schools. Coleman attributed this to school and community norms that encouraged involvement in school, and he theorized that those norms, along with the relationships that developed in those schools, were a form of social capital. This difference in educational attainment was particularly striking for those children coming from the most economically disadvantaged families. In short, he concluded that the availability of social capital was particularly important for children with very limited access to economic capital. (It should be noted that this research was done in the 1960s. Research on public versus private school outcomes in 21st-century America is much less clear-cut—Pianta & Ansari, 2018.)

Both Bourdieu and Coleman saw social capital as being fostered and developed through societal structures (class or schools), but each discussed the *benefits* of social capital primarily in terms of individuals. But this is not the reason for including the concept in this chapter. Social capital can also be understood as an explicitly community construct (Field, 2003; Putnam, 2000).

As is clear in the quote at the beginning of this section, Putnam believes that social capital varies among communities (and societies); some have a lot of social capital and some have very little. And when communities have a great deal of social capital, their members benefit. Putnam said, "By 'social capital' I mean features of social life—networks, norms and trust—that enable participants to act together more effectively to pursue shared objectives" (Putnam, 1996, p. 34).

Putnam is especially concerned with face-to-face associations that strengthen relationships and communication about community life. These may be formal, through community organizations, or informal, through friendships, neighboring, and other social contacts. Both types of association increase social capital (Putnam, 2000).

Social capital exists at multiple ecological levels, including interpersonal relationships, organizations, communities, and societies. It is generally viewed as arising through bonding and bridging relationships (D. D. Perkins et al.,

**bonding social capital**
elements like trust, reciprocity, and shared values within a social network that create group cohesion.

**bridging social capital**
building and maintaining connections between different social networks, establishing links between individuals with different values and experiences.

2002). **Bonding social capital** refers to elements such as reciprocity, trust, and shared norms within a network. This type of social capital relies upon a sense of shared identity and group cohesion, and it can result in a reluctance to address conflict or exclusion of "outsiders."

**Bridging social capital**, by contrast, refers to creating and maintaining links between networks. Bridging ties reach out to a broader set of persons than bonding, and they involve links among people whose life experiences may be very different. Bridging ties are useful especially when diverse groups face a common challenge and need to work together.

A community coalition to promote positive youth development may build bridging social capital by bringing together persons from diverse parts of the locality, such as schools, religious congregations, police, recreation groups, diverse racial or ethnic communities, and youth themselves. Bridging social capital is at work when a group uses new relationships to obtain access to key decision makers in a locality in order to make their concerns heard (M. A. Bond & Keys, 1993; D. D. Perkins et al., 2002). Bonding ties alone seldom accomplish these objectives.

Daniel Kent was working specifically to develop bonding and bridging relationships when he formed Senior Connects, a youth-run nonprofit organization that sent high school and college students into assisted living programs to help elderly residents get connected to the internet. One of his first pupils, Helen Lenke, said:

> Now we don't have to sit around waiting for the undertaker. [Daniel] and his aids were patient, respectful, kind and successful in teaching us with a simple formula of his own to write e-mails, play poker, bridge, watch the news, search for bargains on the Internet, find pictures of my family receiving honors as professors of law and medicine and so much more.

See the Community Psychology in Action feature (Box 6.3) to read more about Daniel and his organization.

Bridging social capital at the community level extends reach or breadth of contacts, access to a diversity of views and resources, and ability to support wider community collaboration. Bonding social capital increases a sense of community and community responsibility. Both are part of social capital.

Social capital can result in important benefits at multiple ecological levels, including at the level of societies and nations. There are many researchers and social commentators, such as Putnam, who believe that social capital is fundamental to the maintenance of a democracy. Pamela Paxton has done research that supports this hypothesis. She analyzed two international data sets, one including 41 countries and one including 101 countries. She concluded that there is a reciprocal relationship between social capital and democracy. Countries with higher levels of democracy generated more associations and higher levels of generalized trust over time. The reciprocal relationship is demonstrated by the finding that high numbers of associations and levels of

**Box 6.3   Community Psychology in Action: Building Social Capital With Senior Citizens Online**

Net Literacy is a student-founded nonprofit where high school and college students comprise 50% of the board of directors and are responsible for all of the actual volunteering services. Over 2,500 student volunteers have given over 200,000 hours of community service, provided internet access to over 150,000 Americans, donated 4,500 computers to schools and nonprofits each year, and have been recognized by two American presidents.

Senior Connects is one of Net Literacy's five core programs. It is an intergenerational program where student volunteers teach senior citizens computer and internet skills in senior centers, community centers, and independent living facilities. Senior Connects believes that highly motivated youths can make a difference in the communities where they reside.

Friendly high school student volunteers teach senior citizens, many of whom are technophobic and have had negative experiences trying to learn computer and internet skills. The "magic" developed by the volunteers includes developing senior-friendly training manuals that contain large font, few technical terms, and many descriptive pictures. Students spend a portion of each of the 8–12 training sessions to learn each senior citizen's broadband value proposition, or what makes it important and compelling for each senior to be able to enjoy the full richness that broadband offers. Some seniors are interested in being able to email friends and family; others pursue their hobbies online; and others appreciate access to news, healthcare information, and online entertainment. The students teach seniors on a one-to-one basis rather than a one-to-many basis and build a relationship with the senior citizens that they are helping. Some seniors "adopt" the student volunteers, and as the seniors progress through the digital divide, the students cross the intergenerational divide. More about the Senior Connects program is at www.seniorconnects.org and more about Net Literacy is at www.netliteracy.org.

**What Do You Think?**

1. How does this example illustrate the concept of bonding capital?
2. How does it illustrate bridging capital?
3. Who do you think benefits from this program? In what ways?

trust in a country supported the development of a democratic system of government (Paxton, 2002).

***Community Psychology and Social Capital.*** Community psychologists have begun to adopt the concept of social capital. For instance, D. D. Perkins and Long (2002) proposed a psychological definition of neighborhood social capital composed of four elements: sense of community, neighboring, citizen participation (covered earlier in this chapter), and sense of collective efficacy (the belief that neighbors acting together can improve community life). They analyzed data from a study of New York City neighborhoods, finding these four elements to be generally interrelated. Sense of community was significantly related to all three other factors.

A recent study using data from 4,120 urban households investigated a different conceptualization of the relationship between some of those variables. A sense of collective efficacy has been associated with positive trends, such as a decrease in violent crime, and other positive outcomes at the individual and neighborhood levels. The study found that level of citizen participation and levels of bonding social capital both predicted sense of neighborhood collective efficacy (C. Collins et al., 2014).

Social capital does have a negative side. One concern is that an emphasis on local social capital (or local sense of community) can lead to underestimating the importance of macrosystem factors. Corporate decisions, losses of federal funding for effective programs such as Head Start, and other macrosystem forces do affect community life. Strengthening local social capital is certainly important for addressing community problems. Yet in many communities, local resources cannot do it all. Broader social change is also important to address social problems and injustices.

Another concern is that social capital is not always a completely "good" thing. Putnam talked about the fact that inner-city gangs possess social capital, but the ways in which they choose to use that social capital are not beneficial to the rest of us (or necessarily to themselves; Putnam, 2000). And Bourdieu (1972/1977), in his original writings on social capital, was explicitly talking about the ways in which social capital supported the maintenance of class differences. There is a great deal of evidence supporting the idea that it is easiest to build social capital in groups that are homogenous in nature. We tend to develop associations with people, and trust them more, when they are like us. Paxton (2007) has done research demonstrating that countries with higher levels of *connected* associations (whose members tend to belong to more than one organization) have higher levels of generalized trust than countries with high levels of *isolated* associations (whose members tend to belong to only that one organization). Thus, social capital at the national level can actually be *negatively* affected by a large number of associations, if those associations are largely isolated. This is true even though those associations might display high levels of social capital within themselves. It just does not translate to the national level.

The exact relationships between all these various constructs is complex and not fully understood, but the impact of social capital, as well as sense of psychological community and sense of collective efficacy, on community and societal health is not in dispute.

# Building Communities

One of the major points of this chapter is that in recent decades we have become very conscious of the communities around us and how our actions can strengthen or weaken them. The information presented in this chapter has very clear implications regarding how we can construct strong communities. Once again, think about the four elements of sense of community proposed by McMillan and Chavis (1986). If you want to build a strong community, you should ensure that the members define the community for themselves, through the development of recognizable community boundaries. The members should develop a set of common symbols, celebrations, and narratives that describe and reflect the meaning they assign the community. The members should set norms that support a sense of personal safety and that ensure all members have a level of influence over the community.

## The Physical and Natural Environments

In addition to the elements of sense of community, the ways in which we construct our physical environment can work to support or destroy a community. There are not many studies of changes in sense of community over time, but one of them demonstrates the negative effects of building a freeway through a community (Lohmann & McMurran, 2009). Sense of community was measured before and after the construction of a freeway through a Los Angeles suburb. Residents in neighborhoods adjacent to the freeway reported a decrease in sense of community over time, compared to the rest of the city. At least part of this decrease is probably related to the fourfold increase in noise levels in their neighborhoods after the freeway was built.

Architects have long understood that how we construct buildings has a direct effect on how the residents interact and on the development of sense of community. A clear example of this can be found in the history of public housing projects in the United States. Low-income public housing in the United States started after World War II. The initial projects were designed as groups of small housing units, each group sharing a common entry point. During the 1960s, new low-income housing was dominated by high-rise apartment buildings. This turned out to have serious negative effects for those communities.

Think about this in terms of neighboring. Neighboring develops because you see the same small group of people every day. Neighboring behaviors are negatively affected by high-rise apartment buildings. When people do not interact with each other, it is impossible for a sense of community to develop. People in high-rise apartment buildings did not feel a sense of connection to the buildings they lived in, and they did not feel safe there. This led to high levels of violence and vandalism, and some of these public housing projects, such as the Robert Taylor Homes in Chicago, became synonymous with urban decay in America (Bradford, 2001). In the 1990s, public planners recognized their mistake and began to replace the high-rise buildings with low-rise apartment buildings and single-family units. But even with all their problems, some residents did develop communities in these high-rise public housing projects, and their displacement from the places that have been their homes for generations has been extremely difficult (Venkatesh, 2002).

Concerns over how neighboring patterns affect community and individual wellness go far beyond concerns with high-rise apartment buildings. Recently, community psychologists and others have advanced the "busy streets" perspective as a way of understanding how elements of the environment affect neighborhoods and neighborhood interactions (Aiyer et al., 2015). Busy streets theory is offered as an alternative perspective to the broken windows theory developed by political scientists as an explanation of the link between neighborhood disorganization and crime (J. Jacobs, 1961). The concept of the broken window was seen as a signal to residents and visitors that the neighborhood was experiencing a breakdown of social control and a resultant process of neighborhood decay, which invited criminal behavior. In contrast, busy streets theory postulates that neighborhoods that are busy—with maintained social spaces, commercial traffic, and visible, positive social interactions—foster social cohesion and social capital (Aiyer et al., 2015; J. Jacobs, 1961).

In addition to the built environment, there is a growing body of evidence that connection to the natural world is an important element of communities. Children living in urban public housing were shown to engage in twice as much play, have twice as much access to adults, and engage in more creative play when their outdoor spaces were rated as high in trees and grass versus low in trees and grass (A. Taylor et al., 1998). Research has also found lower levels of both property and violent crime in inner-city neighborhoods with relatively high levels of trees, grass, and other plants. This relationship held true even though residents were randomly assigned to the buildings and factors such as the size and occupancy rate of the buildings were controlled for. As the researchers concluded, "The greener a building's surroundings were, the fewer crimes reported" (Kuo & Sullivan, 2001, p. 343).

This research hypothesized two major mechanisms through which the presence of plants and trees improves community functioning. The first is on the personal level. There is a growing body of evidence that interaction with green spaces reduces "mental fatigue," increases self-control, and decreases aggressive behavior. People feel calmer and more relaxed when they get to spend time around trees, shrubs, and grass. This mechanism is illustrated in a recent study that demonstrated that preschool children made greater gains in their development of social skills and emotional regulation when exposed to more mature trees and less concrete surfaces at home or at school (J. T. Scott et al., 2018).

The other mechanism is at the community level. When people have access to common spaces with some level of landscaping, they are more likely to spend time in those spaces. This then leads to an increase in neighboring practices and informal surveillance of the community (Kuo et al., 1998).

This mechanism is illustrated by a recent study utilizing the busy streets theory to understand the impact of the Green & Clean program (developed by the Genesee County Land Bank Authority in Flint, Michigan). The program supports community members in maintaining vacant lots in their neighborhoods. Efforts to "green" vacant lots have shown significant neighborhood benefits for the past decade but often involve significant funds spent on professional landscapers for reclamation and maintenance. The Green & Clean program is based on the idea that those same benefits can be achieved through having community members engage in routine maintenance of vacant lots by removing trash, mowing, and weeding. The study compared violent crime counts on 216 streets with vacant lots maintained by community residents to 446 streets with lots that were not maintained. The street segments with maintained lots had almost 40% fewer violent crimes than the street segments with unmaintained lots, and that result was consistent over all 5 years of the study (Heinze et al., 2018).

These are examples of ways in which the built environment and the natural environment can affect a sense of community, particularly in geographically based communities. But what about relational communities? We now turn to two extended examples of communities and community building: online communities and spiritual communities.

## Sense of Community Online

Almost as soon as the internet was developed, social scientists and social commentators became interested in how "community" is manifested online and how involvement in online communities affects wellness. Three decades later, we have a wealth of information related to these questions. An online community may be said to exist when "people carry on public discussions long enough, with sufficient human feeling, to form webs of personal relationships in cyberspace" (Rheingold, 1993, p. xx). Some online communities are tied to an existing locality and build community ties among citizens there (e.g., Craigslist.org or a community Facebook page). Other online communities are purely relational, with membership that can be worldwide. Membership in purely relational online groups, including social networking platforms, newsgroups, gaming sites, and sites developed with the express goal of providing information and support, has demonstrated effects on social identity, social support, sense of community, and well-being (e.g., Blanchard & Markus, 2004; Blight et al., 2017; Dyson et al., 2016; Obst & Stafurik, 2010; O'Connor et al., 2015).

In online mutual help groups, individuals with a shared problem or concern (such as breast cancer or problem drinking) help each other online. This facilitates support among persons unable to attend face-to-face mutual help groups, as well as those who feel especially stigmatized, out of place, or reluctant to attend in person. Some of the largest sites on the internet (in terms of number of visitors) are support groups. Research indicates that helping in online mutual help settings resembles helping in face-to-face groups. For example, an examination of the relationship between well-being and membership in online communities in people living with a physical disability found that membership in disability-specific websites did provide social support and a sense of community for members, and online sense of support and sense of community were linked with measures of wellness, such as personal growth and positive relationships with others (Obst & Stafurik, 2010).

But there is no doubt that online communities can cause harm in addition to support. A recent review of studies investigating the relationship between online discussions and deliberate acts of self-harm found that members of these groups often report a sense of purpose, understanding, and acceptance. Members who join groups seeking support and advice can later become sources of support for others, which can result in increased feelings of competence and usefulness. A few studies found direct beneficial effects on the frequency of self-harming behavior, including using the group as a substitution for self-harm and lower expressions of distress and self-harming behavior over time (Dyson et al., 2016). However, studies also found that some groups included posts normalizing self-harm instead of offering alternative coping strategies, discussions of suicide plans, live depictions of deliberate self-harm, and deliberate provocation and encouragement of self-harm. In one study, 11% of participants stated that belonging to an online group increased their self-harming behavior (C. D. Murray & Fox, 2006).

There have been cases where research and theories from social and community psychology have been deliberately and deceptively used in online communities to incite division and even violence on a national scale. In the country of Myanmar, the military set up fake sites on the internet, and specifically on Facebook, apparently devoted to news or Burmese celebrities. In reality they were used to increase support for the military and to incite division and, ultimately, violence between the country's Buddhist and Muslim populations. Taken together, the fake accounts had 1.3 million followers. The social media campaign has been linked to the 2017 ethnic cleansing of the country's Muslim Rohingya minority, which included murders, rapes, and the forced migration of more than 700,000 people (Mozur, 2018). Facebook has since taken the sites down and said it is taking steps to stop this from happening again.

We still have a great deal to learn about the risks and benefits that result from online communities and about what can be done to support the benefits while decreasing the risks.

## What Do You Think?

1. Are you a member of any online communities, whether it be via social media, playing games, or some other method of interacting with people online? What are the risks and benefits of participating in such a community in your experience?

2. How does your sense of community within online communities compare with the sense you get from more physical communities? Is there any overlap between your online communities and your physical communities? If so, how does this affect your sense of community?

3. Can you think of any ways that your online communities or others could be improved to better reflect the values of community psychology?

# Hope, Spirituality, and Transcendence in Relation to Sense of Community

**sense of the transcendent**
a spiritual experience beyond oneself and one's immediate world.

**hope**
trusting the future will bring better circumstances and that things can and will change in a positive manner. It is essential for motivating community social change.

So far we have discussed sense of community in terms of multiple ecological levels: schools, neighborhoods, organizations, online groups, and nations, among others. But can sense of community extend beyond defined settings? Sarason (1993) noted that sense of community throughout history has often been tied to a **sense of the transcendent**, of a spiritual experience beyond oneself and one's immediate world. He described transcendence as "the need to feel that what one is, was, or has done will have a significance outside the boundaries of one's personal place and time" (Sarason, 1993, p. 188). In this section we explore sense of community as it relates to the concept of transcendence.

**Hope** is the feeling that things do not have to stay the way they are, that the future can be better than the present. We include it in this section in the belief that the experience of hope takes us beyond the limits of our current existence. Hope is an essential element of motivation. You must have some sense that a different future is possible to be motivated to work toward it. Jason and colleagues (2016) investigated the relationship between feelings of hope and sense of community in Oxford Houses, a residential program for people in recovery from substance abuse based upon values of empowerment and collaboration. They found that aspects of sense of community related to commitment, emotional connection, and meaningfulness were predictive of feelings of hope for recovery. One way of looking at those findings is to say that the feeling of being meaningfully connected

**spirituality**
the sense of connection one feels to something beyond themselves and their immediate world that is expressed through beliefs and practices.

**spiritual communities**
religious, spiritual, or faith-based institutions, organizations, or setting that can serve as mediating structures between their members and larger communities.

to something beyond yourself can instill a sense of hope. While there has only been limited research to date on the relationship between hope and sense of community, it seems reasonable to hypothesize that established links between wellness and sense of community and between citizen participation and sense of community could both be mediated by an increased sense of hope.

To date, there has been no research on sense of community that has distinguished the concepts of spirituality and sense of transcendence. **Spirituality** in this book, and to a large degree throughout the community psychology literature, is defined inclusively as beliefs, practices, and communities associated with a personally meaningful sense of transcendence, beyond oneself and one's immediate world. While this definition includes religious traditions that worship an identified deity, it can also include individuals and groups who do not identify as religious (including humanists, agnostics, and atheists) but who also acknowledge and value a sense of transcendence (J. Hill, 2000; Kloos & Moore, 2000). J. Hill (2000, pp. 145–146) defined spirituality as a sense of connection to the human and natural worlds, and awe at mysteries beyond our comprehension. Additional definitions of spirituality include "exploring what it means to be fully human" (McFague, cited in Dokecki et al., 2001, p. 498) and the "search for the sacred" (P. C. Hill & Pargament, 2003, p. 65), while Rasmussen, following theologian Paul Tillich, defined religion as concerning "ultimate meaning in universal life experiences" (T. Moore et al., 2001, p. 490). In this book, we use the inclusive term **spiritual communities** to refer to religious, spiritual, or faith-based institutions, organizations, or settings.

Spiritual communities can serve as mediating structures that help link their members to local, national, and international communities (Todd et al., 2017). They have historically played a strong role in community development and social advocacy (Maton, 2000, 2001; Perisho Eccleston & Perkins, 2019). For example, the U.S. civil rights movement involved many faith-based social change initiatives. Community development for social justice, based in faith communities, has achieved substantive community changes (Perisho Eccleston & Perkins, 2019; Putnam & Feldstein, 2003; Speer et al., 1995). Not surprisingly, many examples of faith-based advocacy arise among members of oppressed populations.

Interfaith groups that are founded specifically to promote faith-based community organizing, such as the Gamaliel Foundation and Faith in Action (formerly the Pacific Institute for Community Organizing), which are highlighted in Chapter 13, are illustrative of the fact that a commitment to social justice and social activism is not the product of any one set of religious beliefs (Todd et al., 2017). Rather, they seem to arise from the sense of transcendence and hope common to most spiritual traditions, which provides the motivation to work for a better, more just world.

# Conclusion

Concepts of community lie at the heart of community psychology yet also involve the questions, issues, and values we have discussed. This chapter is only an introduction to use of these concepts. In later chapters, we discuss in detail other forms of community, such as mutual help groups (Chapter 8), and related topics such as human diversity (Chapter 7), citizen participation in communities (Chapter 9), and community and social change (Chapter 13).

## For Review

### Discussion Questions

1. Review the four elements of a psychological sense of community (Exhibit 6.1) and think about how they may or may not apply to a community to which you belong.

2. Think of a community in which some members might not feel accepted and analyze why that might be the case.

3. Think of a time in your life when you felt distance between yourself and your community. What caused it, and how did that affect your personal well-being? How might other members of your community have been affected?

4. Social capital can be a strong source of support for individuals, communities, and nations. But it can also have a negative side if it only serves to strengthen ties within a group while isolating the members of that group from other groups and the wider community. Can you think of examples of these negative effects of social capital?

5. Compare the pros and cons of geographic communities versus relational communities using specific examples from your own life.

### Key Terms

ecological-transactional model of community, 181
locality-based communities, 182
relational communities, 182
membership, 188
boundaries, 188
common symbols, 189
emotional safety, 189
personal investment, 189

sense of belonging and identification, 189
influence, 190
integration, 190
shared values, 190
exchange of resources, 190
shared emotional connection, 190
neighboring, 192
social support, 192

sense of community responsibility, 193
myth of "we", 200
social capital, 202
bonding social capital, 204
bridging social capital, 204
sense of the transcendent, 211
hope, 211
spirituality, 212
spiritual communities, 212

### Learn More

A detailed summary of the chapter, along with other review materials, is available on the *Community Psychology, Fourth Edition* companion website at http://pubs.apa.org/books/supp/kloos4/.

Each person represents multiple dimensions of diversity, including gender and ethnicity, that intersect in complex ways. Communities are similarly diverse. Respecting this diversity is a core value of community psychology.

iStock.com/FernandoPodolski

# 7 Understanding Human Diversity in Context

## Looking Ahead ‖‖➡

**After reading this chapter you will be able to answer these questions:**

1. Why do community psychologists believe that understanding and recognizing diversity is important?

2. Why is intersectionality important to community research and practice?

3. How does culture influence individuals and communities?

4. What does it mean to have cultural humility and to be culturally competent?

5. How do community psychologists address oppression and social inequity?

## Spaces for Diversity and Inclusion

Let's return to the research project we described in the opening exercise of Chapter 4. You may recall that, in an action research project with university students, community psychologist Urmitapa Dutta (2017) brought together young people from the Garo tribe, which is the largest ethnic group in the Garo Hills region of Northeast India, and young people characterized as nontribal or non-Garo. Long-standing ethnic division and conflict exists between the two groups, yet the young people were able to become a research team that built trust in one another over time. As they engaged in dialogue and reflexive practices, they were able to see themselves in relationship with one another and as having common issues in their community. They were able to foster a space in which they moved toward (rather than away from) existing tensions with a sense of curiosity, and they became more accustomed to experiencing discomfort as part of the learning process. One student reflected on the transformation that occurred over time: "At some point, we realized we all care about our place, that is, Garo Hills, and the tribal versus nontribal distinction became less important." The students began to take on a new identity as action researchers and work toward social inclusion in their region. Another student reflected with a newfound sense of possibility: "At that moment I felt like we can really bring change to the society. At first, I thought we would have to do research only on politicians' visions. But then, I came to understand that we are also thinking of our vision, and that it is about future development."

### What Do You Think?

1. What is needed to foster a space for conversations and collaboration across differences, including different backgrounds and identities? How was this space fostered in the Garo Hills action research project specifically?

2. What would it mean for your class to be such a space? Can you think of another community you belong to in which space for diversity and inclusion could be established? How would the process of fostering space in these settings compare with that in Garo Hills?

## Fostering Brave Spaces: An Invitation to Engage In Diversity Conversations With Courage and Humility

**brave spaces**
spaces in which individuals can proactively engage with and learn from each other despite cultural tension and discomfort.

**cultural humility**
openness to continuous learning and personal growth, curiosity and genuine respect for other cultures and their traditions, a willingness to confront differences in privilege and power, and self-reflection and critique of one's personal and cultural biases.

Talking about diversity and social justice issues can be difficult. Engaging these issues with your professor and classmates may feel uncomfortable, and we hope that this chapter provides some tools for approaching these conversations with curiosity, courage, and humility. As community psychologists who appreciate the strong feelings that these conversations can produce, we aim to foster a **brave space** in which we courageously step into tension and grow more accustomed to experiencing discomfort as we learn together (Arao & Clemens, 2013). This is the type of space that Dutta (2017) fostered with Garo and non-Garo youth, as described in the opening exercise. Having a brave space to discuss diversity and inclusion is important because meaningful change and mutual understandings often emerge in the presence of tension. Dr. Martin Luther King, Jr., famously urged us not to settle for a "negative peace," which is simply the absence of tension, but to press on toward a "positive peace," which is the presence of justice.

As we work to create a brave space, our courage needs to be complemented by humility. The stance of **cultural humility** is one of continuous learning and growth as well as self-awareness and self-reflection in how we engage each other around diversity. To be clear, humility does not mean you abandon deeply held beliefs and values; instead, it represents a willingness to listen and an openness to the possibility of having your perspective challenged or

**pluralism**
the idea that no culture or group should represent the norm; that each individual, group, and culture has a place and must be understood on its own terms; but not assuming that all beliefs and behaviors are okay.

refined. It is also a recognition that even as we engage conversations about diversity with the best intentions, we all will have missteps, and it helps if we are able to be generous with ourselves and one another as we become better at relating.

In our discussions in this chapter, we are also guided by the notion of **pluralism**, which is the idea that no culture or group should represent the norm. Every person, culture, or group has a place, but none is superior. Each must be understood on its own terms. This perspective does not define differences as deficits, instead searching for cultural, community, and human strengths revealed in human diversity (Trickett, 2009). Pluralism does not mean that all ways of doing things are fine, of course, or that one should refrain from drawing any comparisons or conclusions. Instead, a pluralistic perspective requires that one understand the value and meaning of differences and that value judgments are well informed. It also means that there is likely not just one best way to do things. Ultimately, we believe that these conceptual tools—brave spaces, cultural humility, and pluralism—will help you as you engage in discussion on diversity and inclusion.

## What Is Human Diversity?

**intersectionality**
the idea that each person is composed of multiple convergent identities, including culture, race, gender, sexual orientation, socioeconomic status, religion, disability status, and others and these multiple identities can affect power, opportunity, functioning, and access.

It should not be surprising to you now that community psychologists view diversity not simply as a discussion of individual differences; instead, we consider diversity of people in different contexts and between contexts. Depending on the context, we emphasize different dimensions of diversity. A community psychology approach encourages us to view multiple dimensions of diversity in the different contexts in which we live.

Every person is involved when we discuss human diversity. We sometimes encounter among students in the United States the assumption that "diversity" means the study of people other than a White, middle-class, heterosexual norm. Yet each person has a culture, a race, a gender, a gender identity, a sexual orientation, and a place somewhere on each dimension of human diversity—a concept known as **intersectionality**, which we discuss in more detail later in this chapter. And each person interacts with others, each of whom has their own unique diversity profile. Focusing on these multiple dimensions and their intersections, it becomes clear that diversity is an important part of understanding not only differences and similarities *between* individuals and communities but also variation *within* communities. Each community has diversity, and we cannot assume that all members of a group share a similar lived experience. One goal of this chapter is to give you more tools for examining your location, and others' locations, on each dimension of human diversity.

As you may recall from Chapter 1, respect for human diversity is a core value of community psychology. Discussions of diversity are woven throughout this book, as consideration of diversity issues is integral to *all* community research and action. It is critical to effective work as a community psychologist. Yet this chapter represents an opportunity to think more deeply about *how* we take diversity into consideration as we enter into collaborations, define problems, identify strengths, design interventions, and conduct research.

In this chapter, we introduce community psychology conceptions of human diversity. First, we briefly describe some dimensions of diversity within an intersectionality framework. Second, we discuss how persons are socialized into cultural communities, using examples of activity settings to illustrate this process. Third, we examine acculturation and social identities. Fourth, we discuss concepts of oppression, liberation, and decoloniality that explicitly address power in social relationships and social inequities. Finally, we consider what cultural competence means for community psychologists.

## Intersectionality: A Tool for Understanding Human Diversity

In any given situation, many forms of human diversity may be psychologically important. A helpful tool for conceptualizing the interaction of different dimensions of diversity is intersectionality. Intersectionality is an analytic approach to understanding the "meaning and consequences of multiple categories of social memberships" (Cole, 2009, p. 170). Intersectionality theory was initially developed within critical race theory and Black feminist scholarship to highlight the complex forms of oppression Black women experience. In the quote below, Kimberlé Crenshaw, who coined the term "intersectionality," uses a traffic intersection analogy to describe why the discrimination Black women experience cannot be understood simply by an analysis of racism or sexism:

> Consider an analogy to traffic in an intersection, coming and going in all four directions. Discrimination, like traffic through an intersection, may flow in one direction, and it may flow in another. If an accident happens in an intersection, it can be caused by cars traveling from any number of directions and, sometimes, from all of them. Similarly, if a Black woman is harmed because she is in an intersection, her injury could result from sex discrimination or race discrimination. . . . But it is not always easy to reconstruct an accident: Sometimes the skid marks and the injuries simply indicate that they occurred simultaneously, frustrating efforts to determine which driver caused the harm. (Crenshaw, 1989, p. 149)

What Crenshaw argues here is that the experiences of persons who hold multiple social identities that have been marginalized must take into account the different ways oppressions manifest, such as separately and simultaneously.

The potential of an intersectional perspective does not stop with a better understanding of oppression. Intersectionality can also be used to examine

**privilege**
unearned advantages that arise from one's social identity.

**privilege**, unearned advantages one is afforded in a society because of a particular social identity. Moreover, it can reveal how the same individual can possess some identities that confer advantages and others that confer disadvantages. Similar to investigating phenomena at multiple levels of analysis, an intersectionality framework ultimately helps us understand how dimensions of diversity can affect power, opportunity, functioning, and access (Weber, 2010). Intersectionality is even useful for understanding ourselves as community psychologists engaged in practice and research. Specifically, it helps us recognize how our identities may help or hinder us as we participate in different community settings (e.g., based on our race, sexual orientation, or spirituality; Todd, 2017). Last, given community psychology's core values of strength and wellness, intersectionality can help identify dimensions of strengths, resources, and points of intervention (e.g., spirituality, cultural resources, and peer support networks). For instance, Watson and Hunter (2016) have shown that while the "strong Black woman" cognitive schema is associated with some liabilities (e.g., emotional inhibition and reluctance to seek support) for Black women, it also engenders internal strength and perseverance in the face of adversity. In sum, intersectionality helps us appreciate the totality of the person, the fact that we are *all* made up of many important social identities that have consequences for how we do and experience life.

# Key Dimensions of Human Diversity for Community Psychology

The dimensions we discuss here, which are listed in Exhibit 7.1, certainly do not cover all the forms of human diversity, but they do represent concepts frequently addressed in community psychology research and action. Our definitions are brief, designed to provide an orienting overview. Our major point is that human diversity has multiple intersecting dimensions, including dimensions not listed here.

## Exhibit 7.1 Key Dimensions of Diversity for Community Psychology

| | |
|---|---|
| Culture | Sexual Orientation |
| Race | Age |
| Ethnicity | Nationality and Immigration Status |
| Gender | Spirituality and Religion |
| Social Class | Localities |
| Ability/Disability Status | |

**enculturation**
the process of transmitting culture, including language, knowledge, rituals and other behaviors, and social roles and norms for thinking, feeling, and acting.

## Culture

What is culture, and how are cultures diverse? While anthropologists and other social scientists have not settled on a single definition of culture, certain key elements are identifiable (Lonner, 1994). These key elements typically include meanings and experiences shared by a group and transmitted across generations. It does not explain anything to say, "Astrid behaves in a certain way because she is Swedish" (Lonner, 1994, p. 234). To understand cultural influences on Astrid's actions in a certain situation, we need to specify a Swedish cultural element that shapes her choices and actions in that situation. That element must be reflected in other aspects of Swedish culture. These might include a behavioral norm taught to children, a tradition reflected in literature or in religious or political documents, a concept for which the Swedish language has a word, a folk saying, or a routine cultural practice. Culture is often expressed in what adults seek to transmit to children through family socialization practices and formal schooling. The process of transmitting culture is known as **enculturation**. Shared language; everyday routines; social roles; and norms for thinking, feeling, and acting are cultural expressions important to psychologists (Kitayama & Marcus, 1994). In multicultural societies with heterogeneous populations, boundaries between cultural groupings are often somewhat fluid. In all societies, cultures are dynamic and change over time. Also, individuals differ in the extent to which they endorse particular cultural values. Culture is an essential dimension for community psychologists to study (Gomez & Yoshikawa, 2017; O'Donnell, 2005).

Community psychologists look for the impact of culture on communities across multiple levels of analysis (M. J. Kral et al., 2011; Trickett, 2009). That is, cultural influences can be seen in the functioning of individuals and families, organizational practices, and norms of local communities and societies. A contextual, ecological understanding of cultural influences on communities seeks to understand how cultural influences structure community norms and processes for how decisions are made, how conflict is addressed, and how resources are distributed (M. A. Bond & Harrell, 2006). Fully understanding the cultural context of settings requires historical and sociopolitical data that can track patterns of change over time.

### What Do You Think?

1. How do you understand your cultural history and traditions? How have they changed over time?
2. When do you become aware of yourself as a person embedded in culturally specific practices and norms, and when do you think it is possible for your culture to be invisible to you?

## Race, Ethnicity, Gender, and Social Class

Race, ethnicity, gender, and social class have been the dimensions of diversity most often discussed in community psychology research and social action in the United States. As a reflection of the contexts in which community psychology has developed, these dimensions of diversity have been centrally involved in defining and addressing social issues. In other locations (e.g., community psychology in Asia or Africa) or in the future (e.g., community psychology in North America in the next 30 years), different dimensions of diversity may be emphasized.

*Race.* Race is "socially defined on the basis of *physical* criteria" (Van den Berghe, cited in J. M. Jones, 1997, p. 347). Race is not ethnicity, though the two are often confused. People make racial distinctions based on assumptions about observable physical qualities such as skin color or hair texture. As we discuss further in the next section, ethnicity is "socially defined on the basis of *cultural* criteria" (Van den Berghe, cited in J. M. Jones, 1997, p. 358), such as language, national origin, customs, and values, having little to do with physical appearance.

Underlying the definition of race is the assumption that there are biologically distinct groups of individuals and that this distinctiveness is associated with human behavior and capacities (e.g., intelligence; Smedley & Smedley, 2005). Race has long occupied a quasi-biological status in Western psychological thought (Zuckerman, 1990). That quasi-biological definition of race has often provided an intellectual basis for assumptions of racial superiority. Biological and psychological racist assumptions supported, for instance, the eugenics movement, Nazi theories of Aryan superiority, colonialist theories of European superiority, restrictive U.S. immigration laws, and histories of slavery and segregation in the United States and apartheid in South Africa. The damage done to human lives by thinking of race in biological terms makes it particularly important to define race carefully.

Psychologists, anthropologists, and biologists have concluded that biological race differences are not meaningful (American Anthropological Association, 1998; Betancourt & López, 1993; Helms, 1994; J. M. Jones, 2003; Smedley & Smedley, 2005). Human racial groups are biologically much more alike than different. Research from the Human Genome Project found a remarkable amount of genetic similarity among human beings: 99.9% at the DNA level. Leaders from the project concluded, "Those who wish to draw precise racial boundaries around certain groups will not be able to use science as a legitimate justification" (F. S. Collins & Mansoura, 2001, p. 222). Further, most genetic variation exists *within* socially defined racial groups, rather than *between* them. The differences that we observe such as hair texture and skin color occur gradually across geographic regions of origin. Racial differences, as in IQ scores or educational achievement, are attributed to historical, social, and class distinctions rather than biological differences. In an influential review of the literature on race, genetics, and intelligence, Sternberg and colleagues (2005) concluded that "the statement that racial differences in IQ or academic achievement are of genetic origin is, when all is said and done, a leap of imagination" (p. 57).

Yet race does have a psychological and social reality in many societies, as a socially constructed set of categories, status, power, and resources is often stratified according to race (J. M. Jones, 2003; Smedley & Smedley, 2005). Sternberg and colleagues (2005) suggested that while the link between IQ and genetics is a leap of imagination, it is one that is used to justify existing social stratification. Even as racial categories shift over time and across locations, race remains important because racism makes it so. In most contexts within the United States, Whites experience the privilege of not having to pay as much attention to race as members of other racial groups, as they tend to encounter far less racial prejudice and discrimination. On the other hand, persons of color are more frequently made aware of their race. That difference in life experiences and perspective reflects a powerful set of social dynamics. Racial distinctions in U.S. life are based on a history of slavery and segregation and the assumptions of White supremacy that were used to justify them. Today's differences in sociopolitical and economic power are maintained by persistent (often unrecognized) versions of those assumptions of superiority (Sue, 2004).

An example of the significance of race for those of different ethnic or national backgrounds is that in the United States, persons of largely African ancestry include at least three groups: those with long ancestries in the United States dating primarily back to enslavement, those of African–Caribbean or African–Latin American backgrounds, and recent immigrants from various parts of Africa. Yet all share experiences associated with racism in the United States.

No terminology is entirely satisfactory to describe the racial diversity of the United States and many other societies. Use of almost any terminology and definition of race reflects and perpetuates racial oppression in some way (see Birman, 1994; Helms, 1994; and J. M. Jones, 1997, on concepts of race, ethnicity, and similar terms). Yet community psychology, at least in the United States, cannot ignore race, despite the drawbacks of our vocabulary for discussing it (Griffith et al., 2007; Suarez-Balcazar, 1998; Trickett et al., 1994).

***Ethnicity.*** Ethnicity can be defined as a social identity, based on one's ancestry or culture of origin, as modified by the culture in which one currently resides (Helms, 1994; J. M. Jones, 1997). The term is related to the Greek *ethnos*, referring to tribe or nationality. Ethnicity is defined by language, customs, values, social ties, and other aspects of subjective culture. In psychological research, it may refer to a simple demographic category, cultural qualities shared by a group or population, or ethnic identity, the extent to which an individual incorporates ethnicity into one's sense of self (Birman, 1994). It is important to know which is meant in a given study or social context.

Some broad categories often used in U.S. research combine multiple ethnicities. "Hispanic" or "Latino/Latina/Latinx" may refer to persons of Puerto Rican, Cuban, Dominican, Mexican, Spanish, or many other ancestries. Many ethnicities and nationalities exist among Asian Americans. Native Americans represent a diversity of tribal and cultural traditions.

Ethnicity is also not simply nationality: India, for instance, is a very multiethnic nation. Recall the opening exercise in Chapter 4 that featured a participatory action research project with students in the Garo Hills region of Northeast India designed to foster social inclusion in the midst of long-standing ethnic conflict in the region. Even seemingly racially homogeneous countries such as Japan have multiple ethnic groups. In North America, ethnicity often involves an interaction of at least two cultures. Being Chinese American is not simply being Chinese but is defined by the interaction (including conflict) of Chinese and U.S. cultural contexts (Sasao & Sue, 1993).

## What Do You Think?

1. How would you describe your race and ethnicity? Do they seem like different things to you? How do they influence your life, interactions with strangers or friends, life planning, choice of college, and friendships?

2. How many meaningful relationships do you have with others of a different race or ethnicity?

*Gender.* Perceived differences between females and males provide a distinction that has been the basis of socially constructed concepts and definitions of "sexual" differences. Sex is generally assigned at birth; gender is more complex. Gender refers to our understanding of what it means to be assigned sexual categories at birth and how these categories are interpreted and reflected in attitudes, social roles, laws, and the organization of social institutions. For example, how are parenting responsibilities divided? Which jobs do people consider appropriate for whom? More broadly, gender refers to a spectrum of identities beyond male and female.

Gender is not simply a demographic category but represents important psychological and social processes including distribution of resources and power (M. A. Bond & Wasco, 2017; Gridley & Turner, 2010). The lived experience of gender includes expectations for behavior, as well as potential consequences for those who act outside these gendered expectations (Fields et al., 2010; Mankowski & Maton, 2010). During the past 50 years, many have written about or protested limitations in social opportunity that they have encountered with gender norms (e.g., jobs considered inappropriate for one gender, lower rates of pay). Increasingly, community psychologists are developing greater awareness of the gendered nature of settings that privilege one group over others (M. A. Bond & Wasco, 2017). We are also attending to the importance of gender identity and expression, including the experiences of people who identify themselves as transgender or gender nonconforming, living and presenting themselves differently from the sex assigned to them at birth (G. W. Harper & Wilson, 2017; Hoy-Ellis & Fredriksen-Goldsen, 2017). Gender identity is a person's deeply felt, inherent sense of being a girl, woman, or female; a boy, a man, or male; a blend of male or female; or an alternative gender (APA, 2015). It is a concept that emphasizes gender as a spectrum rather than a dichotomy (either-or), and it is interrelated with, but distinct from, sexual orientation. Within a community psychology framework, gender and gender identity are important aspects of one's identity and have an impact on how social problems are defined and addressed.

## What Do You Think?

1. What is your gender and gender identity? How does it influence, for instance, your everyday behavior; your career planning; or your approach to emotions, friendships, or intimate relationships?

2. How does your gender and gender identity compare to societal and cultural norms regarding gender? How could these norms be more representative and respectful of your gender and gender identity?

*Social Class.* While social class may be defined primarily in terms of income or material assets (socioeconomic status or SES), it is usually used to state, either explicitly or implicitly, where one belongs in society. Thus, as a composite concept it also includes occupational and educational status and typically includes assumptions about a person's prospects for the future, occupational aspirations and control, and even where one lives. A multidimensional understanding of social class is important because different dimensions of social class appear to be related to different outcomes of interest (Case et al., 2018). In addition, one's perception of social status (the social class that we perceive we belong to) is an important and sometimes stronger predictor of outcomes such as health than objective assessments of social class such as income or educational attainment.

Social class is a key dimension for community psychology. While often studied only as a demographic descriptor, social class actually marks differences in power, especially economic resources and opportunities (Bullock, 2017; G. Nelson & Prilleltensky, 2010). It influences cultural identity and self-image, interpersonal relationships, socialization, well-being, living environment, educational opportunities, and many other psychological issues (APA, 2006; Bradley & Corwyn, 2002; McLoyd, 1998). Psychologists have only belatedly attended to psychological issues related to social class (Lott & Bullock, 2001; Ostrove & Cole, 2003). Increasingly, community psychologists in the United States recognize social class and growing economic disparities as a critical community context for individual health and well-being (Bullock, 2017).

## What Do You Think?

1. How do socioeconomic factors affect your life? How did they affect the nature and quality of education in your home community, your choice of college, or your experiences in college?

2. Has a need to hold a time-consuming job, or another economic stressor, interfered with your schooling?

## Dimensions of Diversity Receiving Greater Attention in Community Psychology

The dimensions of diversity discussed in this next section represent areas of growing awareness and increased focus in community psychology. These are emerging and generative areas of research and action, driven in part by an increasingly diverse set of researchers and practitioners in community psychology and related fields.

*Ability/Disability Status.* Most persons will experience a physical or mental disability at some time in their lives. However, we often overlook the discrimination and barriers to participation in community life that many persons with disabilities face. While disabilities have implications for physical or cognitive functioning, community psychologists use an ecological lens to see the disabling features of environments and the interactions between persons and their contexts (McDonald et al., 2017). Focusing on the social experience of ability and disability, community psychologists examine how a disability creates life experiences different from those of fully "able" persons (White, 2010). Some persons with disabilities describe feeling invisible or being avoided by others who feel awkward in their presence. Many face negative judgments about their capabilities based solely on assumptions about their disability, which often are not based in fact or knowledge about the individual's abilities. A tendency in society to discriminate based on ableism leads to many barriers for participation in community life as a valued and contributing member. White (2010) has defined ableism as "a non-factual negative judgment about the attributes and capabilities of an individual with a disabling condition" (p. 432). Several community psychologists focus their work on challenging ability-based stigma, limits to opportunity, and accessibility challenges for persons with physical and mental disabilities (e.g., Fawcett et al., 1994; Kloos, 2010; McDonald et al., 2007).

**What Do You Think?**

1. What is your experience of ability and disability? How do your physical and cognitive abilities affect your access to and interactions with different contexts?

2. Does your ability or disability status affect your sense of community in some contexts, whether positively or negatively?

*Sexual Orientation.* Sexual orientation is best understood as a spectrum from exclusively heterosexual to exclusively homosexual, with intermediate points. It refers to an underlying orientation, involving sexual attraction, romantic affection, and related emotions. Because there is widespread social pressure to be heterosexual, sometimes enforced with violence, outward social behavior does not necessarily correspond to an underlying orientation elsewhere along the spectrum (Gonsiorek & Weinrich, 1991; Rivers & D'Augelli, 2001). Sexual orientation is distinct from gender identity, one's sense of being psychologically male or female, and from gender role, one's adherence to social norms for masculinity and femininity (e.g., dress, appearance). Being gay, lesbian, or bisexual is a social identity important for many persons, and the importance of this dimension is increasingly recognized in community psychology (D'Augelli, 2006; G. W. Harper & Wilson, 2017; Lehavot et al., 2009; Wilson et al., 2010).

**What Do You Think?**

1. What is your sexual orientation? How does your orientation affect your everyday life, friendships, career plans, and other choices?

2. Does your sexual orientation have any impact on your sense of community in any contexts? How so?

*Age.* Children, adolescents, and younger and older adults differ in psychological and health-related concerns, developmental transitions, and community involvement (Ozer & Russo, 2017). Similarly, aging also brings changes in relationships and power dynamics for families, communities, workplaces, and society (Cheng & Heller, 2009; Gatz & Cotton, 1994). Community psychology has begun to attend to how age structures the available roles and channels for meaningful participation in communities, focusing on how children and adolescents are included as stakeholders in decision making as well as how aging adults are afforded opportunities to contribute their talents and skills in communities (Cheng et al., 2004; Liegghio et al., 2010).

## What Do You Think?

1. How have you experienced becoming an adult? How has this changed your relationships and the opportunities available to you?

2. How do you think your aging experience compares with how others experience it? How does it compare to societal and community norms about aging?

*Nationality and Immigration Status.* The migration of peoples around the globe is not a new phenomenon, but it continues to grow, with about 250 million people living in a country other than their country of birth in 2015 (International Organization for Migration, 2018). They may be *pushed* to take up residence in a new place because of war or other traumatic events, or they may be *pulled* toward new economic opportunities. Immigrants experience reception in their new host nations and communities differently depending on many factors, including immigrants' nation of origin, class, race, gender, and religion, as well as immigration laws, economics, political rhetoric, and local community norms for receiving newcomers. Regardless of context, many suffer discrimination and hardship, especially recent immigrants. In the United States, deportations of long-term residents have risen over the last few decades, and this has had many harmful effects on individuals, their families, and their communities (Langhout et al., 2018). Community psychologists are interested in working with immigrant communities to better understand immigrants' experiences, develop culturally responsive mental health approaches, and sustain interventions that support individual and community well-being (Birman & Bray, 2017).

## What Do You Think?

1. What is your nationality? What is your birthplace? What is your first language? How do these factors affect your values, career planning, family relationships, and friendships?

2. How many meaningful relationships do you have with others from a different national or linguistic background?

*Spirituality and Religion.* Spirituality and religion concern community psychology because of their importance for personal health and well-being and because of the importance of spiritual institutions and practices in communities (Kelly, 2010; Todd, 2017). As we note in Chapter 6, we use the inclusive terms "spirituality" and "spiritual" to refer to religious traditions and to other perspectives concerned with transcendence. Spirituality and religion often interrelate with culture and ethnicity. It is impossible to understand many cultures without understanding the religious institutions and spiritual practices that affected their history and identity. Religion and spirituality are not simply cultural. Many religions and spiritual traditions are multicultural, and many cultures contain multiple religious and spiritual communities. These interrelationships can be complicated. Community psychologists are increasingly examining the diversity of faith traditions in the United States and around the world. Religion can promote intolerance and injustice, but it also can serve as an empowering setting and site for community organizing and social change (Todd, 2017).

## What Do You Think?

1. Are you religious or spiritual? How does your religion or spirituality affect the way you live and relate to others?
2. How do your religious or spiritual values relate to the values of community psychology?

*Localities.* Differences among localities affect individual lives in many ways, creating differences in life experiences that compose a form of human diversity. Localities are often said to differ along a dimension of rural/suburban/urban communities. An example of how locality affects personal life or community action is that rural areas are often marked by geographic dispersion; limited access to health care and other human services; and stable, insular social networks that can make it difficult to be different or for newcomers or outsiders to establish trust (Bierman et al., 1997, Muehrer, 1997). Transportation is a challenge for almost any rural community innovation.

In contrast, diversity and change are hallmarks of urban life. Skills in understanding multiple forms of human diversity, in establishing new interpersonal relationships, and in adapting to changing circumstances are important in urban life. Relationships between the physical environment and personal life are also different. Finally, disadvantaged urban and rural areas have far fewer economic resources than many suburban and affluent urban ones. This shapes the resources available for schools, human and health services, and key community institutions and organizations.

This is not to say that all urban, rural, or other communities, or their individual members, are alike. Each locality is distinctive, and people have different levels of engagement with the places in which they live, work, and play. Further, the same locality may support some individual identities more than others. For LGBT youth, for example, the local context for "coming out"—disclosing an LGBT identity to others—is critically important. Rates of bullying and victimization associated with "outness" are higher for youth in rural areas and small towns in the United States and in the United Kingdom (Kosciw et al., 2015; Sherriff et al., 2011).

The categories that we have discussed are only general guides to a richness of local and particular communities. In Chapter 5, we look at how neighborhoods serve as an important context for individual development and quality of life, as well as citizen action. In Chapter 6, we examine localities and their relationship to sense of community. We describe individual, family, and cultural connections to particular localities in terms of place attachment, or sense of place. However conceptualized, life experiences in differing localities compose one form of human diversity.

## What Do You Think?

1. Did you grow up primarily in a rural community, a small town, or a large city? How would you describe the neighborhoods where you were raised? How did these contexts enable and constrain your development and well-being?

2. If you have lived in different types of localities, how are they different from or similar to one another?

*Taking an Intersectional Approach.* Before we move on, think a bit further about these dimensions of diversity in your own life. Consider all your responses to the self-reflection questions so far and how all these dimensions define you as a person.

## What Do You Think?

1. Which of these dimensions of human diversity are most important for understanding your experiences growing up in your family and community? Which dimensions are most important for understanding your experiences in college? Which dimensions are most important for people to understand you at work? Which dimensions do you think are most important to consider in understanding your classmates' and coworkers' perspectives?

2. How would you characterize your network of friends in terms of these dimensions? How would you characterize your sources of support, the people to whom you would turn in a crisis?

**social equity**
ensuring that each community has what it needs to thrive while recognizing that disadvantaged communities may require more resources and attention than privileged communities.

**social equality**
treating all communities equally, including the amount of resources and attention they receive.

**social inequity**
when a lack of resources leads to fewer education, health care, and work opportunities for a community, as well as community members' property rights, voting, rights, freedom of speech and assembly, and citizenship being challenged in extreme cases. Lack of opportunities need be considered relative to the availability of those opportunities.

## Social Inequities

Community psychology's value on social justice often leads to an examination of social conditions and opportunities within community settings. One goal many community psychologists work toward is **social equity**, which means ensuring each community has what it needs to thrive. This is a different goal from **social equality**, which refers to treating each community the same. The concept of equity recognizes that some communities have been so disadvantaged and disinvested that they often have unique needs and require *more* attention and resources to thrive than more privileged communities.

Social inequity within and between communities may not be thought of as diversity on an individual level of analysis, but it becomes clearer when diversity is examined at multiple levels of analysis. **Social inequities** occur when the lack of social and economic resources available to particular groups lead to reduced opportunities for education, health care, or work. In more extreme cases, a group's reduced social status can lead to group members having their property rights, voting rights, freedom of speech and assembly, and citizenship challenged. In the United States, disparities in rates of disease have received increasing attention (Lounsbury & Mitchell, 2009; Rapkin et al., 2017; Weber, 2010). These health disparities are often attributed to socioeconomic factors, but recent research has highlighted the social aspects of health disparities due to racism and historical trauma (Gone et al., 2019; Faust et al., 2015). For example, even when level of income is comparable, African Americans have higher rates of heart disease and hypertension (Braveman et al., 2010; Case et al., 2018).

The point here is that inequities exist in relationships, not in abstract principles. That is, from a community psychology viewpoint, a lack of opportunity for education, work, or housing for a particular community or group needs to be compared to the overall availability of those opportunities within a locality and between localities. Community psychologists may investigate the consequences of different social conditions for individuals' educational attainment, disparities in disease and health, and a variety of social issues. Community psychologists may also focus on addressing social inequities in their intervention work as a primary means of promoting well-being and adaptive functioning for individuals of the group identified as experiencing the inequities. Addressing social inequities can be a powerful way of linking the well-being of individuals and communities (Griffith et al., 2007; I. J. Kim & Lorian, 2006).

# Experience of Culture and Dimensions of Diversity: Socialization in Cultural Communities

Whether we like it or not, we come to resemble the people who raised us in many ways. How could it be otherwise? Our families and cultural communities are the place where we learn language, values, and skills in getting along in the world. We learn what is considered smart, beautiful, efficient, and good. We learn what types of people to trust and whom to stay away from. We learn how and when to express different emotions, how to be polite and show respect, and how to disagree. We learn how to make sense of differences in the way people and groups are valued in a society. Although we mature and develop the capacity to become our own persons with our own values and ways of being in the world, this ongoing cultural socialization process is key to understanding part of what makes us who we are as individuals in context. It also helps us understand why we feel so comfortable in some contexts and so uncomfortable in others.

In this section, we examine one key aspect of this cultural socialization process: routine participation in the activity settings of our everyday lives. Remember the concept of *activity settings* that was introduced as a conceptual model of ecological context in Chapter 5. An activity setting is not just a physical setting but also the subjective meanings that develop among setting participants through participation in the setting (O'Donnell & Tharp, 2012). Activity settings draw attention to routine cultural practices and to how the ongoing interactions we have with others in the places we live, learn, work, and play shape our development and understanding of ourselves as individuals. These routine processes shape us; they also sustain and change our cultural communities. Let us consider two examples to illustrate how shared meanings develop from participation in activity settings. In both cases, activity settings serve as nurturing contexts for individual and community well-being within larger dominant cultural frames that devalue these identities. We will come back to these examples later in the chapter as we consider oppression and liberation frameworks, as well as how to design culturally anchored community programs.

## Revitalizing Activity Settings in an Alaska Native Community

The first example comes from Alaska Native community members who partnered with community psychologists to develop interventions that prevent youth suicides. They were moved to act because they saw that young people were suffering without anchoring rituals and socialization practices of Indigenous cultural traditions. Yup'ik leaders described the suicide prevention efforts they developed as a revitalization and reimagining of vital activity settings for individual and community well-being (Ayunerak et al., 2014). In one community, they worked together to reconstitute multifamily community dwellings that had been shut down by missionaries and replaced with single-family houses that were less well suited to the cold, harsh, and rural environment. These revitalized activity settings became spaces for valued community rituals and multigenerational networks that emphasized "how each and every member of the community was needed

Revitalizing activity settings can help communities, like Alaska Native communities, draw on cultural strengths and traditions to address contemporary issues.

and each needed the other" (Ayunerak et al., 2014, p. 95). These reimagined practices were not about recreating a nostalgic vision of the past but rather about adapting strong cultural traditional routines and values to enable new possibilities for survival, growth, and well-being of children and youth in the community.

## Developing Counterspaces as Activity Settings

As you may recall from Chapters 5 and 6, counterspaces can be thought of as activity settings that enhance well-being of marginalized individuals by challenging deficit-oriented societal narratives concerning their identity. Case and Hunter (2012) describe how participation in counterspaces enables people to imagine and develop affirming personal identities and to engage in acts of resistance that affirm parts of themselves devalued in the larger society. Counterspaces also include meaningful communications between participants that provide social support and help individuals navigate oppressive contexts. They might be as small and informal as a home space on a college campus for LGBT persons or as large and formal as a national network of sororities and fraternities for African American students. They can be examined by community psychologists to better understand how marginalized individuals respond adaptively in the face of oppression as well as how to strengthen and create new activity settings that promote well-being.

# Identity Development and Acculturation

*One ever feels his two-ness,—an American, a Negro; two souls, two thoughts, two unreconciled strivings; two warring ideals in one dark body, whose dogged strength alone keeps it from being torn asunder.*

*The history of the American Negro is the history of this strife—this longing to attain self-conscious manhood, to merge his double self into a better and truer self. In this merging he wishes neither of the older selves to be lost. . . . He simply wishes to make it possible for a man to be both a Negro and an American. (Du Bois, 1903/1986, p. 365)*

In this famous passage, W. E. B. Du Bois addresses a conflict of two identities that he could not easily reconcile. His African ancestry and American experience promised mutual enrichment, yet forces of oppression prohibited their merging. Du Bois himself eventually left the United States because racism prevented an integration of these two identities.

Our focus on broad cultural socialization patterns does not fully address how individuals resolve such questions. Further elaboration is needed to focus on a person's multiple social identities and how they develop over time. These social identities are based on race, ethnicity, gender, sexual orientation, religion, and spirituality, or other social or cultural distinctions that influence one's sense of "who I am" and "who I will become." Here we examine two theories that have influenced how community psychologists think about social identities: identity development and acculturation.

## Identity Development Models

Psychologists have proposed models of social identity development for Americans of African, Asian, Latina/o/x, and White ancestry and status; U.S. ethnic minorities in general; feminists; and gay men, lesbians, and persons who are bisexual (e.g., D'Augelli, 1994; Helms, 1994; Phinney, 1990; Rickard, 1990). These models focus on how social identities develop, usually in late adolescence and early adulthood. Some assume a sequence of stages (Helms, 1994; Phinney, 2003), while others describe distinct statuses or attitudes (Sellers et al., 1997).

An examination of early models of ethnic and racial identity point to three stages of identity development among individuals who belong to a social group that has been marginalized (Phinney, 1993). An individual often begins their development with a stage of **unexamined identity**, in which the person identifies with mainstream cultural ideals, ignoring or denying their social group status (e.g., racial, ethnic, gender, or sexual orientation). That is challenged by life experiences that make one's social group status salient (this may involve experiencing or witnessing discrimination or perceiving oneself to be in a minority status).

**immersion**

the second stage of identity development in which an individual becomes more involved in activities in one's own social group, developing a sense of cultural heritage.

**transformed relations**

the third stage of identity development in which, after forming new social identity and committing to their social group, an individual interacts with the larger society in ways that reflect their new social identity.

The person begins to explore their social or cultural status and heritage, forming a new identity around these themes. This often involves a period of **immersion** in the activities of one's own social group. This stage may begin with anger about discrimination by dominant groups but tends to lead to a focus on the strengths of one's social group or cultural heritage.

The individual internalizes the newly formed social identity, strengthening commitment to the social group, before emerging into **transformed relations** with mainstream culture. For instance, for gay men and lesbians, the experiences of "coming out" to others are important developmental steps at this stage (Rosario et al., 2001).

Social identities are especially salient for members of groups that have been oppressed, as they explore the realities of oppression and seek strengths in their own heritages (Birman, 1994; Helms, 1994; Phinney, 2003; Varas-Díaz & Serrano-García, 2003). Yet members of privileged groups also develop social identities as they become aware of human diversity, social boundaries, and injustices (e.g., White identity development; Helms, 1994).

Stage models of identity development have some limitations (Frable, 1997). A person may not go through all the stages, may not go through them in order, or may repeat stages. This suggests that the stages are better understood as states, different ways of viewing the world, but not necessarily in a developmental sequence. These models also may be difficult to apply to individuals who identify as biracial or multiracial or who immigrated to the United States. For example, recent Black immigrants from the Caribbean and Africa have somewhat different notions about race and ethnicity from Blacks who have a longer history in the United States (Waters, 1999). It is also important to consider intersectionality; the reality of intertwining social identities within a single person makes it difficult for some people to think about an identity in isolation (e.g., gender, social class, spirituality; Frable, 1997; Hurtado, 1997).

Newer social identity models address many of these limitations. For example, Sellers and colleagues (1998) proposed and validated a multidimensional model of African American racial identity that focuses on four dimensions of racial identity rather than a hierarchical sequencing of stages. The four dimensions are as follows:

- **Racial salience.** This is the extent to which race is a relevant part of how a person views themselves. This is affected by context, such as being the only person of a race in a classroom or on a job.

- **Racial centrality.** This dimension is more stable across contexts and refers to the degree to which a person typically defines themselves in terms of race. It is how important one's race is to how they see themselves as a person.

- **Regard.** This refers to the views someone has about their race and their perceptions of how others view their race. This dimension accounts for the reality that individuals from marginalized racial groups may hold favorable views of their race while being aware that society might hold unfavorable views of their race.

- **Ideology.** This dimension is the combination of beliefs, opinions, and attitudes a person has about how members of their racial group ought to act. For example, some African Americans may believe that African Americans should make a conscious effort to support African American-owned businesses.

Racial identity can be psychologically advantageous, especially for members of racial minority groups. Many studies have established that higher levels of perceived racial or ethnic discrimination are associated with greater distress, depression, and impaired functioning among African Americans, Latinos, and Asians (e.g., Pascoe & Smart Richman, 2009; Sellers & Shelton, 2003; D. R. Williams & Williams-Morris, 2000). Racial identity researchers have begun to investigate how racial and ethnic identity may act as a buffer from developing psychosocial problems. For instance, in a series of longitudinal studies of African American adolescents and young adults, the centrality of racial identity (i.e., the importance a person places on their racial identity) was a protective buffer when study participants experienced racism and was associated with less alcohol use (Caldwell et. al., 2004; Sellers et al., 2003). Yet the context of these perceived experiences of racism played an important role. When African American adolescents reported more perceived discrimination experiences, they appeared to be at risk for developing more negative images of African Americans themselves and for developing expectations that non-African Americans would hold more negative views of them as African Americans (Seaton et al., 2009). Interestingly, expectations of negative views of African Americans were associated with the reporting of more discrimination experiences, acting as a risk factor for the adolescents (Sellers et al., 2006). However, recognizing racism was also a necessary step in preparing these adolescents to cope with racism (Sellers et al., 2006).

Having a well-developed positive racial identity also appeared to protect students from the psychological effects of racist experiences. African American college students with a well-formed racial identity had lower levels of depression (Yip et al., 2006), and African American adolescents reported better functioning and well-being when they had positive racial identities (Seaton et al., 2006). Future research will focus on understanding the process by which identity develops and the content of the identities that individuals hold (Scottham et al., 2010).

As noted, there are social identity models related to privileged groups. For example, models of White or European American identity in the United States and Canada describe White identity in terms of (a) the perceptions one holds of their racial group as well as of people of color, (b) an awareness of racism and privilege and the feelings of guilt some subsequently experience, and (c) various White supremacy ideologies (Spanierman & Soble, 2010; Spanierman et al., 2009). Many of these models, which are developmental or sequential, assume that a healthy White racial identity involves a person being able to recognize and address racism while possessing an identity free of notions of superiority. For instance, the White Racial Identity Attitude Scale (WRIAS; Helms & Carter, 1990), currently the most widely used assessment of White racial identity, assesses a White person's attitude as they move from being an unaware perpetrator of racism to an aware advocate for social justice. Some critics of the "healthy identity" approach have argued that models such as these are aspirational and may not reflect the attitudes, perspectives, and experiences of all White people (Cleveland, 2018).

An alternative approach to understanding White identity examines the costs of racism to White persons. Todd and colleagues (2010) investigated the emotional responses that White college students had to their perceived Whiteness. They focused on understanding students' responses to interviews and students' essays about how they experience and address racism; in particular, they focused on students' (a) potential for empathy with other racial groups, (b) guilt about White privilege, and (c) racial fear of non-Whites. Their findings suggest that having higher racial fear was associated with more negative emotional responses and distress when discussing how to address racism and White privilege. Conversely, those who had more empathy for persons of different racial backgrounds reported more positive emotions. White guilt was associated with negative emotions, but having more or less guilt was not related to reduced stress when discussing racism and White privilege (Todd et al., 2010). This area of research is only developing, but it holds promise for identifying better ways that racism and discrimination might be addressed, particularly in classrooms.

## Acculturation Models

- A student leaves her native Korea to attend graduate school in Canada.

- A young Diné (Navajo) man must choose between career advancement that would mean leaving his home reservation and weakening ties to his family and culture, or staying home in jobs that will mean less income and prestige.

- An African American student must choose whether to attend a predominantly Black college or a predominantly White one.

**acculturation**
when an individual or group changes because of contact between multiple cultures.

**assimilation**
when an individual or group identifies with their dominant or host culture and loses ties with their culture of origin.

- An Asian American and a Mexican American, college friends, talk a lot about how to balance a future career with loyalty to their families. They realize that they are experiencing differences between mainstream U.S. cultural trends and their own cultural backgrounds.

- Families from several villages leave a civil war in their home country and immigrate to the same city in the United States.

These examples pose a number of questions, three of which we take up here: To what extent do persons continue to identify or maintain relationships with their culture of origin? To what extent do they identify or maintain relationships with the host or dominant culture? How do communities change when they receive persons from other cultures?

**Acculturation** refers to changes in individuals and groups due to contact between two (or more) cultures (Birman et al., 2005; Sonn & Fisher, 2010). "Culture" here is used in a general sense that may also refer to ethnicity, nationality, or other dimensions of diversity. Although psychological acculturation research and interventions have focused primarily on the individual, community psychologists have emphasized an understanding of acculturation as a process that affects individuals and communities (e.g., Birman et al., 2014; Dinh & Bond, 2008). Contact between cultural groups usually involves change by each of them to some extent, although differences in political and economic power can complicate the interaction. Individuals are nested in communities, and an ecological perspective is required to understand acculturation (Salo & Birman, 2015). For some, more than two cultures are involved. In this section we present the more traditional, person-centered models for understanding acculturation and then show how community psychology's interest in context is expanding research and action focused on acculturation.

A terminological note: In some fields, "acculturation" has meant identification with the dominant or host culture and loss of ties to one's culture of origin. Following Berry (1994, 2003) and Birman (1994), we term that loss of one's culture of origin as **assimilation**. Also, remember our discussion of enculturation earlier in the chapter, which refers to developing within one's culture of origin, not changing through relations with another culture (Birman, 1994).

## Psychological Acculturation

In psychological theories, person-centered understandings of acculturation may be behaviorally expressed, for instance, in choices of language, clothing, food, gender roles, child-rearing strategies, or religious affiliation. It may also be internally expressed: One's personal identity, values, emotions, aspirations, and spirituality are grounded in culture. Berry (1994) proposed a model of psychological acculturation to describe experiences of immigrants adjusting

**separation**
when an individual strongly identifies with their culture of origin, develops language and other skills for participating mostly in that culture, lives primarily in communities of that culture, and interacts with the host or dominant culture in limited ways.

to a new (host) culture; it can be extended to address other subordinated, minority, or Indigenous groups. Berry's model assumes that in psychological acculturation, the individual identifies with one or the other culture, with both, or with neither. This leads to the four strategies listed in Table 7.1 and described in the rest of this section (Berry, 2003; LaFromboise et al., 1993). You should understand these four strategies as blending into each other, not as simple, sharply demarcated categories.

*Separation.* Individuals pursue the **separation** strategy if they identify with their culture of origin, develop language and other skills primarily for participating in that culture, live primarily within communities of that culture, and interact with the dominant culture only in limited ways (e.g., work or other economic exchanges). Separation has been a recurrent theme (and one adaptive strategy) in the histories of African Americans, French-speaking Canadians, Native Americans, and immigrants to many countries who live and work in their own ethnic communities. (Separation is not the same as segregation. If members of the dominant culture act in this way, while reserving political, economic, and social power for their group, "segregation" is a more appropriate term.)

*Assimilation.* On the other hand, if individuals give up identifying with their culture of origin to pursue identification with the language, values, and communities of the dominant culture, they are assimilating. Assimilation is an acculturation strategy used by some immigrants, refugees, and similar groups in a new host culture. The idea of the "melting pot" for immigrants to the United States has usually meant assimilation to the dominant Anglo American culture (D. Smith, 2012).

Some form of behavioral (but not internal) assimilation may be the only strategy available under powerful systems of oppression. In such circumstances, some members of a subordinated population may be able to "pass" as a member of the dominant group. However, passing can exact a psychic price, since it involves keeping secrets and maintaining a divided identity. Furthermore, assimilation may be impossible for individuals and groups who

**Table 7.1** Four Acculturative Strategies

| Identification with culture of origin | Identification with dominant culture | |
|---|---|---|
| | Stronger | Weaker |
| Stronger | Biculturality | Separation |
| Weaker | Assimilation | Marginality |

*Note.* Strategies blend into each other. Thus, we have labeled identification with each culture in relative terms: *stronger* and *weaker.* Data from Berry (1994).

**marginality**
when an individual does not or cannot identify with either their culture of origin or the dominant or host culture.

**bicultural integration**
when an individual identifies or participates with both their culture of origin and the dominant or host culture in meaningful ways.

differ from the dominant cultural group in obvious ways such as skin color. The first stage of many ethnic and racial identity development models involves attempts to assimilate by persons of color, who abandon it when they are rebuffed by discrimination (Phinney, 2003).

*Marginality.* **Marginality** occurs if individuals do not or cannot identify with either their culture of origin or the dominant culture. This strategy may not be chosen, but it can result from loss of contact with one's culture of origin combined with exclusion from the dominant culture. It appears to be the strategy usually associated with the greatest psychological distress (Berry & Sam, 1997; Vivero & Jenkins, 1999). Note that this involves not only being marginalized by a dominant culture (something that may happen with separation as well) but also losing contact or participation with one's culture of origin.

*Bicultural Integration.* If individuals identify or participate in meaningful ways with both their culture of origin and the dominant culture, they are using a strategy that Berry (1994) termed "integration" and that others consider "biculturality" (Birman, 1994; LaFromboise et al., 1993). We refer to it as **bicultural integration**.

There are many ways to be bicultural. Some involve strong identification with one's culture of origin and behavioral participation in the dominant culture but not deeper identification with it (Birman, 1994; Ortiz-Torres et al., 2000). This may especially fit the experiences of members of social groups faced with persistent discrimination. For others, particularly immigrant groups, a bicultural strategy may involve identification with one's culture of origin as well as a deepening identification over time with the dominant culture (Birman, 1994; Phinney, 2003).

## The Need for a Contextual Perspective in Acculturation

Two ancient stories from Jewish tradition, familiar to Muslims and Christians as well, illustrate the value of acculturation strategies other than biculturality for a small cultural group within a powerful, oppressive society. Joseph, a Jew sold into slavery in Egypt by his brothers, assimilated into Egyptian society, rose to power, and became the instrument for preserving Jewish culture in a time of famine. Years later, Moses, a Jew reared by Egyptian royalty with little knowledge of his cultural heritage, learned about that heritage and then led a separatist movement and exodus from Egypt. In different ways, both Joseph and Moses helped preserve their culture (adapted from Birman, 1994, p. 281).

What is the most adaptive psychological acculturation strategy? As with Joseph and Moses, that depends on the context (Birman et al., 2014; Trickett, 2009).

Bicultural integration is not necessarily common. For instance, in a study of adolescents whose families had immigrated from Latin America to Washington, DC, most adolescents were highly involved in Hispanic culture and social networks (separation) or in wider American culture and networks (assimilation); few were highly involved in both (Birman, 1998). Among a sample of New York City residents of Puerto Rican ancestry, only about one fourth were bicultural. About one third were involved predominantly in Puerto Rican culture (separation), one fourth were involved predominantly in U.S. culture (assimilation), and the remainder were uninvolved in either culture (marginality; Cortés et al., 1994). Many members of immigrant groups in the United States pursue bicultural strategies, particularly family members born in the United States, but not all do (Phinney, 2003).

Bicultural integration also is not necessarily adaptive: Findings on acculturation and personal adjustment, for adolescents and for adults, are mixed (Birman et al., 2002; Phinney, 2003). From an intersectional perspective, gender, social class, sexual orientation, religiosity, family dynamics, and the qualities of the setting can have an impact on the effects of particular acculturation strategies. A study of Vietnamese refugees who resettled in the United States found that acculturation unfolded differently in different settings, from home spaces with family and friends to the workplace (Salo & Birman, 2015). Both social identity development and acculturation are far more complex processes than we have portrayed in our introduction here. For community psychologists, acculturation must be understood as related to multiple ecological levels (Trickett, 2009) and must include an examination of changes in host settings as well as individuals (Dinh & Bond, 2008).

How do neighborhoods, towns, and regions change with the influx of new residents? What specific qualities of communities or community settings promote appreciation of other communities and cultures and a wider sense of unity and affirmative diversity (J. M. Jones, 1994; Kress & Elias, 2000)? R. S. Smith (2008) examined community adaptations in Utica, New York, a city that has experienced a tremendous amount of immigration and resettlement of refugees during the last 20 years. One in six residents was born outside the United States. Given some rhetoric about immigration, such a wave of immigration might have been feared as "destroying the community" and "taking away jobs." While Utica had some resources for assisting immigrants (e.g., refugee social service agencies) and a history and social norms of helping immigrants (e.g., high levels of volunteering, many citizens whose parents or grandparents were immigrants), such a large influx over a short period of time required many adaptations.

Smith (2008) described clusters of adaptation in Utica, where newcomers actually helped reclaim and improve decaying neighborhoods and where some employers were grateful for a hardworking labor force to help a city that had lost much of its population. In the areas of education and health care, local organizations and institutions appeared to make many accommodations for new residents who left Bosnia, Burma, Somalia, and the Sudan. In the areas of housing and employment, there were fewer adaptations in policies and practices to make interaction more accessible. Smith observed that there were fewer formal roles for social service personnel in housing and employment domains of public life and likely fewer resources dedicated to helping with adaptations for new residents.

Utica has experienced challenges to its accommodation of such a large wave of immigrants. Interviews conducted with community leaders in Utica indicated that there were substantial challenges with transportation; a need for translators in several languages; and different cultural expectations of immigrants for participation in health care, school, and urban life. R. S. Smith (2008) noted that there appeared to be more intergroup conflict among refugee populations than between refugee groups and U.S.-born Uticans. While Smith's study focused on one community, it helps illustrate how a community psychology framework can be applied to understanding acculturation and immigration. Community psychologists are working to develop greater knowledge to better understand community processes and how to support communities' adaptation efforts (Tseng & Yoshikawa, 2008).

## Concepts of Liberation, Oppression, and Decoloniality

*Whenever you feel like criticizing anyone, he told me, just remember that all the people in this world haven't had the advantages that you've had. (Fitzgerald, 1925/1995, p. 5)*

Consider these facts about U.S. society:

- In 2016, women who worked full time earned only 82% of the income of men who worked full time (Bureau of Labor Statistics, 2016).

- Median household income in 2017 for Whites was $65,845, for Hispanics was $49,793 (76% of the White median), and for Blacks was $40,232 (61% of the White median; Census Bureau, 2018).

- Inequality of household income is increasing steadily. From 1979 to 2015, incomes (adjusted for inflation) rose 74% for the highest-earning 20% of the population and 233% for the top 1%, while gains for the lower four fifths of the population were much lower. Because of this trend, there is now great income concentration at the top of the income scale not seen since the 1920s (Center on Budget and Policy Priorities, 2018).

- Upward economic mobility is decreasing; compared with earlier periods, fewer people are now moving from lower income groups into higher ones (Chetty et al., 2017).

**oppression**
occurs in a hierarchical relationship in which a dominant group unjustly holds power and resources, withholding them from one or more other groups.

**dominant or privileged group**
the more powerful group in an oppressive hierarchy.

**oppressed or subordinated group**
the less powerful group in an oppressive hierarchy.

- Wealth (net worth, not yearly income) is highly skewed. The wealthiest 1% of the population control 34.6% of the nation's private assets, and the next 19% own 50.5%. This means that 80% of American households own only 15% of the nation's private wealth (Wolff, 2010).

- Since 1978, American workers have seen pay increases of 11.2%, while CEOs have seen pay increases of 937%. The CEOs of the top 350 U.S. firms earned $15.6 million on average, or 271 times the earnings of a typical worker (Mishel & Schieder, 2017).

- The gap in life expectancy in the United States between the richest and poorest individuals in the United States is 14.6 years for men and 10.1 years for women. Differences in life expectancy across income groups have increased over the last 15 years (Chetty et al., 2016).

- The rate of child poverty in the United States is over 20%, twice as high as in the United Kingdom, Sweden, or France (Smeeding & Thevenot, 2016). (Growing up in sustained poverty places children at higher risk of many problems and illnesses—Bradley & Corwyn, 2002; McLoyd, 1998.) Many low-income families are resilient, but they face daunting money-related challenges.

These and similar differences among persons and families in the United States do not result from cultural factors. They are better understood in terms of power and access to resources. To understand such differences, concepts of liberation and oppression are needed (e.g., M. A. Bond et al., 2000a, 2000b; Montero et al., 2017; G. Nelson & Prilleltensky, 2010; Watts & Serrano-García, 2003).

## Oppression: Initial Definitions

**Oppression** occurs in a hierarchical relationship in which a dominant group unjustly holds power and resources and withholds them from another group (Prilleltensky, 2008; Tatum, 1997; Watts et al., 2003). The more powerful group is termed the **dominant** or **privileged group**; the less powerful is the **oppressed** or **subordinated group**. Oppressive hierarchies are often based on ascribed characteristics fixed at birth or otherwise outside personal control (e.g., sex, race).

For instance, oppressive systems in the United States create a privileged group of White persons and subordinate groups of all others, including African Americans, Latinas/os/x, Asian Americans, and Native Americans. Similarly, men, persons without physical or mental disabilities, heterosexuals, and those with economic power and resources are privileged. Oppressive systems may also create intermediate groups. South African apartheid and British colonialism in India, for instance, created classes such as "Coloured" South Africans

**internalized oppression**
a sense of inferiority developed by members of oppressed or subordinated groups based on beliefs and myths perpetuated by oppressive or privileged groups.

and "Anglo-Indians," subordinated by the dominant class but more privileged than the lowest classes (Sonn & Fisher, 2003, 2010). Class privilege operates along a continuum in many Western societies; middle classes are more privileged than those with lowest incomes, yet they are still less powerful than and often manipulated by the wealthy. In U.S. history, some immigrant groups were only gradually accepted by dominant Anglo American groups. Racial privilege in the United States today often has different effects among diverse persons of color.

Resources controlled by a dominant or privileged group may include economic resources, status and influence, sociopolitical power, interpersonal connections among elites, the power to frame discussion of conflicts (often exerted through media and educational systems), representation in political and corporate offices, and even inequalities in marriage and personal relationships. Perhaps most insidious are ideologies and myths intended to convince members of subordinated groups that they actually are inferior (Hasford, 2016). This sense of inferiority is termed **internalized oppression**.

Members of privileged groups are granted resources, opportunities, and power, not by their own efforts but by oppressive systems (McIntosh, 1998). Members of a privileged class may not recognize or consent to this, yet they are granted the privileges anyway. In the United States, for example, many

Oppressive systems exist globally. Resistance movements to oppression spread internationally as well and influence similarly marginalized groups, such as in this photo of a Black Lives Matter protest in London.

David Mbiyu/Shutterstock.com

**patriarchy**
the system of unearned male power based on long-standing historical beliefs about male superiority and gender role expectations that harms everyone regardless of gender.

White persons oppose racial discrimination, but they are privileged by systems that reliably produce these effects. Similar statements apply to individuals in other privileged groups, such as men, the wealthy, and heterosexuals.

Subordinated groups are denied access to much power and many resources, without their consent. However, they are not powerless. They may resist injustice in many ways, direct and indirect. Think, for example, about contemporary resistance movements such as Black Lives Matter. The strengths of their cultural heritage may provide resources for doing this. Subordinated groups may also develop ways of coping with oppression and protecting themselves (Case & Hunter, 2012). Persons with disabilities, for example, may remove themselves from oppressive environments. They may also create new narratives about themselves that challenge or reframe dominant cultural narratives discounting their capabilities and potential (McDonald et al., 2007). Members of the subordinated group may comply overtly with oppressors and create personal identities revealed only with other members of their group, as "Coloured" South Africans did under apartheid (Sonn & Fisher, 1998, 2003). Remember the concept of *counterspaces* discussed earlier in the chapter. These are settings that are created by persons who are members of oppressed groups to counter deficit notions and stereotypes about themselves and to enhance well-being even in the face of oppression (Case & Hunter, 2012).

Oppressive systems have long historical roots. Those systems, not individuals currently living within them, are the sources of injustice (Freire, 1970/1993; Prilleltensky & Gonick, 1994). For instance, to dismantle sexism, **patriarchy** (the system of unearned male power) is the opponent, not individual men. In fact, patriarchy harms men as well as women, for instance, through the emotional restriction and costly competitiveness of masculine role expectations (O'Neil, 2014). The harm is less for a privileged group than for subordinated groups, of course. Watts (2010) referred to this phenomenon when he wrote about the need for men "to slay Frankenstein." He suggested that oppressive or toxic masculinity is like the creature that Dr. Frankenstein created but could not control. While one may empathize with Dr. Frankenstein's struggles, one may also find him particularly well suited for confronting the harmful creature. In using this evocative metaphor, Watts points out how men are both agents and targets of oppressive masculinity. He shows how dismantling oppression may liberate privileged and oppressed people from a system that dehumanizes both (see also Freire, 1970/1993; Mankowski & Maton, 2010).

In complex societies, multiple forms of oppression exist. Steele (1997) summarized evidence that in the United States, even the best African American students are affected by racial stereotypes, and even the most mathematically talented women are similarly affected by stereotypes about women's mathematical ability. Moreover, the same individual can be privileged by one system yet subordinated by another. In the United States, Black men are oppressed

**tokens**
a small number of individuals from oppressed or subordinated groups who enjoy the privileges of the dominant or host group to make the dominant group seem less exclusionary to the public.

by racism and privileged by sexism, White women are oppressed by sexism and privileged by racism, and working-class and low-income White men are oppressed by socioeconomic classism and privileged by racism and sexism.

## Oppression: Multiple Ecological Levels

The power relationships of the larger society are often mirrored at multiple ecological levels, in macrosystems, communities, organizations, microsystems, and individual prejudices (James et al., 2003; Prilleltensky, 2008).

***Breathing "Smog": Social Myths.*** Oppressive hierarchies are sustained in part by widely accepted myths that rationalize them (Freire, 1970/1993; Prilleltensky & Nelson, 2002; Watts, 1994). Blaming the victims of macrosystem economic forces, such as those who are homeless because of a lack of affordable housing, is one example (Ryan, 1971). As a result, members of dominant groups and even subordinated groups often fail to recognize how systems of oppression are creating injustices. Tatum (1997) likened this process to "breathing smog." After a while, one doesn't notice it; the air seems natural.

One example of "smog" can be a false reading of differences in educational attainment or income. Values of individualism channel our thinking to interpret these as the result of individual effort or ability. This bias is so well established among people in Western nations that it is known as the "fundamental attribution error" in social psychology. Although individual efforts do matter a great deal, it is also true that oppressive systems reward effort and ability among members of the privileged group while often ignoring the same qualities among members of the subordinated group. Recognizing that injustice, especially for members of the privileged group, would call into question cherished beliefs about individual freedom, something that many persons would rather not think about. So, when Whites earn more than other racial groups or when men earn more than women, those in privileged positions are predisposed to interpret those differences in individual terms, ignoring broader factors.

In fact, an oppressive system often works best when a few members of an oppressed group break through to enjoy the privileges of the dominant group. They may be **tokens** accepted only to improve public relations, or perhaps they are the best at assimilating the values and behaviors of the dominant class. Their success seems to offer a lesson about the importance of individual effort, yet it obscures a review of social conditions across levels of analysis. In addition, research shows that these token individuals are often placed in a bind, being held to higher performance standards than members of the privileged group (Ridgeway, 2001).

***The Role of Mass Media.*** Newspapers, magazines, television, cable news, movies, radio, and the internet compose a very influential macrosystem. The presence and status of women, persons of color, and other oppressed groups

**labyrinth**
the array of obstacles that women and minorities must face to achieve success in the workplace, often because White men have more power that they can wield to take advantage of opportunities more readily.

have increased in U.S. mass media in the last half-century. Yet mass media continue to provide misleading images of privileged and oppressed populations.

Often the poor are simply ignored in mainstream news; Wall Street and economic-corporate news are headlined, while unemployment is sporadically mentioned and economic inequality seldom covered. When news stories do cover poverty, they frequently ignore macrosystem factors such as low wages and the lack of affordable housing. Although U.S. drug users and dealers are most often European American men, in news and crime shows they most often appear as urban African American and Latino men. Low-income women also are portrayed negatively (Bullock et al., 2001; Gilliam & Iyengar, 2000).

Gilens (1996) investigated coverage of poverty in major U.S. news magazines, finding that while African Americans accounted for less than one third of persons living in poverty, every person pictured in news magazine stories about the "underclass" was African American. This bias had real effects: Public opinion polls cited by Gilens showed that U.S. citizens consistently overestimated the proportion of poor people who are Black. Additionally, White women are more likely to be portrayed as victims of violent crime than women of color. Persistent exposure to this media content contributes to skewed perceptions concerning the prevalence of crime targeting White women (Parrott & Parrott, 2015).

***The Impact of Social Media.*** Social media (e.g., Facebook, Instagram, Twitter) has become ubiquitous in the last decade, and a great deal of research is focused on understanding the impact of social media on individuals and society. Consider the role of social media in policing, for example. Social media's technologies offer new opportunities for oppressive surveillance and police control, but they also provide the capacity to monitor police and mobilize around perceived injustices, such as brutality or racial profiling (J. P. Walsh & O'Connor, 2018). We are just beginning to understand the complex effects of social media on political engagement. For example, online platforms can be used effectively to organize supporters of a local park conservancy to clean up after a severe storm and to recruit young people into extremist organizations that espouse discrimination and violence. Social media contributes to a rapidly changing landscape, and its complex effects are worth further discussion.

***Institutional Oppression: Workplaces.*** Organizational policies can have discriminatory effects, even when administered by well-meaning individuals. For instance, reliance on standardized test scores in college admissions can exclude otherwise promising students of color and those who are economically disadvantaged.

The multiple barriers, or **labyrinth**, that women face in organizations is another example (Eagly & Carli, 2007). Studies of work communication show that in mixed-sex groups, men talk more, make more suggestions, use more assertive speech and gestures, and influence group decisions more often.

Women are more likely to be interrupted (Hancock & Rubin, 2015) and to experience *mansplaining*, a term that was coined to capture the times when someone speaks condescendingly to someone with the mistaken assumption that they know more about it than the person they are talking to (Solnit, 2008/2012). These routine patterns of communication indicate the use of power in a group, and studies indicate that both women and men accept male leaders who use them competently. Yet when women use these actions to lead assertively, the response is often different. Many men and even women feel discomfort, and emotional backlash is more likely to occur, even if not voiced openly. Assertive women managers, for instance, are more likely to be considered hostile than equally assertive men (Heilman, 2001). The source of discomfort is that assertive women contradict subtle, socially constructed (and unjust) expectations about who can legitimately exercise these forms of power (Carli, 1999, 2001; Ridgeway, 2001; Rudman & Glick, 2001). In other words, assertive women are challenging hierarchical systems of oppression. The discomfort and backlash even among other women indicate that an established system of power and roles is involved, not simply men.

Reviews of psychological research also indicate that women's work performance and leadership, even when identical to men's, still is often rated less positively (Eagly & Carli, 2007). When men and women submit otherwise identical resumes for jobs, men's resumes are often evaluated more positively (Ridgeway, 2001). Even when undergraduate students were asked in several studies to hire a student for a campus job, both male and female raters preferred men over equally qualified women (Carli, 1999).

Pager (2003) conducted a field experiment to test the roles of race and criminal record in hiring. Four male testers answered advertisements for entry-level positions in the Milwaukee area in 2001. Two were White, one presenting credentials with no criminal record and the other presenting otherwise identical credentials but also reporting a (fabricated) felony conviction for selling cocaine and serving 18 months in prison. Two other testers were Black, with the same credentials and manipulation of criminal background. Testers appeared in person to apply for positions (they rotated which individual presented evidence of a criminal record). The pairs applied for a total of 350 jobs. Very few employers actually checked applicants' references; most seemed to accept their self-reports. The dependent variable was the rate of job offers or callbacks for further interviews from employers.

The results showed that Whites received callbacks or offers more than twice as often as Blacks. In fact, Whites reporting a felony drug conviction were more likely to receive call-backs or job offers than Blacks with no criminal record at all (Pager, 2003). Similar studies in other U.S. localities have found similar racial discrimination (Crosby et al., 2003; Quillian et al., 2017).

Many social-psychological studies show that individuals who believe themselves free of prejudice nonetheless can behave in discriminatory ways

**implicit bias**
the mental associations individuals make based on social categories (e.g., race, socioeconomic status, gender) that are often influenced by societal biases.

**ethnocentrism**
understanding or defining communities and community problems using a limited perspective based on the norms and beliefs of one's own group.

(J. M. Jones, 1997, 1998). The widespread discrimination documented by Pager (2003) and others is an institutional and societal issue, not simply an individual matter. Aggregate levels of **implicit bias,** or the mental associations we hold based on social categories, are correlated strongly with aggregate levels of disparities and discrimination in a particular place, such as a nation, city, community, or workplace. We might think of implicit bias not just as a reflection of an individual's internalization of particular stereotypes but also as a "bias of the crowd" that reflects the most widely shared influences of the situation and larger ecological context (Payne et al., 2017). In any society with widespread inequality and systemic prejudice, some systemic and implicit bias would be expected.

***Institutional Oppression: Schools.*** In the United States, schools are often believed to be the pathway to racial integration and upward economic mobility. For some, this is true. Yet schools often simply perpetuate existing racial and class differences (Condron, 2009; Fine & Burns, 2003; Hochschild, 2003; Lott, 2001). One reason is residential racial segregation. In addition, reliance on local funding of schools, combined with great disparities of wealth between school districts, creates much richer opportunities for some students than others. Within schools, tracking of students, largely based on test scores, shunts students of color and those from lower income families disproportionately into lower quality classes that do not prepare students for college or competitive jobs (Lott, 2001; Weinstein, 2002a). Students of color are disproportionately suspended and expelled: While Black students represent 15% of all public school students in the United States, they account for 39% of students suspended (Government Accountability Office, 2018). Further, teachers and schools may not adequately consider many students and their families in terms of the knowledge and resources they bring to the classroom (Gonzalez et al., 2005).

***Intergroup Relations and Individual Prejudices.*** Research on intergroup relations in social psychology demonstrates that as humans, we often hold positive attitudes about our ingroup (whom we see as similar to ourselves) while stereotyping and even holding prejudices about outgroup members (those we see as different). This is an important insight for community psychology, as it reminds us that we are likely to approach a problem and attempt to solve it with an **ethnocentric** understanding or definition of the problem, believing that our own way is best. Examining these ethnocentric assumptions and collaborating across groups are key components of cultural competence, to which we turn later in the chapter.

Members of both dominant and subordinated groups thus may hold stereotypes and prejudices about the other group. However, an insight of the liberation perspective (discussed further in the next section) is that not everyone's stereotypes and prejudices have the same effects. If a person is in a more powerful role (e.g., employer, teacher, police officer, elected official),

**liberation perspective**
a call to action that explains injustices, shines light on the oppressive system, and provides a plan for changing the system and achieving social justice. Exhibit 7.2 reviews the key principles of the liberation perspective.

**decoloniality**
drawing attention to what and whose knowledge counts as legitimate and powerful or as being presented as "other," challenging oppressive conditions around the world, and collaborating with communities historically excluded from action and research.

their biases have greater effects on others. Members of privileged groups have more influence in their organizations, communities, and societies. Members of the subordinated group are not free of prejudices, but theirs are less powerful because their subordinated status limits their influence. For instance, in U.S. society, both Whites and persons of color are likely to hold at least some stereotypes and prejudices about the other. Yet White persons as a group dominate economic, political, and social institutions (e.g., access to employment, housing, education, mortgages, and loans; favorable mass media coverage; political power). The biases of powerful Whites become part of an interlocking set of social arrangements that perpetuate this control of resources: in short, a system of racism (J. M. Jones, 1997). All Whites, even those who oppose racism, benefit from this system; inevitably they are privileged by it. Similar dynamics perpetuate other forms of oppression.

## The Liberation Perspective: A Call to Action

*Liberation in its fullest sense requires the securing of full human rights and the remaking of a society without roles of oppressor and oppressed (Watts et al., 2003, p. 187).*

The **liberation perspective** is not just an intellectual analysis; it is a call to action. It explains injustices and names an opponent: the oppressive system. It also provides an orientation for something positive to work toward. The aim is to change the system, to emancipate both the privileged and the oppressed (Freire, 1970/1993). First-order change in this context would mean the currently oppressed group simply replaces the currently privileged group in power, a reshuffling within the oppressive system. Second-order change dismantles the oppressive system and its inequalities. That is the aim of liberation. Exhibit 7.2 summarizes principles of the liberation perspective.

Members of subordinated groups usually understand the system of oppression better than those who are privileged by it. Frequent participation in relationships where one is privileged dulls the awareness of the privileged person, making injustices seem natural (like breathing smog). Yet the same encounters can lead to insights by the subordinated. For instance, European Americans are seldom forced to confront the existence of racism, while members of other racial groups have perhaps daily experience with it. This means that liberatory efforts need leaders from the subordinated group to sustain awareness of where the real issues lie. Liberation also needs commitment from persons in privileged groups to work toward addressing oppression. Paulo Freire (1970/1993), an important theorist of liberation, holds that three resources are needed for dismantling of oppression:

- critical awareness and understanding of the oppressive system

- involvement and leadership from members of the subordinated group

- collective action; solely individual actions are difficult to sustain against powerful opposition

## Exhibit 7.2  Assumptions and Concepts of the Liberation Perspective

1. Oppression occurs in a hierarchical relationship in which a dominant group unjustly holds power and resources and withholds them from another group.

2. The more powerful group is the dominant or privileged group; the less powerful is the oppressed or subordinated group. A person's group membership is often determined by birth or other factors beyond one's personal control.

3. Resources controlled by a dominant group may include economic resources, status and influence, sociopolitical power, interpersonal connections, and the power to frame public discussion of issues.

4. The oppressive system grants unearned privileges to members of the dominant group, whether or not they recognize or consent to them.

5. The oppressed group resists oppression, directly or indirectly, with the power they have.

6. Multiple forms of oppression exist. An individual may be privileged by one form of oppression and subordinated by another.

7. Oppression involves multiple ecological levels: macrosystems, localities, organizations, interpersonal relationships, and individual prejudices.

8. Social myths rationalize an oppressive system. Tatum (1997) likened this process to "breathing smog": After a while, the workings of the oppressive system seem natural.

9. Because they experience its consequences directly, members of the oppressed group often understand an oppressive system better than members of the dominant group.

10. Any individual may have prejudices, but those of the dominant group are more damaging because they interlock with the power of oppressive systems.

11. Liberation theory is a call to action, to work collectively to dismantle oppressive systems.

12. Oppression dehumanizes both oppressor and oppressed. To truly dismantle it, those who oppose it must aim to liberate both the oppressed group and the dominant group from the oppressive system.

*Note.* Data from Freire (1970/1993), J. B. Miller (1976), G. Nelson and Prilleltensky (2005); Prilleltensky and Gonick (1994), Tatum (1997), Watts (1994), Watts and Serrano-García (2003).

**decentering**
weaving together knowledge and experiences across many communities around the world and beyond academic institutions .

In community psychology, a liberation perspective is increasingly accompanied by a focus on **decoloniality** within our field. Community psychologists, many from the Global South, are addressing oppression by expanding our ecology of knowledge for social emancipation (Sonn, 2016). A decolonial perspective draws attention to *what* and *whose* knowledge counts as legitimate and powerful and to whose understandings and life experiences are constructed as "other." This perspective orients community psychology to challenge oppressive conditions around the world *and* to collaborate with those previously excluded in research and action for liberation and well-being (Montero, 2007; Sonn et al., 2017). It calls on community psychologists, particularly in the United States, to engage in a project of **decentering**, reimagining the field of community psychology as multistranded, weaving together knowledge and experience from inside and outside the university and across many localities and struggles for justice around the world (Dutta, 2016).

# Attending to Diversity in the Practices of Community Psychology

In this book, we view human diversity as both a challenge to address and an asset for improving community psychology work. The concepts in this chapter have a number of implications for community psychology. We first discuss cultural competence among community psychologists and organizations. We next build upon our discussion of collaboration that we began in Chapters 2 and 3. Finally, we consider cultural appropriateness of community programs.

## Cultural Competence Across Levels of Analysis

Community psychologists seek to understand communities by working within them, which often requires competence for working across cultural boundaries. Definitions and descriptions of cultural competence for community researchers and practitioners vary (e.g., Balcazar et al., 2009; Castro et al., 2004; Guerra & Knox, 2008; Harrell et al., 1999; Sasao, 1999) but often contain the following elements (note that several elements parallel the characteristics of bicultural competence described earlier):

- knowledge of and respect for the characteristics, experiences, beliefs, values, and norms of the cultural group with whom one is working

- interpersonal-behavioral skills for working within the culture

- supportive relationships within the culture with whom one is working and in one's own culture

- "a professional stance of informed naiveté, curiosity, and humility" (Mock, 1999, p. 40), involving awareness of one's limited knowledge and a commitment to learn

- awareness of how one's own culture and experiences have shaped one's worldview

- a viewpoint that developing cultural competence is an ongoing process, not an achievement

These qualities involve not only cognitive knowledge and behavioral skills but also attitudes. Those attitudes that are particularly important are related to the concept of cultural humility. Cultural humility is a stance one takes toward working across difference that includes openness to learning and personal growth, a curiosity about other cultures, genuine respect for the strengths of a cultural tradition, a willingness to address differences in privilege and personal experiences with power, and a willingness to engage in self-reflection and critique about one's personal and cultural biases. However, from a community psychology perspective, cultural competence cannot be conceptualized only as an individual level of analysis issue. When community psychologists begin working with people in a new setting, knowing the history of their concerns, challenges, and past social change efforts is critical to culturally sensitive community psychology practice (Guerra & Knox, 2008; Trickett, 2009). Furthermore, reflexive community psychology practice requires examining your own culture as well as the people with whom you are doing the work. Community psychologists working to promote cultural competence will often focus on collaborating with organizations rather than working with individuals alone. For example, Balcazar and colleagues (2009) have developed a training model for supporting cultural competence that emphasizes the importance of organizational context as well as individual attitudes and practices in promoting competence.

The model begins at the individual level, focused on the following training elements: (a) *desire to engage*, referring to the individual's willingness to participate and learn about cultural diversity; (b) *development of critical awareness* of personal biases toward others who are different in any dimension of cultural diversity; (c) *knowledge* of the multiple factors that can influence diversity and *familiarization* with selected characteristics, histories, values, beliefs, and behaviors of members of diverse cultural groups; and (d) *development and practice of skills* for working effectively with other individuals from diverse cultural backgrounds.

In addition, cultural competence is facilitated or hindered by a fifth critical element, the degree of *organizational support* for cultural competence where the service providers work. Organizations have different levels of readiness for training and for discussing issues that may raise conflict. Through their policies, allocation of resources for training, and willingness to change organizational practices, organizations communicate powerful messages to their members about the importance of cultural competence. Taylor-Ritzler et al. (2008) found that individual attitude and knowledge change were possible; however, they also examined organizational practices for changes (e.g., changes in outreach materials that were culturally sensitive and accessible in different languages). They concluded that "cultural competence is a complex process that requires both individual and organizational willingness and commitment to change" (Taylor-Ritzler et al., 2008, p. 89). Viewed as a process, cultural competence takes time and requires continual adaptation and awareness of the multiple factors.

## When Values of Diversity and Community Conflict

As we discussed in Chapter 6, sense of community is a core value of community psychology and one of the most widely used and studied constructs in community psychology. However, sense of community can become problematic when it conflicts with another core value—the value of human diversity. Several commentators have noted that sense of community can come into conflict with diversity because it tends to emphasize group member similarity and appears to be higher in homogeneous communities (e.g., Farrell et al., 2004; Neal & Neal, 2014).

Townley and colleagues (2011) have argued that systematic consideration of a community-diversity dialectic is needed in much community psychology work to identify and address the inherent tension between sense of community and a value in diversity. Reviewing how understanding of diversity figured in their own work on housing environments and well-being, they found that cultural perspectives were required to interpret findings from research on community life in Uganda after displacement in war, experiences of Latino/a immigrants in the U.S. South, and experiences of persons diagnosed with severe psychiatric disorders integrating into neighborhoods. Townley and colleagues found that the values of diversity or community varied for individuals in settings depending on the cultural context. While conflict in community psychology values can be viewed as being problematic, it might be better viewed as a community-diversity dialectic that is an inherent tension and opportunity in multicultural societies (Townley, 2017). For community psychologists, it is critical to understand the manner in which individuals function and achieve a sense of community within diverse environments; each initiative will involve its own unique balancing of these values (Thomas et al., 2015). Considering a community-diversity dialectic in community intervention and research leads us to reexamine our own understanding of the context of our work, of our collaborative relationships, and of potential outcomes (helpful and problematic) in diverse settings.

## When Culture and Liberation Conflict

*Culture, we believe, cannot become a haven for oppression, but must instead be a space where respect for diversity and participation in the development of new values leads all of us closer to health, dignity, and freedom. (Ortiz-Torres et al., 2000, p. 877)*

When cultural traditions contribute to oppression and conflict with liberatory aims, how can this conflict be addressed or resolved? The values and practices of patriarchal cultures prescribe restrictive social roles for women (note that this benevolent sexism is often interpreted as honoring or protecting women) and grant greater authority to men.

Bianca Ortiz-Torres and colleagues (2000) addressed these issues in an article titled "Subverting Culture." As part of an HIV-prevention initiative, their aim was to promote the capability of Puerto Rican women to negotiate use of safer sex precautions with male sex partners. This capacity-building goal conflicted with two cultural values. *Marianismo* defines the culturally feminine role in many Latinx cultures: a vision of the ideal woman as chaste and virginal, nurturant with men yet obedient to them, based on the Christian image of the Virgin Mary. It leads to sexuality being a topic for only private conversation and, often, to young women knowing little about their own sexuality. By extolling virginity, marianismo can be protective against risky sexual behavior. However, its role in suppressing discussion and understanding of sexuality, and its emphasis on obedience to men, also leaves many women less knowledgeable and powerful in sexual situations. *Machismo* defines the masculine role, emphasizing virility and sexual prowess. In sexual situations, the marianismo–machismo combination grants men greater power than women, for whom the contradictory cultural expectations are more difficult (e.g., being chaste vs. pleasing one's partner).

In focus groups and individual interviews, Latina college students (in Puerto Rico and New York City) reported emotional and interpersonal obstacles to discussing safer sex and negotiating with lovers for male condom use. Fears of rejection, feelings of hurt and anxiety, men's assertion that these actions demonstrated a lack of trust, and women's own love for their partners were obstacles mentioned by participants. These are concerns in heterosexual relationships across many cultural communities due to difference in power between men and women as well as gendered social roles and scripts (Peasant et al., 2015).

However, no culture is completely static or unchanging. Women's movements in many cultures have challenged traditions and practices that victimize and disempower women. Moreover, women disadvantaged by cultural values often have cultural resources as well. In the Ortiz-Torres et al. (2000) study, these included social support from other women, the impact of women's movements within the culture, and contact with different gender roles in other cultures. Ortiz-Torres et al. conclude that feminist community psychologists inside Latinx culture can work to promote sexual education and open discussion of women's sexuality, to challenge values and practices that harm women, and to build women's personal negotiating skills and social support. These efforts can use traditional marianismo conceptions of abstinence and of protecting women so that they can build families and serve others. Yet they can also advocate condom use and women's power to make decisions and to negotiate as equals in sexual situations.

Three key conclusions emerge about conflicts between culture and liberation. The first is that cultural values often contain contradictions. Cultural values such as marianismo and machismo have long histories, but so do values for protecting Latina women.

A second point is that cultures are continually evolving in response to external and internal conditions, including contacts with different cultures and diversity within the culture. Efforts for cultural transformation enter a stream of ongoing changes in a culture.

Finally, to be legitimate, cultural transformation needs to be initiated from inside the culture, by its own members. Ortiz-Torres and her colleagues developed their intervention as cultural insiders. Similarly, as you may recall from Chapter 3, Afghan women initiated the Revolutionary Association of the Women of Afghanistan to advocate for women's and wider human rights in their own nation (Brodsky, 2003). For outsiders to impose their conceptions on a culture raises many questions of social justice.

## Designing Culturally Anchored Community Programs

**surface structure**
the observable aspects of a community program, including the race, ethnicity, and gender of its staff, the language(s) used, the choice of cultural elements such as food or music, and the setting.

**deep structure**
the less tangible aspects of a community program, including core cultural beliefs, values, and practices. Historical, psychological, and social knowledge of a culture are required.

Culturally sensitive or appropriate community programs must address many aspects of the culture for which they are designed. These are best developed in genuine collaboration with members of the local culture and community. Writing from a health promotion perspective, Resnicow and colleagues (1999) proposed a useful distinction for describing cultural issues in designing community programs, borrowed from linguistics: the surface structure and deep structure of a community program.

**Surface structure** involves observable aspects of a program: race, ethnicity, and gender of its staff; language(s) used; choice of cultural elements such as food or music; and setting. These elements are important, but surface structure alone may not be enough to make a program effective. For instance, Sasao (1999) found that simply having Asian American staff in a clinical service for Asian Americans did not resolve all cultural differences between therapists and clients. **Deep structure** involves core cultural beliefs, values, and practices. The deep structure of a culture requires historical, psychological, and social knowledge of the culture. For instance, some Latinx and African cultural beliefs emphasize supernatural causes for illness as well as natural causes (Resnicow et al., 1999). These multiple explanations of illness will affect willingness to report symptoms, choice of Indigenous healers or Western health professionals, and many health-related behaviors. A health promotion outreach program for these populations must address those issues.

Remember our initial discussion of how Alaska Native Indigenous communities are collaborating with community psychologists to reinvigorate and reimagine rituals and multigenerational networks that prevent youth suicide. These interventions provide an example of culturally anchored community initiatives, developed by community members, that address both surface and deep structure.

## Conclusion

In countries across the world, populations are becoming increasingly diverse. For example, 39% of the U.S. population is made up of ethnic minorities (Census Bureau, 2017). Furthermore, population estimates suggest that people of color will constitute half of the U.S. population by the year 2045 if current immigration and birth rates continue. As we discussed, growing awareness of human diversity and social inequities in workplaces and community settings has led to new laws (e.g., fair housing and nondiscrimination on the basis of sexuality). Any work done in community settings requires an interest in learning about human diversity and conceptual tools that can guide this lifelong learning.

Two important overall questions remain. First, does this chapter's perspective on human diversity lead to moral relativism, endorsing all value systems (e.g., Nazism, religious intolerance, oppression of women) as equally morally compelling?

Simply put, no. The perspective of this chapter is concerned with understanding human diversity in context. This involves comprehending other persons and cultures in their own terms, especially their strengths. This often leads to discerning one's own assumptions and values and to deeper awareness of both others and oneself. This process is not easy or simple, but only with such pluralistic, contextual understanding can informed, principled moral stances on human problems be built.

Overarching values, such as the seven values we have proposed for community psychology, help address such issues. As we discussed in earlier sections ("When Culture and Liberation Conflict" and "When Values of Diversity and Community Conflict"), action based on principled values such as social justice, by citizens acting collectively within their own culture, can lead to personal and social transformation. Of course, the ways that community psychologists think about social justice or other values are rooted in their own cultural experiences. Yet community psychologists and others working for change, such as the empowerment of women, can ally themselves with members of other cultures or communities who hold similar values within their cultural context.

Second, with all our emphasis on how humans differ across cultural, racial, ethnic, gender, and other boundaries, how can we understand what humans have in common? On what shared basis can multicultural, diverse communities or societies be constructed and sustained?

This question requires some historical perspective. The question may presuppose the desirability of earlier times that seemed harmonious to members of privileged groups, because both they and members of subordinated groups "knew their place." It is also important to note that Western social scientists often have assumed that their concepts and perspective were universal, and later found those ideas were ethnocentric. Perspectives differ on how best to address this question (e.g., Fowers & Richardson, 1996; Hall, 1997; Sue, 2004). Searching for common ground on overarching values may help, as long as we remember that each person's perspective is inevitably limited by their own cultural experiences.

Certainly, there is much that is universal in human experience, but we can understand it only if we also understand how others view that experience differently. As one of psychology's founders, William James, asserted, "There is very little difference between one person and another, but what little difference there is, is very important" (cited in Hall, 1997, p. 650).

## For Review

### Discussion Questions

**1.** How can you contribute to the creation of brave spaces for discussions of diversity?

**2.** As you think about the dimensions of diversity that are important in your own life, are there any that have been missing from our discussion in this chapter? Are there questions that remain for you that you would like to explore further?

**3.** Think back to your responses to the self-reflection questions about dimensions of diversity. How do you think your experiences with these dimensions would influence your approach to community

psychology? What strengths do they provide? Are there any biases or other limitations you might have to address?

**4.** How do contemporary social movements, including Black Lives Matter and #MeToo, represent resistance to injustice and oppression? What do you see as their strengths and limitations as struggles for liberation?

**5.** How would you implement a health promotion program in a way that respects and incorporates the cultural values of a community?

### Key Terms

brave spaces, 215
cultural humility, 215
pluralism, 216
intersectionality, 216
privilege, 218
enculturation, 219
social equity, 229
social equality, 229
social inequity, 229
unexamined identity, 232
immersion, 233

transformed relations, 233
acculturation, 236
assimilation, 236
separation, 237
marginality, 238
bicultural integration, 238
oppression, 241
dominant or privileged
   group, 241
oppressed or subordinated
   group, 241

internalized oppression, 242
patriarchy, 243
tokens, 244
labyrinth, 245
implicit bias, 247
ethnocentrism, 247
liberation perspective, 248
decoloniality, 249
decentering, 249
surface structure, 254
deep structure, 254

### Learn More

A detailed summary of the chapter, along with other review materials, is available on the *Community Psychology, Fourth Edition* companion website at http://pubs.apa.org/books/supp/kloos4/.

Library of Congress Prints and Photographs Division,
Washington, D.C. 20540 USA http://hdl.loc.gov/loc.pnp/pp.print

Fannie Lou Hamer, a leader in the civil rights
movement in the United States, organized
Mississippi's Freedom Summer of 1964. Her work
exemplifies community psychology's values,
including empowerment and citizen participation.

# 8 Empowerment and Citizen Participation

## Looking Ahead →

After reading this chapter you will be able to answer these questions:

**1.** How does an ecological perspective inform the way community psychologists think about empowerment?

**2.** Why do community psychologists value citizen participation as both a means (a path to a goal) and an end (a goal in itself)?

**3.** What are skills that you can develop to become more empowered and engaged as a citizen?

**4.** What are the features that make a setting empowering?

**5.** How does an empowerment perspective inform how community psychologists think about helping relationships?

## Opening Exercise

## Unpacking Assumptions

*If you have come to help me, you are wasting your time. But if you have come because your liberation is bound up with mine, then let us walk together.*

—Lilla Watson, Australian Aboriginal visual artist, activist, and educator, in response to mission workers

*Nobody's free until everybody's free.*

—Fannie Lou Hamer, American civil rights leader, in a speech to the National Women's Political Caucus

Let us look closely at these quotes and how they resonate for you. A bit more context may help. The quote from Lilla Watson comes from her work as an advocate for Aboriginal children and families in Queensland, Australia. Between 1910 and the 1970s, many children of Aboriginal descent were forcibly taken from their families and communities by government agencies and church missions in order to "protect" them and help them assimilate to the majority culture. The stolen generations and their descendants experienced profound suffering, and the Australian government issued a formal apology to Indigenous peoples in 2008.

Fannie Lou Hamer, a leader in the civil rights movement in the United States, organized Mississippi's Freedom Summer of 1964. She endured threats and physical assault as she helped many African Americans become registered to vote. Hamer's quote comes from a speech she gave at the National Women's Political Caucus, an organization that she cofounded in order to increase the number of women in politics and to support women in office. Take a minute to think about your response to each of the following questions.

## What Do You Think?

**1.** Why would Lilla Watson not want help in the form of services for her people?

**2.** What do you think Fannie Lou Hamer meant when she said that no one is free until everyone is free? In what ways is she motivated to be helpful?

**3.** How are these quotes relevant today? More specifically, what roles do you think Lilla Watson might envision for those who walk with her? And what would it look like to work with Fannie Lou Hamer toward more freedom?

In this chapter, we explore these key questions as we think about the roles and relationships that we engage—as community psychologists, but also as students, teachers, parents, youth, elders, neighbors, social workers, researchers, health care professionals, and others—in trying to understand and improve quality of life in our communities. We introduce concepts and tools that can be used to facilitate empowerment processes and outcomes, turning first to grounding definitions of key concepts.

We continue to elaborate the links between individual quality of life and ecological contexts as we focus on power dynamics in relationships, organizations, and communities. This chapter extends the section in Chapter 2 highlighting the concept of empowerment and its key role in defining the field of community psychology. An empowerment perspective changes how we think about problems and solutions and how we work with others. Here we examine *empowerment* in greater detail, beginning with definitions and concluding with a discussion of empowering practices and settings. We also focus on *power*, a concept at the root of empowerment, and *citizen participation* as a strategy for exercising power in community decision making. In Chapter 12, we consider how program evaluation methods can be used to empower individuals and communities, through developing and improving community programs. In Chapter 13, we continue the discussion by focusing on processes of community and social change. Keep in mind, however, that these divisions are due to space limits. In the real world, engaging in empowering settings intertwines with changing communities and macrosystems.

# What Is Empowerment?

**empowerment**
an intentional, ongoing process centered in the local community, involving mutual respect, critical reflection, caring, and group participation, through which people lacking an equal share of resources gain greater access to and control over those resources.

"Empowerment" is a term that has many meanings. It has become a buzzword with varying connotations, used frequently across many different contexts (Cattaneo et al., 2014). Corporations speak of empowering their employees, sometimes with no intent to actually share power (K. J. Klein et al., 2000). International agencies use empowerment language in the context of economic development work that is not necessarily grounded in local knowledge or agendas (Grabe, 2012). Nonprofit organizations in the United States frequently name empowerment as a major goal yet do not often define how advocacy or services are empowering to clients (Kasturirangan, 2008). Physical exercise, meditation, and psychotherapy have been described as empowering; those are better understood in terms of personal growth or individual practice, not empowerment as community psychologists use the term. Scholars have criticized varying, inconsistent usages of the term even within community psychology (Brodsky & Cattaneo, 2013; Riger, 1993). A word that means everything also means nothing distinctive; sometimes it seems that empowerment has suffered that fate.

However, let us look more closely. In community psychology, Rappaport (1981) originally suggested that empowerment is aimed toward enhancing the possibilities for people to control their own lives. He defined **empowerment** as "a process, a mechanism by which people, organizations, and communities gain mastery over their affairs" (Rappaport, 1987, p. 122). Over time, Rappaport and others adopted a more elaborate, community-oriented definition of empowerment proposed by the Cornell Empowerment Group (1989):

> an intentional, ongoing process centered in the local community, involving mutual respect, critical reflection, caring, and group participation, through which people lacking an equal share of resources gain greater access to and control over those resources. (p. 2)

Empowerment in these definitions is accomplished with others, not alone. It involves gaining and exercising greater power (access to resources), and not just the feeling of being in control of one's own life. At the individual level, it includes cognition ("critical reflection" in the Cornell definition above) and emotion ("caring"), as well as the behavior of participation in a group. So, even as individual empowerment is experienced internally as thoughts and feelings, it is also enacted socially and contextually, rather than in isolation. For example, individual empowerment is more likely to occur in some social contexts than others. At the setting level, empowerment includes role relationships marked by mutual influence and reciprocal helping. At the community level, empowerment includes the social norm of broad participation, the presence of coalitions, shared leadership, and inclusive decision making about resources. Rappaport intentionally sought to keep the definition of empowerment open, arguing that a simple definition is likely to limit understanding of its multiple forms.

Empowerment is a multilevel concept: Individuals, organizations, communities, and societies can become more empowered (Rappaport, 1987). A person who becomes more aware and informed, more skeptical of traditional authority, more willing to oppose injustice, and more involved in citizen participation is becoming empowered. A work organization may empower small teams to assume responsibility for day-to-day decisions. Through networking with other groups, a community organization may influence the wider locality. Through advocacy at higher levels of government, a locality may gain a greater control over its affairs. Empowerment also can concern dismantling or resisting oppressive systems of injustice, at macrosystem or other levels.

While empowerment may have radiating effects across levels, empowerment at one level does not necessarily lead to empowerment at other levels. Feeling empowered does not always lead to actual influence in collective decisions. Individuals with more power and control over their lives do not necessarily empower their organizations or communities. Empowering organizations may not be empowered to make changes in the larger community. A powerful organization in which leadership is tightly controlled does not empower its members. Successful empowerment efforts work across multiple levels (D. D. Perkins & Zimmerman, 1995; Zimmerman, 2000). Indeed, recent work in the field examines the connective spaces *between* contexts and *across* levels of analysis, looking toward relational patterns and networks as bridges between individuals, microsystems, and macrosystems (Christens, 2012, 2019; Christens et al., 2014; Langhout et al., 2013).

## The Context and Limits of Empowerment

Empowerment is contextual: It differs across organizations, localities, communities, and cultures because of the differing histories, experiences, and environments of each (Rappaport, 1981). For instance, in a civic group, a person may develop skills for influencing decisions through discussion, teamwork, and compromise. Yet that individual may find these skills ineffective for wielding power in a workplace that rewards directive, task-oriented decision making. The person is thus empowered in the first context but not the second. Even the nature of what empowerment means may be different in these two settings.

A focus on the context of empowerment is critical, not just because empowerment processes may be different across settings and cultural communities but because it leads us to ask key questions: Who is to be empowered, and for what purposes (Berkowitz, 1990)? As discussed previously, empowerment has often been understood in individualistic terms and used to promote personal self-advancement or individual entrepreneurship without regard for one's community or wider society. Empowerment also may be understood

**citizen participation**
the involvement individuals have in community decision-making processes that impact them, having their voices heard and being able to influence these decisions in a democratic manner.

to mean strengthening the position and resources of one's ingroup at the expense of other groups. Examples such as a White supremacy group come to mind. An ecological perspective helps us reflect on the complexities and dilemmas faced in working toward empowerment goals. Recall, for example, our discussion in Chapter 7 of issues of empowering women in patriarchal cultures (Brodsky, 2003; Ortiz-Torres et al., 2000).

Community psychologists are increasingly examining empowerment processes in relation to liberation frameworks and broader social change strategies across a variety of global contexts (Chan et al., 2017; Montero et al., 2017; Watts & Serrano-Garcia, 2003). A study of women's empowerment in rural Nicaragua, for example, addressed pervasive gender inequities that included a lack of access to resources and limiting cultural beliefs about women's capabilities. Empowerment processes in this context included women's access to land ownership and participation in organizations that fostered more progressive ideas about gender, which then led women to experience more control within their relationships and greater individual well-being (Grabe, 2012).

Empowerment is a complex, dynamic process that develops in context and over time. It can deteriorate as well as grow, but it is not reversed by small setbacks (Zimmerman, 2000). It is often best understood by longitudinal and participatory research strategies, as we discussed in Chapters 3 and 4 and to which we will return in Chapter 12. Empowerment often occurs through engagement in settings in which help-giving roles and relationships are marked by reciprocity and expertise is widely distributed. It often involves grassroots groups that are limited in size, possess a positive sense of community, involve members in decision making, and emphasize shared leadership and mutual influence (Maton & Salem, 1995; Rappaport, 1987). Empowerment also may involve linkages among organizations (Zimmerman, 2000) and collective action. We provide examples of empowering practices and settings later in the chapter, but here, to extend our discussion of collective decision making and action, we turn to citizen participation.

## What Is Citizen Participation?

Wandersman (1984) provided a useful definition of **citizen participation**, describing it as "a process in which individuals take part in decision-making in the institutions, programs, and environments that affect them" (p. 339).

Let us unpack this definition. "Institutions, programs, and environments" includes workplaces, hospitals or mental health centers, neighborhoods, schools, religious congregations, and society at large. It also includes grassroots organizations formed for the purpose of influencing larger environments, including neighborhood associations, interfaith coalitions, political action groups, and labor unions. Citizen participation is a process that involves decision making. This does not necessarily mean holding the power to control all decisions but involves making one's voice heard and influencing decisions in democratic ways.

Think about the differences between being a *client* and being a *citizen*. Community psychologists seek guiding conceptual models that emphasize rights, competencies, and collaborative relationships rather than tradition-al medical models that emphasize needs, deficits, and hierarchical doctor–patient relationships. We draw on this distinction in our work with margin-alized or stigmatized groups. For example, in efforts to reduce homelessness and integrate homeless persons with mental illness more fully into communi-ties, practitioners have used a citizenship framework to encourage communi-ty members and organizations to rethink their relationship to homeless per-sons. In thinking about homeless persons as fellow citizens rather than simply as patients or clients who need services, we may place a greater emphasis on helping these individuals contribute to their communities and find a valued niche in society (Ponce & Rowe, 2018; Rowe et al., 2001).

In this example, we see that the concept of citizenship is useful to us as a way of describing persons and groups with whom we work, but citizen-ship as typically understood can also be used to exclude many people from full participation in their communities. Around the world, individuals and groups are too often displaced from their home countries because of violence, war, political upheaval, and economic distress; many of these people are not afforded formal citizenship in the places they live and work. Because of this, scholars have increasingly sought more inclusive notions of citizenship, in-cluding "cultural citizenship" and "global citizenship" as a way of understand-ing community belonging and civic participation (Berryhill & Linney, 2006; Flores & Benmayor, 1997). Many people, in the United States and around the world, are recent immigrants themselves or work with groups and commu-nities that include many individuals facing challenges related to citizenship (remember the discussion in Chapter 6 of the controversies surrounding what it means to be Australian, for example). Expanded notions of citizenship help us work in diverse contexts; they may also help us imagine children and youth with whom we work not just as citizens in the making but also as social agents capable of participating in civic life (Langhout & Thomas, 2010a; Zeldin et al., 2014). For example, in participatory action research with youth (as described in Chapter 3), children show that, with adult support, they are able to exercise the rights and responsibilities of full community members as they investigate real problems and work for meaningful change.

What about the concept of participation? Like empowerment, partici-pation has become quite popular. An influential critique has suggested that in many arenas, from international development efforts to local communi-ty interventions, participation is merely useful rhetoric, a fashionable way of speaking, rather than authentic practice (Arnstein, 1969; Cooke & Kothari, 2001). Community members are increasingly asked to participate in public

**tokenism**
involving community members, particularly those who are marginalized, in a superficial manner to indicate empowerment without actually providing the members with any voice or influence in community decisions.

**participatory practices**
practices that challenge existing processes and hierarchies, provide more opportunities for collaboration, and promote individuals' strengths to better serve the interests of the community and its members.

forums, advisory boards, and so forth, but their voice still may not count when it comes to actual decision making. For example, a high school student might be asked to serve on a local school board or a local resident might be nominated to a community coalition, but that person might then sit at the table (and appear in the picture on the website) without having any real voice or power to affect decisions made by the group. This caution, often referred to as a concern with **tokenism**, seems useful in reminding us that citizen participation is not simply a process of consultation or gaining consent, whereby decision making remains in the hands of a small, powerful group. Participatory strategies require a shift in how decisions are made and a commitment to enact democratic values in meaningful practice (Hickey & Mohan, 2005).

Participatory strategies may truly be valued yet difficult to enact in practice. For example, a human service organization working to reduce poverty might be committed to increasing participatory processes and collaborative decision making, but the staff might find themselves stuck in existing service paradigms that emphasize client over citizen and direct service provider over partner or facilitator. **Participatory practices**—which challenge existing hierarchies, increase possibilities for collaboration, and build upon the strengths of individuals—may run counter to our beliefs and assumptions about expertise and helping. To enact citizen participation, it may be critical for us to be more explicit about the value of participation and the linkages to larger values and shared goals (Bess et al., 2009).

Participation involves influence in making collective decisions in groups, communities, or society. It occurs in a diversity of forms: for instance, serving on a community coalition, writing a letter to the editor, debating the budget at a school board meeting, meeting with government officials to press for an action, testifying at a public hearing, and voting in elections. Each of these forms involves acting in the public sphere, something that many people are hesitant to do. Perhaps that hesitancy comes from myths about engagement in public life (see Exhibit 8.1).

## Citizen Participation in Action

Acts of citizen participation are more effective when done collectively with others and when adequately supported over time (see Wandersman, 2009, for a useful summary of keys to success as well as challenges). The following stories about the Waupun, Wisconsin, youth group and Alison Smith's growing role in community and state affairs illustrate ways of influencing decisions through collective actions.

About 30 sixth graders at the Waupun Middle School in Waupun, Wisconsin, met after class to choose projects they could take on to help their school and community. They divided into small groups to discuss possible service activities. Then the groups presented their ideas to the meeting and the students voted on the list of possibilities. They agreed to take on the top three: raising money for a field trip fund for students whose families could not afford to

**Exhibit 8.1  Myths and Insights About Private Life and Public Life**

**Myth**: Public life is for celebrities, politicians, and activists, people who like to be in the limelight or who want to make waves.

**Insight**: Every day, at school, where we work, where we worship, within civic or social groups, our behavior shapes the public world and is shaped by it. We are all in public life.

**Myth**: It's too depressing to get involved in public life, too easy to burn out.

**Insight**: Public life serves deep human needs: for instance, to work with others or to make a difference. It is as essential as private life.

**Myth**: Public life is always nasty, cutthroat, and all about conflict.

**Insight**: Public life involves encountering differences, but conflict doesn't have to be nasty. When understood and managed well, it can lead to growth for individuals and groups.

**Myth**: Public life is about pursuing one's own selfish interests.

**Insight**: Selfishness and enlightened self-interest aren't the same thing. Understanding how our true interests overlap with those of others comes only through involvement in public life.

**Myth**: Public life interferes with a private life.

**Insight**: Public life often enhances private life, making it more meaningful and enjoyable.

*Note.* Adapted from *The Quickening of America: Rebuilding Our Nation, Remaking Our Lives* (pp. 21, 24, 29, 33, 39), by F. M. Lappe and P. M. DuBois, 1994, Jossey-Bass.

pay the fees, getting new playground equipment for the school, and convincing authorities to install warning lights at a railroad crossing on Edgewood Street, a few blocks away. Only a small sign marked the crossing; brush and mounds of soil obscured the view down the tracks.

Cameron Dary, the sixth grader who led the railroad crossing project, and his fellow students presented their idea to a meeting of the Waupun City Council. Told to collect evidence to support their ideas, they conducted a survey of residents near the crossing. Of 14 residents surveyed, 10 believed the crossing was unsafe, 12 had seen people not stopping, and 13 wanted a better warning device. According to Dary, "Some of the adults thought it might never happen. You could tell by the way they looked they were just waiting for it to fail" (Putnam & Feldstein, 2003, p. 143). However, continued efforts by the youth for over a year led eventually to action: The railroad installed a series of warning signs and removed the debris to clear sight lines at the crossing.

Dary described what it felt like presenting the students' recommendations to the community: "So I went to a town meeting of a couple hundred people, and . . . I voiced my opinions as best I could, red-faced, hesitant, and embarrassed" (Putnam & Feldstein, 2003, pp. 142–144).

That is how Alison Smith began to speak out about community issues. Loeb (1999) tells the story of how she joined the League of Women Voters and became active in environmental issues in her Connecticut town and later in Maine: "I was hesitant at first. I don't have a college degree. I'm more of a behind-the-scenes person. But I've always felt like someone who cares, even if I didn't always know what to do about it" (p. 63).

When the Maine League of Women Voters asked her to collect signatures for the Clean Elections statewide referendum in Maine, she did it: "I just sat at a table with a sign saying 'Do you want to take big money out of politics?' Almost everyone who came over responded and signed" (Loeb, 1999, p. 65). Support for the initiative to establish a voluntary program of full public financing for political campaigns grew statewide, with Alison as one of over a thousand volunteers. "I felt nervous when the League asked me to do new things like speak at press conferences. . . . But I also found that as an ordinary person, I had more credibility than the political professionals" (Loeb, 1999, p. 65).

The Clean Elections Act of 1996 passed with 56% of the vote and became a national model for campaign finance reform. (In 2015, voters in Maine strengthened the initiative, passing another referendum.) Alison Smith reflected on her work: "It gave me a sense that I really can do something just by showing up to further a cause. . . . I'm in it, as I said, to challenge the cynicism and despair, both my own and that of our society" (Loeb, 1999, p. 66).

## What Do You Think?

1. Neither Cameron Dary nor Alison Smith is a community psychologist, but their actions reflect the work of community psychologists. Based on what you have learned so far from this book, do you think knowledge of community psychology would have helped them? How so?
2. How does their work reflect the values of community psychology?
3. Are there similar issues in your community that could be addressed through citizen participation? How so?

## Citizen Participation: A Means or an End?

In these stories, citizen participation is both a means (a path to a goal) and an end (a goal in itself). As a means, participation is often encouraged to improve the quality of a plan or because citizens' commitment to a decision is often greater when they participate in making it (Wandersman & Florin, 2000). As an end, citizen participation is often seen as an essential quality of a democracy (Gaventa & Barrett, 2012).

This means–end distinction is not merely academic. Citizen participation is not always a means to better decisions, particularly if conflicts are not

**power over**
the amount of influence a person or group has over controlling resources and influencing community decisions. This power can be overt or covert and can be used by those with more power in hierarchical, inequal settings to oppress those with less power. Those with less power can exert more power over through acts of resistance.

resolved or valid expertise is ignored. Nonetheless, citizen participation has many advantages. Reviews of field research in organizations show that participation by members usually (but not always) increases the quality of decisions and overall organizational effectiveness. This is true especially if disagreement is seen as a source of information rather than a threat. Studies of voluntary organizations indicate that participation promotes effective leadership and attainment of goals (Bartunek & Keys, 1979; Fawcett et al., 1995; Maton & Salem, 1995; Wandersman & Florin, 2000).

Both empowerment and citizen participation involve exercising power in collective decision making. The principal distinction between them is that participation is a specific strategy or behavior, whereas empowerment is a broader process. Meaningful participation in civic life can be empowering, and lack of opportunities for meaningful participation can be disempowering (Langhout & Thomas, 2010b; Rich et al., 1995).

## Multiple Forms of Power

Understanding empowerment and citizen participation requires considering different forms of power. We introduce three types of power and then look more closely at how power works in social and community life. Our intent is to illuminate often-overlooked sources of power that may help empower citizens and communities. Before reading this section, return to the opening quotes for this chapter and consider these additional questions:

- In settings and relationships in your own life, how do you exercise power? How do others exercise it? Is the use of power different in different settings or relationships? How?

- When do you feel powerless? In what contexts do you experience a lack of power?

- To what extent do your professors have power over you? Do you experience any differences in power in various classes? How? What forms of power can you exercise as a student? What are the limitations of these?

- Now think more broadly about your communities and society. What forms of power exist here? How can someone like you exert power here?

### Power Over, To, and From

One useful framework draws our attention to power in three forms (Riger, 1993; Rudkin, 2003): power over, power to, and power from. **Power over** is the capacity of an individual or group to compel or dominate others through control of valued resources or punishment (French & Raven, 1959; Neal & Neal,

**power to**
the capability individuals and groups have to pursue their own goals and develop their capacities. It can involve individual self-determination.

**power from**
the ability to resist the unwanted power or unwanted demands of others that inhibit one's own needs, which includes resisting oppression and domination by another individual or group.

2011). Power over may enforce a target person's behavioral compliance, but it also invites covert or overt resistance. It may be used in ways that seem gentle but carry a clear implication that if others do not comply, stronger means will follow. It is rooted in patterns of relationships and social structures. For instance, one form of power in organizations is "the ability to issue and enforce a command concerning the use of resources" (M. Levine et al., 2005, p. 382). The ability to determine the annual budget, for example, is created by the organization's structure, regardless of the particular leaders involved. Also, in systems of oppression that we described in Chapter 7, the dominant group has power over, for instance, when social customs and belief systems enable men to occupy more advantageous social positions than women. Power over resembles classical sociological concepts of power (e.g., Giddens et al., 2003). Use of power over involves a hierarchical, unequal relationship and can lead to injustice. Yet it also can be used collectively to promote justice, as when laws compel an end to legal racial discrimination.

**Power to** concerns the ability of individuals or groups to pursue their own goals and develop their capacities. Unlike power over, this can involve self-determination for each person. For example, Nussbaum's (2000, 2011) capabilities framework, which has been adopted by several international development and human rights organizations, emphasizes the power and freedom of individuals to engage in valued social activities and roles. This framework (and attention to the way that capabilities are nurtured in specific contexts, such as those that foster positive youth development) is consistent with the goals of empowering practices (Shinn, 2015). We return to this later in the chapter when we discuss the features of settings that enhance the possibility for people, organizations, and communities to author their own lives more fully. This sort of generative power to may be shared, as it is not conceptualized as a limited commodity or zero-sum game. It is expansive rather than fixed.

**Power from** is an ability to resist the power or unwanted demands of others. It can be used to resist a dominant boss or friend or to resist wider forms of social oppression. Some feminist critiques of patriarchy (which involves power over) focus on how women often use power to and power from to resist domination (hooks, 1984; J. B. Miller, 1976; van Uchelen, 2000).

The workplace is one example setting in which power over, to, and from occur. For instance, a manager may exercise power over by giving orders, by seeking to persuade employees to do what the manager wants, or by delegating decisions to workers (allowing them some power to). Individually or collectively, employees can exercise power to and power from. They can use various persuasive and negotiating strategies to affect managerial decisions and policies. They may circumvent the manager's orders when the manager is not looking or go "over the boss's head" to higher management. At the extreme, they can withdraw their labor (individually quit the job or collectively

**integrative power**
sometimes called "people power," it is the capacity of individuals to collaborate, create and sustain groups, unify under a common cause, and inspire loyalty, allowing them to exhibit power to and power over.

strike). This is not to say that the power of employers and employees is equal. Obstacles to employees' use of power (e.g., difficulties in organizing collective action) are greater than the obstacles employers face. Because employers and employees both hold some form of power, strategies for exercising power depend on the context within the organization (e.g., the presence of nondiscrimination policies) as well as the larger macrosystem (e.g., state "right-to-work" laws). Strategies also depend on how power and resources are defined. In some contexts, collaboration is made possible by more expansive notions of power and resources, while in others, conflict may be necessary to allocate scarce resources in a zero-sum game (C. B. Keys et al., 2017).

## Integrative Power

K. Boulding (1989, p. 25) defined **integrative power** as the capacity to work together, build groups, bind people together, and inspire loyalty. This is sometimes termed "people power"; it is also a realization of power to and/or power from in the framework discussed previously. Mohandas Gandhi and others often have asserted that there exist forms of power stronger and more widespread than violence, powers without which human relationships (families, friendships, and communities) cannot thrive.

People enact these forms of integrative power every day. In a sense, the social sources of integrative power are infinite, unlike finite sources such as money (R. Katz, 1984). Some of the most remarkable forms of integrative power have been based on moral or spiritual principles. Gandhi proposed the concept of *satyagraha*, literally translated as "clinging to truth" or, more broadly, as the power of truth (D. Dalton, 1993, p. 249). Satyagraha was the basis of Gandhi's nonviolent resistance to British colonialism; of the nonviolent demonstrations of the U.S. civil rights movement; and of later nonviolent resistance movements in Poland, South Africa, Chile, and elsewhere (Ackerman & DuVall, 2000; E. Boulding, 2000). It is based on principled, active, openly expressed resistance to oppression, coupled with an appeal to a widely held sense of social justice.

Integrative power also exists in other forms. Labor unions have long used strikes as a form of people power. Boycotts are an exercise of integrative economic power: Colonial Americans boycotted tea to protest British policy, and later Americans boycotted cotton and sugar (made with slave labor) to protest slavery. More recently, we can see the power of organized groups demanding specific changes toward social justice; post-2008 social protest movements led by millennials in the United States (including young immigrant "Dreamers"), the Occupy Wall Street uprising, campus movements protesting sexual assault, and the Black Lives Matter movement continue to reverberate (Milkman, 2017). At the community level, neighborhood associations, support networks, congregations, and mutual help groups rely on integrative power as well.

## Three Instruments of Social Power

Gaventa (1980), a social activist, used concepts of political science to describe **three instruments of social power** or, in other words, three ways that power operates in community and social life (see also Speer & Hughey, 1995, and Culley & Hughey, 2008). These three instruments include the following:

- controlling resources that can be used to bargain, reward, and punish;

- controlling channels for participation in community decisions; and

- shaping the definition of a public issue or conflict.

The story of farm-generated runoff that contaminated the Wallkill River provides examples of these three instruments (Rich et al., 1995, pp. 660–662).

A corporation filed for a permit to use sludge containing human waste on their farm site, which produced grass sod in a rural area along the Wallkill River in upstate New York. Under a temporary permit granted by the state without any local input, sludge dumping began. Local citizens discovered the stench without warning and reacted with understandable anger. The state's Department of Environmental Conservation (DEC) held extensive public hearings on the company's application for a permanent permit before an administrative law judge. These hearings involved hours of testimony from technical experts and local citizens. In theory, all had full input into the DEC decision.

In practice, however, this formal process was distinctly one-sided. The local citizens were assigned seats in rows behind attorneys involved in the case. They did not have the legal training or technical background of the corporation's hired experts and knew neither the legal procedure nor the terminology used routinely during the hearings. They made a number of procedural errors until they hired their own attorney. When many of the local farmers became frustrated with their lack of real input, they used their tractors to block access to the sod farm. They were only temporarily successful.

Perhaps most telling is that citizens' knowledge of local conditions was discounted. Years of accumulated practical experience had shaped their intuitive understanding of things such as the effects of rainwater runoff on streams and the Wallkill River. Yet expert testimony, from consultants who did not live or work in the community, primarily influenced the judge's decision. When that testimony revealed that the corporation's plans met all state regulations, the permit was granted.

Within 5 years, virtually every negative outcome predicted by the local citizens had occurred. Wastes had flowed into the Wallkill River, groundwater became contaminated with toxic cadmium, and illegal hazardous wastes had been stored at the site. DEC sued the operators of the site for repeated violations and finally had to classify the property as a hazardous waste site for later

Environmental health hazards, including water pollution, are concerns for communities globally. Community psychologists can work with residents to define the problem and gain social power for change.

cleanup. Although unsuccessful in this case, local citizens came together to found Orange Environment (named for the county in New York where these events occurred). Orange Environment remains active in community organizing, legal action, and policy advocacy on environmental issues.

The Flint, Michigan, water crisis provides another example. A governor-appointed emergency manager and other leaders in Flint made the decision to switch to a new water source and did not use corrosion controls, resulting in the release of lead and other contaminants into the water supply beginning in spring 2014. Residents in the majority African American city quickly complained of problems, but their concerns were dismissed. Experts assured community members that the water was safe, even as over 100,000 residents were exposed to elevated lead levels in their drinking water (Carrera et al., 2019). Local and national community organizing finally led to a national declaration of emergency in 2016, yet, as of 2019, lead pipes were still being replaced in Flint (Hanna-Attisha, 2018).

Let us look more closely at the ways that power operates in these stories. Gaventa's (1980) first instrument of power is *controlling resources that can be used to bargain, reward, and punish*. This resembles power over. In Flint, the governor-appointed leaders controlled public infrastructure and were

**expert power**
the power related to an individual or group's knowledge, skills, and experiences. Community psychologists rely on their own expert power while also questioning its limits and criticizing expert power used by others to marginalize some individuals and groups.

accountable to the state rather than local citizens; they pursued cost savings over public health. In the Wallkill River example, the company had the money to hire experts and attorneys, to use or circumvent the law, and to overwhelm local opposition. Yet in other contexts, an organized citizenry can effectively threaten punishments such as negative publicity or boycotts, or they can offer attractive compromises.

The second instrument of social power is *controlling channels for participation in community decisions*. Speaking at public hearings, signing petitions, and voting are traditional forms of participation. However, Gaventa (1980) also referred to subtler mechanisms, such as controlling meeting agendas to exclude citizen comments and debate or requiring citizens to hire attorneys to advocate for them. As in our discussion of oppression in Chapter 7, hidden "rules of the game" are used to systematically benefit one group over another (Culley & Hughey, 2008). In the Wallkill River case, this instrument of power was used to limit citizen testimony. In theory, the DEC public hearings offered citizens the chance to participate in and influence a decision that would affect their health and livelihoods. In practice, legal procedures effectively prevented any meaningful citizen participation. Yet in other contexts, an organized opposition can open other channels of participation, such as public demonstrations or use of social media.

Wallkill citizens founded Orange Environment in part to provide legal advocacy when needed for participating in decision making. Orange Environment also provided a site where residents could develop local knowledge and expertise through research and education. Residents learned that technical and legal experts were able to participate and influence decisions in a way that local community members were not. In Flint, residents worked with professionals in the public health and medical community to independently measure lead exposure. They realized that they needed to build and exercise **expert power**, a type of power based on the perceived knowledge, skill, or experience of a person or group.

It is important to note here that community psychologists have paid a great deal of attention to expert power and the role of the professional as the expert (e.g., the attorneys and scientists in the Wallkill River case). Community psychologists have drawn on expert power as researchers and professionals, but we also have criticized the use of expert power to control channels of participation as well as constrain the agency and limit the freedoms of persons in distress (Rappaport, 1977a; Ryan, 1971). Medical doctors and mental health professionals are considered experts, for example, in diagnosing and treating persons with psychological disorders. While a diagnosis of depression or attention-deficit disorder can bring great relief to a person in distress and bring needed resources, it can also stigmatize and limit options.

The power to define and treat what is abnormal can be part of a system of caring but also part of a system of social control and exclusion. For example,

**power of "spin"**
the ability to shape the terms used to define an issue in public discourse. It can be used responsibly to help people understand an issue, but it can also be used to mislead some individuals and groups through lies or censorship that limit their power. It can also be used to amplify one's perspective while minimizing different viewpoints.

McDonald and Keys (2008) examined how research scientists on review boards exclude persons with disabilities from participation in research. They showed how the attitudes of key decision makers limit community access for persons with disabilities. Yet expert power can also be used to offset power, as in mutual help groups, which also offer expertise on psychological difficulties and disorders. They provide a different perspective on illness and recovery for their members and different forms of participation in community. The participatory research methods that we discussed in Chapters 3 and 4 also can be a basis of expert power for communities. The Waupun youth group, described earlier in this chapter, conducted a survey that was instrumental in exerting pressure on city government and the railroad. In Flint, community science has been key to holding government officials accountable and reestablishing trust in the community (Carrera et al., 2019).

The third instrument of power, often overlooked, is *shaping the definition of a public issue or conflict.* Recall our discussions of problem definition throughout this text. We have emphasized the importance of looking across levels of analysis and examining values and assumptions implicit in different definitions of human and social problems. The power to define public problems or issues is often referred to as the **power of "spin,"** or the ability to shape the terms of public debate on an issue (Gaventa, 1980). While this power may be used responsibly, and different definitions of a public issue may arise from genuine disagreement and value differences, Lukes (2005) drew attention to how this power can be used to mislead, whether through outright censorship and disinformation or through various ways of discounting individual or group judgments. It is the power to make one perspective seem natural, normal, important, or rational, while making another perspective seem strange, frightening, irrelevant, or unreasonable. For instance, in the Wallkill River and Flint cases, key decision makers favored technical jargon and scientific expertise while discounting the local, practical knowledge of residents. In a case recounted by Culley and Hughey (2008), powerful stakeholders tried to persuade the residents of Sugar Creek that there was no reason to get involved or worry about chronic oil refinery spills and the contaminants seeping into the area's soil and groundwater. They appealed to the community members' sense of themselves as residents of a "refinery town," with the refinery as a "good neighbor" and economic benefactor.

Communications media play a powerful role in shaping how social issues are defined, but the third instrument of power is not theirs alone. Behind the media are social institutions and interest groups with the money and perceived credibility to make their voices heard and to create the ideas of the media and the public. These dominant beliefs of a community or society, often shared in stories, shape how social issues are interpreted (Rappaport, 2000). An example is Tatum's (1997) metaphor of "breathing smog" for widely accepted social stereotypes (mentioned in Chapter 7). Yet in some situations, citizens who adroitly use the media or word-of-mouth channels also shape public opinion and social imagination (Christens et al., 2007). For example, social media has played a major role in how police violence, particularly toward African Americans, has been viewed. Community members may also share persuasive counternarratives that challenge dominant stereotypes and help themselves and others envision how things could be otherwise (Sonn et al., 2013; Thomas & Rappaport, 1996). Orange Environment used this instrument of power in public advocacy regarding local environmental issues, as did the residents of Sugar Creek. The Community Psychology in Action feature in Box 8.1 describes Marci Culley's experience as an action researcher in Sugar Creek and how local citizens exercised their social power.

---

**Box 8.1** **Community Psychology in Action: Citizen Participation and Power in Sugar Creek, Missouri (continues)**

Marci R. Culley

What does citizen participation "look like" as it unfolds in local communities? To learn more about this, I conducted a qualitative community case study to explore an environmental dispute that occurred in Sugar Creek, Missouri—a small town polluted by a BP refinery. Over decades, residents' concerns and outrage grew. One resident recalled: "People were mad. They'd been lied to for 40 or 50 years. Everything was 'fine,' everything was 'clean,' but yet . . . there was over 200 million gallons of product underneath the neighborhood."

The study evolved from more than 4 years of my involvement as a participant–observer. I explored how federally mandated vehicles for citizen participation facilitated or undermined individual and collective decision making among stakeholders. Specifically, I examined the extent to which these vehicles, and stakeholders' experiences of the participatory processes initiated through them, were shaped by social power dynamics. Findings illustrated how participation was limited and how citizen influence could be manipulated via control of resources, barriers to participation, agenda setting, and shaping conceptions about what participation was possible. I learned a great deal from my work in this community. Three findings are particularly instructive for citizen participation efforts everywhere.

First, while participatory processes may on the surface appear open and collaborative, they can, nonetheless, contain significant power imbalances. In this case, subtle forms of power were often used by government and industry officials to marginalize community residents' views. As one regulator noted, existing environmental policy requires that regulators "pretty much work with the responsible party, in this case, BP." One federal health official lamented: "Communities are given the wrong impression . . . that they have more 'say' than they actually do."

Second, a profound disconnect often exists between stakeholders regarding the fairness and effectiveness of formal participatory processes. In this case, industry and government officials generally believed such processes worked well and that all stakeholders' views were considered fairly. As one regulator put it, such processes "allowed for a somewhat level playing field." However, citizens viewed these processes as mere window dressing, serving only to rationalize a preordained outcome. For example, citizens routinely characterized the formal public meetings as a "dog and pony show" that provided a way for government and industry officials to "get their propaganda out" and "feather their own bonnet."

---

**Box 8.1 Community Psychology in Action: Citizen Participation and Power in Sugar Creek, Missouri (continued)**

Third, the most successful forms of community influence often exist beyond formal structures. Here, such influence emerged from "unofficial" avenues for citizen participation (e.g., email campaigns, use of news media, organized demonstrations). Such mechanisms were much more likely than formal avenues to result in desired outcomes and to leave citizens with the feeling that they had been "heard." As one community activist noted,

> We weren't participating in a function that was established and [where] perimeters were drawn . . . and absolutely, we made a huge difference. It came down in the public's lap to affect change on this site . . . those civil actions that we undertook are the single most important thing that's happened here as far as moving this [investigation] along.

Citizens everywhere can be inspired by their story.

**What Do You Think?**

1. How are the three instruments of power illustrated in this example?
2. Compare this example with the Wallkill and Flint examples. What are the similarities and differences in each of these cases?
3. How do these examples illustrate concepts discussed in earlier chapters? For example, how do they illustrate the importance of an ecological framework and multiple levels of analysis?

## Summary Thoughts on Power

What is power, in terms useful to community psychologists?

Power is not a purely internal state, such as simply feeling powerful, inspired, or confident. Holding power involves capacity to exert actual influence on decisions (C. B. Keys et al., 2017; Riger, 1993). Power is best understood as a dimension, not an all-or-none dichotomy. Seldom is a person or group all-powerful or entirely powerless. Those who hold greater power will resist change, yet others may be able to use alternative sources of power. Even small acts may reflect some degree of power. Persons and groups with little or no capacity to compel may find ways to resist the powerful. We do not discount the differences in power in oppressive systems but seek to call attention to sources of power that citizens can use.

Power is best understood in relationships (Neal & Neal, 2011; Serrano-García, 1994). Patterns of relationships in families, settings, communities, and societies are typically self-sustaining, resulting in stubborn social regularities (see Gruber & Trickett, 1987; Tseng et al., 2002; and recall our discussion of social regularities from Chapter 5). Yet they can change, shifting in both predictable and unpredictable ways. Power also is contextual: You may hold power in some circumstances (e.g., influencing decisions in a student group) but not elsewhere (e.g., in a job where you have little voice in decisions).

Exercising power, or having an impact on decisions, requires control of some resources, and ultimately at least some capacity to compel those who resist, so that they go along or compromise. Many resources can empower communities, and personal willingness to get involved and work with others can help mobilize them (recall the examples that began this chapter). Integrative power is demonstrated at a variety of levels, from neighbors coming together to create safer playgrounds to grassroots groups influencing international policies on climate change. But how does this "people power" develop over time?

## How Do Citizens Become Empowered Leaders in Their Communities?

Use the following example from Loeb (1999) to begin to think about how this might happen. What are key aspects of this change process?

At a community organizing meeting at her church, Virginia Ramirez raised her hand. "I have this problem. This neighbor lady of mine died because it was too cold and they wouldn't fix her house. I want someone to do something about it" (Loeb, 1999, p. 16).

"What are *you* going to do about it?" the community organizer asked (Loeb, 1999, p. 16). Angered, Virginia left the meeting. A few days later, an organizer came to Virginia's home. Virginia let her in only because the organizer was a nun. The organizer asked only why Virginia was so angry. She responded with stories not only about her neighbor but also of poor schools and overt racism. Eventually Virginia agreed to hold a meeting of neighbors in her home.

Virginia had never run a meeting, but discussion turned quickly to neighborhood problems: poor housing, poor sewers, and few city services. Together the group researched documents at city hall and discovered that city funds for repairing houses in their neighborhood had been diverted to build a street in an affluent area. When they went to a city council meeting to complain, Virginia froze:

> I didn't remember my speech. I barely remembered my name. Then I . . . realized that I was just telling the story of our community. So I told it and we got our money back. It was hard. . . . But I began to understand the importance of holding people accountable. (Loeb, 1999, p. 17)

The community organizers encouraged Virginia to continue learning, to make her involvement in social causes more effective. They helped her reflect on each step of participation and learn new skills. Virginia earned her GED and eventually finished college. Her husband objected strenuously at first. When he yelled at her for studying instead of cleaning house and fixing supper, she trembled, but she told him, "I'm preparing for my future. If you don't like it, that's too bad, because I'm going to do it. I'm sorry, but this is a priority"

(Loeb, 1999, p. 19). Slowly and reluctantly, he accepted and even began to take pride in her accomplishments.

Virginia became a community organizer, supervising volunteers in health education outreach and training members of her church and community, especially women, to speak out. She has negotiated with politicians and business leaders to promote community development and better jobs and has testified before the U.S. Senate about an innovative job-training program she helped develop. Through it all, her faith has sustained her personally and directed her efforts (Loeb, 1999).

One way to understand citizen participation and empowerment is to study how it develops and is sustained over time, among individuals-in-communities like Virginia Ramirez. For instance, Watts and colleagues (2003) studied sociopolitical development among 24 African American youth and young adult activists in New York, Chicago, and San Francisco. From another perspective, Angelique and Culley (2014) studied long-term antinuclear citizen activism at the Three Mile Island nuclear plant near Harrisburg, Pennsylvania, the site of an environmental disaster in 1979 that was the worst commercial nuclear accident in U.S. history. Both approaches used qualitative methods that allowed thick description of participants' experiences over time.

In both studies, individuals initially accepted the social and political status quo but increasingly recognized social injustice. They began to see how community and personal events involved power, which benefited only members of dominant groups. For Virginia Ramirez, the process began when she recognized the social injustice behind her neighbor's death. For participants in the Watts et al. (2003) study, this involved experiences of racism. For Angelique and Culley's (2014) participants, it involved a specific provocation—a large-scale nuclear accident that threatened their community. Events like these can lead citizens, however reluctantly, to begin speaking out and confronting those they hold responsible.

One of the long-term activists in the Three Mile Island study, Paula K., a stay-at-home mom, said: "I graduated from high school in '65 and at that time the Vietnam War was in full swing, and I was disgusted by the protesters. I mean how DARE they question our government" (Angelique & Culley, 2014, p. 215). But she then went on to describe how her "need to understand" motivated her to attend town meetings in various townships:

> I went to probably about four or five meetings and . . . I noticed that when the same question was asked in one township, it was answered [by the industry and regulators] with a different answer than it was in Middletown or Highspire . . . the realization hit me that one of two things was happening. They really either didn't know and they were fudging it . . . or they were lying . . . and neither one was comforting to me. (Angelique & Culley, 2014, p. 215)

Through their participation in social action, empowered leaders emerged. They experienced conflicts, gained insights from critical reflections, and ben-

**critical awareness**
the knowledge of
how power and
political forces can
change, improve, or
interrupt community
and personal life. It
includes knowledge
of and questioning
oppressive hierarchies
and how social myths
maintain them. Critical
awareness arises
from life experiences,
reflections on those
experiences, and
dialogue with others.

efited from support and mentorship. They developed an awareness of power relationships in their communities and a sense that these relationships could be transformed by citizens working together. These developmental insights are useful, but they are only one standpoint for understanding how participation, empowerment, and community intertwine. Another perspective is to study the qualities of empowered persons.

## Personal Qualities for Citizen Participation and Empowerment

*Empowerment appears not to be a spectator sport. (B. McMillan et al., 1995, p. 721)*

In the research we review in this section, six personal qualities seem common among empowered persons engaged in citizen participation (see also reviews by Berkowitz, 2000, and Zimmerman, 2000):

- critical awareness,

- participatory skills,

- sense of collective efficacy,

- sense of personal participatory efficacy,

- participatory values and commitment, and

- relational connections.

But remember that empowerment is contextual. It develops in a specific setting, community, and culture and is strongly influenced by those contexts. Thus, the list of qualities that we describe below is suggestive, but we do not expect it to be characteristic of empowered persons in all circumstances.

*Critical Awareness.* **Critical awareness** is an understanding of how power and sociopolitical forces affect personal and community life (Freire, 1970/1993; Zimmerman, 2000). Serrano-García (1994) listed two cognitive elements: "critical judgment about situations [and] the search for underlying causes of problems and their consequences" (p. 178). One form of critical awareness is understanding hierarchies of oppression, dominant and subordinated groups, and social myths that sustain such hierarchies of power (Moane, 2003; Watts et al., 2003). The feminist motto "the personal is political" is an expression of critical awareness.

Critical awareness emerges from three sources: life experiences with injustices, reflection on those experiences and lessons learned, and dialogue with others. It begins with questioning the legitimacy of existing social conditions and existing authority, and learning to see problems as social practices that can be changed, not as the natural order of the world. It proceeds with answering questions such as the following: Who defines community

**participatory skills**
a person's ability to communicate, organize, solve problems, and identify and obtain material and social resources to address community issues.

problems? How are community decisions made? Whose views are respected and whose are excluded? Who holds power and how do they use it? How can these be challenged?

Consider the following story told by Anderson Williams, program director at Community Impact! Nashville:

> In 2003, a 16-year-old high school sophomore had just begun to work with our organization. As I sat and talked with her, she began making broad generalizations about "black folk" (black herself) and her frustrations with "their" behavior. She started throwing around the now popular adjective "project" (herself a public housing resident) to describe the negative behaviors of those around her. Knowing something of the history of the particular housing project where she lived, I sent her to the library to do some research on the history of that development. About 6 hours later, I called her and had to pick her up. She was so enthralled and excited because she found that many of the behaviors and actions she was complaining about had also been prevalent when "the projects" were completely full of white people. She was amazed. She presented this research to her peers, and thus we began the discussion of "systems" in the lives of our young people. (A. Williams, 2007, p. 813)

This story, along with the stories of Virginia Ramirez, Alison Smith, and the Waupun youth, illustrates critical awareness. Remember how the research that Virginia Ramirez's group did, documenting that money had been diverted from services for their neighborhood, deepened their critical awareness of how a city decision had affected their lives and where to focus their action. These stories also illustrate the role of collaborative change agents who support reflection and analysis of life experiences.

***Participatory Skills.*** To be effective in citizen participation, one also needs competencies and **participatory skills**, including communication, organizing, and problem-solving skills. Increasingly, technical skills are useful. For example, long-term environmental activists at Three Mile Island made a commitment to learn about energy technologies and ecological relationships (Angelique & Culley, 2014).

Skills for identifying and mobilizing resources are particularly important. Resources include tangible factors such as time, money, skills, knowledge, and influential allies. They also include less tangible qualities such as legitimacy or status in the community, the talents and ideas of community members, their personal commitment to community change, and social support. Social resources include shared values as well as the shared rituals and stories that illustrate those values (Rappaport, 1995). Many of the psychological and social resources involved in empowerment (e.g., social support, commitment, knowledge) are not scarce but are multiplied through working together (R. Katz, 1984; Rappaport, 1987). These skills can be learned, as the stories of Alison Smith and Virginia Ramirez especially illustrate.

**sense of collective efficacy**
the belief that coming together and working collaboratively will lead to social change and improve community life.

**sense of personal participatory efficacy**
an individual's level of belief and confidence in their ability to engage in effective citizen participation and impact community decisions. It is contextual in nature, meaning that it can feel more effective in some settings than others.

*Sense of Collective Efficacy.* **Sense of collective efficacy** is the belief that citizens acting collectively can be effective in improving community life (Bandura, 1986; D. D. Perkins & Long, 2002). Critical awareness and behavioral skills alone seldom lead to action unless persons also believe that collective action will lead to constructive changes (Saegert & Winkel, 1996; Zimmerman, 2000).

Others defined this simply as collective efficacy. Our term *"sense of* collective efficacy" explicitly marks this as a belief, or an individual cognition. Belief in collective efficacy usually arises along with personal experience in citizen participation and opportunities to build relationships of trust with other citizens (C. Collins et al., 2014). Sense of collective efficacy is contextual: A person may believe that citizens can collectively influence community decisions in one situation but not in another (Bandura, 1986; Duncan et al., 2003; D. D. Perkins & Long, 2002).

In quantitative studies of U.S. urban neighborhoods, citizens with stronger beliefs related to critical awareness, collective efficacy, or both participated more in community organizations and experienced a stronger sense of community (D. D. Perkins & Long, 2002; D. D. Perkins et al., 1996; Speer, 2000). Neighborhoods with higher levels of collective efficacy had lower crime rates (Snowden, 2005). M. J. Kral and Idlout (2008) found that a sense of collective efficacy served as a foundation for mental health and wellness in rural Canadian Indigenous communities. Suicide prevention and healing efforts were integrally tied to the collective power and intergenerational wisdom of local communities.

*Sense of Personal Participatory Efficacy.* **Sense of personal participatory efficacy** is an individual's belief that they personally have the capacity to engage effectively in citizen participation and influence community decisions. At its strongest, this includes confidence that one can be an effective leader in citizen action. This is not simply feeling empowered; it must also be connected to behavioral participation. It is a contextual belief; one can feel more effective in some situations than in others. It is thus a specific form of self-efficacy (Bandura, 1986). Virginia Ramirez and Alison Smith grew in both sense of collective efficacy and sense of personal participatory efficacy.

Research has often concerned similar concepts of sociopolitical control, perceived control, and political efficacy (Zimmerman, 2000). (Again, we added "sense of" to make explicit the cognitive focus.) Such beliefs have been linked to citizen participation among residents of a neighborhood near a hazardous waste site, among residents of urban neighborhoods, and in other circumstances (Speer, 2000; Zimmerman, 2000). However, context makes a difference: In one study, involvement in a community service experience led college students to increased feelings of political commitment but a *decreased* sense of political efficacy (Angelique et al., 2002). Perhaps these students discovered community and social forces that were not as changeable as they had originally expected.

Qualitative studies of community activists have found that long-term citizen participation was sustained by optimism: enjoyment of challenges, can-do spirit, and excitement about the work (Berkowitz, 1987; Colby & Damon, 1992). In these studies, experienced citizen activists also attributed setbacks to temporary or situational causes, not personal failures, and sought to learn from them. They celebrated successes, and they accepted adversity with humor. These optimistic ways of thinking seem related to personal efficacy beliefs about participation.

***Participatory Values and Commitment.*** Beliefs about efficacy are not enough to motivate citizen action. Participation is often initiated and sustained by commitment to deeply held values. Citizen action is also a fully embodied practice, with commitments often experienced emotionally, as work of the heart as well as the head (Langhout, 2015). Qualitative studies and other accounts have often found that commitment sustained citizen participation and empowerment (Berkowitz, 1987; Colby & Damon, 1992; Loeb, 1999; Moane, 2003; Nagler, 2001; Schorr, 1997). For some, this involved spiritual faith and practices; for others, it centered on a secular commitment to moral principles such as social justice and ensuring a future for our children and the larger planet (Angelique & Culley, 2014). Spiritual support for community involvement included a sense of innate value within everyone, a sense of "calling" to the work, and a certainty of the work's spiritual necessity. Beliefs that enabled taking risks included a certainty that "God will provide" and a "willing suspension of fear and doubt" as participants began new challenges. A capacity for forgiveness in the rough and tumble of community decision making was also important (Colby & Damon, 1992, pp. 78–80, 189–194, 296). Virginia Ramirez, who became a community organizer, and others in her church illustrate a spiritual basis for participatory commitment.

Moane's (2003) account of empowerment in the Irish women's liberation movement included building personal strengths in creativity and spirituality and having a larger, positive vision of liberation. Berkowitz (1987) found what he called "traditional virtue" among many local activists: caring for others, integrity, persistence, and commitment (p. 323). Colby and Damon (1992) found similar commitments to justice, harmony, honesty, and charity. Schorr's (1997) review of effective community organizations found that many of them promote a shared group climate based on spiritual or secular ideals that provide shared meaning and purpose related to community change.

***Relational Connections.*** Empowerment and citizen participation occur not in a social vacuum but rather in the context of interpersonal relationships and networks (Christens et al., 2014). They involve a wide variety of relational connections with others, including both bonding and bridging ties (Putnam, 2000; recall these from Chapter 6). They also include social support and mentoring for participation, neighboring, and participating in community organizations (Kieffer, 1984; Moane, 2003; Putnam & Feldstein, 2003; Speer & Hughey, 1995). Relational connections were essential for Virginia Ramirez, Alison Smith, and the Waupun youth in their development as citizen leaders. They had a strong sense that they could not have done the work without the support of others.

As a reminder, our list is merely suggestive; there is no single profile of empowered persons or citizen activists (Berkowitz, 2000; Zimmerman, 2000). Communities and settings also shape empowerment and citizen participation.

## Sense of Community and Citizen Participation in Neighborhood Organizations

Neighborhood organizations illustrate how grassroots citizen participation and empowerment intertwine with sense of community (see also Chapter 6). For instance, volunteer block associations offer many opportunities for participation in neighborhood decisions. (A "block" in this sense includes the two facing sides of a street, one block long.) Block associations address a variety of neighborhood issues such as zoning, housing, neighborhood appearance, crime, traffic, and recreation. They form mediating structures between individual residents and city governments. In studies in New York City, resident perceptions of problems on the block decreased over time on blocks with an association and increased on those without one (Wandersman & Florin, 2000).

Community psychologists have studied citizen participation in block associations and larger neighborhood organizations in several U.S. cities: Nashville, New York City, Baltimore, and Salt Lake City. Citizen participation is usually measured as a variable ranging from attending meetings, through increasing involvement in association tasks, to association leadership. Samples in all four cities were multiracial, multiethnic, and of lower to middle income (Chavis & Wandersman, 1990; Florin et al., 1992; Florin & Wandersman, 1984; D. D. Perkins & Long, 2002; D. D. Perkins et al., 1990, 1996; D. Unger & Wandersman, 1983, 1985; Wandersman & Florin, 2000).

In general, these studies demonstrated the interrelationships of five key factors: sense of community for the neighborhood; informal neighboring, such as talking with neighbors or watching someone's house while they are away; initial dissatisfaction with neighborhood problems; sense of collective efficacy regarding working through the neighborhood organization; and extent of citizen participation in neighborhood organizations.

These findings suggest a pathway of citizen participation similar to the findings of the developmental studies (Kieffer, 1984; N. A. Peterson & Reid, 2003; Watts et al., 2003) that we described earlier: embeddedness in a community, recognition of challenges there, a sense that these challenges can be addressed collectively, and a spiraling pattern of participation in a grassroots organization and strengthening sense of efficacy. While the process is often initiated by neighborhood problems, high levels of crime can inhibit participation (Saegert & Winkel, 2004). Longitudinal analyses of the New York City data indicated that participation led to increased feelings of efficacy (Chavis & Wandersman, 1990). More recent research has also connected sense of community, social capital, and participation in grassroots organizations (C. Collins et al., 2014). Of course, not every person, organization, or locality follows this pattern, but these factors are often involved.

These studies demonstrate that sense of community, neighboring, and citizen participation are resources for communities, even those with fewer material resources. These resources involve not simply individuals but individuals-in-communities.

## Empowering Practices and Settings

> When I returned to Atlanta [after long involvement in the civil rights movement and serving as ambassador to the United Nations], I wanted nothing to do with politics. Some of the women in Ebenezer Baptist Church wanted me to run for mayor. I was very reluctant, but one of them told me, "We need for you to do this. And we made you." I told her, "That's funny, I thought Martin [Luther King, Jr.] made me." "Oh, no" she replied. "We made him, too." (Andrew Young, speech to the Society for Community Research and Action, June 2001)

As this passage indicates, Ebenezer Baptist Church in Atlanta was a key setting in the civil rights movement (and, as its members hoped, Andrew Young did become mayor of Atlanta). To fully understand citizen participation and empowerment, we must learn more about how community settings like this one empower citizens and foster citizen participation. We must understand better the empowering practices that transform role relationships within settings (Rappaport, 1995) and the conditions that help change disempowering and nonempowering settings into empowering ones (Maton, 2008).

This section on empowering practices and settings is intended to provide tools for observing and for acting with others in your community. Remember that collaborative change agents may be found in a variety of roles, including students, teachers, grandparents, youth leaders, scientists, artists, and (insert *your* most challenging roles here!). We begin this section with a brief discussion of empowering practices and then provide a distinction between empowering and empowered settings, offer examples of empowering community practices and settings, and identify key features of these practices and settings. In Chapter 13, we turn to a discussion of how empowered community settings and organizations can influence their communities and societies.

**empowering practices**
collaborative efforts that lead to more empowering settings and organizations. Community psychologists focus on daily activities that maintain or change role relationships within in a community, focusing on how diverse experiences and strengths are developed and affirmed in everyday routines.

# Empowering Practices

How can you or I, as someone trying to work for change, engage in **empowering practices**, in which we collaborate with others to create more empowering settings and organizations? Community psychologists have sought to be facilitators who stay out of the spotlight in processes of organizational and community change. Yet this relative inattention to our role and how it is negotiated over time has often obscured how we do our work as researchers and practitioners. Leaders in the field have consistently argued that the "how" is often more important than the "what," and we are now beginning to articulate and fully value our work as practitioners. For example, D'Augelli (2006) examined his role as a community psychologist in empowering lesbian, gay, and bisexual people in a rural university community. He noted the challenge of organizing and gaining visibility when individuals had well-grounded fears about what would happen to them as they came together publicly and created new resources in the community. In examining successes over time, he found that those with more social power had to take the lead and take risks.

Several community psychologists are currently exploring the role of community psychologists in empowering practice. The first ever Summit on Community Psychology Practice was held in 2007; a new global community psychology practice journal was launched in 2009; and practitioners, researchers, and educators are working together to better articulate the theoretical and practical training needed to work as community psychologists in community settings (Christens et al., 2015; Faust et al., 2017; Francescato et al., 2007; Langhout, 2015; Meissen et al., 2008).

While it is important to examine our own role as collaborative change agents, a focus on empowering practices is more generally a concern with the routine activities that maintain or transform role relationships within settings. It is a concern with the way professional helpers and experts approach their work, as facilitators and partners (Gone, 2007, 2008) and as teachers and learners (Horton & Freire, 1990). It leads us to an examination of the opportunities for reciprocal helping, for mutual influence, for collaboration, for decision making, and for creating change. An emphasis on empowering practices focuses our attention on how diverse experiences, strengths, and capacities are developed and affirmed in routine dialogue and communication (Ullman & Townsend, 2008). In other words, we begin to look closely at how the relational context across multiple levels serves as a foundation for empowering settings (Christens, 2012; J. Neal, 2014). We turn now to further discussion of these empowering settings and illustrations.

# Empowering and Empowered Community Settings

Communities and community settings can be described as empowering or empowered (N. A. Peterson & Zimmerman, 2004; Zimmerman, 2000).

**empowering
settings**

settings that
encourage member
participation and
sharing of power in
group decisions and
actions.

**empowered
settings**

settings that utilize
power to influence
the macrosystem level
and impact broader
social and community
change.

**Empowering settings** foster member participation and sharing or power in group decisions and actions. They serve as viable and vital relational communities (Maton, 2008). **Empowered settings** exercise power in the wider community or society, influencing decisions and helping create community and macrosystem change.

Becoming an empowered setting or organization often requires creating empowering opportunities for members and citizens (B. McMillan et al., 1995). But being empowering and being empowered do not always go together. Organizations that exclude rank-and-file members from any real decision-making power may nonetheless be powerful forces in communities and societies. For instance, Putnam (2000) noted the rise in the United States of national advocacy organizations that rely on mail and online fundraising, use mass media and lobbying to exercise power, and lack active local chapters.

In addition, some organizations that empower their members choose not to seek wider influence. A mutual help group or spiritual setting, for instance, may empower its members to participate in decision making within the group. Yet many of these settings are not concerned with influencing communities or society. The individualistic focus of psychology, even sometimes in community psychology, has meant that until recently, the study of empowerment focused on individual processes of empowerment. Thus, when settings or organizations were considered, researchers attended to factors that were empowering for individuals, not how citizen organizations gained and exercised power in community or society (N. A. Peterson & Zimmerman, 2004; Riger, 1993). That focus is now broadening to study how empowered community settings wield wider influence (Maton, 2008). This is consistent with Rappaport's (1987) original emphasis on empowerment at multiple levels (Zimmerman, 2000).

Next, we turn to stories that illustrate empowering community practices and settings. As you read about Family Violence Coordinating Councils, the Highlander Research and Education Center, and the Riot Youth LGBTQ+ Theater Group, think about what makes them empowering to participants.

## Family Violence Coordinating Councils as Empowering Contexts

Coordinating councils bring together representatives from multiple stakeholder groups, including criminal justice, health, education, social services, and other community groups, to grow community awareness of how to combat intimate partner violence and support policies that increase the safety of survivors. For example, they may work to improve the accessibility of orders of protection, which are associated with declines in violence and survivors' reported fear of their partners. The councils engage in collaborative problem solving that leads to criminal justice system reform and greater long-term community health (N. E. Allen et al., 2013). For example, they may collectively engage in efforts to place advocates in the courthouse so that they are more accessible to survivors, create informational brochures that help survivors know what to expect in seeking an order of protection, or create specialized courts with judges who are familiar with intimate partner violence and resources for survivors. Councils work by empowering their members to act as change agents in the community (Javdani & Allen, 2011). Features of councils that are empowering have included effective leadership, a positive council climate featuring democratic participation, effective strategies for conflict resolution, and a sense of shared mission. Interestingly, councils are perceived by members as more empowering when members also perceive higher levels of support from their own home organizations.

## Highlander Research and Education Center: An Empowering Setting

Many are familiar with the story of Rosa Parks, who helped give birth to civil rights movements in the United States in the 1950s and 1960s. An African American woman, she refused to give up her seat on the bus to a White passenger, which was an act of civil disobedience during a time of legalized segregation and racial discrimination in the United States. Many of us are less familiar with the context of her action. Rosa Parks, along with Martin Luther King, Jr., and many other civil rights leaders, had received extensive training in democracy education and community organizing at the Highlander Folk School, now known as the Highlander Research and Education Center, in Tennessee. There, civil rights organizers also learned what have become well-known freedom songs, such as "We Shall Overcome," which was adapted by Highlander staff from an old African American hymn. The songs were then sung at rallies, at marches, and in jails across the South. They sustained and nurtured the nonviolent protestors who sang them; they also disconcerted those who used violence against them. Septima Clark, a civil rights organizer participating in a training session, recalled a raid by local police at Highlander. Blacks and Whites were watching a film together when the police burst in. According to Clark, one of the police

> jerked the plug out of the wall, while one of the teenagers made up a new verse to "We Shall Overcome." She started singing, and everyone followed: "We are not afraid, we are not afraid tonight." He say, "you can sing, but don't sing too loud." They had numbers of verses to it, and they sang them all. It made the police feel nervous. (S. Clark, 1986, p. 57)

Clark was arrested for violating segregation laws and spent the night in jail. She recalled,

> I had to sit up there, and the only thing I could think of was I'd sing, "Michael Row the Boat Ashore." We had a workshop and Harry Belafonte had been there, teaching us "Michael Row." So I just sat up there and sang that, until they came to get me out of that room. (p. 58)

At Highlander, Septima Clark and others also developed a successful strategy for voter education across the South. This strategy, known as Citizenship Schools, helped many African Americans learn to read so that they could pass the literacy tests required to become eligible voters in the South at the time. Originally founded in the 1930s to train labor organizers, Highlander continues to focus on democracy education and justice. Its current areas of focus are environmental justice in the Appalachian region and youth leadership development. Highlander uses an empowerment approach, believing that the answers to the problems facing society lie in ordinary people, like Septima Clark and Rosa Parks, coming together to share their experiences and learn from one another. Those shared experiences, as they say, "so often belittled and denigrated in our society," have grounded their empowering popular education and research practices and continue to drive social change.

### Riot Youth: An LGBTQ+ Theater Group

LGBTQ+ youth routinely experience bullying, discrimination, and hostile school environments. Gay–straight alliances (GSAs) have been one successful strategy to build safer school environments and empower youth, but less attention has been paid to other strategies outside of schools for supporting LGBTQ+ youth. Wernick and colleagues (2014) shared the story of a group called Riot Youth, made up of LGBTQ+ and allied youth who were based out of the Neutral Zone, a youth-driven teen center in Ann Arbor, Michigan. They

Empowering settings promote group solidarity, member participation, and collaboration.

iStock.com/FG Trade

established a theater group called Gayrilla Theater to share the results of a participatory action research project that investigated the climate for LGBTQ+ youth in local public high schools. They used scripted theater performances delivered to adult stakeholders and hosted question-and-answer sessions with adults who came to the performances (e.g., administrators, teachers, parents, health workers, elected officials). They also used theater games within the group to cultivate youth empowerment. In interviews and focus groups, the young people participating in Riot Youth shared their experiences of isolation and powerlessness before participation in the group. Storytelling in informal theater games with peers and in more structured, formal narrative performances allowed them to share their experiences and connect to a common struggle. The youth were recognized as experts in their own lives with important contributions to make and stories to tell. Individually, they developed the self-confidence and practical skills to advocate for themselves. Collectively, they developed leadership skills and cultivated their collective power to make changes in their schools as part of a larger advocacy campaign (Wernick et al., 2014).

## What Do You Think?

1. What do the Family Violence Coordinating Councils, the Highlander Research and Education Center, and the Riot Youth LGBTQ+ Theater Group have in common? What are the key differences?

2. Besides empowerment, what values of community psychology do these settings exhibit? How so?

3. Can you think of another community that would benefit from an empowering setting like the three examples just described? If you were to work with others to create an empowering setting within this community, how would it compare and contrast with those examples?

## Features of Empowering Practices and Settings

What qualities of community organizations empower their members? We have assembled nine key features of empowering practices and settings (listed in Exhibit 8.2). These were identified in case studies of community settings; personal accounts of community psychologists; and reviews of research on effective neighborhood organizations, community coalitions, and organizational empowerment (M. A. Bond, 1999; M. A. Bond & Keys, 1993; Christens et al., 2014, Foster-Fishman et al., 2001; Maton, 2008; N. A. Peterson & Zimmerman, 2004; Speer & Hughey, 1995; Wandersman & Florin, 2000; Wolff, 2001). Some factors first identified as important in community settings focused on personal development (Maton & Salem, 1995) also have proved to be important in settings concerned with citizen participation in community decisions. Our list is suggestive; others might choose a different list from the many important factors.

We suggest, as a study aid, organizing these nine factors into three groups: those primarily concerned with group solidarity, with member participation, and with diversity and collaboration (see Exhibit 8.2). Of course, these three functions overlap to some extent, and we encourage you to organize them in a way that makes sense to you.

***Promoting a Strengths-Based Belief System.*** Empowering community settings promote principles or beliefs that define member and organizational goals, provide meaning and inspiration for action, develop strengths, and promote optimism in the face of setbacks. Shared community events, rituals, and narratives embody core values and strengthen sense of community as well as personal commitment to the group. Highlander is founded on a clear set of strengths-based values, including a belief in democracy. Myles Horton (1990), one of the founders of Highlander, put it this way:

> If you believe in democracy, which I do, you have to believe that people have the capacity within themselves to develop the ability to govern themselves. You've got to believe in that potential, and to work as if it were true in the situation. (p. 131)

Another clearly articulated principle is that the key to change is found in everyday people's experiences. These shared experiences, as well as hopes

---

**Exhibit 8.2  Nine Features of Empowering Practices and Settings**

**Solidarity**

1. Promoting a strengths-based belief system
2. Fostering social support
3. Developing leadership

**Member Participation**

4. Providing participatory niches, opportunity role structures
5. Keeping a focus on tasks and goals
6. Making decisions inclusively
7. Rewarding participation

**Diversity and Collaboration**

8. Promoting diversity
9. Fostering intergroup collaboration

and dreams for a better future, are often given form at Highlander in story-telling, singing, and art making, as they take seriously the role of the arts in individual and social transformation (Greene, 1995; Sarason, 1990; Thomas & Rappaport, 1996; Thomas et al., 2015).

*Fostering Social Support.* Empowering settings attend to the quality and nature of interpersonal relationships in a setting and promote exchange of social support among members (L. D. Brown et al., 2008; Maton, 2008). Social support is key to the work of Riot Youth, where traditionally isolated youth share stories, learn from one another, and exchange information and resources (Wernick et al., 2014). A case study of effective faith-based community advocacy organizations found that one-to-one meetings among members helped build mutual support and identified issues for action (Speer et al., 1995). Social support and interpersonal ties among members also build organizational solidarity and power for influencing the wider community (Putnam & Feldstein, 2003; Speer & Hughey, 1995).

*Developing Leadership.* Empowering settings have committed leaders who articulate a vision for the organization, exemplify interpersonal and organizational skills, share power, and mentor new leaders (Maton, 2008; Maton & Salem, 1995). Sharing leadership and developing new leaders were also important in Riot Youth. Leadership development is central to the mission and work of Highlander, where individuals continue to develop organizational and leadership skills in civil rights as well as economic and environmental justice.

*Providing Participatory Niches, Opportunity Role Structures.* Empowering organizations create roles and tasks that offer opportunities for members to become involved and assume responsibility: participatory niches (Speer & Hughey, 1995) or opportunity role structures (Maton, 2008; Maton & Salem, 1995). Coordinating councils provide opportunities for individuals to act as change agents in their community. Often, empowering settings are also *underpopulated settings* that promote member participation (Barker, 1968; Schoggen, 1989; recall this concept from Chapter 5). Participatory niches promote recruitment and training of individuals for roles needed by the setting, increase members' leadership skills, and strengthen their interpersonal ties within the group.

Members bring diverse skills to a community organization: for example, assertion, emotional sensitivity, financial management, writing, planning events, securing volunteers, or remodeling dilapidated office space. Knowledge of cultures, languages, or community history may be useful. Social networks and connections, prestige or legitimacy as community leaders, and other social resources are important. An empowering organization has leaders and members who identify and engage such resources (Foster-Fishman et al., 2001; N. A. Peterson & Zimmerman, 2004).

In opportunity role structures, members also develop skills within an organization. Power comes not just from participation but also from opportunities to develop the necessary skills and competencies in order to be able to have real influence in settings. Youth participation in governance of nonprofit organizations and schools provides an illustration. Young people aging out of foster care in New Jersey, for example, participated in a youth advisory board in which they developed the skills to effect change in the state foster care system (Forenza, 2016).

S. D. Evans (2007) reflected that many young people are waiting to be invited to join as full and active community participants but need adults in schools and youth-based organizations to support and challenge them to do so. Educational research supports this view that youth engagement is fostered in authentic learning experiences and positive relationships. Students become engaged when asked to participate in meaningful and valuable activities (Rahm, 2002). Community-based service learning illustrates this type of student engagement in authentic learning practices, which allows students to take what they need to become competent in a particular skill or way of thinking (Seely Brown & Duguid, 1993). Experienced leaders and peers can serve as skilled partners who scaffold learning and development within an organization (Lave & Wenger, 1991). They can also act as guides who introduce and model new ideas to newer members.

***Keeping a Focus on Tasks and Goals.*** Many citizens prefer to become involved in community organizations that get things done, with clear goals and productive meetings (Wandersman & Florin, 2000). In addition, such organizational structure increases the capacity of the organization to make an impact in its community (N. E. Allen, 2005; Foster-Fishman et al., 2001). This includes having organizational goals and specific objectives for action, meeting agendas, time limits, and leaders who can summarize lengthy discussions and clarify choices to be made.

***Making Decisions Inclusively.*** This is the essence of citizen participation: widespread, genuine power and voice for citizens in making organizational decisions and plans. Community coalitions function best when decisions are inclusive (Foster-Fishman et al., 2001). The best predictor of effectiveness of an intimate partner violence council (as perceived by its members) was an inclusive climate of shared decision making, in which members from many community agencies and groups actively participated (N. E. Allen, 2005; Javdani & Allen, 2011).

***Rewarding Participation.*** Community groups rely on volunteers. If those volunteers do not find their involvement rewarding, or if the personal costs are too high, they will leave. If they find involvement rewarding, they will often become more involved. Empowering community settings provide rewards

**boundary spanning**
bridging mechanisms that connect different groups within an organization, foster the understanding of one another, and strengthen collaborative efforts.

for citizen participation that outweigh its costs (Prestby et al., 1990; see also Kaye, 2001; Kaye & Wolff, 1997). Lappe and DuBois (1994) found that rewards U.S. citizens obtained from community involvement included taking pride in accomplishment; discovering how much one has to contribute; working with those who share concerns and hopes; learning new skills; knowing efforts will help create a better world; and enjoying better communities, schools, jobs, housing, and medical care.

Barriers to participation include competing demands on time and energy, finding child care, feeling out of place, and unpleasant meetings (e.g., rambling discussions, unproductive conflict).

*Promoting Diversity.* Empowering community organizations value member diversity, which can broaden the skills, knowledge, resources, legitimacy, and social connections available to the setting. For community coalitions and other organizations that seek to represent multiple parts of a community, diversity is essential.

However, promoting diversity does not end with a diverse membership list. Often more difficult is the work of building an atmosphere of genuine inclusion of all viewpoints. When powerful community leaders or professionals (who are used to speaking out and being heeded) dominate discussion, the group must find ways to enable less powerful members to speak out, support each other, and influence decisions.

Promoting diverse participation includes having several members from a disenfranchised group, not just one token member. It also includes taking time to discuss issues of diversity and making organizational language inclusive (e.g. recognizing the presence of women or youth). Finally, diversity is not fully realized until the leadership, not simply the membership, is diverse (Foster-Fishman et al., 2001; Goodkind & Foster-Fishman, 2002). In nonprofit and educational settings, for example, this means that teachers, case managers, and administrators reflect the diversity of participants.

*Fostering Intergroup Collaboration.* Promoting diversity can generate challenges for a setting. Community members share an overall sense of community but also have identifications with other groups within or outside the community (Wiesenfeld, 1996). This also is true of organizations. Diversity multiplies the number and types of groups to which individuals in an organization feel committed; this is often valuable for organizational learning, growth, and adaptation to changes in the environment. But a viable setting also needs commitment to the organization itself. Thus, the challenge may be framed as developing *bonding* ties while also promoting *bridging* ties (Putnam, 2000; recall this from Chapter 6). The concept of bridging mechanisms, or **boundary spanning**, as it is understood in organizational psychology (D. Katz & Kahn, 1978), refers to relationships that connect groups within an organization, helping each understand the other and building capacity for collaboration. Boundary spanning is critical to the work of coordinating councils for intimate partner violence and other community coalitions.

Organizations also need to develop practices and member skills in identifying, discussing, managing, and resolving conflicts (Chavis, 2001; Foster-Fishman et al., 2001). This was a key element to an empowering climate for coordinating councils. An important skill is recognizing when systems of oppression are involved, not simply interpersonal styles. Conflict often is a useful resource: for learning about problems and for creative ideas for action. It is often helpful to reframe conflicts as shared problems, not simply blame others, and to search for shared values or goals based on the organization's belief system.

## Conclusion

Understanding and promoting citizen participation and empowerment is challenging. Verbal commitment to the principle of empowerment does not guarantee active individual or organizational commitment to empowering practices. Across a variety of employment, educational, and health care settings, disparities exist between organizational ideals and routine ways of accomplishing tasks and meeting goals (Gruber & Trickett, 1987).

Further, citizen participation and empowerment are realized differently among diverse contexts and communities. Professional helpers and experts cannot assume that good intentions or well-designed programs will empower others. In making these assumptions, we more likely resemble the person wasting their time with their offers to help. Instead, as Lilla Watson suggests in the opening quote, we may walk with others as facilitators and partners, teachers and learners in a process of reciprocal helping, collaboration, and community change. These processes are not simple.

## For Review

### Discussion Questions

**1.** Return to the quotes at the beginning of the chapter. How has your understanding of these quotes changed after engaging with the concept of empowerment from a community psychology perspective?

**2.** What are the challenges you would anticipate in a professional helping role, for example, as a teacher, social worker, nurse, or doctor, in adopting an empowerment approach in your work?

**3.** How might you apply what you have learned about empowerment and citizen participation in your own life? Are there settings in which you could engage in empowering practices and develop your participatory and leadership skills?

## Key Terms

empowerment, 259
citizen participation, 261
tokenism, 263
participatory practices, 263
power over, 266
power to, 267
power from, 267

integrative power, 268
three instruments of social power, 269
expert power, 271
power of "spin", 272
critical awareness, 277
participatory skills, 278

sense of collective efficacy, 279
sense of personal participatory efficacy, 279
empowering practices, 283
empowering settings, 284
empowered settings, 284
boundary spanning, 291

## Learn More

A detailed summary of the chapter, along with other review materials, is available on the *Community Psychology, Fourth Edition* companion website at http://pubs.apa.org/books/supp/kloos4/.

Natural disasters like Hurricane María represent major stressors for individuals and communities, particularly for marginalized communities who do not receive adequate assistance.

JEAN-FRANCOIS Manuel/Shutterstock.com

# 9 Understanding Stress and Coping in Context

## Looking Ahead III➡

After reading this chapter you will be able to answer these questions:

1. What are risk and protective factors, and how do they relate to stress?

2. What are the advantages of an ecological model of stress and coping over traditional models?

3. What is coping, and how can our understanding of coping inform the development of interventions?

4. What are the different forms of social support, and how are they helpful?

## Opening Exercise

## When a Natural Disaster Becomes a Humanitarian Crisis

In September 2017, Hurricane María devastated Puerto Rico. It was the strongest, costliest, and deadliest hurricane in the island's history. María claimed the lives of over 2,900 people and resulted in damages in excess of $91 billion. The hurricane system was so big that it wrought destruction and fatalities in several Caribbean islands, including Dominica, the Dominican Republic, Guadeloupe, Haiti, and the U.S. Virgin Islands, and extended into the U.S. state of North Carolina. While the impact of the storm was wrenching across these areas, the scale and scope of the destruction and disruptions in Puerto Rico were especially overwhelming. The aftermath of this natural disaster became a humanitarian crisis that is still ongoing and negatively affecting the health and well-being of most of the citizens of Puerto Rico. Many people were left without water, food, electricity, and shelter. Hospital systems did not have power or water and were overwhelmed with need. Schools were closed for several months. Many roads were impassable even after some government aid became available. Food and first aid could not be easily distributed, and phone and media networks were largely offline. It is not surprising that many people developed symptoms of depression, anxiety, and posttraumatic stress disorder. And those that already had health problems had them exacerbated.

This humanitarian crisis was compounded by several factors. First, the local government's capacity to respond to a natural disaster was insufficient and further diminished because the island was recovering from the effects of Hurricane Irma, which had struck two weeks prior. María was a much bigger storm and overwhelmed much of the infrastructure needed to sustain well-being and respond to disasters. The federal government's response was tardy and inadequate. The Puerto Rico Electric Power Authority (PREPA) was managing an already susceptible power grid because of the agency's mounting debt, budget and workforce cuts, aging power plants, and inadequate safety systems. This made it possible for María to effectively destroy the power grid, leaving approximately 95% of the island without electricity. It took PREPA nearly 1 year to restore electricity throughout the island. The island's water system was similarly vulnerable. According to the National Resource Defense Council, 70% of the island had water that did not meet the minimum standards of the Safe Drinking Water Act. As a result, 2 weeks after the hurricane, nearly half of the population was without clean water.

The challenges Puerto Rico faced in the aftermath of Hurricane María were not solely or simply due to issues of local mismanagement or political corruption, as some have claimed. There has been a long history of mainland U.S. federal policies that have stunted Puerto Rico's economic development. Perhaps the clearest evidence of this is the federal government's longstanding reluctance to provide debt

relief to Puerto Rico and support its efforts to address infrastructure development. Austerity measures meant to contain debt effectively hindered efforts to upgrade the island infrastructure. It has been debated to what extent such policies may be due to racist stereotypes and colonial attitudes toward a territory that uses Spanish as a first language. Although Congress appropriated at least $136.1 billion in disaster relief funds, only a fraction of that amount has been disbursed by 2020. Much of the recovery aid has gone to outside contractors who had been given federal contracts. One estimate suggested that only 20% of federal funds released has actually contributed to the local economy. Residents have seen failures at all levels of government and systems meant to prevent problems and provide care.

While many factors have hampered Puerto Rico's recovery, there have been some that have helped it. After María struck the island, residents immediately began to work together to clear roads of debris and fallen trees. In addition, when emergency aid to the island was delayed, local residents formed brigades to deliver food and water to inaccessible and remote parts of the island. Community organizations on and off the island brought generators and solar panels to businesses, homes, and schools. Puerto Ricans on the U.S. mainland raised money to assist in the recovery effort. Puerto Ricans have also demanded a say from the local government in how disaster relief funds are used. From ordinary citizens to urban planners, nonprofit leaders, and community organizers, Puerto Ricans have sought to inform the government's long-term economic and disaster recovery plan. Though the road to recovery may be long, Puerto Ricans have begun to mobilize their resources and talents to help begin the process of rebuilding their lives and society.

**What Do You Think?**

1. What makes natural disasters like Hurricane María particularly stressful? Can some of these stressors be prevented?

2. What makes someone vulnerable to developing health problems after a natural disaster?

3. How would you cope in a situation like the one described above?

4. How do natural disasters become humanitarian crises and community calamities?

5. What are some things that can reduce the negative impact of these events?

# Stress and Coping: An Ecological-Contextual Model

This chapter marks a transition point in the book. In our examples and discussion, we begin to apply the conceptual tools of community psychology that were introduced in the previous eight chapters to the prevention of life problems and the promotion of well-being. This chapter introduces a few more critical ways of thinking about how interventions might be developed and then presents examples of how they can be applied. In particular, we (a) discuss choices in when, how, and where to intervene and (b) expand the kinds of outcomes we might want to promote to go beyond a traditional focus of avoiding illness and harm to promoting resilience and well-being. This chapter prepares you to make choices in the models of intervention that are presented in Chapters 10–13. As discussed in Chapters 1 and 2, how a problem is defined will guide how you choose the best approach to change.

A community psychology view of stress and coping emphasizes how persons are embedded in multiple contexts. We show in this chapter how community psychology can intersect and complement counseling and clinical psychology approaches to create a more comprehensive approach to health care and promotion of well-being. We focus on contextual and community processes in coping with stressors; details of individual-level cognitive and emotional coping processes are well presented in more individually oriented textbooks and resources (e.g., Nevid & Rathus, 2016; Straub, 2019). However, it is important to note that we believe that both community-contextual and clinical-individual perspectives are needed for understanding the dynamic experiences and outcomes of stress and coping. In responding to stressful situations, individual and contextual processes are intertwined.

To help introduce community psychology ways of thinking about intervention, Figure 9.1 illustrates the conceptual model of this chapter. It identifies key processes and outcomes, relationships among them, and choice points for constructive interventions. It is based on work of Barbara Dohrenwend, Rudolf Moos, and Abraham Wandersman and associates (Dohrenwend, 1978;

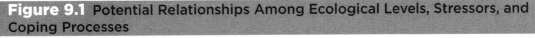

**Figure 9.1** Potential Relationships Among Ecological Levels, Stressors, and Coping Processes

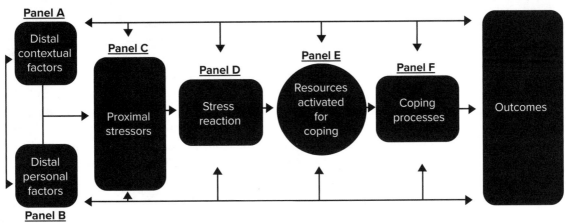

Moos, 2002; Wandersman, Morsbach, et al., 2002). We present the model to stimulate your own thinking about the contexts of stress and coping processes involved in responding to life's challenges. Each shape in the model represents a different possibility for addressing stressors or promoting better coping. The arrows of the model suggest connections between different components. To keep the model from becoming too complex, we use single lines to note theoretical connections; in predictive statistical models, we would need to use more arrows to represent multiple processes involved in contextual influences on stress and coping. Thus, the figure is best used as a starting point for thinking about stressors, coping, and outcomes in a more ecological and contextual way.

In this chapter, we draw case examples from our research and intervention work related to discrimination, homelessness, and natural disasters. However, this model can be a useful way of thinking about how people respond to a wide range of stressors and stressful situations. Stress and coping play out differently in different contexts and for different persons. Contextual factors in responding to stressors are part of a dynamic process that can influence how stress is experienced, which resources are available, which resources are used, and which outcomes become the focus of coping efforts.

## Risk and Protective Factors

In applying our ecological model to stress and coping, we distinguish between *risk factors* that are correlated with problem outcomes and *protective factors* that are associated with avoiding problems or promoting well-being (you may remember that we also used this distinction in Chapter 5 in discussing links between neighborhoods and individual and collective well-being). We also use our ecological model represented in Figure 9.1 to conceptualize how risk and protective factors can exist at multiple levels of analysis, from individual qualities to macrosystem forces.

Risk factors are characteristics of individuals and situations that are thought to increase the likelihood that a person will experience problematic outcomes, like personal distress, mental disorders, or behavior problems. For example, children who have a parent with a chronic illness could have multiple factors that put them at increased risk for developing their own problems. The ill parent may be unable to help the children with schoolwork, take the children to friends' houses, or go to school for activities or programs. The children may also receive less attention from a second parent who needs to attend to the sick parent's care and to work to cover the family's costs. Neither parent may be able to maintain regular contact with their children's teachers. The children's reactions may range from disappointment to frustration to anger and behavior problems. The children's learning and academic outcomes may suffer. Furthermore, the illness may affect the family's income and health care expenses. Older children may worry about their genetic vulnerability for contracting a similar illness. Thus, a parent's illness, although only one of many factors in the family's life, may be related to academic or social problems for the children and to the family's economic and social well-being. Each of these factors may contribute to the development of specific risk processes that can be the focus of an intervention.

An accumulation of risk factors can create situations that make people vulnerable for developing problematic outcomes. In the example discussed, if a parent's chronic illness leads to decreased support from parents, reduced income, and more distress in the family, it is not hard to imagine how this may make it hard for children to do well at school and how it may affect their coping. Of course, not all children whose parents have a chronic illness will develop mental health or academic problems. Risk factors do not always lead to problematic situations. The same risk factors may affect children in each family differently, depending on their development, access to support outside their family, or relationships with peers. For some, recognizing the risks may activate coping. For others, the accumulation of risk may be overwhelming and create feelings of helplessness. Thus, exposure to risk factors is not the whole story about stress and coping.

Protective factors, in contrast, provide resources for coping and often represent strengths of persons, families, and communities. An ecological approach to coping looks for potential strengths at different levels of analysis that can buffer people from stressors rather than focusing only on potential risks. Protective factors may include *personal qualities* such as a parent's optimism or spirituality; *interpersonal resources* such as friends who offer to help; *community resources* such as support from religious congregations, school programs, or recreational opportunities; and *macrosystem resources* such as access to affordable health care, child care, or home nursing. The availability of such protective factors can nurture protective processes whereby people use the resources to buffer the impact of stressors they encounter. As presented in Chapter 6, a positive sense of community and social capital in neighborhoods and organizations can be protective factors for coping with stressful situations.

In our example of a family with a parent who has a chronic illness, suppose this family had several caring relatives or friends who were available to help the family and encourage the children. Add a caring school environment and a teacher who realizes these children need some special help. Furthermore, a worksite with policies of flexible hours and livable wages for the healthy parent could reduce economic hardship. At a macrolevel, access to affordable health insurance and family leave legislation can protect the family's financial situation while they are coping with medical emergencies. With these protective influences, the risk of negative outcomes for these children may be significantly reduced.

Building capacity for protective processes and strengths can be a primary focus of intervention efforts themselves. For instance, adolescents "at risk" for having academic problems often thrive as their personal strengths are identified, enhanced, valued, and linked to areas of difficulty (DuBois, 2017). Community psychology has a long-standing interest in focusing on strengths of individuals and settings that can develop those strengths (Cowen & Kilmer, 2002; J. G. Kelly, 1970b; Rappaport et al., 1975). In community psychology, strengths are defined at multiple ecological levels beyond the individual, including those of cultural traditions, neighborhoods, organizations, and friendship networks (D. D. Perkins et al., 2004). In addition, community and preventive interventions bolster abilities in social and emotional competencies (e.g., DuBois, 2017; Shinn & Yoshikawa, 2008), particularly for those who have experienced social disadvantage. From a community psychology perspective, protective factors need to be conceptualized within an ecological model in which cultural traditions can be a protective resource (e.g., Hartmann et al., 2019; Wexler et al., 2013). This can help us achieve a more complete understanding of how strengths of persons and communities can affect stress and coping outcomes.

***How Can Knowledge About Risk and Protective Factors Be Useful for Interventions?*** Within this ecological model, interventions may be designed (a) to reduce exposure to risk factors, (b) to enhance protective factors and experiences, or (c) to combine both strategies. Putting risks or strengths into context requires having a theory for how these factors may contribute to processes that can affect a person's life. It is not enough to note a statistical probability of increased vulnerability or protection. An intervention needs to have a plan for when, where, how, and with whom to intervene. These theories can

**distal factors**
factors that contribute to the probability of a problem or that protect against a problem but are not directly visible or obvious; these factors are more "distant" from an individual.

be tested, researched, and refined for interventions rather than simply identifying a greater or less likelihood of having problems.

## Distal and Proximal Factors

We begin explaining the theory behind Figure 9.1 by observing that factors affecting stress include those that put people at greater risk for having a problem and those that could serve to protect people from developing a problem. Furthermore, risk and protective factors can be proximal to our lived experience and our awareness, or they may be perceived to be more removed or distal to a person's experience. We will use our ecological levels of analysis framework to think about how factors at different levels might increase risk for or protection from the development of problems.

**Distal factors** are contributors to or buffers against a problem that may not be readily observable or obvious. In one way they are more distant from the expression of a problem; however, like roots on a plant, they can be very much connected to the development of a problem even though they are not readily visible. Distal factors are *not* direct triggers of a problem but are better thought of as (a) vulnerabilities that increase the likelihood of a problem developing or (b) buffers that decrease the likelihood. For example, an economic recession is a distal factor (*macrolevel*) that may reduce financial resources for employers (*organizational level*). In turn, these organizations lay off employees, directly affecting how their families cope (*microlevel*). With this increased stress, problematic individual outcomes such as increased substance abuse or developing depression may occur (*individual level*). While distal factors are more distant from an individual when explaining a problem, they are never conceptually far away from a potential impact on an individual, using the linkages across multiple ecological levels. As we have argued in earlier chapters, a complete conceptualization of the development of a problem needs to include distal levels of analysis as well as individuals and small groups.

Distal factors can also be *personal*, that is, located within the person but not readily observable. A common example is a having a genetic vulnerability to disease. Without testing, the reality of genetic vulnerability is distant from our understanding of why someone has problems, but this reality has very immediate effects. This personal distal risk factor may make one more vulnerable to a problem but, by itself, would not result in the development of a problem. Combined with other distal factors (e.g., losing a job), stress may trigger a process whereby the vulnerability would be expressed as illness. Many distal, predisposing factors for health conditions include these kinds of personal vulnerabilities. Figure 9.1 encourages us to use an ecological levels of analysis framework to consider both contextual and personal distal factors of a problem.

As stated above, distal factors can involve risk or protection. This theory would also expect distal protective factors to be present in most people's lives.

**proximal factors**
factors that directly contribute to a problem or the buffering against a problem; these factors are "closer" to the individual, with the individual usually being more aware of their link to the development or prevention of a problem.

At a macrosystem level, cultures, for instance, can influence us in ways that may be risky (e.g., expectations for thinness that can lead to eating disorders) or protective (e.g., belief systems that might help us cope with loss of a loved one). While we are all embedded in culture, we are not always aware of how it shapes our experience. On an individual level, a person may have personal traits that increase risk of stress (e.g., anxiousness) or strengths that promote hardiness to stressful circumstances.

**Proximal factors** can also confer risk or protection and are closer to the individual. That is, people are usually aware of their link to the development or avoidance of a problem. Within our ecological levels of analysis framework, proximal factors are most often classified as being at an individual, interpersonal, or small group level of analysis. Proximal factors are often thought of as directly contributing to a problem or providing a resource that can be directly used for coping. In Figure 9.1, *proximal stressors* trigger a challenge or a problem that requires coping responses. Examples include a recent conflict with someone or losing your job. In Figure 9.1, *resources activated for coping* are proximal if the person turns directly to these for help in coping, such as seeking social support from friends.

**What Do You Think?**

1. Which distal factors act as protective factors for your well-being?
2. Which distal factors could be risk factors?
3. Did you list more risk or more protective factors? If you listed one type of factor more than the other, why do you think that is?
4. How are these distal factors linked to your proximal stressors?

**distal contextual factors**
ongoing societal or community conditions, including cultural beliefs and traditions, that can interact in various domains of life. They can promote strength and resilience, but they can also create stressors.

## Working Through the Ecological-Contextual Model

To help explain our ecological framework of stress and coping, we will take apart the model we presented earlier and build it up piece by piece. In Figure 9.2, Panels A and B depict the distinct yet interrelated influences of distal contextual and personal factors.

*Distal Contextual Factors.* **Distal contextual factors** include ongoing conditions at a societal or community level of analysis that may interact in various life domains. Cultural traditions, beliefs, practices or rituals, and institutions can provide meaning and strength in difficult times. Yet they also can create stressors, for instance, in the ways that many cultures' views about gender roles foster unequal workloads and limit opportunities for women. In a multicultural society, cultural influences include those from a dominant culture as well as those of other cultures. For example, immigrants often need

**Figure 9.2** Distal and Proximal Factors Contributing to Stress Reactions

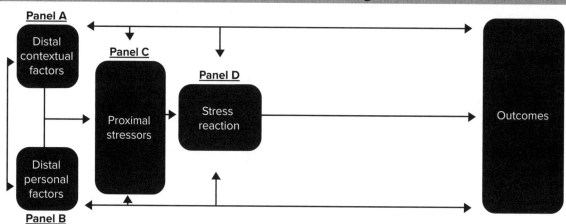

to negotiate cultural expectations from both their culture of origin and where they live currently. Economic conditions at multiple levels, from global to local, also introduce both stressors and opportunities. Social and political forces affect individuals, for instance, in the form of discrimination or through policies that limit it. An ongoing environmental hazard, such as toxic waste near a community, poses both biological and psychological risks. As we discussed in Chapters 5 and 6, neighborhood processes such as violence, sense of community, or informal neighboring can influence individual well-being. Finally, the dynamics of family life and of interpersonal relationships provide both stressors and resources for individuals.

Distal contextual risk factors tend to be chronic stressors that involve long-term processes that can affect access to resources and cause accumulation of disadvantage over years and decades (Shinn & McCormack, 2017). In the opening exercise, the U.S. policies that hampered economic growth and development in Puerto Rico, the local government corruption, and the inadequate infrastructure were distal contextual risk factors that increased the likelihood of a humanitarian crisis in the aftermath of Hurricane María. Other general examples of distal contextual risk factors include poverty, racism, stigma, environmental pollution, noise, crowding, neighborhood crime, and lack of health care (Dupéré & Perkins, 2007; G. W. Evans, 2004; Rasmussen et al., 2004; H. Turner, 2007). Poverty, viewed as a prolonged and persistent situation of low resources to meet needs, is often understood among many developmental psychologists as the biggest risk factor for problematic outcomes (Leventhal et al., 2005). (Note that within our model, income problems due to a sudden job loss would be labeled a proximal stressor.) The effects of chronic environmental conditions may be cumulative, such as the combined effects of poverty, crowding, and a chronic illness. Ongoing family conditions,

**distal personal factors**
aspects of an individual that are generally not observable, such as biological factors, personality traits, thought patterns, and personal life experiences.

**proximal stressors**
situations or events that characterize a threatened or actual loss of resources; they can differ in duration, severity, quantity, personal meaning and impact.

such as parental alcoholism or chronic illness, may be both chronic stressors for the affected family member and contextual factors for the children in such families that increase their risk of dysfunction (Barrera et al., 1995; Ozer & Russo, 2017).

## Distal Personal Factors

**Distal personal factors** are aspects of an individual that are generally not readily observable. They may include genetic and other biological factors; personality traits such as shyness, optimism, or extraversion; learned cognitive patterns such as attributions about the source of problems; and continuing effects of prior life experiences such as child maltreatment. As with contextual factors, distal personal factors may act as stressors or resources and play a risk or protective role. Dispositional optimism, for example, promotes a positive appraisal of stressors and effective coping (Connor-Smith & Flachsbart, 2007; Scheier et al., 2001). Since these personal factors are well covered in other sources about stress and coping, we do not review them in detail here. Our emphasis is on the contextual factors that have received less attention in stress and coping research (Dohrenwend, 1978).

We should note that the boundary between contextual and personal factors is permeable and fluid. A chronic illness, for example, is not only a personal issue. The personal impact of the illness is influenced by sociocultural interpretations of the illness, how disabling it is considered to be, and how individuals with that illness are expected to behave. Although family dynamics are contextual, they interact closely with a wide range of personal factors. The important point about this model is that we need to look at both contextual and personal factors in understanding the effects of stress and coping. See Exhibit 9.1 for illustrative examples of distal factors.

Distinguishing between distal contextual and distal personal factors helps in designing interventions. Interventions to reduce the prevalence of bulimia nervosa, for instance, might focus on distal contextual factors such as mass media depictions of excessive thinness as always desirable for women, or they might use university-level social marketing approaches (e.g., a public service advertising campaign in dorms and student organizations) to educate students about the risks of chronic, stringent dieting. Individual interventions could focus on reducing personal risk factors, including individual eating practices and body image.

## Proximal Stressors

Panel C in Figure 9.2 represents **proximal stressors**, events or situations that represent a threatened or actual loss of resources (Hobfoll, 1998; Lazarus & Folkman, 1984). They are risk factors that vary in duration, severity, quantity, personal meaning, and impact. In addition, the boundary between proximal

**Exhibit 9.1 Examples of Distal Factors in Coping**

**Contextual**

- Cultural traditions, practices
- Economic conditions
- Social, political forces
- Environmental hazards
- Neighborhood processes
- Setting social climates
- Social regularities
- Family dynamics

**Personal**

- Biological, genetic factors
- Personal temperaments, traits
- Patterns of thinking
- Chronic illness or similar conditions
- Ongoing effects of prior life experiences

**major life events**
events that are stressful and demand sizable kinds of change; examples include marriage and the birth of a child ("entrances") or the death of a loved one, divorce, or unemployment ("exits").

stressors and distal chronic stressors is not always simple. For instance, traumatic events such as an assault or combat may evoke distress for years following the incident. We present here six types of proximal stressors to illustrate our framework, recognizing that these categories overlap to some extent and other useful categories exist:

- major life events
- life transitions
- daily hassles
- disasters
- minority-related and acculturative stressors
- vicious spirals

In our model, potential stressors are first presented as antecedents, before appraisal and coping. However, stressors and coping responses shape each other to some extent (see feedback arrows in Figure 9.1). For instance, binge drinking to deal with a stressful situation can create additional stressors at work and in personal relationships.

***Major Life Events.*** Holmes and Rahe (1967) pioneered the study of the impact of **major life events**. Their Social Readjustment Rating Scale is a standardized list of stressful life events such as grieving, divorce, and job loss. Each event is assigned, based on empirical studies, a point value to estimate the amount of change or adjustment it requires of the individual. The sum of these points has been used to represent an individual's degree of exposure to stress. Similar to estimating how much stress a bridge can bear and not collapse, this approach to understanding proximal stressors expects that an

**life transitions**

transitions that present challenges for coping as part of regular human development; these transitions can include the need to adapt to change, aquire new skills, and adopt new roles.

accumulation of stressful events will likely lead to the development of psychological problems.

Correlations of life-events scores and outcomes have been relatively modest, accounting for only 9%–10% of the variance (i.e., only 10% of negative outcomes are associated with major life events; Hobfoll & Vaux, 1993; Zautra & Bachrach, 2000). Community psychology research has shown a number of shortcomings of the original life-events approach and potential advantages of refinements (Sandler et al., 2000). While stressors are defined as events requiring adaptive change, there are differences in the kinds of change that they demand. Life-events lists typically include both "entrances," such as marriage or the birth of a child, which are usually seen positively, and "exits," such as death of a loved one or unemployment. Studies indicate that exits tend to have a stronger association with psychological distress and illness than entrances (Thoits, 1983; Vinokur & Selzer, 1975). Furthermore, standardized lists of life events are not sensitive to the cultural and personal meaning of those events to the individual (Green et al., 2006; Mirowsky & Ross, 1989). Divorce, for example, is given a single score, regardless of its cultural acceptability or the variability of its impact. Finally, uncontrollable and unpredictable events (e.g., a major car accident) have been found to be particularly stressful, yet these dimensions are not measured by most life-events scales (Thoits, 1983). Continuing community psychology research will help us understand how variation in major life event stressors can lead to different outcomes.

*Life Transitions.* Within a stress and coping model, **life transitions** are expected to present challenges for coping. These transitions produce enduring changes in a person's life context, requiring the learning of new skills or assumption of new roles. Life transitions occur as part of regular human development (e.g., becoming an adolescent, an adult, or a senior) and as part of life circumstances (e.g., taking a job with new responsibilities, becoming a parent). Recall the transition for you when you entered college or graduate school. What challenges did that life transition present to you? Perhaps you had to expand your academic, time-management, or decision-making skills. Perhaps your network of friends or your relationships with loved ones changed. Did the transition lead to new insights about yourself or new insights about others? The effects of a life transition are contextual. Each transition requires its own combination of coping skills; each has its own cultural-social meaning (e.g., attitudes about divorce), and persons bring different personal and social resources to the transition.

Some community psychologists focus on understanding regular life transitions as a point of intervention to promote healthy development of children. Transitions from elementary to middle and high school can be stressful, especially in large school systems that diminish individual contacts between students and staff. Seidman and associates studied multiracial samples of

**daily hassles**
everyday challenges on a short-term, smaller scale than major life events. Examples include traffic, family arguments, and workplace conflicts.

**daily uplifts**
everyday mood-lifters on a short-term, smaller scale than major life events. Examples include an act of kindness from a coworker or a phone call from a loved one.

**microaggressions**
commonplace actions or incidents of indirect, subtle, or unintentional discrimination toward a member of a marginalized group. These are experienced as slights, insults, or demeaning incidents.

low-income adolescents in New York City; Baltimore; and Washington, DC. After the transition to junior high school, students' grades, preparation for school, involvement in school activities, social support from school staff, and self-esteem all dropped. Engagement with peers increased, but this was not necessarily constructive, because students reported that peers' values were becoming more antisocial (E. Seidman et al., 1994). At the transition to high school, similar but less negative effects occurred (E. Seidman et al., 1996). Similar effects occurred among low-income, mainly Hispanic students in Chicago, where students moved directly from elementary school to high school. Decreases occurred in students' grades; attendance; and perceptions of support from family, peers, and school staff (Gillock & Reyes, 1996). Declines in academic engagement are especially serious given the developmental importance of the early adolescent years (E. Seidman et al., 2004). These studies document a loss of resources for many youth. Social support from adults, especially at school, decreases.

*Daily Hassles.* A third strategy for documenting proximal stressors is to focus on challenges encountered in everyday experience, or **daily hassles**. In contrast to a major life events approach, the study of daily hassles and uplifts applies the life-events approach to short-term, smaller scale events (Kanner et al., 1981; Kilmer et al., 1998). Examples of daily hassles include family arguments, traffic jams, and conflicts at work. Consistent with a community psychology approach that examines potential risks and protective processes, the approach of Kanner and colleagues also includes measurement of daily uplifts. **Daily uplifts** are the small, commonplace, mood-lifting things that can occur day to day, such as the kind gesture of a coworker or a phone call from a friend.

Psychological research on racism shows how a distal contextual condition may create multiple specific proximal stressors. Harrell (2000) studied racism-related stress among a multiracial sample of U.S. students and African American community members. They measured a variety of stressors. Specific racism-related life events, such as being harassed by police or being unfairly rejected for a loan, were infrequent but stressful. While major life events related to discrimination are certainly stressful, research has documented the cost of "low-level" hassles related to racism and discrimination. **Microaggressions** are similar to daily hassles but are focused on the daily hassles resulting from discrimination toward minorities based on their race, gender, or sexual orientation (Sue, 2010). Racial microaggressions have been defined as "brief and commonplace daily verbal, behavioral, or environmental indignities, whether intentional or unintentional, that communicate hostile, derogatory, or negative racial slights and insults toward people of color" (Sue et al., 2007, p. 271). This research also emphasizes how it is stressful to witness racism that is targeted toward others in one's group, such as regularly encountering low expectations for youth of color, community violence, and chronic inequalities of

**disasters**

a form of proximal stressor, these are extremely disruptive events that affect entire communities, regions, or nations. They include natural disasters, technological disasters, and mass violence.

**minority-related and acculturative stressors**

stressful events or circumstances due to the experience of being a member of a group that is marginalized in society.

income and material resources. Symptoms of depression, anxiety, and psychological trauma were correlated with each type of stressor, especially with daily microaggressions (Harrell, 2000; Prelow et al., 2004; Sue, 2010). Responses to microaggressions might include efforts to change distal contextual influences through antiracist social action or efforts to change proximal factors through personal relationships and organizational practices. Sue and colleagues (2019) proposed a strategy of *microinterventions* that spans levels of analysis to make racist events visible, to engage allies to mitigate the harm of the microaggressions, to educate those committing or allowing these events, and to encourage support for the persons experiencing the microaggressions.

*Disasters.* These proximal stressors are regularly examined by community psychologists. **Disasters** affect entire communities, regions, or nations. They include *natural disasters* such as hurricanes and floods (e.g., Hurricane María in the opening exercise), *technological disasters* such as an accident at a nuclear power plant, and *mass violence* such as terrorism and war (Norris et al., 2002, 2008). Reviewing 160 empirical studies involving 60,000 disaster victims, Norris and her colleagues found that the meaning of a disaster makes a difference: Mass violence had more damaging psychological consequences than natural or technological disasters. Moreover, prior social context makes a difference: Negative effects of disasters were usually stronger among children, women, ethnic minorities, and people in developing rather than developed nations. Those exposed to more severe situations, those who had more prior problems, and those with fewer resources reported greater problems.

Furthermore, Norris and colleagues (2002, 2008) found that in any disaster, problems are intertwined and tend to cluster together. Those who report mental health problems tend to also have problems related to physical health, family distress, fragmented social networks, property loss, and dislocation. How does this clustering of risk factors happen? We suggest that an ecological view is needed to understand such accumulation of risk factors and processes as well as potential points of intervention to promote healthy coping.

*Minority-Related and Acculturative Stressors.* The experience of being a member of a group that is marginalized in society is a unique type of stressor that can affect one's health and well-being (R. Clark et al., 1999; Harrell, 2000). These **minority-related and acculturative stressors** can be a frequent or even daily occurrence. Recall our discussion of microaggressions as a daily hassle. Someone may live in an area or work at a job where they are constantly the target of racism, sexism, or religious bigotry. Research suggests that the more one perceives discrimination against themselves or others from their group, the more likely they are to report poorer physical and mental health (Pascoe & Smart Richman, 2009; Pieterse et al., 2012).

Racism scholarship by James Jones (1972), Shawn Utsey and Joseph Ponterotto (1996), and Shelly Harrell (2000) suggests that minority-related

**vicious spirals**

when the loss of one resource leads to additional losses; a downward pattern of many stressors that then multiply the effects of risk factors. They are especially common for those who have few resources to begin with.

stressors can be distinguished by the ecological level at which they occur. Institutional minority-related stressors are systems, policies, and practices that result in the unfair treatment of a group. Racial profiling by law enforcement agencies is an example of this. Individual minority-related stressors are discriminatory behaviors enacted by individuals, including racial and gendered microaggressions as well as hate crimes. Cultural minority-related stressors occur when the cultural practices, values, ways of knowing, and contributions of one group are cast as superior to others. White nationalism and supremacy, which assume the superiority of European culture over others, are an example of this. Also, the fact that members of racial minority groups often experience that the contributions of their groups are undervalued or devalued in American society reflects cultural racism. Recall our discussion on decoloniality in Chapter 7. The decolonization perspective is, in part, a response to the reality that Eurocentric values, ideals, and ways of knowing are upheld as normative even among non-European groups and nations.

Acculturative stressors are stressful events or circumstances related to navigating multiple cultures (Berry, 1970). For recent immigrants, such stressors may take the form of challenges such as learning a new language and the cultural mores and expectations of the host society. For the children of these individuals, acculturative stressors often involve balancing the traditional cultural expectations of their parents against the values of society. For instance, female children of recent immigrants may feel familial pressure to conform to gender roles that place an unequal burden on them to preserve their family's traditions and to sacrifice their personal goals to better their family's standing. In the larger society, however, they receive messages to pursue their own dreams and that they have a right to equitable and egalitarian relationships with men. Such tensions have psychological costs. Research on acculturative stress suggests that greater acculturative stress is associated with more psychological distress (Berry, 1970; Berry & Sam, 1997). We discuss the challenges of acculturation in more detail in Chapter 7.

*Vicious Spirals.* **Vicious spirals** are cascading patterns among multiple stressors that compound the effects of risk factors. These spirals are set in motion when the loss of one resource triggers other losses (Hobfoll, 1998; Thorn & Dixon, 2007). Imagine the case of a single mother who loses her car because it was in an accident and she cannot afford to repair it. Without transportation, she may be unable to get to work, which results in the loss of her job. She can no longer afford child care, which makes finding a new job even more difficult. Perhaps she cannot afford medications needed for herself or her children. These setbacks also undermine her self-esteem and belief in her ability to cope. If the loss of resources is profound, she may lose her housing and need shelter. Vicious spirals are particularly common for those with fewer material, social, or personal resources. In the example of our single mother, a

**stress reactions**
the instant response a person has when they face a stressor. Reactions can vary from mild irritation to critical health issues, and they can take many forms—physical, emotional, social, etc. One stress reaction can often trigger another, creating a cycle of stress.

**eustress**
stress that has a positive, adaptive effect and can be beneficial or productive, such as by instilling hope and meaning into a bad situation.

vicious spiral might be interrupted by accessing one of several resources: an understanding employer, a community short-term loan fund, a relative who can provide child care, or a friend with car repair skills. An early intervention such as provision of child care might stop the spiral long enough for her to get back on her feet.

***Stress Reactions.*** The next component of our ecological model of stress and coping includes the immediate reactions persons have when they encounter stressors. These reactions may range from mild irritation to serious health problems. The personal experience of stress includes physiological (e.g., racing heart, elevated cortisol, elevated blood pressure), emotional (e.g., anxiety, agitation, depression), behavioral (e.g., alcohol use, seeking help), cognitive (e.g., appraisal of threat and meaning of a stressor, excessive worry), and social (e.g., social withdrawal) components. These **stress reactions** are interdependent and often cyclical. When a dangerous threat is imminent, brain structures and neural pathways react instantaneously, allowing little time for rational consideration. In a less dangerous circumstance, there is more time for reflection and planning. As shown by Panel D in Figure 9.2, the stress reaction will be more influenced by the proximal stressors and, in turn, will have a greater influence on outcomes. In some situations, an increase in proximal stressors may initiate stress responses that could be viewed as positive experiences, such as rising to meet a challenge. At higher levels of analysis, organizations and localities can be understood as having stress reactions that require changes in functioning when they encounter proximal stressors. While the analogy to individual stress does not exactly translate to organizations, they must also mobilize resources to respond to potential threats (e.g., a major factory will close in a small town—how do the businesses that depend on potential lost customers react to this stress?). In response to stressors, organizations may also encounter impaired functioning (e.g., poor decision making, poor communication, disruption of relationships among co-workers, isolation from other organizations) or rise to meet challenges that they face (e.g., creation of new working relationships by using bridging social capital as discussed in Chapter 6). Detailed descriptions of stress reactions can be found in Folkman and Moskowitz (2004), Goleman (1995), and Somerfield and McCrea (2000).

It is important to note that not all stress reactions are distressing. The focus of this chapter is on stress reactions that place us at risk for impaired health and well-being. That said, some stress is beneficial and even productive. For example, the Yerkes-Dodson law suggests that while too little or too much physiological arousal is associated with poor performance on a task, moderate arousal is associated with peak performance. Thus, experiencing some stress is more adaptive than experiencing no stress or too much stress. Some refer to the positive aspects of the stress reaction as **eustress.** States of eustress can include a sense of hope and meaning (D. L. Nelson & Simmons, 2003).

**material resources**
physical items used in daily life that meet personal and basic needs and provide opportunities to achieve objectives.

**social-emotional competencies**
individual qualities that include self-regulation skills that are needed for personal connection with others; examples include empathy, developing relationships, managing conflict, etc.

## Resources Activated for Coping

The next component of our ecological stress and coping model includes resources that can be used to buffer the effect of stressors or to support the development of personal strengths. To handle stressors, individuals often mobilize available resources for coping (Panel E in Figure 9.3). It is important to note that resources are involved at many points in our ecological model: Contextual and personal protective factors are resources, stressors are defined by their threats to resources, and interventions often provide resources. Simply having resources available does not lead to positive coping outcomes; a person needs to *activate* resources for coping. In this model, resources activated for coping are proximal resources. These resources include the following:

- material resources
- social-emotional competencies
- social settings
- cultural resources
- social support
- mutual help groups
- spiritual resources

*Material Resources.* **Material resources** are tangible objects used to address personal needs and in daily life (e.g., money, car, shelter, food, clothing). Many stressors are related to insufficient material resources, whose effect on psychological outcomes is greater than many realize. As discussed already, employment, transportation, and affordable quality housing are resources that can circumvent vicious spirals induced by job loss or divorce. In addition to meeting basic needs, material resources may provide opportunities for accomplishing goals. Material resources can create access to education (e.g., tuition, books, labs) that helps students develop skills to obtain jobs and build careers.

*Social-Emotional Competencies.* **Social-emotional competencies** are personal qualities that include self-regulation skills: managing emotions, motivations, cognitions, and other intrapersonal processes (Goleman, 1995). Social competencies are needed to connect with others and make use of the resources they offer. Empathy involves accurate understanding of the emotions of others. In a sample of highly stressed, low-income urban children in the United States, empathy was related to resilience and adjustment (Hoyt-Meyers et al., 1995). Making personal connections, building relationships, and managing conflicts are crucial among both adults and children (Elias et al., 2007). Assertiveness has

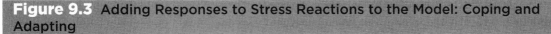

**Figure 9.3** Adding Responses to Stress Reactions to the Model: Coping and Adapting

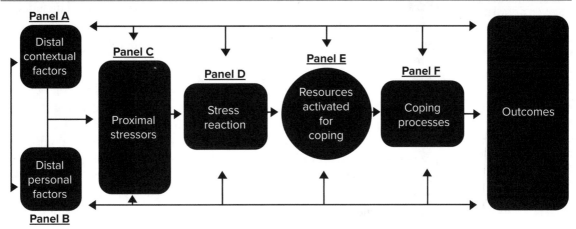

**social settings**
communal contexts where people interact such as youth groups, mutual help organizations, and religious congregations that provide social resources for community members.

**cultural resources**
traditions, rituals, and beliefs from one's culture that provide ways to understand stressors and models for copying with them.

been associated with a number of positive outcomes for children, including the ability to resist drug use (Rotheram-Borus, 1988). As discussed in Chapter 10, social and emotional competencies are a major focus of prevention-promotion programs in community psychology and related fields.

*Social, Cultural, and Spiritual Resources.* Social resources often reflect the idea stated in the African proverb "It takes a village to raise a child." **Social settings** such as youth groups, mutual help organizations, and religious congregations can be coping resources. For persons who belong to a group that is marginalized, counterspaces can be another coping resource. **Cultural resources** include traditions, rituals, and beliefs that provide systems of meaning for interpreting stressors, examples of skillful coping, and guides to coping choices. Religious writings, widely read stories, and folk sayings are examples of these. The rituals of bereavement in any culture provide resources to those who have lost loved ones. Later in this chapter, we discuss social support, mutual help, and social aspects of spiritual resources.

## Coping Processes

In our ecological stress and coping model, Panel F of Figure 9.3 represents responses or strategies that a person uses to reduce stress (Moos, 2002). Coping is a dynamic process that fluctuates over time according to the demands of the situation, the available resources, and a person's ongoing appraisal and emotions. The literature on coping responses is extensive. Researchers have classified coping strategies and styles along a number of descriptive dimensions, such as approach-avoidance, cognitive-behavioral, and prosocial-antisocial (Folkman & Moskowitz, 2004; Hobfoll, 1998; Lazarus & Folkman, 1984; Moos, 1984, 2002; D. H. Shapiro et al., 1996). Here, we briefly discuss a few key concepts.

**cognitive appraisal**
the ongoing assessment of a situation or event in order to evaluate its meaning. This also entails reappraisal, which involves revisiting and perhaps changing one's interpretation of an event.

*Cognitive Appraisal.* During a stress reaction, **cognitive appraisal** is the ongoing process of constructing the meaning of a stressful situation or event (Lazarus & Folkman, 1984). The most relevant aspects of appraisal include the extent to which the situation is seen as challenging or threatening, expected or unexpected, and largely controllable or not. Appraisal of stressors or resources may change over time.

*Reappraisal.* During coping processes, reappraising or "reframing" a problem involves altering one's perception of the situation or its meaning (Lazarus & Folkman, 1984; Watzlawick et al., 1974). It may include changing one's view of the stressor's intensity, identifying unrecognized resources, or finding opportunities for growth or meaning in the situation. For example, you might reappraise a stressful circumstance as an opportunity to learn new skills or reframe an appraised threat as a challenge. People who have lost a job might reinterpret their situation as an opportunity for changing careers or seeking

Communities provide their members important resources for coping, including material, emotional, and spiritual resources. Community psychologists work to ensure that these resources are available to all communities.

**problem-focused coping**

a coping response where the individual addresses the problem directly by making and implementing a plan to change the situation in order to cope.

**emotion-focused coping**

a coping response where the individual addresses the feelings that accompany the stressors and outcomes.

**meaning-focused coping**

a coping response where the individual determines the significance in the stressor by reappraising it, which can result in personal growth and learning.

**virtuous spirals**

when increased access to coping resources and the successful utilization of these resources can build upon each other to create an upward pattern of growth by diminishing risk and encouraging health functioning.

further education. Cultural values and social support influence which reappraisals are perceived as realistic or constructive.

*Categories of Coping.* Empirically based studies have usually found three general categories of coping responses (Folkman & Moskowitz, 2004). **Problem-focused coping** involves addressing a problem situation directly, especially by making a plan to change the situation and following that plan. Changing how one studies for tests, making a plan to improve one's diet, or learning interviewing skills to search for a new job would be examples. **Emotion-focused coping** addresses the feelings that accompany the stressors. Typically, this approach seeks to reduce anxiety or increase emotional support from friends or family. **Meaning-focused coping** involves finding significance in the stressor by reappraising it, especially if this leads to growth or learning of important lessons. It may be based on deeper values, whether secular or spiritual, as when suffering is interpreted as leading to growth. These categories may overlap, as when a person seeks emotional support from a friend.

From an ecological perspective, coping is contextual. Wise coping choices are based on the context and the person: There is no coping style or strategy that is always superior. Societal and cultural factors, gender and other forms of diversity, ecological level (e.g., community, neighborhood, family), and the stressor itself must all be taken into account.

*Virtuous Spirals.* Earlier we noted how stressors may sometimes trigger each other in a vicious downward spiral. However, adaptive coping may initiate a very different cascade: a **virtuous spiral** in which resources are increased, successes build on each other, and the stressor is transformed into a catalyst for growth (Hobfoll, 1998). In a virtuous spiral, access to coping resources and the ability to utilize the resources can have a multiplicative effect, reducing risk and promoting functioning. Persons in long-term recovery from substance abuse who have previously hit rock bottom in a vicious spiral often describe how they were able to use coping resources and opportunities as a result of their steps to get sober, get support from peers and sponsors, and repair relationships. Many describe being thankful for "hitting bottom" because their lives are much better than they were before a vicious spiral associated with substance abuse consumed them. New opportunities for work, a career, and a fulfilling life appear as virtuous spirals of opportunity open doors to new resources.

*Positive Emotions.* The presence of positive emotions such as joy, contentment, pride, and love can also trigger upward spirals toward resilience and well-being. Barbara Fredrickson's (1998, 2001) broaden-and-build theory maintains that unlike negative emotions, which constrain our ability to respond adaptively to stressful situations, positive emotions expand our "thought-action repertoires,"

**posttraumatic growth**

positive psychological outcomes resulting from experiencing suffering or facing challenging situations or events, such as a greater appreciation for life.

**wellness**

a state of positive health outcomes and personal well-being.

stimulating novel and adaptive mindsets and ways of coping. Thus, positive emotions help build our intellectual, social, and psychological coping resources.

***Posttraumatic Growth.*** For some people, virtuous spirals occur in the aftermath of traumatic experiences themselves and not necessarily because of the adaptive coping responses that follow them. That is, the experience of suffering and grappling with suffering sometimes leads to positive outcomes. Researchers refer to this as **posttraumatic growth**, the positive psychological change that results from struggling with highly challenging circumstances (Tedeschi & Calhoun, 2004). Positive changes may include a greater appreciation for life and changed priorities, better and more satisfying relationship with others, a greater sense of personal strength, the perception of new possibilities and paths in life, and increased spirtualty. These outcomes suggest that posttraumatic growth is not a coping mechanism per se but "an experience of improvement that for some persons is deeply profound" (Tedeschi & Calhoun, 2004, p. 4). Studies have found posttraumatic growth among members of a number of groups including combat veterans, survivors of sexual assault and abuse, persons with chronic health conditions, and refugees (see Tedeschi & Calhoun, 2004).

## Coping Outcomes

Traditionally, psychologists have studied coping outcomes by measuring reductions of maladaptive functioning. Problematic outcomes include psychological or physical disorders, raised levels of distress, or personal problems classified as dysfunction or clinical disorders (Folkman & Moskowitz, 2004). However, this perspective on coping is limited in two ways. First, it focuses on avoiding negative coping outcomes more than the possibility of promoting positive outcomes. Second, it tends to focus on individuals in isolation rather than also studying how individual functioning is related to broader ecological levels (families, organizations, communities, and societies). From a community psychology perspective, the promotion of well-being and positive outcomes is as important as avoiding negative outcomes. Thus, we refine our ecological model of stress and coping one more time to reflect two different sets of outcomes. In Figure 9.4, Panel G concerns positive coping outcomes and their relationship to broader ecological levels, while Panel H concerns distress, dysfunction, and disorders.

**Wellness** is not simply the absence of symptoms of disorder or of distress; it is the experience of positive outcomes in health and subjective well-being (Cowen, 1994, 2000a; G. Nelson & Prilleltensky, 2010). Life and job satisfaction, positive affect, self-esteem, social connection, and academic achievement represent desired wellness outcomes that go beyond mere absence of symptoms (Cicchetti et al., 2000; Prilleltensky, 2012).

**resilience**
the ability to adapt positively and behave capably after experiencing hardships, trauma, or other stressful events.

**Resilience** is an individual's capacity to adapt successfully and function competently despite exposure to stress, adversity, or chronic trauma (Bonanno, 2004; Masten, 2001). In Chapter 10, we discuss in more detail the Kauai longitudinal study that has helped inform how community psychologists understand resilience. Resilience appears to be a common coping process. Many people experience distress due to a stressor (e.g., death of a loved one) but recover their prior level of functioning without clinical intervention. Some are able to maintain stable levels of healthy functioning in the face of stressors, with little or no emotional distress or physical symptoms at all. Resilience arises from the interplay of environmental and individual factors (Luthar et al., 2000; Werner, 1993). Serrano-García (2020) provided a critical review of how "resilience" has been used to describe Puerto Rico's situation after Hurricane María. She observed that a focus on "thin resilience," meaning individuals' extraordinary capacity to persevere, was most frequent and is too often lifted up as a justification for governmental decisions about providing fewer resources. She advocates instead for a conceptualization of community resilience "defined as community capacities for adaptation and the availability

**Figure 9.4** Expanding Outcomes of Stress and Coping

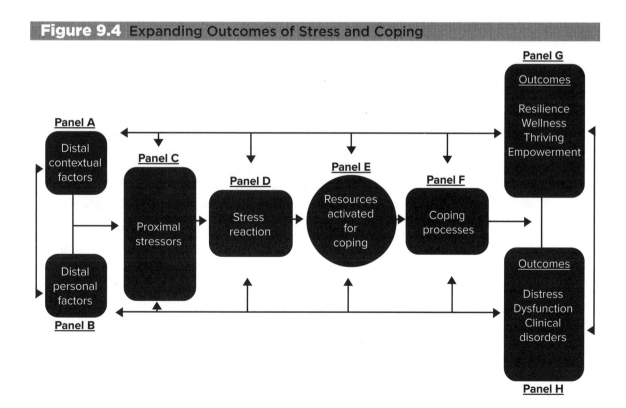

**thriving**
positive growth development in the face of adversity that leads an individual to function better than they did before their adverse experience.

and mobilization of social capital within an environment characterized by change, uncertainty, and unpredictability" (Serrano-García, 2020, p. 4).

Recognizing environmental influences, consistent with a community psychology perspective, suggests pathways for action involving multiple ecological levels, not just individuals. Community psychology research on natural disasters has proposed that communities as well as individuals can have a capacity for resilience, such as a community that "bounces back" after a flood (Velázquez et al., 2017).

*Thriving.* For some individuals, an encounter with adversity initiates a process of growth that takes them beyond their prior level of functioning. This positive outcome is referred to as **thriving** (Ickovics & Park, 1998). It may be thought of as "resilience plus": in the face of stressors, not only holding one's ground but growing through the experience. For instance, Abraído-Lanza and colleagues (1998) studied thriving among Latinas with chronic illness living in impoverished neighborhoods. Thriving in response to stressors often involves meaning-focused coping, access to coping resources, and the ability to mobilize scarce resources.

*Empowerment.* Wiley and Rappaport (2000) defined empowerment as gaining access to valued resources. Recall our discussion of empowerment in Chapter 8. It is important to recognize that empowerment involves actually gaining power in some way, not simply the feeling of being in control of one's life decisions (Zimmerman, 2000). For instance, empowerment occurs when a person with a serious mental illness is able to understand and advocate for their rights, gain more control in treatment planning, and make decisions about where to live and work. Empowerment can also occur at multiple levels of analysis. For example, mutual help groups bring together persons with common challenges in coping with a specific problem, sharing their resources and promoting positive outcomes for individuals and the broader collective. The growing awareness of the group's empowerment can lead to effective advocacy and obtaining resources that support other positive outcomes of coping.

*Distress, Dysfunction, Clinical Disorders.* Panel H of Figure 9.4 includes problematic outcomes of coping. These outcomes range from symptoms of mental disorders to outcomes that are problematic but not considered clinical disorders. These include high levels of distress, irritability, or dysfunctional behaviors in family or work relationships such as neglect, hostility, or even violence. Many psychological outcomes experienced by college students (e.g., anxiety about grades), by families (e.g., dissatisfaction with a marriage), and in workplaces (e.g., frustration over limited job opportunities) involve distress or dysfunction that is important, and painful, but these outcomes are not considered mental disorders. Coping research related to clinical interventions has focused on avoiding symptoms of disorders (e.g. depression, anxiety, PTSD, substance abuse) that can result from maladaptive coping, overwhelming exposure to stressors, and insufficient coping resources.

***Coping Is Dynamic and Contextual.*** Look back at Figure 9.4 for a moment; notice the feedback cycles and arrows. Outcomes are not end states but simply one more step in the cyclical processes of coping. Outcomes can affect stressors and resources for future coping. Outcomes are best understood as snapshots in ongoing processes of living. Our coping processes and the stressors we encounter are dynamic, changing over time, and vary in the diverse contexts in which we live.

## Interventions to Promote Coping

A primary purpose for developing the conceptual model presented in Figure 9.1 is to think about how and where community psychologists might work with others to improve coping outcomes and reduce exposure to risk factors. Community psychologists refer to actions taken to affect outcomes as *interventions*. Interventions can be targeted at each level of analysis and might be initiated by health, educational, or social service professionals; researchers; public leaders; or concerned citizens. Through the next five chapters, we discuss in detail different interventions implemented and/or supported by community psychologists.

Using our ecological model of stress and coping, community psychologists can conceptualize a range of possibilities for better targeted and more holistic interventions (Yoshikawa & Shinn, 2002). As we discuss in later chapters, interventions need to be selected to fit the definition of the problem, the level of analysis used for the problem definition, and available resources. The model also illustrates how community psychologists, clinical psychologists, and others who implement social interventions might work together to produce synergistic results.

Planning interventions requires considering several dimensions (Domlyn & Wandersman, 2019; Wandersman, Morsbach, et al., 2002). *Timing* concerns the point of intervention in the ecological model: Is the goal to influence distal factors, proximal stressors, stress reactions, resource activation, and/or coping strategies? *Ecological level(s)* concerns the intervention focus (e.g., individual, microsystem, organizational, locality, macrosystem). *Content* goals of the intervention might include increasing awareness (a goal of many psychotherapies and of consciousness-raising in liberation movements), behavior change, skill building, social support, spiritual facilitation (as in twelve-step groups), advocacy for individuals or families, changing social policy, or other goals. The *value system* inherent in the intervention is critical to its nature and effectiveness. For instance, community efforts by expert helpers to reduce environmental stressors might not be as effective for neighborhood residents as an approach emphasizing their citizen participation and empowerment. A major point of this chapter is that many stressors cannot be addressed by individual coping alone (Wong et al., 2006). For instance, job stress often is rooted in organizational and macrosystem conditions that require collective action. Improved individual coping skills alone cannot change these conditions.

In Figure 9.5, we have commented on the types of interventions that are most appropriate for addressing each component of our ecological model of stress and coping. From left to right, interventions range from more global to more individual in scope. The figure includes both community and clinical approaches to intervention. In our discussion to follow, we leave clinical treatments to other sources and focus on interventions most relevant to community psychology. As shown in Figure 9.5, community psychologists think broadly about the types of interventions that can support coping.

*Social Policy and Advocacy.* Improvements in the well-being of large numbers of persons involve changing laws, organizational practices, social programs, and funding decisions that affect resources for coping. These interventions can be understood as addressing stressors and distal factors in coping. Targets of advocacy may be government officials, private sector or community leaders, or media and the public. Advocacy may involve working to raise public awareness of an issue: for instance, gaining media attention for the needs of homeless families in your community. It may involve social action: for instance, protesting cuts in mental health or youth development programs or holding a Take Back the Night rally to call attention to violence against women.

Advocacy can be supported by community research. Community and developmental psychologists joined to promote a strengths-building perspective in U.S. government policies regarding children, youth, and families (Maton et al., 2017) and supporting community members in advocacy (Kornbluh et al., 2016). Furthermore, a group of community psychologists pooled their expertise to develop a resource guide for how communities can prepare for and respond to natural disasters (Velázquez et al., 2017). They not only created this guide but have also built relationships with funders and government agencies to see that it is field tested, refined, and then distributed among organizations that are early responders to natural disasters. We discuss approaches to community and social change in detail in Chapter 13.

*Organizational Consultation.* Human services, schools, and work sites are less effective when organizational problems create too many stressors. Community and organizational psychologists consult with these settings, seeking to change organizational policies and practices. These may include altering employees' roles, decision-making processes, or communication. Consultation may deal with issues such as work-family relationships, human diversity, and intergroup conflict. These interventions may lessen stress, increase social support, promote employee job satisfaction, or help make services more effective for clients (e.g., Boyd, 2015; Trickett et al., 2000).

**Figure 9.5** Potential Relationships Among Stressors, Coping Processes, and Community Psychology Interventions at Different Ecological Levels

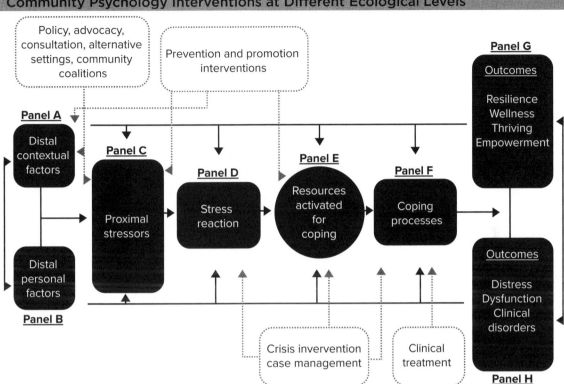

*Alternative Settings.* At times, the shortcomings of an agency, clinic, or other setting may be so great that citizens or professionals decide to form an alternative setting to provide interventions. Charter schools and self-help organizations provide examples of citizens coming together to address distal factors and stressors that they felt were not being adequately addressed by conventional services. For instance, when many community agencies failed to recognize the needs of domestic violence and rape victims, concerned women formed women's shelters and rape crisis centers. At first these settings had very little funding or outside support, but they have grown into an established part of many communities. The Community Lodge (discussed in Chapters 2 and 5) and Oxford House (discussed in Chapter 1) are examples of alternative, supportive housing created by those concerned about the well-being of persons with mental illness or substance abuse problems. Alternative settings can provide citizens important choices of services and values systems (Cherniss & Deegan, 2000; Reinharz, 1984). Some alternative settings can also function as counterspaces. Before the formation of ethnic studies departments and programs on university campuses, cultural centers met the desire of racial and ethnic minority students to learn about their cultural history. These settings also functioned as refuges from the onslaught of discrimination occurring on campuses in the 1960s as well as launching pads for protests and other forms of social action against racism (Stovall, 2005).

***Community Coalitions.*** Community coalitions bring together representatives from a local community to address issues such as preventing drug abuse or promoting health or youth development. Often, coalitions are created by coordinating the work of groups who were already committed to addressing an issue but who had not been working together. An effective coalition brings together citizens from many walks of life to discuss community issues and work toward shared goals. It also builds collaboration among multiple agencies, whose separate funding streams and agendas often create a fragmented community service system. For example, community coalitions have increased the rates of immunization of young children, effected community changes in drug abuse and domestic violence, and helped decrease levels of local gang violence (N. E. Allen, 2005; Wolff, 2014). We discuss this approach in detail in Chapter 13.

***Prevention and Promotion Programs.*** Prevention and promotion programs are carefully designed interventions that seek to reduce the incidence of personal problems in living and illness or to promote health and personal development (see box in top center of Figure 9.5). Examples include school-based programs to promote social-emotional competence, family-based programs to strengthen parenting or promote resilience, and community-wide efforts to promote exercise or prevent drug abuse (DuBois, 2017). Many prevention/promotion programs have grown out of collaboration between community coalitions, schools, and researchers. These programs may strengthen coping skills or other protective factors also addressed in clinical treatment, but they focus on intervention before problems appear. We discuss these approaches in detail in Chapters 10 and 11.

Moving to the bottom center of Figure 9.5, we next discuss community approaches more closely related to clinical treatments.

***Crisis Intervention.*** After the September 11, 2001, terrorist attacks in the United States, over 1 million New Yorkers received public education or individual counseling through Project Liberty, a public disaster mental health program (Felton, 2004). The most promising crisis-intervention approaches immediately after traumatic events focus on providing emotional support, practical assistance, and information about coping and on encouraging later use of one's own sources of support and treatment if needed (McNally et al., 2003). These are consistent with a community-ecological perspective. For mental health professionals, skills for responding to disasters include helping persons and families deal with multiple problems; working with community resources such as schools, workplaces, and religious congregations; and using mass media to provide information (Felton, 2004). Moreover, programs must be tailored to the specific culture, needs, and resources of a community (Aber, 2005). Community psychologists have long advocated for the training of paraprofessionals and community members for similar outreach that might reduce the impact of stress reactions. Paraprofessionals can also promote the use of coping resources before dysfunction and the development of clinical symptoms (DeWolfe, 2000; Rappaport, 1977a). As we discuss in Chapter 12, community psychologists also evaluate the effectiveness of programs, such as crisis intervention. While crisis intervention can be helpful (K. Jones et al., 2009), in some cases crisis-intervention approaches have been found to increase long-term distress rather than ameliorate it (Gist & Lubin, 1989).

***Case Management.*** To increase the availability of coping resources within agencies, professional treatment is often complemented with innovations in case management and client advocacy. These interventions focus on both practical needs (e.g., housing) and psychological issues (e.g., decision making, social support). For example, community psychologists concerned about housing resources for persons who were homeless developed a new approach to providing housing. Rather than expecting persons to prove that they were ready to live in housing by working their way through a shelter system, Pathways to Housing in NYC developed a "housing first" program that put homeless persons with mental illness directly into apartments (Padgett et al., 2016). The housing-first approach makes available specialized case management and treatment options through Assertive Community Treatment (G. Bond et al., 1990) involving multidisciplinary teams (e.g., nurse, psychiatrist, case manager, vocational specialist, substance abuse counselor) that visit tenants in their apartments to respond to a variety of needs. This approach has demonstrated that helping homeless persons find suitable independent housing, and then helping them develop a treatment plan once in housing, is more effective than transitional housing approaches (e.g., having persons demonstrate their "housing readiness" by living in increasingly less supervised housing). Outcomes include more days housed, reduction in service use, and more cost-effective interventions (Gulcur et al., 2003; Tsemberis et al., 2004).

Although the discussion of coping interventions is brief, our purpose is to provide examples of the richness of intervention options and entry points available to address stress and coping. In the next three sections, we describe in detail three important community-based resources for coping: social support, mutual help organizations, and spirituality and religious settings. These areas of community psychology research and practice have implications for personal coping and professional services.

| Box 9.1 | **Changing Perspectives: Expanding How You Think About Stress and Coping** |
|---|---|

Think of an important stressful experience in your life. For instance, it may have been a single event: a serious illness, injury, or failing an important test. It may have been a life transition: beginning college or graduate school, changing jobs, or losing a loved one. It may be an ongoing or long-term situation: growing up in poverty; having a chronic illness; experiencing discrimination or harassment; or having to balance several demanding roles such as mother, wife, student, and worker. It may be an experience that fits none of these categories well. Write down your stressful event and refer to Figure 9.5. Consider the following questions about your experience:

- What was stressful about it for you?
- Was it a short-term or a long-term situation?
- What things did you do to cope with this experience? (Panels E and F)
- What distal factors may have contributed to the experience? (Panels A and B)
- What resources helped you cope with this stressful experience? Are there other resources that might have been helpful?
- What were the outcomes of the experience? (Panels G and H)
- What could have been done to address distal factors before you had the experience?
- How did the experience affect you as a person? How did you change?

# Social Support

Social support is a key resource for strengthening coping and well-being. Social support is an intuitive concept for many of us. As community psychologists understand social support, it represents a collection of social, emotional, cognitive, and behavioral processes occurring in relationships and social networks. Understanding how it works in our lives requires careful conceptualization and research. For this chapter, we provide a brief introduction to this naturally occurring resource for coping that can be bolstered or diminished by policy and interventions.

Interest in social support soared in the 1980s after research showed that it was associated with lower levels of personal distress and illness, even in the presence of stressful challenges. Research in a variety of disciplines found that social support was correlated with decreased anxiety, depression, distress, and physical illness among children, adolescents, and adults. It also has been correlated with stronger cardiovascular and immune functioning, academic performance, parenting skills, and job and life satisfaction. However, later research has indicated that its effects are complicated by many interacting factors, and some negative effects of supportive relationships have become clearer (Saegert & Carpiano, 2017).

**generalized support**
help and caring that are continued over time and that offer basic security for living and coping; not focused on a particular stressor.

**perceived support**
a measurement of the value or availability of support determined by an individual's subjective judgment.

**specific support**
also called enacted support, it is help that is tailored to an explicit stressor that is actively present in an individual's life, such as advice, monetary support, or emotional encouragement.

## Generalized and Specific Support

**Generalized support** is sustained over time, providing the individual with a secure base for living and coping. It is not tailored to one specific stressor and does not necessarily involve behavioral helping in a specific situation. It is most clearly measured in terms of **perceived support**, in which research participants are asked about the general quality or availability of support in their lives (Barrera, 1986, 2000). Generalized support thus involves an assessment of the presence of meaningful others in one's life (Barrera, 2000; Cohen, 2004). It especially refers to experiences of caring and attachment in close personal relationships, such as a strong marriage, parent–child relationship, or friendship. It is there in some form all the time.

**Specific support**, or *enacted support*, is behavioral help provided to people coping with a particular stressor. It may be emotional encouragement, information or advice, or tangible assistance such as loaning money. Because it concerns distress already present in the recipient's life, specific support is discernible only when a person needs it and is tailored to a specific stressor (Barrera, 2000). This kind of support is received rather than only perceived.

Generalized and specific support can intertwine. Stressors such as job loss require both. A close relationship often provides both. Other relationships may involve less caring and more instrumental support, but that too is helpful. It is important to note that perceived support and specific support are different. For instance, if you are having trouble in a demanding psychology course, a caring friend helps, but so does a tutor. An empirical review of 23 research studies that compared perceived general and enacted specific support suggests that these types of support had an average correlation of 35% (Haber et al., 2007).

## The Relationship Context of Support

Social support occurs not in a vacuum but within relationships with others. It is shaped by the dynamics in those relationships. In a number of studies, having close, confiding, reciprocal relationships has been linked to higher levels of social support and to less loneliness and greater life satisfaction (Barrera, 2000; Terry & Townley, 2019). Yet it is also true that relationships can create stressors as well as provide support. Researchers have studied many support relationships; we will focus on a few examples.

*Families as Contexts.* Family members, particularly parents and spouses, are important sources of support, both generalized and specific. Compared with other sources, they often involve greater commitment and personal knowledge of the individual. However, they also involve greater obligation for reciprocity and greater potential for conflict, and they may not be useful for every stressor.

Trotter and Allen (2009) studied the role of social support from family and friends for 45 women who had experienced domestic violence in the past 12 months. Perhaps not surprisingly, the results of this qualitative study suggest that the reactions of families and friends were not always perceived as supportive. Only 22% of the women reported that responses from family and friends were uniformly supportive; these included assistance with obtaining a safe living situation, emotional support, and other practical aid. The majority of women experienced mixed support (78%) that included negative reactions of jeopardizing safety (25% of sample), limited or no emotional support (50% of sample), and limited practical help (33% of the sample). Trotter and Allen concluded that mobilizing support from families and friends can be instrumental in addressing stressors arising from domestic violence but also that programs need to determine the nature of the perceived and specific support that families and friends will provide, or the programs may unintentionally put these women at greater risk.

***Natural Helpers and Mentors.*** Natural helpers and mentors are sources of informal support in a community. Some people become natural helpers because their jobs lead to conversations with personal-emotional meaning, such as beauticians and bartenders (Cowen et al., 1981). Mentors are older or more experienced persons (other than one's parents) who support and guide younger, less experienced persons (Lyons et al., 2019; Rhodes & DuBois, 2008). Mentors may occur naturally in one's social network or be provided through a program such as Big Brothers Big Sisters. Reviews of research on mentoring programs for youth found only modest positive effects for mentoring but also identified characteristics of highly effective mentoring relationships that can be built into future mentoring programs (Lyons et al., 2019; Rhodes & Dubois, 2008). Mentoring programs were most helpful with youth in disadvantaged and risky environments.

***Relationships as Stressors.*** Of course, relationships can create stressors as well as support (Saegert & Carpiano, 2017). Studies of persons who were HIV-positive revealed that depressive symptoms were associated with relationship conflicts with others (Fleishman et al., 2003). A study of adolescent mothers found that depression was lower when more support was received but greater when those same relationships involved criticism, conflict, and disappointment (Rhodes & Woods, 1995). These occurred because the women all experienced a simultaneous stressor, many individuals sought support, and the shared resources of the group were strained. In other contexts, if support is required over an extended time, for an illness or other chronic problem, conflict often occurs as supporters tire (Kohn-Wood & Wilson, 2005). Providing support to others takes energy and time. Interventions have been developed to help promote social support among caregivers for whom old networks of support may not be sufficient for the stresses of caring for a loved

**multidimensional relationships**

associations where the two people involved take on multiple role relationships and the responsibilities and activities of these roles. An example is someone who is both a friend and a neighbor.

**unidimensional relationships**

associations that are limited to one role, such as a classmate you only ever see in class.

**density**

a measurement of one's social network determined by the relationship ties between network members.

one with a chronic illness. Studying support in the context of relationships helps clarify its positive and negative effects.

## Social Support Networks

Social support occurs within networks of relationships. Researchers analyze social networks in terms of many variables related to social support. We focus on three: multidimensionality, density, and reciprocity.

*Multidimensionality.* **Multidimensional relationships** are those in which the two persons involved do a number of things together and share a number of role relationships. Multidimensional relationships exist when a coworker is also a friend that we see socially or when we share multiple interests and activities with neighbors. **Unidimensional relationships** are confined to one role: One sees a coworker only at work; neighbors who are not friends. As a student, you have a multidimensional relationship with a classmate who is also a neighbor or who is involved in the same organization. With a person you know only in class, you share a unidimensional relationship.

Because a multidimensional relationship means we see the other person more often, forming and deepening friendships is easier. Multidimensional ties are more resilient. For instance, loss of a job effectively means the end of unidimensional relationships with coworkers, whereas multidimensional relationships would survive. However, unidimensional relationships also are valuable for linking with a broader number of people (recall the strength of weak ties and bridging social capital, in Chapter 6).

*Density.* Your social network contains relationships that your network members have with each other, which is called **density**. A high-density network exists when many ties exist between network members; for instance, when most network members are friends of each other. Residents of small towns and some urban neighborhoods often live in high-density networks. A low-density network exists when few of the members are closely connected to each other. A person with many friends in different settings who do not know each other has a low-density network. A high-density network and a low-density network could have the same number of persons, but those persons are more interconnected in the high-density network.

High-density networks usually offer greater consensus on norms and advice (B. J. Hirsch et al., 1990) and often quicker help in a crisis because the network members are more interconnected. However, low-density networks often hold a greater diversity of persons with a greater variety of skills and life experiences. Thus, they can provide a diversity of resources needed during life transitions such as divorce, bereavement, or entering college (Hobfoll & Vaux, 1993; Wilcox, 1981). In such transitions, too much density within one's network may inhibit the development of new roles and personal identities or adaptation to changed circumstances.

*Reciprocity.* Social networks also vary in the extent to which the individual *both* receives support from others and provides it to others. Reciprocity of support may be the most important aspect of friendship across the lifespan (Hartup & Stevens, 1997).

In studies of self-help groups and of a religious congregation, Maton (1987, 1988) found that reciprocity of support was associated with greater psychological well-being. When individuals both provided and received support, well-being was higher. Among those who mostly provided or mostly received support and those who did little of either, well-being was lower. Maton's findings refer to overall reciprocity in one's social network, not to reciprocity within each dyadic relationship. An individual may primarily provide support to one person while primarily receiving support from another yet have an overall balance of providing and receiving.

### What Is the Role of Reciprocity in Professional Supportive Relationships?

When examining helping relationships, how important is reciprocity of support? Typically, relationships with doctors, therapists, or other health professionals do not have expectations of reciprocity. Some community psychologists have become concerned about small social support systems of persons with long histories of psychiatric treatment (Kloos, 2020; G. Nelson et al., 2014). Often, persons with serious and persistent mental illness have relied on the mental health system to meet many of their needs; resources such as housing, transportation, employment, and even socializing with peers typically are managed by mental health workers. In such cases, persons with mental illness have greatly reduced opportunity to give support as well as receive it.

In community psychology research and action, community psychologists are called to look for how their work can be collaborative and have elements of reciprocity in their professional relationships (see Chapters 1 and 3). Collaboration with mutual help organizations has been one approach advocated by community psychologists interested in promoting availability of nonprofessional helping capacities in communities and changing professional systems of care (G. Nelson et al., 2017).

# Mutual Help Groups

Mutual help groups, which include mutual assistance or self-help groups and mutual support groups, are voluntary associations of persons who share a life situation or status that produce challenges for coping in their environments. In many cases, these groups are also alternative settings formed to address shortcomings in existing resources for addressing stressors. Examples include formal organizations such as Alcoholics Anonymous (AA), an international support organization for persons who have problems with alcohol, or less formal groups of bereaved persons in a local community. Mutual help organizations

**mutual assistance groups**
self-help groups facilitated by a peer where the participants share a similar concern, such as Alcoholics Anonymous.

have had tremendous growth across the world over the last 40 years (Borkman et al., 2005; G. Nelson et al., 2017). Over 1,200 mutual help organizations exist worldwide, each with a network of local groups (Chinman et al., 2002). Mutual help groups are usually affiliated with parent organizations and are not isolated microsystems (Borkman, 1991; Pistrang et al., 2008).

In a representative sample of U.S. citizens, 7% of adults reported attending a mutual help group within the past year, and 18% have done so within their lifetimes (Kessler et al., 1997). A smaller but significant portion of Canadians have reported using mutual help (Gottlieb & Peters, 1991). It is likely that these numbers have grown since the last formal surveys. The number of self-help initiatives outnumbers mental health agencies and organizations in the United States (Goldstrom et al., 2006). The proportion of the adult population in mutual help groups appears equal to that engaged in psychotherapy (Munn-Giddings & Borkman, 2017). In just over 60 years, the first widely recognized mutual help organization, AA, has grown from the meeting of two founders to a worldwide organization with thousands of local groups. A majority of those seeking help for alcoholism in the United States attend AA meetings (Munn-Giddings & Borkman, 2017).

Mutual help groups vary in the degree to which members direct the group. **Mutual assistance groups**, or self-help groups, are facilitated by a person experiencing the focal concern and do not have professional involvement (e.g., groups like AA). Some mutual support groups include supportive roles for professionals (e.g., providing referrals), but it is important to note that the term "mutual support" refers to groups that are peer led. Some mental health professionals have sought to use distinctive features of mutual support to create professionally led peer support groups (e.g., peer counseling groups in high schools; Reach to Recovery, a group for women with breast cancer; Borkman, 1990; Salem et al., 2008). There is some debate about whether these professionally facilitated groups retain the critical ingredients of the mutual support experience (Salem et al., 2008; Segal, 2018). However, self-help advocates have correctly predicted that collaboration between professionals and self-help groups would increase (Munn-Giddings & Borkman, 2017; Riessman & Banks, 2001). For simplicity, and to focus on the communal aspect of these settings, we use the term "mutual help," although readers should keep in mind the diversity of groups.

## Distinctive Features of Mutual Help Groups

Mutual help groups have five distinctive features (Pistrang et al., 2008; Riessman, 1990):

- a focal concern: a problem, life crisis, or issue common to all members;
- peer relationships rather than, or in addition to, a professional-client relationship;

**helper therapy principle**
the belief that helping others will also support one's own well-being.

**experiential knowledge**
wisdom from someone who has direct personal experience managing the focal concern.

**community narratives**
a shared story among participants that explains the focal problem, draws meaning from it, helps participants to transform owe's identity, and provides a clear path to recovery or coping.

- reciprocity of helping: each member both receives and provides help;

- experiential knowledge used for coping; and

- a community narrative that embodies the experiences and wisdom of its members.

Mutual help is based on peer relationships. It involves an exchange of helping based on interpersonal norms of reciprocity rather than a professional service provided for a fee. Each member both provides aid and receives help. Thus the helping relationship is symmetrical, unlike the asymmetrical professional-client relationship. It also involves the **helper therapy principle** (Riessman, 1990): Providing aid to others promotes one's own well-being. For instance, GROW, a mutual help group for persons with mental illnesses, emphasizes the principle "If you need help, help others" (Maton & Salem, 1995, p. 641). In addition, needing and receiving aid for one's problems is less stigmatizing if everyone in the group shares similar concerns and if one expects to provide aid also.

Another distinctive element of mutual help is the type of knowledge that is most respected and used for helping. **Experiential knowledge** is based on the personal experiences of group members who have coped with the focal concern, often for years (Borkman et al., 2016). This practical, "insider" knowledge is shared in mutual help group meetings. Professional expertise is valuable in many contexts, but professionals usually do not have direct, daily, personal experience in coping with the focal problem.

Mutual help groups offer **community narratives**, expressing in story form a description and explanation of the focal problem and an explicit guide to recovery or to coping (we discuss these narratives in Chapter 6). The group's belief system, rituals, and mutual storytelling provide ways to make meaning of life experiences, to transform one's identity, and to promote coping. As members become committed to the group, they interpret their own life stories and identities in terms similar to the community narrative. This is especially a concern of spiritually based twelve-step groups (Humphreys, 2000; Rappaport, 1993, 1995).

Professional mental health treatment and mutual help can be complementary forms of helping (Chinman et al. 2002; Segal, 2018). Professional treatment offers, for instance, scientific and clinical knowledge of symptoms and treatments and is especially useful in assessing and treating complicated problems. Mutual help offers the benefits of peer relationships, helping others, and experiential-practical knowledge, at very low or no cost. Members of Schizophrenics Anonymous groups in Michigan clearly distinguished between expertise of group members and leaders and expertise of mental health professionals, yet members valued both (Salem et al., 2000). However, not all professionals are willing to support the use of mutual support to address life problems (Salzer et al., 1994; Segal, 2018). In a survey of mental health and rehabilitation professionals in Connecticut, those with more professional experience and those with personal or family experience with mental disabilities viewed mutual help groups more positively than other professionals and were more likely to refer clients to them (Chinman et al., 2002).

Mutual help groups are not helpful for everyone. Knowledge, personal contact, and discretion are helpful when professionals refer clients to specific mutual help groups. However, those caveats are also true for referrals to professionals. A consensus statement by leading researchers called for strengthening ties between drug abuse treatment professionals and self-help groups (Humphreys et al., 2004). Professionals or students can attend mutual help group meetings to initiate mutual understanding and collaboration.

## Online Mutual Help

Online mutual help groups provide a resource to those with privacy concerns or those who cannot attend face-to-face groups (Figeuroa Sarriera & Gonzalez Hilario, 2017; Kral, 2006). Online mutual help groups can be effective in addressing depression and problem drinking (J. F. Kelly et al., 2019; Pistrang et al., 2008). Klaw et al., (2000) found that online group interactions generally resembled interactions in face-to-face groups. Interestingly, these studies found gender involvement was different online. Unlike in face-to-face groups, men more often used the online depression group, and women the online problem-drinking group. An online professionally moderated support group effectively engaged Asian American male college students in discussing ethnic identity issues, whereas face-to-face groups with similar aims had failed (Chang et al., 2001). These findings indicate that persons reluctant to participate in face-to-face groups are more willing to join online groups and can receive similar benefits there. Although research on these interventions is still relatively new, several reviews have concluded that there are beneficial outcomes for adults who use internet-based self-help (Kral, 2006; Ybarra & Eaton, 2005).

Online groups are more accessible for individuals who are less able to leave home. W. Campbell and colleagues (2016) developed a web-based intervention to address problem drinking. They recruited 189 heavy drinkers to participate in the study where participants were randomly assigned to the web-based intervention, in-person mutual aid group, or both. Interestingly, they did not find a difference between modalities; both the web-based application and the in-person mutual support groups were helpful. Initial concerns with online mutual support revolved around whether the technical skills needed to navigate and participate and the cost of having a computer would prohibit people from participating. In the last 20 years, the availability and knowledge of how to use these technologies have increased greatly, although there are still inequities regarding who has access to internet, smartphones, or computers.

It should also be noted that most of the participants in the study already had some familiarity with in-person mutual aid through Alcoholics Anonymous. This may have helped prepare them to utilize the web-based intervention.

Online groups also are helpful for persons with chronic health conditions (Kingod et al., 2017). As we noted earlier, persons with health conditions that limit mobility may particularly benefit. In early randomized experiments, online social support programs for HIV-positive persons, women with breast cancer, and adults with Type 2 diabetes were effective in providing support (Barrera et al., 2002; J. A. Lewis et al., 2018). A systematic review of 13 qualitative studies of peer online groups for people with chronic health problems focused on the experience of participating and what was valued by participants (Kingod et al., 2017). Reviewers identified four broad themes: (a) *illness-associated identity work*, (b) *social support and connectivity*, (c) *experiential knowledge sharing*, and (d) *collective voice and mobilization*. These themes describe how the peer-to-peer groups helped individuals navigate daily concerns related to their condition and provided support for asking how people "make it" without having to talk with medical staff. Participants discussed day-to-day coping, posted helpful information, and had real-time chat rooms. These interactions appear to have strengthened social ties for many participants and assisted them in exchanging pragmatic knowledge that was not available in their medical care. In some cases, these online mutual support groups helped raise awareness of issues and build collective responses. In terms of policy, some researchers now argue that online mutual support needs institutional support because it constitutes a medium that can reach many people who otherwise may not receive this valuable nonmedical support.

## Mutual Help Outcomes

Empirical evaluations of mutual help programs have documented their potential in helping members make changes in their lives (den Boer et al., 2004; Kingod et al., 2017; Kryouz et al., 2002; Pistrang et al., 2008). For example, research with GROW, a mutual help group for persons with mental illness, found that weekly attendees of meetings experienced more positive changes in psychological, interpersonal, and community adjustment than infrequent attendees. Compared with matched controls, GROW members spent less than half as many days in psychiatric hospitalization over a 32-month period (Maton & Salem, 1995; Rappaport, 1993). In general, persons with psychiatric disabilities who participate in mutual help groups (not just GROW) have lower symptom levels and hospitalization rates, shorter hospital stays, and enhanced positive functioning and social networks (Chinman et al., 2002).

Studies of participants in AA and similar twelve-step groups have generated similar findings (J. F. Kelly, 2003). Humphreys and colleagues (1994) followed 439 men and women with an alcohol abuse problem in the San

Francisco area over 3 years. Those more involved with AA over the 3-year period were more likely to develop active coping strategies, including less use of alcohol. AA participants also develop greater friendship resources, especially support from others committed to abstinence (Chinman et al., 2002; Humphreys & Noke, 1997).

It is important to note that mutual help groups are not for everyone. Dropout rates are significant (also an issue for professional treatment), and mutual help alone may not be enough for some especially complicated problems (Humphreys, 1997). Moreover, some mutual help groups welcome diversity in their membership and address social injustices underlying some personal problems, whereas others do not (Rapping, 1997).

However, thinking of mutual help only as a treatment method overlooks much of its value (Munn-Giddings & Borkman, 2017). One joins a mutual help group for an extended period, perhaps for life. Membership incurs responsibility not only for working on one's own concerns but also for helping others. For example, Oxford Houses, a mutual help, self-governed, communal living arrangement for persons in substance abuse recovery, have counteracted neighbors' concerns about living near a "halfway house" by focusing on improving the community around them, as well as themselves (Doogan et al., 2019). Rappaport (1993) argued that a more revealing view of such groups is that they are normative communities, providing a sense of belonging, identification with the group, and mutual commitment: a psychological sense of community.

## Spirituality and Coping

Long before psychology was organized, many people turned to spiritual practices and religious communities for support in times of stress. In times of suffering or loss, but also in times of joy and of deeply felt commitment, people have used spiritual resources to understand their lives, to receive and give support, or to experience the transcendent. A spiritual perspective can help make sense of the incomprehensible, unfathomable, and uncontrollable (Todd, 2017). This can be especially meaningful when one faces limitations in the ability to cope, such as when Western cultural and psychological assumptions about controlling outcomes in one's life fall short.

Spirituality and religion offer distinctive personal and social resources for coping. Personal resources include a spiritual relationship with God or other transcendent experience, a set of beliefs that provides meaning in life and may promote coping, and specific coping methods such as prayer and meditation. Social resources include membership and support within a religious congregation or other spiritual setting (including spiritually based mutual help groups) and a sense of belonging (Mammana-Lupo et al., 2014; Pargament, 2008).

However, the personal and social impact of religion and spirituality can also be negative (Hebert et al., 2009). In a survey of U.S. women who had experienced domestic violence, one half of respondents reported negative experiences with religion (Pargament, 1997). Spirituality and religion can create or worsen stressors, such as when a person interprets a stressor in a spiritual way that prevents helpful coping or when personal conflicts with a congregation are not resolved (Pargament, 1997). Among a sample of resilient African American single mothers, some found that involvement in a religious community offered "protection and blessing" (Brodsky, 2000, pp. 213–214), while others found spiritual solace and strength outside religious congregations or avoided them.

Of course, religious beliefs, institutions, and cultural forms of spirituality have much larger purposes than existing solely as resources for coping (Todd, 2017). Their usefulness for coping must be understood within those larger aims. Spirituality involves a sense of transcendence, of going beyond oneself and daily life (J. Hill, 2000; J. G. Kelly, 2002; Sarason, 1993). Spiritual persons often view their relationship with God or a spiritual realm as distinct from other relationships. Spirituality cannot be reduced simply to coping resources

Spiritual and religious traditions are meaningful for members and can expand coping resources and outcomes.

Rawpixel.com/Shutterstock.com

(Mattis & Jagers, 2001). Our focus here on coping concerns only part of the meaning of spirituality.

## Empirical Research on Spirituality and Coping

Empirically, how do spiritual and religious factors affect coping outcomes? Pargament's (1997) classic review of empirical studies of spirituality, religion, and coping has shaped how community psychologists think about spirituality and coping. Of course, people do not need to be religious or spiritual to develop coping skills. Pargament's point was that religious and spiritual dimensions of coping had been overlooked. Participants in these studies were mostly North American adults, including persons with chronic and terminal illnesses, bereaved widows and children, victims of automobile accidents and of floods, Whites and Blacks, heterosexuals and gay men, and senior citizens. Most who indicated religious involvement were Christian. However, a growing research literature has documented the benefits of religion and spirituality for coping of people across religious beliefs (e.g., E. Lee & Chan, 2009; Rosmarin et al., 2009; Tarakeshwar et al., 2003). Researchers measure a variety of coping outcomes, including psychological distress and well-being as well as health.

Spiritual-religious coping practices include prayer, meditation, a sense of a personal relationship with God or other transcendent experience, framing stressors in spiritual terms, engaging in spiritual practices and rituals, and seeking support from congregation members. Both religious and nonreligious persons may use these practices for coping. Pargament's (1997) review documented five general findings about what spiritual-religious coping can add to psychology's understanding of coping:

- Spiritual-religious coping may be particularly important for coping with stressful, largely uncontrollable situations among those who identify as religious or spiritual.

- Spiritual-religious coping was empirically related to positive coping outcomes even after accounting for the influence of nonspiritual coping methods.

- Spiritual-religious coping methods that were most related to positive outcomes included (a) perception of a spiritual relationship with a trustworthy and loving God, (b) activities such as prayer, (c) religious reappraisal promoting the sense that growth can come from stressful events, and (d) receiving support from fellow members of a religious congregation.

- While there are many positive relationships between religion, spirituality, and coping, studies are beginning to show patterns of negative religious coping. Negative effects have included self-blame, a view of a harsh and severe deity, and lack of support from one's religious congregation.

- Persons with low incomes, the elderly, ethnic minorities, women, and the widowed were more likely to find religion and spirituality useful for coping than other groups. What these groups seem to have in common is less access to secular sources of power and resources that can be used to address their problems.

Religion and spirituality are important for understanding coping and community life for many people and for understanding that the effect may be positive or negative (Todd, 2017). The most distinctive coping contributions may occur when other resources are lacking or when stressors are uncontrollable (Pargament, 1997, 2008). Mattis and Jagers (2001) proposed a framework to understand affective, cognitive, and behavioral mechanisms through which religion and spirituality shape individual, family, and communal relationships among African Americans. Sabina and colleagues (2012) studied help-seeking behavior by Latina women who had experienced sexual violence. They found that positive religious coping (e.g., "I work together with God as partners") was associated with more help seeking among family and friends. However, negative religious coping (e.g., "I wonder whether God has abandoned me") was associated with seeking professional help but also with less likelihood of sharing experiences with family. The importance of the development of religious identity is another area of scholarship, especially as it relates to coping and competence (Kress & Elias, 2000).

Community psychologists are beginning to develop an empirical foundation to understand stress and coping across diverse cultural contexts and religious experiences beyond Judeo-Christian traditions. For instance, Tarakeshwar and colleagues (2003) have studied religious practices of Hindus and identified four pathways for religious expression: devotion, ethical action, knowledge, and physical restraint/yoga. They found that these pathways were predictive of well-being and positive coping. Dockett studied the convergence of Buddhism and several core community psychology concepts such as prevention and health promotion, empowerment, understanding people in context, linking individuals to higher levels of analysis, promoting collective wellness, and sense of community (Dockett, 1999, 2003; Dockett et al., 2003). Hazel and Mohatt (2001) conducted a collaborative research project with Native Alaskan leaders to understand how their spirituality can be a resource for well-being and incorporated into a substance abuse prevention program.

## Conclusion

In this chapter, we provided an ecological model of the relationships between stress and coping. In particular, we examined the importance of understanding the context of stress and coping for selecting interventions that can prevent negative outcomes and promote positive outcomes. This model also outlines processes and resources relevant to coping, highlighting community-based resources. However, we do not assume that these concepts fully reflect the complex reality of coping or the diversity of resources and interventions that can be used. We encourage you to consider what else needs to be included and to diagram your own ecological model of coping.

## For Review

### Discussion Questions

**1.** How does the ecological-contextual model of stress and coping presented in this chapter expand your understanding of how mental health problems can develop?

**2.** How does this model expand *where* and *when* to address health problems and social problems?

**3.** What is the role of social support in an ecological-contextual model of stress and coping?

**4.** Looking at the panels in Figure 9.5, where are citizen participation and empowerment relevant? Where are social support and mutual help relevant?

**5.** How might the ecological-contextual model of stress and coping change how mental health professionals think about their work?

### Key Terms

distal factors, 300
proximal factors, 301
distal contextual factors, 301
distal personal factors, 303
proximal stressors, 303
major life events, 304
life transitions, 305
daily hassles, 306
daily uplifts, 306
microaggressions, 306
disasters, 307

minority-related and acculturative stressors, 307
vicious spirals, 308
stress reactions, 309
eustress, 309
material resources, 310
social-emotional competencies, 310
social settings, 311
cultural resources, 311
cognitive appraisal, 312
problem-focused coping, 313

emotion-focused coping, 313
meaning-focused coping, 313
virtuous spirals, 313
posttraumatic growth, 314
wellness, 314
resilience, 315
thriving, 316
generalized support, 323
perceived support, 323
specific support, 323
multidimensional relationships, 325

## Learn More

A detailed summary of the chapter, along with other review materials, is available on the *Community Psychology, Fourth Edition* companion website at http://pubs.apa.org/books/supp/kloos4/.

Prevention of problems and promotion of community members' capacities to address their concerns are common strategies for community psychologists to promote health, resilience, and collective wellness.

Photo by Bret Kloos, reprinted with permission.

# 10 Key Concepts in the Science of Prevention and Promotion

## Looking Ahead  ||▶

**After reading this chapter you will be able to answer these questions:**

1. Why did some psychologists in the mid-20th century become frustrated with an individual-level, treatment-oriented approach to promoting well-being?

2. What are the benefits of prevention compared with treating a problem after it has started, both for individuals and for communities?

3. What does the term "resiliency" mean, and how does it relate to the concepts of prevention and promotion?

4. What are some common elements of effective prevention programs?

5. How can we assess the value of prevention programs?

## Opening Exercise

## The Broad Street Pump

In 1854, a cholera epidemic struck London. Cholera was a relatively new (the first cholera pandemic began in 1816) and deadly disease. An outbreak in 1832 had killed more than 55,000 people in Great Britain, and in 1849 cholera claimed 14,137 victims in London alone. In 1852, the disease struck again. At the time, it was commonly believed that cholera, like other diseases, was spread through miasma (bad air). The mystery about the nature of the disease added to the fear and panic. The only way people knew to escape the disease was to flee the towns and cities in which it appeared. And for many people, especially the poor, leaving was not an option. A physician in London, John Snow, published a pamphlet disputing the miasma theory and suggesting that cholera was reproduced in the human body and spread through food or water (he did not know which). Suppose you were John Snow in London in 1854. What could you do to stop the cholera epidemic? Could these deaths be prevented?

What John Snow did was to develop a new approach to thinking about epidemics. He took

**The Broad Street Pump (continued)**

a map of London and plotted the location of the homes in which 578 people had died from cholera. He went to those homes and spoke to the family members of the people who had died. He found that almost all the people who died had got their drinking water from the Broad Street pump. On his now famous map, he plotted the position of 13 water pumps, showing graphically the relationship between the pump on Broad Street and the cholera deaths. He took this information to a committee of city officials, who removed the handle from the Broad Street pump the next day. The cholera epidemic subsided (S. Johnson, 2006).

John Snow is now considered one of the founders of epidemiology, and his work in identifying the source of the 1854 London cholera epidemic is considered one of the events that launched the field of public health. This story also plays a central role in the development of community psychology because of what it teaches us about prevention. First, even if you do not know how to cure a problem, you may still be able to prevent it. Second, you do not need to know the cause of a problem to prevent it; you just need to understand something about the mechanisms through which the problem is transmitted or sustained. Third, you can often prevent a problem by changing some aspect of human behavior. And fourth, while individual behavior change can contribute to prevention, complete prevention of a problem often relies upon public action.

These lessons have been fundamental to the development of prevention science, as well as its application to emotional, behavioral, and cognitive disorders.

## What Do You Think?

1. Did John Snow's work require a change in perspective? How would you describe that change?

2. There was a great deal of resistance to John Snow's theory that cholera had nothing to do with "bad air." Why do you think he encountered so much resistance? What did he need to do to change people's minds?

3. At what ecological level was his intervention directed? How do you think this related to the resistance his ideas faced?

# Prevention and Promotion Are All Around You

In the previous chapters, we presented concepts that community psychologists use to understand individuals and communities. In this chapter and the next, we convey how community psychology's values, concepts, and tools can be used in the context of preventing problem behaviors and mental health difficulties and promoting sound mental health and social competence. In this chapter, we outline key concepts and give some examples of prevention programming. In Chapter 11, we review in detail how to implement prevention/promotion innovations in a variety of contexts.

Prevention and promotion efforts are ubiquitous. Parents, teachers, health workers, police officers, safety inspectors, public officials, and many others spend a great deal of their time in prevention efforts. Every time a

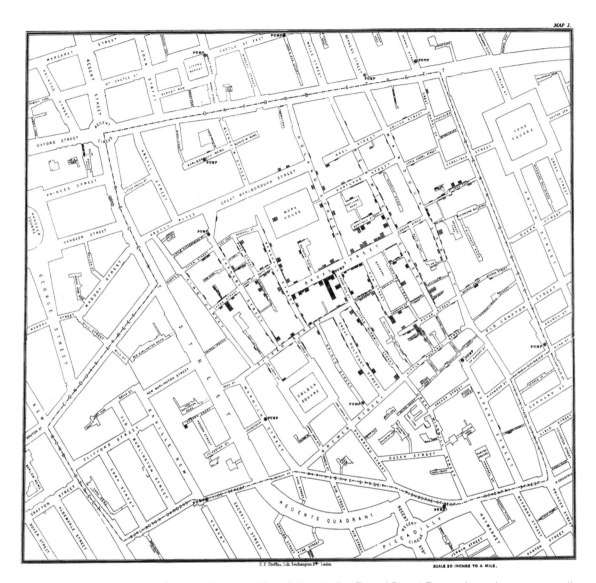

John Snow's map of the cholera epidemic and its relation to the Broad Street Pump shows how community well-being is impacted by environmental factors that community psychologists can then target.

parent tells their child to wear a helmet and look both ways before crossing the street on a bike, their intent is to prevent a harmful outcome. The majority of prevention work is not done by community psychologists or by psychologists at all. It is conducted by everyone, both as a part of their occupations and as a part of their everyday lives. As we mentioned in Chapter 1, community psychology has had a "peculiar success" in having its approaches widely adopted even though the field itself is not well known (Snowden, 1987). This is particularly true of prevention science. Since its founding, the field has been

**prevention**
taking steps to ensure a negative event does not occur, rather than having to deal with the negative impact of that event.

interdisciplinary and collaborative, so much so that its members and their work in prevention and promotion appear in many places, including law, education, government, public health, social work, the corporate world, and several fields of psychology (especially developmental, health, organizational, school, and clinical). Further, members of other disciplines often collaborate on research and interventions that appear as part of collections of work in community psychology. In this chapter, we help you recognize some of the work community psychologists are doing in prevention and promotion, alongside the work of practitioners in other disciplines and in various countries. We then discuss some successful prevention and promotion programs that illustrate the ideas we present in this chapter.

## What Is Prevention?

**Prevention** is a commonsense concept that derives from Latin words meaning "to anticipate" or "before something to come." The language of prevention is found in all aspects of public endeavor. Although the idea of prevention can be found throughout the written history of humankind, the idea that prevention concepts could be systematically applied to mental disorders has a very recent history.

In 1959, George Albee looked at the number of people in the United States who could benefit from mental health counseling in a given year. Then he looked at the number of mental health clinicians the country could produce. His analysis showed that there could never be a sufficient number of clinicians trained to provide all the needed mental health services for the population. Consider the implications of this extraordinary finding. Therapeutic resources were scarce and would realistically remain scarce. If we continued to rely upon a one-on-one, professional-to-patient method for providing psychotherapy, then U.S. society would never be able to train enough professionals to provide therapy to everyone who needed it. And, not incidentally, we would not be able to pay for it.

Another issue raised by Albee's (1959) findings concerns the way in which scarce treatment resources are distributed. A series of epidemiological studies (Hollingshead & Redlich, 1958; Myers & Bean, 1968) showed a strong relationship between socioeconomic status, ethnicity, and services received. Members of poor and minority groups were more likely to receive severe diagnoses, to receive medication rather than psychotherapy, and to be seen in groups rather than individually. The preferred clients were those most like the therapists—male, Caucasian, verbally articulate, and successful.

Psychologists working in the 1950s saw research saying the following: (a) Psychotherapy may not work. (b) Even if it does work, we can't provide it to everyone who needs it. (c) Even if we could provide it, it is not equally available for all groups. These people looked at this research and said, "There has to be a better way."

**promotion**
encouraging positive, healthy behaviors to replace maladaptive behaviors that could lead to problems.

Now we go back to our opening exercise, the story of John Snow and the beginning of the public health model. The public health model is based upon the idea that no disease has ever been eradicated through the treatment of its victims. John Snow did not develop a cure or even a more effective treatment for cholera. Instead, he prevented new occurrences of the disorder (the *incidence* of the disorder, in public health terms). Mental health professionals began thinking about what it would mean to apply this concept to cognitive, emotional, and behavioral disorders. Our need for psychotherapy would be greatly decreased if we could prevent problems in living from arising to begin with.

## What Is Promotion?

Although community psychology has embraced the concept of prevention, there is another aspect of the concept that merits consideration: **promotion**, which involves developing and reinforcing positive behaviors to replace maladaptive behaviors that could lead to problems. For example, when we implement a program to decrease the incidence of child abuse, the goal is not limited to stopping parents from abusing their children. We want to support parents in developing positive parenting skills. Divorce prevention programs are not really about preventing divorce; the goal is to support the development of healthy, successful marriages. These examples focus on developing desired competencies, skills, and abilities. Overall health and quality of life become the goals, more than simply preventing psychiatric disorders or types of problem behaviors. Cowen (1991, 2000a) championed the term *wellness* to describe the overall goal of preventive efforts. Although wellness refers to life satisfaction or gratification in living, it is, like most of the concepts in this book, ecological and transactional in nature. Cowen's views have become central to how community psychologists think about prevention of disorder and promotion of competence and wellness.

# Concepts for Understanding Prevention and Promotion

In this section, we describe the historical progression of concepts from prevention of disorder, to promotion of competence, to ideas of strengths and thriving. In so doing, we define and illustrate key concepts in the contexts in which they are used.

## Primary, Secondary, and Tertiary Prevention

There is a rich history to the concept of prevention, rooted in the field of public health and the mental hygiene movement of the early 20th century (Heller et al., 1984; Spaulding & Balch, 1983). However, Gerald Caplan is recognized as the individual whose use of the term "prevention" made it a part of the

**primary prevention**
to reduce potentially harmful circumstances before they have a chance to create difficulty.

**secondary prevention**
actions that are taken as initial signs of a disorder or difficulty appear; also known as "early intervention."

**tertiary prevention**
actions that are taken to decrease the intensity, length, and lasting effects of mental health or behavioral disorders; these programs usually encompass a group of people and are offered at the systems level.

mental health lexicon. Caplan (1964) made a distinction between the following three types of prevention.

*Primary Prevention.* **Primary prevention** is an intervention given to entire populations when they are not in a condition of known need or distress. The goal is to lower the rate of new cases (from a public health perspective, to reduce the incidence) of disorders. Primary prevention intervenes to reduce potentially harmful circumstances before they have a chance to create difficulty. Examples of this are such things as vaccinations, fluoridating water, and providing programs to build decision-making and problem-solving skills to children in preschool. Similarly, primary prevention also can be thought of as being applied to all persons in a given setting, regardless of potential need (e.g., all fifth graders in preparation for transition to middle school, all first-year college students).

*Secondary Prevention.* **Secondary prevention** is an intervention given to populations showing early signs of a disorder or difficulty. Another term for this is "early intervention." This concept is a precursor of current notions of being "at risk," which we discuss later. Examples of secondary prevention are programs targeted to children who experience an uncomfortable level of shyness, children who are beginning to have academic difficulty, or adults who are getting into conflicts with coworkers on the job.

Secondary prevention presupposes some method of determining which individuals are at risk. Identifying such individuals creates a potential for stigmatization, both because they do not currently have a disorder and because they might never develop one. Improving methods of risk identification represents an important area of work in community psychology.

*Tertiary Prevention.* **Tertiary prevention** is an intervention given to populations who have a mental health or behavioral disorder, with the intention of reducing its intensity and duration and limiting the long-term negative effects caused by the disorder. These types of programs are aimed at preventing additional problems and improving the mental health and quality of life of the people affected. People leaving long-term mental health treatment, substance abuse treatment, or prison need to come back to a family, a home, a job or education program, and support systems tailored to their needs. Tertiary prevention, as it is currently practiced, is a strategy for a whole group of people, not just individuals, and is often seen at a systems level.

## Universal, Selective, and Indicated Preventive Measures

A report by the National Academy of Medicine (Mrazek & Haggerty, 1994) had great influence on our thinking about prevention. Its main conceptual contribution is the idea of universal, selective, or indicated measures or methods for prevention, and you may see these terms used if you continue

**universal preventive measures**
similar to primary prevention, these are interventions provided to an entire population group even though these populations are usually not in distress.

**selective preventive measures**
interventions provided to a population of individuals who carry an above-average risk to develop a mental health or behavioral disorder.

**indicated preventive measures**
interventions provided to those individuals who are associated with high risk for development of mental health or behavioral disorders, particularly if they demonstrate initial symptoms but have not been fully diagnosed with a disorder.

your investigations into prevention science. While this framework is similar to Caplan's, it differs in that none of the populations described have yet experienced a disorder. Instead, the distinction is based upon the level of risk or distress the members of the population experience.

*Universal Preventive Measures.* **Universal preventive measures** are interventions designed to be offered to everyone in a given population group, and they typically are administered to populations that are not in distress. This is similar to primary prevention.

*Selective Preventive Measures.* **Selective preventive measures** are interventions designed for people at above-average risk for developing behavioral or emotional disorders. That risk may be based on their environment (e.g., low income, family conflict) or personal factors (e.g., low self-esteem, difficulties in school). These risk characteristics are associated with the development of particular disorders but are not symptoms of the disorder itself.

*Indicated Preventive Measures.* **Indicated preventive measures** are interventions directed toward individual people who are considered at high risk for developing a disorder in the future, especially if they show early symptoms of the disorder. However, they do not meet criteria for full-fledged diagnosis of a mental disorder.

Interestingly, the National Academy of Medicine report (Mrazek & Haggerty, 1994) places mental health promotion (including concepts related to competence and wellness) into a separate area, distinct from prevention. The editors viewed self-esteem and mastery as the main focus of mental health promotion, with competence, self-efficacy, and individual empowerment all terms commonly used in describing such efforts. The National Academy of Medicine report defined its focus in terms of whether or not an approach prevents a specific disorder, not in terms of competence enhancement.

## Prevention of Disorder and Promotion of Wellness and Competence

Earlier in this chapter, we presented Cowen's (1991, 2000a) view that the goal of intervention should be not just the prevention of disorder but rather the enhancement of wellness and competence as well. He, and many others who share his viewpoint, believed that the goal of merely preventing disorders was setting our sights too low. Rather than a goal of having people and families minimally functional, our goal should be to ensure that they are functioning to their fullest potential.

Among prevention scientists and public policymakers, there is a continuing debate about where the emphasis of time and resources is best placed: on prevention or promotion. In addition, within these areas there are varying options for emphasis (e.g., based on age, socioeconomics, gender, or ethnicity).

Convincing spokespersons of different points of view arise periodically, and this debate is ongoing. In general, the debate can be framed between proponents of prevention of disorder and those believing that promotion of wellness and social competence should be emphasized.

Advocates of the prevention view argue that we are learning a great deal about how to prevent specific disorders such as depression, suicide, conduct disorders, and schizophrenia. Research should be directed toward isolating and reducing the operation of risk factors most closely targeted with specific disorders. This view is most likely to be associated with selective and indicated interventions, based on the National Academy of Medicine report (Mrazek & Haggerty, 1994).

Advocates for promotion note that many people may not experience psychological well-being despite not having specific disorders. We know a great deal about how to promote sound health and social competence, drawing in part from interventions in public health in such areas as prevention of cardiovascular disease, from school settings in areas such as social and emotional skill building, and from workplace efforts to increase organizational effectiveness. Research should be directed toward identifying and understanding the factors that promote health, wellness, and competence in daily living. These will differ in different living environments, cross-culturally and internationally.

In reality, it is often difficult to separate the two goals of health promotion and problem prevention. Several prevention scientists have argued that the distinction between prevention and promotion is particularly baseless when discussing child development. Children who do not drop out of school, do not abuse substances, are not involved in juvenile delinquency, and delay becoming parents may still have problems developing into healthy, happy, and well-functioning adults. Thus, programs that focus solely on preventing those negative outcomes will not be designed to ensure optimal development (Weissberg et al., 2003). Programs that are aimed at the prevention of a specific problem may be focused on perceived deficits in the population, ignoring community psychology's focus on strengths and building competencies. In fact, strictly focused prevention programs may not be as effective as intervention with a broader health promotion focus. The distinction between the two types of programs becomes even more confused when you realize that health promotion programs are often evaluated in terms of specific prevention goals, basically because those types of goals are easier to specify and measure.

The goals of preventing specific disorders and promoting wellness and competence are not mutually exclusive, and the techniques used to pursue them may be the same in particular circumstances. There are strong parallels with physical health, where health-promoting activities such as a sound diet are valuable and may also serve to prevent such problems as cardiovascular disease but may not have specific preventive effects on specific conditions or illnesses. This issue may become a factor in the politics of prevention and promotion programs. Since the goals of prevention programs are generally easier to understand, and evaluate, than the goals of promotion programs, they may receive greater support among policymakers and funding agencies. However, as you will see later in this chapter, many programs that are designed as prevention programs actually end up having broader, health promotion effects.

## Promotion of What? Building Resiliency

In 1955, one of the most remarkable longitudinal studies in the history of developmental psychology began on the island of Kauai. Emmy Werner and her colleagues followed 698 children, every child born on the island that year, for 40 years. The children were multiracial, and a full 30% experienced one or more risk factors in their lives, such as prenatal or birth complications, poverty, family violence, divorce, or parents with psychopathology or low education. One of the first important findings to arise from this study was that two

Emmy Werner's research found that the more risk factors children are exposed to, the more negative outcomes they face. However, they also build resilience, a process community psychologists can support.

iStock.com/YinYang

**cumulative-risk hypothesis**
the theory that multiple risk factors during childhood when taken all together raise the likelihood of negative mental and behavioral health outcomes exponentially.

**resiliency**
the ability of some individuals to overcome adverse conditions and experience healthy development.

thirds of the children who experienced four or more of these risk factors in the first 2 years of life developed learning disabilities, behavior disorders, delinquency, or mental health problems before adulthood (Werner, 1996, 2005). This finding, and others like it, helped lead to the **cumulative-risk hypothesis** (Rutter, 1979). This hypothesis recognizes that almost all children can deal with one risk factor in their lives without it increasing their risk of negative outcomes. Most children can handle two risk factors. But when you get up to four risk factors, the chances of a negative outcome increase exponentially. It is not the presence of risk in a child's life that results in negative outcomes; it is the level of cumulative risk.

But in the over 40 years since this study began, many people, including Emmy Werner, have decided that the findings on cumulative risk are not the most important thing we learned from it. Instead, much of Werner's work has focused on the 30% of the children exposed to four or more risk factors who did not develop behavior or learning problems:

> One out of three of these children grew into competent, confident and caring adults. They did not develop any behavior or learning problems during childhood or adolescence. They succeeded in school, managed home and social life well, and set realistic educational and vocational goals and expectations for themselves. By the time they reached age 40, not one of these individuals was unemployed, none had been in trouble with the law, and none had to rely on social services. Their divorce rates, mortality rates and rates of chronic health problems were significantly lower at midlife than those of their same sex peers. Their educational and vocational accomplishment were equal to or even exceeded those of children who had grown up in more economically secure and stable home environments. (Werner, 2005, pp. 11–12)

## What Do You Think?

**1.** Why might Emily Werner and others believe that the children who experienced multiple risk factors but reached adulthood without major problems have more to teach us than the children who experienced serious difficulties?

**2.** How might you explain the outcomes of those children from an individualistic perspective? How might you explain them from a structural perspective?

**3.** What do you think we have to learn about prevention and promotion from this research?

Werner termed these children who overcame multiple risk factors to become "competent, confident and caring adults" *resilient*, and the study of resiliency became the focus of her research. **Resiliency** refers to the ability of some individuals to overcome adverse conditions and experience healthy development. Werner and her colleagues identified factors that served to protect children exposed to multiple risk factors from negative outcomes. These protective factors (summarized in Table 10.1) have also been identified by other researchers (Garmezy, 1985; Masten & Powell, 2003; Rutter & Sroufe, 2000).

One of the important things to note about this table is the ways in which the factors interrelate and affect one another. Children with a positive outlook on life and an adaptable, social personality find it easier to form and maintain positive relationships. The presence of prosocial organizations in a community, and the ability of children (or adults) to access those services, provides opportunities for the development of positive relationships. The presence of high-quality health care and social services in a community might mean that there are programs that teach appropriate parenting skills (we talk about some of those programs later). And the existence of strong, supportive relationships outside the family helps support positive parenting.

Before we leave the story of the Kauai Longitudinal Study, you might be interested in hearing about the 70% of the children exposed to four or more

**Table 10.1** Examples of Attributes of Individuals and Their Contexts Often Associated With Resilience

| | |
|---|---|
| Individual differences | Cognitive abilities (IQ scores, attentional skills, executive functioning skills) |
| | Self-perceptions of competence, worth, confidence (self-efficacy, self-esteem) |
| | Temperament and personality (adaptability, sociability) |
| | Self-regulation skills (impulse control, affect and arousal regulation) |
| | Positive outlook on life (hopefulness, belief that life has meaning, faith) |
| Relationships | Parenting quality (including warmth, structure and monitoring, expectations) |
| | Close relationships with competent adults (parents, relatives, mentors) |
| | Connections to prosocial and rule-abiding peers (among older children) |
| Community resources and opportunities | Good schools |
| | Connections to prosocial organizations (e.g., clubs, religious groups) |
| | Neighborhood quality (public safety, collective supervision, libraries, recreation centers) |
| | Quality of social services and health care |

*Note.* From Masten and Powell, 2003. Reprinted with permission from Cambridge University Press.

risk factors who did not display resiliency in childhood. These children all displayed significant behavioral or mental health problems by age 18. They experienced school failure, drug abuse, teen pregnancy, delinquency, and mental or emotional disorders. But when Werner and her colleagues followed up with these people at ages 32 and 40, the majority were doing fine in middle age. They had stable employment, were happy with their relationships, and were productive members of their communities. What the researchers found, and what has been documented in other longitudinal studies of resiliency, is that for the majority of these troubled teens, the *opening of opportunities* in early adulthood led to significant improvement in functioning by middle age (Werner, 2005, p. 12). These opportunities included education, vocational and educational opportunities provided through the military, geographic relocation, a good marriage (often a second marriage), and conversion to a religion that provided membership in a strong and active faith community. For some participants in the study, surviving a life-threatening experience served as an opportunity to evaluate their lives and make positive changes.

Masten and Powell (2003) emphasized that resilience arises from what they termed *ordinary magic* (p. 15). While these individuals are facing extraordinary adversity (think about what exposure to four or more risk factors means in the

From 'The Gardens Community Garden, Haringey,' by Department for Communities and Local Government. Licensed under CC BY-ND 2.0. Adapted with permission.

Just as gardeners work to provide a healthy environment for all their plants, community psychologists work to develop communities where everyone can thrive.

life of a child), they overcome that adversity through resources and relationships that are part of normal, everyday life. Professional intervention was found to play a very small role in the lives of resilient individuals (Werner, 2005).

The research on risk and protective factors, resiliency, and ordinary magic has resulted in a rich field devoted to exploring ways to decrease the presence of risk factors and increase the presence of protective factors in the lives of all children. The goal is not just to decrease the prevalence of disorders and problem behaviors but rather to develop strengths, support positive development, and promote resilience and thriving. Increasingly, this is becoming the goal of the majority of the programs described in this chapter and the next, even if the original intent of the program was narrowly defined as the prevention of a specific problem.

In Chapter 8, we presented a model of risk and protective processes in coping, in which the positive outcomes are resilience, wellness, thriving, and empowerment. That model could easily be used to describe processes and intended outcomes in prevention and promotion. The goal is to use the research on specific risk and protective factors to ensure that everyone in a community has a chance to experience the ordinary magic that helps people thrive.

## Putting It All Together: Addressing Risk and Protective Factors on a Community Level

Research on identifying specific risk and protective factors has flourished since the Kauai study—see for example the Casale et al. (2015) study of risk and protective factors among impoverished teens and their caregivers in South Africa, which is described in Chapter 4. But those lists of factors do not provide a coherent framework upon which to base interventions. In 1982, George Albee developed a formula to illustrate that the presence of risk factors alone did not definitively lead to behavioral and emotional disorders. Rather, it was the cumulative effect of those risk factors and the presence of protective factors that predicted whether disorder would arise. The protective factors had a direct impact on the effect of the risk factors. The formula was also meant to be used as a framework for potential points of prevention interventions.

Albee's equation only included two categories of risk factors (physical vulnerability and stress) and three categories of protective factors (coping skills, social support, and self-esteem). Maurice Elias (1987) argued that Albee's equation could too easily be interpreted solely at an individual level (although this is not what Albee intended). Community psychology calls for ways of examining the risk and protective processes for populations and communities, not just for individuals. In order to reflect this emphasis, Elias extended Albee's formula to explicitly include risk and protective factors in organizations, communities, and societies. He did this by including two new risk factors (risk factors in the environment and stressors in the environment) and three new protective factors (positive socialization practices, social support resources, and opportunities for connectedness). You saw a detailed explanation of this type of modeling illustrating the role of distal and proximal risk and protective factors related to stress and coping in Chapter 9 (see Figure 9.2).

In recent years, the research focus on the promotion of wellness, resilience, and thriving has given rise to two prominent models, Positive Youth Development (PYD) and the Social Development Strategy (SDS). Both models focus on identifying strategies to strengthen the ordinary magic in communities in order to promote the healthy development of children and youth by changing the contexts of children's lives. While there has been some debate about the relative merits of each model, arising largely from their different theoretical beginnings, more recent discussions recognize their fundamental commonalities (Catalano et al., 2002). The goal of both models is to promote a supportive environment for everyone living there. Table 10.2 summarizes the common elements of these models.

While both of these models are specific to children and adolescents, the general understanding of risk and protective factors is also relevant to adults. Take a look at the social development strategies in Table 10.2. The presence of these protective factors would be equally important for an adult who is in recovery from substance abuse, who recently lost a job, or who just left an abusive relationship. Communities that provide substantive and structural protective factors—that provide a supportive environment for growth and wellness—support well-being at all stages of the lifespan.

**Table 10.2** Common Elements of Positive Youth Development and Social Development Strategy

| Social development strategy | Positive youth development |
| --- | --- |
| Opportunities for meaningful involvement | Youth are given useful roles in the community. |
| Skills to master opportunities | Youth are supported in developing a commitment to learning and social competencies. |
| Recognition for accomplishments and effort | Community values youth. |
| Bonding to positive influences | Support from family and other adult relationships. |
| Healthy beliefs and clear standards for behavior | Families, schools, neighborhoods, and peers have clear standards and high expectations for youth. |

Our understanding of risk and protective factors is far from complete. A critical example is the risk posed for people of color from racism and discriminatory racial encounters. Recent efforts have been able to document the deep and encompassing nature of the negative effects of experiencing racism and have identified protective processes to combat that risk. Sociopolitical development is a process employed by parents to help their children develop a framework for understanding racist encounters and to develop a positive ethnic identity and sense of self-efficacy, which can help promote coping and well-being (Anderson & Stevenson, 2019). Both Positive Youth Development and the Social Development Strategy would benefit from incorporating this work.

## Applying Knowledge of Risk and Protective Factors in Your Community

Imagine yourself moving into a new home, where you find a garden. There are weeds choking the plants, the soil is dry and rocky, and many of the plants are weak and struggling. But some—just a few—are thriving. You have never gardened before, but you spend time in the garden. You read gardening books and talk to neighbors who have successfully raised a wide variety of plants in conditions much like yours. And then you work. You test the soil, look at the sunlight, and measure the amount of water each part of the garden receives. Then you enhance the soil with compost, remove enough weeds to provide space for the plants you want, and ensure that each plant is receiving enough sunlight and water. As you work, you realize that you aren't trying to take care of each plant individually; your goal is to provide all the elements for a healthy garden. If your garden as a whole is taken care of, the chances of each individual plant thriving are greatly increased.

This is the fundamental point concerning how community psychologists think about risk and protective factors in your community. We are not just focused on eliminating the weeds or supporting any individual plant. We recognize that there will always be weeds in our garden. Rather than focusing inventions at the individual level, we look for ways to strengthen the organizations and communities—the gardens—in which we all live. By understanding the risk factors and strengthening the protective factors, we hope to create a community environment where everyone has a chance to thrive.

The point of understanding risk and protective factors is not to think of one as outweighing or canceling out the other. Rather, the idea is that identifying risk factors can lead you to multiple points for intervention (refer to Chapter 9 and Figure 9.2 for additional examples of this). And the purpose of those interventions is not solely to eliminate the risk factors but to actively transform what were risk factors into protective factors.

Figure 10.1 is meant to be a graphic portrayal of these ideas. Risk factors and protective factors exist at multiple ecological levels (see Chapter 1). In this illustration, the risk factors are examples of those commonly affecting young children. The shapes represent points of intervention. They are actual evidence-based programs and activities that we discuss later in this chapter, as well as in Chapters 11 and 13. The final column shows the protective factors that have been shown to be enhanced as a result of those interventions.

This is an ecological-transactional model, a concept we introduced you to in Chapter 6. It is ecological in that we locate the risk and protective factors at specific ecological levels, and it is transactional in the recognition that those settings are transformed by the interventions. That is the goal of assessing and addressing risk and protective factors, and the goal of the field of community psychology: not just to assist some people but to transform settings for the benefit of everyone.

Although the model anchors particular risk factors in specific ecological levels, it is important to realize that the risk factors could be located at other levels, with subsequent changes in how we understand the issue. For example, a lack of affordable housing could be viewed as a locality-specific problem. Defining the problem as locality specific might suggest that we look at local zoning practices or local approaches to developing affordable housing projects. But defining it as a macrosystem problem, as we do in this model, provides both a different definition of the problem and a different intervention. We discuss affordable housing further in Chapter 13.

The proliferation of arrows in the figure is evidence based and deliberate. The arrows also highlight the transformational nature of this work. Interventions at a community level, when done well, support one another and amplify one another's effects. For example, promoting self-regulation skills in children is most effective when those skills are taught and supported across settings. That is why self-regulation skills are linked to home-visiting programs, skills-based parenting programs, and social-emotional learning programs (which are generally school-based) in our model. We could have added an arrow between the protective factors of self-regulation and effective parenting to illustrate the point that warm, effective parenting is key to the development of self-regulation skills in children and that effective parenting is easier when children have those skills (Rosanbalm & Murray, 2017).

Notice that community coalitions are centrally placed in the figure. That is because building effective coalitions is key to the successful implementation of a risk and protective factor approach to community change. Two examples of effective programs for strengthening communities through coalition formation and the implementation of evidence-based programs are the Communities That Care program and the Search Institute's Developmental

**Figure 10.1** An Example of How Community Psychologists Conceptualize Risk and Intervention at Multiple Ecological Levels to Strengthen Protective Factors That Promote the Well-Being of Young Children

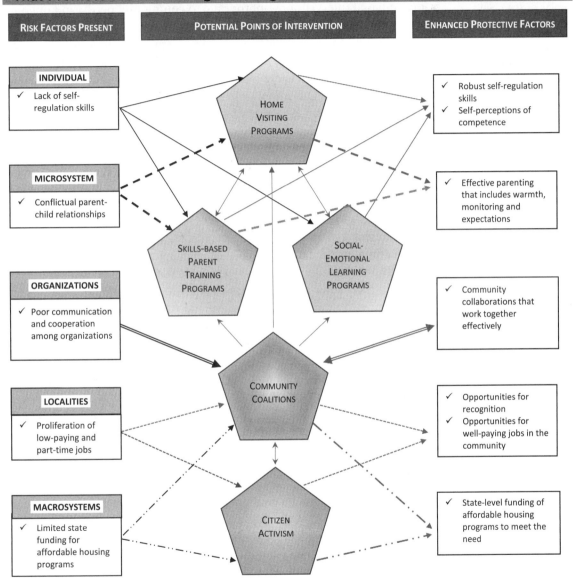

**developmental assets**

factors within the child; the child's family; or the child's school, neighborhood, or community that promote healthy child and youth development.

Assets approach. The Search Institute utilizes PYD, and Communities That Care utilizes SDS. Both programs emphasize the importance of community coalitions, the assessment of community resources, a focused search for evidence-based interventions appropriate to community needs, and ongoing evaluation of the effectiveness of their efforts.

The Search Institute (2004) reviewed existing research and conducted extensive research of their own to develop a list of 40 developmental assets. **Developmental assets** are factors within the child; the child's family; or the child's school, neighborhood, or community that promote healthy child and youth development (Scales et al., 2004). Internal assets include a strong commitment to learning, positive values, social competencies, and a positive identity. External assets include supportive relationships, opportunities for prosocial involvement, clear boundaries and expectations for behavior, and opportunities for constructive use of time. Many of the developmental assets identified in the research reflect the factors related to resiliency listed in Table 10.1. You can see detailed descriptions of these assets as they apply to different age ranges on the Search Institute's website (https://www.search-institute.org/).

The Search Institute has a survey available that coalitions can administer to youth in their communities to determine which developmental assets are strongly represented in their community and which are weak or absent. The coalition then uses the results of that assessment to develop an action plan to promote positive youth development. While the Search Institute is the organization most strongly identified with the developmental assets approach, there are other organizations, such as the Community Asset Development for Youth program at Michigan State University, that also use the PYD model.

The Communities That Care (CTC) program was developed by David Hawkins and Richard Catalano. CTC uses an approach similar to a developmental assets approach but includes both risk factors and protective factors in their assessment. A large longitudinal study that randomly assigned 24 communities to either the CTC intervention group or a control group has been repeatedly evaluated. While evaluation results over the years have been mixed, the latest evaluation, 10 years after baseline when program participants were 21 years old, found positive long-term reductions in substance use (49%), antisocial behavior (18%), and engagement in violence (11%; Oesterle et al., 2018). More information about CTC can be found on their website (https://www.communitiesthatcare.net).

Both of these programs begin with an assessment of the developmental assets or risk and protective factors currently existing in your community. The programs then guide you in selecting and implementing interventions that are targeted to the specific needs of your community. This holistic, strengths-based approach to community assessment and intervention clearly reflects the values and philosophy of community psychology.

# Do Prevention Programs Work?

**effect size**
a quantitative way to determine the effectiveness of a program by reporting the strength of the effect of an intervention.

**best practices approach**
a qualitative way to understand effectiveness by analyzing current best practice research and conducting site visits to further discover and examine common characteristics that could lead to continued and future success.

The short answer to this question is yes, they do. But, as with research regarding the efficacy of psychotherapy, research in prevention science has moved beyond the basic question "Does it work?" to sophisticated questions such as "How well does it work, for whom, under what conditions, and what are the mechanisms that account for its effects?" Clear answers are a precursor to making sound decisions about prevention programming, policy, and funding. However, deriving such answers can be difficult.

One of the major tools in finding answers to those questions is meta-analytic techniques. Meta-analyses compare the findings of all studies done on a given topic that meet certain methodological criteria (e.g., comparison of parent training programs and control groups in randomized field experiments, all of which used similar dependent variables). Experimental, quantitative studies of prevention programs often compute a statistical estimate of **effect size**: the strength of the effect of that intervention (independent variable) on the chosen outcomes (dependent variables). There are many ways of presenting information regarding effect sizes. For example, the statement, "The children participating in the intervention demonstrated an increase of 10 percentage points on their test scores, while children in the control group demonstrated no such increase," is a description of the strength of the effect of the intervention. In a quantitative meta-analysis, the average effect size is computed for a set of similar programs tested in multiple studies and is generally presented as a statistic between 0 and 1. Although not without controversy (e.g., Gurevitch et al., 2018; Trickett, 1997), meta-analysis is one useful tool for broad analyses of the effectiveness of prevention programs.

Another tool for deriving an understanding of what makes for effective prevention programming is the **best practices approach**. This approach focuses on qualitative analyses. In a best practice approach, the focus is on studying a specific type of program that has been empirically shown to be effective across multiple settings and on gleaning from further studies of those settings the procedures that effective programs of that type have in common. Some best practice analyses are conducted through a review of the available research, while others involve actual site visits and qualitative research much more detailed and descriptive than what is usually found in journal articles.

So what does all this research tell us? There is a great deal of information generated by this research, and it is extremely difficult to summarize. We try to summarize it later in this section, but first we would like to give you an idea of what some of the meta-analytic findings look like.

## Meta-Analyses of Prevention Programs

There have been many meta-analyses of prevention programs published in the literature. Generally, they focus on one area of prevention. For example, one of the earliest meta-analytic studies of prevention programs was conducted by Durlak and Wells in 1997. They examined 177 primary prevention programs directed at children and adolescents. Their conclusions, which have many qualifiers that are best read in the original study, are that 59%–82% of participants in a primary prevention program surpassed the average performance of those in control groups. This indicates clear superiority of prevention groups to controls. Durlak and Wells (1998) conducted a second meta-analysis on 130 secondary or indicated prevention programs for children who were experiencing early signs of difficulty such as persistent shyness, learning difficulties, and antisocial behavior. The average participant in these programs was better off than 70% of the control group members. These programs were especially effective for children whose externalizing behaviors put them at risk of conduct disorders and delinquency, for which later treatment is difficult.

Other meta-analytic studies have reviewed the following prevention areas and demonstrate significant effects for prevention programming:

- prevention of childhood and adolescent depression (Fisak et al., 2011; Horowitz & Garber, 2006; Stice et al., 2009)

- school bullying prevention programs (Gaffney et al., 2018; Merrell et al., 2008)

- teen pregnancy and subsequent teen pregnancies (Corcoran & Pillai, 2007; Smith Battle et al., 2018)

- childhood and adolescent drug use (C. H. Brown et al., 2007; Das et al., 2016; Tobler et al., 2000)

- programs implemented in infancy and early childhood (Manning et al., 2010)

- mentoring programs (DuBois et al., 2002; Raposa et. al., 2019)

- social and emotional learning programs for children (R. Taylor et al., 2017; Weissberg & Durlak, 2006)

While quantitative meta-analyses are, and will continue to be, an important part of our understanding of effective prevention programs, it can be difficult to translate their findings into clear guidelines for designing or implementing programs. For that, we need to add the descriptive piece provided by best practices analyses. The past 20 years have been extremely productive in combining information from these two approaches. Table 10.3 summarizes 10 principles for effective prevention and promotion programs. We return to this table later in the chapter, where we present specific examples of effective prevention programs.

**Table 10.3** Principles of Effective Prevention/Promotion Programs

| Principle | Definition |
| --- | --- |
| Theory driven and evidence based | Programs have a theoretical justification, address risk and protective factors identified in research, and have empirical support of efficacy. |
| Comprehensive | Programs provide multiple interventions in multiple settings to address interrelated goals. |
| Appropriately timed | Programs are provided before the onset of a disorder, at an appropriate developmental stage for the participants, or during important life transitions. |
| Socioculturally relevant | Programs are culturally sensitive and incorporate cultural norms when appropriate. |
| Behavioral and skills based | Programs include a strong behavioral component that focuses on the acquisition of specific skills and ensures opportunities for practicing those skills. |
| Sufficient dosage | Programs are of a sufficient length and intensity to ensure the desired effects and have subsequent booster sessions to reinforce these effects when appropriate. |
| Positive relationships | Programs specifically promote the development of positive relationships to provide mentoring and social support. |
| Second-order change | Programs include a focus on changes in setting and communities, including changes in formal policies and specific practices and developing resources for positive development. |
| Support for staff | Programs provide appropriate training for staff and ongoing support to ensure effective implementation and evaluation. |
| Program evaluation | Programs have ongoing processes to ensure continual evaluation and improvement, assessment of outcomes, and assessment of community needs. |

*Note.* This table is adapted from work by Nation et al. (2003), Weissberg et al. (2003), and Zins et al. (2004).

## Are Prevention Programs Cost-Effective?

When people are first presented with the data regarding the effectiveness of prevention programs, a common response is, "Sure, this all sounds good, but it must be expensive. We just can't afford it." Successfully implementing a prevention or promotion program requires significant human resources in terms of time, dedication, and effort. We discuss these resource requirements in detail in Chapter 11, but in this section we want to specifically discuss monetary costs. While some prevention and promotion programs cost very little money

**cost-effectiveness analysis**
an evaluative process used to determine if the value of an intervention, program, or service justifies its cost; research has been limited because it is difficult to conduct, and evaluations are complicated.

to implement, many of them are quite expensive. Is the statement "We just can't afford it" a good reason for not implementing prevention programs?

**Cost-effectiveness analyses** essentially view prevention/promotion programs as an investment, and the analyses are trying to determine the return on that investment. Research on the cost-effectiveness of prevention programs has been ongoing for almost as long as the programs have been evaluated, but interest in this question has been particularly critical in recent decades. Even with this surge in interest, and the intense need for information on cost-effectiveness to inform policy decisions, the body of good cost-effectiveness evaluations is still very small. The reason for this is clear; these evaluations are extremely complex and very hard to conduct.

One type of cost-effectiveness analysis compares several programs with similar goals to determine how economically efficient each program was in reaching that goal. The question is this: If we have several programs that have each been shown to be effective in preventing a particular problem, which will lower the incidence of the problem for the least amount of money?

An example of this type of research was conducted by the RAND Corporation in an influential analysis of the California three-strikes law. Three-strikes laws are mandatory-sentencing laws that send individuals convicted of a third felony conviction to prison for life. California passed the United States' most sweeping three-strikes law in 1994 (it was subsequently modified in 2000). In 1996, the Rand Corporation published an analysis of the cost-effectiveness of the three-strikes law compared with four types of prevention programs: home visits and day care in early childhood, parenting training programs, monetary incentives for high-risk students to graduate from high school, and intensive supervision of delinquent juveniles. The analysis consisted of estimating the number of serious crimes each initiative could be reasonably expected to prevent and then calculating the cost of each program per serious crime prevented. Programs with lower costs per crime prevented were more economically efficient. The analysis showed that both parent training and graduation incentives prevented serious crimes at a much lower cost than the three-strikes law (P. Greenwood et al., 1998). As the authors of the study point out, the three-strikes law is more effective at preventing crime than the prevention programs (the law is 100% effective in preventing "participants" from committing future crimes), but it does so at a much higher cost than the four prevention programs.

That type of analysis, however, leaves out a great deal of information. For example, what about the money society saves by not having to incarcerate the successful graduates of the prevention programs? And what about the benefits to society of having those individuals become wage-earning (and tax-paying) members of society rather than prison inmates? The majority of cost-effectiveness studies are not just interested in the relative economic efficiency of different types of programs; they want to address the basic question

**cost-benefit analysis**
a comparison of the costs spent to implement an intervention against the economic benefits gained. It must also address the complex question of how much money was saved by preventing something that did not happen.

of whether or not prevention programs result in an overall economic benefit for society. Are the economic benefits greater than the program costs? These types of analyses involve some type of **cost-benefit analysis**: a comparison of the costs of implementing an intervention against the monetary benefits gained. They are often expressed as a return on an investment. For each dollar spent, how much money was eventually saved because of the intervention? These types of analyses are not easy to do. Evaluation of prevention programs overall is made difficult by the fundamental problem of measuring an event that did not occur. Cost-benefit evaluations are made even more complex because they must address the question, how much money was saved because an event did not occur?

Calculating the basic monetary costs of the cost-benefit equation often seems fairly simple. Most programs either publish or can easily compute program costs per person served (although even this can get quite challenging for many programs). Calculating the monetary benefits of prevention programs is much more difficult. Generally, these benefits fall into one of two categories: (a) services the program participants will not need because of the success of the program and (b) monetary benefits to society in terms of wages earned and taxes paid by program participants that they otherwise would not have earned or paid. Services that prevention program participants may not need because of the success of the program include educational services, mental health services (including foster care and hospitalization), physical health services (e.g., treatment for health problems related to smoking, drug use, or obesity), criminal justice system costs, and welfare programs.

To illustrate these points, let us look at the High Scope/Perry Preschool Project, a program designed to prevent conduct disorder and other behavior disorders in adolescence. The original program provided high-quality, academically based day care to children born into poverty. The children were enrolled in the program starting at ages 3 and 4. The 123 children were all African American and were randomly assigned to either the intervention group or a control group. The most recent results from the program were collected when the participants were 40 years old. Data were collected from 97% of the participants who were still living. A cost-benefit analysis found that the general public gained $12.90 for every $1 spent on the program (Belfield et al., 2006). Athough other analyses have found a lower rate of return, the general finding that the program benefits outweigh program costs holds true over multiple analyses (Heckman et al., 2009; Schweinhart et al., 2005).

Another example of this kind of analysis was done in relation to the Communities That Care program discussed earlier in this chapter. This independent analysis found that there is a savings of $4.95 for every $1 invested in CTC programming. The savings come from decreased costs in law enforcement, medical and mental health treatment, and other public services that would have occurred if the program had not been in place, as well as increased income among participants due to the prevention of substance abuse (Washington State Institute for Public Policy, 2018b).

The Washington State Institute for Public Policy regularly conducts cost-benefit analyses of intervention programs, which can be found on its website (https://www.wsipp.wa.gov/). We recommend visiting the website for more, easily searchable examples of these types of analyses.

In addition to giving insight into questions such as which programs are most economically efficient at achieving the same outcomes and which programs generate economic benefits that outweigh the program costs, economic analyses can also shed light on the selection of program components. If you look back at Table 10.3, you will see that one of the principles of effective prevention programming is that the program is comprehensive and provides multiple interventions across multiple settings. But just because multiple components increase positive effects does not necessarily mean that the increased cost of those additional components is economically justified. Cost-effectiveness analyses can help answer those questions.

A large, and growing, body of research demonstrates not only that prevention programs work but also that the ones that have demonstrated positive results generate economic benefits to society that far outweigh their costs. In general, targeted programs are more economically efficient than universal programs, and programs that are implemented in early childhood provide greater lifetime benefits. As a discussion of economic analyses of early childhood prevention programs concludes:

> The fundamental insight of economics when comparing early childhood policies with other social investments is that a growing body of program evaluations shows that early childhood programs have the potential to generate government savings that more than repay their costs and produce returns to society as a whole that outpace most public and private investments. (Kilburn & Karoly, 2008, p. 11)

The great thing about cost-effectiveness analyses is that everyone who is serious about data-based decision making cares about them. Researchers and organizations spend a great deal of time and effort thinking about the complexities of these analyses and the best way to analyze the data in order to inform good public policies. The sad thing about cost-effectiveness analyses is that they so rarely actually have an effect on public policy. We discuss this sad phenomenon further in Chapter 13.

## Examples of Successful Prevention and Promotion Programs

In this section, we present examples of prevention and promotion programs that have significant empirical evidence of success. We chose these programs to illustrate the ideas regarding prevention science that we covered in the first part of this chapter. Additional examples of successful programs are presented in the next chapter. We also provide you with resources to help you locate other empirically supported programs that you may wish to consider for adaptation in your community.

First, we review programs in HIV/AIDS prevention to illustrate some of the basic points of prevention science that we discussed at the beginning of this chapter. These programs are designed to change the behavior of individuals but are provided in community settings and have their major impact on the behavior of individuals in relationships. Then we discuss parent training programs, which were developed to prevent child and adolescent behavior disorders. These programs are designed to affect the microsystem of the family by improving parenting practices and parent-child relationships. While these programs focus on changing the behavior of parents, the goal is to change the microsystem of the family and the behavior of children. Finally, we examine programs designed to prevent bullying in schools. These programs target the microsystem of the school, rather than individuals, as their level of intervention. While each of these programs was designed to prevent a specific problem (HIV infection, conduct disorder, and school bullying), as you shall see, in practice they all have clear promotion effects.

## Prevention of HIV/AIDS Infection: Promoting Healthy Sexual Behaviors

For an explicit illustration of many of the concepts discussed in this chapter, let us take a look at the field of HIV/AIDS prevention. The story of HIV prevention began when public health officials first became aware that some strange things were occurring in the health of gay men in the United States in 1981. It is estimated that, by this time, there were already at least 100,000 cases of HIV infection spread across five continents (Mann, 1989). This illustrates an important point of prevention science that we have not yet discussed: There must be public recognition of a problem before prevention efforts will begin.

In June 1982, the Centers for Disease Control published an article suggesting that the syndrome was caused by an infectious agent that was transmitted through sexual activity (CDC, 1982a). The name "AIDS" (acquired immune deficiency syndrome) was first suggested in July of that year, and in September the CDC published the first proper description of AIDS (CDC, 1982b). It was not until 1984 that HIV was identified as the virus that causes AIDS, and it was not until January 1985 that the first blood test for HIV was licensed.

But this lack of knowledge about the cause of AIDS did not stop the development of prevention efforts. By the end of 1982, a number of voluntary organizations had arisen, particularly in gay communities, to deal with the growing AIDS crisis. Several of these organizations began promoting safe-sex practices as a way of stopping the spread of AIDS in their communities (Berridge,

1996). The first needle exchange program was established in Amsterdam in 1984 (National Institute on Drug Abuse, 1988). By 1988, the first descriptions of AIDS/HIV prevention programs were being published.

Remember John Snow and the lessons we learned from how he dealt with the cholera epidemic?

- Even if you do not know how to cure a problem, you may still be able to prevent it.

- You do not need to know the cause of a problem to prevent it; you just need to understand something about the mechanisms through which the problem is transmitted or sustained.

- You can often prevent a problem by changing some aspect of human behavior.

- While individual behavior change can contribute to prevention, complete prevention of a problem often relies on public action.

All of these lessons are illustrated by the history of HIV prevention. While we now have better treatments for HIV infection, there is no cure or vaccine. Effective prevention programs were being implemented even before the human immunodeficiency virus was identified as the cause of AIDS. The reason this was possible was because it was known, very early on, that whatever was causing AIDS was most likely spread through sexual contact and, probably, through blood. We did not know the cause or have a cure, but we *did* have some ideas about the mechanism through which the disorder was transmitted, and this allowed effective prevention programs to be developed.

While modifying the behavior of individuals is obviously key to preventing the spread of HIV, managing the AIDS epidemic was heavily dependent on public action. First, there had to be public recognition of the problem and recognition that the problem was not limited to small subsets of the population (men who have sex with men, women who have sex with those men, intravenous drug users, or hemophiliacs). This required public action to track the spread of the disease and to educate citizens and legislators about the epidemic. It also required public action to fund the research, medical services, public education programs, and prevention programs necessary to fight the disease.

The CDC currently identifies 41 interventions as demonstrating best evidence for reducing HIV risk (CDC, 2019b). Most of those programs are indicated prevention programs—they are directed toward populations that are already engaged in behaviors that put them at a higher risk of being exposed to HIV. We describe one here, the AMIGAS (Amigas, Mujeres Latinas, Informándonos, Guiándonos, y Apoyándonos Contra el Sida; Friends, Latina Women, Informing Each Other, Guiding Each Other, and Supporting Each

Other Against AIDS) program, which demonstrates many of the points of this chapter (Wingood et al., 2011).

Take a minute to look back at Table 10.3, the principles of effective intervention programs. Although those principles were developed primarily through reviews of effective prevention programs with children and adolescents, many of the principles are reflected in the AMIGAS program, which was developed to work with adult women. The program is theoretically based. It was developed using concepts from both social cognitive theory and theories of gender and power. It is designed to address risky behaviors and protective factors that have been identified in the research, and it has been empirically supported. The program is timed to identify a group engaging in a risky behavior (unprotected vaginal sex) but before the development of HIV infection. The program has clear implications for developing a positive sense of self and improved healthy sexual relationships. It is behaviorally based, focusing on teaching specific skills.

The program is also designed to be sensitive to and to build upon the cultural norms of the ethnic minority women it serves. In Chapter 7 we introduced you to the idea that cultural norms can, in some cases, become "a haven for oppression" rather than a source of respect and support for all members of that culture (Ortiz-Torres et al., 2000, p. 877). Ortiz-Torres et al. (2000) addressed the cultural values of *marianismo* and *machismo*, which affect ideas of acceptable masculine and feminine behavior in many Latina/o/x cultures. Those cultural expectations can make it difficult for women in those cultures to discuss and negotiate safe-sex practices with their male sex partners. The AMIGAS program is specifically designed to acknowledge and respect those cultural values while emphasizing that those values can support the discussion and utilization of safe-sex practices in sexual relationships.

The program comprises four sessions that are presented in a small-group format and are delivered in Spanish by Latina health educators. The program begins not by talking about HIV or healthy sexual behaviors but with a discussion of the power, strength, and beauty of Latina women and of the cultural norms around family and sexual relationships. The second session focuses on healthy sexual relationships and female anatomy. The third session focuses on HIV, including videos of Latina women living with HIV; an exploration of cultural beliefs about HIV; and information about safe-sex practices including condom use, abstinence, and having fewer sexual partners.

One interesting point of the AMIGAS evaluation study is that since HIV infection is a relatively rare occurrence, the program was not specifically evaluated on its effectiveness in preventing the spread of HIV, which was the explicit goal of the program when it was developed. Instead, the program has been evaluated on its ability to decrease unprotected vaginal sex and to promote condom use, which also has the effect of preventing other STDs and unwanted pregnancies. So what began as a program with an explicit prevention focus is actually functioning as a health promotion program. The promotion of healthy sexual behaviors obviously has effects far beyond the prevention of HIV.

HIV/AIDS continues to be an epidemic that affects all racial/ethnic groups in all parts of the world (CDC, 2019a). As powerful medical interventions have changed the course of the disease, prevention efforts seem to have become routinized and driven by less urgency. Wolitski (2003) reported an upsurge of "safe-sex fatigue" and "AIDS burnout." This leads prevention messages to be ignored, thereby increasing health risks and perpetuating the epidemic. This highlights the important point that there is never one single best response to a problem. Rather, a diversity of approaches, addressing different populations, cultures, and aspects of problem, along with an emphasis on promoting overall healthy behavior, is needed to intervene in complex problems such as HIV infection.

## Prevention of Childhood Behavior Disorders: Promoting Positive Parenting

One of the clearest examples of effective prevention programming in the literature has to do with parenting practices. Research in developmental psychology, and particularly research on resiliency factors, has long emphasized the primary role that warm, accepting parenting behaviors, coupled with clear, consistent supervision and discipline, play in the development of happy, healthy children (Baumrind, 1991; Werner, 1996). Behaviorally based parent training programs have been shown in numerous reviews to be very effective in reducing problem behaviors in young children (including aggression, oppositional behaviors, and hyperactive behaviors). These reductions in early childhood are then empirically linked to the prevention of problems in adolescence, such as school failure, substance abuse, and delinquency (Center for Substance Abuse Prevention, 1998; Kumpfer & Alvarado, 2003; Leijten et al., 2019).

It is important to note that these results do not apply to *parent education programs*, which have not been shown to result in measurable behavior change in children. Parent education programs typically focus on providing parents with information about child rearing, such as ideas for effective communication and information about normative behavior in childhood, but they often do not teach specific parenting skills. While parents generally report feeling that the programs where helpful, evaluations of these programs fail to demonstrate any change in the behavior of the children of those parents (Kumpfer & Alvarado, 2003).

Behaviorally based parent training programs focus on specific skills training for parents. Information is presented, but the programs' primary content centers on the acquisition of new parenting skills. The main emphasis is on improving parent-child interactions by teaching parents to engage in positive play with their children, give frequent reinforcement for good behavior, ignore most unwanted behavior, clearly communicate expectations, and set clear consequences. The skills most closely related to positive results are use of positive reinforcement (specifically praise) and the use of natural and logical consequences for poor behavior (Leijten et al., 2019).

One of these programs is the Triple P—Positive Parenting Program (Prinz et al., 2009; Sanders, 1999). Triple P takes an explicit public health approach to improving parent-child relationships, preventing child behavior disorders and child maltreatment, and improving family life. The program was developed as a universal prevention program. The overarching goal is to provide all parents in a community with the level of parenting support that they need, with different levels of intervention provided for families with different needs.

Triple P offers programs at five different levels, analogues to the universal, selective, and indicated prevention measures described earlier in this chapter. These programs are geared toward parents of children ages 0–12. Level 1 is a community media campaign designed to provide basic information about positive parenting techniques and services available to everyone in a community. Level 2 is for parents of children with mild behavior problems such as regular temper tantrums and involves one or two consultation sessions. Level 3 is for parents dealing with a moderate, ongoing, specific behavior problem. It involves both individual and group sessions. Level 4 is for parents of children with serious behavior problems. This level lasts for 8–10 sessions and is focused on teaching, practicing, and reinforcing the specific parenting skills that have been demonstrated to be effective in reducing behavioral disorders in children. Level 5 is for families with complex parenting challenges, such as partner conflict, or factors that indicate the risk of child maltreatment. There are also programs for parents of children with developmental disabilities and parents of teenagers.

Programs range from information-only to online, large-group, small-group, and one-on-one interventions. Triple P has been implemented, at various levels, in at least 25 countries, and the materials are available in four languages. It has a strong training component for providers, emphasizing understanding of and training in fidelity to the program. Components of the program have been evaluated multiple times, in multiple settings, around the world.

Referring to Table 10.3, you can see that the Triple P program incorporates, at least to some degree, every principle of effective prevention programs. The program was developed by a team at the University of Queensland in Australia, and they have been modifying and expanding the program in response to both their own evaluations and new advances in prevention science for decades.

There have been several cost-effectiveness evaluations of Triple P. One recent evaluation focused on two Level 4 interventions with the parents of children who met diagnostic criteria for conduct disorder (Sampaio et al., 2018). One intervention was presented in a group format and the other was one on one. Both formats were cost-effective when the cost and benefits of treatment were compared to the lifetime costs associated with a diagnosis of conduct disorder. Of particular interest is that Triple P has been found to be cost-effective at a universal level, with a benefit-to-cost ratio of $10.05 gained for every $1 spent when all five levels are offered to a complete population (Prinz et al., 2009; Washington State Institute for Public Policy, 2018a).

## Prevention of Bullying and School Violence: Promoting Safe School Climates

*For 2 years, Johnny, a quiet 13-year-old, was a human plaything for some of his classmates. The teenagers badgered Johnny for money, forced him to swallow weeds and drink milk mixed with detergent, beat him up in the rest room and tied a string around his neck, leading him around as a "pet." When Johnny's torturers were interrogated about the bullying, they said they pursued their victim because it was fun. (Newspaper clipping cited in Olweus & Limber, 2010, p. 124)*

Bullying-related behaviors are prevalent worldwide, with about 246 million children experiencing school violence or bullying in some form every year (United Nations Educational, Scientific and Cultural Organization, 2017). Incidence of school bullying specifically varies widely across countries and studies, with estimates as low as 10% and as high as 65%. The negative effects of bullying are far ranging and affect both victims and perpetrators (Zych et al., 2015). But school bullying can be prevented. A recent meta-analysis of prevention programs around the world found that those programs reduce bullying perpetration by 19%–20% and victimization by 15%–16% (Gaffney et al., 2018).

Just as there is a wide variation in school bullying rates across countries, rates also vary widely by school. In some schools, these problems are far less frequent than in others. Bullying can be conceptualized in ecological terms, using the individual- and environmental-level prevention equations presented earlier (Albee, 1982; Elias, 1987). Key preventive influences on both of these problems are positive sources of relatedness and connectedness in both school and home life; supportive friends, family members, and other caring adults; and coping skills to deal with frustrations, setbacks, stress, and conflict and to accurately perceive emotional cues in oneself and others. Bullying prevention requires multilevel ecological approaches to intervention (Ttofi et al., 2008; Zins et al., 2007).

Community psychologists are among those asking how it happens that certain schools are organized so that their levels of violence are lower than those of other schools. The following conditions have been identified as con-

Effective bullying prevention programs focus on understanding and changing the school environment.

ducive to low rates of school violence (Felner & Adan, 1988; Hawkins & Lam, 1987; Pepler & Slaby, 1994; Zins et al., 2007):

- School courses are perceived as highly relevant to students' lives.

- School rules and structures allow students some control over what happens to them at school.

- School discipline policies are viewed as firm, fair, clear, and consistently enforced.

- A rational reward structure in the school recognizes students for their achievement.

- Strong and effective school governance exists with strong principal leadership.

- Ongoing, positive contacts occur between students and adults.

- The curriculum includes education in social and emotional competencies.

These characteristics are the foci of a growing number of school-based prevention/promotion programs. The largest preventive effects with regard to bullying come from comprehensive school-wide efforts that create a climate of nonacceptance of bullying, a positive social norm of disclosure, a track record of effective action in response to threats and incidents, and curriculum-based training in social-emotional competencies (Elias & Zins, 2003; Zins et al., 2007). Firm, clear, school-wide policies, referral procedures, and staff training must exist to deal effectively with student reports of problems. Next, we discuss one approach that has shown success in some contexts.

In 1983, three young boys committed suicide in northern Norway, most likely as a result of severe bullying. The Norwegian Ministry of Education started a national campaign to address bullying in schools. The Olweus Bullying Prevention Program (OBPP) was developed in response to that campaign (Limber et al., 2018; Olweus & Limber, 2010; Olweus et al., 1999). OBPP has several core components, which have been identified by research as being central to the program's success. These include the use of a survey to identify the type and intensity of bullying in a school and to identify the areas and settings in the school where bullying is most likely to occur. After analysis of the survey data, the school holds a conference day with parents, teachers, and administrators to discuss the results of the survey and to decide how to use those results to implement the program in their school. Implementation is overseen by a coordinating committee made up of administrators, teachers, parents, and students.

A core component of intervention is increased teacher supervision of hot spots for bullying that were identified in the survey. These generally include the lunch room and the playground. For example, since children generally take only 10 minutes to eat lunch, but lunch lasts for 20–30 minutes, schools in the program often have board games available in the lunchroom, and teachers direct students to those games when they are finished eating. On the playground, teachers are supported in identifying and intervening in situations that could lead to bullying, such as "play fighting." Students are directed into prosocial, structured play and are provided with more games and play equipment. The intervention also involves regular class meetings with students, clear classroom and school-wide rules against bullying, and serious talks with students and parents when bullying occurs.

While the program does have core components, it also allows for a great deal of flexibility because each school determines the specifics of how the program will be implemented. Because of this flexibility, the program can be implemented with children in a variety of developmental stages and in different cultures. As with parent training programs, the main focus of OBPP is on changing the behavior of adults (teachers) and changing the climate of the setting in order to change the behavior of the children. In essence, Olweus's approach creates a school with different patterns of social interaction and a different environmental feeling.

The first evaluations of the program in Norway demonstrated decreases in bullying of up to 50%, but subsequent evaluations found decreases of only 23%–38% (Olweus, 1997; Olweus & Limber, 2010). A recent evaluation of the program in 210 schools in Pennsylvania found an overall decrease in bullying behaviors of 3% over a 2-year period (Limber et al., 2018). Given the large sample size, that number suggests that 2,000 fewer students were bullied during that period compared to if the program had not been implemented. Effects varied between schools and were larger for schools that had implemented the program over a longer period of time. The evaluation did not assess the fidelity of program implementation.

The importance of implementation fidelity is illustrated by an evaluation of OBPP in the United States involving 13 inner-city schools over 4 years (Black, 2007). The program was evaluated on the number of observed instances of bullying, rates of reported bullying, and fidelity to the core components of the program. Overall, the schools saw an average decrease in bullying behaviors of 25.5% over the 4 years of the program.

The researchers found that only a few schools managed to implement the program with a high degree of fidelity for 4 years and that the success of the program was directly related to the degree of the fidelity of implementation (Black, 2007). The main factor that ensured fidelity was the existence of key people in the school (a principal, a school nurse, and a group of teachers) who were strongly committed to the program. Schools that had difficulty maintaining fidelity or that could not maintain the program at all were marked by frequent changes in staffing and administration and other forms of internal change or crises.

We discuss issues of program fidelity in detail in the next chapter, where we also introduce you to another type of school-based prevention and promotion program called Social and Emotional Learning (SEL). Although SEL programs have much broader aims than antibullying programs, the skills they teach and the changes in school climate that they promote should theoretically have the effect of reducing school violence.

# The Implementation and Sustainability of Programs

As you have seen, answering the question "Does prevention work?" is much like answering the questions "Does surgery work?" or "Does education work?" The answer is yes, but it must be qualified by knowing how well interventions are implemented. More refined questions are appropriate: "Is this program being implemented as designed, in accordance with theory and research?" and "How does it work with specific populations and contexts?"

Thus, another emerging area for research and action concerns actual implementation of prevention/promotion initiatives in local contexts. As we have noted throughout this chapter, ideas and approaches may work very well in one organization, locality, culture, or other context yet not be applicable in another. Interventions identified as effective by empirical research in multiple settings, even when backed by meta-analytic findings or best practices and supported by lessons learned in certain situations, must be adapted to the local and particular dynamics and resources of each setting. Community psychologists and other prevention advocates are continuously learning about the importance of carefully considering implementation plans in context. An equal concern now is how to sustain effective prevention/promotion initiatives even after they have been brought to the point of adequate implementation. We take up these matters in detail in Chapter 11.

# For Review

## Discussion Questions

1. Think about the Kauai Longitudinal Study. What are the key findings from this study? Do any of those key findings resonate with you when you think of your own life? Think of periods of adversity you have faced. Do you think those experiences have helped you build resiliency?

2. Think of the three example programs presented in this chapter (AMIGAS, Triple P—Positive Parenting Program, and the Olweus Bullying Prevention Program). Review the principles of effective prevention programming presented in Table 10.3. How are the programs similar in implementation of those principles? How do they differ?

3. Is there a problem in a community you care about that you thought about while reading this chapter? Based upon your reading, what ideas do you have about how to address the problem? Would your approach involve the development of a community coalition? Who would be involved?

4. John Snow had a hard time convincing people in power that he had an effective idea to prevent cholera. Which of the arguments presented in this chapter were most effective in convincing you that prevention and health promotion are powerful tools for improving communities and the lives of the people who live there? Was the discussion of cost-effectiveness and cost-benefit analyses important to you?

## Key Terms

prevention, 340
promotion, 341
primary prevention, 342
secondary prevention, 342
tertiary prevention, 342
universal preventive measures,
    343

selective preventive measures,
    343
indicated preventive measures,
    343
cumulative-risk hypothesis,
    346
resiliency, 346

developmental assets, 354
effect size, 355
best practices approach, 355
cost-effectiveness analysis,
    358
cost-benefit analysis, 359

## Learn More

A detailed summary of the chapter, along with other review materials, is available on the *Community Psychology, Fourth Edition* companion website at http://pubs.apa.org/books/supp/kloos4/.

Proper implementation of health promotion programs is essential, ensuring that they are tailored to meet the cultural needs of communities as they grow and change.

Vladimir Konstantinov/Shutterstock.com

# 11 Implementing Prevention and Promotion Programs

## Looking Ahead IIII➡

**After reading this chapter you will be able to answer these questions:**

**1.** Why do community psychologists (and others involved in prevention and promotion programs) emphasize innovation and adaptation of programs rather than just implementation?

**2.** What systems need to be in place in order to ensure successful implementation of a program?

**3.** Why is setting capacity an important element in program implementation? What aspects of capacity should be assessed when adopting a prevention program? What can be done to build capacity?

**4.** What is meant by "fidelity to key components," and why is that concept important when deciding how to adapt a program to a specific setting?

## Opening Exercise

## Prevention in Your Future

Imagine that someday you are working as the activities director for your local community center. Your boss tells you that, as part of your job responsibilities, you will serve on a community board trying to support community members living with chronic mental disorders. When you attend your first meeting, you find that the board is currently focusing on community supports for people transitioning from hospitalization to independent living, and by the time you leave your first meeting, you find that you are on a subcommittee charged with investigating ways of working with those community members to provide supported employment opportunities.

Or imagine that you work as a school counselor in a middle school. One day your principal calls you into her office and says that she thinks incidences of violence are increasing in the school, and she is concerned that the school staff members are increasingly relying on the police to deal with aggressive students.

Prevention in Your Future (continued)

She wants you to investigate other ways of intervening in, or hopefully preventing, school violence.

Or maybe you are the president of the parent–teacher association at your child's school. The mayor calls you because the city was awarded a grant to investigate ways of preventing child abuse in your community. The first step in the grant is to set up a community board to oversee the process. The mayor wants a parent on the board and someone gave him your name.

## What Do You Think?

**1.** What would you do in these situations?

**2.** Based on what you have learned so far, how do you think community psychologists would do this work?

**3.** What kinds of information, support, and resources do you think you would need if you found yourself in one of these situations?

Every day, people with no background in prevention work, community psychology, or even any aspect of mental health are finding themselves faced with preventing some problem in their community. Many of you reading this textbook will someday be in a situation like this, as a parent, community member, working professional, or community psychologist. The purpose of this chapter is to provide you with a guide for effectively addressing these situations.

# Introduction to Prevention: Program Implementation Is Challenging

In this chapter, we explore how prevention science is implemented in real-life settings. As you will see, it is not easy. While the theory and research you read about in Chapter 10 form the basis of this chapter, they are not enough to guarantee successful replication of prevention and promotion programs.

This chapter is a summative chapter, in the sense that information from every other chapter in this book can be applied to the material covered here. We make some of those links in this chapter, but we encourage you to make others yourself. Program implementation is community-based work, and it is a cornerstone activity that defines the field of community psychology. As we engage in this work, and the social change work discussed in Chapter 13, we have an ethical obligation to reflect upon the core values of the field introduced in Chapter 1 and to ensure that our work embodies those values: individual and family wellness, sense of community, respect for human diversity, social justice, empowerment and citizen participation, collaboration and community strengths, and empirical grounding.

Community and preventive psychologists have learned a great deal about the art and science of implementing preventive efforts. Bringing good ideas and sound procedures of the kind you read about in Chapter 10 into high-quality, enduring practice is possible. The challenge can be likened to the difference between reviewing for a test in the library and actually taking the test or the difference between pitching in the bullpen and facing live batters in a stadium with a huge crowd roaring on every pitch. Performance in the practice situation does not always match what can be demonstrated under real-world conditions. These challenges are made clear in the following study, which investigated the effectiveness of community-based substance abuse prevention programs.

In 2005, a group of researchers published a meta-analysis of results from 46 drug prevention programs funded by the U.S. Substance Abuse and Mental Health Services Administration (SAMHSA). A wide variety of programs were involved, but all were focused on the prevention of child and adolescent substance abuse and all targeted high-risk youth. Some programs focused on in-class instruction about substance abuse; others were designed to teach children specific skills, such as how to refuse offers of drugs and alcohol; and still others were recreation oriented. The evaluations covered a total of 5 years over 46 sites around the United States. The meta-analysis included the computation of effect size, a statistic that, in most cases, ranges from 0 to 1. The results were extremely disappointing. The mean effect size over all the sites was only 0.02, almost 0. Even more discouraging, at 21 of the 46 sites, the effect sizes were negative, indicating that the comparison groups demonstrated less substance abuse than the participant groups after the intervention (Derzon et al., 2005).

What happened? These programs all had displayed some kind of promising result in demonstration projects. That was why SAMHSA was willing to fund this large dissemination project. But when they tried to implement the programs in a variety of community contexts, those promising results disappeared. Or did they? Can you think of any reasons why the program failed to show positive results in real-world settings?

Some of the differences in effectiveness could be attributed to differences in the programs. For instance, the study found that programs that were behavioral and skills based and those that were based upon a coherent theory were among the most effective (refer to Table 10.2 in Chapter 10). Programs that just provided information about substance abuse were not effective. But these programmatic differences did not completely explain the overall lack of positive results. Even the behavioral, theory-based programs showed a great deal of variability in effectiveness.

**implementation**
the process of executing a program in a real-life setting. Implementation science is a discipline dedicated to studying the best methods of delivering programs.

When the evaluators dug deeper, they discovered two things. First, at many of the sites, the control groups were not really control groups. Many of those children actually were being exposed to some sort of drug abuse prevention or intervention program; they just were not in the program being evaluated. And second, the programs were implemented in very different ways at the different sites. For example, the sites differed in how well the goals and procedures of the program were integrated into the day-to-day functioning of the organization. The researchers wanted to know how well the program would have worked if all the control groups had been true control groups and if the programs had been implemented consistently across settings. When they statistically controlled for these factors, the overall comparison of intervention to control groups was statistically significant, and the estimated effect size across all 46 sites rose to 0.24 (Derzon et al., 2005).

These discouraging results concerning attempts to disseminate promising prevention and promotion programs in real-life settings are not unique. But successful dissemination of prevention and promotion programs has taken place. What has been found is that program implementation itself must be the subject of serious research. The goal of this chapter is to provide you with the information you need to successfully implement prevention programming in your community. As we hope we showed in Chapter 10, there are many exciting and important advances in prevention science. In this chapter, we want to show you how those advances can be used to benefit your community. We also describe two example prevention programs in detail: social-emotional learning and home-visiting programs. But first let us define what we mean when we discuss implementation and take a look at the research linking implementation quality to program outcomes. Then we will talk about the models that are used in the field of implementation and dissemination research.

# It's Not Just Program Implementation, It's Program Innovation

Developing an intervention that shows positive results in small-scale, highly controlled settings, while not an easy task, may actually be the simplest part of prevention science. The complexities involved in the adoption of those interventions across multiple, diverse settings have made implementation science the fastest growing subfield in prevention science. **Implementation** refers to how a program is delivered in a real-life setting. Research into how a program gets from experimental development to widespread implementation has grown and changed immensely over the past 50 years. Implementation science is currently the fastest growing area in the field of prevention science and is arguably the most important. We will introduce current theories and research in implementation science shortly, but first it is helpful to understand how our understanding of program implementation has evolved.

**scaling up**
the process of expanding a program's original concept to a more widespread application.

# A Brief History of Approaches to Program Implementation

Historically, concepts of how best to transfer effective educational programs and adapt them to new host settings have evolved through four stages (RMC Research Corporation, 1995):

- **Cookbook:** In the 1970s, it was believed that programs had to be thoroughly documented, ideally in "kits" that could be followed precisely, step by step.

- **Replication:** Later, model programs were replicated by training staff in the methods used by program developers and then bringing these methods back to specific settings to be carried out as similarly as possible, but with some room for adaptation to the setting.

- **Adaptation:** By the late 1980s, models were understood to require adaptation to the unique context of the host site, ideally by having the developer serve as a consultant in making the necessary changes.

- **Invention/Innovation:** Recently, models have been seen as sources of ideas and inspiration rather than procedures to replicate or adapt. There is emphasis on creating a program tailored to the unique circumstances at a given time, using ideas gleaned from best practices literature.

When we say that implementing prevention programs in real-life settings is as much an art as it is a science, we do not mean that one is more important than the other. Scientific methods must underlie implementation efforts, something that did not happen in the cookbook approach that was used in the 1970s. Handing a community specific instructions for implementing a program, giving little to no ongoing support while community members do their best to follow those instructions, and then asking (or more often, requiring) them to document how well they completed the task just did not work. Prevention programs cannot just be replicated, or even adapted, to a local setting. There must be true innovation involved in every implementation. But that innovation must be based on real knowledge. Here is where an ecological understanding of settings, community, and diversity is so helpful.

The process of going from original development of an innovation to its widespread implementation is sometimes referred to as **scaling up** (Schorr, 1997). That process represents the core of this chapter. Combining this work with a community psychology perspective, we can identify four stages of program development and implementation:

- **Experimental Development:** A program demonstrates its effectiveness under small-scale, optimal, highly controlled conditions, compared to a control group.

**research-to-practice models**
focus on the desire of researchers and policymakers to "push" communities and organizations to adopt evidence-based programs (e.g., "Research shows this is effective, now how do we adapt it to real life?").

**community-centered models**
focus on the desire of community members to identify and successfully adopt programs that they believe fit the unique needs, strengths and values of their community (e.g., "These are the issues in our community, now how do we find programs that address these needs and successfully adopt them?").

- **Technological Application:** A program demonstrates effectiveness under real-world conditions, similar to the conditions for which it is eventually intended, but still under the guidance of its developers.

- **Diffusion of Innovation:** A program is adopted by other organizations or communities and demonstrates effectiveness under real-world conditions when not under the direct scrutiny and guidance of its developers.

- **Widespread Implementation:** The diffusion stage brings the program to a few communities only. Implementation becomes widespread when a program continues to show its effectiveness in a wide variety of settings and is transferred from its developers to new implementers, who in turn conduct further program diffusion. The program has widespread impact only when this final stage occurs.

What exactly is happening when we try to diffuse our knowledge of successful prevention and promotion programs into widespread practice? Numerous researchers, funding sources, policy developers, and community members have tried to answer that question, with only partial success. Often this is discussed in terms of the "gap" between prevention research and practice, and several models have been developed to explain that gap. The models generally have been of two types: research-to-practice models and community-centered models.

**Research-to-practice models** focus on the desire of researchers and policymakers to "push" communities and organizations to adopt evidence-based programs. Program developers have put a great deal of effort and resources into demonstrating that their approach to dealing with a particular problem is effective, and now they want people to use it. Research-to-practice models ask the question "We know what works, so now how do we get it successfully adopted in real-life settings?" **Community-centered models** come from a somewhat different perspective. Communities need to be able to answer the question "How do we find programs that will work for our issues in our community, and then how do we successfully adopt them?" (Saul et al., 2008).

As we hope you will see in this chapter, this split between the two types of models is actually a false dichotomy. The primary goal of both types is to help generate information that will support the successful implementation of prevention research. Where they differ is on which perspective they take: that of the researcher or that of the community. Increasingly, the role of the community is being prioritized. As Robin Miller and Marybeth Shinn (2005) pointed out, it is quite likely that communities have already developed, on their own, effective prevention programs. Miller and Shinn suggested that prevention scientists look for examples of these indigenous prevention efforts and learn from them. One major benefit from this approach is the fact that indigenous prevention efforts are likely to fit community capacity and community values

**prevention synthesis and translation system** highlights the issues related to accessing helpful prevention approaches and stresses the need to locate, combine, and explain this information in a way that is helpful for program adopters.

**prevention support system** consists of the ability of organizations and communities to deliver the support necessary to adopt new innovations, including all aspects involved in developing capacity.

in ways that programs developed under controlled research conditions cannot match.

As community psychologists, we emphasize the need to understand the community perspective, and in this chapter we emphasize that successful program implementation must be based on a community-based participatory action research approach (see Chapter 3). Community members must be involved in every step, from defining the problem through deciding how well the program is working. This shift, from an emphasis on the role of researchers to an emphasis on the role of communities, has had a major impact on how community psychologists view themselves. As Roger Weissberg (2019) wrote about his lifelong work with social and emotional learning programs (discussed later in this chapter):

> I started my career using a *researcher-practitioner* model in which my university colleagues and I took the lead in conceptualizing, designing, implementing, evaluating and disseminating programs. . . . Increasingly, I think a *practitioner-researcher* model can have a greater impact, with more emphasis on how to implement ideas in the real world. (p. 68)

## An Integrative Model

One model that successfully integrates the research-to-practice and community-centered models is the interactive systems framework for dissemination and implementation (ISF), which attempts to describe the key elements and relationships involved in the implementation process (Flaspohler et al., 2012; Wandersman et al., 2008). The model describes three systems:

- the prevention synthesis and translation system,
- the prevention support system, and
- the prevention delivery system.

This model is not meant to describe the stages or processes involved in program dissemination and implementation; rather, it describes the systems that need to be in place in order for those processes to be successful.

The **prevention synthesis and translation system** addresses the fact that information regarding promising prevention approaches is often difficult to access. It is published in multiple journal articles, often in specialized language, and without the level of detail necessary for program adoption. This system acknowledges the need for someone to find all that information, synthesize it, and translate it into a form that is useful for potential adopters. We introduce you to some organizations attempting to serve as this system later in the chapter.

The **prevention support system** addresses the ability of organizations and communities to provide the support necessary to successfully adopt new innovations. This system is best understood in terms of capacity building.

**capacity**
possessing the resources, knowledge, and ability to achieve a goal.

**general capacity**
the skills and resources needed to accomplish any type of program.

**innovation-specific capacity**
the skills and resources needed to implement a specific program in addition to general capacity of an organization. This capacity needs to be developed as dictated by the innovation.

**prevention delivery system**
includes the groups (organizations, communities, or governmental agencies) that are involved in implementing the new program or innovation in a real-life setting.

**Capacity**, as we are using the term, refers to having the resources, knowledge, and ability to accomplish something. For the purposes of program implementation, it includes both **general capacity** (the ability to get anything done) and **innovation-specific capacity** (the ability to successfully implement a specific program). No community setting will have, or can be expected to have, all of the capacity required for a new innovation. That capacity must be developed. The prevention support system includes all the aspects of the setting that are involved in building capacity for the intervention. This concept of capacity is so important that we discuss it in further detail later in this section.

The **prevention delivery system** describes the groups (organizations, communities, or governmental agencies) that are actually implementing the new program or innovation. Are these systems able to apply the capacity they have to engage in the activities necessary for successful implementation?

As shown in Figure 11.1, the three systems interact and inform each other and are influenced by larger, macrosystem forces, such as the existing theory and research; current organizational, community, or governmental policies; the availability of funding; and the social and political climate. The systems also all influence each other; there is a reciprocal relationship between them. The prevention support system can build capacity in a setting, and that capacity in turn can support a more robust prevention support system. All of that can then result in a more specific and effective translation of the innovation to that setting.

The importance of providing support for program adopters is a good example of this figure. Research into the implementation of programs, such as the ones discussed in Chapter 10, consistently points to the need for significant training and technical support for adopters of a prevention program. Each program needs to specify exactly what support and training needs to be provided to whom and at what point in the implementation process that information needs to be provided to program adopters, in a format that is easy to understand and use. That is the role of the prevention synthesis and translation system. Think back to the Olweus Bullying Prevention Program (OBPP). A well-designed prevention synthesis and translation system ensures that the program is widely available and that the materials provided to implement the program are comprehensive, detailed, and engaging. OBPP provides a school-wide guide and teacher guide for implementation of the program as well as a school-wide bullying survey and specific classroom curriculum materials.

The prevention support system then uses that information to build organizational capacity. This often involves identifying funding to pay for support and consultation from the people who have developed the program or from others who have implemented it successfully. OBPP recommends that schools implementing the program contract with a trained OBPP consultant or have someone from the school district attend training to become a consultant.

**Figure 11.1** The Interactive Systems Framework for Dissemination and Implementation

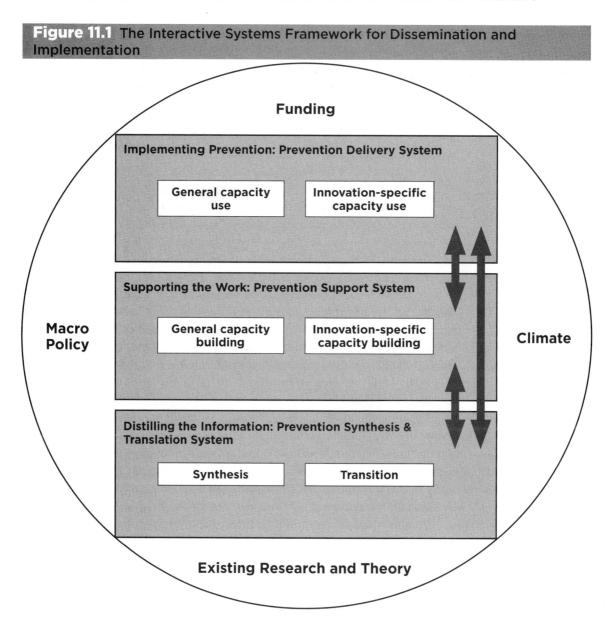

Once that capacity is built, the prevention delivery system ensures that everyone involved in providing the program is appropriately trained and supported. When a school adopts the OBPP, its parents, teachers, and administrators must all understand the link between school environment and bullying; how to administer a survey and analyze the results to better understand how, when, and where bullying is present in their school; and how to use those results to customize interventions that will work for them.

The arrows linking the systems in Figure 11.1 show that the knowledge gained by all three systems as they address this issue informs the existing research and theory. Later in this chapter, we provide additional examples as we use the ISF model to understand the successful dissemination and implementation of specific prevention programs and will be referring back to this figure.

Support for some aspects of the ISF model comes from a very interesting meta-analysis specifically investigating the issue of program implementation (Durlak & DuPre, 2008). The research involved a review of five meta-analyses covering 483 studies, as well as a review of an additional 59 studies that specifically studied the effect of program implementation on program outcomes.

The basic finding from this research is simple but profound. Sites that demonstrated better program implementation (specifically closer fidelity to the original program and higher dosage levels) had effect sizes 2–3 times higher than sites demonstrating poorer program implementation (Durlak & DuPre, 2008). The researchers then went on to look specifically at which factors had the greatest effect on the implementation process. They list 23 factors that were each identified as affecting program implementation in at least five of the articles they reviewed. Those 23 factors were grouped into four categories. By far, the largest portion of the factors, 11 out of 23, related to the organizational capacity of the prevention delivery system. An abbreviated version of this list is included in Table 11.1.

**Table 11.1** Factors Affecting the Implementation Process

| | |
|---|---|
| **Community-level factors** | The current state of prevention theory and research |
| | Politics, funding, and policy considerations |
| **Provider characteristics** | Adopters' perceptions of the need for the program |
| | Adopters' assessment of their ability to implement the program |
| **Innovation characteristics** | Compatibility of the program with the setting |
| | Degree to which the program can be adapted to the needs of the setting |
| **The prevention delivery system: organizational capacity** | Positive work climate |
| | Norms supporting change |
| | Shared decision-making processes |
| | Open communication |
| | Strong leadership that is supportive of the program and the people directly implementing it |

*Note.* Adapted from Durlak and DuPre (2008).

**readiness**
the degree to which one is prepared and willing to tackle a goal based on motivation, general capacity, and innovation-specific capacity.

The ISF model has been widely used and evaluated since its inception. One result is a much deeper understanding of the importance of the prevention support system. Part of that understanding is that having the capacity to implement an innovation is never enough. Capacity is a complex and limited resource. Look back at Figure 11.1. The word "capacity" is used four times in that figure, in reference to the general and innovation-specific capacity of the setting that is already available to use to implement the innovation and the general and innovation-specific capacity that could be built through a robust prevention support system.

But capacity alone does not determine implementation success; there must also be the motivation to expend that capacity to reach a specific goal. As a result of this understanding, the prevention support system has been expanded to include the concept of **readiness**. Readiness is defined as the result of a multiplicative relationship between motivation and capacity (Scaccia et al., 2015; V. C. Scott et al., 2017). The following formula represents the concept of readiness in mathematical terms:

Readiness = Motivation × (General Capacity + Innovation-Specific Capacity)

Assessing a setting's readiness to implement an intervention can be key to determining your starting point. It is basically seeking the answers to two questions: Is this something that you want to do, and do you have the resources to do it? Methods for assessing setting readiness are currently an emerging area of research (V. C. Scott et al., 2017).

## Elements of Successful Implementations

The ISF model identifies the systems that need to be in place in a setting for successful program implementation. In this section, we describe some specific program elements that have been identified as fundamental to successful program implementation. In an influential review of best practices in program implementation, Durlak and DuPre (2008) discussed eight different aspects of implementation (five of which are based on work by Dane & Schneider, 1998):

- **Fidelity:** How closely is the design of the original program maintained?

- **Dosage/intensity:** How often and how frequently is the program presented?

- **Quality:** How well are the components of the program presented?

- **Participant responsiveness:** How engaged are the participants?

- **Program differentiation:** Were there clear theoretical and practical distinctions between this program and other interventions?

- **Monitoring of control/comparison conditions:** Were the control participants exposed to any other type of intervention?

- **Program reach:** How many of the intended participants were actually enrolled in the program?
- **Adaptation:** What aspects of the program were adapted to fit the specific context of the setting?

Our understanding of the science of implementation is still developing, and this list is only preliminary. However, it is still a useful way of thinking about implementation issues that need to be addressed. Each of these aspects of implementation can be measured separately. For example, to measure program reach in a program designed for teen mothers, you could do two things. First, you could check to ensure that all the participants enrolled in the program were teen mothers. And, second, you could look at public health data regarding the number of teen mothers in your area and compare that number to the number of participants in your program. To measure participant responsiveness, you could look at attendance in the program (if participants are not actively involved in a program, they often will just stop attending). You could also ask the participants to rate how enjoyable and interesting they found the program.

Unfortunately, even though all these aspects can be measured, it is rare that all of them are. Only a minority of programs monitor implementation issues at all (although that number is growing), and those that do tend to limit their focus to a few issues such as fidelity, dosage/intensity, and program reach. In the next section, we discuss the role of assessment and evaluation in program implementation success.

## Evaluation as a Means to Better Implementation

The chances are great that, at some point in your life, you will have some role to play in the implementation of a prevention and promotion program. Stakeholders in these programs include children, adolescents, parents, schools, community and health organizations, police, policymakers, service providers and clients, and other community members. Extensive resources will be devoted to the program, and there will be great hopes for a positive impact. Earlier we presented a number of elements that you need to be aware of in order to ensure an effective implementation. But how do you know whether you have a good support system in place? How do you know whether you are reaching your intended participants, and whether they are engaged in the program? How do you know whether the program is being implemented with fidelity to key components, but with appropriate adaptations for your unique setting?

As we hope the questions above point out, you cannot wait until a program has been fully implemented in order to evaluate the outcomes. There is nothing so frustrating as an outcome evaluation of a resource-intensive

**theory of change**
a group's concept of how an intervention will lead to an intended outcome. This theory can be broad at the beginning but be expanded and more detailed as a community intervention continues to be applied and addressed.

intervention that concludes that the intervention did not have the intended impact. That is particularly true when the evaluation tells you nothing about why the program did not produce the expected results or when, perhaps worse, it pinpoints a problem that was present in the early stages of implementation and could have been addressed at that point, if only you had known about it.

In Chapter 12, we introduce you to two approaches to evaluation that can be used together to help avoid these scenarios: formative evaluation and Getting To Outcomes. Both of these approaches emphasize the point that assessment and evaluation must begin at the beginning, preferably before you choose an intervention. These approaches should be seen more as an implementation process than an evaluation process. The goal is not to find out whether your program is successful but rather to supply you with ongoing information you can use to improve the program and, thereby, increase both your knowledge and chances of success. The idea is to foster a culture in which reflection by team members is emphasized and evaluation is seen as a tool for continuous improvement of the program and its implementation rather than a judgement of the success of the program or the individuals involved (V. C. Scott et al., 2020).

Every group engaged in selecting and implementing a community intervention is continually developing a **theory of change**, their idea of how their intervention is going to bring about the desired result. A theory of change may start as overarching theory based on a shared understanding of elements in the setting that give rise to or prevent specific problems. An example might be "If we increase involvement in supervised after-school activities, we can decrease delinquent behavior by adolescents in our community." But as work proceeds, the overarching theory will expand and become more detailed, specifying why and how each program component will have an impact, such as "If we provide free transportation, more teens will be involved in after-school programs."

When an intervention is not showing the expected results, the problem can often be categorized as a theory failure or an implementation failure. Adopting a formative evaluation approach can help you (a) develop a theory of change, (b) expand and modify that theory with real-time, contextualized data as you implement your program, and (c) help you identify and distinguish between theory failure and implementation failures while you still have an opportunity to address them (V. C. Scott et al., 2020).

In Chapter 12, we will discuss in more detail how a formative evaluation approach and evaluation tools, such as Getting To Outcomes, can help ensure that you are continually generating the knowledge needed to inform innovative implementation. These approaches are strongly participatory in nature, and they are iterative: The knowledge that you generate through the assessments is continually used to make improvements to the program and implementation process, which then leads to further assessment. In the next section, we describe a general framework for this process.

## Community-Based Participatory Action Research in Program Implementation

Effective program implementation requires that you understand the context in which you are working and that you are continually making program adaptations to fit the reality of your setting. The adaptations must be based on empirical knowledge, not just of your setting and of your chosen program but also of the details of that ongoing interaction between the program and the setting. You gain that empirical knowledge through a participatory action research paradigm.

As we discussed in Chapter 3, there are many models for ensuring that research projects, including implementation projects, are participatory in nature. You can rely on an existing structure; develop new connections between existing organizations, committees, and individuals; or develop a completely new coalition specifically to implement this program. However you choose to do it, keep in mind that developing some sort of structure and process to ensure that all key stakeholders have a collaborative role to play is central to successful program implementation and to developing the community capacity required for organizational or community change. True community work involves strengthening the capacity of the community. After the intervention has been implemented successfully, the community members should have increased skills and, ideally, there should be formal and informal processes in place to pass these skills on to others. As one further point, remember that when you are discussing problems or settings involving children or adolescents, they should be viewed as key stakeholders and specifically have a role in the collaboration (Kennedy et al., 2019; Langhout & Thomas, 2010b). The importance and effectiveness of including children and adolescents in participatory action research is discussed further in Chapter 3.

Participatory action research is a collaborative cycle of activities in which research (assessment) continually informs action (implementation). The reverse is also true. Action informs research. Both of the programs we highlight in this chapter—social-emotional learning and home-visiting programs—have benefited extensively from knowledge gained during implementation. The organizing principles of a participatory action research cycle of program implementation can be generally summarized in the following activities:

- Problem identification and definition

- Assessment of the setting

- Reviewing available interventions

- Assessing the fit between the intervention and the setting

**iatrogenic effects**
unintended, harmful consequences of what is planned as a helpful intervention.

- Training and support of staff

- Developing the evaluation process

- Implementing, adapting, and sustaining

The process of action research is cyclical and ongoing. It does not stop at the last bullet point; it repeats the whole process. Think back to the discussion of Kelly and Trickett's four ecological principles in Chapter 5: interdependence, cycling of resources, adaptation, and succession (J. G. Kelly, 1966; Trickett, 1984). The last principle, succession, states that the first three principles will continually change over time. There will be multiple and ongoing changes in the relationships among the various aspects of the setting, the resources available, and the ways in which the setting and the innovation are continually adapting to each other. It is only through continual assessment processes that you can be aware of these changes and respond thoughtfully to them.

While some interventions provide a specific framework for these activities, there are also models for program development, implementation, and evaluation that can be applied in any setting that is attempting to implement prevention activities. One of these models is called Getting To Outcomes, which we introduce here and discuss in more detail as an approach to evaluation in Chapter 12. The activities described in this section, where they are discussed specifically in terms of program implementation, are closely aligned with the steps of the Getting To Outcomes approach (Wandersman et al., 1999).

The rest of this chapter is structured around specific prevention activities, but before we begin, we want to discuss one important aspect of evaluation that often gets overlooked: the need to evaluate for consequences you did not expect.

## Evaluate for Unintended Consequences

Ongoing evaluation is important not only because it provides data for continual program innovation but also because even the best designed programs can have unintended consequences, sometimes negative ones. These unintended, harmful consequences of what is planned as a helpful intervention are called **iatrogenic effects**. Ideas that seem exciting and full of promise at the outset may not work, or even if they are effective in some ways and in some circumstances, they may be ineffective or even harmful in others. These unintended negative effects may never be seen unless we specifically look for them.

An excellent example of a prevention program with iatrogenic effects is the Scared Straight program. In the 1970s, inmates serving life sentences in Rahway State Prison in New Jersey began a program that they believed would help deter young people from a life of crime. Juvenile defenders were brought to the prison with the explicit intention of scaring them. They were given a brutal view of life in prison, including graphic stories of rape and murder. The program resulted in a documentary that claimed a 94% success rate (A. Shapiro, 1978), and as a result, the program was widely replicated.

The replications also reported success rates between 80% and 90%. Unfortunately, none of the evaluations included control groups or random assignment. In 1982, the program in Rahway was evaluated using a control group and random assignment, and a different picture emerged. This evaluation found that juveniles who went through the program were actually more likely to be arrested than those in the control group (Finckenauer, 1982). Instead of deterring juveniles from crime, it was increasing their risk. The program was having the opposite of the intended effect. Numerous other well-designed studies in multiple settings came to the same conclusion (Petrosino et al., 2003; Schembri, 2009). Research suggests that the reason the program actually increases criminal behavior is because it reinforces attitudes and behaviors that are associated with criminality, such as the belief that aggression is an effective way to control other people.

Serious scientific investigation of negative effects from prevention programs (and other types of behavioral interventions) is still in the beginning stages, and there are no formal procedures for identifying safety concerns (such as the procedures monitored by the U.S. Food and Drug Administration for identifying potentially harmful medications). There are some preliminary reviews of potentially harmful therapies, with specific programs such as Scared Straight listed (Lilienfeld, 2007). But it is still largely up to practitioners to ensure that they are monitoring for negative effects.

In the rest of this chapter, we explain how you can use knowledge of all of these concepts to guide successful implementations of prevention and promotion programs. To illustrate this process, we use two examples of programs that have been successfully disseminated.

# Examples of Successful Dissemination

In this section, we introduce two types of prevention programming that have been widely disseminated with largely successful results: social-emotional learning programs and home-visiting programs. We then use examples of these types of programs throughout the rest of the chapter to discuss some general principles of program implementation, which we hope will serve as a guide in your own efforts to support effective prevention and promotion programming in your community.

## Social-Emotional Learning Programs

Social-emotional learning (SEL) programs are school-based programs designed to foster social and emotional learning in children. SEL interventions are theoretically grounded on the concept of Positive Youth Development (PYD) and are specifically identified as promotion programs, even though they have been effective in preventing some negative outcomes (see Chapter 10 for more on PYD programs). SEL refers to a set of skills that allows children, adolescents, and adults to successfully understand and moderate their own emotions and to show empathy and understanding for others. That knowledge and those skills then support the ability to set and achieve positive goals for oneself, to make responsible decisions, and to develop and maintain positive relationships with others (Weissberg et al., 2015). SEL programs are based on research demonstrating that those skills can be taught to children and supported through directed, school-wide organizational change (Elias et al., 1997; Weissberg et al., 2015).

Figure 11.2 gives a graphic display of the theory behind SEL programs and the mechanisms through which they work. The specific skills taught are listed in the SEL Competencies box, but other elements of the model describe the ecological context in which learning is taking place. Take a moment and compare it to the list of factors associated with resiliency (Table 10.1) and the diagram demonstrating the potential for interventions to transform risk factors into protective factors (Figure 10.1) in Chapter 10. As you can see, SEL programs are designed specifically to increase the strength and presence of protective factors in children's lives.

iStock.com/monkeybusinessimages

Social-emotional learning (SEL) programs exemplify successful program implementation because they work to change the culture of schools while also instilling in children positive social and emotional skills.

**Figure 11.2** School-Related Factors Predicting Academic Life and Success

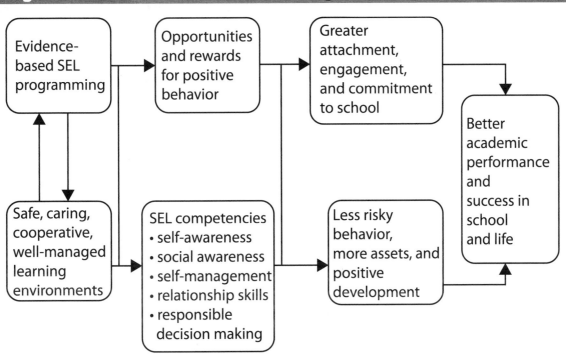

*Note.* SEL = social-emotional learning.

There are a wide variety of SEL programs available. Virtually all of the most successful programs focus on building student skills in key areas. Although most programs involve a large component of classroom instruction, it is widely recognized that effective SEL programming is a school-wide effort. The level of intervention is the school, and the goal is to institute a school culture in which SEL skills are recognized, valued, taught, and supported. Their components and procedures have been carefully studied and identified. The Collaborative for Academic, Social, and Emotional Learning (CASEL) was established to promote the adoption of SEL programs from preschool through high school. CASEL provides extensive resources to help in the adoption of SEL programs at the organization's website (https://casel.org).

SEL programs can make a difference. A recent meta-analysis included evaluations of 82 SEL programs affecting 97,406 students from kindergarten to high school (R. Taylor et al., 2017). The programs were located in multiple countries, among diverse populations, and were all universal applications (children were not selected for the intervention). The meta-analysis focused on follow-up data collected from 8 months to 18 years after the intervention. There were significant gains in SEL skills and attitudes at follow up across the programs. Participation in an SEL program was also significantly associated with increased prosocial behavior; better academic performance; and decreased conduct problems, emotional distress, and drug use. Some programs even demonstrated a positive effect on outcomes such as safe-sex behaviors and high school graduation. It is likely that more programs might have had these effects; they just were not measured. SEL programs have also been found to be cost-effective, with an average return of $11 for every $1 invested, according to one robust study of six SEL programs (Belfield et al., 2015).

One important point to take away from the research on SEL school-based programming is that SEL is a universal measure, not a selective or indicated one. This is true for many promotion-focused programs. The goal of CASEL, and other organizations that support SEL, is to someday see educational systems around the world in which SEL is seen not as an intervention but rather as a fundamental and integral part of learning itself.

## Home-Visiting Programs

Home-visiting programs involve having a trained staff person visit pregnant women and new mothers in their homes. Generally, the programs are intensive, involving weekly to monthly visits for up to 2–5 years. Visits focus on providing parenting information and support for the mothers. The goals of the programs are to support healthy child development, increase positive parenting and parent-child interactions, and prevent child maltreatment. Home-visiting programs are extremely popular and are supported by both private and public funding. The major funder in the United States is the Maternal, Infant, and Early Childhood Home Visiting Program, which is provided by the U.S. Department of Health and Human Services. The department funds programs in every state and five U.S. territories and, through those programs, provided services to 80,000 families in 2017 (Department of Health and Human Services, 2017). The programs also exist in many other countries.

There are at least 20 separate programs based on the core components of the home-visiting model. A recent review of the research focused on follow-up data from four of the most popular programs (follow-up time periods ranged from kindergarten to age 21). The review found evidence of positive effects on child development and school performance; family economic self-sufficiency; juvenile delinquency, family violence, and crime; maternal health; child health; child maltreatment; and parenting. The actual results varied within and between programs. Cost-benefit analyses generally show benefits exceeding costs, particularly among programs focused on disadvantaged families and when lifetime benefits were calculated. Most of the benefits arose from greater earnings and less reliance on government support programs in the participating families (Michalopoulus et al., 2017).

Two of the programs included in that analysis have been extensively disseminated and are referenced frequently in this chapter. The Nurse-Family

Partnership is a nonprofit agency that supports the dissemination of a program that grew out of David Olds's Prenatal/Early Infancy Project (www.nursefamilypartnership.org). Healthy Families America is a national program that initially developed as an extension of the Hawai'i Healthy Start program (www.healthyfamiliesamerica.org).

## What Do You Think?

1. What general themes and goals do the SEL programs and the home-visiting programs have in common? Are there any key differences?

2. What community psychology values do these programs reflect? Do they reflect these values differently?

3. Why do you think these programs might have been so successful? What essential elements do you think are needed for effective prevention program implementation?

iStock.com/monkeybusinessimages

Home-visiting programs are another example of successful program implementation because they conduct thorough, individualized needs assessments for families and empower pregnant and new mothers.

# Applying What We Know in Program Implementation

The research literature on SEL and home-visiting programs provides numerous examples of how the ISF model, elements of successful implementation, and a community-based participatory action research approach are central to successful program implementation. In this section of the chapter, we review the research on those two programs organized according to the participatory action research activities listed earlier in the chapter.

## Problem Identification and Definition

The first activity in our general model of participatory action research for program implementation is the identification and definition of the problem or area of concern. We say "problem or area of concern" to point out that prevention efforts do not always have to be directed toward a specific problem area. Communities may instead wish to work on strengthening existing resources and health promotion activities in their community or organization. As discussed in Chapter 10, these two goals often overlap.

A problem cannot be effectively addressed until it is widely identified as a problem. This relates directly back to the concept of community readiness and is an important piece of the prevention support system in the ISF model. It points out that communities and organizations must be motivated to reach a goal before resources will be dedicated toward reaching that goal. Problem identification and definition are key parts of this process. Communities generally mobilize around issues that are already recognized. But developing momentum to address a little-known issue is possible. Form coalitions with like-minded individuals, do your research on the problem and its effects in your community, and then talk about it. Write letters to the local newspapers, ask to speak to the city council and other legislative bodies, and present to as many groups as you can (e.g., church groups, PTAs, school boards, community groups, the chamber of commerce). These activities may be particularly important when your goal is to address health promotion or positive youth development rather than prevent a specific problem.

Once there is some general level of agreement that the problem or area of concern is an important one, a common understanding of the problem needs to be developed. This is the process of problem definition. Think back to the discussion of problem definition in Chapters 1 and 3. How a problem is defined will directly affect how that problem is addressed. A fundamental example of this is the fact that a problem must be defined as something that *is preventable* before stakeholders will begin to consider prevention opportunities. There may be public recognition of a problem, but if that public recognition includes the belief that the problem is inevitable, then there will be no energy or resources available for prevention programming. Poverty is a good

**setting context**
includes all features of a pertinent environment, such as cultural traditions and norms; the historical experiences of that environment; the abilities, objectives, and apprehensions of the individuals; and all aspects of community capacity.

**community and organizational capacity**
the resources present in a setting that would be available to help implement a new program or other types of innovation. Resources can exist at the individual, organizational, or community level.

example of a societal problem that is considered by many to be inevitable. We discuss this issue more in Chapter 13.

But the issue of problem definition goes beyond just instilling a general belief that a particular problem is preventable. The way the problem is defined has a huge impact on what possible interventions will be considered. SEL programming is a good example of this. Suppose there is a school district with high levels of disruptive behavior in the classrooms; high levels of bullying, violence, and vandalism; and low levels of academic achievement. There are many ways those problems could be understood. For example, if the problem is defined as being caused by aggressive, out-of-control children who are impossible to teach, then the solution chosen may be to increase police presence in the schools so those children can be arrested and removed when they cause trouble. If the problem is defined as being caused by poor teachers and inept administrators, then the obvious solution is to fire those poorly performing personnel. If the problem is defined as being caused by a lack of resources in the schools, then the preferred solution might be to funnel more money to the school district. But if the problem is defined in terms of school climate and a lack of opportunity for children to learn prosocial behaviors and self-regulatory skills, then SEL programming starts to seem like a good idea.

## Assessment of the Setting

The next step in the action research cycle is to assess the resources and organizational capacity of the setting. This is an assessment of the prevention support system in the ISF model and of community and organizational readiness. It is also a necessary step to ensure that you understand the setting in which you are working. From a community psychology perspective, there must be an ecological match, or fit, between the goals and methods of a program and the values and resources of the setting context in which it is being implemented. **Setting context** is a complex concept. It refers to all aspects of the relevant setting, including cultural traditions and norms; the skills, goals, and concerns of the individuals; historical issues in that setting (e.g., prior experiences with similar innovations); and all the elements of community capacity. It would be difficult to overestimate the importance of community capacity in our discussion of program implementation. As stated earlier, 11 of the 23 factors identified as affecting program implementation by Durlak and DuPre (2008) were related to the organizational capacity of the prevention delivery system.

In a broad sense, **community and organizational capacity** refers to the resources present in a setting that would be available to help implement a new program or other types of innovation. Capacity can refer to individual-level resources (e.g., skills, education, motivation), organizational-level resources (e.g., clarity of mission, ability to attract funding, a cohesive staff), or community-level resources (e.g., strength of linkages among various groups, sense of community, history of other successful innovations). Community-level capacity can be seen as related to the concept of social capital we discussed in Chapter 6.

As discussed earlier, and as shown in Figure 11.2, many implementation models differentiate between innovation-specific capacity and general capacity. Innovation-specific capacity refers to the motivation, skills, and resources that are necessary to implement a specific program. General capacity refers to the skills, characteristics, and overall level of functioning necessary to implement any type of program. Both types of capacity exist at individual, organizational, and community levels (Flaspohler et al., 2008; Wandersman et al., 2008). An assessment of capacity should take place before the selection of any program.

An assessment of a community's innovation-specific capacity, for example, might tell you that a home-visiting program based on the Nurse-Family Partnership model will not work because your community is already experiencing a shortage of nurses and it would be impossible to hire enough for the program. In this case, you might want to consider a different model of home visiting. It may be that there is no need to identify an external program to prevent a problem; the community may already have existing programs that are working but need to be strengthened (R. Miller & Shinn, 2005).

Look back at Table 11.1. One element of organizational capacity that has repeatedly been found to be central to the implementation process is strong leadership that is supportive of the program and the people who will be implementing it. A study of SEL programs conducted by CASEL found that *strong, clear leadership* in the setting is key to successful implementation. Active administrative support for the program was critical for school commitment, for adoption and sustaining of the program by teachers and other staff, for obtaining money and other resources, and for explaining the program to parents and community members (Elias et al., 1997). When administrative turnover occurred, programs with strong leadership proceeded with minimal disruption, usually because program developers engaged new administrators and offered program consultation to school staff. Sustainability can take a long-term emotional toll on even its most committed members if the program is in a constant state of reinvention or uncertainty.

There is one important point about community and organizational capacity that is becoming increasingly clear in the research on program implementation. When your assessment shows that existing capacity levels make it doubtful that a specific program can be successfully adopted, the most useful intervention may be to focus on increasing community capacity. Some research suggests that, rather than focusing efforts on trying to address specific problems, the most beneficial approach is to focus on building community strengths (R. Miller & Shinn, 2005). Formative evaluation and Getting To Outcomes both focus on developing processes that have been linked to organizational capacity, such as shared decision-making processes and open communication. We present examples of community organizations that have successfully accomplished this in Chapter 13.

## Reviewing Available Interventions

Once you have defined your problem and have a basic understanding of your setting, you have to select an intervention. In this chapter, we encourage you to follow certain steps: Assess your setting, clarify goals, and review the available programs to select one appropriate for your goals and setting. Unfortunately, this recommended process of assessment, review, and selection is not always followed. A review of how various states select specific home-visiting programs found that most states did not engage in any type of systematic evaluation of available programs. Generally, only one program was considered, often the program that was most popular nationally at the time (Wasserman, 2006). Think about that for a moment, reflecting on the issues of context discussed earlier. Do you think that a program selected based on popularity, with little consideration of how it would fit with a particular setting, has much chance of success?

The most prevalent approach to selecting an intervention is to review the available evidence-based programs. As you have seen in Chapter 10, there is a wealth of research on effective prevention programs and many, many organizations devoted to helping you choose an evidence-based prevention program that fits your goals and settings. In addition to the organizations we have already mentioned, such as CASEL and the Maternal, Infant, and Early Childhood Home Visiting Program, other highly regarded organizations include the following:

- Blueprints for Healthy Youth Development (www.blueprintsprograms.org)

- Substance Abuse and Mental Health Services Administration (SAMHSA) National Registry of Evidence-Based Programs and Practices (www.samhsa.gov/nrepp)

- Office of Juvenile Justice and Delinquency Prevention Model Programs Guide (www.ojjdp.gov/mpg)

These organizations are addressing the prevention synthesis and translation system of the ISF model that we introduced at the beginning of this chapter. Their goal is to provide clear information regarding these programs to as wide an audience as possible. They want to help bridge the gap between research and practice by synthesizing the sometimes dense and complex information from research articles and presenting it in a useful format for the general public. This, of course, is also the goal of the program developers themselves.

These organizations are not trying to promote one specific program. They reflect a community-centered model of implementation by taking the community perspective. The websites do not assume that there is one best program to address any specific problem. Rather, the developers of these sites assume that only the members of the community can make an informed decision concerning what programs will best meet the needs of that community. The goal of those websites is to provide community members with as much information as possible about evidence-based prevention programs, in order to ensure that the communities can make informed decisions.

This task is not an easy one. If you look at the Blueprints for Healthy Youth Development website and click on their programs listing, you will see that the organization has reviewed over 1,500 youth promotion programs. At the time of this writing, 17 programs met the organization's strict criteria to be identified as a model program and another 70 met the criteria for promising programs. While we recommend that you consider programs identified as model programs by one of these organizations, there are concerns with the evidence-based program approach, specifically concerns with expecting replication of previous evaluation results when bringing interventions to scale and, relatedly, with ensuring a fit between the intervention and the setting (Wandersman et al., 2016). As stated earlier, sometimes developing programs that demonstrate results in small-scale, controlled conditions may turn out to be the easiest step in the prevention science process. From those small-scale results, it is impossible to predict how the program will perform in diverse settings with less controlled conditions. Yet funders and other stakeholders expect the same results. This is a particular problem when the program selected does not match resources, values, or culture of a setting. These issues are addressed further in our discussion of the Getting To Outcomes approach to program implementation and evaluation in Chapter 12, but for now let us discuss the important question of program and setting fit.

As helpful as these organizations are, they cannot determine what program is right for a particular context. As stated in Table 11.1, the community members must determine both the compatibility of the program with the setting and the degree to which the program can be adapted to the needs of the setting. In order to do that, community members must have a clear idea of the specific challenges and goals that exist in their setting. For example, there are a large number of evidence-based SEL programs, and they differ in important ways. Some focus on changing school climate, others on teaching specific skills. Some are designed for after-school programs; many others are classroom based. Some have clear links to educational goals, such as literacy skills. And all of them have implicit cultural biases. Only through a collaborative assessment of the setting and the available programs can communities determine what program is most likely to work for them.

**core components**
aspects of a program that are critical to the program's identity and effectiveness and need to be implemented with adherence to their original design when adapting the program to a new setting.

**adaptive components**
aspects of a program that can be modified to fit the culture or practical limitations of a new setting when adapting a program; also referred to as key characteristics.

*Core and Adaptive Components.* In order to successfully engage in program adaptation, those implementing the program must know what the core components of the program are and maintain fidelity to those; everything else is open to adaptation to the setting context. Developers of prevention/promotion programs understand the need to specify the key components of their programs, especially when they transfer their initiatives to new host settings. Two types of components have been identified. **Core components** are crucial to the identity and effectiveness of the program and need to be transferred with fidelity and care. **Adaptive components** may be altered to fit the social ecology or practical constraints of the new host setting (Price & Lorion, 1989). Some researchers also use the term "key characteristics" to refer to the adaptive components of the program. These include things such as specific activities or delivery methods (e.g., the exact video tapes used, the examples chosen to illustrate a point). For example, many major prevention programs, including both examples highlighted in this chapter, specify that the presence of a structured curriculum of some sort is a core component for program success. But the details of what is covered in the curriculum can vary widely, even between programs of the same general type.

This need to be clear on the difference between core and adaptive components is illustrated by the research on home-visiting programs. The programs differ greatly on such things as the goals of the program, the frequency and duration of home visits, the population served, the background of the home visitors, and whether the home visits are tied to other services, such as high-quality center-based day care (Howard & Brooks-Gunn, 2009). Some programs begin home visits at birth; others begin prenatally. The visits can be weekly, biweekly, monthly, or of variable frequency over a period of time anywhere from 3 months to 5 years. The visitors can be nurses, master's-level psychologists, college graduates, or paraprofessionals (individuals with relevant experience but no formal education or training). Given this variability, how can you determine what the core components are?

Most organizations developed to support the implementation of specific programs are fully aware of the need to clarify core components and go to great lengths to ensure fidelity to those components. Home-visiting programs are no exception. Although there is no widely recognized list of core components for home-visiting programs in general, specific programs have worked to identify them, which can be seen on their websites.

Researchers have been working for decades to identify a set of core components common to general types of prevention programs, and they still have not completely succeeded. It is common in the literature to have a core component clearly specified for a general type of program, without specifying exactly what form that component should take. For example, as we have already mentioned, all home-visiting programs agree that programs should have in place a method for assessing which families are most likely to benefit from the program. Home visitation, at least as it is implemented in the United States, is designed as a targeted intervention. But exactly who should be targeted in a specific community? The answer to that question varies depending on the goals of the program and the setting. Home-visiting programs have been shown, in various studies, to demonstrate their strongest effects for specific populations, such as first-time teenage mothers, mothers with low psychological resources, and immigrant families, particularly Latinx families (Astuto & Allen, 2009; Howard & Brooks-Gunn, 2009). Which program you choose will depend on whether you have a particular population you wish to target.

Another component of home-visiting programs that may be considered adaptive is the issue of the qualifications necessary to be a home visitor. In general, the research supports the use of professional home visitors (i.e., nurses, social workers, or mental health counselors) rather than paraprofessionals for maximum beneficial effects (Howard & Brooks-Gunn, 2009). However, some evaluations have found positive effects with paraprofessionals (DuMont et al., 2008). Taking into account issues of context, there could easily be reasons why a community would choose to use paraprofessionals in a home-visiting program. The community members may feel strongly that the program should employ individuals local to community, which might make it difficult to hire enough visitors with professional degrees. There may also be important issues of cultural match between the visitors and the participant population that would make paraprofessionals a more appropriate choice for your community.

Another example of these points from the SEL literature is from a case study of an elementary school in the Chicago area, the Cossitt School. Starting in 1994, the school began researching SEL programs and eventually chose the Child Development Project (CDP) as the program they wished to implement. CDP had over a decade of research supporting its effectiveness in a variety of school settings. The school made a long-term commitment to the program and dedicated a great deal of time and resources into training the teachers and educating the whole school community about the program. But the training and education was not limited to just that specific program. Teachers, administrators, and others began reading about multiple aspects of SEL, and as they did, their understanding of what they were doing, and how they were doing it, changed. As the Cossitt School principal, Mary Tavegia, said, "We still do components of the program. But we've been trying to pull knowledge and best practices from everything we've read and learned about SEL" (CASEL, 2006, p. 8). As the school staff began to feel that they clearly understood the core components of SEL programs in general and could see that they were successfully implementing those components, they became comfortable in adapting other aspects of the program to better fit the needs of their school.

## Assessing the Fit Between the Program and the Setting

Defining the problem and selecting a program with empirical evidence of preventing that problem, while essential, is not enough to ensure successful adoption. Regardless of the program's primary goals, it must also clearly address the mission of, and most pressing goals of, the setting and the people who inhabit that setting. Settings such as schools, workplaces, and governmental organizations face multiple pressures. They often have various constituent groups, with various needs that those groups expect the settings to address. These needs are often competing, leading to conflicting priorities for the setting. Sometimes a regulatory agency or other constituency with authority over the setting will mandate that a particular goal become a priority for the setting. In order for a prevention program to be successful, it must adapt to the priorities of the setting.

Earlier, we said that the assessment of context includes recognition of the values of the community or organization. If the values espoused by the potential prevention program do not fit with the values of the setting (or the values of the funding organization), there is little chance that the program will be successfully implemented. Before this determination is made, however, there should be a careful assessment of the core components of the program to see whether those are actually in opposition to the values of the setting. If the core components are congruent with the values of the setting, other concerns with the program will probably be amenable to adaptation.

One aspect of context that must be taken seriously if a program is to be successfully disseminated is the skills and goals of the staff who implement it. Skilled staff members in any setting take pride in their craft and view their work with a sense of ownership. To gain their approval, an innovation must fit their values and identity: for instance, a police officer's sense of what police work involves. At the same time, an innovation must also offer something new that increases the staff's sense of effectiveness. Staff members of different ages, ranks in the organization, or levels of seniority may support or resist an innovation, depending on how they understand their work and roles.

Almost all people have seen innovations come and go in their settings. And the longer they have been in that setting, the more experience they have with this process. That experience may be positive. They may have seen a problem in their community or organization effectively addressed through an innovation that was sustained over the long term. Or the experience may have been negative. They may have felt that a potentially positive innovation was not given enough support and died away. Or perhaps they felt that an innovation was forced on them even though it was completely inappropriate for their setting. Some people may live or work in settings that have been subject to an almost continuous cycle of "innovations," none of which have lasted for more than a year or two. These people in particular may be burned out on the whole idea of innovation and convinced that there is nothing truly different anyone can offer them.

The need to understand and meet the goals and priorities of the setting is illustrated by the experiences of the developers of the Social Decision Making and Social Problem Solving (SDM/SPS) Program, a model SEL program. The organizers, from the Rutgers Social-Emotional Learning Lab, implemented the program in an urban, economically disadvantaged school setting. The district was under unprecedented pressure to meet mandates to raise standardized test scores. Those efforts crowded out programs directed at social-emotional and character development (Elias & Kamarinos, 2003).

In order for SEL programs to be successfully adopted by such school districts, it is critical that the programs demonstrate a direct relationship to state and local mandates governing those schools. In this case, the success of the program implementation was based on the fact that the five skill areas of SEL (see Figure 11.2) were aligned with academic standards explicitly named and monitored in the district's goals.

Like most SEL programs, the SDM/SPS program has a set curriculum. To meet the needs of the district, that curriculum had to be meshed with the various mandates the district was facing, especially concerning literacy. A series of topical modules to build readiness skills was created for Grades K–1, as well as a supplemental small-group intervention for young students with early reading difficulties (Elias & Kamarinos, 2003). This innovation demonstrated to the district that SEL programs could be used to address the academic mandates they were facing.

## Training and Support of Staff

One clear core component for any program is the need to provide significant training and ongoing support for the individuals implementing the program. Both areas of prevention programming highlighted in this chapter emphasize the need for significant training of the people who will be delivering the program. If you look at the model elements specified by the Nurse-Family and Healthy Families America home-visiting programs—available on their websites (www.nursefamilypartnership.org and www.healthyfamiliesamerica.org)—you will see that both organizations emphasize the importance of training for the visitors. In addition, they both emphasize the need for significant supervision of the visitors, even going so far as to present guidelines regarding the number of visitors each supervisor should have on their caseload.

Even with the focus on training provided by the model programs, there is still concern that home visitors, who can have a wide variety of educational backgrounds, may be lacking specific skills and the support necessary to implement them (Michalopoulos et al., 2015). This is one reason why the Maternal, Infant, and Early Childhood Home Visiting Program of the U.S. Health Resources and Services Administration has provided significant fund-

**small wins**
minor yet concrete changes that can lead to a pattern of accomplishment and feeling of momentum.

ing since 2009 to support additional training for home visitors. A recent initiative based on the Interactive Systems Framework was successful in identifying a particular need for increased skills in relationship building, communication, and cultural competence. The team then used ISF principles to develop and implement a training program for home visitors. That program has been shown to result not only in an increased sense of self-efficacy among home visitors but also in improved communication around sensitive topics in a randomized trial (Schultz et al., 2019).

Training by itself, however, cannot ensure successful implementation. There must be planning, before the beginning of the implementation of the program, to develop processes to support the individuals involved in the day-to-day provision of the program. In particular, staff must feel that their work is valuable and acknowledged. When discussing Albee's (1982) and Elias's (1987) prevention equations in Chapter 10, we talked about the protective benefits of settings that provided opportunities for recognition of positive, prosocial behavior. This protective factor does not just apply to children. It is important for adults as well and should be kept in mind when designing the structures that will support the implementation of a program. Processes need to be in place to recognize *small wins* so that the members of the setting can see and celebrate successes of the program early on.

Weick (1984) mustered evidence from social and cognitive psychology for the conclusion that when extensive changes are required of humans in organizations, their sense of being threatened rises, as does their resistance to change. When the proposed change seems smaller, the perceived threat is smaller, risks seem tolerable, allies are easier to attract, and opponents are less mobilized. **Small wins** is Weick's term for limited yet tangible innovations or changes that can establish a record of success and sense of momentum.

In a home-visiting program that begins prenatally, one small win that could be tracked is the number of prenatal care appointments the clients successfully complete. This is a measure that has been shown to be positively affected by these programs, it is data that should be kept as part of any program evaluation, and it is an achievement that the home visitors will recognize as important (particularly if they are health professionals). Progress on this measure should be extremely visible. For example, a chart could be put in a room where the program staff regularly meet, and each home visitor could indicate on the chart whenever a pregnant client keeps a prenatal care appointment. The chart may sound like an approach that would be used with children, but trust us: Adults need these visible celebrations of success too.

## Implementing, Innovating, and Sustaining Programs

In this chapter, we have emphasized the idea that, to be successful, programs cannot just be implemented in a cookbook fashion. They must be informed by the unique strengths, values, and practices of their setting. We take the

**longitudinal**
taking place over a length of time.

**institutionalized**
established as part of a setting's routine functioning.

specific position that successful program implementation must involve some level of program innovation. We believe that the current state of the research supports the conclusion that, while core components must be identified and adhered to, programs must be adapted to the specific context in which the program is being implemented.

Many of the challenges of implementation that we discuss in this section relate back to concerns about core components, context, and program selection. This emphasizes again the need for a participatory action research approach to program implementation. If you do your groundwork in understanding your setting and understanding your program, implementation will be much easier. But the process is ongoing; you must be continually collecting information and using that data to adjust and improve your program.

As we hope was clear from our discussion of the interaction between individuals and their environments in Chapter 5, adaptation is not a one-way street. While the program is adapting to the setting, the setting is also changing and adapting to the program. Program adaptation takes place over time; it must be **longitudinal** in nature. This idea is similar to Kelly's principle of succession—the fact that settings and social systems change over time (Trickett et al., 1972). An innovation takes place in a setting with a history and culture. To be effective, it must change that setting in some way (Tornatzky & Fleischer, 1986). To be lasting, it must become part of that history and culture, not dependent on an influential leader or a few staff members, all of whom will eventually leave the setting. It must be **institutionalized**, made a part of the setting's routine functioning.

Moreover, any effective prevention/promotion innovation must be repeated or elaborated periodically for effect. One-shot presentations or activities seldom have lasting impact. Teaching a child to read is a multiyear effort, from identifying letters to reading novels (Shriver, 1992). Should it be any surprise that learning social-emotional skills or developing attitudes that limit risky behavior cannot be done quickly?

In order for a program to be institutionalized, it must be integrated into the ongoing activities of the setting; it cannot be seen as something "extra." The CASEL evaluation of social and emotional learning programs found that sustained programs were integrated with other courses and into the mainstream of the school day and routine. This included use of the program in reading, health, and social studies, as well as in school assemblies, school discipline and resolution of conflicts among students, and expectations for playground and lunchroom behavior. Integration takes place over a period of years and includes the program becoming a regular part of the school budget; external funding is often available only for a few years or can change over time (Elias et al., 1997).

The CASEL evaluation also found that sustained implementation required ongoing professional development about the program among teams of committed staff (teachers and others). This required some staff to become

**emic perspective**
a perspective grounded in and arising from the community itself.

program advocates and role models. Sustainability is more likely when professional development is continual and implementers have a constantly deepening understanding of the theoretical principles and pedagogy upon which the program is based. When teams of implementers with a deep commitment to the program work together, they can often maintain program momentum even during times of turnover. Most important, deep understanding of program principles allows implementers to adapt programs in response to changing circumstances yet maintain key program elements. While a surface understanding of the program may be sufficient for a setting to adopt it, in order for the program to be institutionalized, multiple members of the setting must have a deep understanding of the program and its core components and must be able to teach others about it.

McLaughlin and Mitra (2001) analyzed the staying power of school reforms over a 5-year period and found that deep learning of theory and planned, proactive training of staff and administrators were important factors. Initial support for an innovation by administration and staff was less important than predicted, if the innovation had a clear, feasible path of implementation and its benefits were soon apparent. Lessons about sustaining innovations in schools are similar to those in other workplaces. Administrative energy and direction are essential for sustainability, but overcoming turnover requires an educated, committed workforce. Administrative commitment, deep involvement of the workforce in ongoing change (especially at a face-to-face microsystem level), and innovations that address integral parts of the organization's mission foster sustainability (Elias & Kamarinos, 2003).

## Cultural Diversity in Program Implementation

Throughout this chapter we have emphasized the need to understand the community or setting in which you are working and to adapt programs to the values, strengths, and self-identified needs of the community. In Chapter 7, we explored the different dimensions of human diversity and how those dimensions intersect and affect the contexts in which we live. Nowhere is the importance of community-based participatory approaches so clear as in the area of cultural diversity. Program implementation and adaptation needs to proceed from an **emic perspective** (a perspective grounded in and arising from the community itself), and the process needs to be directed by the voices of the community members. This is in contrast to an *etic perspective*, where the program implementation is directed by a person or group from outside the community (such as the developers of the program or a university research team).

While this is true for all communities and settings, it is particularly true of communities with a history of colonization. Let us look at this in the context of a specific issue in a specific group of communities: suicide prevention in Native American/Alaska Native communities.

## Suicide Prevention Program in Native American/Alaska Native Communities

Like so many of the discussions in this book, this one starts with the idea of problem definition. Problem definitions are rooted in historical perspective and cultural values. For Native American communities, many of the mental health problems seen on some reservations, such as substance abuse and depression, are the direct result of historical attempts by European Americans to destroy Native American cultures, traditions, and religions (Gone & Alcántara, 2007). The framework of decoloniality describes a movement away from imposed understandings and processes and toward Indigenous knowledge and practices. From this perspective, there are clear problems with the uncritical adoption of interventions derived from European American culture. Those problems were described in an ethnographic interview conducted by community psychologist Joseph Gone (2007) with a member of the Fort Belknap Indian Community whom Gone referred to as "Traveling Thunder":

> That's kind of like taboo. You know, we don't do that. We never did do that. If you look at the big picture—you look at your past, your history, where you come from—and you look at your future where the Whiteman's leading you, I guess you could make a choice: Where do I want to end up? And I guess a lot of people want to end up looking good to the Whiteman. Then it'd be a good thing to do: Go [to the] white psychiatrists in the Indian Health Service and say, "Rid me of my history, my past, and brainwash me forever so I can be like a Whiteman." (p. 294)

The central role of problem definition is clear here. If substance abuse, depression, and suicide in Native American communities are defined by those communities as resulting from the decimation of their culture, values, and spirituality by the dominant American culture, then adopting an intervention from that dominant culture can never be seen as a solution. Rather, it would be a continuation of the problem (Gone, 2007; Gone & Alcántara, 2007).

From this perspective, any successful intervention or prevention program would have to be developed from the spiritual and cultural traditions of that specific community. Since the fundamental problem is not depression but rather the forced separation of community members from traditional approaches to understanding the world, then interventions should be judged by how well they attempt to address that fundamental problem.

The recognition that suicide-prevention programming in Native American communities needs to be informed by this conceptualization of the problem is becoming widely recognized. In fact, a guide to suicide prevention among Native American and Alaska Native youth, published by the U.S. Department of Health and Human Services (2010), lists historical trauma as a risk factor and cultural continuity as a protective factor.

This recognition, however, does not mean that this culturally anchored definition of the problem has been reflected in evidence-based prevention programming. In fact, the whole concept of "evidence-based" programming can be seen in some communities as an attempt to force the dominant cultural values of science onto communities that do not necessarily share those values (Gone & Alcántara, 2007). This means that every aspect of the participatory action research cycle, from definition and assessment through implementation and evaluation, must be informed by, and congruent with, the values of the community.

An example of this kind of work is Promoting Community Conversations About Research to End Suicide (PC CARES; Trout et al., 2018). The program is based on a series of conversations in Alaskan Indigenous communities (learning circles). The learning circles are facilitated by Alaska Natives familiar with the scientific research on suicide prevention. The research is presented not as something for communities to adopt but rather as a means to begin a discussion of how youth suicide is conceptualized in their communities and culture and how the history, beliefs, values, and resources of the community can inform and support effective interventions. For example, a common medical approach to dealing with an adolescent with thoughts of suicide is hospitalization and intensive treatment. In the rural communities of Alaska, that often means hospitalization 500 miles away. That approach can be quite successful in preventing an immediate suicide. But if the community's understanding of youth suicide is that it is linked to the breakdown of intergenerational mentorship resulting from colonization, then removing youth from their communities can only exacerbate the problem (Trout et al., 2018).

These examples reflect the integration of cultural values at a *deep structural level* rather than just on a *surface level* (see Chapter 7 for additional discussion of these concepts). Including cultural references in a program is a surface-level change that is likely to have little or no effect on the effectiveness or appropriateness of a program for a particular community. Integration on a deep level requires an in-depth understanding of a community's values, history, and practices, and ensuring that those factors serve as a fundamental basis for the theory and implementation of a program. For additional descriptions and reflections on this type of work with Alaskan Indigenous communities, see the special issue of the *American Journal of Community Psychology* on this topic (J. Allen & Mohatt, 2014).

## What Do You Think?

1. How do these suicide-prevention programs exemplify community psychology's core values?

2. Think back to the SEL and home-visiting programs. How do these programs compare with the programs used with Alaskan Indigenous communities? What are some key differences, particularly when it concerns implementation methods?

3. Imagine you are a participating in a similar program with Indigenous peoples who do not share your cultural background. How would you ensure that your efforts are effective, are respectful of the community, and reflect the values of community psychology?

## Putting It All Together

Perhaps you have read all this and concluded, "But I want to do it all!" You want a home-visiting program to promote healthy infant development and parent–child attachment, you want SEL programs in your local schools, and you want a community-wide, multilevel parenting program to reduce rates of child maltreatment. Plus, you want some of the other programs you read about in Chapter 10.

In other words, you want to strengthen your whole community, not just address specific problems piecemeal. Well, first of all, the evidence supports you. All of these programs have their largest effects when they are systematically applied in conjunction with other programs and services. Home-visiting programs, for example, demonstrate some of their largest effects when they are offered in conjunction with high-quality day care and when they focus on connecting families with other services in the community (Astuto & Allen, 2009). In fact, one of the most serious criticisms of the Hawai'i Healthy Start program was that the home visitors did not connect the families with other services, and this is considered to be an important factor in their poor program results (Howard & Brooks-Gunn, 2009).

Doing it all, while obviously impossible in a literal sense, is still not out of the collective reach of communities. In Chapter 13, we talk about community change initiatives and the importance of community coalitions in ongoing community change. Community coalitions have their most positive effects when they address issues in their community as a whole, rather than specific problems. They also work longitudinally, engaging in a long-term process of community assessment and program implementation and adaptation. So, in the long term, these community members are attempting to "do it all" for their communities. Specific models for these types of community coalition initiatives include the Communities That Care and Developmental Assets programs discussed in Chapter 10.

After reading this chapter, you also may be wondering, if prevention and promotion programs are so effective, why don't we seem to see results on a national level? For example, if SEL programs are so effective and are implemented in so many schools, why is the American public school system still in such trouble? Why aren't things getting better? The basic answer to that question is that forces such as poverty, politics, and state and federal policies have huge effects on the functioning of schools. These large effects are going to affect evaluations of school performance on a national level much more than the implementation of SEL programming (for a recent discussion of some of these issues, see Ravitch, 2010). We discuss efforts to address some of those macrolevel factors in Chapter 13. But we would like to emphasize here that discouragement at a national level is no reason for discouragement at a local level. You may not be able to significantly improve the whole American public school system, but you can still improve the schools in your communities.

## For Review

### Discussion Questions

1. In the discussion questions for Chapter 10, we asked you to think about a problem in a community that you care about and how you might work to address that problem. How have the implementation guidelines and examples presented in this chapter added to or modified your previous answer?

2. In this chapter, we have emphasized the importance of moving beyond a cookbook mindset of strictly adopting a manual for an evidence-based prevention program. Instead, there should always be a component of innovation in program implementation. What does this mean? How does it relate to community capacity, community values, and core components?

3. This chapter presented numerous examples of prevention program implementation. Which examples stood out for you? Can you analyze why these examples were important for you personally?

### Key Terms

implementation, 375
scaling up, 376
research-to-practice models, 377
community-centered models, 377
Prevention Synthesis and Translation System, 378
Prevention Support System, 378

capacity, 379
general capacity, 379
innovation-specific capacity, 379
Prevention Delivery System, 379
readiness, 382
theory of change, 384
iatrogenic effects, 386
setting context, 393

community and organizational capacity, 393
core components, 397
adaptive components, 397
small wins, 401
longitudinal, 402
institutionalized, 402
emic perspective, 403

### Learn More

A detailed summary of the chapter, along with other review materials, is available on the *Community Psychology, Fourth Edition* companion website at http://pubs.apa.org/books/supp/kloos4/.

Mentoring programs like GirlPOWER! are effective at promoting healthy behaviors by empowering children and adolescents.

# 12 Program Development, Evaluation, and Improvement

## Looking Ahead

After reading this chapter you will be able to answer these questions:

1. How does evaluation occur in our everyday life?

2. Why does the notion of results-based accountability evoke anxiety for some program stakeholders?

3. What are the three types of evaluation, and what purpose does each serve?

4. What are the linkages among program development, evaluation, and improvement?

5. How can evaluations be guided by the values of community psychology?

## Opening Exercise

## Evaluating the DARE Drug Prevention Program

If you went to public school in the United States in the past 30 years or know any other children who did, there is a good chance that you have experience with an adolescent substance abuse prevention program called DARE (Drug Abuse Resistance Education). DARE involves police officers visiting classrooms in local schools to present a curriculum over several weeks. Officers present information on the dangers of drug use and teach refusal skills to help participating students resist peer pressure to use drugs. The program was originally based on a zero-tolerance policy regarding drug use, and students were encouraged to sign pledges stating that they would not use drugs. Students who complete the program receive certificates, T-shirts, and other materials that promote a "just say no to drugs" message.

If you participated in a DARE program, take a moment to think back. What do you remember about the program? Did you enjoy it? Do you think it helped prevent adolescent substance abuse in your school or community?

**Evaluating the DARE Drug Prevention Program (continued)**

Have your thoughts about the program changed in the years since your participation? If you did not participate in a DARE program, what have you heard about it? Does it seem to be effective at preventing adolescent drug use from what you know?

DARE was started in 1983 by the Los Angeles Police Department in cooperation with the Los Angeles Unified School District. Over the years, it has developed a number of different curricula targeting different grades and topics (such as prescription drug abuse). DARE is taught in most school districts across all 50 states and in 54 countries, reaching millions of school children and training over 12,000 law enforcement officers globally (DARE, 2008). It continues to be the most popular school-based drug-use prevention program in the United States. However, a number of evaluations of school curricula originally delivered by DARE provided only limited evidence of its effectiveness. For instance, results from a longitudinal evaluation of the program showed only a modest effect on students' drug use immediately following the intervention, and there was no evidence of effect on drug use 1 or 2 years after receiving DARE instruction. In addition, evaluations indicated that DARE programs had only limited positive effects on secondary variables of interest, such as self-esteem, and no effect on social skills variables, such as resistance to peer pressure (Ennett et al., 1994, p. 113). Negative evaluations continued to pile up over the years. By 1998, a report to the National Institute of Justice concluded that DARE was ineffective, and in 2001 the Surgeon General of the United States placed DARE in the "Does Not Work" category of prevention programs (Satcher, 2001; Sherman et al., 1998).

## What Do You Think?

1. How do these ineffectual results fit with your experience of the program? If you had a positive experience with DARE, why do you think your experience differs from the overall effectiveness research? If you did not have a positive experience, what about the program made it less effective for you?

2. Based on the key concepts and implementation guidelines you learned about in Chapters 10 and 11, why do you think DARE is ineffectual overall? How could the DARE program be improved, if at all? What qualities discussed in previous chapters would make for a more effective adolescent drug-prevention program?

In this chapter, we discuss how evaluation is used to help develop and improve the effectiveness of programs such as DARE. The primary goal of this chapter is to introduce you to the concept of evaluation and specific models that you can use to evaluate and improve community interventions. We will come back to DARE, but first, we want to make the point that you already know a great deal about evaluation because you do it all the time, perhaps without even being fully aware of when and how you are doing it.

# Evaluation in Everyday Life

Evaluation is not just an activity performed by social scientists. We all engage in what is essentially program evaluation, and we do it every day. When you go to a new restaurant or watch your favorite sports team, you are engaged in evaluation. In a restaurant, you think about the quality of the service, the quality of the food, the cost, and the atmosphere. If the service was slow, the food was nothing special, and the cost was high, you probably would not dine there again. And you will probably "disseminate your results." If a friend asks you about your experience with the restaurant, you will give both your data (poor service, mediocre food, and high price) and your overall evaluation (don't bother going there).

When you watch your favorite sports team, you are thinking about the individual performance of the players (in that game, over the season, and in previous seasons), the team's performance against the opposing team in the past, the quality of the coaching, and perhaps the cost to the team of recruiting individual players. You will probably also consider the context in which the game is being played. Some contextual factors you might consider are the weather, if the team is playing at home or away, whether the team has had a chance to rest since their last game, and popular opinion about the team's chances of winning. With a sports team, your evaluation and the data you consider will probably depend a great deal on your goals for the team. If the team is performing much better than the previous season, with a number of talented new players and a new coach, your evaluation is likely to be positive, even if the team does not have an outstanding season. If you are evaluating a child's soccer team, then there will be different goals and contextual factors to consider than with a professional sports team, but there will be some similarities as well. For instance, weather will still be an important factor to consider—perhaps for different reasons—but the main goal is to have the players learn to get along well and have fun, with every child having an opportunity to play. Thus, the team's actual performance may have little to do with your evaluation of their success.

While evaluation activities can sometimes result in a yes or no decision (e.g., the case of the restaurant when you decide not to return there), they are more likely to result in decisions regarding steps to take to foster improvement, as with your favorite sports team. Most sports fans do not give up on their favorite teams just because they have a losing season, and certainly coaches and owners do not. Instead, they spend a great deal of time reviewing their evaluation data to decide how to help the team improve. Evaluation aimed at improving outcomes (known as formative evaluation) is of increasing interest to community practitioners. In this chapter, we discuss this type of evaluation, in addition to more traditional forms of evaluation.

The DARE program is an example of a prevention program that was not properly modified in the face of extensive critical evaluations.

# Rationale for Program Evaluation

### It Seemed Like a Good Idea, but Is It Really Working? (Results-Based Accountability)

**opportunity cost**
the loss of potential gain or value when one alternative is selected over others.

**results-based accountability**
the need to evaluate a program in order to show proven results.

The DARE program illustrates the importance of comprehensive program evaluation. DARE uses a great deal of public resources (its funding sources are state and federal agencies, in addition to corporations and foundations) and a relatively large amount of classroom time that could be used for other educational purposes. Further, there is an **opportunity cost** (missed or lost value that results from pursuing one option over another): School districts that implement DARE are not implementing other available programs, which might be more effective in preventing adolescent substance abuse.

With the DARE program as a case in point, consider that each year, millions of taxpayer dollars, charitable contributions, and grants by philanthropic foundations are invested to improve living conditions and community outcomes. Citizens across the nation volunteer time and effort to promote social justice. Even paid staff members in community organizations often choose to work for a low salary in order to promote individual and collective wellness. Is that money, time, and effort making a difference? In other words, is it a valuable investment? Government, nonprofit, and private sectors are being challenged to show results. The responsibility to demonstrate program results through evaluation is commonly referred to as **results-based accountability**. At first, this can be a frightening prospect to people who oversee and coordinate community programs. Below are some common complaints and fears about program evaluation (compiled by the Grosvenor Performance Group, n.d.):

- Evaluation can create anxiety among program staff.

- Staff may be unsure how to conduct evaluation.

- Evaluation can interfere with program activities or compete with services for scarce resources.

- Evaluation results can be misused and misinterpreted, especially by program opponents.

Imagine yourself as a board member of a foundation who has to make funding decisions about community programs. You get many more requests for funding than you could possibly fund. It makes sense to ask grantees, "How can we know whether your program, supported by our grant money, actually accomplishes its goals?" Schorr (1997) described several types of responses to this question often given by nonprofit organizations and government agencies:

- **Process and outputs.** "Our agency sees 200 eligible clients yearly in the 20 parent education programs we offer, and our two licensed staff are funded by your grant." This is probably the most typical answer, with detailed documentation of programs or services provided and resources expended. However, simply providing services does not mean that those services are effective. Services may be misdirected, thus not addressing the real problem. They may be well planned but not strong or well funded enough to make a difference. They may have unintended side effects. Hopeful but undocumented expectations underlie many community programs.

- **Trust and values.** "Trust us. What we do is so valuable, so complex, so hard to document, so hard to judge, and we are so well-intentioned that the public should support us without demanding evidence of effectiveness. Don't let the bean counters who know the cost of everything and the value of nothing obstruct our valiant efforts to get the world's work done." However, if program funding is determined by trust, then citizens and decision makers don't know the process of how the program works and don't know whether there are any results.

- **Results-based accountability.** "The number of hospital readmission rates have declined in our community ever since the major healthcare system deployed community nurses to provide in-home visits, an evidence-based approach to improving community health outcomes." Using program evaluation, agency staff and evaluators can show that a specific program achieved its intended effects. They can also modify it to become even more effective. However, agency staff are often not trained to do evaluation. Also, what happens if the evaluation shows that the program does not have its intended results? Will the program be given a chance to improve, and the resources it needs to do so?

You can see a number of these themes in the responses of the DARE directorship to the negative evaluation results. The 1998 report from the National Institute of Justice states that "D.A.R.E. proponents challenge the results of the scientific D.A.R.E. evaluations. Officials of D.A.R.E. America are often quoted as saying that the strong public support for the program is a better indicator of its utility than scientific studies" (Sherman et al., 1998, p. 191). Rather than using the evaluation results to strengthen the program, DARE proponents initially rejected the validity of the results.

But that is not the end of the DARE story. Even with the disappointing evaluation results, there were good reasons not to simply eliminate the DARE program. DARE has something other programs do not have: extremely successful national and international prevention support and delivery systems. Remember our discussion of these systems as part of the Interactive Systems Framework for Dissemination and Implementation in Chapter 9? DARE has shown for decades that police officers can be successfully trained to provide the program as designed (officers receive a minimum of 80 hours of training) and that schools and police departments working together can implement the program with high fidelity to the intended audience (Merrill et al., 2006). As you might recall from Chapter 10, effective, large-scale prevention support and delivery systems are something that many evidence-based programs have not been able to develop, and the fact that DARE has managed to develop them is an important finding.

In addition, the full DARE program includes curricula developed for elementary through high school students. The elementary school curriculum is the one most often evaluated, but there is less research discussing the effectiveness of the middle and high school level curricula. Finally, remember our discussion of efficacy versus effectiveness studies in Chapter 11? Efficacy studies are generally conducted under controlled conditions, while the program is still under development, and are designed to test whether or not the program is capable of producing positive results. Effectiveness studies are done in a variety of settings, often with much less control, and are designed to test whether or not the program can produce positive results under real-life conditions. Many programs that have been successful in efficacy studies have failed to replicate those results in effectiveness studies. Because of the unique circumstances around its development, the DARE program essentially never had any efficacy studies and went straight to the harder standard of effectiveness.

DARE officials did begin to acknowledge that there were problems with their program, and they began making modifications and developing new

**critical friend**
a supportive person who provides feedback about program implementation that is honest and constructive, encouraging program practitioners to recognize their biases and identifying strengths, weaknesses, and emotionally sensitive issues.

programs through use of evaluation feedback. In 2008, DARE adopted a new evidence-based middle school curriculum developed by researchers at Pennsylvania State University and Arizona State University. The program, called "keepin' it REAL," was included in the SAMHSA (2014) National Registry of Evidenced-Based Programs and Practices. Multiple national reports and journals have favorably reported on the DARE keepin' it REAL curriculum (e.g., Christie et al., 2017; Office of the Surgeon General, 2016). The keepin' it REAL program has been shown to reduce substance use at a rate that was 72% higher than the control group (Kulis et al., 2007).

The DARE story illustrates some important themes:

- evaluations about the effectiveness of a program can lead to program improvement efforts;

- whether programs work and for whom should influence data-informed decision making in communities (e.g., while early substance abuse prevention education is a good idea, follow-up booster approaches in high-risk years should also be considered); and

- program development, program evaluation, and program improvement need to be linked so that data can inform decisions.

If program evaluation and program development are linked, even initially disappointing results might lead to systematic improvements in a program and to data-informed decisions about what strategies to implement with whom.

In the next section, we discuss associations among program development, program evaluation, and program improvement.

## Linkages Among Program Development, Evaluation, and Improvement

Since the 1960s, the field of program evaluation has developed concepts and methods, based on the methods of the social sciences, to study program theory and implementation. This chapter uses many of these basic program evaluation concepts. However, we focus on approaches that make program evaluation user-friendly and accessible to a wider audience.

Professional evaluators are trained to think causally. They recognize that an intervention or prevention activity should be based on a theory of change (see Chapter 11). For social scientists, this type of thinking becomes so automatic that it is easy to forget that it is not universal. Program practitioners often benefit from having a **critical friend** to help them identify their underlying assumptions about a program theory, goals, and an implementation plan. A critical friend is someone who is encouraging and supportive but who also provides candid feedback that may be uncomfortable or difficult to hear.

**logic model**
a visual diagram that illustrates how a program will work to fill a community need by illustrating connections between community conditions, inputs, activities, outputs, outcomes, and impacts.

**conditions**
identify the needs of a program; examples include risk factors, community issues, and organizational challenges that the program will tackle.

**inputs**
the various resources available to address the conditions.

**activities**
the tasks and actions that are completed to address the conditions; also known as program of intervention.

**outputs**
the immediate product of a program's activities.

**outcomes**
direct, short-term results or changes related to the program activities.

**impacts**
indirect, long-term results or changes related to the program that impact the community at large.

A critical friend speaks truthfully, but constructively, about weaknesses, problems, and emotionally sensitive issues.

We offer an example on the value of thinking about causal links: A common community prevention activity is sponsoring a Red Ribbon Awareness Campaign. A local group wants to significantly reduce alcohol, tobacco, and other drug (ATOD) use by getting citizens to display red ribbons. Why would wearing a red ribbon lead to reductions in ATOD use? The logic may be that a red ribbon stimulates awareness of the hazards of substance use, which then either reduces one's own consumption of alcohol or stimulates the idea of designating a sober friend to drive. Questioning the connections between the display of red ribbons and the goal of reducing drunk driving requires critical thinking about cause and effect. It is important for school and community practitioners to use causal thinking and to, as much as possible, develop a causal model (theory of change) for a community program. The theory of change can be refined into a **logic model** and used to guide the program evaluation. The logic model is a graphic representation of how the program works. Its primary purpose is to illustrate the logical connections between the conditions that contribute to the need for a program in a community (conditions); the involved resources (inputs); the activities aimed at addressing these conditions (activities); and the expected immediate (outputs), short-term (outcomes), and longer term (impacts) results of the activities.

Figure 12.1 illustrates a six-step logic model that can be applied to program evaluation. **Conditions** specify the needs of a program. They include risk factors or processes, community problems, or organizational difficulties that the program seeks to address. **Inputs** are the resources involved in addressing the conditions. **Activities**, sometimes referred to as a program of intervention, specify the tasks and things that are done to address each condition. One or more activities can aim to solve each of the conditions (e.g., development of manuals, implementation of trainings, advocacy). **Outputs** are indicators that program activities were conducted (e.g., number of participants reached, percentage of participant engagement). **Outcomes** refer to direct, short-term results from the activity (e.g., changes in knowledge or attitudes about substance use among program participants, changes in local laws or organizational policy). **Impacts** of the program capture the distal (indirect, longer term) results of the activities on the community at large. For example, impacts on ATOD use might include lowering alcohol abuse and other forms of drug abuse in a community as well as related consequences, such as lower crime and better personal health. The six logic model circles are linked together with lines that show the expected logical relationships among them based on the program theory of change.

In Figure 12.2, we show the relationship between the logic model and program development, evaluation, and improvement efforts. The first row depicts the six steps of the logic model. The middle row illustrates key stages in program

**Figure 12.1** Program Logic Model

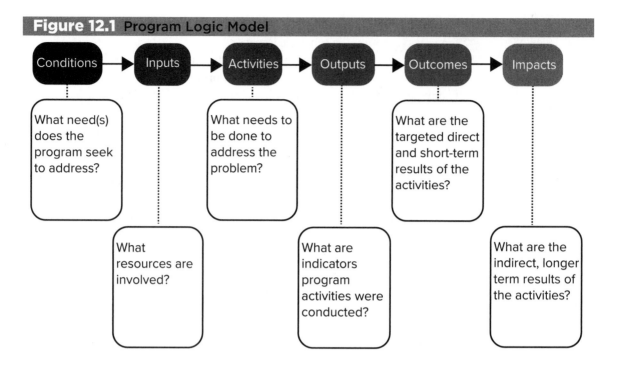

development. We overview the stages of program development here and discuss them in greater depth later in this chapter (see Getting To Outcomes). First, an assessment is conducted to determine the needs of the program (*needs assessment*). This stage reflects the *conditions* of the logic model. The next two stages involve developing a plan to address identified needs (*program planning*) and putting the plan into action (*implementation*). These two program development stages are linked to *inputs* and *activities* of the logic model. Finally, evaluations are used to monitor program implementation and determine the results of program activities. While depicted as the last stage of program development in Figure 12.2, evaluation activities are most optimally conducted during and after implementation. We will return to this concept of evaluation in the next section. The *evaluation* stage is associated with the last three steps of the logic model (*outputs*, *outcomes*, and *impacts*). All stages of program development ideally involve engagement from program recipients and other stakeholders. The bottom row of Figure 12.2 shows how program evaluation relates to the logic model and to program development, specifically the use of three types of evaluation (*process evaluation*, *formative evaluation*, and *summative evaluation*) to measure and monitor program goals. A feedback loop occurs between evaluation and both the logic model and program development, such that evaluation findings are used to inform changes to program theory and implementation. In the next section, we discuss the three types of evaluation depicted in the bottom row of Figure 12.2.

**Figure 12.2** Linking Program Development, Evaluation, and Improvement to Your Program Logic Model

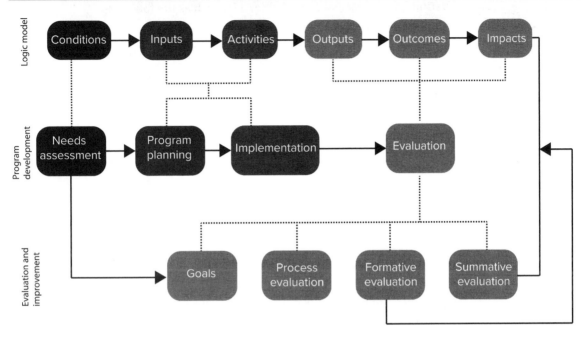

## Three Types of Evaluation

**process evaluation**
the assessment of the implementation part of a program; focuses on studying the program's activities to find out what worked well and what didn't work as well.

In program evaluation, we are often concerned with two major points: (a) *Did the program work?* (summative evaluation) and (b) *Why or why not?* (process evaluation). More recently, community-based program evaluation researchers and practitioners have begun examining an additional question: (c) *What changes are needed to the intervention to make it work better?* (formative evaluation). This section describes these three types of evaluations—process evaluation, formative evaluation, and summative evaluation—in detail.

### Process Evaluation

A **process evaluation** is used to document and monitor the implementation of a program. It involves examining the activities of a program and assessing aspects of how those activities were put into practice. A process evaluation is typically guided by the following broad questions:

- What aspects of the program worked well?

- What aspects of the program did not work or worked less well?

**formative evaluation**
an assessment that takes place while a program is being implemented and provides information for making program improvements.

Answering these questions involves asking *who* was supposed to do *what* with *whom* and *when* was it to be done. It also involves examining implementation issues (discussed in Chapter 11), such as the following:

- **Fidelity.** What were the intended and actual activities of the program? What factors (intentionally or unintentionally) contributed to deviations from the intended activities?

- **Program Reach.** How many of the intended participants were actually enrolled in the program?

- **Participant Responsiveness.** How engaged were the participants?

- **Quality.** How well were components of the program implemented?

In the context of an alcohol and drug prevention program, the process evaluation might examine the rates of participation and program completion and the effectiveness of program facilitators/trainers in delivering the prevention program curriculum.

A process evaluation serves several purposes. First, monitoring program activities helps organize program efforts. It ensures that all parts of the program are conducted as planned. It also helps program staff allocate resources judiciously, for example, not spending most of the program's money on only one activity or target group when resources are needed for multiple activities and groups. Second, information in a process evaluation provides accountability to ensure program staff are implementing the set of agreed-upon activities. Accountability may be to administrators, funders, boards of directors, and other stakeholders. Third, a process evaluation can help program staff decide whether or not the effects of a program can be assessed. For example, if a program has been in existence for only a short time and you have implemented only the third activity of a seven-activity program, then it is premature to assess program outcomes. Fourth, sometimes conditions change and what was planned isn't what actually happens. Process evaluation helps keep track of such changes. Answering process evaluation questions before, during, and after the planned activities documents what actually happened. Lastly, after a summative evaluation of outcomes and impacts, the process evaluation can provide information about why the program worked or did not work. By providing information on what was done and who was reached, program planners can better understand the reasons why a program achieved a particular set of outcomes. Process evaluation information also can provide insight for future improvements and for sharing practical tips with others planning similar programs.

## Formative Evaluation

A **formative evaluation** is a rigorous assessment method designed to identify potential and actual influences on the progress and effectiveness of im-

**summative evaluation**
a collective summary of the effects of a program.

**outcome evaluation**
an examination of the instant, short-term effects of a program on its participants or recipients; includes both output and outcomes data.

**impact evaluation**
an examination of the long-term effects of a program on its participants or recipients to compare the final effects with the planned outcomes.

plementation activities for the purposes of program improvement (Stetler et al., 2006). While a formative evaluation relies on process evaluation data, it differs by objective. The aim of a formative evaluation to facilitate mid-course program improvement, whereas the aim of a process evaluation is simply to monitor implementation activities. A formative evaluation helps with identifying and addressing emergent challenges (Scott et al., 2020). It is guided by the following broad questions:

- What aspects of the program need to be improved?

- How can improvements be made?

Sample formative evaluation questions in the context of an alcohol and drug prevention program might include the following:

- What aspects of the substance abuse prevention training program effectively engaged participants (e.g., training facility, instructor delivery style, training format)?

- What aspects of the training design could be improved to strengthen the program?

- What unanticipated challenges emerged?

- What steps would be useful to take before future trainings to prepare for these challenges?

## Summative Evaluation

**Summative evaluation** assesses the bottom line, or effects, of a program. These effects are generally examined according to time: short term (outcome evaluation) and long term (impact evaluation). An **outcome evaluation** examines the immediate, short-term effects of a program on its participants or recipients. It involves output and outcomes data. Output data capture indicators of activity completion (e.g., number of trainings held, number of individuals trained). Outcomes data measure the direct effects of the program activities, such as the degree to which a drug-use prevention program increased knowledge of drugs and the perceived risk of using drugs. Evidence of program outcomes for a drug-abuse prevention program could include increased awareness of drug dangers or improved scores on a measure of social skills for resisting pressure to use drugs. **Impact evaluation** is concerned with the ultimate effects of a program and whether they matched the desired outcomes. In alcohol and other drug prevention programs, the ultimate effects might include reduction in overall drug use (prevalence), reduction in rate of new high school students starting drug use (incidence), decreases in drunk-driving arrests, and decreases in school disciplinary actions for drug or alcohol offenses.

(Of note, the field of evaluation uses the terms "outcomes" and "impacts" as they are described in this chapter. The field of public health reverses these terms and uses the term "outcomes" to mean long-term indicators and "impacts" to mean short-term indicators.) Exhibit 12.1 illustrates how the three types of evaluation can be used to measure program goals.

### Evaluation Data Collection Methods

Process, formative, and summative evaluations typically involve mixed-methods data collection that includes quantitative and qualitative approaches. Hayes and colleagues (2016) have developed a three-prong mixed-methods framework for data collection referred to as the *inquiry-observation-reflection (IOR) framework*. The *inquiry* frame involves actively seeking information using an explicit, concise, "evaluator question, participant answer" format (e.g., surveys, brief feedback forms). The *observation* frame involves collecting data on naturally occurring activities in the past or present (e.g., reviewing meeting products, observing a partnership meeting). In the *observation* frame, the evaluators' questions may not be sent to activity participants before the activity. The *reflection* frame encourages participants to reflect deeply on an issue or experience. It uses a structured narrative approach (e.g., critical moments reflection methodology via interviews and focus groups, case studies) to obtain multiple stakeholder input on the questions of interest. The IOR framework has conceptual roots in developmental evaluation and uses strategies articulated by the Medical Research Council (G. F. Moore et al., 2015; Patton, 2006). The data collection methods used in the IOR evaluation framework overlap with the methods used in community-based research (see Chapter 4).

## Case Example: Development, Evaluation, and Improvement of a Mentoring Program

In this section, we further illustrate program evaluation concepts by applying them to mentoring programs.[1] Specifically, we review GirlPOWER!, a program developed to empower young adolescent girls, particularly those from low-income and ethnic minority backgrounds, so that they grow up to become strong, successful women.

### Overview of Mentoring Programs

Mentoring relationships generally involve an older, more experienced person (the mentor) and a younger, less experienced person (the mentee). The mentor helps develop the character, confidence, and competence of the mentee or assists the mentee in reaching goals, while also displaying trust, empathy, and companionship; modeling positive behavior; and serving as an advocate

---

[1] The material for this section was primarily written by Bernadette Sanchez of DePaul University.

**Exhibit 12.1** **Example Evaluation of Program Goals (continues)**

Identify Goals and Desired Outcomes

## A. Make a list of the primary goals of the program.

Ask yourself: "What are we trying to accomplish?"

**Examples:**

Decrease adolescent use of alcohol, tobacco, and other drugs.

Decrease rates of accidents, illness, and other drug-related conditions.

Decrease drug-related arrests.

## B. Determine groups to involve (stakeholders).

Ask yourself: "Whom are we trying to reach? For each group, how many persons do we want to involve?"

**Examples:**

Local citizens (all residents of locality)

Parents in training course (20 families in first year)

Adolescents in Grades 7–9 in school (500 in first year)

Local stores selling tobacco (25 stores)

## C. Clarify the set of desired outcomes.

Ask yourself: "As a result of this program, how would we like participants to change? What would they learn? What attitudes, feelings, or behaviors would be different?"

**Examples:**

Increase citizen knowledge of drug-related issues.

Increase citizen commitment to action on these issues.

Increase parents' skills in communicating with children about drug use.

Increase teens' skills in resisting pressure to use drugs.

Decrease local sales of tobacco to minors.

Process Evaluation

## A. What activities were implemented?

Ask yourself: "What did we do to implement this program?"

**Examples:**

1. Public awareness campaign: TV, radio, newspapers (ads, letters, columns, brochures, interviews)

2. Public meetings: schools, religious congregations, etc.

3. Curriculum and materials in school health classes

4. Dramatic skits in schools by student team

5. Parent communication skills training (six sessions)

**Exhibit 12.1** **Example Evaluation of Program Goals (continued)**

For each activity, reflect on key implementation issues (e.g., dose, program reach).

| Activity number | Activity length (hours) | Attendance (estimated number of individuals reached) | Percentage of attendance goal |
|---|---|---|---|
| 1 | 23 | 1,590 | 65% |
| 2 | 100 | 400 | 80% |
| 3 | 10 | 625 | 80% |
| 4 | 12 | 880 | 90% |
| 5 | 25 | 230 | 25% |

Total duration of all activities: 170 hours

Total attendance at all activities: 3,725 persons

### Formative Evaluation

**B. What can you learn from this experience? How can the program be improved?**

What topics or activities were planned but not delivered? Why were these not accomplished?

**Examples:**

Tobacco sales testing not completed because training and logistics took longer than planned.

Public awareness campaign was launched at only three of the four desired ZIP codes because there were challenges with community engagement and divergences in political views about best practices for reducing substance use among minors.

Who was missing that you had hoped to have participate in the program?

**Examples:**

Youth, parents from high-risk family and neighborhood environments

Not enough business, civic, and religious leaders

What explanations can you give for any discrepancy between the planned and actual participation?

**Examples:**

Competing news events overshadowed some media campaigns.

Courses, materials for youth need to be more appealing.

What feedback can be used to improve the program in the future?

**Examples:**

Skits were a hit, use that format more.

Identify potential student and community leaders, involve them.

Involve youth, parents from high-risk environments in planning.

Improve "teen appeal" of course materials.

**Exhibit 12.1  Example Evaluation of Program Goals (continued)**

**Summative Evaluation**

**C. What results did the program achieve?**

| Desired outcome | Measure |
|---|---|
| **1.** Increased citizen knowledge of drug abuse issues | Scores on survey of knowledge |
| **2.** Increased citizen commitment to action to prevent drug abuse | Number of volunteers for antidrug activities |
| **3.** Increased parent communication skills with teens regarding drug abuse | Self-report survey of parental skills before and after training sessions |
| **4.** Increased student resistance | Teacher ratings, student questionnaires on resistance skills before and after training |
| **5.** Decreased sales of tobacco | Number of times clerks were willing to sell to underaged kids when teen assessment teams attempted purchases before and after behavioral intervention |

| Desired impact | Measure |
|---|---|
| **1.** Decreased drug-related traffic accidents, arrests | Police records: number of drug-related accidents, arrests before and after program |
| **2.** Decreased school disciplinary actions related to drug use | School records: number of drug-related disciplinary actions before and after program |
| **3.** Decreased incidence of drug-related conditions, accidents | Hospital records: number of drug-related emergency room visits; number of admissions for drug-related conditions before and after program |

*Note.* Adapted from Linney and Wandersman (1991).

for the mentee (DuBois & Karcher, 2005; Rhodes, 2002; Rhodes & DuBois, 2008; Rhodes et al., 2006; Spencer, 2006). Studies show that mentoring is related to adolescents' increased positive social and psychological development (e.g., DuBois & Silverthorn, 2005; Karcher, 2008), school achievement (e.g., DuBois & Silverthorn, 2005; Sánchez et al., 2008), and career development (e.g., Klaw & Rhodes, 1995), and to less substance use and delinquency (e.g., Zimmerman et al., 2002). However, evaluations show that the effects of mentoring are modest (Eby et al., 2008; Jolliffe & Farrington, 2007).

Many evaluations of mentoring programs focus on whether or not mentoring works. In other words, does mentoring make a difference in the lives of young people (summative evaluation)? It is important to consider the processes that are taking place in these mentoring programs in order to understand what contributes to these outcomes (process evaluation), why program effects are modest (process evaluation), and how to improve outcomes (formative evaluation).

## How Does Mentoring Work?

To understand how mentoring promotes positive youth development (topic discussed in Chapter 10), researchers have examined the characteristics of these relationships. Mentor–mentee relationship length, frequency of contact, amount of time spent together, and relationship quality are known to be important (Herrera et al., 2007; Jolliffe & Farrington, 2007). Additionally, there is evidence to suggest that youth mentoring leads to greater benefits when it is complemented with other support services (Jolliffe and Farrington, 2007; Kuperminc et al., 2005). Complementary interventions included employment programs, educational programs, counseling, and behavioral modification.

## Evaluation in Practice: GirlPOWER!

GirlPOWER! is an innovative mentoring program for ethnic minority, low-income, young adolescent girls, who are paired with adult women volunteers. This program was part of Big Brothers Big Sisters of Metropolitan Chicago (BBBSMC), and it supplemented the one-on-one mentoring relationship model that is typical in the Big Brothers Big Sisters program. In GirlPOWER!, girls and their female mentors met regularly (at least monthly) in a group with several other female mentoring pairs for 1 year. Mentor–mentee pairs were also expected to meet regularly on their own outside the GirlPOWER! program. GirlPOWER! is described in more detail in DuBois et al. (2008).

A number of steps were taken in the development of the GirlPOWER! program, which was led by a team of researchers. First, the researcher team interviewed various stakeholders, including parents, youth, mentors, and staff, to determine the goals and topics that should be addressed in the mentoring program as well as how the program should be implemented. Second, the researchers reviewed the relevant theoretical, empirical, and intervention literature. Then, a pilot program was implemented based on the previous two steps, and the program was revised based on feedback from participants.

The overarching goal of GirlPOWER! is to facilitate the development of strong and lasting mentoring relationships that empower girls to grow into healthy and successful women. The program has more specific measurable goals in the areas of health promotion (e.g., exercise, nutrition), risk behavior prevention (e.g., substance use, violence), education (e.g., academic success, career exploration), and positive youth development (e.g., self-esteem, problem solving, ethnic identity).

In order to assess the degree to which the program was successfully achieving its goals and desired outcomes, researchers conducted process, formative, and summative evaluations. Several different stakeholders in the program were surveyed in an attempt to get feedback about their satisfaction with the current program and to elicit suggestions for improvement. These stakeholders included mentors, mentees, parents, and the staff who ran the program. In addition, worksheets were completed by program staff to document important program components (e.g., mentor recruitment, training, supervision).

Process evaluation results showed that mentors and youth found GirlPOWER! to be generally fun and helpful. For example, some participants reported that they enjoyed the structured opportunities for mentors and youth to interact and that the topics in the GirlPOWER! sessions served as seeds for further discussion in their own time. They also liked spending time with other mentors and youth during the sessions. Participants also provided suggestions for program improvement. They stated that they wanted more time during the GirlPOWER! sessions to engage in activities and explore topics in depth to allow for spontaneous and creative interactions between mentors and youth. Further, in the beginning of the program, attendance was, on average, about 50%, so efforts were made by staff to increase attendance.

A summative evaluation was conducted by using an experimental design. Twenty mentor–youth pairs were randomly assigned to GirlPOWER! while 20 mentor–youth pairs were randomly assigned to the traditional one-on-one mentoring program provided by BBBSMC. All mentors and youth were surveyed at the beginning of the program, during the program, and at the end of the program. Mentoring relationship quality and a variety of youth developmental outcomes were measured. Comparisons of the two groups showed that, overall, participants in the GirlPOWER! mentoring program had better quality mentoring relationships than their counterparts in the traditional mentoring program. Further, GirlPOWER! youth reported more health knowledge, more parental support, better peer self-esteem, and higher academic aspirations and motivation than their peers. However, there were no differences between the two groups in other outcomes, such as grades, ethnic identity, other self-esteem areas, and aggression. Longer term impacts were not assessed.

Since GirlPOWER! targeted a wide array of youth outcomes, perhaps more focused efforts needed to be made in program development and implementation to influence some of the areas where positive results were not observed. For example, if increasing grades was a goal, then tutoring services might have been necessary to change grades. Another example is that ethnic identity was covered in only one component of a workshop. Perhaps spending more time on this topic would have made a difference in girls' ethnic identity. Further, each monthly workshop was focused on a specific topic (e.g., culture, self-esteem). A lack of continuity about topics may have resulted in the lack of positive outcomes for those areas of interest. Reflecting on process and outcomes data with program stakeholders (i.e., participants, researchers/

evaluators, funders, program implementation staff) can help identify strategies for program improvement and sustainability. Initiating these conversations during program implementation, rather than only after program completion, can surface midprogram improvement opportunities and facilitate collaborative decision making.

## Making Continuous Improvements to the GirlPOWER! Mentoring Program

Traditionally, program evaluation has been concerned with whether an established program is working, and why. However, the traditional program evaluation approach does not study how to develop an effective program in the first place. Continuous quality improvement (CQI) of programs relies on the use of evaluation data to plan and implement program modifications. Many barriers prevent program planners and staff from using such feedback well.

First, programs may use an outside evaluator, a person with no stake in the success or failure of the program (who is thus presumably more objective). Such an approach can set up an us-versus-them relationship that can limit the quality and usefulness of the evaluation findings. (Recall from Chapter 3 the importance of relationships between researchers and communities studied.) While possibly more objective, an external evaluator has a limited understanding of the program and implementation setting compared to program staff. Yet program practitioners often believe that they do not have the time, resources, or expertise to conduct their own evaluation. Second, program evaluation usually provides evaluation feedback at the end of program implementation without opportunities for midcourse corrections. Therefore, program staff members often view evaluation as an intrusive process that results in a report card of success or failure but no useful information for program improvement. A third, related barrier is the general perception of evaluation research and findings as too complex, too theoretical, or not user friendly. Sharing program evaluation results in a way that is accessible (understandable) to program staff and community stakeholders is an important aspect of effective evaluations. Program evaluation can, and should, provide important information about processes and outcomes. This information is important but is much more meaningful if community program staff and participants understand how and why the program outcomes were or were not produced. If the outcomes were positive, stakeholders can pinpoint some of the processes that led to program success. Conversely, if the outcomes were less than expected, stakeholders can identify what needs to be improved.

In the next section, we turn to a specific kind of evaluation (Empowerment Evaluation) that places evaluation directly in the hands of community members. This type of evaluation was developed in response to limitations in traditional forms of evaluation.

**What Do You Think?**

1. What values of community psychology are illustrated in the GirlPOWER! example? Review Chapter 1 to refresh your understanding of each of the eight core values.

2. What are strengths of the evaluation approach described in the example? What are limitations to how the program was evaluated?

3. Think back to one or more of the programs presented in Chapters 10 and 11. How does the GirlPOWER! program compare and contrast with those programs?

# Empowerment Evaluation

**empowerment evaluation**
an evaluation approach designed for community members to monitor and evaluate their own performance.

**Empowerment evaluation** (EE) is an evaluation approach designed for community members to monitor and evaluate their own performance. It aims to increase the probability of achieving program success by (a) providing program stakeholders with tools for assessing the planning, implementation, and self-evaluation of their program, and (b) mainstreaming evaluation as part of the planning and management of the program/organization (Wandersman, Snell-Johns, et al., 2005, p. 28).

This evaluation approach draws on all three types of evaluation (process, formative, and summative), but it particularly emphasizes formative evaluation (i.e., data collection to inform program improvements). EE grew out of discussions of "new" and evolving roles for evaluators. This evaluation approach is designed to encourage the self-determination of program practitioners and proactively surface midcourse opportunities for strengthening program implementation (e.g., Fetterman, 2001; Fetterman & Wandersman, 2005; Linney & Wandersman, 1991). In EE, the evaluator takes on a participant–conceptualizer role by codesigning and participating in the evaluation. This is markedly different from traditional evaluator roles whereby the evaluator is external to the program being assessed. In this way, EE breaks down barriers inherent in traditional evaluation methods and values, promoting the objectives of empowerment and citizen participation discussed in Chapter 8 (Fetterman, 1996).

Empowerment evaluators collaborate with community members and program practitioners to determine program goals and implementation strategies. They serve as facilitators or coaches and build the capacity of community members and program staff to conduct evaluations, stressing the importance of using evaluation data to inform ongoing program improvement. They work with program staff to achieve their program goals by providing them with tools for assessing and improving the planning, implementation, and results of their own programs. EE is well suited as an evaluation approach when the primary goal of the evaluation is to place evaluation tools in the hands of program participants and staff members to help programs achieve favorable results. If the primary goal of the evaluation is to examine whether a program worked, according to a predetermined theory and without influence from the evaluator, then the hands-off stance of traditional evaluation is more likely to be a suitable approach.

## Principles of Empowerment Evaluation

EE shares some values and methods with other approaches to evaluation, including traditional evaluation and EE's close relatives (collaborative evaluation, participatory evaluation, and utilization-focused evaluation). However, it is the set of EE principles (see Exhibit 12.2) considered in their entirety that distinguishes EE from other evaluation approaches. Developed by two individuals who have helped shape the field of community psychology (David Fetterman and Abraham Wandersman), this evaluation approach is guided by principles that overlap with the values of community psychology (see Chapter 1) and participatory action research (see Chapter 3).

## Empowerment Evaluation in Action

*Case Example 1: Foundation for the Future.* Established by Boys and Girls Club of Metro Spartanburg, South Carolina, the Foundation for the Future (FFF) is a community partnership created to provide additional community services to families of Boys and Girls Club members who were exposed to multiple risk factors (e.g., poverty, lack of family support). The FFF partnership was founded on the belief that existing organizations and programs in the community could achieve more by working together than they each could by operating independently. Those programs include fine arts programs, a Junior Achievement program, a Parents as Teachers program for parents of young children, and a Parent University program for parents of Boys and Girls Club members. A major FFF component was an enhanced after-school program. Although each agency had its own unique set of desired outcomes, the partnership was unified around the overall goal of increasing families' sense of belonging, usefulness, influence, and competence.

The FFF initiative capitalized on evidence-based programs that already existed in the Spartanburg area. The evaluation contract stated that the first objective of the evaluation team was to help establish and maintain an effective self-evaluation system. To fulfill this task, the evaluation team worked

**Exhibit 12.2** Ten Principles of Empowerment Evaluation (continues)

### Principle 1: Improvement

Empowerment evaluators want programs to succeed. Toward that end, EE values improvement in people, programs, organizations, and communities.

### Principle 2: Community Ownership

Empowerment evaluators believe that evaluation is most likely to lead to program improvement when the community is empowered to exercise its authority to make decisions that direct the evaluation process. In EE, the stakeholders, with the assistance of the empowerment evaluators, conduct the evaluation and put the evaluation findings to use.

### Principle 3: Inclusion

Empowerment evaluators believe that the evaluation of a program or organization benefits from having stakeholders and staff from a variety of levels involved in planning and decision making. Being inclusive is distinct from how people make their decisions as a group, such as democratic forms of participation (see Principle 4).

### Principle 4: Democratic Participation

The definition of EE assumes that stakeholders have the capacity for intelligent judgment and action when supplied with appropriate information and conditions. Democratic participation also (1) underscores the importance of deliberation and authentic collaboration as a critical process for maximizing use of the skills and knowledge that exist in the community and (2) emphasizes that fairness and due process are fundamental parts of the EE process.

### Principle 5: Social Justice

Empowerment evaluators believe in, and have a working commitment to, social justice: a fair, equitable allocation of resources, opportunities, obligations, and bargaining power (Prilleltensky, 1999). EE is well suited for most programs and populations that are interested in improving their performance. Not all programs identify directly with social justice as part of their mission. However, EE advocates believe that almost any program that is designed to help people and communities at any level (individuals, families, neighborhoods) and domain (e.g., education, health, economic) ultimately contributes to the larger goal of social justice.

### Principle 6: Community Knowledge

In EE, community-based knowledge and wisdom are also valued and promoted. EE embraces local community knowledge and believes that people typically know their own problems and are in a good position to generate their own solutions.

### Principle 7: Evidence-Based Strategies

EE values the role of science and evidence-based strategies and believes that a review of relevant evidence-based or best practice interventions is important to consider early in the process of designing and/or selecting a program to address a community need. Just as EE respects the work of the community and its knowledge base, it also respects the knowledge base of scholars and practitioners who have provided empirical information about what works in particular areas (e.g., prevention, treatment).

---

**Exhibit 12.2  Ten Principles of Empowerment Evaluation (continued)**

**Principle 8: Capacity Building**

Evaluation capacity building refers to individual-, program-, and organizational-level growth in capability to conduct evaluations that results from learning during the evaluation process (Patton, 2008, p. 90). Empowerment evaluators believe that when stakeholders learn the basic steps and skills involved in conducting program evaluation, they are in a better position to shape and improve their lives and the lives of those who participate in their programs.

**Principle 9: Organizational Learning**

Improvement is enhanced when there is a process that encourages learning (organizational learning) and an organizational structure that encourages learning (a learning organization). Empowerment evaluations are most effective when nested in the context of an organizational learning culture.

**Principle 10: Accountability**

EE provides an innovative vehicle for helping programs be accountable to themselves, and to the public, by generating process- and outcome-oriented data within an evaluation framework that heightens an organization's sensitivity to its responsibility to the public and to itself.

*Note.* This description of the EE principles is an abbreviated description excerpted from Wandersman, Snell-Johns, et al. (2005, pp. 29–38).

---

closely with FFF member organizations to develop individual evaluation plans and products. However, the major responsibility for the evaluation belonged to FFF staff (not the evaluators). This is consistent with EE principles of community ownership, inclusion, democratic participation, and capacity building.

One FFF objective was to improve student scores on standardized tests in schools, which would be accomplished by after-school programs at the Boys and Girls Clubs. The programs included a daily homework-completion hour and a program for educational and career development. Local Boys and Girls Clubs committed to having over one third of their weekly programs in these areas, and staff prepared weekly tracking reports on programs. An outcome evaluation compared 334 program participants in multiple FFF programs with a group of 836 similar students on an annual standardized test in schools. FFF participants outperformed the comparison group in English, math, social studies, and science. The largest program effects involved students who moved from the lowest scoring category into the basic proficiency category, although positive effects were seen at multiple levels. In Box 12.1, Greg Tolbert, president of the Boys and Girls Club of the Upstate, expounds on the impact of EE on the Foundation for the Future program.

**Box 12.1   Community Psychology in Action: A Community-Based Organization Director's Perspective on Empowerment Evaluation (continues)**

Greg Tolbert, President of the Boys and Girls Club of the Upstate

Our adventure with Empowerment Evaluation began in 1998 as part of a 5-year, $2 million grant from a local foundation. We learned how to plan, implement, and measure our programs and partnerships. We set out to enhance and expand our impact on children in high-poverty schools and their families through our school-based Boys and Girls Club model and community partnerships. Today, we continue implementing within the values of EE. The results speak for themselves. When we started the initiative, our community's youth issues were high school dropout, juvenile crime, and teen pregnancy. Today, our graduation rates have never been higher, our teen pregnancy rates have never been lower, and our county has the lowest juvenile crime rate in the state, holding consistently low for 4 years now. The issues facing our youth have transformed to obesity, college-going academic trajectory, and workforce readiness.

Over the 20 years since institutionalizing EE principles, the program has focused almost $35 million on Upstate children and families in nine school districts and 23 public schools. We have earned almost $15 million in 21st Century Community Learning Center grants. Our parents have contributed over $890,000 in monetary donations since 2012. We have spent over $5.5 million closing the opportunity gap for our children, bringing in specialized program partners and providing extracurricular opportunities that would otherwise be scarce for our populations.

Our programs have been measured by numerous grantors and within Boys and Girls Clubs of America's National Youth Outcomes Initiative (NYOI). Here's what Boys and Girls Clubs of America shared in a recent letter: "In 2018, your Club Experience data registered in the Top 5% of all 797 organizations that participated in NYOI across the country."

When we started Foundation for the Future, our clubs were serving only the poorest urban populations in our community. The needs of those adult family members and the preschool siblings of our club members were dire. Case management, intervention programming, and home visitation typified our partner programming for these older and younger family members.

Our growth strategy was to cover the highest need schools and communities first and then grow out into the rural schools. Today, all but two of our first expansion schools have been closed because of population decline, and our program coverage is much more diverse, split between urban and rural communities. Today's families need affordable, outcome-focused youth development after school that provides a nutritious, balanced evening meal. We meet those needs each day for over 1,100 young people in 11 clubs.

Young adults need career guidance and work experiences that provide earnings for college, and they need work schedules that accommodate class schedules and study time. Our most recent program partnership developed the Teachers Up Apprenticeship program, which now includes over 100 part-time staff in our clubs. This U.S. Department of Labor–registered apprenticeship meets those identified needs of young adults, enabling them to become credentialed as Youth Development Specialists in about 2 years. We are intentionally pointing young people to careers in teaching and building their connectedness to high-poverty student populations. Many of our staff have gone on to be teachers, and many more are already on track to be teachers in the future.

**Box 12.1 Community Psychology in Action: A Community-Based Organization Director's Perspective on Empowerment Evaluation (continued)**

As we look back and outwardly into our community, we can see the impact beyond kids and schools. Our alumni are returning to tell their stories and share their lives with us as staff, board members, volunteers, and program champions. We've even had two Harvard graduates come out of one of our first expansion sites.

As we look out to the future, we envision a time soon to come when our program, measuring implementation with EE discipline, has spread to other communities in ways that minimize bureaucracy, maximize accessibility, enhance impact, and sustain financially without significant grant and philanthropic support. As we have evolved over the past 20 years, we are excited about what is possible for the next 20.

**What Do You Think?**

1. What are similarities and differences between the GirlPOWER! and the Boys and Girls Club programs? Think about the aims, target audience, program design, and evaluation approach of each.

2. Identify three outcomes described by Greg Tolbert in the Boys and Girls Club example. For each, describe how you might measure the outcome. What evaluation method(s) are necessary? Refer to the inquiry-observation-reflection framework at the beginning of the chapter to inform your response.

Foundations for the Future is an initiative by the Boys and Girls Club that was tailored through careful evaluations to empower and support families and children exposed to multiple risk factors.

s_bukley/Shutterstock.com

# Getting To Outcomes: A 10-Step Approach to Results-Based Accountability

Empowerment evaluation sounds good and is attractive to many funders and practitioners, but how does one actually put EE to use? Using the EE philosophy, Wandersman and colleagues (1999, 2000) developed a 10-step approach to results-based accountability called Getting To Outcomes (GTO). GTO provides a systematic framework that can be used by empowerment evaluators to work with program staff to codesign the evaluation components of a program. GTO can also be used by program staff for systematic program development (see the middle row of Figure 12.2 earlier in this chapter).

## The 10 GTO Accountability Questions

Whether beginning a new program or continuing an existing one, program practitioners can start thinking about program effectiveness and program improvement by answering the 10 GTO accountability questions. Each GTO question is linked to a set of assessment questions and tools to facilitate systematic program planning, implementation, and evaluation. The answers to each question lead to the next question—this is a form of what is called "data-informed decision making."

The 10 GTO questions encourage program stakeholders to be thoughtful about the process of program selection, development, evaluation, and improvement. GTO Questions 1–5 help program staff choose the best fitting program, and GTO Questions 6–10 help the program staff implement, improve, and sustain the program. The next section includes a brief description of each GTO question. With careful consideration of each question and its answers, an organization can significantly increase the likelihood that it will achieve desired outcomes.

*Question 1: What are the needs and resources in your organization/school/community/state?* (Needs/Resources Assessment) How do you know you need a program? Often, programs are selected because they are popular or have been implemented at other local sites rather than because they have been demonstrated to effectively prevent a specified problem in your setting. For example, Kaskutas and colleagues (1991) described the experience of a guidance counselor who was working on a project as part of an interagency collaboration: "I discovered, after two months of planning a drug [prevention] group [for] the senior high kids in the project who were non-working, that there *were* no senior high kids in the project who didn't have jobs!" (p. 179). Therefore, there was no need for the program.

In order to determine which types of programs are needed in a given community, school, or other agency, a planning strategy called a needs assessment is often used (Altschuld, 2010; Soriano, 1995). This assessment is designed to gather information about the issues most in need of improvement or intervention in a community or organization (e.g., youth violence, alcohol and drug abuse). A good needs assessment also includes a resource assessment and identification of individual, organizational, and community strengths that can be used to address community needs. Assets may include individual talents; microsystems that can offer social support for persons involved in the program; and organizations that can provide funding, a meeting space, or a venue for public discussion of program goals. A resource assessment also provides a counterpoint to a needs assessment. The identification of community problems involved in a needs assessment is balanced by an assessment of community strengths (Kretzmann & McKnight, 1993).

***Question 2: What are the goals, target population, and desired outcomes (objectives) for your organization/school/community/state?*** (Goals). After the needs and resources for a program have been determined, it is essential to specify the goals of the program, the target group(s) of the program, and the desired outcomes. This question involves the following:

- developing a broad statement that describes what you want to accomplish in the long term.

- identifying the group of people on whom the program will focus and describing how the program will help them change.

- writing objectives in concrete terms that can be measured. What will change, for whom, by how much, and by when? How will the change be measured?

Working through this step helps focus the program on your target population and objectives. It makes it possible to judge the "success" of the program at a later point based on whether or not it meets specific near-term objectives or makes progress toward meeting long-term objectives.

***Question 3: Which evidence-based interventions can be used to reach your goal?*** (Best Practices) Once program personnel have decided that there is a need to address a specific program and have developed their goals and desired outcomes, how will they achieve them? Strategies will need to be put in place to achieve those outcomes. Decisions need to be made on which program or intervention to use. For example, administrators of school and community programs are showered with glossy mailings advertising multimedia curriculum products for programs such as violence prevention, sex education, and substance abuse prevention. How should they decide which program to choose? This decision is frequently based on convenience or availability. Does one rely on the program used last year, regardless of success, or use the program that can be borrowed for free from another source, or maybe use the program advertised at the last convention? It is important to keep in mind that although convenience and availability are important, they do not ensure program effectiveness.

A goal of prevention science is to provide two kinds of information. One is empirical findings (usually quantitative) about the effectiveness of programs in attaining identified goals. Another is information (usually qualitative) about best practices, the elements and methods of programs that work best for a particular type of problem within a particular type of population (recall this idea from Chapters 10 and 11). These types of knowledge are useful in answering the question of what program to select. To be effective, programs need to be based on a theory of the target problem and be tied to current and relevant research. Science and best practice knowledge help not only in program selection but also in program planning and implementation. Several federal agencies, such as the Center for Substance Abuse Prevention and the U.S. Department of Education, have websites with information about evidence-based programs.

### Question 4: How does the intervention fit with other programs already being offered? (Fit) Will this program enhance, interfere with, or be unrelated to other programs that are already offered? Will it be part of a comprehensive and coordinated package or just a new program in a long list of programs?

When designing a new program, it is important to be sure that it aligns well with the community's needs as well as the available services already in place (Elias, 1995). When a new program is to be implemented in a school or other community setting, a primary consideration should be to make sure that the new intervention will enhance existing efforts. To reduce duplication, practitioners should be familiar with preexisting programs in their school or community.

### Question 5: What capacities do you need to put this intervention into place with quality? (Capacities) Organizational capacity consists of the resources that the organization possesses to direct and sustain the prevention program (Flaspohler et al., 2008). Some model programs may be too difficult or resource intensive for an organization to deliver. In GTO, organizational capacities to assess include having (a) adequate numbers of staff with appropriate credentials and experience to implement the program, (b) clearly defined staff roles and strong staff commitment to the program, (c) strong program leadership by leaders who understand the program, and (d) adequate funding and technical resources for the program or a plan to get them. At this stage, it is also important to assess the willingness (motivation) of program staff to implement the intervention.

### Question 6: How will this intervention be carried out? (Plan) What are the steps that program personnel will take to carry out the program? During

this planning stage, program developers must identify how they will implement the program. Outlining how a program will be implemented includes determining specific steps to carry out the program, identifying and training personnel to carry out each of these steps, and developing a timeline or schedule for this plan. Program staff should specify what will happen during scheduled program activities and where these activities will take place. All of these components must be clearly defined in order to plan and implement a program effectively.

**Question 7: How will the quality of implementation be assessed?** (Implementation, process, and formative evaluation) This question can be answered by thinking about the following:

- What activities were actually implemented (versus what was planned)?

- Was the program implemented on time?

- What was done well (e.g., with fidelity to the best practice program you selected)?

- Did the program participants match the population that the program intended to reach?

- What midcourse corrections should be made?

These questions are addressed through a process and formative evaluation and often involve eliciting feedback from program staff and participants. Answering these questions provides insight into the strengths and weaknesses of implementation for program planning in both the near and distant future.

**Question 8: How well did the intervention work?** (Outcome evaluation) At the end of a program (intervention period), an outcome evaluation is conducted to assess the effectiveness of the program. This involves gathering evidence about the outcomes and impact of the program. Example supporting questions for the outcome evaluation include the following:

- Did the program have the desired effects and proposed outcomes?

- Were there any unanticipated consequences?

**Question 9: How will continuous quality improvement strategies be incorporated?** (Improve/Continuous Quality Improvement) Many programs are repeated. Given that no program is perfect, what can be done to improve the program's effectiveness and efficiency in the future? If the process and outcomes of a program are well documented, the potential to learn from previous implementation efforts is enormous. Keeping track of program components that worked well ensures that such components will be included in the future. Assessing what program components did not work provides the opportunity for improvement to future implementation cycles.

Lessons about what went well with a program and what areas can use improvement come from informal sources, such as personal observations and verbal reports from participants and staff members, or formal sources, such as participant-satisfaction measures and evaluations of the program process and outcomes. However it is gathered, information for program improvement is obtained from the answers to Questions 1–8.

### Question 10: If the intervention (or a component) is successful, how will the intervention be sustained? (Sustain) After service providers have gone through the time, energy, and money to develop a successful program, what will they do to see it continued? Unfortunately, this is a commonly neglected question in prevention programming. Even when programs have successful outcomes, they are often not continued because there is a lack of funding, staff turnover, or loss of momentum. Lerner's (1995) review of prevention programs for youth development concluded that there are numerous effective programs to prevent risks and problem behaviors, but unfortunately, these programs were rarely sustained over time.

Goodman and Steckler (1989) defined *institutionalization* as developing community and organizational supports for health promotion and prevention programs so that they remain viable in the long term. They identified factors related to successful institutionalization, such as identifying resources and making program components accessible and user friendly to host organization staff. K. Johnson and colleagues (2004) reviewed the literature on sustainability and developed a model that identified factors related to sustaining not only a program but also the organization that implements the program (e.g., a coalition).

GTO is designed to be used iteratively. Even for an effectively implemented, thoroughly institutionalized program, staff members routinely revisit the GTO questions. Figure 12.3 illustrates that GTO is (a) continuous, (b) results oriented, and (c) amenable to being used at any stage of the life cycle of a program. In the next section, we return to the topic of youth substance use prevention to provide a community-based case example of GTO in practice.

## Using Getting To Outcomes to Prevent Underage Drinking: GTO in Action

For many people, the heaviest drinking period in their life is before they reach the age of 21. Some youth will emerge in their 20s and reduce their drinking to only limited occasions. For others, drinking will lead to addiction, injury, death, or other adverse life experiences, including sexual assaults, violence, and diminished personal life opportunities.

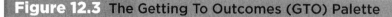

**Figure 12.3** The Getting To Outcomes (GTO) Palette

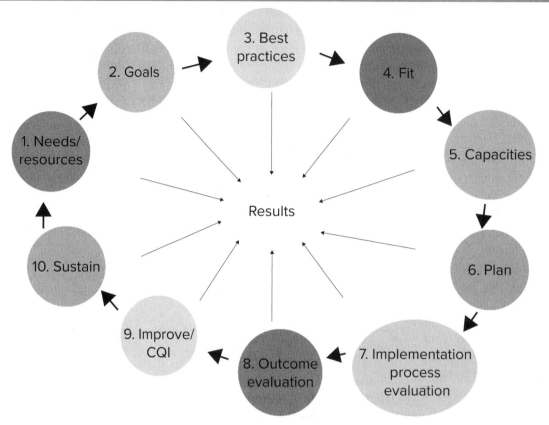

GTO was initially a written guide published by the RAND Corporation in 2004 to help individuals conduct drug and alcohol prevention programs (Chinman et al., 2004). It was developed by reviewing multiple literatures on planning, implementation, and program evaluation and then distilling down key points that could be more easily understood by community-based practitioners (Wandersman et al., 2000). Tools—or worksheets—were added to the guide to prompt users to make and record key decisions.

The following example[2] illustrates how a group of concerned parents used the 10 GTO accountability questions to prevent underage drinking. Their efforts resulted in the South Carolina Alcohol Enforcement Team, which has since influenced similar statewide prevention programs.

---

[2] Portions of the following section are adapted from an excerpt of *Preventing Underage Drinking*, by Pamela Imm, Matthew Chinman, Abraham Wandersman, David Rosenbloom, Sarah Guckenburg, and Roberta Leis (RAND, 2007). Permission for use has been granted by RAND. While the excerpt is older and does not reflect the latest intervention strategies and best practices—including the active inclusion of youth in preventive efforts for preventing underage drinking—it is a valuable abbreviated case illustration of how communities can use GTO in the context of preventing underage drinking.

*Background.* A female high school student was hosting a party at her house after the homecoming football game. A deputy came upon her house during a normal patrol and noticed that a large number of cars surrounded the house. The deputy called for backup and entered the house. Tickets were issued to approximately 40 high school students. Some students managed to escape by hiding in the woods or fleeing in their vehicles. A number of parents were concerned about the way the incident was handled, and it became a point of major public controversy in the community.

As a result of this incident, there was a great deal of discussion in the community about the role of police in underage drinking. A small group of concerned parents, school administrators, teachers, law enforcement, and community leaders developed an initial working group that evolved into a larger community coalition to combat underage drinking as a community problem. The community coalition utilized the GTO accountability questions in order to plan, implement, and evaluate their comprehensive plan to reduce underage drinking.

*Community Mobilization.* Following the homecoming party where law enforcement became involved, the chairperson of the school district convened an initial group of key stakeholders, including members of law enforcement agencies, teachers, guidance counselors, parents, and members of the local alcohol and drug abuse agency (see Chapter 13 for more on coalitions). The group continued to organize by developing a regular meeting schedule, forming subcommittees, and formalizing procedures to become a structured community coalition. This included mechanisms for establishing bylaws, determining membership on subcommittees, conflict-resolution procedures, and strategies for communication and coordination. In addition, the coalition recognized that in order to understand the genuine underlying needs and conditions of their school district and surrounding neighborhoods, they needed to begin a formal assessment process.

### Program Development, Evaluation, and Improvement Process
#### Step 1. Assess Needs/Resources
One of the first activities of the newly formed coalition was to conduct needs and resources assessments in the school district that included input from youth, merchants, and law enforcement. Members of the local alcohol and drug abuse agency conducted several focus groups of middle and high school youth. One clear result was that alcohol was very easy for the youth to obtain, and they had little fear that law enforcement, their parents, or school administrators would catch them. As a result, law enforcement and local merchants were surveyed to gather some additional information. The results indicated that neither group knew the South Carolina underage drinking laws very well, that law enforcement did not believe that enforcing underage drinking laws was really worth

their time, and that the merchants had little knowledge about how to properly conduct ID checks for alcohol sales. Additional results included the following:

- Approximately 28% of minors could buy alcohol in convenience stores in the targeted areas.

- 64% of 12- to 18-year-old students said that it would be "very easy" or "fairly easy" to get beer or malt liquor in the targeted areas.

- The majority of youth questioned believed that they would be "very un-likely" to be caught by law enforcement for underage drinking.

Results of surveys from law enforcement and local merchants included the following:

- The majority of officers answered only 20% of the questions about laws related to underage drinking correctly.

- Merchant groups (e.g., bartenders, cashiers) reported a need for additional training in proper identification and the legal responsibility for alcohol sales by merchants.

- Most merchants reported that they would attend a free training on alcohol sales, if offered.

One major resource was the community coalition, which was becoming larger and more representative of the population. In addition, the school board and school district personnel (e.g., school nurse, teachers) were interested in considering what actions the school board might take to address related needs. Law enforcement agencies faced issues regarding jurisdiction, interpretation of laws, and uninformed magistrates. Fortunately, the community coalition was able to secure funding through the South Carolina State Incentive Grant (funded by the Center for Substance Abuse Prevention) to begin addressing the needs identified.

### Step 2. Set Goals

The community coalition decided that the goal should be an effort to reduce youth access to alcohol by targeting the attitudes and behavior of law enforcement officials and merchants. To achieve the outcomes in reducing access, there would need to be changes in the behaviors of law enforcement and merchants. For example, merchant knowledge of laws regarding underage drinking would increase by 20% after merchant training, as measured a survey before and after training.

### Step 3. Select Best Practices

A review of evidence-based literature was conducted, and the following research-based findings were used to plan and implement an initiative to address underage alcohol use. Information was obtained from the Pacific Institute of Research and Evaluation and its Underage Drinking Enforcement and Training Center. The following summary reviews evidence-based principles related to underage drinking:

- Environmental strategies targeted at availability, accessibility, and social norms have shown to be the most effective at reducing underage alcohol use.

- The most effective strategies create environments in which the opportunities to drink are fewer and the temptations weaker. Some of these include the following:

  » policy-level changes, including consequences for the youth attempting to buy and the merchants selling to youth;

  » laws against adults who buy for minors or allow them to drink in their homes;

  » enforcement of laws that is consistent and representative of adequate sanctions and punishment; and

  » settings that promote a strong normative message that excessive drinking is not typical or widely accepted behavior.

A variety of environmental strategies were selected as part of the community's comprehensive plan. Several of the strategies used were the following:

- compliance checks (underage youth attempt to buy alcohol)

- party patrols (patrolling of neighborhoods where parties are suspected)

- traffic stops (establishing probable cause for traffic violations)

- traffic safety checkpoints (checking for drivers' licenses, open container violations, or other safety violations)

- casual contact (contacting the community stakeholders)

- merchant education (to increase knowledge about underage alcohol sale laws and data)

**Step 4.  Determine Fit**

Before finalizing the underage drinking plan primarily designed to reduce underage access to alcohol, the community coalition examined how its potential strategies fit with existing interventions to reduce underage alcohol use among youth. Data from the resource assessment indicated that there were some individually oriented programs for youth (e.g., health classes in school); however, there were no systematic environmental interventions designed to influence behaviors of law enforcement officials and merchants. Because key members of the community (e.g., law enforcement, community coalitions, businesses) were involved early in the process, they became strong supporters of the plan to reduce underage drinking (i.e., good fit among key partners). This assisted with issues around community readiness and ensuring that the strategies would be pursued in a culturally competent manner. The coalition readily determined that the fit was beneficial because the community wanted a solution to the problem (i.e., a good-values fit), and the involvement of law enforcement was viewed as advantageous. The coalition also knew that there were some strategies in the underage drinking plan that might be controversial (e.g., sobriety checkpoints), but they decided to move forward with pursuing these activities since law enforcement was such a strong ally.

### Step 5. Assess Current Capacities

The community coalition examined what capacities they possessed to develop a comprehensive plan that would help reduce youth access to alcohol. Because they knew that the goal was to reduce youth access to alcohol and that law enforcement and merchants would be the primary target populations, they considered their current capacities and what needed to be strengthened:

- **Human.** Continued buy-in from school personnel, undercover cooperating informants, merchant educators, project coordinators, and law enforcement coordinators.

- **Fiscal.** Funding was adequate, but continued state and national training opportunities were needed.

- **Technical.** Best practice resources, access to evaluation expertise, law enforcement expertise (including surveillance), and public awareness efforts.

- **Structural.** Continued efforts to gain buy-in from the community and champions in law enforcement who would remain committed to the effort over a long period of time.

### Step 6. Develop a Plan

The community developed a plan for implementing the compliance check component only. Officers would receive training on how to conduct compliance checks from the Pacific Institute for Research and Evaluation. Before beginning any compliance checks, a clear protocol had to be established for what to do when a clerk sold alcohol to a minor. A five-person Alcohol Enforcement Team (AET) and volunteer undercover youth planned to conduct approximately 20 compliance checks per month for a 10-month time period. The plan was endorsed by the AET liaison, a lead officer who serves as a liaison between the AET team, the sheriff's department, and the ATOD agency. He is ultimately responsible for overall operations, including planning, coordination of efforts, and documentation.

### Step 7. Implement and Conduct Process and Formative Evaluation

A process and formative evaluation was conducted to monitor and improve implementation of the plan. These evaluations included a schedule of completion, a tool to measure implementation, and the person responsible for carrying out each task. Careful monitoring revealed that although the average number of compliance checks for the 10-month period was at 125% (more than anticipated), no compliance checks were conducted during two months. The holiday season, including vacation time for the AET officers, contributed to the lack of compliance checks in December 2003. In April 2004, issues of financial obligations emerged, so officers could not perform their duties without knowing how they would be paid. These issues were resolved fairly quickly, but they did result in no operations in April 2004.

### Step 8. Conduct Outcome Evaluation

A number of desired outcomes were achieved. For example, the rate of underage youth who were able to "buy" liquor in the compliance checks was reduced from 38% before the strategies (GTO 3–5) were implemented to 10% after 1 year (73% decrease). Clearly, youth were less able to purchase alcohol.

### Step 9. Conduct Continuous Quality Improvement

The coalition members used a CQI tool to organize all the feedback from the evaluation to facilitate changes. The feedback included information from law enforcement, merchants, and youth. Some insights from the evaluation included the following:

- There was a need to increase support from community stakeholders, particularly merchants. Proposed strategy: Examine evidence-based strategies for recruiting merchants and develop a plan to target and enroll merchants in the program.

- There was a need for more compliance in rural areas where evaluation data showed that the rate did not decrease as significantly as it did in the city. Proposed strategy: Engage in discussions with the planning team. Identify anticipated barriers to implementing additional rural compliance checks and solutions for addressing anticipated barriers.

- Law enforcement officers had complaints about requisite paperwork. Proposed strategy: Meet with officers to better understand their views and experiences with completing program documents.

### Step 10. Sustain the Program

Emphasis was placed on obtaining positive outcomes and securing additional funding to sustain the program. Utilizing the Getting To Outcomes method ensured that the staff planned, implemented, and evaluated the initiative in a way that increased the likelihood of achieving positive results for future funding opportunities. Specifically, Lexington/Richland Alcohol and Drug Abuse Council (LRADAC) managed to secure funding for the AET through a state incentive grant. This funding allowed the continued functioning of the AET initiative. The likelihood of continued sustainability of the AET initiative was also increased as a result of several recognitions and awards received by the AET. In August 2004, the AET received "exemplary" status for innovative programs at the National Prevention Network Conference in Kansas City, Missouri. This award, presented to only five programs in the nation, is awarded by several national agencies, including the Center for Substance Abuse Prevention, the National Association of State Alcohol and Drug Abuse Directors, and the Community Anti-Drug Coalitions of America. In addition, the AET was presented with the Law Enforcement Partnership of the Year Award, a national recognition presented by their law enforcement peers. These awards led to increased ownership of, and commitment to, the AET model, thereby contributing to sustainability efforts. The positive outcomes led to various funding and acknowledgements, including a $100,000 Drug-Free Communities grant awarded by the Office of National Drug Control Policy and administered by SAMHSA. In addition, various in-kind donations, including space and meeting times from the Lexington police department and the Lexington school district, were obtained. Furthermore, the state of South Carolina adopted the model and is awarding funds to additional counties to replicate the AET model. Taking an Empowerment Evaluation approach helped build the capacity of program staff for evaluation and improvement activities, which are critical sustainability issues in addition to funding.

## Developments in GTO

As part of the first GTO study, a quasi-experimental trial from 2002 to 2005 (Chinman et al., 2008), RAND added face-to-face training and ongoing technical assistance to the existing written guide to increase GTO's impact. From then on, in all subsequent studies, the GTO approach provided three supports: (a) the GTO manual (tailored to a variety of content domains, including drug and alcohol prevention); (b) face-to-face training; and (c) ongoing, on-site, proactive technical assistance.

In early quasi-experimental (Chinman et al., 2008) and randomized controlled trials (Acosta et al., 2013; Chinman et al., 2009), GTO has been found to improve the capacity of individual practitioners and the performance of alcohol and drug prevention programs. A later randomized trial comparing community-based organizations (Boys and Girls Clubs) implementing a teen pregnancy prevention evidence-based program (Making Proud Choices) to similar clubs augmented with GTO support showed that GTO sites had better capacity, performance, fidelity, and youth outcomes than clubs not using GTO (Chinman et al., 2013; Chinman, Acosta, Ebener, Malone, & Slaughter,

2016). These results were replicated in a subsequent randomized trial with the same design (Chinman et al., 2018). The original GTO workbook for substance abuse prevention won the 2008 Outstanding Publication Award from the American Evaluation Association.

GTO has been applied to multiple content areas, including teen pregnancy prevention, underage drinking prevention, and Positive Youth Development (Chinman, Acosta, Ebener, Sigel, & Keith, 2016; D. Fisher et al., 2006; Imm et al., 2007). The key to GTO's capacity building is asking practitioners to be active learners. GTO establishes expectations and gives opportunities and guidance for practitioners to carry out for themselves the implementation best practices that GTO specifies.

## Conclusion

Chelimsky (1997) described three purposes of evaluation:

- program development (e.g., information collected to strengthen programs or institutions),

- accountability (e.g., measurement of results or efficiency), and

- broader knowledge (e.g., increasing understanding about factors underlying public problems).

Traditional evaluation is primarily oriented to the second purpose. The methods explained in this chapter expand the focus to include the first and second purposes and can inform research concerning the third (Wandersman et al., 2004). However, this does not preclude more traditional evaluation approaches (Fetterman, 2001). The value of any evaluation approach depends on the purpose of the evaluation (Chelimsky, 1997; Patton, 2008; Rossi et al., 2018).

As we have discussed in this chapter, program evaluation concepts can be incorporated into program planning, implementation, and improvement. When this is done, the boundaries between program development and program evaluation are blurred for the sake of improving the program and increasing the probability of successful results. GTO is an example of this approach. Although the GTO emphasis, so far, has been on the accountability of practitioners who receive money for prevention (or treatment or education), Wandersman (2003) noted that the accountability questions also apply to funders and to researchers or evaluators. Strong partnerships between evaluators, program staff, funders, and community stakeholders contribute to results-based accountability and increase the likelihood of achieving and sustaining desired outcomes (Scott et al., 2020). For example, when funders consider developing a new initiative, the questions of how they know they need a new initiative, how it will use science and best practices, how it will fit with other initiatives, and so on should be asked and answered. For evaluators, the same questions would concern whether a new or intensified evaluation process is needed or justified, how well it will fit with existing evaluation procedures, and how best practices for program evaluation will be used in planning this evaluation. Regardless of the evaluation type (formative, process, and/or summative), it is valuable to consider the evaluation needs of all relevant stakeholders. This involves including participants, to the extent that is feasible, in the development and prioritization of the evaluation questions and methods. Ideally, considering the needs, values, and questions pertinent to all stakeholders is done at the beginning of the evaluation.

As societies, funders, and citizens become more concerned about accountability and results for schools, health care, human services, and related areas, evaluation can lead to fear and resistance or to openness, honesty, empowerment, and improvement. Evaluation and accountability need not be feared—if we work together for results. Results-based accountability requires us to understand program evaluation and how programs can be improved to achieve their goals. When evaluation is done well, it can strengthen a program's quality as well as its ability to resist critics.

## For Review

## Discussion Questions

1. What are three reasons for conducting program evaluations? What type of evaluation (process, formative, or summative) would you use for each reason?

2. Why might program staff be opposed to evaluation activities? What would you say to program staff who are resisting efforts to evaluate the program?

3. Identify a prevention program of interest (e.g., preventing substance abuse or suicide on a college campus, preventing high school dropout, preventing global warming). Then, use the six steps of a logic model described in this chapter (see Figure 12.1) to create a theory of change for the identified prevention program. Why is the prevention program needed? What resources and activities are critical for the program? What immediate, short-term, and long-term outcomes would the program seek to achieve?

4. Think of a current issue you care about in a community of which you are a member (e.g., gun violence, voter engagement in local elections, social connectedness on campus, access to health care). Using the 10 steps of GTO, how would you work to address the issue?

## Key Terms

opportunity cost, 411

results-based accountability, 411

critical friend, 414

logic model, 415

conditions, 415

inputs, 415

activities, 415

outputs, 415

outcomes, 415

impacts, 415

process evaluation, 417

formative evaluation, 418

summative evaluation, 419

outcome evaluation, 419

impact evaluation, 419

empowerment evaluation, 427

## Learn More

A detailed summary of the chapter, along with other review materials, is available on the *Community Psychology, Fourth Edition* companion website at http://pubs.apa.org/books/supp/kloos4/.

An unknown street artist completes artwork on a building in Santiago, Chile, demonstrating a creative form of direct action that can empower a community.

iStock.com/scottnz

# 13 Improving Society Through Community Action

## Looking Ahead

**After reading this chapter you will be able to answer these questions:**

**1.** What does the term "social change" mean in the context of community psychology, and why is it considered fundamental to the field?

**2.** What are some community organizing approaches that people can use to bring about meaningful change in their communities?

**3.** Why are ethical conflicts particularly prevalent in social change efforts, and how can a grounding in community psychology values help negotiate those conflicts?

**4.** Why do community psychologists focus on public policy as a central avenue for effecting social change and social justice?

## Opening Exercise

# Two Stories of Social Justice Through Community Organizing

**Community Development in Camden**

Ron Evans has lived in Camden, New Jersey, his whole life. In 2009, Camden had the highest violent crime rate in the United States, which was more than 5 times the national average. Over 40% of Camden residents had household incomes below the national poverty line. Evans helped found Camden Churches Organized for People, which worked with other community organizations to arrange a public meeting where 1,500 people met with the governor of New Jersey. The purpose of the meeting was to push for legislation that eventually provided $175 million in recovery funds to Camden. Three years later, Ron helped survey Camden residents to ask them how well they thought the recovery program was working. The answer was "Not very well" (Ott, 2005). The residents thought that the majority of the recovery money was going to large-scale development projects rather than to efforts that would benefit long-term residents.

As Ron explains the situation, "We asked ourselves, 'How could we spend this money in a way that would benefit the people?' What we came up with is that the people who've committed to stay in Camden should be the ones who benefit."

Another public meeting was held that brought 500 people to meet with the New Jersey state treasurer to propose a forgivable loan program that would allow residents up to $20,000 to rehabilitate their homes. New Jersey started the Camden Home Improvement Program, which originally allocated $7.5 million for forgivable home-improvement loans to long-term Camden residents. The program has been demonstrated to affect more than just the loan recipients. As neighbors of loan recipients see home improvement in their neighborhood, they tend to improve their homes as well. An evaluation of the program found that, as a result of the Camden Home Improvement Program, home values increased significantly in the neighborhoods targeted by the program (J. Chisholm, personal communication, April 23, 2010).

### Olive Groves Versus Power Plants

Olive trees are central to the culture of Turkey. Olive oil and the olive fruit are part of the everyday diet in the country, and Turkey is a major exporter of both. In 2014, the Kolin Group of Companies made plans to build a coal power plant in village of Yirca. They were going to destroy the village's olive grove to build it. Twenty-four members of the village sued to stop the power plant, and they were granted a legal stay. Kolin ignored the stay and illegally sent in bulldozers to raze the grove. They destroyed 13 trees before being stopped by villagers who stood in front of the machines to stop them. But Kolin's bulldozers soon returned with a security force to restrain the villagers. The encounter turned violent, and this time 6,000 trees were cut down (Tashea, 2015).

Mustafa Akın, Yirca's elected leader, gave an emotional interview on Turkish television, saying, "Surely those who did this eat olives. They use olive oil on their dinner tables. How can they eat olives now?" The interview captured the attention of the nation and of the local member of parliament. The subsequent outrage stopped not only the Kolin plant but also a proposed national law that sought to make it legal to seize olive groves to build power plants.

What would you do if you were in a situation similar to those described above? All of us have had the experience of coming face to face with something in our communities, our societies, our nations, that just makes us say, "This is wrong. We can do better than this." These people did something. And in the process, they changed their communities, their societies, and themselves.

### What Do You Think?

1. Why do you think these two examples of community organizing were successful?

2. Do you see any similarities between the two stories?

3. Have you ever been involved in a community organizing campaign to address a specific problem? What was your experience like?

The small Turkish village of Yirca acting to protect its olive trees, an important part of Turkish culture, from destruction by a major corporation represents the power of communities to create social change.

## Why Should We Attempt Social Change?

*Things alter for the worse spontaneously, if they be not altered for the better designedly.*

*—Francis Bacon*

**social change**
a complex, long-term process by which human interactions and relationships transform cultural and social institutions.

Change is inevitable. Our world will change, whether we want it to or not. In this book we have promoted the idea of consciously examining and directing those change processes to ensure that when change does occur, it results in stronger, healthier, and more effective organizations, neighborhoods, communities, and societies. These settings will then be better able to support healthy functioning in the people who live and work there. With this goal in mind, we want to invite you to explicitly think about the concept of applying science to **social change** and social justice. Social change can be defined as the transformation of cultural and social institutions.

Historically, the application of science to achieve social change has been a point of debate. Some of these concerns were focused on the idea of scientists as social engineers—ones with no personal stake in the communities they were "researching." In no sense does the field of community psychology support the idea of an isolated intellectual dictating to a community what social policies or practices that community should adopt. That approach would constitute a violation of many of the fundamental values of the field, particularly the idea that communities have a basic right to self-determination.

However, we also believe, strongly, that science gains value through application. As an example, think of the iterative process of the ISF model as illustrated in Chapter 11 (see Figure 11.1). Research is translated to communities, who generate new knowledge as they go through the implementation process, which is then used to inform the research base. Community psychology is an applied field. As we hope we have emphasized throughout this book, science and practice inform each other. Scientific research is continually used to inform business practice and the political process; why should it not be used to advance social change and justice?

Social change is a long-term process, and thus it is useful to view it through the lens of the participatory action-research cycle (as discussed in Chapters 3 and 11). Social change involves second-order change in communities and societies, not just adding a new program or resource. This means, among other things, that resources and power are being redistributed (remember the discussion of ecological principles from Chapter 4). These changes can result in conflict and unintended effects.

When you are discussing change at this level, the solutions you propose can easily generate new, unintended problems. As noted by the community psychologist Julian Rappaport (1981), today's solutions often become tomorrow's problems. There are always multiple, divergent solutions to a particular problem, each with its own costs and benefits. Communities are rarely homogenous, and the very presence of diversity in a community logically suggests that what might be good for one group in a community may actually be harmful for another. How you define the problem has a major impact on what you see as an appropriate solution, and part of your action-research cycle should always involve periodically reexamining your problem definition (remember our discussion of this issue in Chapters 1 and 11).

It sometimes seems to students of psychology that community and social change is exceedingly difficult, beyond their capabilities. In fact, social change occurs around us all the time. In every act of living, we involve ourselves in dynamic processes of change at many ecological levels. Community psychology's different approach and scope provides tools to see where it is possible to institute change and skills to make those changes successfully. By the end of this chapter, we hope that you will see how often Margaret Mead's oft-quoted adage about changing the world comes true, and how you can become involved:

> Never doubt that a small group of thoughtful, committed citizens can change the world. Indeed, it's the only thing that ever has. (Margaret Mead, as quoted in D. Keys, 1982, p. 79)

**community organizing**
coordinated, cooperative work undertaken by community residents to improve their community and achieve social change.

**Community organizing** refers to coordinated, cooperative work conducted by community residents with the goal of improving their community. The goal of community organizing is to achieve social change. In this chapter, we introduce several community organizing approaches, including community development, consciousness raising, direct action, community coalitions, and consultation. Then we turn to a discussion of a specific aspect of social change, public policy. We discuss the relationship between prevention science and public policy, using crime policy in the United States as an example. Finally, we present two examples of problems, which require that attention be paid to public policy, poverty and homelessness.

# Community Development

**community development**
a process whereby government, nonprofit organizations, volunteer associations, or public-private partnerships ameliorate or prevent adversities and develop strengths in a community's economic, political, social, or physical environment.

**Community development** is defined in the community psychology literature as "a process whereby government, nonprofit organizations, volunteer associations, or public-private partnerships ameliorate or prevent adversities and develop strengths in a community's economic, political, social, or physical environment" (D. D. Perkins et al., 2004, p. 325). The people and organizations described in the opening exercise were all engaged in community development. Almost everyone engages in some type of community development during their lives, and some people choose it as their vocation. The explicit goal of organizations like the Highlander Center (discussed in Chapter 8) is to train and empower citizens to become effective organizers for community development efforts. The personal qualities for citizen participation and empowerment and the empowering practices presented in Chapter 8 relate directly to this work.

From a community psychology perspective, community development is most effective when it is based on a multilevel, strengths-based perspective; addresses issues of social inequity and social justice; and is based on collaborative relationships in the community (D. D. Perkins et al., 2004). The most effective community development projects are those that address multiple domains of community adversity. These include improving the economic environment through supporting the development of local businesses and good jobs; improving the political environment through coalition building to empower and engage the community and its members in the political process and decisions that affect them; improving the social environment through strengthening community assets to prevent crime and increase neighboring activities; and improving the physical environment through rehabilitating deteriorating buildings, increasing public transportation, and addressing environmental hazards (D. D. Perkins et al., 2004).

Community development projects have, at their core, the development of community and social capital. If you remember from Chapter 6, *social capital*

**consciousness raising**
increasing citizens' critical awareness of social conditions that affect them and energizing their involvement in challenging and changing those conditions. This is achieved by developing awareness of personal experiences of systemic oppression.

refers to the features of social life in a community (networks, norms, and relationships) that allow the members of the community to work together effectively to achieve shared goals. *Community capital* is a broader term, encompassing both social capital and infrastructure, investment, and the elements of organizational capacity discussed in Chapters 10 and 11. Increasing these tangible and intangible resources in a community serves not only to improve community life in the short term but also to strengthen the community's capacity to effectively address challenges in the future.

At its core, community development is concerned with increasing community resources and the empowerment of community members. Those resources could be jobs, infrastructure, strengthened relationships among individuals and organizations, or increased access to the political process. Community development efforts can increase tangible resources in communities (e.g., good jobs, schools, parks, health facilities), but they also increase less tangible, but equally important, resources such as social capital and a sense of personal and collective efficacy for community residents.

## Consciousness Raising and Community Readiness

**Consciousness raising** involves increasing citizens' critical awareness of social conditions that affect them and energizing their involvement in challenging and changing those conditions (Freire, 1970/1993). Consciousness is raised as individuals become aware of personal experiences with systematic oppression of any sort such as racism, classism, or ageism. These experiences can take place in private or public contexts (e.g., home, workplace, school, place of worship, retail store). However, consciousness raising is not solely cognitive or emotional. New personal understanding is connected to working with others and actions for change. Action and reflection feed each other.

Consciousness raising is directly related to the idea of problem definition but focuses on the processes underlying the recognition and understanding of a problem (think back to our discussions of problem definition in Chapter 11). Power dynamics such as those discussed in Chapter 8 play a central role in this process. A major example of the impact of power inequity in problem recognition is demonstrated when a group in power insists that a problem identified by a disempowered group does not actually exist. There is no imperative to address a problem that you refuse to acknowledge exists. The organizers of the Black Lives Matter movement are an example of a group that has effectively made use of social media to force recognition of the existence of institutional racism in the U.S. criminal justice system (Milkman, 2017). The goal of the online movement was not to promote any specific legislative or even social agenda (although it has given rise to some of those efforts). Rather, it was to publicly name a problem that was unrecognized, ignored, and hidden.

**community readiness**
the degree to which a locality recognizes a problem and is willing to devote resources to address or prevent it.

Even when recognition of the problem does exist, conceptualization of the causes and best ways to address the problem will often vary widely. Community members need to be willing to engage in some level of consciousness raising if they are to be open to new understandings of phenomena such as racism, colonization, social power, and economic iniquities.

Let's look at this process as it can work in a community. From this lens, consciousness raising involves bringing diverse groups with diverse viewpoints together. The goal is to develop a shared understanding of the structural forces that affect their community. Through the respectful sharing of individual stories, a new, common viewpoint can arise, even among community members who begin the conversations feeling a huge divide that could never be crossed. An example of recent work in this area in the United States is the Hands Across the Hills project, which works to address the growing political divide in America by engaging communities in structured dialogue and is described in more detail in Box 13.1 (see also https://www.handsacrossthehills.org/).

The intended result of consciousness raising is an increase in **community readiness**, which refers to the degree to which a locality recognizes a problem and is willing to devote resources to address or prevent it (see Chapter 11 for a discussion of this concept at the organizational level). Community readiness also involves an assessment of community capacity to address a problem, which often results in community development efforts specifically to increase that capacity. Although consciousness raising can contribute to community readiness, these terms refer to separate concepts, and consciousness plays a relatively small role in promoting readiness. There are many other factors that contribute to community readiness, including motivation and community capacity for change (see the discussion of these concepts in Chapter 11).

---

**Box 13.1  Community Psychology in Action: Hands Across the Hills**

After the 2016 election in the United States, the country seemed to be facing an unprecedented political divide. That is still true as of the time of this writing. But there have been attempts to cross that divide. One of those is the Hands Across the Hills project, which brought together residents of deeply conservative Letcher County, Kentucky, and strongly progressive Leverett, Massachusetts. The participants visited each other's communities to talk, share, and learn about each other. The goal was to meet "face to face with others who voted differently than us, eliminating the voices of politicians and the media, who seek to divide us, to see us as enemies, red versus blue."

The encounters included structured dialogues, shared meals, music, staying in each other's homes, and exploring each other's communities. The result was that the participants now see each other as friends, with common values that bridge political differences. They are currently working on common projects, including an oral history project, a youth exchange, and a speakers' bureau. In 2018 the project was awarded the Melanie Greenberg Award for domestic peace building.

**What Do You Think?**

1. How is this project an example of consciousness raising? How would raising consciousness then lead to community readiness, and how could this readiness be translated into community action? What other factors might lead to community readiness in this case?

2. What do you see as the possible long-term impacts of this project? Are there any important limitations to this project or any significant challenges it could face in the long term? How could those limitations or challenges be addressed from a community psychology perspective?

## Direct Actions

**direct actions**
identify specific obstacles to community development and then create constructive, nonviolent, public conflict to hold powerful entities (people or organizations) responsible for removing those obstacles.

Grassroots groups use direct actions to offset the power of organized money with the power of organized people (*integrative power*, as discussed in Chapter 8; Alinsky, 1971). **Direct actions** identify specific obstacles to community development and then create constructive, nonviolent, public conflict to hold powerful entities (people or organizations) responsible for removing those obstacles. They differ from public protests in that they publicly identify specific actions that they demand specific individuals take in order to address a problem in the community.

The organization AIDS Coalition to Unleash Power (ACT UP) was formed in 1987 specifically to engage in direct actions to address the lack of public response to the AIDS crisis. One of its most successful actions was held at the Food and Drug Administration (FDA), where members successfully shut down the offices for a day. The action was peaceful but confrontational. ACT UP members blocked doorways and hallways and chanted slogans such as "hey, hey FDA, how many people have you killed today?" They presented specific demands regarding the FDA drug approval process that would allow faster and more equitable access to experimental drugs. Within a year, government agencies dealing with AIDS began to include AIDS activists in their planning and decision-making processes (Crimp, 2011).

Direct action has a long history, reflected by labor movements in many countries, including Gandhi's movement to decolonize India and gain independence and the U.S. civil rights movement. Direct action also is illustrated in the examples at the beginning of the chapter. Direct action efforts can range from confronting local legislators about irregularities in funding to standing down bulldozers attempting to remove olive groves. The effectiveness of direct action methods in attaining their immediate goals depends on the context, but in the right circumstances, they can lead to surprising changes.

Saul Alinsky's (1971) classic *Rules for Radicals* delineated direct action principles. To effectively oppose organized, powerful interests, citizens must identify their capacities (the strengths of community group members and their potential to act together) and the capacities of the opposing group or community institution. In addition, they need to identify a situation that dramatizes the need for change and that calls forth citizens' strengths. It is best if that situation is something their opponents have never encountered before and cannot dominate.

Direct actions involve power and conflict (see Chapter 9). If powerful elites limit citizen participation in a decision, strategic choice of a direct action can assert citizen views and frame the issue in their terms. For these reasons, direct actions can be an important tool when addressing issues of social justice. The "accountability meetings" of the PICO approach are an example of direct actions and are an integral part of their work. The direct actions draw power from an organized community making specific demands of specific targets.

From a community psychology perspective, this aspect of direct actions (making specific demands of specific targets) is a necessary one. Direct actions involve highly visible, emotionally charged events that generally require some level of public risk on the part of the participants. If all of that occurs without some tangible result, the participants can become discouraged with the whole idea of community involvement. Their sense of personal and collective efficacy is damaged. Having a clear expectation for the outcome of the social action event, one that is based upon sound research and for which specific individuals can be held accountable, greatly increases the probability that the event will be successful in the eyes of the participants. And when a social action event is perceived as successful, it builds a collective sense of self-efficacy and social capacity.

***Revisiting the Opening Exercise: Examples of Direct Action.*** The two cases described at the beginning of this chapter depict people who decided to do something about the problems they saw in their communities. They wanted to promote social change. They did so through an approach referred to as direct action, and they both had guidance from their association with larger organizations. In Camden, Ron Evans and Camden Churches Organized for People were associated with a national organization called Faith in Action (formally called the PICO Network) that provided training in conducting direct action campaigns. In Turkey, the villagers worked with Greenpeace Turkey, which helped file the lawsuit, provided consultation, and worked to focus national attention on what was happening to the olive groves.

Faith in Action is a national network of local faith-based groups in the United States. The focus on religious congregations for community organizing is based on the fact that, for many disadvantaged communities, religious organizations provide one of the few stable gathering places. In addition, congregations provide a means for gathering people based on shared positive values of social justice, rather than anger regarding a specific local issue. Faith in Action works with congregations of all faiths and denominations, and the local Faith in Action organizations often develop relationships with other community organizations. Faith in Action supplies intensive leadership training in using democratic processes to identify issues of concern to community residents and effectively address those issues.

While there are many community organizations that do the same type of work as Faith in Action, we are focusing on that organization in this chapter because a group of community psychologists have written about them extensively. Paul Speer, Joseph Hughey, and associates worked with community organizations and studied the processes and outcomes of their methods (Speer, 2008; Speer & Hughey, 1995; Speer et al., 1995). Their community organizing strategies combine building strong interpersonal and community relationships with "pressure-group tactics" to influence government and community leaders and institutions.

***A Direct Action Model for Creating Social Change.*** Direct action proceeds through a cycle of community organizing:

1. Assessment

2. Research

3. Mobilization/Action

4. Reflection

In the initial phase, *assessment*, members of the community organization meet one-to-one with citizens to define community issues and to develop working partnerships that strengthen the group. This stage builds interdependence and mutual support.

In the second phase, *research*, organization members meet as a whole to identify the most pressing community issue for the group, based on their conversations with citizens. Members gather further information on that issue, from interviews, searching documents, or other sources. A key goal is to identify contradictions between stated policies and actual practices of government, business, and community services.

The third phase, *mobilization/action*, follows. Organization members meet to decide on an action plan and a person or office to be targeted to discuss community changes. If preparatory meetings with an official do not succeed, a public "accountability meeting" is arranged with that official. The key function of the meeting is to confront the target official, presenting the reality of the community problem and actions that citizens demand to resolve it. Meetings often have brought together city officials with large groups of well-informed citizens making clear, focused demands (due to the extensive groundwork conducted by the organization). They often result in commitments being made by the target official.

**community coalitions**
a group of representatives from local organizations or constituencies who work together to focus on solving community issues by identifying problems and developing action plans. They can be both drivers and outcomes of community development.

It is a potent experience of citizen power, especially for a public official, to face a unified crowd of hundreds of citizens making clear demands for a policy change. Moreover, the community organization hosts the public meeting and carefully scripts its agenda, thus exercising the second and third instruments of power discussed in Chapter 8: channeling participation to maximize the strength of citizen voices and framing the issues for discussion.

The final phase, *reflection*, returns to the one-to-one relationships where the cycle began, to evaluate outcomes and lessons learned. These themes are then discussed in meetings of the whole organization. The organizations also monitor the keeping of promises made by the target officials and institutions. The organization begins the cycle again with a new assessment phase.

While the work of Greenpeace Turkey in Yirca did not follow each step of this model, it did begin with individual conversations with community members and moved on to public mobilization and action. Thus it is an example of a direct action approach (Tashea, 2015).

***Overview of the Direct Action Approach.*** The effectiveness of the direct action approach has been demonstrated in more than these three communities. Speer and Hughey's (1995) studies of organizations in one Midwestern U.S. city showed that they effectively mobilized citizens and produced specific changes in the policy and practices of city government and other organizations. Several psychological factors contribute to the effectiveness of these organizations: strong interpersonal networks; mutual support; an institutional and values base in religious congregations; and participatory niches (recall this from Chapter 8) created by rotating offices and identifying emerging leaders, targeting specific issues and institutions for change, and mobilizing large meetings to make specific demands. With these tools, organizations representing low-income communities can influence powerful private and public institutions. PICO's commitment to supporting the development of emerging community leaders can be seen in their current work with youth leaders (Speer, 2008).

The relationship between Paul Speer and his colleagues and PICO demonstrates the way in which research is informed by practice and vice versa. By developing a relationship with and observing organizations such as PICO, community psychologists learn a great deal about effective community organizations. They then can disseminate that information, and community organizers around the world can learn from the best practices of others working in the field.

## Community Coalitions

Effective community coalitions have been identified as a driving force behind successful efforts to address community problems. **Community coalitions** are made up of representatives from organizations or constituencies who come together and work toward a common goal (Butterfoss, 2007). Take another look at Figure 10.1 in Chapter 10. Community coalitions play a central role in that figure, with links to multiple interventions and positive outcomes at multiple ecological levels. Effective community coalitions can be seen both as a mechanism through which community development occurs and as a powerful outcome of community development in their own right through their impact on increasing community capacity.

Coalitions may involve citizens, community organizations (e.g., community agencies, schools, government, religious congregations, businesses, media, grassroots groups), or, most often, both. Coalitions agree on a mission and write and implement action plans. Those plans may involve action by the coalition itself or by affiliated organizations and may lead to changes in policies or to development of community programs. Coalitions have become a popular and often effective means for strengthening citizen participation and catalyzing community change (Bess, 2015; C. Harper et al., 2014; Oesterle et al., 2018; V. Shapiro et al., 2015; Wolff, 2010).

The Communities That Care movement, which was introduced in Chapter 10, provides an example of a program based on the development of community coalitions. Its mission is community-wide action to foster positive youth development and promote psychosocial competence, including many concepts that we emphasized in Chapters 10 and 11. The Communities That Care coalition model involves developing a local coalition to match prevention/promotion methods backed by empirical research with local community needs and resources (L. D. Brown et al., 2010; Hawkins et al., 1992; Oesterle et al., 2018). Family Violence Coordinating Councils, introduced in Chapter 8, are another example of a coalition-based intervention, in that case addressing the problem of intimate partner violence (N. E. Allen et al., 2013; Javdani & Allen, 2011). What are some examples of other coalitions?

Community coalitions need to put a lot of work into determining how they will function. A community coalition must make choices about its mission, whether it will have a narrow or broad focus, who the members will be, how decisions will be made, whether the coalition will work within existing social structures or attempt to engage in social change, how the coalition will be funded, and how conflict will be negotiated. A community psychologist and leader in the community coalition movement, Tom Wolff, has summarized much of the existing practitioners' wisdom about them in various sources (Wolff, 2001, 2004, 2010).

Empirical research on the qualities of effective community coalitions and the processes through which they demonstrate impact is growing. Research and theory on this topic strongly suggest that coalitions should be viewed in terms of their impact on already existing intervention systems (Bess, 2015; C. Harper et al., 2014; V. Shapiro et al., 2015). For example, the existence of Communities That Care coalitions has been shown to result in a greater likelihood of communities adopting a science-based approach to prevention

(V. Shapiro et al., 2015). Likewise, Family Violence Coordinating Councils have been shown to result in systems-level change such that the development of councils statewide was linked to an increase in the issuance of orders of protection, a recognized best practice in the field of intimate partner violence (N. E. Allen et al., 2013).

This emphasis on the impact of coalitions on systems-level change and increases in community capacity demonstrates that coalitions can result in benefits related to their original specified goals and beyond. A recent network study of a youth violence-prevention coalition documented impacts on organizations that did not belong to the coalition as well as ones that did (Bess, 2015). Research and theory development into the coalition characteristics and community conditions that lead to these systems-level changes is an emerging area of interest that has the potential to greatly improve our understanding of community development and community change.

## Consultation as a Community Development Tool

Community psychologists in both practice and academic settings, as well as professionals from many other fields, often work directly with community coalitions and organizations to enhance their ability to engage in community development. This approach involves professionals working as consultants with workplaces, for-profit or nonprofit, to make changes in the organization's policies, structure, or practices. To qualify as community or social change, this must alter the organization, not simply individual workers, and be connected to wider changes in community or society. In other words, the consultation must result in second-order change, not just surface-level changes. Organizational consulting may change organizational policies; alter roles, decision making, or communication in the organization; or deal with organizational issues such as work-family relationships, understanding human diversity, and intergroup conflict.

Organizational consultation, as conceptualized in community psychology, is grounded in an ecological and contextual understanding of the specific organizations involved (Trickett et al., 2000). For this reason, all of the ecological principles discussed in Chapter 5 are fundamental to consultative work. Issues of power and empowerment (see Chapter 8) are also key to organizational change, and helping an organization become empowered could be a specific goal of the consultation process.

The consultative relationship goes both ways, as we hope we have made clear throughout our discussions. While organizations are learning from consultants, the consultants are also learning through their work with the organizations. Consultants can then play a role in disseminating that information so that others can learn from it. Reviews of organizational concepts and approaches in community psychology include Boyd and Angelique (2002), Shinn and Perkins (2000), and Trickett et al. (2000).

**public policy**
the laws, regulations, and policies established by a government or public institution. Changing public policy is an essential mechanism for achieving social change in communities and in society at large.

***Ethical Concerns in Community Development Work.*** Consultation on community development projects raise complex and fundamental ethical dilemmas. These projects involve multiple constituencies with unequal levels of power and deal with complex community issues often anchored in deep histories of social injustice, racism, and/or colonization. In Box 13.2, these ethical dilemmas are explored in a discussion of Sarah Suiter's work with a community development project in the Dominican Republic.

Effective community change initiatives must take a long-term perspective (Schorr, 1997). The community initiatives described throughout this book are often the products of years of effort. When decisions are made through genuine citizen participation, time is a necessary resource. Initiatives that build slowly and steadily, with citizen input, are likely to be sustained even if conditions change because their participatory base is solid.

There are no exact formulas for community change (Alinsky, 1971). Each community and community issue involves a unique mix of resources, obstacles, allies and opponents, means and ends, intentions, and unanticipated consequences. Community change initiatives are an art, but a collective art, involving personal relationships and shared successes and failures. In the next section, we discuss an avenue for change at both the community and societal levels—public policy.

# Public Policy

The definition of **public policy** used in this chapter is a broad one, including such things as tax policy, traffic laws, local ordinances, and the regulations regarding how those policies are carried out. The dress code at the local public school is a public policy, as is the policy of a state's child health care program to only accept typed applications submitted in person. By this definition, all of the PICO members in our opening examples were engaged in public policy work.

Public policy work involves conducting research and seeking to influence public decisions, policies, or laws. To develop recommendations regarding public policy and to act on those recommendations draws upon all the aspects of community and prevention science discussed in this book and all of the community-organizing techniques presented earlier in this chapter. It often involves persuading government officials but may include influencing leaders in the private sector, journalists, or others. It especially involves framing how a social issue is understood. Remember the importance of problem definition when you are doing public policy work. This work generally seeks to persuade with information (especially research findings) and reasoned arguments, but it may also involve more confrontational approaches such as direct action.

Policy research and advocacy may be focused on legislative, executive, or judicial branches of government, at local, state or provincial, national, or

**Box 13.2 Community Psychology in Action: Ensuring That Community Voices Are Heard**

Sarah Suiter's work was centered in seven communities of Haitian immigrants and their decedents that were marked by extreme poverty, poor health, social discrimination, and political marginalization. A constitutional court decision in 2013 stripped citizenship from over 210,000 people who were born in the Dominican Republic but whose parents or grandparents had immigrated from Haiti sometime after 1929. This decision left the immigrant communities (known as *bateyes*) with few jobs or other economic resources, no government support or services, and no political capital to address the situation.

The project Suiter worked on involved an extensive needs assessment on behalf of a foundation (a non-governmental organization [NGO]) that had a positive history of funding health-related community development projects in the bateyes (Suiter, 2017). The needs assessment process was intentionally collaborative, with strong representation from the three main stakeholders: the foundation, the community members, and the research team. Serious issues in relation to clean water, economic development, and access to affordable, healthy food were identified. All parties agreed that those problems should form the basis for the foundation's strategic priorities. The ethical dilemma arose during the process of determining how to meet those goals, specifically about which parties in the collaboration held the most expertise in making those decisions.

Suiter uses the example of providing clean, potable water for the communities. While other communities in the DR had water provided by the government, the bateyes did not. The funding organization wanted to raise funding in the United States, contract with NGOs in the United States with expertise in water projects, and recruit volunteers from the United States to implement the project. The research team agreed with raising the money in the United States but wanted to identify a Latin American NGO to manage the project and pay community members for the work involved in implementation (which would have resulted in much needed jobs in the community). The community members had a different vision. They wanted the foundation and the researchers to use their standing to put pressure on the government to provide the infrastructure for clean water, just as was provided for other communities in the country (Suiter, 2017).

Suiter refers to a "community psychology values toolbox" when describing how her team approached this dilemma. When faced with this dilemma, they relied on the values presented in Chapter 1 to guide their actions and decision making. Instead of presenting the solution her team eventually supported, we challenge you to review those values and consider how they might have informed her team.

### What Do You Think?

1. Why do you think the three partners in the needs assessment (the funders, the evaluators, and the community members) preferred different approaches to the problem of getting clean water?

2. Which approach do you think would result in the most efficient use of the foundation's funds? Which would result in the greatest gains in community social capital (i.e., community empowerment and collective self-efficacy)? Which approach would best serve the goal of social justice?

3. What other community psychology values do you think you might consider if you were involved in resolving this dilemma?

international levels. Examples of policy advocacy by community psychologists include expert testimony in public interest lawsuits, filing "friend of the court" briefs in court cases, serving on advisory commissions (e.g., the Federal Interagency Council on Homelessness), contacts with lawmakers or government officials, testimony in legislative hearings on proposed bills, interviews or writing for mass media, working with advocacy organizations such as the Children's Defense Fund or the National Mental Health Association, working as a staff member for legislators or in executive or judicial branches of government, and even serving as an elected official, from the local school board to wider office (Maton, 2016; Mayer & Davidson, 2000; Melton, 1995, 2000; Meyers, 2000; Shinn et al., 2001; Solarz, 2001; Toro, 1998). The community research we have cited in this book offers many examples of policy-relevant studies and findings. Several qualities of community psychology equip it especially for policy concerns: concern with both research and action, emphasis on multiple ecological levels, and participatory approaches to working with citizens.

Policy advocacy is often based on policy research, which is conducted to provide empirical information on social issues. An early instance of research-based public advocacy was the use of social science research findings in the 1954 Supreme Court desegregation case *Brown v. Board of Education*. Psychological research was also used for community mental health reforms and early childhood programs such as Head Start (Phillips, 2000).

A more recent example is the publication of a policy statement by the Society for Community Research and Action on the effects of deportation on families and communities (Langhout et al., 2018), detailed in Box 13.3.

Public policy is a particularly important avenue for social change because many such policies exist at the macrosystem ecological level (see Chapter 1). Impacts at the macrosystem level will have impacts for every other ecological level. Those of you who have taken sociology, and particularly those who have taken a class specifically in social stratification, should be well aware of the effect of macrolevel social forces on individual well-being. Structural forces shape who you are, what you believe, how you behave, and what opportunities you have. As a quick example of this, just imagine how different your life would have been if you have been born in poverty, to HIV-infected parents, in a part of Ethiopia stricken by famine. But this recognition of the power of structural forces does not mean we are mere robots. We can consciously examine those structural forces, and we can change them.

Let us start with an example of prevention research that has specific policy implications.

## Crime Policy: Punishment Versus Prevention

Crime policy may be the clearest example of why it is important to systematically examine our public policies. All modern societies have laws defining criminal behavior and procedures for enforcing those laws. We also have a

## Box 13.3 Changing Perspectives: Informing Immigration Policy

In December 2017, community psychologist Regina Langhout received an inquiry from an attorney who had a client facing deportation. His client had been brought to the United States as a young child. He was granted permanent residency, married a U.S. citizen, and had children and grandchildren who were all U.S. citizens. But many years prior, he had been convicted of a crime that made him eligible for deportation.

The attorney was looking for a summary of research demonstrating the harmful effects of deportation on families and communities. The research existed, but lawyers simply did not have a way to present the results of that research to judges during deportation hearings. Regina did not know of anything he could use, so she took the request to the Immigration Justice Interest Group of the Society for Community Research and Action, but none of the members knew of any such summary either. So they decided to write one themselves.

Close to 10% of U.S. families with children include someone without citizenship, and 5.9 million children who are U.S. citizens have a caregiver who could be at risk for deportation. The policy brief describes, among other impacts, research demonstrating the following (Langhout et al., 2018):

- decreased household income, increased food insecurity, less stable housing, and less stable child care among families who lost a family member to deportation

- fear of deportation present years after an immigration raid, even among those who were not at risk of deportation and were not directly affected by the initial raid

- decreased community involvement, including visits to public spaces such as parks and involvement in schools and churches

- increased mistrust of local police departments and an associated decreased willingness to report crimes

The brief is currently being utilized in the legislative system, which could result in a demonstrated impact on case law and local, state, and federal legislation in the United States.

### What Do You Think?

1. What impacts could deportation have at multiple ecological levels—beyond the individual level—and in different communities, including families and other groups?

2. Do you think that impacts at the family and community levels should be considered when developing immigration policy? How might you address those impacts if you were helping develop this policy?

3. Aside from public policy, what other kinds of community action described earlier in the chapter could address immigration and deportation issues? What would be the benefits and limitations of these actions compared to public policy initiatives?

large and long-standing body of research regarding the effects of crime policies. So, for example, we know the following:

- Moderate punishments consistently enforced have the greatest deterrent effects.

- Any type or length of incarceration can increase the chances of recidivism when compared to diversion programs such as community service and restorative justice programs.

- Treatment for drug abusers is a more cost-effective approach to dealing with drug-related offenses than incarceration.

- Among previously incarcerated individuals, increased education leads to decreased recidivism.

- Among previously incarcerated individuals, those who have maintained close ties with their families have decreased recidivism.

Immigration reform is an important topic in public policy debates, one that needs to be addressed at multiple ecological levels.

lev radin/Shutterstock.com

Each of these specific statements is related to research findings that have been well established for decades (see Sherman et al., 1998, and R. Wright, 1996, for reviews). Incarceration is damaging to individuals, leaving them alienated, with few positive social supports and limited economic resources. Even individuals who are incarcerated for extremely short time periods experience increased alienation and recidivism compared to individuals who committed the same offenses but were not incarcerated. In addition, increasing the severity of punishment does little to increase deterrent effects. Let us compare existing crime policy in the United States to these research findings.

The United States incarcerates a greater number of its own citizens than any other country in the world and accounts for 20% of the total worldwide prison population (Institute for Criminal Policy Research, n.d.). Of every 100,000 adults in the United States, 920 are in jail or prison and another 1,400 are on probation or parole. That means that 1 in 38 adults in the United States is living under the supervision of the correctional system, and 1 out of every 109 American adults is incarcerated (Bureau of Justice Statistics, 2019). Those numbers are actually a significant improvement from 2006, when 1 out of every 31 adults was under the supervision of the correctional system and 1 out of every 100 was behind bars.

Those incredibly high rates were fueled by several factors, such as the War on Drugs, which greatly escalated in the 1980s, and various "get tough on crime" initiatives designed to increase the severity of punishment, including mandatory minimum sentencing guidelines and the three-strikes laws discussed in Chapter 10. This high rate of incarceration has continued, even as the violent crime rate in the United States has decreased significantly from 758 violent crimes per 100,000 people in 1991 to a rate of 383 per 100,000 people in 2017 (Federal Bureau of Investigations, 2018).

Crime policy has specific social justice implications. Minority populations in the United States, particularly African American populations, are disproportionately represented in the criminal justice system and in prison populations, far beyond what would be expected given differences in criminal offenses between different ethnic groups. This disproportionate representation has far-reaching, negative effects not only on the individuals themselves but also on their families and communities (Alexander, 2010; Cochran et al., 2018; Haskins & McCauley, 2019). While there are obviously pragmatic, economic, and social welfare reasons for being concerned about the state of crime policy, the serious social justice implications add urgency to the situation.

The cost of this mass incarceration is immense, at least $80 billion a year. And that only includes direct spending on correctional systems. If you include other expenses, such as court costs, policing expenses, and the money families spend supporting incarcerated family members, the true cost could be over $180 billion (Wagner & Rabuy, 2017). Prisons are meant to keep the public safe by preventing future crimes. Is it possible to meet this goal without the high costs of incarcerations? The research clearly says yes.

The discussion of cost-benefit analyses in Chapter 10 included reference to the Washington State Institute for Public Policy, which has focused on providing cost-benefit analyses of multiple prevention and treatment programs based on existing research studies. One of the goals in developing the database was to help the Washington state government make informed decisions about which programs to fund. The institute provides cost-benefit analyses of 33 programs that have the stated goal of reducing or preventing juvenile delinquency. Thirteen of those programs are rated as having a 90% or better chance that the benefits of the program will exceed the costs. One program, Education and Employment Training, has a 100% chance of benefits exceeding costs, with a return of $40.25 in benefits for every $1 spent on the program (Washington State Institute for Public Policy, 2018c).

For programs with a stated goal of reducing or preventing involvement in the adult criminal justice system, results indicate that 20 programs had a 90% or better chance of benefits exceeding costs. Four of those programs are specifically focused on keeping drug offenders out of prison and providing treatment services instead. Three of those programs involve providing education programs to incarcerated individuals, with opportunities for postsecondary education having a 100% chance of benefits exceeding costs and a return of $19.80 in benefits for every $1 spent on the program (Washington State Institute for Public Policy, 2018d).

In our discussion of cost-benefit analyses in Chapter 10, we said that the sad thing about cost-effectiveness analyses is that they so rarely actually have an effect on public policy. This depressing point is particularly salient when discussing crime policy. For example, you may have noticed that education programs show particularly good results in the cost-benefit analyses discussed above. The research on the positive impact of education on recidivism goes back to 1924 and has been consistent for almost 100 years (Silva, 1994).

While those findings relate to all levels of education, a particularly contentious point of crime policy in the United States has to do with higher education, specifically Pell Grants. Pell Grants are a federal program designed to make higher education affordable to low-income students. Since 1972, when the program started, Pell Grants were available to eligible incarcerated individuals, just as they were to all eligible students in the United States. These grants helped fund programs where colleges and universities provided courses and full degree programs in prisons. In 1994, federal legislation was passed as part of the "tough on crime" initiatives of that decade that made inmates ineligible for Pell Grants. This meant that incarcerated individuals were denied access to the most long-standing effective means of preventing recidivism at the very point when the United States was rapidly expanding the prison population.

That policy change has been repeatedly challenged by organizations and individuals familiar with the research. For example, a recent meta-analysis by the RAND Corporation found that individuals who participated in post-secondary education programs while incarcerated were 23% less likely to return to prison than other prisoners (Bozick et al., 2018). In 2015, the U.S. Department of Education began the Second Chance Pell pilot program, which allowed 67 colleges and universities to offer Pell-funded secondary education programs in prison. Based on data from that program, it is estimated that reinstating Pell Grant availability for incarcerated individuals would have cascading effects, providing states with a better educated workforce, providing formally incarcerated individuals and their families with an estimated $45.3 million increase in earnings in just the first year after release from prison, and saving $365.8 million in incarceration costs each year due to reduced recidivism (Oakford et al., 2019).

This example illustrates an important point about policy advocacy. The impact of social science research on policy making is generally much broader than just advocating for a specific regulation. Instead, policy advocacy often involves educating policy makers, influencing their overall perspective on an issue. The researchers and organizations involved in crime prevention worked persistently to publicize the evidence about postsecondary education and its beneficial impact on recidivism rates. They needed to change the public and legislative perspective away from the view that Pell Grants are an individual benefit that incarcerated individuals do not deserve toward one that recognized Pell Grants as a public prevention and wellness improvement program that yields significant benefits for the nation when offered to incarcerated individuals. This shift of perspective can take years of work. As of this writing, the U.S. Congress is considering adopting the Restoring Education and Learning Act (REAL Act), which is a bipartisan bill to restore access to Pell Grants to incarcerated individuals, a quarter of a century after they were first taken away.

## Macrolevel Change: Public Policy Regarding Poverty

Poverty is a social issue with pragmatic, economic, social welfare, and social justice implications. The fact that poverty is correlated with almost every conceivable negative outcome humans can face is well established. People who live in poverty have poorer nutrition, poorer health, less education, and shorter lifespans than people who are not living in poverty. This is true even in wealthy, developed countries where poverty is defined relative to the median income. For a review of the effects of poverty on child development, see Huston and Bentley (2010).

It is difficult to find anyone who does not agree that poverty is a serious problem, but there is little agreement on what to do about it. All developed countries have a long history of public policy efforts to decrease poverty, decrease income inequality, and support the development of a middle class. In the United States, those policies include the public school system (starting in the early 1800s), public funding of land-grant colleges and universities (starting in 1854), the Homestead Act of 1862, antitrust legislation (starting at the end of the 19th century), the first progressive income tax in 1913, the New Deal legislation of the 1930s (including the Social Security System and unemployment insurance), the GI Bill of Rights (starting after World War II), and the Great Society programs (starting in 1964) including instituting health insurance (in the form of Medicare and Medicaid) for the elderly and the poor.

There were significant problems with the design and application of many of these programs. For example, the Homestead Act, while providing unprecedented opportunities for African Americans, women, and recent immigrants to own land, also ultimately resulted in large transfers of land to corporations and a massive loss of tribal lands and rights for Native Americans (Freund, 2013; M. Jacobs, 2017). The GI Bill of Rights, while designed at the federal level to be nondiscriminatory, ended up being administered at the state level and resulted in widespread discrimination against African American veterans in many areas (Humes, 2006; S. Turner & Bound, 2003).

Even with these serious problems, these programs were undeniably successful in reducing poverty in the United States. The U.S. Census Bureau first began collecting data on poverty rates in 1959. That year, the U.S. poverty rate was 22.4%. In 2018 (the last year for which data were available at the time of this writing), it was 11.8% (Census Bureau, 2020, Table 2). Just looking at the overall decrease in the poverty rate, however, masks some important differences among groups of Americans.

In 1959, the poverty rate for Americans less than 18 years of age was 27.3%. The rate for Americans 65 and older was 35.2%, and the rate for Americans ages 18–64 was 17%. Poverty disproportionately affected children and the elderly. Rates for all three groups declined from 1959 until about 1969, when child poverty was at 14%, poverty in the elderly was at 25.3%, and poverty for nonelderly adults was 8.7%. Since then, poverty among the elderly has continued to show a general decline and in 2018 was 9.7%. In contrast, after sharp decreases in the 1960s and early 1970s, child poverty began to rise again and is currently 16.2% (Census Bureau, 2020, Table 3; see Figure 13.1).

Poverty in general, and child poverty in particular, is a serious public problem in the United States. Both of these concerns are related to the even larger, overarching issue of income inequality. Income inequality is measured by the difference between the households with the highest income and those with the lowest income. In the United States, income inequality decreased significantly after World War II, as households at all levels experienced relatively equal gains in income. That trend stopped in the late 1970s, and currently the United States is ranked 39 out of 157 countries in our level of income inequality (with a lower ranking indicating a higher level of inequality), according

**Figure 13.1** Historical Poverty Rates in the United States

*Note.* Data from Census Bureau (2020).

to the CIA World Factbook (CIA, n.d.). There is more income concentrated in the highest earning American households now than at any time since the 1920s (C. Stone et al., 2018).

How wealth is distributed in a society is a function of many factors, most importantly the basic structure of the economy and the tax system. As with social change and social policy, the distribution and redistribution of wealth is occurring, and will continue to occur, regardless of our actions. We encourage you to consciously examine these processes in your society.

***Defining the Problem.*** Before we can determine the best policy approach for fighting poverty, we must go back to the issue of problem definition. What approach you choose to take to deal with the problem of income inequality depends very much upon how you define the problem. For example, if your understanding of child poverty is that poverty is correlated with increased risk factors and decreased protective factors in children's lives, then your answer will be to focus on ameliorating the effects of poverty on the lives of children. In this case you might work to implement prevention and wellness-promotion programs, such as the home-visiting and social-emotional learning programs discussed in Chapters 10 and 11 and Head Start, which have the goal of enhancing the development of children living in poverty.

If your understanding of the problem is that families with young children are particularly vulnerable to poverty, then you might focus your efforts on providing supports for those families. Programs such as the Supplemental Nutrition Assistance Program (SNAP; formerly known as "food stamps") and housing vouchers, for example, have the goal of reducing the number of children living in poverty by providing increased resources to families with children.

Finally, if your understanding of the problem is that increased income inequality in a country leads to increased numbers of people living in poverty, then your answer might be to promote economic policies that result in the reduction of income inequality and thus decrease the incidence of poverty throughout a society. An example of this type of policy in the United States is the Earned Income Tax Credit.

In the rest of this section, we discuss examples of these last two groups of policies and the effect on poor families. First, let us get a picture of what one of these families might look like by examining the living costs for a hypothetical single parent with two children ages 3 and 4 who lives in Chicago, Illinois.

***Poverty in a Single-Parent Family.*** In 2019, the poverty guideline for a three-person household in the United States was $21,330 (Health and Human Services Department, 2019). The minimum wage is $7.25 an hour (which has not been raised in a decade and has no scheduled increases in the future despite the fact that the cost of living has increased since that time). If a single parent with two children worked full time (40 hours a week for 52 weeks a year), the family's gross income would be $15,080, not enough to lift them out of poverty. Their income would even be less if a family member got sick and the parent had to miss work. Let us assume that our single parent is lucky enough to have a job that pays $10.26 an hour, $3 an hour over the federal minimum wage and the lowest salary that is needed to earn more than the federal poverty level.

While this person would not be liable for any income tax, they would still have to pay 7.65% of their gross income for Social Security and Medicaid (Federal Insurance Contributions Act tax, FICA). The U.S. Department of Agriculture estimates that a thrifty parent of two young children (ages 3 and 4) could feed all three of them for about $381 a month, assuming that all meals are prepared at home (Department of Agriculture, 2019). The 2019 Fair Market Rent for a two-bedroom apartment in Chicago is $1,820 a month (ZIP code 60614). This includes rent and utilities and varies widely depending on geographic location (Department of Housing and Urban Development, 2019). In 2016, the last year for which data are available, the average cost of child care for a 4-year-old in Illinois was $797 per month (Economic Policy Institute, 2016). Our family is lucky that both children are out of infancy since Illinois is one of 33 states where infant care costs more per year than in-state tuition for a year at one of the state's 4-year public colleges (Economic Policy Institute, 2016).

In Illinois, this family will qualify for the All Kids health insurance program, with no premiums and only negligible copays for the parent's care. And they will qualify for SNAP benefits, giving them access to food. SNAP is a federal program that is administered by the states, so benefits can vary a great deal according to geographic location. In 2018, the maximum SNAP benefit in Illinois was $505 for a family of three, which would result in our family receiving $505 a month or $6,060 a year (Illinois Department of Health and Human Services, 2018). Table 13.1 presents a sample budget worksheet, illustrating the flow of money for this single parent and the family's end-of-year financial situation.

So even without spending a penny on transportation, clothes, or necessary items like toilet paper and soap, this family is already facing an annual deficit of $19,772, which translates to a loss of about $1,648 per month. This is why many economists calculate that for a family to live safely while meeting their basic needs, they need an income that is twice the federal poverty level (Mishel et al., 2009). Many families are in the same situation as our single parent of two. In 2017, 38% of American family households with children had income at or below twice the poverty threshold for their families (Census Bureau, 2018, Table 5). Unfortunately, as you can see from our example, for many Americans, having a job is no guarantee that they can support their families. In 2017, 35% of wage earners made less than $20,000 (less than the parent in our example; Social Security Administration, 2017).

***Public Policies for Preventing Homelessness.*** Perhaps you looked at the estimated housing costs for our family and thought that, unless they could find cheaper housing, they were in danger of homelessness. This is a valid

**Table 13.1** Sample Annual Budget for a Single Parent With Two Children

| Description | Income (money in) | Expenses (money out) | Overall balance |
|---|---|---|---|
| Gross income | $21,341 | | $21,341 |
| SNAP | $6,060 | | $27,401 |
| FICA | | $1,633 | $25,768 |
| Rent and utilities | | $21,840 | $3,928 |
| Food | | $4,572 | −$644 |
| Child care | | $19,128 | −$19,772 |
| Total | $27,401 | $47,173 | −$19,772 |

*Note.* SNAP = Supplemental Nutrition Assistance Program; FICA = Federal Insurance Contributions Act.

concern. In Chapter 1 we used the issue of homelessness to illustrate the conceptual shift we hoped you would make while reading this book, which involves understanding that societal issues are caused by a variety of factors at multiple ecological levels and not solely because of individuals' actions or life choices. We presented research demonstrating that while individualistic explanations of homelessness have some validity (issues such as mental illness, substance abuse, and domestic violence), structural issues that exist only at the community and societal level have much more explanatory power. We asked you to consider a shift in perspective from an individual to a community understanding of homelessness, specifically to the idea that the fundamental cause of homelessness in a society has nothing to do with the characteristics of individuals; it is a lack of affordable housing.

Homelessness presents a powerful example of the role that community psychologists, and all those who believe in community change, can play in public policy and human welfare. Community psychologist Marybeth Shinn has joined many other social scientists in advocating, with research supporting their contentions, that homelessness must be understood fundamentally as a problem of access to affordable housing. While these researchers do support specific types of legislation, their message has focused fundamentally on this shift in problem definition. Policy makers, at local, state, and national levels, are increasingly speaking and acting from this perspective. This shift in perspective is occurring after years of work, and the "influence is more on ways of thinking" about policy issues than on particular research findings or programs (Shinn, personal communication, September 22, 2004).

As the collective research on homelessness has become more conclusive, the recommendations from social scientists have become more specific. The first conclusion is that the single most effective policy approach to eliminating homelessness is to provide affordable housing (generally in the form of subsidized housing) for every family. The second conclusion is a matter of perspective, related to the shift in defining homelessness as a community-level rather than an individual-level issue. Research has increasingly supported the idea that, if you want to intervene successfully in the multiple problems faced by people and families who are without a stable residence, then meeting their housing needs must come first (Tsemberis, 2010).

The Section 8 Housing Choice Vouchers program is an example of a subsidized housing program. The program is administered by local housing authorities, so the details may vary by locality, but the program is designed to provide vouchers to cover the difference between 30% of a participant's income and the local rental costs. The program can be linked to specific housing projects, or the renter can use the voucher to find housing anywhere in the community. Allowing the renter to find housing anywhere in a community or having public housing policies that require new units of affordable housing to be spread throughout the community are both approaches that can help eliminate areas of concentrated poverty. The program requires participants to spend 30% of their income because most economists agree that housing costs (rent plus utilities) that total less than one third of a family's income are affordable.

Housing subsidy programs such as Section 8 are an amazingly effective way of ending family homelessness. In a report for the National Alliance to End Homelessness, Shinn (2009) says, "In every study that examined this issue, subsidized housing—with or without any additional services—has helped families to leave shelters and stay out" (p. 4). This statement has only gained validity since that report (Gubits et al., 2018).

The Family Options Study was a 3-year-long study of over 2,200 families including over 5,000 children who were recruited after spending at least 7 nights in a crisis homeless shelter. The study was conducted under the auspices of the U.S. Department of Housing and Urban Development (Gubits et al., 2018). The families were randomly assigned to either long-term subsidized housing (a housing voucher), project-based transitional housing, rapid rehousing, or usual care (the families were given shelter care and given information about resources, but they needed to seek out those resources on their own). The study was evaluated at three points: baseline, 20 months after assignment, and 37 months after assignment. The results were clear. While all interventions were helpful, long-term housing subsidies resulted in the greatest impact, including reduced psychological distress, intimate partner violence, food insecurity, and sleep and behavior problems in children.

The second homelessness policy point upon which there is widespread agreement has to do with the order in which services should be supplied to the homeless. Homeless families, as a group, have fewer serious and chronic problems than individuals who are homeless. In fact, homeless families are essentially identical to poor families who have housing (Shinn, 2009). There are, however, a subset of poor families, and an even larger group of homeless individuals, who have a wide variety of problems such as mental illness and substance abuse. Traditional approaches to working with these people were based on the idea that these problems needed to be dealt with before stable housing could be achieved. A large body of research now supports the opposite perspective; if stable housing is provided first, it becomes easier to address the other problems (Gubits et al., 2018; Tsemberis, 2010).

Even among homeless persons with serious mental illness, programs that put housing first are more effective and less costly. These programs place homeless persons with mental illness in subsidized housing first and then offer other treatment and support services, rather than requiring them to receive mental health treatment in transitional housing programs before becoming eligible for their own housing (Gulcur et al., 2003).

A significant problem with the current Section 8 housing voucher program is that the number of eligible families far exceeds the number of available vouchers. Communities keep extensive wait lists, but even getting on a wait list is difficult. Only about 20% of households that qualify receive a voucher, and another 20% get on to a wait list. The other 60% of qualifying households are not even on a wait list (Scally et al., 2018).

Let's assume that the single parent with two children discussed earlier is one of the fortunate ones who receives a voucher. A voucher would reduce their expenses for rent and utilities to 30% of their gross income, or $6,402. This reduces their annual deficit to $4,334, which results in a monthly deficit of about $361 (see Table 13.2).

Even in this budget, our family is facing a monthly deficit of over $300. Now think about all the things that are not included in the budget so far. Not only do they need to pay for clothes, transportation, and basic household expenses such as soap; we also expect them to be saving for retirement, the children's education, emergency expenses, and perhaps a down payment on their own home. Next, we will discuss a program designed not to decrease our family's expenses but rather to increase their income: the Earned Income Tax Credit.

***Making Work Pay: The Earned Income Tax Credit.*** In 1975, the United States introduced the Earned Income Tax Credit (EITC). The EITC was designed to "make work pay" for even low-income workers. This federal income tax program is quite possibly the single most effective tax policy designed to reduce poverty (and income inequality) the country has ever implemented. The program works by providing low-income families a refundable tax credit.

**Table 13.2** Sample Annual Budget for a Single-Parent Family With a Section 8 Housing Voucher

| Description | Income (money in) | Expenses (money out) | Overall balance |
|---|---|---|---|
| Gross income | $21,341 | | $21,341 |
| SNAP | $6,060 | | $27,401 |
| FICA | | $1,633 | $25,768 |
| Rent and utilities (after Section 8 housing voucher) | | $6,402 | $19,366 |
| Food | | $4,572 | $14,794 |
| Child care | | $19,128 | −$4,334 |
| Total | $27,401 | $31,735 | −$4,334 |

*Note.* SNAP = Supplemental Nutrition Assistance Program; FICA = Federal Insurance Contributions Act.

The size of the credit is substantial. For example, in 2019 the credit could be up to $5,828 for a single parent with two children earning $18,500 a year. The amount of the credit goes down after that, but single parents with two children earning up to $50,162 or married couples earning up to $55,952 receive some portion of the credit. The credit is refundable, which means that any amount left over after it is used to offset income tax owed is refunded to the families. The credit is designed to supplement the income of those working in low-paying jobs to ensure they actually earn enough to support their families. Since the credit only applies to earned income, it is designed to encourage employment, and there is evidence that it has worked that way. Studies have repeatedly concluded that expansions of the federal EITC have reduced welfare use among single mothers by increasing employment and earnings (Gao et al., 2009; Hoynes & Patel, 2015; Lim, 2009; Ziliak, 2009).

The EITC improves the circumstances of our family a great deal. The parent would receive the maximum federal credit of $5,828, and, since with their low income they would owe no income tax, all of that money would be refunded. As of 2018, 29 states had implemented their own refundable ETIC, which operate in addition to the federal program and have been shown to have their own positive effects (National Conference of State Legislatures, 2019). In Illinois, our sample family would most likely receive an additional $900 from the state EITC.

Temporary Assistance for Needy Families (TANF) is a federal block-grant program administered by the states. There is wide variability among the benefits offered by the states, but Illinois uses part of its TANF funds to partially fund a Child Care Assistance Program (CCAP). Similar to the Section 8 HUD housing vouchers program, CCAP calculates a copay amount for qualifying families and then CCAP pays the remainder of the day care provider's fees. Our family qualifies for the full CCAP benefit, with a weekly copay of just $89 per month, plus any remaining fees from the provider. For this budget, we will assume that there are no additional fees.

Adding these programs into the budget leaves our family with $20,454 to pay for all their other expenses for the year, a much more reasonable situation than the previous scenarios (see Table 13.3).

Significant aspects of this budget are not guaranteed. The CCAP in Illinois has experienced some upheaval in recent years, with funding cuts to the program and a freeze on the amounts the state will pay to providers. This has resulted in fewer service providers participating in the program and more day cares with fees higher than the state reimbursement rate. And, as stated earlier, even though our family qualified for a housing voucher, demand for these vouchers exceeds the supply and it is more than likely that a family will not receive one, or at least not for 1 year or more (Department of Housing and Urban Development, n.d.). Since housing and child care were by far the most expensive items in our family's budget, leaving them without assistance

**Table 13.3** Sample Annual Budget for a Single-Parent Family With a Section 8 Housing Voucher, Federal and State EITC, and CCAP Assistance

| Description | Income (money in) | Expenses (money out) | Overall balance |
|---|---|---|---|
| Gross income | $21,341 | | $21,341 |
| SNAP | $6,060 | | $27,401 |
| FICA | | $1,633 | $25,768 |
| Rent and utilities (after Section 8 housing voucher) | | $6,402 | $19,366 |
| Food | | $4,572 | $14,794 |
| Child care (with CCAP assistance) | | $1,068 | $13,726 |
| Federal EITC | $5,828 | | $19,554 |
| Illinois state EITC | $900 | | $20,454 |
| Total | $34,129 | $13,675 | $20,454 |

*Note.* SNAP = Supplemental Nutrition Assistance Program; FICA = Federal Insurance Contributions Act; CCAP = Child Care Assistance Program; EITC = Earned Income Tax Credit.

for either of expenses makes their financial position fall right back into an untenable situation.

An interesting aspect of the EITC, and tax credits for low- and middle-income families in general, is the effect these programs have had on current public discussions of tax policy in the United States. The Tax Policy Center (2018) calculated that about 44% of U.S. households paid no income tax in 2018, largely because of programs such as the EITC. The vast majority of the households that paid no income tax still paid significant amounts of other taxes (e.g., payroll taxes, sales tax). But those points did not stop an analyst from the Heritage Foundation, who said, "We have 50 percent of people who are getting something for nothing" (Ohlemacher, 2010).

Think about this statement. Do you think it is an accurate description of programs that are designed to ensure that full-time workers can adequately support their families? What impact do you think quotes such as that one (which was widely reported) have on the public perception of programs such as the EITC and on other efforts to reduce income inequality?

The good news is that, increasingly, the social and policy issues in the United States discussed in this section—income inequality, low wages, lack of affordable housing, and the high cost of day care—are gaining widespread recognition as problems resulting from structural forces rather than individual deficits. A recent report from the American Enterprise Institute and the Brookings Institute was specifically labeled "a consensus plan for reducing poverty," because of the bipartisan nature of the workgroup that developed the plan (L. Aber et al., 2015). Several of the policy recommendations in that plan are interventions and policies discussed in this book, including effective parenting education programs, increased access to high-quality preschool programs, social-emotional learning programs, and increasing the EITC.

## Conclusion

This chapter is not just about social change; it is about developing strong communities and considering our roles in participating in those communities. Each of the activities described in this chapter develops community capital and community leadership. But these activities take time. There are multiple roles to play in social change initiatives, and they all count on community members being willing to make a long-term commitment. Change does not take place overnight, and unfortunately it is easy (and understandable) to become frustrated with the inevitable setbacks. But the democratic process we have tried to describe in this chapter is not free; it takes vigilance and work.

If you are inspired to become involved in community or wider social change, an excellent place to learn about practical action steps is the Community Toolbox website (https://ctb.ku.edu/en), developed by community psychologists to offer an online, accessible resource for citizens.

## For Review

### Discussion Questions

1. We discussed several approaches to social change, including community organizing, direct action, and consciousness raising. Think of groups you know of that work to achieve social change. Which of these approaches do they use? How effective do you think they have been, and why?

2. Have you ever been involved in a social change effort? Which approaches did you use, and how effective were they?

3. A number of social justice issues are discussed in this chapter, including housing, poverty, child care, institutional racism, immigration, the criminal justice system, and health care. Which of those issues are personally important to you? Did this chapter give you any ideas about how you might work to address that issue in your community?

## Key Terms

social change, 450

community organizing, 452

community development, 452

consciousness raising, 453

community readiness, 454

direct actions, 455

community coalitions, 458

public policy, 461

## Learn More

A detailed summary of the chapter, along with other review materials, is available on the *Community Psychology, Fourth Edition* companion website at http://pubs.apa.org/books/supp/kloos4/.

Youth action on climate change in response to inaction among politicians shows the power that communities can have in the fight for social change.

Disobey Art/Shutterstock.com

# 14 Emerging Challenges and Opportunities: Shifting Perspective to Promote Change

## Looking Ahead ⅠⅠⅠ➡

**After reading this chapter you will be able to answer these questions:**

**1.** How can you balance the urgency of the need for change and a commitment to sustained effort required to achieve most community and social change?

**2.** Which personal qualities are helpful in promoting community and social change?

**3.** What emerging issues could shape community psychology in the future?

**4.** How will you use the strategies and perspectives from this book to help improve your community?

## Opening Exercise

## When to Act

Hurricane María had cut a devastating path across the Caribbean while wildfires in Washington and British Columbia made it hard to breathe. Such storms and fires had become annual events. News reports were full of examples of glaciers receding and agricultural crops being more vulnerable to drought or flooding. For those born after 2000, they had heard about sea level rise and climate change getting worse each year but had seen little action to address it. In 2017, a group of teenagers began organizing to protest inaction on climate change and its effects on the most vulnerable. They were dissatisfied by the slow pace of action to address climate change. Furthermore, elected officials and the broader public had largely ignored the voices of youth in conversations about climate change even though the youth would bear the burden of inaction.

Unlike most past movements, they used social media to organize across wide

**When to Act (continued)**

geographic areas of the United States to create a youth-led movement to raise awareness about climate change and create a sense of urgency to try to get policy makers and the broader public to act. From two original founders, the organization Zero Hour grew to a leadership group of 20 people who were connected across the country. They developed a broad platform of issues and demands. These include (a) disrupting standard practices that use fossil fuels and consume too many resources; (b) providing food, water, and housing for all; (c) reducing energy consumption; and (d) restoring ecosystems (Zero Hour, n.d.). In the summer of 2018, Zero Hour organized a lobbying day in Washington, DC, that met with 40 federal lawmakers. Two days later they organized a march that had 25 sister marches around the world. In 2019, they held a Youth Climate Summit in Miami. They have also joined a lawsuit, *Juliana v. the United States*, that was first filed in 2015. In the suit, the plaintiffs argue that the federal government is violating their constitutional rights to life, liberty, and property by promoting fossil fuel production and failing to take action on climate change. It is not yet clear whether these efforts to promote social change will achieve the outcomes listed on the organizers' platform. However, their ability to mobilize so many youth, meet with legislators, and command so much media attention is remarkable.

## What Do You Think?

1. What allowed these teens to act on their concerns on such a broad scale?
2. What would encourage you to act on issues that are of great concern to you?
3. What do you think the group should do next to achieve their goals?
4. Which principles or strategies from community psychology might be helpful?

In Chapter 1, we demonstrated how community psychology represents an alternative framework for understanding and addressing social problems. In each of the chapters that followed, we considered how community psychology perspectives can lead to examining relationships between ecological levels of analysis rather than only looking for individuals' deficits or individual explanations for social problems (e.g., people who are homeless because they have an addiction or are lazy). Furthermore, by defining problems differently, community psychology can consider a wider array of possible interventions, not only seeking to address problems but also considering ways to prevent them and to promote well-being. These changes in perspective encourage community stakeholders to look for resources within their communities and possibilities for collaborative action to address problems. We have emphasized the pragmatism of community psychology by considering problems across levels of analysis, involving local stakeholders, and appreciating the potential resources of human diversity in addressing social problems. Even though engaging a number of stakeholders can be challenging, it is more likely to lead to a comprehensive solution than social change efforts that overlook or exclude a wide variety of community perspectives. Balancing commitments to research and action, community psychology's approaches to social intervention can lead to a variety of intervention strategies, as well an assessment of their effectiveness: community organizing, creating and improving prevention programs, health promotion strategies, and changing public policy. These chapters document that there are many ways to do community psychology.

For this final chapter, we ask you to consider how these ideas and strategies for change can be resources for you as a person concerned about your neighborhood, schools, workplace, and community. These resources can help change organizations, localities, and communities to support individual and collective well-being. They are also resources for people choosing careers in human services, education, and health care. We start the chapter by considering opportunities for using community psychology perspectives as an engaged citizen. We discuss the development of personal qualities that are encouraged for people engaged in community and social change efforts. Next, we discuss emerging directions and challenges for community psychology research and action. We present a few examples of interventions that demonstrate the promise of community psychology for addressing emerging issues. Some of you may be interested in pursuing a career in community psychology or related fields. For those interested, we describe opportunities for training in community psychology that can prepare you for social change careers. We conclude with a final exercise to encourage you to reconsider different ways that you might use your insights from studying community psychology to promote well-being in your communities.

## Promoting Community and Social Change

We have spent our careers working with students and community partners to help them work toward positive changes in their communities. In fact, most of the examples of community change that we described in this book were partnerships between community members and a community psychologist. We begin this chapter focused on how community psychology's approaches to defining and addressing problems are relevant for people advocating for their communities and for people working in human services.

### Opportunities for Citizens

Without formal training in community psychology or without collaborating with community psychologists, citizens get involved in community organizing by raising awareness about social issues, mobilizing advocacy groups, and developing programs to address their concerns. From North American and

**seizing the day**
being ready and willing to collaborate and take effective action to implement social change when the time comes.

other viewpoints, democratic forms of government aspire to balance power among diverse, competing interests, with systems of checks and balances often divided among branches and levels of government. For this to work effectively, citizens need to be informed about issues and have avenues for addressing them. When such avenues are blocked or unavailable, there is a tradition in North America of creating new settings to address concerns and work toward action (e.g., civil rights, First Nations and Indigenous rights, and women's liberation movements). Conceptualizing citizen action across levels of analysis, there are opportunities to get involved at neighborhood, local, and higher levels of government. As a citizen, you can help redefine problems, push for evidence of effectiveness of intervention strategies, and demand a place at the table in deciding how problems are addressed. Recall the examples of the school children in Wisconsin in Chapter 8 that changed local policy and the neighbors in Camden, New Jersey, in Chapter 13 that changed how community development money was distributed.

While democratic structures have many strengths, it can be challenging to muster sufficient agreement within a community that a social problem exists, much less consensus about how to respond. To mobilize communities to action, a social issue (e.g., drug abuse, homelessness, poverty, racism) often must assume crisis proportions. In most cases, the work to address the issues has long predated when they are labeled as "crises." As presented in Chapters 1 and 2, citizens and decision makers can adopt a *participant–conceptualizer* model of community psychology to consider levels of analysis in problem definitions and work toward long-term solutions rather than quick fixes in response to the crisis. Work toward social change requires sustained effort and partnerships. However, as examples in this book suggest, we need to be prepared for the difficulties in sustaining long-term changes, especially with changing political conditions (Langhout, 2015; Riger, 1993; Schorr, 1997). We should expect setbacks and disappointment during sustained efforts to achieve community change.

Citizen action on community issues requires a balance of acting when opportunities arise, being creative and persistent when encountering resistance, and a long-term commitment to action. The history of social and community change illustrates the value of two seemingly contradictory ideas about time in relation to intervention: *seizing the day* and *taking the long view*. Early in the history of community psychology, J. G. Kelly (1970b) articulated the importance of both for citizens and community psychologists.

For citizens, **seizing the day** means being prepared to work with others using effective methods to push for change when opportunities arise. In social change efforts, it is not uncommon to struggle to raise awareness of a problem or ineffective efforts to address a problem. When moments arise when there is greater awareness or even consensus to "do something," we need to be prepared to act. This can involve using direct action skills reviewed in Chapter 13

**taking the long view**
understanding that implementing social and community change takes a long time and continued persistence, even after some substantial changes have been achieved.

(e.g., community organizing and targeted protest with specific requests to address community violence). It might involve using established health prevention and promotion programs reviewed in Chapters 10–12 (e.g., antibullying programs in schools, promoting physical activity) that have research evidence of effectiveness and are adapted to be culturally relevant and responsive to your community. Being familiar with concepts from this course can prepare you to act when others in your community are engaged and ready. Seizing the day usually involves taking advantage of opportunities for learning. For example, when awareness about an issue is raised through an effective campaign, stories of success, or common concern about a problem, you can be ready to introduce strategies and evidence-supported programs. Some of these opportunities may arise through community events, direct action to demand civic accountability, social media, and news coverage (J. G. Kelly, 1970b). Change does not happen because consciousness has been raised; as presented in Chapters 10–13, it requires a sustained campaign of planned, collective action. We need to be prepared to act. Applying lessons from Chapter 6 on understanding community, most action to improve communities involves bonding social capital in building support with those in your community and bridging social capital when you build partnerships with persons that you do not know but who have common experiences and purposes. As suggested in Chapter 8's discussion of empowerment and citizen participation, seizing the day means speaking out and acting as a group of citizens and communities whenever possible.

**Taking the long view** recognizes that ongoing, long-term commitments needed to promote social and community change will take time and require persistence (Tseng et al., 2002). In a world of instant messaging, social media, and 24-hour news cycles, it is easy to conclude that nothing can be done about complex social or community problems that do not change quickly. However, this view misses a fundamental reality: Social change is occurring all around us, every day. Don Klein, a founder of community psychology in the United States, mused in a 1995 interview that when he began his career in the 1950s, it was inconceivable that someday smoking would be widely considered a health problem and banned in many public places. Yet that is today's reality (D. C. Klein, 1995). In the 1950s and 1960s in the United States, African American college students took practical steps to resist segregation and, together with others in their communities, conducted sit-ins, voter registration, and other actions of the civil rights movement, against violent opposition and seemingly insurmountable odds (J. Lewis, 1998). Although substantial changes have been achieved, such as political representation and integration of sports, cultural institutions, and social institutions, their highest aims have yet to be realized. In 2020, work to gain and protect equality for racial and ethnic minorities continues, addressing issues such as reforming a criminal justice system that disproportionately imprisons Black and Latinx men and women, confronting police brutality, working to end voter disenfranchisement and other actions that limit access to voting, and addressing social inequities associated with poorer health outcomes and earlier deaths for Native American men and women. In the long view, achievements must be recognized, but the work is never done.

Similarly, as we celebrate 100 years of women's suffrage in the United States in 2020, we are reminded that women's movements have spanned decades in their efforts to address injustice and create more opportunities for women. Scholars of modern women's movements in North America and Europe have described three waves of feminism dating back to the 1900s (Riger, 2017). The first wave focused heavily on the right to vote and saw the beginnings of legalization of contraceptives. Emerging in the late 1960s, a second wave of the movement sought to include more women of color and address social inequities in more nations, including domestic violence. Many shelters and community initiatives to address domestic violence and rape-crisis centers were organized by community leaders during this period. Similarly, the birth control pill, as well as many legal initiatives (e.g., Title IX and the Equal Rights Amendment in the United States), date back to this period. A third wave of the movement emerged in the 1990s that sought to address layers of oppression based on intersectional perspectives on gender, race, and class. While previous movements had accomplished some change, proponents of the third wave felt that a new approach was needed to challenge entrenched oppression for women (e.g., prevalence of sexual harassment, dismissing women's perspectives in legislation). The focus of change efforts expanded to challenge broader systems of oppression (e.g., marriage equality) while encouraging more examination of diversity of viewpoints of what well-being and freedom meant for women. A fourth wave of feminism may be emerging to directly challenge injustice and amplify women's voices with direct action through media sources. Long-held concerns about bodily autonomy and equal pay for equal work have not yet been adequately addressed. The #MeToo and #SayHerName movements have used social media to raise awareness about the injustices of sexual assault and police brutality against Black women but also to organize, resist, and compel policy makers to respond. Women's movements are transforming societies around the world, addressing rights to education, rights to health, self-determination, and freedom from violence. These and other examples illustrate that citizens' efforts to work for social change are pervasive and that their proponents need to be persistent. Recall the discussion in Chapter 13 of the social change that congregation members and community activists were doing all around the United States. Most communities have seasoned social change advocates that have developed social capital and experience that can be helpful in navigating when to seize the day and when to do the long-term preparatory work that prepares communities for quick action when opportunities arise.

## Community Psychologists' Readiness to Participate in Social Change

For community psychologists, being prepared to seize the day means being involved and active in the communities where they live (J. G. Kelly, 1970b). This viewpoint emphasizes the "participant" part of being a *participant–conceptualizer*. This includes building relationships with people involved in community change and supporting their efforts. When an opportunity to collaborate arises, community psychologists can offer their perspectives on change strategies, knowledge of effective programs, and research/evaluation skills to support the efforts of community leaders. Alternatively, community psychologists could get directly involved as citizens: participating in community organizations, addressing local issues, attending community events, and helping develop or organize local resources. Community psychologists can, through research and advocacy, offer their skills and position to call attention to the views and experiences of those who have less power and have been marginalized (S. D. Evans et al., 2017; Langhout, 2016; Rappaport, 1981). Seizing the day means speaking out and taking action, alongside citizens and organizations, at critical moments when the voices of citizens can shape change efforts.

Taking a long view on social change means planning for sustained involvement, long-term partnerships, and perseverance. It means learning the histories of communities and attempts to address the social concern; those histories influence the issues of the day (Tseng et al., 2002). It can benefit from understanding historical swings of perspective and power, which influence how social and community issues are addressed (Levine & Levine, 1992). Moreover, taking a long view on social change involves continuing commitment, perhaps for years, attending carefully to the process of that work, such as personal-emotional relationships and power dynamics (Case, 2017; J. G. Kelly, 1970b, 1990; Langhout, 2015; Primavera & Brodsky, 2004). It can mean making a commitment to helping communities build their capacity to address concerns. Taking the long view can mean devising, implementing, evaluating, and refining community interventions that can offer sound, scientific evidence of effectiveness in addressing clearly defined objectives. By doing that, we can provide empirically supported approaches that are not only tailored to local context but also more likely to weather the changes of social, political, and economic climates than interventions that have popular appeal but little efficacy. Finally, it means articulating core values in ways that sustain persons and communities through setbacks and challenges (J. G. Kelly, 2010; Tseng et al., 2002). In these ways, community psychologists can continue to pursue community and social transformation despite changes in the current social context.

## Personal Qualities That Are Helpful in Working for Community and Social Change

Soon after the outset of the field of community psychology, James G. Kelly (1971) described eight desirable personal qualities for the development of community psychologists. We have found that these qualities were also held by most of the effective community partners that we have worked with. As we describe an updated version of these qualities below, we encourage you to think about the qualities that you have already developed and those that are emerging for you:

- a clearly identified area of expertise

- creating an eco-identity

- valuing diversity and inclusion

- coping effectively with varied resources

- commitment to risk taking

- metabolic balance of patience and zeal

- giving away the spotlight

- emotional accountability in community work

These qualities remain an insightful, useful summary for today's community psychologists (Langhout, 2015). They are also a helpful guide for anyone involved in working for change in their communities. In many ways, they summarize several important themes of this book. We discuss these qualities as helping to shape the development of people interested in taking a community psychology approach to working for social change.

*A Clearly Identified Area of Expertise.* A community psychologist or a citizen leader must demonstrate skills and knowledge that will be useful to a change effort. It is critical that community partners recognize what your contribution can be to the effort. This is particularly relevant when one is joining an effort from outside the community. These contributions might be leadership skills such as community organizing and coalition building. They could involve someone skilled in communication or who has special knowledge of or experience with the issue. For citizens with specialized training and community psychologists, there are technical skills that may be critical for a change effort: participatory research; program evaluation; policy analysis; advocacy; grant writing; or proficiency as a consultant, workshop leader, or another role. Where possible, knowledge and skills can be developed with community members. That is, a community psychologist or citizen with special skills can share their expertise as a resource for the development of others and not simply serve as an expert.

***Creating an Eco-Identity.*** The work of community change involves immersing oneself in a community, identifying with it, and caring about it. It means understanding the ecology of the community: its resources, challenges, adaptation, patterns of interdependence, and histories. The understanding is both cognitive and emotional. This kind of emotional engagement with a community supports enduring commitment, deeper understanding, and respecting its members' choices.

***Valuing Diversity and Inclusion.*** This quality goes well beyond passive support for diversity to embracing diversity, promoting opportunities for inclusion, and working toward equity. As discussed in Chapter 7, it includes examining one's own biases and practicing cultural humility. It involves seeking out and relating to people who may be very different from oneself and understanding how those differences are resources for the community even when they involve conflict. It also involves understanding differences among community members and looking for ways to include a range of perspectives and resources in addressing community interests.

***Coping Effectively With Varied Resources.*** From a community psychology viewpoint, all community members are potential resources for change efforts and have resources, but these may not be visible in community life. It becomes essential for engaging others to identify their skills, knowledge, and other resources that have not been recognized by their peers and to draw on these while working together. For community psychologists, this also involves stepping out of the professional/expert role to collaborate with citizens as true partners, respecting their skills and insights.

***Commitment to Risk Taking.*** Seeking positive community change typically involves being an advocate for a cause or person. This often requires taking sides with a marginal or unpopular cause. It means standing with persons or groups with less power or less social capital against more powerful interests. It may involve risking failure, such as advocating a course of action before knowing whether it will succeed. This risk taking is not impulsive but a deliberate decision and an expression of one's values for the community.

***Metabolic Balance of Patience and Zeal.*** To remain engaged in a community, one needs to feel passionate about the values and goals of one's work but also to be patient with the time required for community change. Knowing when to speak out and when to be silent is an art to be learned, as is finding ways to sustain oneself through successes and failures. Recall the discussion of seizing the day and taking the long view earlier in this chapter. One key to maintaining a balance of patience and zeal is to seek out and nurture supportive

**affective ontology**
the emotional understanding of being human; considering what it means to be human and how that sentiment impacts one's knowledge and actions.

relationships with people who share the same goals. Together you can promote learning about the community and risk taking in one's work. That may involve a network of personal relationships or a community setting or group.

A second element of maintaining balance is cultivating an awareness of the emotions involved in community work (Case, 2017; Langhout, 2015). Videos of interviews with early community psychologists in the United States revealed their emotions that were not visible in their journal articles or books (J. G. Kelly, 2003). These included anger that propelled advocacy, pride and sense of personal connection with a community setting, joy when injustice was confronted, the excitement of finding like-minded allies, the ability to laugh about the ironies of community work, and a mixture of pride and loss when a community was ready to pursue its own future, saying goodbye to the psychologist. Emotions can express values, energize commitment, and strengthen community solidarity. Community psychology needs to be passionate because the work demands it. It also demands that we recognize our emotions, the self-care needed to process them, and the care for others needed in doing the work.

*Giving Away the Spotlight.* Most community change efforts will involve many people. The goals are to strengthen community resources, work with community partners, and accomplish positive community change. Seeking or basking in personal recognition interferes with the long-term pursuit of those goals. It is important to celebrate successes but also to share the credit.

*Emotional Accountability in Community Work.* Regina Langhout (2015) updated Kelly's discussion of personal qualities that are desirable in working toward social change. She observed that while these qualities described above are helpful in thinking about how to approach community-based work, the realities of doing the work require emotional engagement with the issues and the people. "This is necessary because in the face of exhausting events, it is love for the community, toughness, and risk taking that helps community psychologists to persevere" (Langhout, 2015, p. 268). She argued that we need to acknowledge and learn from our affective responses to community work. She referred to this as **affective ontology** of understanding what it is to be human, which has parallels to other schools of philosophy and politics regarding what is considered valid knowledge and how we make decisions. You may recall that we discussed Langhout (2015) and Fernández (2018b) addressing the emotional side of their work in Chapter 3. Emotions of fear, shame, anger, guilt, and anxiety often arise in conflicts and difficult work; this is to be expected because nearly every relationship has conflict. However, if we do not acknowledge and prepare for our emotional responses in community-based work, we may unintentionally impede that work. These negative emotions can end up preserving the status quo when they lead people to avoid addressing conflicts and pushing for change. Further, emotions can be manipulated in community conflict in ways that seek to silence dissent or prevent questioning the accountability of those in power. Courage to address conflict is viewed not as an impulsive act but as intentional action rooted in long-held values, relationships, and planned action. Similarly, more positive emotions can encourage action and can be celebrated, but under certain conditions, they may lead us to hold on to the status quo too long.

Langhout (2015) observed that our experiencing of emotions in community work is an indication that we are engaged in the work and that we need to honor our emotional responses. Recognizing emotions in our lives and those of our community partners (i.e., affective ontology) can be a tool for social change efforts (i.e., affective politics; D. B. Gould, 2009). Langhout argued that we need to analyze our emotional responses and use them for better understanding. Our emotions can serve as an index of whether our action is consistent with our values. Our ethical decisions cannot use competencies or values alone but must consider our emotional responses along with values, competencies, and standards in context of the larger issue (e.g., "Could I lose funding for the project by speaking out about social injustice? Will I lose friendships by taking this stand? How would my career by affected if I speak out?"). Case (2017) provided a thoughtful discussion of the need for reflexivity when navigating ethically important moments in projects with community members, particularly when the researcher has the potential to undermine the conduct of the study and/or the well-being of the participants. If a decision is unduly influenced by unacknowledged fear, it may not be consistent with your values and cause unintended harm.

Reflexivity in community psychology practice and research requires an acknowledgment of our emotions and a balancing of our values and professional and personal commitments. It can encourage us to take risks and to persevere when projects encounter difficulties. Acknowledgment of our affective life is required to build relationships with community partners and to sustain personal well-being. Langhout (2015) argued that community psychologists need to make visible their emotions for others to realize that this work takes heart. She also contended that we need to analyze our emotional responses and our social position in relationships with communities to be accountable.

## What Do You Think?

1. Which personal qualities valued by community psychologists in working toward social change apply to you and your aspirations for seeking social change?

2. How could you seize the day in your communities to work for change?

3. How could you use the wisdom of taking the long view to sustain your efforts to work for change?

4. Have you observed other personal qualities that are needed to work for change?

# Emerging Trends in Community Psychology

Now we consider emerging trends that are shaping the development of community psychology today. Commentators on contemporary life often remark on the tremendous changes taking place in many communities. One would expect that these changes will require responses and may change how community psychology thinks about itself and conducts its work. Some of these include the changing demographics all around the world, the increasing globalization in workplaces, growing social inequities in our communities, and the necessity of learning new technologies to navigate daily life. Furthermore, levels of conflict, expressions of intolerance, and violence appear to have increased. Some issues such as climate change, discrimination, and growing inequities appear overwhelming for any one individual to address. Efforts to counter the negative aspects of community changes can be hard and even disheartening. These transformations in our communities certainly present challenges and opportunities for community psychology in promoting well-being and social justice. We draw from the field of community psychology to help us navigate these challenges. As discussed in Chapters 1–3 and 7, a firm grounding in reflexive practice helps us examine our actions. As we build collaborations, community psychology values and ethics can help us make decisions about how to navigate these changes and where to dedicate our efforts. We argue that an increased use of community psychology paradigms and skills can help us understand how communities are changing. Community psychologists focus, to a greater extent than practitioners of other disciplines, on being linking agents: linking stakeholders, linking resources to address problems, linking research questions across levels of analyses, and linking research and action. In the next section, we consider broad trends among community psychologists who are navigating these changes.

## Broadening Commitment to Social Justice and Social Action

In community psychology, many trends are coalescing to bring increased energy to advocacy for social justice, liberation, and social transformation. As we discussed in Chapter 2, community psychology has long been concerned about conditions that are perceived as unjust or unfair (e.g., M. A. Bond et al., 2017; Langhout, 2015; Ryan, 1971). However, the field is building more sophisticated understandings of how social justice theory can inform its interventions. For example, considerations of social justice have been particularly important in choices of *with whom* prevention and health promotion interventions are conducted; these have emphasized a distributive justice concerned with access to resources and how community psychology interventions might be used to connect people with resources (Lykes, 2017; Rappaport, 1977b). Empowerment initiatives emphasize understandings of procedural justice focusing on (a) how interventions are carried out and (b) participation by persons who have often been left on the margins of society (Fondacaro & Weinberg, 2002; Rappaport, 1981). Social justice concerns have begun to be incorporated into evaluative criteria of scientific work by critical community psychologists (e.g., S. D. Evans et al., 2017; G. Nelson & Prilleltensky, 2010). From this perspective, the merit of science and intervention needs to reflect on assumptions about power and legitimacy of knowledge and action within the work. Critical community psychologists have pushed the field to examine these power assumptions in light of social justice values (e.g., distributive justice and procedural justice) rather than assuming that scientific discoveries are absolute truths that do not have implications for social justice.

The example of social psychologist and Jesuit priest Ignacio Martín-Baró's work in El Salvador has been influential in broadening social justice concerns of community psychology across the world. Martín-Baró worked to promote mental health and well-being by confronting oppression. He studied the psychosocial roots of civil war in 1980s El Salvador and the effects of overcrowding among poor Salvadorans (Portillo, 2012). Along with colleagues, he created radio programs to promote community development in rural areas. His efforts to address needs of persons living in poverty and social inequities of these conditions attracted attention of the government, which worked to curtail or stop such activities. Martín-Baró persuasively argued that an emphasis on social justice reminds us to identify oppressive conditions and work toward creating access to resources (material, social, and personal) for all citizens. Moreover, it requires an understanding of macrosystems, even global forces, and how they link to individuals' well-being. For example, he was very critical of how support from the United States for the government of El Salvador was fomenting violence and exacerbating poor social conditions and poor health for citizens in his country. He organized his thoughts about how psychology could be used to challenge oppression and named it *liberation psychology* (Martín-Baró, 1986). Martín-Baró's work also reminds us that this work can be courageous. By using psychology and advocacy to raise awareness of the needs of powerless Salvadorans, he challenged the power of the government and its supporters. He pursued this work even though his life had been threatened; paramilitary groups often threatened those who opposed the government and had a slogan: "Be a patriot, kill a priest" (Portillo, 2012, p. 81). Unfortunately, Martín-Baró was murdered in 1989 at the Universidad de CentroAmericana in San Salvador with five other scholar-priests, their housekeeper, and the housekeeper's daughter on account of their social activism (Portillo, 2012). However, the legacy of their work continues through the social justice, community-engaged efforts of many social-community psychologists.

A variety of social justice-informed interventions have been documented in community psychology articles and conferences. Common among these approaches are a commitment to work alongside those most harmed by inequities, to focus efforts on the psychosocial and political systems that do the most harm, and to engage in research and social action to promote equitable allocation of resources and control over decisions affecting one's life (S. D. Evans et al., 2017). For example, Lykes (2017) has written about her 30 years of involvement in liberatory action research with local communities in Guatemala, South Africa, Northern Ireland, and the United States. Working with Maya women as coresearchers, Lykes and colleagues (2003) created opportunities for the women to tell the stories of the human cost of armed conflict in villages across Guatemala. In producing a book with pictures and stories of loss and resistance, the research helped create legitimacy for their calls for justice, challenging the government's accounts and even generating some revenue for women involved through sales of the book. Community psychology researchers and practitioners have applied these concepts to address issues of economic hardship and homelessness (Israel & Toro, 2003; Shinn & McCormack, 2017). Such efforts have included increasing awareness of the psychological effects of economic inequities, working with homeless parents to empower them to speak out for their children's interests with schools, and creating ways for businesses and community groups to provide resources for homeless children.

As we have discussed throughout the text, renewing commitment to social justice can be seen in community psychology theory, research, and teaching. Community psychology theorists have drawn upon critical race theory (e.g., Hope et al., 2019; Langhout, 2016), feminist theory (Langhout, 2016; J. M. Silva and The Students for Diversity Now, 2018), decolonial studies (Cruz & Sonn, 2011; Dutta, 2018; Seedat & Suffla, 2017), and critical psychology (S. D. Evans et al., 2017; Prilleltensky & Nelson, 2009) to deepen understanding of how commitments to social justice change how we understand our work, which questions we ask, and how we can be accountable. These theorists challenge us to critically reflect on our position in doing research, the questions we ask, and whom we work alongside. Such reflexive examinations of social justice have informed research such as reexamining what is meant as racial justice (Sonn, 2018) or institutional and cultural discrimination (Hope et al., 2019). Recommitments to social justice using these self-critiques have also begun to influence how community psychology is taught and practiced: for example, by creating classrooms that engage perspectives of students who have been overlooked or marginalized to connect with material in more substantive ways and apply their learning to their concerns, such as campus activism (J. M. Silva and The Students for Diversity Now, 2018).

An emphasis on social justice in community psychology is not new, of course. Many community psychologists had dedicated themselves to working toward social justice through their community science. Consider the work of community psychologists who have been recognized as providing outstanding examples of using community psychology approaches to research and action to advance social justice.

## Examples of Innovative Social Justice Research and Practice

***Black Scholars Matter.*** As a graduate student, Dominique Thomas was concerned about the social climate for Black college students who studied at universities where most students were White. Although some scholarship had noted challenges for Black students, there was not a reliable measure of racial social climate that could be used to compare whether settings were more or less supportive, more or less stressful, or more or less challenging. Combining community psychology values of social justice and empiricism, Thomas designed a study that used qualitative and quantitative methods to understand the challenges faced by Black students and then developed a survey instrument to measure those challenges and campus racial climate, specifically for African American students. The resulting measure includes three subscales: Institutional Factors, Experiences and Perceptions, and Student Interracial Interactions (D. Thomas, 2018). Thomas's work is an exemplar of using community psychology perspectives and values. His rigorous methodology and careful attention to engaging research participants produced a measure that can help advance the field theoretically, provides a tool for action, and offers a guide for future research.

***Criminal Justice Responses to Sexual Assault.*** As we presented in the opening exercise of Chapter 1, criminal justice systems have overlooked, ignored, or been indifferent to the experiences of sexual assault, although the consequences of the crime can have long-term physical and psychological problems for the victim. This might include warehousing DNA evidence; it might be a prosecutor that refuses to try a case or an investigating officer who challenges the account of the victim who makes a report. However, research by Jessica Shaw and colleagues (2017) documented that most sexual assaults do not move from the investigation stage to the prosecution stage. If a case is judged to not have sufficient evidence, it disappears, to be stored in files or warehouses. But how can a determination be made about the evidence if it is never tested? Shaw questioned the justification for why investigations were routinely being dismissed without using the evidence. Although media reports and previous research suggested that law enforcement investigations vary in how thoroughly they investigate sexual assault, little was known about why so much evidence went untested. Shaw and colleagues analyzed the police records of 248 sexual assault cases chosen at random from the large number of untested, warehoused DNA evidence kits found in a police storage facility. Their careful analysis of records documents that law enforcement personnel drew upon traditional rape myths regarding what qualifies as "real" rape and who can be raped in order to justify their response to sexual assault. Furthermore, the researchers found that many instances where law enforcement justified inaction in an investigation because of rape myths that were focused on the behavior of the victim. Thus, the victim was blamed for law enforcement personnel's inaction in sexual assault case investigations. This research achieved national attention and led to efforts to develop protocols for testing evidence and for training investigators and efforts to increase accountability. Although the research has had a large impact, more work needs to be done to change systems to be more responsive and sensitive to victims and to prevent assaults.

Women's rights and sexual assault are among the many important issues that can be addressed through community social action.

# Challenges and Opportunities in Local-Global Connectedness

There is growing dialogue about the diversity of community psychology across the world. Over half of the members of professional community psychology organizations live outside the United States. Given community psychology's emphasis on understanding the ecology of settings (remember Chapter 5), it is not too surprising that different regions have emphasized different aspects of community psychology (e.g., social justice, social intervention, research). Different emphases in community-based research, action, and theory derive, in part, from the local realities that community psychologists face and the global challenges that are experienced in each locale.

As discussed in Chapter 2, the development of community psychology in each country has its own unique story. Some community psychologies have been aligned with providing alternatives to mental health systems while others are focused on changing social conditions and social action. This, also, is not surprising. We have found that different regions have different demands, different social conditions, and different resources to address them. Reviews of international community psychology suggest a diversity of approaches and intervention traditions that are tailored for the local ecologies of a region's communities. There is substantial overlap in core values of these community psychologies across countries, as well as a variety of emphases in community psychology research and action that are suited for local conditions (Reich et al., 2017). The development of community psychology around the world can be seen in the regular community psychology conferences that occur in Australia/New Zealand, Europe, Japan, and Latin America. There are community psychology textbooks and journals developed specifically for these different regions: Italian, Japanese, Portuguese, Latin American Spanish, European Spanish, and different English media for Australia, the British Isles, Canada, and the United States.

Within the United States and Canada, there is also growing awareness of the diversity of community psychology in different regions. In the last 15 years, the Society for Community Research and Action (SCRA), the professional organization for community psychologists in the United States and many in Canada, has created new working groups based on awareness of the diversity of interests among community psychologists, including the SCRA Task Force on Disaster, Community Readiness, and Recovery; Criminal Justice; Immigrant Justice; Indigenous Interest Group; Organization Studies; and Transformative Change in Community Mental Health. The focus of community psychology practitioners and researchers varies greatly by their location. Although the majority of community psychologists have focused on urban areas, there is awareness of the value of community psychology approaches to addressing problems of rural areas; slightly less than 20% of the U.S. population lives in

**community-diversity dialectic**
the discussion arising from the productive tension between two seemingly conflicting concepts that should be seen as interdependent and essential to community development.

rural areas (Census Bureau, n.d.). Rural community psychology interventions focus, to a greater extent, on barriers to participation in services, such as access to resources, less developed service systems, higher costs, and lack of transportation (Mulder et al., 1999). Development of internet resources has potential for overcoming some of these barriers (Ybarra & Eaton, 2005).

Community psychology journals increasingly contain culturally anchored research and interventions (Langhout & Thomas, 2010a). We have highlighted a number of these throughout this book. These trends in published work and in membership are examples of a growing trend in the field, in which community psychology is (belatedly) recognizing how its values and perspective can lead to including the voices of diverse persons in the field. Ten years after the founding of community psychology in the United States, the students and teachers were still primarily male and primarily White (Gridley & Turner, 2010; T. Moore, 1977). However, entering the third decade of the 21st century, many more women and persons of color have held leadership positions in professional organizations and in training programs. As with much of social change, it has been the participation of persons of color and women that has been instrumental in making these changes happen. Greater inclusion of diverse perspectives has had transformative effects on how community psychologists conduct research, collaborate with community members, design interventions, and conceptualize their work. Greater representation of the diversity of experiences and perspectives in community psychology is a work in progress.

As we observed in Chapter 7, attending to the values of diversity and community can require the need for new approaches to intervention and collaboration. Townley and colleagues have argued that a **community-diversity dialectic** forms a creative tension for the field that will be critical for its development in the next decade (Townley, 2017; Townley et al., 2011). Both concepts are needed to understand human communities and should be seen as being interdependent. Promoting community and promoting inclusion of diversity will likely require different levels of attention in different settings. It can be easy to privilege one over the other. This is a primary challenge for balancing local and global connectedness. For community psychology, it is important to foster genuine understanding and respect for (a) the many forms of human diversity and (b) the many challenges to human connection and belonging represented in sense of community. This may require a broader examination of what we mean by "community" (S. D. Evans et al., 2017). We need to conduct careful research to deepen that understanding of each; there is much to learn. At the same time, it is also important to articulate widely shared human ideals, and the particular ideals of community psychology, so that in relationships we can understand both ourselves and others.

As we argued in Chapter 2 about the development of community psychology, we all are affected by social forces, and the field of community psychology

**globalization**
the process of interaction and centralization among companies and governments across national boundaries by international trade, technology, and investment.

**indigenization**
the recognition of traditional values and communal bonds among members of native ethnic cultures and local communities.

continues to evolve. The prospects of globalization and increasing connectedness were touted in the late 1990s and early 2000s, particularly by businesses and neoliberal politicians. In the 2010s, the challenges of increased global connectedness continued to be addressed and neoliberal globalization became increasingly contested (S. D. Evans et al., 2017). Marsella (1998) proposed that a "global-community psychology" study the links between economic and political forces of globalization, the development and destruction of diverse cultures and local communities, and how these are related to the psychological functioning of families and individuals. In particular, he was concerned about the tension between two opposing viewpoints: "globalization from above and indigenization from below" (Marsella, 1998, p. 1284). Within his framework, **globalization** refers to the centralizing effects of market capitalism, advertising, mass media, and values of individualism and economic output. **Indigenization** refers to consciousness of traditional collective values and community bonds of indigenous ethnic cultures and local communities. Of course, there exists a diversity of local peoples, with a diversity of responses to the different aspects of globalization. Yet the interface of globalizing markets and traditional cultures does influence individual and community life across the world. Indigenous resistance to globalization has increased as local communities seek to conserve their identities and values. With an increased focus on social justice, critical scholarship, and reflexive practice, more community psychologists are reexamining their initiatives to work with individuals and communities addressing the tensions between indigenization and globalization.

Most contemporary globalization proponents have emphasized economic advantages of interdependent markets but have not developed many initiatives consistent with community psychology values, such as social justice, well-being, empowerment, and prevention (S. D. Evans et al., 2017; Reich et al., 2017). There is a need for community psychology's perspectives to recognize and promote the diversity of world cultures, seek to understand them on their own terms, and accept that Western psychological principles are only one form of psychology among many. Increased connectivity between distant parts of the world creates opportunities for community psychology to engage in dialogues and action that support social change. However, that poses several challenges for the field: increased understanding of the experiences of diverse peoples, even more participatory approaches to research, learning from community psychologists outside the United States, and careful consideration of how to apply core community psychology values in action.

*Decolonialism.* A broadened understanding of social justice for our current times has spawned debates about how community psychology's commitment to social justice can be renewed and updated. One particularly influential strand, decolonial scholarship, is shaping current developments in the field.

**decolonialism**
a process that requires conscious examination, acknowledgment, and undoing of unearned privilege resulting from historical and current inequality. It examines and challenges the patterns and hierarchies of power that were caused by colonialism, including how knowledge from various communities is produced and valued, as well as the limitations of our current knowledge.

We introduced this concept in Chapters 2 and 7 but present a more detailed discussion here. Led by many scholars and activists from the Global South, community psychologists around the world gathered in Durban, South Africa, in 2016 to question how we think about social justice in research, action, and teaching. Drawing from theory and critical scholarship, **decolonialism** is a "process of examining and undoing unearned privilege resulting from historical and present day injustice" (J. M. Silva and The Students for Diversity Now, n.d., p. 2). According to Dutta (2016), "a decolonial approach then involves striving toward a vision of human life that is not configured by the imposition of specific societal ideals (especially the genealogy of European intellectualism) over others" (p. 331). A decolonial approach in community psychology includes a reexamination of assumptions about how "to do" community psychology, how knowledge is produced, and what community partnerships can look like. In particular, our models for how to research, authority in decision making, and modes of helping were created in eras when countries, mostly from the Global North, claimed other countries as possessions to gather materials and benefit themselves. Colonies were normally not seen to be as advanced in science, medicine, manufacturing, arts, and structures of civil society, and the viewpoints of those living in the colonies were discounted. Colonizers considered it better to import modes of knowing and doing from the more "civilized" countries. Based in critical scholarship, decolonialism investigates "long-standing patterns of power that emerged as a result of colonialism, but that define culture, labor, intersubjective relations, and knowledge production well beyond the strict limits of colonial administrations" (Maldonado-Torres, 2007, p. 243). In many regions of the Global South, assumptions about how to do research has promoted vigorous debate about how knowledge is produced, whose knowledge is valued, and what the limits of our knowledge have been (Dutta, 2016).

For example, Sonn (2018) described a multiyear effort to create an alternative setting where immigrants from Africa living in an Australian city could gather and support each other when they encountered discrimination and exclusion. It is not surprising that, with higher rates of stress from racial discrimination, community conflict, and difficult living conditions, some immigrants developed physical and mental health problems and became more isolated. Rather than focusing on standard explanations from health professionals for these problems, community leaders created a setting to gather and actively engage African immigrants in creating art and self-expression. For some, this may seem like an unusual way to address people's economic or health needs, but from a decolonial perspective, it was important to create space for individuals who had been marginalized to express their views and experiences, connect with others, and identify resources that could address their needs. By creating opportunities for leadership and reciprocal helping, their participation in community life could give voice to their concerns that had been unheard by the social service system. Sonn played a role in facilitating critical dialogue with staff and government agencies about how their assumptions about services or the problems of African immigrants could be problematic. Service providers learned that they needed to listen more to the immigrants' perspectives to figure out how to be responsive to their needs. Sonn wanted to decenter the expectations of service providers from their own experiences so that they could learn about those of the immigrants. However, without creating an alternative setting, the immigrants would not have had the collective voice to advocate for a different view of their experience, their potential, and what they would find helpful. The conversations to take a new perspective were made possible by taking an empowering approach to engagement and challenging the dominant cultural understandings of why African immigrants had problems living in this Australian city. Perhaps not surprisingly, Sonn has also documented how engagement in these activities led to improvements in mental health and economic well-being.

Researchers are called to take account of how their positions of power and privilege shape how they view a research collaboration and to make these positions more transparent to have a more fruitful dialogue with community partners (Langhout, 2015). In terms of teaching, modes for engaging students are being considered that promote questioning. As a process, decolonial perspectives can push students to challenge their assumptions and discard their apathy to develop a sense of activism (Fernández, 2018a; J. M. Silva and The Students for Diversity Now, 2018). The emphases on understanding power, engaging in reflexive practice, and building relationships with stakeholders have commonalities with community psychology. In the coming years, we will be better able to assess the impact of decolonial scholarship on the ongoing development of community psychology.

## Collaborative and Participatory Research and Action

One of the most distinctive contributions of community psychology to the social sciences is the promotion of concepts and practical strategies for culturally anchored, truly collaborative action research that promotes genuine citizen participation in making decisions. Throughout this book, especially in Chapters 3, 8, and 13, we have highlighted examples of collaborative, participatory work (see also Jason et al., 2004; Lykes, 2017). Not all participatory-collaborative approaches are the same. Even within community psychology and closely related fields, approaches such as community coalitions, empowerment evaluation, participatory action research, and culturally anchored research are based on differing values and worldviews (Trickett & Espino, 2004). This diversity of ideals and practices provides many rich resources and options for promoting community collaboration and participation. It also provides the basis for many future conversations about their differences, strengths, and limitations as applied in real-life community contexts.

Since communities are diverse, it also is likely that different conceptions of collaboration and citizen participation will be useful in different communities.

Like the recent development of more sophisticated frameworks for advancing social justice in community psychology, more detailed frameworks are beginning to be articulated for collaborative approaches to research and action. For example, Schensul and Trickett (2009) pushed the field to consider how collaborative action can be conceptualized across levels of analysis. Langhout (2016) and Dutta (2016) pushed the field to learn from community partners rather than center its efforts on methodology and theory of standard research. While research can help identify the conditions under which different types of intervention may have greater effects, collaborative and participatory research processes can lead to knowledge and models of helping that are more sustainable for community partners. Further, intervention activities can be coordinated across levels of analysis to facilitate empowerment of collaborative partners. Models for collaboration and participatory action research are also being reexamined and adapted to fit the contexts of the projects (Langhout, 2016; Sonn, 2018). The application of collaborative and participatory methods with different populations will require adaptation and evaluation of methodological assumptions.

Langhout and Thomas (2010a) devoted a special issue of the *American Journal of Community Psychology* to the examination of how frameworks for participatory action research and collaboration need to be adapted to work with children. They suggest that several assumptions need to be reexamined to facilitate participatory action research with children: children's capabilities and likely expansion of expectations for children as social actors, the kinds of research deemed "appropriate" done with children if an understanding of their capabilities is expanded, and the epistemological frameworks used for learning about children's lives. Finally, limitations of participatory and collaborative methods will likely vary by context and need to be explicitly examined (Lykes, 2017). For children research partners, limitations will likely be encountered when considering the realities of the social structures in which they live, the time needed to build collaborative relationships, and the deeply embedded power and ethical issues that can converge when children are viewed as social actors in domains outside traditional children's settings (e.g., public policy deliberations).

A joint program of UC Berkeley and Clinica de Salud del Valle de Salinas provides an example of how participation needs to be a commitment from researchers and a partnership with youth. The university and clinic staff engaged a group of Latino youth in Salinas, California, who were concerned about chemical exposure in this farm worker community (Ramirez et al., n.d.). They helped form the CHAMACOS Youth Council to learn about issues of environmental health and justice. Through discussion and development of the youth council, the youth decided to conduct a research project about the potential exposure to chemicals through personal care products and cosmetics. This was not a standard youth project. The youth were concerned about family members and wanted answers. By adopting a participatory research approach, the UC Berkeley and Clinica de Salud staff talked with youth about the project and what they wanted to do. They talked about the training they would need to carry it out. It might have been easier for the staff to conduct such a research project themselves, but they were committed to a participatory process, so the youth council developed the project with staff support. To gain support for the project, the staff served as supervisors of the training and implementation. The youth council recruited 100 girls to participate in a study of the use of personal care products. They surveyed girls about their uses of personal care products and had participants use low-chemical alternatives for 3 days. By comparing urine samples collected before and after trying the alternative products, they found reductions of 25%–45% in harmful chemicals that have been associated with cancer and other health problems. The participation with the health clinic and university gave the youth some credibility in speaking about their findings. From a participatory perspective, the staff needed to be careful about letting the youth voices report the findings and advocate for change. The youth council decided to use these findings to educate other teens about chemicals in personal care products and look for ways to change policies.

Tebes (2018) notes that changes in the field, many of which were described in the previous sections, challenge the philosophical underpinnings of how we understand science as a method of knowledge production. He observes that science increasingly consists of interdisciplinary team-based research to address complex social, biomedical, public health, and global challenges. He refers to this movement as participatory team science that engages public stakeholders on science teams as coproducers of knowledge in contrast to traditional approaches to science that emphasize objectivity and maintaining separation from the research topic. Tebes questions the position of researchers as objective and separate from social phenomena, pointing out that researchers have values and biases and support broader community structures by focusing on some topics and avoiding others. Tebes does not view participatory approaches as a problem for science, although they can change timeframes and include different responsibilities for researchers to meaningfully include community partners. In Tebes's view, the coproduction of knowledge in team science can produce better understanding and can promote justice better than traditional models of supposedly objective science removed from public comment or accountability. His views are consistent with the role of a community psychologist as participant–conceptualizer, as discussed in Chapters 2 and 3.

The importance and usefulness of participatory approaches is also reflected in many fields (e.g., public health, anthropology, social work). Increasingly, it is expected that community members have active roles in research and intervention efforts in their communities. There is still a need for wider acceptance of the concept that community members have a central role to play throughout the action research cycle, from program conceptualization through implementation and evaluation, but progress has been made. In addition, there is growing awareness across disciplines that programs must be adapted to local contexts and that cookbook implementation of model programs is not an effective approach.

**What Do You Think?**

1. What are the biggest challenges you see for your community?
2. What resources do we have to address them? Think about tangible and intangible resources.
3. How will these challenges shape the ongoing development of community psychology?

# Becoming a Community Psychologist

### Careers Related to Community Psychology

It is an interesting paradox that there are many more jobs well suited for community psychologists' skills than there are positions advertised for community psychologists. Community psychology practice skills make students very competitive for many jobs. In *Diverse Careers in Community Psychology*, a recent book focused on career pathways taken by students who earned a community psychology degree, Viola and Glantsman (2017) reported on the experience of over 400 community psychologists. Their survey found that most persons with community-oriented degrees did not have a problem finding a job that valued their skills. For some, their first jobs were not those that they had envisioned when they began their studies. For others, their career paths took unexpected but very valued turns when they discovered opportunities to use their skills in new settings. McMahon and Wolfe (2017) suggested that job seekers need to become familiar with possible job titles, to be creative and open in their job searches, and to be prepared to educate potential employers about their training and job skills. They suggested that resumes should be customized to highlight community practice skills and experiences. Viola and Glantsman (2017) reported that more than half of the 400 community psychologists they surveyed found their jobs through networking, especially by focusing on community practice competencies rather than "marketing" their degrees. See Chapter 2 to review the community practice skill competencies that many graduate programs include in their training.

Training in community psychology typically provides a range of experiences and skills that prepare students for careers in practice settings as well as teaching in college and universities. These include smaller local community-based organizations and large national nonprofit organizations. It was estimated in 2010 that there were more than 1.6 million nonprofits in the United States (McMahon & Wolfe, 2017). The majority of these were in health care, education, and social welfare programs. Community psychologists may work designing programs to promote well-being or prevent problems. They may use their expertise to build local coalitions to implement programs or evaluate the reach, inclusion, and effectiveness of programs. Health care organizations also need employees with these skills; community psychologists work in hospital systems, health clinics, and government agencies monitoring health of community members. Educational systems were one of the earliest areas of emphasis for community psychologists, and many continue this work today. They can address a range of issues from parent engagement to preventing school bullying, addressing the needs of homeless students, and supporting pregnant and parenting teens. Many of these programs may be funded by charitable foundations that employ community psychologists to help design grants; build capacities of community members; or bring community members together to identify the needs, resources, and priorities in a community. Skills in research, evaluation, program development, policy making, and consultation are especially useful in working from the positions noted above. Many smaller agencies do not have employees with these areas of expertise and are interested in hiring consultants to help them meet the needs for accountability and reporting that their funders require. Community psychologists may start their own consultation business or consult as part of their current position. Finally, there are a large number of community psychologists working in a range of academic settings, from liberal arts colleges to state universities and large research universities. Some dedicate their careers to teaching, some to research. Most work outside the university using their community practice skills to collaborate with community partners. With an academic position as a starting point, many create unique combinations of service, teaching, and research.

In this book, we have presented many examples of roles for community psychologists that involve the core values of the field. It is important to note that a single community psychologist cannot act in every role, be an expert in every community psychology practice skill, or focus in equal depth on every value in every decision. We need to work together as a field and with community partners. Some might primarily pursue social justice, empowerment, and citizen participation. Others may primarily pursue promotion of wellness, prevention, and sense of community. Some may focus on building the empirical knowledge base for action while others involve themselves in community or wider social action itself. Through collaborations with other community psychologists, human service professionals, and citizens, more complete enactment of community psychology values and interventions can be realized.

As the variety of concepts and action approaches in this book indicates, we view community psychology as a big tent, bringing together psychologists, citizens, and others with shared values, but also with many ways of acting on those values in communities. That variety can be a strength. Its contradictions can foster discussions that deepen understanding. Another useful metaphor for the field of community psychology is a conversation, in which multiple views are articulated, considered, modified through consideration of other views, and developed over time. We seek to create space to exchange and hear diverse views and heed the advice of Rappaport's (1981) rule: "When everyone agrees with you, worry" (p. 3).

## Graduate Training in Community Psychology

After taking this course, some of you may be interested in specializing in community psychology. Of course, you do not need an advanced degree in community psychology to be involved in efforts to improve your community. But graduate training in community psychology can provide focused training in how you (a) assess problems and resources to address them; (b) choose, adapt, or develop interventions; and (c) evaluate evidence about the need for and the effectiveness of social interventions. For many professional positions in human services, policy, or government or for academic positions, an advanced degree is required. Similarly, an advanced degree is expected for those involved in research careers. To test your interest in a research career, it is possible to work as a research assistant as a student or after you have graduated. In fact, working in a research lab or in supervised community interventions is a good way to get experience for your graduate school applications.

Universities across the United States and Canada offer graduate training. A listing of community psychology training programs is periodically updated at the SCRA website (http://www.scra27.org/resources/educationc/academicpr). Master's programs typically take 2 years to complete for full-time students, although evening part-time courses are often available for those completing a degree while working a full-time job. PhD programs typically take 5–6 years to complete and place more emphasis on research. PsyD programs also take about 5 years to complete but have more of an emphasis on community psychology practice. In most programs, there is a combination of coursework, practice, and community placements to develop your skills. There is much diversity in the emphases and opportunities of community psychology training programs. It is important to find a good match for your interests. There are master and doctoral programs that emphasize training

## A Final Exercise: Where Will You Use Community Psychology?

To maintain its vitality and relevance, the field of community psychology needs new community partners, new activists, and new researchers. To *seize the day*, the field of community psychology needs to engage youth in our communities and their visions for change. To sustain campaigns for change, change efforts can benefit from engaging supportive elders who fought to create space to address concerns and have learned some hard lessons from past challenges (Langhout, 2015). It may not be easy to find a balance between the immediacy of the need for change and a commitment to sustained effort that draws upon a depth of collective experience, but doing so can generate unique solutions. The viewpoints of new generations can bring passion and a sense of immediacy to efforts to improve our communities because their concerns are often not tied to the traditions (and limitations) of past efforts. This is a strength: It promotes questioning assumptions, enables fresh perspectives and innovative practices to emerge, and helps focus on the issues of the day. At the same time, seasoned community leaders, if they are willing to listen and share their views in collaborative ways, can offer the wisdom of personal experience and growth over time. New lessons can be difficult to understand at first, but new awareness can emerge in the rough and tumble of community action and sustained partnerships that work through misunderstandings, opposition, painful experiences, and failure (Sarason, 2003b). In coming to understand the complexities of community and social life, all of us are students, including community psychologists. In our view, both the visions of youth and the wisdom of experience are too valuable to overlook.

As you pause at the end of this book, we encourage you to briefly reflect on what you have learned in this course and how it might be useful for you. Think about a specific domain of your life and the community-based challenges that you may encounter (e.g., family life/interpersonal relationships, home/neighborhood, work/school, health care). If you do not see challenges for yourself currently, what challenges do you observe as you move around your community? Choose one challenge to focus on and consider these questions:

- How do you define this challenge?
- What is your understanding at different ecological levels of analysis?
- How does taking a critical perspective about power and social regularities lead to new understandings of which change strategies you might choose?
- What resources are available for addressing this challenge?
- With whom would you collaborate to address this challenge?
- How would you choose and implement an intervention strategy?
- What type of change are you seeking to make?
- How would you decide whether the intervention was effective?
- What more do you want to know?

in clinical-community, social-community, and interdisciplinary approaches to community intervention, as well as community psychology-focused programs. In addition, training programs may specialize in addressing particular concerns (e.g., substance abuse, prevention of health problems, working with community coalitions) or the concerns of particular populations (e.g.,

iStock.com/franckreporter

Communities can create meaningful social change through multiple, collaborative approaches that are not just limited to public protests.

children, families, ethnic minorities, persons with disabilities). For doctoral study, the match between your interests and those of an advisor is particularly important. If you are considering graduate study of any type, we encourage you to talk with your professors to learn how you can better prepare for your applications.

## Concluding Thoughts

We hope that after working through the material presented in these chapters, you have a better understanding of community psychology. In particular, we expect that you have a greater appreciation of how individual, family, organizational, community, and societal levels of analysis are intertwined in the development of social issues. We hope that you have a willingness to consider the many sides of social issues, respecting the value of empirical inquiry and the perspectives of human diversity in understanding and addressing these issues. We imagine that many of you now have a greater awareness of your own values. Further, we hope that this book has played a role in preparing you to embrace opportunities for citizen engagement that can change your communities for the better. We came to community psychology because it engaged our minds, our values, and our lives. We hope that this book did that for you, too.

## For Review

## Discussion Questions

1. As discussed in Chapters 6 and 7, how does understanding diversity in communities inform your approach to working toward social change?

2. As discussed in Chapters 5 and 8, how does your understanding of settings, social regularities, power, and empowerment inform your approach to social change?

3. As discussed in Chapters 1, 3, 4, and 10–12, how would you balance community psychology values of social justice and empiricism when implementing a prevention program that could contribute to community change?

4. As discussed in Chapters 2, 9, and 13, which strategies will you choose to address your concerns? Will they be top-down, bottom-up, or both? Will they address a problem or promote a strength?

5. As discussed throughout the book, how will you assess the effectiveness of your efforts and whose voices are included?

## Key Terms

seizing the day, 483
taking the long view, 484
affective ontology, 489

community-diversity
 dialectic, 497
globalization, 498

indigenization, 498
decolonialism, 499

## Learn More

A detailed summary of the chapter, along with other review materials, is available on the *Community Psychology, Fourth Edition* companion website at http://pubs.apa.org/books/supp/kloos4/.

# REFERENCES

Aber, J. L. (2005, June). *Children's exposure to war and violence: Knowledge for action* [Keynote address]. Biennial Meeting of the Society for Community Research and Action, Champaign-Urbana, IL.

Aber, L., Butler, S., Danziger, S., Doar, R., Ellwood, D. T., Gueron, J. M., Haidt, J., Haskins, R., Holzer, H. J., Hymowitz, K., Mead, L., Mincy, R., Reeves, R. V., Strain, M. R., & Waldfogel, J. (2015). *Opportunity, responsibility, and security: A consensus plan for reducing poverty and restoring the American dream.* American Enterprise Institute / Brookings Working Group on Poverty and Opportunity. https://www.brookings.edu/wp-content/uploads/2016/07/Full-Report.pdf

Abraído-Lanza, A., Guier, C., & Colon, R. (1998). Psychological thriving among Latinas with chronic illness. *Journal of Social Issues, 54*(2), 405–424. https://doi.org/fnvcd3

Ackerman, P., & DuVall, J. (2000). *A force more powerful: A century of nonviolent conflict.* Palgrave.

Acosta, J., Chinman, M., Ebener, P., Malone, P. S., Paddock, S., Phillips, A., Scales, P., & Slaughter, M. E. (2013). An intervention to improve program implementation: Findings from a two-year cluster randomized trial of Assets-Getting To Outcomes. *Implementation Science, 8*(1), 87. https://doi.org/10.1186/1748-5908-8-87

Addams, J. (1910). *The spirit of youth and the city streets.* University of Illinois Press.

Aiyer, S. M., Zimmerman, M. A., Morrel-Samuels, S., & Reischl, T. M. (2015). From broken windows to busy streets: A community empowerment perspective. *Health Education & Behavior, 42*(2), 137–147. https://doi.org/10.1177/1090198114558590

Albee, G. W. (1959). *Mental health manpower trends.* Basic Books.

Albee, G. W. (1982). Preventing psychopathology and promoting human potential. *American Psychologist, 37*(9), 1043–1050. https://doi.org/10.1037/0003-066X.37.9.1043

Albee, G. W. (1996). [Untitled videotape interview]. In J. G. Kelly (Ed.), *The history of community psychology: A video presentation of context and exemplars.* Society for Community Research and Action. https://vimeo.com/69635912

Alexander, M. (2010). *The new Jim Crow: Mass incarceration in the age of colorblindness.* The New Press.

Alinsky, S. (1971). *Rules for radicals: A practical primer for realistic radicals.* Random House.

Allen, J., & Mohatt, G. V. (2014). Introduction to ecological description of a community intervention: Building prevention through collaborative field based research. *American Journal of Community Psychology, 54*(1–2), 83–90. https://doi.org/10.1007/s10464-014-9644-4

Allen, N. E. (2005). A multi-level analysis of community coordinating councils. *American Journal of Community Psychology, 35*(1–2), 49–63. https://doi.org/10.1007/s10464-005-1889-5

Allen, N. E., & Javdani, S. (2017). Toward a contextual analysis of violence: Employing community psychology to advance problem definition, solutions, and future directions. In M. A. Bond, I. Serrano-García, & C. B. Keys, (Eds.), *APA handbook of community psychology: Vol. 2. Methods for community research and action for diverse groups and issues* (pp. 327–343). American Psychological Association. https://doi.org/10.1037/14954-019

Allen, N. E., Todd, N., Anderson, C., Davis, S., Javdani, S., Bruehler, V., & Dorsey, H. (2013). Council-based approaches to intimate partner violence: Evidence for distal change in the system response. *American Journal of Community Psychology, 52*(1–2), 1–12. https://doi.org/10.1007/s10464-013-9572-8

Allen, N. E., Watt, K., & Hess, J. (2008). A qualitative study of the activities and outcomes of domestic violence coordinating councils. *American Journal of Community Psychology, 41*(1–2), 63–73. https://doi.org/10.1007/s10464-007-9149-5

Altschuld, J. (2010). *The needs assessment kit.* Sage.

American Anthropological Association. (1998, May 17). *Statement on "race."* http://www.aaanet.org/stmts/racepp.htm

American Psychological Association. (2006). *Report of the APA Task Force on Socioeconomic Status.* http://www.apa.org/pi/ses/resources/publications/task-force-2006.pdf

American Psychological Association. (2015). Guidelines for psychological practice with transgender and gender nonconforming people. *American Psychologist, 70*(9), 832–864. https://doi.org/10.1037/a0039906

American Psychological Association. (2017a). *Ethical principles of psychologists and code of conduct* (2002, amended effective June 1, 2010, and January 1, 2017). https://www.apa.org/ethics/code/index.aspx

American Psychological Association. (2017b). *Multicultural guidelines: An ecological approach to context, identity, and intersectionality.* https://www.apa.org/about/policy/multicultural-guidelines.pdf

Anderson, R. E., & Stevenson, H. C. (2019). RECASTing racial stress and trauma: Theorizing the healing potential of racial socialization in families. *American Psychologist, 74*(1), 63–75. https://doi.org/10.1037/amp0000392

Anderson, S., Currie, C. L., & Copeland, J. L. (2016). Sedentary behavior among adults: The role of community belonging. *Preventive Medicine Reports, 4,* 238–241. https://doi.org/10.1016/j.pmedr.2016.06.014

Angelique, H. L., & Culley, M. R. (2014). To Fukushima with love: Lessons on long-term antinuclear citizen participation from Three Mile Island. *Journal of Community Psychology, 42*(2), 209–227. https://doi.org/10.1002/jcop.21605

Angelique, H., & Mulvey, A. (2012). Feminist community psychology: The dynamic co-creation of identities in multilayered contexts. *Journal of Community Psychology, 40*(1), 1–10. https://doi.org/10.1002/jcop.20515

Angelique, H. L., Reischl, T. M., & Davidson, W. S., II. (2002). Promoting political empowerment: Evaluation of an intervention with university students. *American Journal of Community Psychology, 30*(6), 815–833. https://doi.org/10.1023/A:1020205119306

Appelbaum, P. S. (1999). Law & psychiatry: Least restrictive alternative revisited: Olmstead's uncertain mandate for community-based care. *Psychiatric Services, 50*(10), 1271–1280. https://doi.org/10.1176/ps.50.10.1271

Arao, B., & Clemens, K. (2013). From safe spaces to brave spaces: A new way to frame dialogue around diversity and social justice. In L. Landreman (Ed.), *The art of effective facilitation: Reflections from social justice educators* (pp. 135–150). Stylus.

Arnstein, S. R. (1969). A ladder of citizen participation. *Journal of the American Institute of Planners, 35*(4), 216–224. https://doi.org/10.1080/01944366908977225

Astuto, J., & Allen, L. (2009). Home visitation and young children: An approach worth investing in? *Social Policy Report, 23*(4), 1–24. https://doi.org/dvsb

Ayunerak, P., Alstrom, D., Moses, C., Charlie, J., Sr., & Rasmus, S. M. (2014). Yup'ik culture and context in Southwest Alaska: Community member perspectives of tradition, social change, and prevention. *American Journal of Community Psychology, 54*(1–2), 91–99. https://doi.org/10.1007/s10464-014-9652-4

Baker, E. (1970, December). *Developing community leadership.* https://americanstudies.yale.edu/sites/default/files/files/baker_leadership.pdf

Balcazar, F. E., Suarez-Balcazar, Y., & Taylor-Ritzman, T. (2009). Cultural competence: Development of a conceptual framework. *Disability and Rehabilitation, 31*(14), 1153–1160. https://doi.org/b4qvk7

Bandura, A. (1986). *Social foundations of thought and action: A social cognitive theory.* Prentice Hall.

Banks, S., Armstrong, A., Carter, K., Graham, H., Hayward, P., Henry, A., Holland, T., Holmes, C., Lee, A., McNulty, A., Moore, N., Nayling, N., Stokow, A., & Strachan, A. (2013). Everyday ethics in community-based participatory research. *Contemporary Social Science, 8*(3), 263–277. https://doi.org/10.1080/21582041. 2013.769618

Barker, R. (1968). *Ecological psychology.* Stanford University Press.

Barker, R., & Gump, P. (Eds.). (1964). *Big school, small school.* Stanford University Press.

Barr, S. M., Budge, S. L., & Adelson, J. L. (2016). Transgender community belongingness as a mediator between strength of transgender identity and well-being. *Journal of Counseling Psychology, 63*(1), 87–97. https://doi.org/10.1037/cou0000127

Barrera, M., Jr. (1986). Distinctions between social support concepts, measures, and models. *American Journal of Community Psychology, 14*(4), 413–445. https://doi.org/10.1007/BF00922627

Barrera, M., Jr. (2000). Social support research in community psychology. In J. Rappaport & E. Seidman (Eds.), *Handbook of community psychology* (pp. 215–245). Kluwer/Plenum. https://doi.org/10.1007/978-1-4615-4193-6_10

Barrera, M., Jr., Glasgow, R., McKay, H., Boles, S., & Feil, E. (2002). Do internet-based support interventions change perceptions of social support?: An experimental trial of approaches for supporting diabetes self-management. *American Journal of Community Psychology, 30*(5), 637–654. https://doi.org/10.1023/A:1016369114780

Barrera, M., Jr., Li, S. A., & Chassin, L. (1995). Effects of parental alcoholism and life stress on Hispanic and non-Hispanic Caucasian adolescents: A prospective study. *American Journal of Community Psychology, 23*(4), 479–507. https://doi.org/10.1007/BF02506965

Bartunek, J. M., & Keys, C. B. (1979). Participation in school decision making. *Urban Education, 14*(1), 52–75. https://doi.org/10.1177/0042085979141005

Bateman, H. V. (2002). Sense of community in the school. In A. Fisher, C. Sonn, & B. Bishop (Eds.), *Psychological sense of community: Research, applications, and implications* (pp. 161–179). Kluwer/Plenum. https://doi.org/10.1007/978-1-4615-0719-2_9

Bathum, M. E., & Baumann, L. (2007). A sense of community among immigrant Latinas. *Family & Community Health, 30*(3), 167–177. https://doi.org/10.1097/01.FCH.0000277760.24290.de

Battjes, R. J., & Pickens, R. W. (Eds.). (1988). *Needle sharing among intravenous drug abusers: National and international perspectives* (National Institute on Drug Abuse Research Monograph Series 80). National Institute on Drug Abuse. https://archives.drugabuse.gov/sites/default/files/monograph80.pdf

Baum, A., & Fleming, I. (1993). Implications of psychological research on stress and technological accidents. *American Psychologist, 48*(6), 665–672. https://doi.org/10.1037/0003-066X.48.6.665

Baumrind, D. (1991). Parenting styles and adolescent development. In R. M. Lerner, A. C. Peterson, & J. Brooks-Gunn (Eds.), *Encyclopedia of adolescence* (Vol. 11, pp. 746–758). Garland.

Belenky, M., Clinchy, B., Goldberger, N., & Tarule, J. (1986). *Women's ways of knowing: The development of self, voice, and mind.* Basic Books.

Belfield, C., Bowden, A. B., Klapp, A., Levin, H., Shand, R., & Zander, S. (2015). The economic value of social and emotional learning. *Journal of Benefit-Cost Analysis, 6*(3), 508–544. https://doi.org/10.1017/bca.2015.55

Belfield, C. R., Nores, M., Barnett, S., & Schweinhart, J. (2006). The High/Scope Perry Preschool Program: Cost-benefit analysis using data from the age-40 followup. *Journal of Human Resources, 41*(1), 162–190. https://doi.org/10.3368/jhr.XLI.1.162

Bell, J. (1995). *Understanding adultism: A key to developing positive youth-adult relationships.* The Freechild Project. https://www.nuatc.org/articles/pdf/understanding_adultism.pdf

Bellah, R., Madsen, R., Sullivan, W., Swidler, A., & Tipton, S. (1985). *Habits of the heart: Individualism and commitment in American life.* Harper & Row.

Bendezú, J. J., Pinderhughes, E. E., Hurley, S. M., McMahon, R. J., & Racz, S. J. (2018). Longitudinal relations among parental monitoring strategies, knowledge, and adolescent delinquency in a racially diverse at-risk sample. *Journal of Clinical Child & Adolescent Psychology, 47*(Suppl. 1), S21–S34. https://doi.org/10.1080/15374416.2016.1141358

Benjamin, L. T., Jr., & Crouse, E. M. (2002). The American Psychological Association's response to *Brown v. Board of Education*: The case of Kenneth B. Clark. *American Psychologist, 57*(1), 38–50. https://doi.org/10.1037/0003-066X.57.1.38

Bennett, C., Anderson, L., Cooper, S., Hassol, L., Klein, D., & Rosenblum, G. (1966). *Community psychology: A report of the Boston Conference on the Education of Psychologists for Community Mental Health*. Boston University.

Berger, P. L., & Neuhaus, R. J. (1977). *To empower people: The role of mediating structures in public policy*. American Enterprise Institute for Public Policy Research.

Berkowitz, B. (1987). *Local heroes*. Lexington Books.

Berkowitz, B. (1990). Who is being empowered? *Community Psychologist, 23*(3), 10–11.

Berkowitz, B. (1996). Personal and community sustainability. *American Journal of Community Psychology, 24*(4), 441–459. https://doi.org/10.1007/BF02506792

Berkowitz, B. (2000). Community and neighborhood organization. In J. Rappaport & E. Seidman (Eds.), *Handbook of community psychology* (pp. 331–357). Kluwer/Plenum. https://doi.org/10.1007/978-1-4615-4193-6_14

Bernard, J. (1973). *The sociology of community*. Scott, Foresman.

Berridge, V. (1996). *AIDS in the UK: The making of policy, 1981–1994*. Oxford University Press. https://doi.org/cb628q

Berry, J. W. (1970). Marginality, stress and ethnic identification in an acculturated Aboriginal community. *Journal of Cross-Cultural Psychology, 1*(3), 239–252. https://doi.org/cwbxff

Berry, J. W. (1994). An ecological perspective on cultural and ethnic psychology. In E. Trickett, R. Watts, & D. Birman (Eds.), *Human diversity: Perspectives on people in context* (pp. 115–141). Jossey-Bass.

Berry, J. W. (2003). Conceptual approaches to acculturation. In K. Chun, P. Organista, & G. Marin (Eds.), *Acculturation: Advances in theory, measurement and applied research* (pp. 17–37). American Psychological Association. https://doi.org/10.1037/10472-004

Berry, J. W., & Sam, D. L. (1997). Acculturation and adaptation. In J. W. Berry, M. Segall, & C. Kagitçibasi (Eds.), *Handbook of cross-cultural psychology*: Vol. 3. *Social behavior and applications* (pp. 291–326). Allyn & Bacon.

Berryhill, J. C., & Linney, J. A. (2006). On the edge of diversity: Bringing African Americans and Latinos together in a neighborhood group. *American Journal of Community Psychology, 37*(3–4), 155–156. https://doi.org/10.1007/s10464-006-9012-0

Bess, K. (2015). Reframing coalitions as systems interventions: A network study exploring the contribution of a youth violence prevention coalition to broader system capacity. *American Journal of Community Psychology, 55*(3–4), 381–395. https://doi.org/10.1007/s10464-015-9715-1

Bess, K., Fisher, A., Sonn, C., & Bishop, B. (2002). Psychological conceptions of community: Theory, research, and application. In A. Fisher, C. Sonn, & B. Bishop (Eds.), *Psychological sense of community: Research, applications and implications* (pp. 3–22). Kluwer/Plenum. https://doi.org/10.1007/978-1-4615-0719-2_1

Bess, K., Prilleltensky, I., Perkins, D., & Collins, L. (2009). Participatory organizational change in community-based health and human services: From tokenism to political engagement. *American Journal of Community Psychology, 43*(1–2), 134–148. https://doi.org/10.1007/s10464-008-9222-8

Betancourt, H., & López, S. R. (1993). The study of culture, ethnicity, and race in American psychology. *American Psychologist, 48*(6), 629–637. https://doi.org/10.1037/0003-066X.48.6.629

Beyers, J. M., Bates, J. E., Pettit, G. S., & Dodge, K. A. (2003). Neighborhood structure, parenting processes, and the development of youths' externalizing behaviors: A multilevel analysis. *American Journal of Community Psychology, 31*(1–2), 35–53. https://doi.org/10.1023/A:1023018502759

Bhana, A., Petersen, I., & Rochat, T. (2007). Community psychology in South Africa. In S. M. Reich, M. R. Riemer, I. Prilleltensky, & M. Montero (Eds.), *International community psychology: History and theories* (pp. 377–391). Springer. https://doi.org/10.1007/978-0-387-49500-2_21

Bierman, K., Cole, J. D., Dodge, K. A., Greenberg, M. T., Lochman, J. E., McMahon, R. J., & the Conduct Problems Prevention Research Group. (1997). Implementing a comprehensive program for the prevention of conduct problems in rural communities: The Fast Track experience. *American Journal of Community Psychology, 25*(4), 493–514. https://doi.org/10.1023/A:1024659622528

Biglan, A., Ary, D., Koehn, V., Levings, D., Smith, S., Wright, Z., James, L., & Henderson, J. (1996). Mobilizing positive reinforcement in communities to reduce youth access to tobacco. *American Journal of Community Psychology, 24*(5), 625–638. https://doi.org/10.1007/BF02509717

Binder, S. B., Baker, C. K., & Barile, J. P. (2015). Rebuild or relocate? Resilience and postdisaster decision-making after Hurricane Sandy. *American Journal of Community Psychology, 56*(1–2), 180–196. https://doi.org/10.1007/s10464-015-9727-x

Birman, D. (1994). Acculturation and human diversity in a multicultural society. In E. J. Trickett, R. J. Watts, & D. Birman (Eds.), *Human diversity: Perspectives on people in context* (pp. 261–283). Jossey-Bass.

Birman, D. (1998). Biculturalism and perceived competence of Latino immigrant adolescents. *American Journal of Community Psychology, 26*(3), 335–354. https://doi.org/10.1023/A:1022101219563

Birman, D., & Bray, E. (2017). Immigration, migration, and community psychology. In M. A. Bond, I. Serrano-García, & C. B. Keys, (Eds.), *APA handbook of community psychology: Vol. 2. Methods for community research and action for diverse groups and issues* (pp. 313–326). American Psychological Association. https://doi.org/10.1037/14954-018

Birman, D., Simon, C., Chan, W., & Tran, N. (2014). A life domains perspective on acculturation and psychological adjustment: A study of refugees from the former Soviet Union. *American Journal of Community Psychology, 53*(1–2), 60–72. https://doi.org/10.1007/s10464-013-9614-2

Birman, D., Trickett, E. J., & Buchanan, R. (2005). A tale of two cities: Replication of a study on the acculturation and adaptation of immigrant adolescents from the former Soviet Union in a different community context. *American Journal of Community Psychology, 35*(1–2), 83–101. https://doi.org/10.1007/s10464-005-1891-y

Birman, D., Trickett, E. J., & Vinokurov, A. (2002). Acculturation and adaptation of Soviet Jewish refugee adolescents: Predictors of adjustment across life domains. *American Journal of Community Psychology, 30*(5), 585–607. https://doi.org/10.1023/A:1016323213871

Bishop, B., Coakes, S., & D'Rozario, P. (2002). Sense of community in rural communities: A mixed methodological approach. In A. Fisher, C. Sonn, & B. Bishop (Eds.), *Psychological sense of community: Research, applications and implications* (pp. 271–290). Kluwer/Plenum. https://doi.org/10.1007/978-1-4615-0719-2_14

Black, S. (2007). Evaluation of the Olweus bullying prevention program: How the program can work for inner city youth. In D. L. White, B. C. Glenn, & A. Wimes (Eds.), *Proceedings of Persistently Safe Schools: The 2007 National Conference on Safe Schools* (pp. 25–36). Hamilton Fish Institute, George Washington University.

Blanchard, A., & Markus, L. (2004). The experienced "sense" of a virtual community: Characteristics and processes. *The Data Base for Advances in Information Systems, 35*(1), 64–79. https://doi.org/10.1145/968464.968470

Blight, M., Ruppel, E., & Schoenbauer, K. (2017). Sense of community on Twitter and Instagram: Exploring the roles of motives and parasocial relationships. *Cyberpsychology, Behavior, and Social Networking, 20*(5), 314–319. https://doi.org/10.1089/cyber.2016.0505

Bonanno, G. A. (2004). Loss, trauma, and human resilience: Have we underestimated the human capacity to thrive after extremely aversive events? *American Psychologist, 59*(1), 20–28. https://doi.org/10.1037/0003-066X.59.1.20

Bond, G., Witheridge, T., Dincin, J., Wasmer, D., Webb, J., & De Graaf-Kaser, R. (1990). Assertive community treatment for frequent users of psychiatric hospitals in a large city: A controlled study. *American Journal of Community Psychology*, *18*(6), 865–891. https://doi.org/10.1007/BF00938068

Bond, L. A., Belenky, M. F., & Weinstock, J. (2000). The Listening Partners program: An initiative toward feminist community psychology in action. *American Journal of Community Psychology*, *28*(5), 697–730. https://doi.org/10.1023/a:1005149821279

Bond, M. A. (1989). Ethical dilemmas in context: Some preliminary questions. *American Journal of Community Psychology*, *17*(3), 355–359. https://doi.org/10.1007/BF00931043

Bond, M. A. (1999). Gender, race, and class in organizational contexts. *American Journal of Community Psychology*, *27*(3), 327–355. https://doi.org/10.1023/A:1022229926119

Bond, M. A., & Harrell, S. P. (2006). Diversity challenges in community research and action: The story of a special issue of *AJCP*. *American Journal of Community Psychology*, *37*(3–4), 247–255. https://doi.org/10.1007/s10464-006-9013-z

Bond, M. A., Hill, J., Mulvey, A., & Terenzio, M. (Eds.). (2000a). Special issue part I: Feminism and community psychology. *American Journal of Community Psychology*, *28*(5).

Bond, M. A., Hill, J., Mulvey, A., & Terenzio, M. (Eds.). (2000b). Special issue part II: Feminism and community psychology. *American Journal of Community Psychology*, *28*(6).

Bond, M. A., & Keys, C. B. (1993). Empowerment, diversity, and collaboration: Promoting synergy on community boards. *American Journal of Community Psychology*, *21*(1), 37–57. https://doi.org/10.1007/BF00938206

Bond, M. A., Serrano-García, I., & Keys, C. B. (2017). Community psychology for the 21st century. In M. A. Bond, I. Serrano-García, C. B. Keys, & M. Shinn (Eds.), *APA handbook of community psychology: Vol. 1. Theoretical foundations, core concepts, and emerging challenges* (pp. 3–20). American Psychological Association. https://doi.org/10.1037/14953-001

Bond, M. A., & Wasco, S. (2017). Gender as context: A framework for understanding and addressing gendered qualities in settings. In M. A. Bond, I. Serrano-García, C. B. Keys, & M. Shinn (Eds.), *APA handbook of community psychology: Vol. 1. Theoretical foundations, core concepts, and emerging challenges* (pp. 369–385). American Psychological Association. https://doi.org/10.1037/14953-018

Borkman, T. (1990). Self-help groups at the turning point: Emerging egalitarian alliances with the formal health care system? *American Journal of Community Psychology*, *18*(2), 321–332. https://doi.org/10.1007/BF00931307

Borkman, T. (Ed.). (1991). Self-help groups [Special issue]. *American Journal of Community Psychology*, *19*(5).

Borkman, T., Karlsson, M., Munn-Giddings, C., & Smith, C. (2005). *Self-help organizations and mental health: Case studies*. Skondal Institute and University.

Borkman, T. J., Stunz, A., & Kaskutas, L. A. (2016). Developing an experiential definition of recovery: Participatory research with recovering substance abusers from multiple pathways. *Substance Use & Misuse*, *51*(9), 1116–1129. https://doi.org/10.3109/10826084.2016.1160119

Boulding, E. (2000). *Cultures of peace: The hidden side of history*. Syracuse University Press.

Boulding, K. (1989). *Three faces of power*. Sage.

Bourdieu, P. (1977). *Outline of a theory of practice* (R. Nice, Trans.). Cambridge University Press. https://doi.org/10.1017/CBO9780511812507 (Original work published 1972)

Boyd, N. M. (2015). Organization theory in community contexts. *Journal of Community Psychology*, *43*(6), 649–653. https://doi.org/10.1002/jcop.21767

Boyd, N. M., & Angelique, H. (2002). Rekindling the discourse: Organization studies in community psychology. *Journal of Community Psychology*, *30*(4), 325–348. https://doi.org/10.1002/jcop.10011

Boyd, N. M., & Nowell, B. (2017). Testing a theory of sense of community and community responsibility in organizations: An empirical assessment of predictive capacity on employee well-being and organizational citizenship. *Journal of Community Psychology, 45*(2), 210–229. https://doi.org/10.1002/jcop.21843

Boyd, N. M., Nowell, B., Yang, Z., & Hano, M. C. (2018). Sense of community, sense of community responsibility, and public service motivation as predictors of employee well-being and engagement in public service organizations. *American Review of Public Administration, 48*(5), 428–443. https://doi.org/10.1177/0275074017692875

Bozick, R., Steele, J., Davis, L., & Turner, S. (2018). Does providing inmates with education improve postrelease outcomes? A meta-analysis of correctional education programs in the United States. *Journal of Experimental Criminology, 14*(3), 389–428. https://doi.org/10.1007/s11292-018-9334-6

Bradford, H. D. (2001). What went wrong with public housing in Chicago? A history of the Robert Taylor Homes. *Journal of the Illinois State Historical Society, 94*(1), 96–123.

Bradley, R., & Corwyn, R. (2002). Socioeconomic status and child development. *Annual Review of Psychology, 53*, 371–399. https://doi.org/10.1146/annurev.psych.53.100901.135233

Brady, L., Fryberg, S., & Shoda, Y. (2018). Expanding the interpretive power of psychological science by attending to culture. *Proceedings of the National Academy of Sciences, 115*(45), 11406–11413. https://doi.org/10.1073/pnas.1803526115

Braveman, P., Cubbin, C., Egerter, S., Williams, D., & Pamuk, E. (2010). Socioeconomic disparities in health in the United States: What the patterns tell us. *American Journal of Public Health, 100*(Suppl. 1), S186–S196. https://doi.org/10.2105/AJPH.2009.166082

Brewer, M. (1997). The social psychology of intergroup relations: Can research inform practice? *Journal of Social Issues, 53*(1), 197–211. https://doi.org/fmhxqd

Bringle, R., & Hatcher, J. (2002). Campus-community partnerships: The terms of engagement. *Journal of Social Issues, 58*(3), 503–516. https://doi.org/10.1111/1540-4560.00273

Brodsky, A. (1996). Resilient single mothers in risky neighborhoods: Negative psychological sense of community. *Journal of Community Psychology, 24*(4), 347–363. https://doi.org/dxhd75

Brodsky, A. (2000). The role of religion in the lives of resilient, urban, African American, single mothers. *Journal of Community Psychology, 28*(2), 199–219. https://doi.org/cjwn3h

Brodsky, A. (2003). *With all our strength: The revolutionary association of the women of Afghanistan.* Routledge.

Brodsky, A. (2009). Multiple psychological senses of community in Afghan context: Exploring commitment and sacrifice in an underground resistance community. *American Journal of Community Psychology, 44*(3–4), 176–187. https://doi.org/10.1007/s10464-009-9274-4

Brodsky, A., & Cattaneo, L. B. (2013). A transconceptual model of empowerment and resilience: Divergence, convergence and interactions in kindred community concepts. *American Journal of Community Psychology, 52*(3–4), 333–346. https://doi.org/10.1007/s10464-013-9599-x

Brodsky, A., & Faryal, T. (2006). No matter how hard you try, your feet still get wet: Insider and outsider perspectives. *American Journal of Community Psychology, 37*(3–4), 191–201. https://doi.org/10.1007/s10464-006-9015-x

Brodsky, A., Loomis, C., & Marx, C. (2002). Expanding the conceptualization of PSOC. In A. Fisher, C. Sonn, & B. Bishop (Eds.), *Psychological sense of community: Research, applications and implications* (pp. 319–336). Kluwer/Plenum. https://doi.org/10.1007/978-1-4615-0719-2_16

Brodsky, A., Mannarini, T., Buckingham, S., & Scheibler, J. (2017). Kindred spirits in scientific revolution: Qualitative methods in community psychology. In M. A. Bond, I. Serrano-García, & C. B. Keys, (Eds.), *APA handbook of community psychology: Vol. 2. Methods for community research and action for diverse groups and issues* (pp. 75–90). American Psychological Association. https://doi.org/10.1037/14954-005

Bronfenbrenner, U. (1979). *The ecology of human development: Experiments by nature and design.* Harvard University Press.

Brown, C. H., Guo, J., Singer, L. T., Downes, K., & Brinales, J. (2007). Examining the effects of school-based drug prevention programs on drug use in rural settings: Methodology and initial findings. *Journal of Rural Health, 23*(s1), 29–36. https://doi.org/fwrf4s

Brown, L. D., Feinberg, M. E., & Greenberg, M. T. (2010). Determinants of community coalition ability to support evidence-based programs. *Prevention Science, 11*(3), 287–297. https://doi.org/10.1007/s11121-010-0173-6

Brown, L. D., Shepherd, M. D., Merkle, E. C., Wituk, S. A., & Meisson, G. (2008). Understanding how participation in a consumer-run organization relates to recovery. *American Journal of Community Psychology, 42*(1–2), 167–178. https://doi.org/10.1007/s10464-008-9184-x

Brown v. Board of Education, 347 U.S. 483 (1954). https://www.oyez.org/cases/1940-1955/347us483

Buck, J. (2017). Retention remedy: Building a sense of community through appreciative inquiry. *Nursing Management, 48*(4), 9–12. https://doi.org/dqvk

Buckingham, S. L., Brodsky, A. E., Rochira, A., Fedi, A., Mannarini, T., Emery, L., Godsay, S., Miglietta, A., & Gattino, S. (2018). Shared communities: A multinational qualitative study of immigrant and receiving community members. *American Journal of Community Psychology, 62*(1–2), 23–40. https://doi.org/10.1002/ajcp.12255

Bullock, H. (2017). The widening economic divide: Economic disparities and classism as critical community context. In M. A. Bond, I. Serrano-García, C. B. Keys, & M. Shinn (Eds.), *APA handbook of community psychology: Vol. 1. Theoretical foundations, core concepts, and emerging challenges* (pp. 353–368). American Psychological Association. https://doi.org/10.1037/14953-017

Bullock, H., Wyche, K., & Williams, W. (2001). Media images of the poor. *Journal of Social Issues, 57*(2), 229–246. https://doi.org/10.1111/0022-4537.00210

Bulsara, M., Wood, L., Giles-Corti, B., & Bosch, D. (2007). More than a furry companion: The ripple effect of companion animals on neighborhood interactions and sense of community. *Society & Animals, 15*(1), 43–56. https://doi.org/10.1163/156853007X169333

Bureau of Justice Statistics. (2019). *Prisoners in 2017.* http://www.bjs.gov/index.cfm?ty=pbdetail&iid=6546

Bureau of Labor Statistics. (2016, January 15). *Women's earnings 83 percent of men's, but vary by occupation.* U.S. Department of Labor. https://www.bls.gov/opub/ted/2016/womens-earnings-83-percent-of-mens-but-vary-by-occupation.htm

Burlew, A. K. (2003). Research with ethnic minorities: Conceptual, methodological, and analytical issues. In G. Bernal, J. Trimble, A. K. Burlew, & F. Leong (Eds.), *Handbook of racial and ethnic minority psychology* (pp. 179–197). Sage. https://doi.org/10.4135/9781412976008.n9

Butterfoss, F. D. (2007). *Coalitions and partnerships in community health.* Jossey-Bass.

Bybee, D., & Sullivan, C. (2002). The process through which an advocacy intervention resulted in positive change for battered women over time. *American Journal of Community Psychology, 30*(1), 103–132. https://doi.org/10.1023/A:1014376202459

Caldwell, C. H., Kohn-Wood, L. P., Schmeelk-Cone, K. H., Chavous, T. M., & Zimmerman, M. A. (2004). Racial discrimination and racial identity as risk or protective factors for violent behaviors in African American young adults. *American Journal of Community Psychology, 33*(1–2), 91–105. https://doi.org/bq7hwm

Camic, P., Rhodes, J., & Yardley, L. (Eds.). (2003). *Qualitative research in psychology: Expanding perspectives in methodology and design.* American Psychological Association. https://doi.org/10.1037/10595-000

Campbell, R. (2016). "It's the way that you do it": Developing an ethical framework for community psychology research and action. *American Journal of Community Psychology, 58*(3–4), 294–302. https://doi.org/10.1002/ajcp.12037

Campbell, R., & Morris, M. (2017a). Complicating narratives: Defining and deconstructing ethical challenges in community psychology. *American Journal of Community Psychology*, *60*(3–4), 491–501. https://doi.org/10.1002/ajcp.12177

Campbell, R., & Morris, M. (2017b). The stories we tell: Introduction to the special issue on ethical challenges in community psychology research and practice. *American Journal of Community Psychology*, *60*(3–4), 299–301. https://doi.org/10.1002/ajcp.12178

Campbell, R., Patterson, D., & Bybee, D. (2011). Using mixed methods to evaluate a community intervention for sexual assault survivors: A methodological tale. *Violence Against Women*, *17*(3), 376–388. https://doi.org/10.1177/1077801211398622

Campbell, R., Shaw, J., & Gregory, K. (2017). Giving voice—And the numbers, too: Mixed methods research in community psychology. In M. A. Bond, I. Serrano-García, & C. B. Keys, (Eds.), *APA handbook of community psychology: Vol. 2. Methods for community research and action for diverse groups and issues* (pp. 139–153). American Psychological Association. https://doi.org/10.1037/14954-009

Campbell, R., & Wasco, S. (2000). Feminist approaches to social science: Epistemological and methodological tenets. *American Journal of Community Psychology*, *28*(6), 773–791. https://doi.org/10.1023/A:1005159716099

Campbell, W., Hester, R. K., Lenberg, K. L., & Delaney, H. D. (2016). Overcoming addictions, a web-based application, and SMART Recovery, an online and in-person mutual help group for problem drinkers, part 2: Six-month outcomes of a randomized controlled trial and qualitative feedback from participants. *Journal of Medical Internet Research*, *18*(10), e262. https://doi.org/10.2196/jmir.5508

Caplan, G. (1961). *An approach to community mental health*. Grune and Stratton.

Caplan, G. (1964). *Principles of preventive psychiatry*. Basic Books.

Caplan, N., & Nelson, S. (1973). On being useful: The nature and consequences of psychological research on social problems. *American Psychologist*, *28*(3), 199–211. https://doi.org/10.1037/h0034433

Carli, L. L. (1999). Gender, interpersonal power, and social influence. *Journal of Social Issues*, *55*(1), 81–99. https://doi.org/10.1111/0022-4537.00106

Carli, L. L. (2001). Gender and social influence. *Journal of Social Issues*, *57*(4), 725–741. https://doi.org/10.1111/0022-4537.00238

Carling, P. J. (1995). *Return to community: Building support systems for people with psychiatric disabilities*. Guilford Press.

Carrera, J., Key, K., Bailey, S., Hamm, J., Cuthbertson, C., Lewis, E., Woolford, S., DeLoney, E., Greene-Moton, E., Wallace, K., Robinson, D., Byers, I., Piechowski, P., Evans, L., McKay, A., Vereen, D., Sparks, A., & Calhoun, K. (2019). Community science as a pathway for resilience in response to a public health crisis in Flint, Michigan. *Social Sciences*, *8*(3), 94. https://doi.org/10.3390/socsci8030094

Casale, M., Cluver, L., Crankshaw, T., Kuo, C., Lachman, J., & Wild, L. (2015). Direct and indirect effects of caregiver social support on adolescent psychological outcomes in two South African AIDS-affected communities. *American Journal of Community Psychology*, *55*(3–4), 336–346. https://doi.org/10.1007/s10464-015-9705-3

Case, A. D. (2014). *More than meets the eye: Exploring a Black cultural center as a counterspace for African American college students* [Doctoral dissertation, University of Illinois at Urbana-Champaign]. Illinois Digital Environment for Access to Learning and Scholarship. http://hdl.handle.net/2142/50395

Case, A. D. (2017). Reflexivity in counterspaces fieldwork. *American Journal of Community Psychology*, *60*(3–4), 398–405. https://doi.org/10.1002/ajcp.12196

Case, A. D., Eagle, D. E., Yao, J., & Proeschold-Bell, R. J. (2018). Disentangling race and socioeconomic status in health disparities research: An examination of Black and White clergy. *Journal of Racial and Ethnic Health Disparities*, *5*(5), 1014–1022. https://doi.org/10.1007/s40615-017-0449-7

Case, A. D., & Hunter, C. D. (2012). Counterspaces: A unit of analysis for understanding the role of settings in marginalized individuals' adaptive responses to oppression. *American Journal of Community Psychology*, *50*(1–2), 257–270. https://doi.org/10.1007/s10464-012-9497-7

Case, A. D., & Hunter, C. D. (2014). Counterspaces and the narrative identity work of offender-labeled African American youth. *Journal of Community Psychology*, *42*(8), 907–923. https://doi.org/10.1002/jcop.21661

Case, A. D., Todd, N. R., & Kral, M. J. (2014). Ethnography in community psychology: Promises and tensions. *American Journal of Community Psychology*, *54*(1–2), 60–71. https://doi.org/10.1007/s10464-014-9648-0

Castro, F. G., Barrera, M., Jr., & Martinez, C. R., Jr. (2004). The cultural adaptation of prevention interventions: Resolving tensions between fidelity and fit. *Prevention Science*, *5*(1), 41–45. https://doi.org/fpttwq

Catalano, R. F., Hawkins, J. D., Berglund, M. L., Pollard, J. A., & Arthur, M. W. (2002). Prevention science and positive youth development: Competitive or cooperative frameworks? *Journal of Adolescent Health*, *31*(6), 230–239. https://doi.org/fq2sx3

Cattaneo, L. B., Calton, J. M., & Brodsky, A. (2014). Status quo versus status quake: Putting the power back in empowerment. *Journal of Community Psychology*, *42*(4), 433–446. https://doi.org/10.1002/jcop.21619

Caughey, M. O., O'Campo, P., & Brodsky, A. (1999). Neighborhoods, families, and children: Implications for policy and practice. *Journal of Community Psychology*, *27*(5), 615–633. https://doi.org/cq43d4

Census Bureau. (n.d.). *Rural America*. https://gis-portal.data.census.gov/arcgis/apps/MapSeries/index.html?appid=7a41374f6b03456e9d138cb014711e01

Census Bureau. (2017). *American Community Survey demographic and housing estimates: 2017* [Table]. U.S. Department of Commerce. https://data.census.gov/cedsci/table?d=ACS%205-Year%20Estimates%20Data%20Profiles&table=DP05&tid=ACSDP5Y2017.DP05

Census Bureau. (2018, September 12) *Income and poverty in the United States: 2017*. U.S. Department of Commerce. https://www.census.gov/library/publications/2018/demo/p60-263.html

Census Bureau. (2020, April 6). *Historical poverty tables: People and families–1959 to 2018*. U.S. Department of Commerce. https://www.census.gov/data/tables/time-series/demo/income-poverty/historical-poverty-people.html

Center for Substance Abuse Prevention. (1998). *Preventing substance abuse among children and adolescents: Family-centered approaches. Prevention Enhancement Protocol System (PEPS)* (DHHS Publication No. SMA 3223). U.S. Government Printing Office.

Center on Budget and Policy Priorities. (2018). *A guide to statistics on historical trends in income inequality*. https://www.cbpp.org/research/poverty-and-inequality/a-guide-to-statistics-on-historical-trends-in-income-inequality

Centers for Disease Control and Prevention. (n.d.). *U.S. Public Health Service study at Tuskegee*. https://www.cdc.gov/tuskegee/timeline.htm

Centers for Disease Control and Prevention. (1982a, June 18). A cluster of Kaposi's sarcoma and pneumocystis carinii pneumonia among homosexual male residents of Los Angeles and Orange counties, California. *Morbidity and Mortality Weekly Report*, *31*(23), 305–307.

Centers for Disease Control and Prevention. (1982b, September 24). Current trends update on acquired immune deficiency syndrome (AIDS)—United States. *Morbidity and Mortality Weekly Report*, *31*(37), 507–508, 513–514.

Centers for Disease Control and Prevention. (2019a). *Centers for Disease Control and Prevention HIV prevention progress report, 2019*. https://www.cdc.gov/hiv/pdf/policies/progressreports/cdc-hiv-preventionprogressreport.pdf

Centers for Disease Control and Prevention. (2019b). *Compendium of evidence-based interventions and best practices for HIV prevention*. https://www.cdc.gov/hiv/research/interventionresearch/compendium/rr/complete.html

Central Intelligence Agency. (n.d.). The *world factbook: Distribution of family income—GINI index*. https://www.cia.gov/library/publications/the-world-factbook/rankorder/2172rank.html

Chamberlin, J. (1978). *On our own: Patient-controlled alternatives to the mental health system*. McGraw-Hill.

Chan, W. Y., Cattaneo, L. B., Mak, W. W. S., & Lin, W.-Y. (2017). From moment to movement: Empowerment and resilience as a framework for collective action in Hong Kong. *American Journal of Community Psychology*, *59*(1–2), 120–132. https://doi.org/10.1002/ajcp.12130

Chang, T., Yeh, C. J., & Krumboltz, J. D. (2001). Process and outcome evaluation of an on-line support group for Asian American male college students. *Journal of Counseling Psychology*, *48*(3), 319–329. https://doi.org/10.1037/0022-0167.48.3.319

Chavis, D. M. (2001). The paradoxes and promise of community coalitions. *American Journal of Community Psychology*, *29*(2), 309–320. https://doi.org/10.1023/A:1010343100379

Chavis, D. M., & Wandersman, A. (1990). Sense of community in the urban environment: A catalyst for participation and community development. *American Journal of Community Psychology*, *18*(1), 55–81. https://doi.org/10.1007/BF00922689

Chelimsky, E. (1997). The coming transformation in evaluation. In E. Chilemsky & W. Shadish (Eds.), *Evaluation for the 21st century: A handbook* (pp. 1–26). Sage. https://doi.org/10.4135/9781483348896.n1

Cheng, S.-T., Chan, A. C. M., & Phillips, D. R. (2004). Quality of life in old age: An investigation of well older persons in Hong Kong. *Journal of Community Psychology*, *32*(3), 309–326. https://doi.org/10.1002/jcop.20003

Cheng, S.-T., & Heller, K. (2009). Global aging: Challenges for community psychology. *American Journal of Community Psychology*, *44*(1–2), 161–173. https://doi.org/10.1007/s10464-009-9244-x

Cherniss, C., & Deegan, G. (2000). The creation of alternative settings. In J. Rappaport & E. Seidman (Eds.), *Handbook of community psychology* (pp. 359–377). Kluwer/Plenum. https://doi.org/10.1007/978-1-4615-4193-6_15

Chetty, R., Grusky, D., Hell, M., Hendren, N., Manuca, R., & Narang, J. (2017). The fading American dream: Trends in absolute income mobility since 1940. *Science*, *356*(6336), 398–406. https://doi.org/10.1126/science.aal4617

Chetty, R., Stepner, M., Abraham, S., Lin, S., Scuderi, B., Turner, N., Bergeron, A., & Culler, D. (2016). The association between income and life expectancy in the United States, 2001–2014. *Journal of the American Medical Association*, *315*(16), 1750–1766. https://doi.org/10.1001/jama.2016.4226

Chinman, M., Acosta, J., Ebener, P., Driver, J., Keith, J., & Peebles, D. (2013). Enhancing quality interventions promoting healthy sexuality (EQUIPS): A novel application of translational research methods. *Clinical and Translational Science*, *6*(3), 232–237. https://doi.org/10.1111/cts.12031

Chinman, M., Acosta, J., Ebener, P., Malone, P. S., & Slaughter, M. E. (2016). Can implementation support help community-based settings better deliver evidence-based sexual health promotion programs? A randomized trial of Getting To Outcomes. *Implementation Science*, *11*(1), 78. https://doi.org/dwgf

Chinman, M., Acosta, J., Ebener, P., Malone, P. S., & Slaughter, M. E. (2018). A cluster-randomized trial of Getting To Outcomes' impact on sexual health outcomes in community-based settings. *Prevention Science*, *19*(4), 437–448. https://doi.org/10.1007/s11121-017-0845-6

Chinman, M., Acosta, J. D., Ebener, P., Sigel, C., & Keith, J. (2016). *Getting To Outcomes: A guide for teen pregnancy prevention*. RAND Corporation. https://doi.org/10.7249/TL199

Chinman, M., Hunter, S. B., Ebener, P., Paddock, S. M., Stillman, L., Imm, P., & Wandersman, A. (2008). The Getting To Outcomes demonstration and evaluation: An illustration of the prevention support system. *American Journal of Community Psychology*, *41*(3–4), 206–224. https://doi.org/10.1007/s10464-008-9163-2

Chinman, M., Imm, P., & Wandersman, A. (2004). *Getting To Outcomes 2004: Promoting accountability through methods and tools for planning, implementation, and evaluation*. RAND Corporation.

Chinman, M., Kloos, B., O'Connell, M., & Davidson, L. (2002). Service providers' views of psychiatric mutual support groups. *Journal of Community Psychology, 30*(4), 349–366. https://doi.org/10.1002/jcop.10010

Chinman, M., Tremain, B., Imm, P., & Wandersman, A. (2009). Strengthening prevention performance using technology: A formative evaluation of interactive Getting To Outcomes. *American Journal of Orthopsychiatry, 79*(4), 469–481. https://doi.org/10.1037/a0016705

Chipuer, H. M., & Pretty, G. M. H. (1999). A review of the Sense of Community Index: Current uses, factor structure, reliability, and further development. *Journal of Community Psychology, 27*(6), 643–658. https://doi.org/b86hj3

Chirowodza, A., van Rooyen, H., Joseph, P., Sikotoyi, S., Richter, L., & Coates, T. (2009). Using participatory methods and geographic information systems to prepare for an HIV community-based trial in Vulindela, South Africa. *Journal of Community Psychology, 37*(1), 41–57. https://doi.org/10.1002/jcop.20294

Christens, B. D. (2012). Toward relational empowerment. *American Journal of Community Psychology, 50*(1–2), 114–128. https://doi.org/10.1007/s10464-011-9483-5

Christens, B. D. (2019). *Community power and empowerment.* Oxford University Press. https://doi.org/10.1093/oso/9780190605582.001.0001

Christens, B. D., Connell, C. M., Faust, V., Haber, M. G., & the Council of Education Programs. (2015). Progress report: Competencies for community research and action. *Community Psychologist, 48*(4), 3–9.

Christens, B. D., Hanlin, C. E., & Speer, P. W. (2007). Getting the social organism thinking: Strategy for systems change. *American Journal of Community Psychology, 39*(3–4), 229–238. https://doi.org/10.1007/s10464-007-9119-y

Christens, B. D., Inzeo, P. T., & Faust, V. (2014). Channeling power across ecological systems: Social regularities in community organizing. *American Journal of Community Psychology, 53*(3–4), 419–431. https://doi.org/10.1007/s10464-013-9620-4

Christie, C., Baker, C., Cooper, R., Kennedy, P. J., Madras, B., & Bondi, P. (2017). *The president's commission on combating drug addiction and the opioid crisis* [Final report]. The President's Commission on Combating Drug Addiction and the Opioid Crisis.

Cicchetti, D., & Lynch, M. (1993). Toward an ecological/transactional model of community violence and child maltreatment: Consequences for children's development. *Psychiatry, 56*, 96–118. https://doi.org/10.1080/00332747.1993.11024624

Cicchetti, D., Rappaport, J., Sandler, I., & Weissberg, R. P. (2000). *The promotion of wellness in children and adolescents.* Child Welfare League of America.

Clark, D. (2004). *Stonewall: The riots that sparked the gay revolution.* St. Martin's Press.

Clark, K. (Ed.). (1953). Desegregation: An appraisal of the evidence [Special issue]. *Journal of Social Issues, 9*(4).

Clark, K., Chein, I., & Cook, S. (2004). The effects of segregation and the consequences of desegregation: A (September 1952) social science statement in the *Brown v. Board of Education of Topeka* supreme court case. American Psychologist, 59(6), 495–501. https://doi.org/10.1037/0003-066X.59.6.495 (Reprinted from "The effects of segregation and the consequences of desegregation" [Appendix to the appellants' briefs in *Brown v. Board of Education of Topeka, Kansas*; *Briggs v. Elliot*; and *Davis v. Prince Edward County, Virginia*. Signed by 29 other social scientists], September 22, 1952)

Clark, R., Anderson, N. B., Clark, V. R., & Williams, D. R. (1999). Racism as a stressor for African Americans: A biopsychosocial model. *American Psychologist, 54*(10), 805–816. https://doi.org/df7srj

Clark, S. (1986). *Ready from within: Septima Clark and the civil rights movement.* Wild Trees Press.

Cleveland, R. (2018). *A study of White racial identity development, meaning, experience, and expression in elite, White males* [Doctoral dissertation, George Washington University]. George Washington ScholarSpace. https://scholarspace.library.gwu.edu/etd/c821gk02r

Coalition for Community Living. (n.d.). *Fairweather Lodge—Frequently asked questions*. Retrieved December 16, 2019, from https://www.theccl.org/Fairweather-Lodge

Cochran, J. C., Siennick, S. E., & Mears, D. P. (2018). Social exclusion and parental incarceration impacts on adolescents' networks and school engagement. *Journal of Marriage and the Family*, *80*(2), 478–498. https://doi.org/10.1111/jomf.12464

Cohen, S. (2004). Social relationships and health. *American Psychologist*, *59*(8), 676–684. https://doi.org/dxbvbz

Colby, A., & Damon, W. (1992). *Some do care: Contemporary lives of moral commitment*. Free Press.

Cole, E. R. (2009). Intersectionality and research in psychology. *American Psychologist*, *64*(3), 170–180. https://doi.org/10.1037/a0014564

Coleman, J., & Hoffer, T. (1987). *Public and private schools: The impact of communities*. Basic Books.

Collaborative for Academic, Social, and Emotional Learning. (2006). *Cossitt School case study*. https://web.archive.org/web/20100705223217/http://www.casel.org/downloads/cossitt_casestudy.pdf

Collier-Thomas, B., & Franklin, V. P. (Eds.). (2001). *Sisters in the struggle: African American women in the civil rights–Black power movement*. NYU Press.

Collins, C., Neal, J., & Neal, Z. (2014). Transforming individual civic engagement into community collective efficacy: The role of bonding social capital. *American Journal of Community Psychology*, *54*(3–4), 328–336. https://doi.org/10.1007/s10464-014-9675-x

Collins, F. S., & Mansoura, M. K. (2001). The human genome project: Revealing the shared inheritance of all humankind. *Cancer*, *91*(Suppl. 1), 221–225. https://doi.org/bmxsm9

Collins, S. E., Clifasefi, S. L., Stanton, J., the LEAP Advisory Board, Straits, K. J. E., Gil-Kashiwabara, E., Rodriguez Espinosa, P., Nicasio, A. V., Andrasik, M. P., Hawes, S. M., Miller, K. A., Nelson, L. A., Orfaly, V. E., Duran, B. M., & Wallerstein, N. (2018). Community-based participatory research (CBPR): Towards equitable involvement of community in psychology research. *American Psychologist*, *73*(7), 884–898. https://doi.org/10.1037/amp0000167

Comas-Díaz, L., Lykes, M. B., & Alarcón, R. (1998). Ethnic conflict and the psychology of liberation in Guatemala, Peru, and Puerto Rico. *American Psychologist*, *53*(7), 778–792. https://doi.org/10.1037/0003-066x.53.7.778

Condron, D. J. (2009). Social class, school and non-school environments, and Black/White inequalities in children's learning. *American Sociological Review*, *74*(5), 685–708. https://doi.org/d7wmp6

Connor-Smith, J. K., & Flachsbart, C. (2007). Relations between personality and coping: A meta-analysis. *Journal of Personality and Social Psychology*, *93*(6), 1080–1107. https://doi.org/frf2r2

Cooke, B., & Kothari, U. (2001). *Participation: The new tyranny?* Zed Books.

Cope, M. R., Currit, A., Flaherty, J., & Brown, R. B. (2016). Making sense of community action and voluntary participation—A multilevel test of multilevel hypotheses: Do communities act? *Rural Sociology*, *81*(1), 3–34. https://doi.org/10.1111/ruso.12085

Coppens, N., Page, R., & Thou, T. (2006). Reflections on the evaluation of a Cambodian youth dance program. *American Journal of Community Psychology*, *37*(3–4), 175–182. https://doi.org/10.1007/s10464-006-9018-7

Corcoran, J., & Pillai, V. K. (2007). Effectiveness of secondary pregnancy prevention programs: A meta-analysis. *Research on Social Work Practice*, *17*(1), 5–18. https://doi.org/cj3q7k

Cornell Empowerment Group. (1989). Empowerment and family support. *Networking Bulletin*, *1*, 1–23.

Cortés, D. E., Rogler, L. H., & Malgady, R. G. (1994). Biculturality among Puerto Rican adults in the United States. *American Journal of Community Psychology*, *22*(5), 685–706. https://doi.org/10.1007/BF02506900

Coulton, C., Korbin, J., Chan, T., & Su, M. (2001). Mapping residents' perceptions of neighborhood boundaries: A methodological note. *American Journal of Community Psychology*, *29*(2), 371–383. https://doi.org/10.1023/A:1010303419034

Cowen, E. L. (1973). Social and community interventions. *Annual Review of Psychology*, *24*, 423–472. https://doi.org/10.1146/annurev.ps.24.020173.002231

Cowen, E. L. (1991). In pursuit of wellness. *American Psychologist*, *46*(4), 404–408. https://doi.org/10.1037/0003-066X.46.4.404

Cowen, E. L. (1994). The enhancement of psychological wellness: Challenges and opportunities. *American Journal of Community Psychology*, *22*(2), 149–179. https://doi.org/chqb7j

Cowen, E. L. (2000a). Community psychology and routes to psychological wellness. In J. Rappaport & E. Seidman (Eds.), *Handbook of community psychology* (pp. 79–99). Kluwer/Plenum. https://doi.org/10.1007/978-1-4615-4193-6_4

Cowen, E. L. (2000b). Prevention, wellness enhancement, Y2K and thereafter. *Journal of Primary Prevention*, *21*(1), 15–19. https://doi.org/10.1023/A:1007041011360

Cowen, E. L. (2000c). Psychological wellness: Some hopes for the future. In D. Cicchetti, J. Rappaport, I. N. Sandler, & R. P. Weissberg (Eds.), *The promotion of wellness in children and adolescents* (pp. 477–503). Child Welfare League of America Press.

Cowen, E. L., & Kilmer, R. (2002). "Positive psychology": Some plusses and some open issues. *Journal of Community Psychology*, *30*(4), 449–460. https://doi.org/10.1002/jcop.10014

Cowen, E. L., McKim, B. J., & Weissberg, R. P. (1981). Bartenders as informal, interpersonal help-agents. *American Journal of Community Psychology*, *9*(6), 715–729. https://doi.org/10.1007/BF00896251

Cowen, E. L., Pedersen, A., Babigian, H., Izzo, L. D., & Trost, M. A. (1973). Long-term follow-up of early detected vulnerable children. *Journal of Consulting and Clinical Psychology*, *41*(3), 438–446. https://doi.org/10.1037/h0035373

Crenshaw, K. (1989). (1989). Demarginalizing the intersection of race and sex: A Black feminist critique of antidiscrimination doctrine, feminist theory and antiracist politics. *University of Chicago Legal Forum*, *1989*(1), Article 8. https://chicagounbound.uchicago.edu/cgi/viewcontent.cgi?article=1052&context=uclf

Creswell, J., & Creswell, D. (2018). *Research design: Qualitative, quantitative, and mixed methods approaches* (5th ed.). Sage.

Crimp, D. (2011, December 6). Before Occupy: How AIDS activists seized control of the FDA in 1988. *The Atlantic*. https://www.theatlantic.com/health/archive/2011/12/before-occupy-how-aids-activists-seized-control-of-the-fda-in-1988/249302/

Crosby, F. J., Iyer, A., Clayton, S., & Downing, R. A. (2003). Affirmative action: Psychological data and the policy debates. *American Psychologist*, *58*(2), 93–115. https://doi.org/10.1037/0003-066X.58.2.93

Cruz, M. R., & Sonn, C. C. (2011). (De)colonizing culture in community psychology: Reflections from critical social science. *American Journal of Community Psychology*, *47*(1–2), 203–214. https://doi.org/10.1007/s10464-010-9378-x

Cubbin, C., Kim, Y., Vohra-Gupta, S., & Margerison, C. (2020). Longitudinal measures of neighborhood poverty and income inequality are associated with adverse birth outcomes in Texas. *Social Science & Medicine*, *245*, 112665. https://doi.org/10.1016/j.socscimed.2019.112665

Culley, M. R., & Hughey, J. (2008). Power and public participation in a hazardous waste dispute: A community case study. *American Journal of Community Psychology*, *41*(1–2), 99–114. https://doi.org/10.1007/s10464-007-9157-5

Dalton, D. (1993). *Mahatma Gandhi: Nonviolent power in action*. Columbia University Press.

Dalton, J. H., & Wolfe, S. M. (2012). Competencies for community practice. *Community Psychologist*, *45*(4), 7–14.

Dan, A., Campbell, R., Riger, S., & Strobel, M. (2003). Feminist panel: Discussing "Psychology constructs the female." In J. G. Kelly (producer, director), *Exemplars of community psychology* [DVD set]. Society for Community Research and Action.

Dane, A. V., & Schneider, B. (1998). Program integrity in primary and early secondary prevention: Are implementation effects out of control? *Clinical Psychology Review, 18*(1), 23–45. https://doi.org/b7m38p

Danzer, A. M., & Danzer, N. (2016). The long-run consequences of Chernobyl: Evidence on subjective well-being, mental health and welfare. *Journal of Public Economics, 135*, 47–60. https://doi.org/10.1016/j.jpubeco.2016.01.001

DARE. (2008). *2008 annual report.*

Das, J. K., Salam, R. A., Arshad, A., Finkelstein, Y., & Bhutta, Z. A. (2016). Interventions for adolescent substance abuse: An overview of systematic reviews. *Journal of Adolescent Health, 59*(4)(Suppl.), S61–S75. https://doi.org/f88gbg

D'Augelli, A. R. (1994). Lesbian and gay male development: Steps toward an analysis of lesbians' and gay men's lives. In B. Greene & G. Herek (Eds.), *Contemporary perspectives in gay and lesbian psychology* (Vol. 1, pp. 118–132). Sage. https://doi.org/10.4135/9781483326757.n7

D'Augelli, A. R. (2006). Coming out, visibility, and creating change: Empowering lesbian, gay, and bisexual people in a rural university community. *American Journal of Community Psychology, 37*(3–4), 365–376. https://doi.org/10.1007/s10464-006-9043-6

David, E. J. R., Schroeder, T. M., & Fernandez, J. (2019). Internalized racism: A systematic review of the psychological literature on racism's most insidious consequence. *Journal of Social Issues, 75*(4), 1057–1086. https://doi.org/10.1111/josi.12350

De Groot, J. I. (2018). *Environmental psychology: An introduction.* John Wiley & Sons.

den Boer, P. C. A. M., Wiersma, D., & van den Bosch, R. J. (2004). Why is self-help neglected in the treatment of emotional disorders? A meta-analysis. *Psychological Medicine, 34*(6), 959–971. https://doi.org/10.1017/S003329170300179X

Denzin, N. K., & Lincoln, Y. S. (Eds.). (1994). *Handbook of qualitative research.* Sage Publications.

Department of Agriculture. (2019, April). *Official USDA food plans: Cost of food at home at four levels, U.S. average, March 2019.* https://fns-prod.azureedge.net/sites/default/files/media/file/CostofFoodMar2019.pdf

Department of Health and Human Services. (2010). *To live to see the great day that dawns: Preventing suicide by American Indian and Alaska Native youth and young adults.* DHHS Publication SMA (10)-4480, CMHS-NSPL-0196, Center for Mental Health Services, Substance Abuse and Mental Health Services Administration.

Department of Health and Human Services. (2017). *Maternal, infant, and early childhood home visiting program: Partnering with parents to help children succeed.* https://mchb.hrsa.gov/sites/default/files/mchb/MaternalChildHealthInitiatives/HomeVisiting/pdf/programbrief.pdf

Department of Housing and Urban Development. (n.d.). *HUD's Public Housing Program.* http://portal.hud.gov/portal/page/portal/HUD/topics/rental_assistance/phprog

Department of Housing and Urban Development. (2018). *2018 annual homeless assessment report to Congress.* https://files.hudexchange.info/resources/documents/2018-AHAR-Part-1.pdf

Department of Housing and Urban Development. (2019). *Fair market rates.* https://www.huduser.gov/portal/datasets/fmr/fmrs/FY2019_code/select_Geography.odn

Derzon, J. H., Sale, E., Springer, J. F., & Brounstein, P. (2005). Estimating intervention effectiveness: Synthetic projection of field evaluation results. *Journal of Primary Prevention, 26*(4), 321–343. https://doi.org/b88s9p

DeWolfe, D. J. (2000). *Training manual for mental health and human services workers in major disasters* (2nd ed.). U.S. Department of Health and Human Services.

Dinh, K. T., & Bond, M. A. (2008). The other side of acculturation: Changes among host individuals and communities in their adaptation to immigrant populations. *American Journal of Community Psychology, 42*(3–4), 283–285. https://doi.org/10.1007/s10464-008-9200-1

Dockett, K. H. (1999, June). *Engaged Buddhism and community psychology: Partners in social change* [Presentation]. Biennial Meeting of the Society for Community Research and Action, New Haven, CT.

Dockett, K. H. (2003). Buddhist empowerment: Individual, organizational, and societal transformation. In K. H. Dockett, G. R. Dudley-Grant, & C. P. Bankart (Eds.), *Psychology and Buddhism: From individual to global community* (pp. 173–196). Kluwer Academic/Plenum.

Dockett, K. H., Dudley-Grant, G. R., & Bankart, C. P. (2003). *Psychology and Buddhism: From individual to global community*. Kluwer Academic/Plenum.

Dohrenwend, B. S. (1978). Social stress and community psychology. *American Journal of Community Psychology*, 6(1), 1–14. https://doi.org/10.1007/BF00890095

Dokecki, P. R., Newbrough, J. R., & O'Gorman, R. T. (2001). Toward a community-oriented action research framework for spirituality: Community psychological and theological perspectives. *Journal of Community Psychology*, 29(5), 497–518. https://doi.org/10.1002/jcop.1033

Domlyn, A. M., & Wandersman, A. (2019). Community coalition readiness for implementing something new: Using a Delphi methodology. *Journal of Community Psychology*, 47(4), 882–897. https://doi.org/10.1002/jcop.22161

Doogan, N. J., Light, J. M., Stevens, E. B., & Jason, L. A. (2019). Quality of life as a predictor of social relationships in Oxford House. *Journal of Substance Abuse Treatment*, 101, 79–87. https://doi.org/10.1016/j.jsat.2019.03.006

Du Bois, W. E. B. (1986). The souls of black folk. In N. Huggins (Ed.), *W. E. B. Du Bois: Writings* (pp. 357–548). Library of America. (Original work published 1903)

DuBois, D. L. (2017). Prevention and promotion: Toward an improved framework for research and action. In M. A. Bond, I. Serrano-García, & C. B Keys (Eds.), *APA handbook of community psychology: Vol. 1. Methods for community research and action for diverse groups and issues* (pp. 233–252). American Psychological Association.

DuBois, D. L., Holloway, B. E., Valentine, J. C., & Cooper, H. (2002). Effectiveness of mentoring programs for youth: A meta-analytic review. *American Journal of Community Psychology*, 30(2), 157–197. https://doi.org/10.1023/A:1014628810714

DuBois, D. L., & Karcher, M. J. (2005). Youth mentoring: Theory, research, and practice. In D. L. DuBois & M. J. Karcher (Eds.), *Handbook of youth mentoring* (pp. 2–12). Sage Publications. https://doi.org/10.4135/9781412976664.n1

DuBois, D. L., & Silverthorn, N. (2005). Natural mentoring relationships and adolescent health: Evidence from a national study. *American Journal of Public Health*, 95(3), 518–524. https://doi.org/10.2105/AJPH.2003.031476

DuBois, D. L., Silverthorn, N., Pryce, J., Reeves, E., Sánchez, B., Silva, A., Ansu, A. A., Haqq, S., & Takehara, J. (2008). Mentorship: The GirlPower! program. In C. W. LeCroy & J. E. Mann (Eds.), *Handbook of preventive and intervention programs for adolescent girls* (pp. 326–365). Wiley. https://doi.org/10.1002/9781118269848.ch11

Dudgeon, P., Mallard, J., Oxenham, D., & Fielder, J. (2002). Contemporary Aboriginal perceptions of community. In A. Fisher, C. Sonn, & B. Bishop (Eds.), *Psychological sense of community: Research, applications and implications* (pp. 247–267). Kluwer/Plenum. https://doi.org/10.1007/978-1-4615-0719-2_13

Dudley Street Neighborhood Initiative. (n.d.). *DSNI historic timeline*. Retrieved December 16, 2019, from https://www.dsni.org/s/DSNI-Historic-Timeline-56ea.pdf

DuMont, K., Mitchell-Herzfeld, S., Greene, R., Lee, E., Lowenfels, A., Rodriguez, M., & Dorabawila, V. (2008). Healthy Families New York (HFNY) randomized trial: Effects on early child abuse and neglect. *Child Abuse & Neglect*, 32(3), 295–315. https://doi.org/10.1016/j.chiabu.2007.07.007

Duncan, T. E., Duncan, S. C., Okut, H., Strycker, L. A., & Hix-Small, H. (2003). A multilevel contextual model of neighborhood collective efficacy. *American Journal of Community Psychology*, 32(3–4), 245–252. https://doi.org/cqtdbg

Dupéré, V., & Perkins, D. D. (2007). Community types and mental health: A multilevel study of local environmental stress and coping. *American Journal of Community Psychology, 39*(1–2), 107–119. https://doi.org/10.1007/s10464-007-9099-y

Durkheim, É. (1993). *The division of labor in society* (G. Simpson, Trans.). Free Press. (Original work published 1893)

Durlak, J. A., & DuPre, E. P. (2008). Implementation matters: A review of research on the influence of implementation on program outcomes and the factors affecting implementation. *American Journal of Community Psychology, 41*(3–4), 327–350. https://doi.org/gqg

Durlak, J. A., & Wells, A. M. (1997). Primary prevention mental health programs for children and adolescents: A meta-analytic review. *American Journal of Community Psychology, 25*(2), 115–152. https://doi.org/10.1023/A:1024654026646

Durlak, J. A., & Wells, A. M. (1998). Evaluation of indicated preventive intervention (secondary prevention) mental health programs for children and adolescents. *American Journal of Community Psychology, 26*(5), 775–802. https://doi.org/10.1023/A:1022162015815

Dutta, U. (2016). Prioritizing the local in an era of globalization: A proposal for decentering community psychology. *American Journal of Community Psychology, 58*(3–4), 329–338. https://doi.org/10.1002/ajcp.12047

Dutta, U. (2017). Creating inclusive identity narratives through participatory action research. *Journal of Community & Applied Social Psychology, 27*(6), 476–488. https://doi.org/10.1002/casp.2328

Dutta, U. (2018). Decolonizing "community" in community psychology. *American Journal of Community Psychology, 62*(3–4), 272–282. https://doi.org/10.1002/ajcp.12281

Dyson, M. P., Hartling, L., Shulhan, J., Chisholm, A., Milne, A., Sundar, P., Scott, S. D., & Newton, A. S. (2016). A systemic review of social media use to discuss and view deliberate self-harm acts. *PLOS ONE, 11*(5), e0155813. https://doi.org/10.1371/journal.pone.0155813

Eagly, A. H., & Carli, L. L. (2007). *Through the labyrinth: The truth about how women become leaders.* Harvard Business School Press.

Eagly, A. H., & Riger, S. (2014). Feminism and psychology: Critiques of methods and epistemology. *American Psychologist, 69*(7), 685–702. https://doi.org/10.1037/a0037372

Eby, L. T., Allen, T. D., Evans, S. C., Ng, T., & DuBois, D. L. (2008). Does mentoring matter? A multidisciplinary meta-analysis comparing mentored and non-mentored individuals. *Journal of Vocational Behavior, 72*(2), 254–267. https://doi.org/10.1016/j.jvb.2007.04.005

Economic Policy Institute. (2016). *The cost of childcare in Illinois.* https://www.epi.org/child-care-costs-in-the-united-states/#/IL

Edgerton, J. W. (2000). [Untitled videotape interview]. In J. G. Kelly (Ed.) *The history of community psychology: A video presentation of context and exemplars.* Society for Community Research and Action. https://vimeo.com/69635912

Edwards, R., Jumper-Thurman, P., Plested, B., Oetting, E., & Swanson, L. (2000). Community readiness: Research to practice. *Journal of Community Psychology, 28,* 291–307.

Elias, M. J. (1987). Establishing enduring prevention programs: Advancing the legacy of Swampscott. *American Journal of Community Psychology, 15*(5), 539–553. https://doi.org/10.1007/BF00929908

Elias, M. J. (1995). Primary prevention as health and social competence promotion. *Journal of Primary Prevention, 16*(1), 5–24. https://doi.org/10.1007/BF02407230

Elias, M. J., & Kamarinos, P. (2003, August 8). *Sustainability of school-based preventive social- emotional programs: A model site study* [Presentation]. Meeting of the American Psychological Association, Toronto, Canada.

Elias, M. J., Parker, S. J., Kash, V. M., & Dunkelblau, E. (2007). Social-emotional learning and character and moral education in children: Synergy of fundamental divergence in our schools? *Journal of Research in Character Education*, 5(2), 167–181.

Elias, M. J., & Zins, J. E. (Eds.). (2003). *Bullying, peer harassment, and victimization in the schools: The next generation of prevention.* Haworth.

Elias, M. J., Zins, J. E., Weissberg, R. P., Frey, K., Greenberg, M., Haynes, N., Kessler, R., Schwab-Stone, M., & Shriver, T. (1997). *Promoting social and emotional learning: Guidelines for educators.* Association for Supervision and Curriculum Development.

Ellis, L. A., Marsh, H. W., & Craven, R. G. (2009). Addressing the challenges faced by early adolescents: A mixed-method evaluation of the benefits of peer support. *American Journal of Community Psychology*, 44(1–2), 54–75. https://doi.org/10.1007/s10464-009-9251-y

Ennett, S. T., Rosenbaum, D. P., Flewelling, R. L., Bieler, G. S., Ringwalt, C. L., & Bailey, S. L. (1994). Long-term evaluation of drug abuse resistance education. *Addictive Behaviors*, 19(2), 113–125. https://doi.org/10.1016/0306-4603(94)90036-1

Evans, G. W. (2004). The environment of childhood poverty. *American Psychologist*, 59(2), 77–92. https://doi.org/10.1037/0003-066X.59.2.77

Evans, S. D. (2007). Youth sense of community: Voice and power in community contexts. *Journal of Community Psychology*, 35(6), 693–709. https://doi.org/10.1002/jcop.20173

Evans, S. D., Duckett, P., Lawthom, R., & Kivell, N. (2017). Positioning the critical in community psychology. In M. A. Bond, I. Serrano-García, and C. B. Keys (Eds.) *APA handbook of community psychology: Vol. 1. Theoretical foundations, core concepts, and emerging challenges* (pp. 107–127). American Psychological Association. https://doi.org/10.1037/14953-005

Evans, S. D., Hanlin, C., & Prilleltensky, I. (2007). Blending ameliorative and transformative approaches in human service organizations: A case study. *Journal of Community Psychology*, 35(3), 329–346. https://doi.org/10.1002/jcop.20151

Fairweather, G. W. (1979). Experimental development and dissemination of an alternative to psychiatric hospitalization. In R. Munoz, L. Snowden, & J. G. Kelly (Eds.), *Social and psychological research in community settings* (pp. 305–342). Jossey-Bass.

Fairweather, G. W. (1994). [Untitled videotape interview]. In J. G. Kelly (Ed.), *The history of community psychology: A video presentation of context and exemplars.* Society for Community Research and Action.

Fairweather, G. W., Sanders, D., Cressler, D., & Maynard, H. (1969). *Community life for the mentally ill: An alternative to institutional care.* Aldine.

Farrell, S. J., Aubry, T., & Coulombe, D. (2004). Neighborhoods and neighbors: Do they contribute to personal well-being? *Journal of Community Psychology*, 32(1), 9–25. https://doi.org/10.1002/jcop.10082

Faust, V., Christens, B., Sparks, S., & Hilgendorf, A. (2015). Exploring relationships among organizational capacity, collaboration, and network change. *Psychosocial Intervention*, 24(3), 125–131. https://doi.org/10.1016/j.psi.2015.09.002

Faust, V., Haber, M., Christens, B., & Legler, R. (2017). Intersections of competencies for practice and research in community psychology. *Global Journal of Community Psychology Practice*, 8(1), 1–13. https://doi.org/10.7728/0801201708

Fawcett, S. B., Paine-Andrews, A., Francisco, V., Schulz, J., Richter, K., Lewis, R., Williams, E., Harris, K., Berkley, J., Fisher, J., & Lopez, C. (1995). Using empowerment theory in collaborative partnerships for community health and development. *American Journal of Community Psychology*, 23(5), 677–697. https://doi.org/10.1007/BF02506987

Fawcett, S. B., White, G., Balcazar, F., Suarez-Balcazar, Y., Mathews, R., Paine-Andrews, A., Seekins, T., & Smith, J. (1994). A contextual-behavioral model of empowerment: Case studies involving people with physical disabilities. *American Journal of Community Psychology, 22*(4), 471–496. https://doi.org/10.1007/BF02506890

Federal Bureau of Investigation. (2018) *Crime in the United States, 2017*. https://ucr.fbi.gov/crime-in-the-u.s/2017/crime-in-the-u.s.-2017

Feinberg, M., Greenberg, M., & Osgood, D. W. (2004). Readiness, functioning, and perceived effectiveness in community prevention coalitions: A study of Communities That Care. *American Journal of Community Psychology, 33*(3–4), 163–176. https://doi.org/10.1023/B:AJCP.0000027003.75394.2b

Felner, R., & Adan, A. (1988). The School Transition Environment Project: An ecological intervention and evaluation. In R. Price, E. Cowen, R. Lorion, & J. Ramos-McKay (Eds.), *Fourteen ounces of prevention* (pp. 111–122). American Psychological Association. https://doi.org/10.1037/10064-009

Felton, C. (2004). Lessons learned since September 11th 2001 concerning the mental health impact of terrorism, appropriate response strategies and future preparedness. *Psychiatry: Interpersonal and Biological Processes, 67*(2), 147–152. https://doi.org/10.1521/psyc.67.2.147.35957

Fernández, J. S. (2018a). Decolonial pedagogy in community psychology: White students disrupting White innocence via a family portrait assignment. *American Journal of Community Psychology, 62*(3–4), 294–305. https://doi.org/10.1002/ajcp.12282

Fernández, J. S. (2018b). Toward an ethical reflective practice of a *Theory in the flesh*: Embodied subjectivities in a youth participatory action research mural project. *American Journal of Community Psychology, 62*(1–2), 221–232. https://doi.org/10.1002/ajcp.12264

Fernández, J. S., Nguyen, A., & Langhout, R. D. (2015). "It's a puzzle!" Elementary school-aged youth concept-mapping the intersections of community narratives. *International Journal for Research on Extended Education, 3*(1), 24–38. https://doi.org/10.3224/ijree.v3i1.19579

Fetterman, D. (1996). Empowerment evaluation: An introduction to theory and practice. In D. Fetterman, S. Kaftarian, & A. Wandersman (Eds.), *Empowerment evaluation: Knowledge and tools for self-assessment and accountability* (pp. 3–46). Sage. https://doi.org/10.4135/9781452243573.n1

Fetterman, D. (2001). *Foundations of empowerment evaluation*. Sage.

Fetterman, D., & Wandersman, A. (Eds.). (2005). *Empowerment evaluation principles in practice*. Guilford Press.

Fiala, W., Bjorck, J., & Gorsuch, R. (2002). The Religious Support Scale: Construction, validation, and cross-validation. *American Journal of Community Psychology, 30*, 761–786. https://doi.org/10.1023/A:1020264718397

Field, J. (2003). *Social capital*. Routledge.

Fields, A. M., Swan, S., & Kloos, B. (2010). "What it means to be a woman": Ambivalent sexism in female college students' experiences and attitudes. *Sex Roles, 62*(7–8), 554–567. https://doi.org/10.1007/s11199-009-9674-9

Figueroa Sarriera, H. J., & Gonzalez Hilario, B. (2017). Emerging technologies: Challenges and opportunities for community psychology. In M. A. Bond, I. Serrano-García, C. B. Keys, & M. Shinn (Eds.), *APA handbook of community psychology: Vol. 1. Methods for community research and action for diverse groups and issues* (pp. 469–484). American Psychological Association. https://doi.org/10.1037/14953-024

Fike, K. J., Ceballo, R., & Kennedy, T. M. (2019). The role of academic mentors for Latino/a adolescents exposed to community violence. *Journal of Community Psychology, 47*(6), 1329–1346. https://doi.org/10.1002/jcop.22189

Finckenauer, J. (1982). *Scared Straight and the panacea phenomenon*. Prentice-Hall.

Fine, M., & Burns, A. (2003). Class notes: Toward a critical psychology of class and schooling. *Journal of Social Issues, 59*(4), 841–860. https://doi.org/dmgqsg

Fine, M., Torre, M. E., Boudin, K., Bowen, I., Clark, J., Hylton, D., Martinez, M., Roberts, R. A., Smart, P., & Upegui, D. (2003). Participatory action research: From within and beyond prison bars. In P. M. Camic, J. E.

Rhodes, & L. Yardley (Eds.), *Qualitative research in psychology: Expanding perspectives in methodology and design* (pp. 173–198). American Psychological Association. https://doi.org/10.1037/10595-010

Fisak, B. J., Jr., Richard, D., & Mann, A. (2011). The prevention of child and adolescent anxiety: A meta-analytic review. *Prevention Science, 12*(3), 255–268. https://doi.org/b7872j

Fisher, A., & Sonn, C. (2002). Psychological sense of community in Australia and the challenges of change. *Journal of Community Psychology, 30*(6), 597–609. https://doi.org/10.1002/jcop.10029

Fisher, D., Imm, P., Chinman, M., & Wandersman, A. (2006). *Getting To Outcomes with developmental assets: Ten steps to measuring success in youth programs and communities*. Search Institute.

Fitzgerald, F. S. (1995). *The great Gatsby*. Simon & Schuster. (Original work published 1925)

Flaherty, J., Zwick, R., & Bouchey, H. (2014). Revisiting the Sense of Community Index: Confirmatory factor analysis and invariance test. *Journal of Community Psychology, 42*(8), 947–963. https://doi.org/10.1002/jcop.21664

Flaspohler, P., Duffy, J., Wandersman, A., Stillman, L., & Maras, M. A. (2008). Unpacking capacity: An intersection of Research-to-Practice models and Community-Centered models. *American Journal of Community Psychology, 41*(3–4), 182–196. https://doi.org/10.1007/s10464-008-9162-3

Flaspohler, P., Lesesne, C. A., Puddy, R. W., Smith, E., & Wandersman, A. (2012). Advances in bridging research and practice: Introduction to the second special issue on the interactive system framework for dissemination and implementation. *American Journal of Community Psychology, 50*(3–4), 271–281. https://doi.org/10.1007/s10464-012-9545-3

Fleishman, J. A., Sherbourne, C. D., Cleary, P. D., Wu, A. W., Crystal, S., & Hays, R. D. (2003). Patterns of coping among persons with HIV infection: Configurations, correlates, and change. *American Journal of Community Psychology, 32*(1–2), 187–204. https://doi.org/fkpphz

Flores, W. V., & Benmayor, R. (1997). *Latino cultural citizenship: Claiming identity, space, and rights*. Beacon Press.

Florin, P. R., Chavis, D., Wandersman, A., & Rich, R. (1992). A systems approach to understanding and enhancing grassroots organizations: The Block Booster Project. In R. Levine & H. Fitzgerald (Eds.), *Analysis of dynamic psychological systems: Methods and applications* (Vol. 2, pp. 215–243). Plenum. https://doi.org/10.1007/978-1-4615-6440-9_9

Florin, P. R., & Wandersman, A. (1984). Cognitive social learning and participation in community development. *American Journal of Community Psychology, 12*(6), 689–708. https://doi.org/10.1007/BF00922619

Folkman, S., & Moskowitz, J. T. (2004). Coping: Promises and pitfalls. *Annual Review of Psychology, 55*, 745–774. https://doi.org/d3gc4p

Fondacaro, M., & Weinberg, D. (2002). Concepts of social justice in community psychology: Toward a social ecological epistemology. *American Journal of Community Psychology, 30*(4), 473–492. https://doi.org/10.1023/A:1015803817117

Forenza, B. (2016). Opportunity role structure, social support, and leadership: Process of foster youth advisory board participation. *Journal of Community Psychology, 44*(7), 904–918. https://doi.org/10.1002/jcop.21817

Foster-Fishman, P., Berkowitz, S. L., Lounsbury, D. W., Jacobson, S., & Allen, N. A. (2001). Building collaborative capacity in community coalitions: A review and integrative framework. *American Journal of Community Psychology, 29*(2), 241–261. https://doi.org/10.1023/A:1010378613583

Foster-Fishman, P., Nowell, B., Deacon, Z., Nievar, M. A., & McCann, P. (2005). Using methods that matter: The impact of reflection, dialogue, and voice. *American Journal of Community Psychology, 36*(3–4), 275–291. https://doi.org/10.1007/s10464-005-8626-y

Foster-Fishman, P., Nowell, B., & Yang, H. (2007). Putting the system back into systems change: A framework for understanding and changing organizational and community systems. *American Journal of Community Psychology, 39*(3–4), 197–215. https://doi.org/10.1007/s10464-007-9109-0

Fowers, B. J., & Richardson, F. C. (1996). Why is multiculturalism good? *American Psychologist*, *51*(6), 609–621. https://doi.org/10.1037/0003-066X.51.6.609

Fowler, P., & Todd, N. (2017). Methods for multiple levels of analysis: Capturing context, change, and changing context. In M. A. Bond, I. Serrano-García, & C. B. Keys, (Eds.), *APA handbook of community psychology: Vol. 2. Methods for community research and action for diverse groups and issues* (pp. 59–74). American Psychological Association. https://doi.org/10.1037/14954-004

Frable, D. (1997). Gender, racial, ethnic, sexual, and class identities. *Annual Review of Psychology*, *48*, 139–162. https://doi.org/10.1146/annurev.psych.48.1.139

Francescato, D., Arcidiacono, C., Albanesi, C., & Mannarini, T. (2007). Community psychology in Italy: Past developments and future perspectives. In S. M. Reich, M. Riemer, I. Prilleltensky, & M. Montero (Eds.), *International community psychology: History and theories* (pp. 263–281). Springer. https://doi.org/10.1007/978-0-387-49500-2_13

Fredrickson, B. L. (1998). What good are positive emotions? *Review of General Psychology*, *2*(3), 300–319. https://doi.org/10.1037/1089-2680.2.3.300

Fredrickson, B. L. (2001). The role of positive emotions in positive psychology: The broaden-and-build theory of positive emotions. *American Psychologist*, *56*(3), 218–226. https://doi.org/10.1037/0003-066X.56.3.218

Freeman, H. L., Fryers, T., & Henderson, J. H. (1985). *Mental health services in Europe: 10 years on*. WHO Regional Office for Europe.

Freire, P. (1993). *Pedagogy of the oppressed* (Rev. ed.). Continuum. (Original work published 1970)

French, J. R. P., & Raven, B. (1959). The bases of social power. In D. Cartwright (Ed.), *Studies in social power* (pp. 150–167). Institute for Social Research.

Freund, J. (2013). The Homestead Act of 1862: The first entitlement program. *Journal of the West*, *52*(2), 16–21.

Fryer, D., & Fagan, R. (2003). Toward a critical community psychological perspective on unemployment and mental health research. *American Journal of Community Psychology*, *32*(1–2), 89–96. https://doi.org/10.1023/A:1025698924304

Gaffney, H., Ttofi, M. M., & Farrington, D. P. (2019). Evaluating the effectiveness of school-bullying prevention programs: An updated meta-analytical review. *Aggression and Violent Behavior*, *45*, 111–133. https://doi.org/10.1016/j.avb.2018.07.001

Gallón, A. (2017, April 6). When neighbors played volleyball over the U.S.-Mexico border fence. *Univision*. https://www.univision.com/univision-news/culture/when-neighbors-played-volleyball-over-the-u-s-mexico-border-fence

Gao, Q., Kaushal, N., & Waldfogel, J. (2009). How have expansions in the Earned Income Tax Credit affected family expenditures? In J. Ziliak (Ed.), *Welfare reform and its long-term consequences for America's poor* (pp. 104–139). Cambridge University Press. https://doi.org/10.1017/CBO9780511605383.005

Garmezy, N. (1985) Stress-resistant children: The search for protective factors. In J. E. Stevenson (Ed.), *Recent research in developmental psychology* (pp. 213–233). Pergamon.

Gatz, M., & Cotton, B. (1994). Age as a dimension of diversity: The experience of being old. In E. J. Trickett, R. J. Watts, & D. Birman (Eds.), *Human diversity: Perspectives on people in context* (pp. 334–355). Jossey-Bass.

Gaventa, J. (1980). *Power and powerlessness: Quiescence and rebellion in an Appalachian valley*. University of Illinois Press.

Gaventa, J., & Barrett, G. (2012). Mapping the outcomes of civic engagement. *World Development*, *40*(12), 2399–2410. https://doi.org/10.1016/j.worlddev.2012.05.014

Gearhart, M. C. (2019). Preventing neighborhood disorder: Comparing alternative models of collective efficacy theory using structural equation modeling. *American Journal of Community Psychology*, *63*(1–2), 168–178. https://doi.org/10.1002/ajcp.12317

Gergen, K. (1973). Social psychology as history. *Journal of Personality and Social Psychology*, *26*(2), 309–320. https://doi.org/10.1037/h0034436

Gergen, K. (2001). Psychological science in a postmodern context. *American Psychologist, 56*(10), 803–813. https://doi.org/10.1037/0003-066X.56.10.803

Giddens, A., Duneier, M., & Appelbaum, R. (2003). *Introduction to sociology* (4th ed.). Norton.

Gilens, M. (1996). Race and poverty in America: Public misperceptions and the American news media. *Public Opinion Quarterly, 60*(4), 515–541. https://doi.org/10.1086/297771

Gilliam, F. D., Jr., & Iyengar, S. (2000). Prime suspects: The influence of local television news on the viewing public. *American Journal of Political Science, 44*(3), 560–573. https://doi.org/10.2307/2669264

Gillock, K. L., & Reyes, O. (1996). High school transition-related changes in urban minority students' academic performance and perceptions of self and school environment. *Journal of Community Psychology, 24*(3), 245–261. https://doi.org/fjwpnz

Gist, R., & Lubin, B. (1989). *Psychosocial aspects of disaster.* John Wiley & Sons.

Glidewell, J. (1994). [Untitled videotape interview]. In J. G. Kelly (Ed.), *The history of community psychology: A video presentation of context and exemplars.* Society for Community Research and Action. https://vimeo.com/69635912

Glover, M., Dudgeon, P., & Huygens, I. (2005). Colonization and racism. In G. Nelson & I. Prilleltensky (Eds.), *Community psychology: In pursuit of liberation and well-being* (pp. 330–347). Palgrave Macmillan.

Goldston, S. (1994). [Untitled videotape interview]. In J. G. Kelly (Ed.), *The history of community psychology: A video presentation of context and exemplars.* Society for Community Research and Action. https://vimeo.com/69635912

Goldstrom, I. D., Campbell, J., Rogers, J. A., Lambert, D. B., Blacklow, B., Henderson, M. J., & Manderscheid, R. W. (2006). National estimates for mental health mutual support groups, self-help organizations, and consumer-operated services. *Administration and Policy in Mental Health and Mental Health Services Research, 33*(1), 92–103. https://doi.org/dxqb2z

Goleman, D. (1995). *Emotional intelligence.* Bantam.

Gomez, C., & Yoshikawa, H. (2017). A community psychology approach to structure and culture in family interventions. In M. A. Bond, I. Serrano-García, C. B. Keys, & M. Shinn (Eds.), *APA handbook of community psychology: Vol. 1. Theoretical foundations, core concepts, and emerging challenges* (pp. 337–352). American Psychological Association. https://doi.org/10.1037/14953-016

Gone, J. P. (2007). "We never was happy living like a Whiteman": Mental health disparities and the postcolonial predicament in American Indian communities. *American Journal of Community Psychology, 40*(3–4), 290–300. https://doi.org/10.1007/s10464-007-9136-x

Gone, J. P. (2008). Encountering professional psychology: Re-envisioning mental health services for Native North America. In L. J. Kirmayer & G. G. Valaskakis (Eds.), *Healing traditions: The mental health of Aboriginal peoples in Canada* (pp. 419–439). UBC Press.

Gone, J. P. (2011). The red road to wellness: Cultural reclamation in a Native First Nations community treatment center. *American Journal of Community Psychology, 47*(1–2), 187–202. https://doi.org/10.1007/s10464-010-9373-2

Gone, J. P., & Alcántara, C. (2007). Identifying effective mental health interventions for American Indians and Alaska Natives: A review of the literature. *Cultural Diversity & Ethnic Minority Psychology, 13*(4), 356–363. https://doi.org/10.1037/1099-9809.13.4.356

Gone, J. P., Hartmann, W. E., Pomerville, A., Wendt, D. C., Klem, S. H., & Burrage, R. L. (2019). The impact of historical trauma on health outcomes for indigenous populations in the USA and Canada: A systematic review. *American Psychologist, 74*(1), 20–35. https://doi.org/10.1037/amp0000338

Gone, J. P., Hartmann, W. E., & Sprague, M. G. (2017). Wellness interventions for indigenous communities in the United States: Exemplars for action research. In M. A. Bond, I. Serrano-García, & C. B. Keys (Eds.), *APA handbook of community psychology: Vol. 2. Methods for community research and action for diverse groups and issues* (pp. 507–522). American Psychological Association. https://doi.org/10.1037/14954-030

Gonsiorek, J. C., & Weinrich, J. D. (1991). The definition and scope of sexual orientation. In J. C. Gonsiorek & J. D. Weinrich (Eds.), *Homosexuality: Research implications for public policy* (pp. 1–12). Sage. https://doi.org/10.4135/9781483325422.n1

Gonzales, N. A., Cauce, A. M., Friedman, R. J., & Mason, C. A. (1996). Family, peer, and neighborhood influences on academic achievement among African-American adolescents: One-year prospective effects. *American Journal of Community Psychology, 24*(3), 365–387. https://doi.org/10.1007/BF02512027

Gonzalez, N., Moll, L. C., & Amanti, C. (2005). *Funds of knowledge: Theorizing practices in households, communities, and classrooms.* Lawrence Erlbaum Associates.

Goodkind, J., & Deacon, Z. (2004). Methodological issues in conducting research with refugee women: Principles for recognizing and re-centering the multiply marginalized. *Journal of Community Psychology, 32*(6), 721–739. https://doi.org/10.1002/jcop.20029

Goodkind, J., & Foster-Fishman, P. (2002). Integrating diversity and fostering interdependence: Ecological lessons learned about refugee participation in multiethnic communities. *Journal of Community Psychology, 30*(4), 389–409. https://doi.org/10.1002/jcop.10012

Goodman, R. M., & Steckler, A. (1989). A model for the institutionalization of health promotion programs. *Family & Community Health, 11*(4), 63–78. https://doi.org/dwgd

Gottlieb, B. H., & Peters, L. (1991). A national demographic portrait of mutual aid participants in Canada. *American Journal of Community Psychology, 19*(5), 651–666. https://doi.org/10.1007/BF00938037

Gould, D. B. (2009). *Moving politics: Emotion and ACT UP's fight against AIDS in Chicago.* University of Chicago Press.

Gould, S. J. (1981). *The mismeasure of man.* Norton.

Government Accountability Office. (2018, March 22). *K-12 education: Discipline disparities for Black students, boys, and students with disabilities.* https://www.gao.gov/products/gao-18-258

Grabe, S. (2012). An empirical examination of women's empowerment and transformative change in the context of international development. *American Journal of Community Psychology, 49*(1–2), 233–245. https://doi.org/10.1007/s10464-011-9453-y

Green, B. L., Chung, J. Y., Daroowalla, A., Kaltman, S., & DeBenedictis, C. (2006). Evaluating the cultural validity of the Stressful Life Events Screening Questionnaire. *Violence Against Women, 12*(12), 1191–1213. https://doi.org/cz9wdk

Greene, M. (1995). *Releasing the imagination: Essays on education, the arts, and social change.* Jossey-Bass.

Greenfield, T., Stoneking, B., Humphreys, K., & Bond, J. (2008). A randomized trial of a mental health consumer-managed alternative to civil commitment for acute psychiatric crisis. *American Journal of Community Psychology, 42*(1–2), 135–144. https://doi.org/10.1007/s10464-008-9180-1

Greenwood, P., Model, K., Rydell, C. P., & Chiesa, J. (1998). *Diverting children from a life of crime: Measuring costs and benefits.* RAND Corporation.

Greenwood, R. M., Manning, R. M., O'Shaughnessy, B. R., Vargas-Moniz, M. J., Loubière, S., Spinnewijn, F., Lenzi, M., Wolf, J. R., Bokszczanin, A., Bernad, R., Källmén, H., Ornelas, J., & the HOME-EU Consortium Study Group. (2019). Homeless adults' recovery experiences in housing first and traditional services programs in seven European countries. *American Journal of Community Psychology.* Advance online publication. https://doi.org/10.1002/ajcp.12404

Gridley, H., & Turner, C. (2010). Gender, power, and community psychology. In G. Nelson & I. Prilleltensky (Eds.), *Community psychology: In pursuit of well-being and liberation* (2nd ed., pp. 389–406). Macmillan.

Gridley, H., Turner, C., D'Arcy, C., Sampson, E, Madyaningrum, M. (2017). Community-based interventions to improve the lives of women and girls: Problems and possibilities. In M. A. Bond, I. Serrano-García, & C. B. Keys (Eds.), *APA handbook of community psychology: Vol. 2. Methods for community research and action for diverse groups and issues* (pp. 539-554). American Psychological Association. https://doi.org/10.1037/14954-032

Griffith, D. M., Childs, E. L., Eng, E., & Jeffries, V. (2007). Racism in organizations: The case of a county public health department. *Journal of Community Psychology*, *35*(3), 287–302. https://doi.org/10.1002/jcop.20149

Grosvenor Performance Group. (n.d.). *10 reasons not to evaluate your program.* https://www.grosvenor.com.au/resources/9-reasons-program-managers-shouldnt-evaluate-their-programs/

Gruber, J., & Trickett, E. J. (1987). Can we empower others? The paradox of empowerment in the governing of an alternative public school. *American Journal of Community Psychology*, *15*(3), 353–371. https://doi.org/10.1007/BF00922703

Gubits, D., Shinn, M., Wood, M., Brown, S. R., Dastrup, S. R., & Bell, S. H. (2018). What interventions work best for families who experience homelessness? Impact estimates from the Family Options Study. *Journal of Policy Analysis and Management*, *37*(4), 835–866. https://doi.org/10.1002/pam.22071

Guerra, N. G., & Knox, L. (2008). How culture impacts the dissemination and implementation of innovation: A case study of the Families and Schools Together program (FAST) for preventing violence with immigrant Latino youth. *American Journal of Community Psychology*, *41*(3–4), 304–313. https://doi.org/10.1007/s10464-008-9161-4

Gulcur, L., Stefancic, A., Shinn, M., Tsemberis, S., & Fischer, S. N. (2003). Housing, hospitalization, and cost outcomes for homeless individuals with psychiatric disabilities participating in continuum of care and housing first programmes. *Journal of Community & Applied Social Psychology*, *13*(2), 171–186. https://doi.org/10.1002/casp.723

Gurevitch, J., Koricheva, J., Nakagawa, S., & Stewart, G. (2018). Meta-analysis and the science of research synthesis. *Nature*, *555*(7695), 175–182. https://doi.org/10.1038/nature25753

Haber, M., Cohen, J., Lucas, T., & Baltes, B. (2007). The relationship between self-reported received and perceived social support: A meta-analytic review. *American Journal of Community Psychology*, *39*(1–2), 133–144. https://doi.org/10.1007/s10464-007-9100-9

Haertl, K. (2005). Factors influencing success in a Fairweather model mental health program. *American Journal of Psychiatric Rehabilitation*, *28*(4), 370–377. https://doi.org/10.2975/28.2005.370.377

Haertl, K. (2007). The Fairweather mental health housing model—A peer supportive environment: Implications for psychiatric rehabilitation. *American Journal of Psychiatric Rehabilitation*, *10*(3), 149–162. https://doi.org/10.1080/15487760701508201

Haertl, K. (2016). Utilization-focused evaluation: Ten-year outcomes of a Fairweather model mental health program—Implications for occupational therapy. *American Journal of Occupational Therapy*, *70*(4) (Suppl. 1), 7011510196p1. https://doi.org/10.5014/ajot.2016.70s1-po2033

Hall, C. C. I. (1997). Cultural malpractice: The growing obsolescence of psychology with the changing U.S. population. *American Psychologist*, *52*(6), 642–651. https://doi.org/10.1037/0003-066X.52.6.642

Hancock, A. B., & Rubin, B. A. (2015). Influence of communication partner's gender on language. *Journal of Language and Social Psychology*, *34*(1), 46–64. https://doi.org/10.1177/0261927X14533197

Hanna-Attisha, M. (2018). *What the eyes don't see: A story of crisis, resistance, and hope in an American city.* One World Press.

Harper, C., Kuperminc, G., Weaver, S., Emshoff, J., & Erickson, S. (2014). Leveraged resources and systems changes in community collaborations. *American Journal of Community Psychology*, *54*(3–4), 348–357. https://doi.org/10.1007/s10464-014-9678-7

Harper, G. W., Bangi, A., Contreras, R., Pedraza, A., Tolliver, M., & Vess, L. (2004). Diverse phases of collaboration: Working together to improve community-based HIV interventions for adolescents. *American Journal of Community Psychology*, *33*(3–4), 193–204. https://doi.org/10.1023/B:AJCP.0000027005.03280.ee

Harper, G. W., Lardon, C., Rappaport, J., Bangi, A., Contreras, R., & Pedraza, A. (2004). Community narratives: The use of narrative ethnography in participatory community research. In L. A. Jason, C. Keys, Y. Suarez-Balcazar, R. Taylor, & M. Davis (Eds.), *Participatory community research: Theories and methods in action* (pp. 199–217). American Psychological Association. https://doi.org/10.1037/10726-011

Harper, G. W., & Wilson, B. D. M. (2017). Situating sexual orientation and gender identity diversity in context and communities. In M. Bond, I. Serrano-García, & C. Keys (Eds.), *APA handbook of community psychology: Vol. 1. Theoretical foundations, core concepts, and emerging challenges* (pp. 387–402). American Psychological Association. https://doi.org/10.1037/14953-019

Harrell, S. P. (2000). A multidimensional conceptualization of racism-related stress: Implications for the well-being of people of color. *American Journal of Orthopsychiatry*, *70*(1), 42–57. https://doi.org/10.1037/h0087722

Hartmann, W. E., Wendt, D. C., Burrage, R. L., Pomerville, A., & Gone, J. P. (2019). American Indian historical trauma: Anticolonial prescriptions for healing, resilience, and survivance. *American Psychologist*, *74*(1), 6–19. https://doi.org/10.1037/amp0000326

Hartup, W. W., & Stevens, N. (1997). Friendships and adaptation in the life course. *Psychological Bulletin*, *121*(3), 355–370. https://doi.org/bzghzr

Hasford, J. (2016). Dominant cultural narratives, racism, and resistance in the workplace: A study of the experiences of young Black Canadians. *American Journal of Community Psychology*, *57*(1–2), 158–170. https://doi.org/10.1002/ajcp.12024

Haskins, A., & McCauley, E. (2019). Casualties of context? Risk of cognitive, behavioral and physical health difficulties among children living in high-incarceration neighborhoods. *Journal of Public Health*, *27*(2), 175–183. https://doi.org/10.1007/s10389-018-0942-4

Hastings, J. F., & Snowden, L. R. (2019). African Americans and Caribbean Blacks: Perceived neighborhood disadvantage and depression. *Journal of Community Psychology*, *47*(2), 227–237. https://doi.org/10.1002/jcop.22117

Hawe, P. (2017). The contribution of social ecological thinking to community psychology: Origins, practice, and research. In M. A. Bond, I. Serrano-García, C. B. Keys, & M. Shinn (Eds.), *APA handbook of community psychology: Vol. 1. Theoretical foundations, core concepts, and emerging challenges* (pp. 87–105). American Psychological Association. https://doi.org/10.1037/14953-004

Hawkins, J. D., Catalano, R. F., & associates. (1992). *Communities that care: Action for drug abuse prevention*. Jossey-Bass.

Hawkins, J. D., Jenson, J., Catalano, R., Fraser, M., Botvin, G., Shapiro, V., Brown, C., Beardslee, W., Brent, D., Leslie, L., Rotheram-Borus, M., Shea, P., Shih, A., Anthony, E., Haggerty, K., Bender, K., Gorman-Smith, D., Casey, E., & Stone, S. (2015). Unleashing the power of prevention. *NAM Perspectives*, *5*(6). https://doi.org/10.31478/201506c

Hawkins, J. D., & Lam, T. (1987). Teacher practices, social development, and delinquency. In J. D. Burchard & S. N. Burchard (Eds.), *Prevention of delinquent behavior* (pp. 241–274). Sage.

Hayes, H., Scott, V., Abraczinskas, M., Scacciam, J., Stout, S., & Wandersman, A. (2016). A formative multi-method approach to evaluating training. *Evaluation and Program Planning*, *58*, 199–207. https://doi.org/f8z39w

Hazel, K. L., & Mohatt, G. V. (2001). Cultural and spiritual pathways to sobriety: Informing substance abuse prevention and intervention for Native American communities. *Journal of Community Psychology*, *29*(5), 541–562. https://doi.org/10.1002/jcop.1035

Hazel, K. L., & Onaga, E. (2003). Experimental social innovation and dissemination: The promise and its delivery. *American Journal of Community Psychology*, *32*(3–4), 285–294. https://doi.org/10.1023/B:AJCP.0000004748.50885.2e

Health and Human Services Department. (2019). *Annual update of the HHS poverty guidelines*. https://www.federalregister.gov/documents/2019/02/01/2019-00621/annual-update-of-the-hhs-poverty-guidelines

Hebert, R., Zdaniuk, B., Schulz, R., & Scheier, M. (2009). Positive and negative religious coping and well-being in women with breast cancer. *Journal of Palliative Medicine*, *12*(6), 537–545. https://doi.org/10.1089/jpm.2008.0250

Heckman, J. J., Moon, S. H., Pinto, R., Savelyev, P. A., & Yavitz, A. (2009). *The rate of return to the High/Scope Perry Preschool Program* (National Bureau of Economic Research Working Paper No. 15471). https://doi.org/bcgzzw

Heilman, M. (2001). Description and prescription: How gender stereotypes prevent women's ascent up the organizational ladder. *Journal of Social Issues*, *57*(4), 657–674. https://doi.org/10.1111/0022-4537.00234

Heinze, J. E., Krusky-Morey, A., Vagi, K. J., Reischl, T. M., Franzen, S., Pruett, N. K., Cunningham, R. M., & Zimmerman, M. A. (2018). Busy streets theory: The effects of community-engaged greening on violence. *American Journal of Community Psychology*, *62*(1–2), 101–109. https://doi.org/10.1002/ajcp.12270

Heller, K., & Monahan, J. (1977). *Psychology and community change.* Dorsey.

Heller, K., Price, R., Reinharz, S., Riger, S., & Wandersman, A. (1984). *Psychology and community change* (2nd ed.). Dorsey.

Helm, S. (2003, June 4–7). *Rural health in Molokai: Land, people and empowerment* [Presentation]. Biennial Meeting of the Society for Community Research and Action, Las Vegas, NM.

Helms, J. E. (1994). The conceptualizations of racial identity and other "racial" constructs. In E. J. Trickett, R. J. Watts, & D. Birman (Eds.), *Human diversity: Perspectives on people in context* (pp. 285–310). Jossey-Bass.

Helms, J. E., & Carter, R. T. (1990). White Racial Identity Attitude Scale (Form WRIAS). In J. E. Helms (Ed.), *Black and White racial identity: Theory, research, and practice* (pp. 249–251). Greenwood.

Herrera, C., Grossman, J. B., Kauh, T. J., Feldman, A. F., & McMaken, J. (2007). *Making a difference in schools: The Big Brothers Big Sisters school-based mentoring impact study.* Public Private Ventures.

Hickey, S., & Mohan, G. (2005). *Participation: From tyranny to transformation? Exploring new approaches to participation in development.* Zed Books.

Hill, J. (1996). Psychological sense of community: Suggestions for future research. *Journal of Community Psychology*, *24*(4), 431–438. https://doi.org/ch9w8c

Hill, J. (2000). A rationale for the integration of spirituality into community psychology. *Journal of Community Psychology*, *28*(2), 139–149. https://doi.org/crfhjk

Hill, P. C., & Pargament, K. I. (2003). Advances in the conceptualization and measurement of religion and spirituality: Implications for physical and mental health research. *American Psychologist*, *58*(1), 64–74. https://doi.org/10.1037/0003-066x.58.1.64

Hillier, J. (2002). Presumptive planning: From urban design to community creation in one move? In A. Fisher, C. Sonn, & B. Bishop (Eds.), *Psychological sense of community: Research, applications and implications* (pp. 43–67). Kluwer/Plenum. https://doi.org/10.1007/978-1-4615-0719-2_3

Hirsch, B. J., Engel-Levy, A., DuBois, D. L., & Hardesty, P. (1990). The role of social environments in social support. In B. R. Sarason, I. G. Sarason, & G. Pierce (Eds.), *Social support: An interactional view* (pp. 367–393). Wiley.

Hobfoll, S. E. (1998). *Stress, culture, and community: The psychology and philosophy of stress.* Plenum. https://doi.org/10.1007/978-1-4899-0115-6

Hobfoll, S. E., & Vaux, A. (1993). Social support: Social resources and social context. In L. Goldberger & S. Breznitz (Eds.), *Handbook of stress: Theoretical and clinical aspects* (2nd ed., pp. 685–705). Free Press.

Hochschild, J. (2003). Social class in public schools. *Journal of Social Issues*, *59*(4), 821–840. https://doi.org/10.1046/j.0022-4537.2003.00092.x

Hollingshead, A., & Redlich, F. (1958). *Social class and mental illness: A community study.* Wiley. https://doi.org/10.1037/10645-000

Holmes, T. H., & Rahe, R. H. (1967). The social readjustment rating scale. *Journal of Psychosomatic Research*, *11*(2), 213–218. https://doi.org/cw7wzk

hooks, b. (1984). *Feminist theory: From margin to center.* South End Press.

Hope, E. C., Gugwor, R., Riddick, K. N., & Pender, K. N. (2019). Engaged against the machine: Institutional and cultural racial discrimination and racial identity as predictors of activism orientation among Black youth. *American Journal of Community Psychology, 63*(1–2), 61–72. https://doi.org/10.1002/ajcp.12303

Horowitz, J. L., & Garber, J. (2006). The prevention of depressive symptoms in children and adolescents: A meta-analytic review. *Journal of Consulting and Clinical Psychology, 74*(3), 401–415. https://doi.org/bzf78v

Horton, M. (1990). *The long haul: An autobiography*. Doubleday.

Horton, M., & Freire, P. (1990). *We make the road by walking: Conversations on education and social change*. Temple University Press.

Howard, K. S., & Brooks-Gunn, J. (2009). The role of home-visiting programs in prevention child abuse and neglect. *The Future of Children, 19*(2), 119–146. https://doi.org/10.1353/foc.0.0032

Hoy-Ellis, C., & Fredriksen-Goldsen, K. (2017). Depression among transgender older adults: General and minority stress. *American Journal of Community Psychology, 59*(3–4), 295–305. https://doi.org/10.1002/ajcp.12138

Hoynes, H., & Patel, A. (2015). *Effective policy for reducing inequality? The Earned Income Tax Credit and the distribution of income* (NBER Working Paper No. 21340). https://www.nber.org/papers/w21340 https://doi.org/10.3386/w21340

Hoyt-Meyers, L., Cowen, E. L., Work, W. C., Wyman, P. A., Magnus, K., Fagen, D. B., & Lotyczewski, B. S. (1995). Test correlates of resilient outcomes among highly stressed second- and third-grade urban children. *Journal of Community Psychology, 23*(4), 326–338. https://doi.org/djb7hc

Hughes, D., & DuMont, K. (1993). Using focus groups to facilitate culturally anchored research. *American Journal of Community Psychology, 21*(6), 775–806. https://doi.org/10.1007/bf00942247

Hughes, D., & Seidman, E. (2002). In pursuit of a culturally anchored methodology. In T. A. Revenson, A. R. D'Augelli, S. E. French, D. L. Hughes, D. Livert, E. Seidman, M. Shinn, & H. Yoshikawa (Eds.), *Ecological research to promote social change: Methodological advances from community psychology* (pp. 243–255). Kluwer Academic/Plenum. https://doi.org/10.1007/978-1-4615-0565-5_10

Humes, E. (2006). How the GI Bill shunted Blacks into vocational training. *Journal of Blacks in Higher Education, 53*, 92–104.

Humphreys, K. (1996). Clinical psychologists as psychotherapists: History, future, and alternatives. *American Psychologist, 51*(3), 190–197. https://doi.org/10.1037/0003-066x.51.3.190

Humphreys, K. (1997). Individual and social benefits of mutual aid self-help groups. *Social Policy, 27*(3), 12–19.

Humphreys, K. (2000). Community narratives and personal stories in Alcoholics Anonymous. *Journal of Community Psychology, 28*(5), 495–506. https://doi.org/b5xr9g

Humphreys, K., Finney, J. W., & Moos, R. H. (1994). Applying a stress and coping framework to research on mutual help organizations. *Journal of Community Psychology, 22*(4), 312–327. https://doi.org/d5nfgb

Humphreys, K., & Noke, J. M. (1997). The influence of posttreatment mutual help group participation on the friendship networks of substance abuse patients. *American Journal of Community Psychology, 25*(1), 1–16. https://doi.org/10.1023/A:1024613507082

Humphreys, K., & Rappaport, J. (1993). From the community mental health movement to the war on drugs: A study in the definition of social problems. *American Psychologist, 48*(8), 892–901. https://doi.org/10.1037/0003-066X.48.8.892

Humphreys, K., Wing, S., McCarty, D., Chappel, J., Gallant, L., Haberle, B., Horvath, A. T., Kaskutas, L. A., Kirk, T., Kivlahan, D., Laudet, A., McCrady, B. S., McLellan, A. T., Morgenstern, J., Townsend, M., & Weiss, R. (2004). Self-help organizations for alcohol and drug problems: Toward evidence-based practice and policy. *Journal of Substance Abuse Treatment, 26*(3), 151–158. https://doi.org/b8rnc9

Hunter, A., & Riger, S. (1986). The meaning of community in community mental health. *Journal of Community Psychology, 14*(1), 55–71. https://doi.org/d897kz

Hurtado, A. (1997). Understanding multiple group identities: Inserting women into cultural transformations. *Journal of Social Issues, 53*(2), 299–327. https://doi.org/10.1111/j.1540-4560.1997.tb02445.x

Huston, A., & Bentley, A. (2010). Human development in societal context. *Annual Review of Psychology, 61*, 411–437. https://doi.org/10.1146/annurev.psych.093008.100442

Ickovics, J., & Park, C. (Eds.). (1998). Thriving: Broadening the paradigm beyond illness to health [Special issue]. *Journal of Social Issues, 54*(2).

Illinois, O. (June 7, 2018). *Child-care chaos.* https://www.oneillinois.com/stories/2018/4/25/ccap?rq= Child Care Assistance Program

Illinois Department of Health and Human Services. (2018). *Supplemental nutrition assistance program.* https://www.dhs.state.il.us/OneNetLibrary/27897/documents/Brochures/124.pdf

Imm, P., Chinman, M., Wandersman, A., Rosenbloom, D., Guckenburg, S., & Leis, R. (2007). *Using the "Getting To Outcomes" approach to help communities prevent underage drinking.* RAND Corporation.

Institute for Criminal Policy Research. (n.d.). *World prison brief.* http://www.prisonstudies.org/world-prison-brief-data

International Organization for Migration. (2018). *World migration report.* United Nations Migration Agency.

Iscoe, I., Bloom, B., & Spielberger, C. (Eds.). (1977). *Community psychology in transition: Proceedings of the national conference on training in community psychology.* Hemisphere.

Isenberg, D. H., Loomis, C., Humphreys, K., & Maton, K. (2004). Self-help research: Issues of power sharing. In L. A. Jason, C. Keys, Y. Suarez-Balcazar, R. Taylor, & M. Davis (Eds.), *Participatory community research: Theories and methods in action* (pp. 123–137). American Psychological Association. https://doi.org/10.1037/10726-007

Israel, N., & Toro, P. A. (2003). Promoting local action on poverty. *Community Psychologist, 36*(4), 35–37. https://www.scra27.org/files/1513/9016/0105/tcp03.Number4.pdf

itlmedia. (2009, June 30). *A Stormé life* [Video]. YouTube. https://youtu.be/XgCVNEiOwLs

Itzhaky, H., Zanbar, L., Levy, D., & Schwartz, C. (2015). The contribution of personal and community resources to well-being and sense of belonging to the community among community activists. *British Journal of Social Work, 45*(6), 1678–1698. https://doi.org/10.1093/bjsw/bct176

Jacobs, J. (1961). *The death and life of great American cities.* Random House.

Jacobs, M. (2017). Reproducing White settlers and eliminating natives: Settler colonialism, gender, and family history in the American West. *Journal of the West, 56*(4), 13–24.

Jagers, R. J., Mustafaa, F. N., & Noel, B. (2017). Cultural integrity and African American empowerment: Insights and practical implications for community psychology. In M. A. Bond, I. Serrano-García, & C. B. Keys, (Eds.), *APA handbook of community psychology: Vol. 2. Methods for community research and action for diverse groups and issues* (pp. 459–474). American Psychological Association. https://doi.org/10.1037/14954-027

Jahoda, M. (1980). *Current conceptions of positive mental health.* Arno Press. (Original work published 1958)

Jahoda, M., Lazarsfeld, P., & Zeisel, H. (1971). *Marienthal: The sociography of an unemployed community.* Tavistock. (Original work published 1933)

James, S. E., Johnson, J., Raghavan, C., Lemos, T., Smith, M., & Woolis, D. (2003). The violent matrix: A study of structural, interpersonal, and intrapersonal violence among a sample of poor women. *American Journal of Community Psychology, 31*(1–2), 129–141. https://doi.org/10.1023/A:1023082822323

Jason, L. A., Keys, C., Suarez-Balcazar, Y., Taylor, R., & Davis, M. (Eds.). (2004). *Participatory community research: Theories and methods in action.* American Psychological Association. https://doi.org/10.1037/10726-000

Jason, L. A., Olson, B. D., Ferrari, J. R., & Lo Sasso, A. T. (2006). Communal housing settings enhance substance abuse recovery. *American Journal of Public Health, 96*(10), 1727–1729. https://doi.org/10.2105/AJPH.2005.070839

Jason, L. A., Olson, B. D., & Harvey, R. (2015). Evaluating alternative aftercare models for ex-offenders. *Journal of Drug Issues, 45*(1), 53–68. https://doi.org/10.1177/0022042614552019

Jason, L. A., Stevens, E., & Light, J. (2016). The relationship of sense of community and trust to hope. *Journal of Community Psychology, 44*(3), 334–341. https://doi.org/10.1002/jcop.21771

Jason, L. A., Stevens, E., & Ram, D. (2015). Development of a three-factor psychological sense of community scale. *Journal of Community Psychology, 43*(8), 973–985. https://doi.org/10.1002/jcop.21726

Javdani, S., & Allen, N. E. (2011). Councils as empowering contexts: Mobilizing the front line to foster systems change in the response to intimate partner violence. *American Journal of Community Psychology, 48*(3–4), 208–221. https://doi.org/10.1007/s10464-010-9382-1

Javdani, S., Singh, S., & Sichel, C. E. (2017). Negotiating ethical paradoxes in conducting a randomized controlled trial: Aligning intervention science with participatory values. *American Journal of Community Psychology, 60*(3–4), 439–449. https://doi.org/10.1002/ajcp.12185

Johnson, K., Hays, C., Center, H., & Daley, C. (2004). Building capacity and sustainable prevention innovations: A sustainability planning model. *Evaluation and Program Planning, 27*(2), 135–149. https://doi.org/fdrfg9

Johnson, S. (2006). *The ghost map: The story of London's most terrifying epidemic—And how it changed science, cities and the modern world.* Riverhead Books.

Joint Commission on Mental Health and Mental Illness. (1961). *Action for mental health: Final report.* Basic Books.

Jolliffe, D., & Farrington, D. P. (2007). *A rapid evidence assessment of the impact of mentoring on re-offending: A summary.* Home Office.

Jones, J. M. (1994). Our similarities are different: Toward a psychology of affirmative diversity. In E. J. Trickett, R. J. Watts, & D. Birman (Eds.), *Human diversity: Perspectives on people in context* (pp. 27–45). Jossey-Bass.

Jones, J. M. (1997). *Prejudice and racism* (2nd ed.). McGraw-Hill.

Jones, J. M. (1998). Psychological knowledge and the new American dilemma of race. *Journal of Social Issues, 54*(4), 641–662. https://doi.org/cgqcf8

Jones, J. M. (2003). Constructing race and deconstructing racism: A cultural psychology approach. In G. Bernal, J. Trimble, K. Burlew, & F. Leong (Eds.), *Handbook of racial and ethnic minority psychology* (pp. 276–290). Sage. https://doi.org/10.4135/9781412976008.n14

Jones, K., Allen, M., Norris, F. H., & Miller, C. (2009). Piloting a new model of crisis counseling: Specialized crisis counseling services in Mississippi after Hurricane Katrina. *Administration and Policy in Mental Health and Mental Health Services Research, 36*(3), 195–205. https://doi.org/fg3v8n

Kaniasty, K., & Norris, F. H. (1995). In search of altruistic community: Patterns of social support mobilization following Hurricane Hugo. *American Journal of Community Psychology, 23*(4), 447–477. https://doi.org/10.1007/BF02506964

Kanner, A. D., Coyne, J. C., Schaefer, C., & Lazarus, R. S. (1981). Comparison of two modes of stress measurement: Daily hassles and uplifts versus major life events. *Journal of Behavioral Medicine, 4*(1), 1–39. https://doi.org/10.1007/BF00844845

Karcher, M. J. (2008). The study of mentoring in the learning environment (SMILE): A randomized evaluation of the effectiveness of school-based mentoring. *Prevention Science, 9*(2), 99–113. https://doi.org/10.1007/s11121-008-0083-z

Kaskutas, L., Morgan, P., & Vaeth, P. (1991). Structural impediments in the development of community-based drug prevention programs for youth: Preliminary analysis from a qualitative formative evaluation study. *International Quarterly of Community Health Education, 12*(3), 169–182. https://doi.org/dgpvqp

Kasturirangan, A. (2008). Empowerment and programs designed to address domestic violence. *Violence Against Women, 14*(12), 1465–1475. https://doi.org/10.1177/1077801208325188

Katz, D., & Kahn, R. L. (1978). *The social psychology of organizations.* Wiley.

Katz, R. (1984). Empowerment and synergy: Expanding the community's healing resources. In J. Rappaport, C. Swift, & R. Hess (Eds.), *Studies in empowerment: Steps toward understanding and action* (pp. 210–226). Haworth Press.

Kaye, G. (2001). Grassroots involvement. *American Journal of Community Psychology*, *29*(2), 269–275. https://doi.org/10.1023/A:1010382714491

Kaye, G., & Wolff, T. (Eds.). (1997). *From the ground up: A workbook on coalition building and community development*. AHEC/Community Partners.

Kelly, J. F. (2003). Self-help for substance-use disorders: History, effectiveness, knowledge gaps, and research opportunities. *Clinical Psychology Review*, *23*(5), 639–663. https://doi.org/c8btr6

Kelly, J. F., Hoffman, L., Vilsaint, C., Weiss, R., Nierenberg, A., & Hoeppner, B. (2019). Peer support for mood disorder: Characteristics and benefits from attending the Depression and Bipolar Support Alliance mutual-help organization. *Journal of Affective Disorders*, *255*, 127–135. https://doi.org/ggvf5v

Kelly, J. G. (1966). Ecological constraints on mental health services. *American Psychologist*, *21*(6), 535–539. https://doi.org/10.1037/h0023598

Kelly, J. G. (1970a). Antidotes for arrogance: Training for community psychology. *American Psychologist*, *25*(6), 524–531. https://doi.org/10.1037/h0029484

Kelly, J. G. (1970b). Toward an ecological conception of preventive interventions. In D. Adelson & B. Kalis (Eds.), *Community psychology and mental health* (pp. 126–145). Chandler.

Kelly, J. G. (1971). Qualities for the community psychologist. *American Psychologist*, *26*(10), 897–903. https://doi.org/10.1037/h0032231

Kelly, J. G. (Ed.). (1979). *Adolescent boys in high school: A psychological study of coping and adaptation.* Erlbaum.

Kelly, J. G. (1986). Context and process: An ecological view of the interdependence of practice and research. *American Journal of Community Psychology*, *14*(6), 581–589. https://doi.org/10.1007/bf00931335

Kelly, J. G. (1990). Changing contexts and the field of community psychology. *American Journal of Community Psychology*, *18*(6), 769–792. https://doi.org/10.1007/BF00938064

Kelly, J. G. (2002). The spirit of community psychology. *American Journal of Community Psychology*, *30*(1), 43–63. https://doi.org/10.1023/A:1014368000641

Kelly, J. G. (Producer, Director). (2003). *Exemplars of community psychology* [Film; DVD set]. Society for Community Research and Action.

Kelly, J. G. (2010). More thoughts: On the spirit of community psychology. *American Journal of Community Psychology*, *45*(3–4), 272–284. https://doi.org/10.1007/s10464-010-9305-1

Kelly, J. G., Azelton, S., Burzette, R., & Mock, L. (1994). Creating social settings for diversity: An ecological thesis. In E. J. Trickett, R. J. Watts & D. Birman (Eds.), *Human diversity: Perspectives on people in context* (pp. 424–450). San Francisco: Jossey-Bass.

Kelly, J. G., Ryan, A. M., Altman, B. E., & Stelzner, S. P. (2000). Understanding and changing social systems: An ecological view. In J. Rappaport & E. Seidman (Eds.), *Handbook of community psychology* (pp. 133–159). Kluwer Academic/Plenum. https://doi.org/10.1007/978-1-4615-4193-6_7

Kennedy, H., DeChants, J., Bender, K., & Anyon, Y. (2019). More than data collectors: A systematic review of the environmental outcomes of youth inquiry approaches in the United States. *American Journal of Community Psychology*, *63*(1–2), 208–226. https://doi.org/10.1002/ajcp.12321

Kessler, R. C., Mickelson, K. D., & Zhao, S. (1997). Patterns and correlates of self-help groups membership in the United States. *Social Policy*, *27*(3), 27–46.

Keys, C. B., McConnell, E., Motley, D., Liao, C., & McAuliff, K. (2017). The what, the how, and who of empowerment: Reflections on an intellectual history. In M. A. Bond, I. Serrano-García, C. B. Keys, & M. Shinn (Eds.), *APA handbook of community psychology: Vol. 1. Theoretical foundations, core concepts, and emerging challenges* (pp. 213–231). American Psychological Association. https://doi.org/10.1037/14953-010

Keys, D. (1982). *Earth at omega: Passage to planetization*. Branden Press.

Kieffer, C. (1984). Citizen empowerment: A developmental perspective. In J. Rappaport, C. Swift, & R. Hess (Eds.), *Studies in empowerment: Steps toward understanding and action* (pp. 9–36). Haworth.

Kilburn, M. R., & Karoly, L. A. (2008). *The economics of early childhood policy: What the dismal science has to say about investing in children*. RAND Corporation. http://www.rand.org/pubs/occasional_papers/2008/RAND_OP227.pdf

Kilmer, R. P., Cowen, E. L., Wyman, P. A., Work, W. C., & Magnus, K. B. (1998). Differences in stressors experienced by urban African American, White, and Hispanic children. *Journal of Community Psychology*, *26*(5), 415–428. https://doi.org/fgwxpq

Kim, I. J., & Lorion, R. P. (2006). Introduction to special issue: Addressing mental health disparities through culturally competent research and community-based practice. *Journal of Community Psychology*, *34*(2), 117–120. https://doi.org/10.1002/jcop.20087

King, M. L., Jr. (1968). The role of the behavioral scientist in the civil rights movement. *American Psychologist*, *23*(3), 180–186. https://doi.org/10.1037/h0025715

Kingod, N., Cleal, B., Wahlberg, A., & Husted, G. R. (2017). Online peer-to-peer communities in the daily lives of people with chronic illness: A qualitative systematic review. *Qualitative Health Research*, *27*(1), 89–99. https://doi.org/10.1177/1049732316680203

Kitayama, S., & Marcus, H. R. (Eds.). (1994). *Emotion and culture: Empirical studies of mutual influence*. American Psychological Association. https://doi.org/10.1037/10152-000

Klaw, E., Huebsch, P. D., & Humphreys, K. (2000). Communication patterns in an on-line mutual help group for problem drinkers. *Journal of Community Psychology*, *28*(5), 535–546. https://doi.org/bqjmnv

Klaw, E. L., & Rhodes, J. E. (1995). Mentor relationships and the career development of pregnant and parenting African-American teenagers. *Psychology of Women Quarterly*, *19*(4), 551–562. https://doi.org/bb4qr3

Klein, D. C. (1995). [Untitled videotape interview]. In J. G. Kelly (Ed.), *The history of community psychology: A video presentation of context and exemplars*. Society for Community Research and Action.

Klein, D. C., & Lindemann, E. (1961). Preventive intervention in individual and family crisis situations. In G. Caplan (Ed.), *Prevention of mental disorders in children* (pp. 283–306). Basic Books.

Klein, K. J., Ralls, R. S., Smith-Major, V., & Douglas, C. (2000). Power and participation in the workplace. In J. Rappaport & E. Seidman (Eds.), *Handbook of community psychology* (pp. 273–295). Kluwer Academic/Plenum. https://doi.org/10.1007/978-1-4615-4193-6_12

Kloos, B. (2010). Creating new possibilities for promoting liberation, well-being, and recovery: Learning from experiences of psychiatric consumers/survivors. In G. Nelson & I. Prilleltensky (Eds.), *Community psychology: In pursuit of well-being and liberation* (2nd ed., pp. 453–476). Macmillan.

Kloos, B. (2020). Addressing community-based challenges arising from mental health problems: Learning from experiences of psychiatric consumers/survivors. In M. Riemer, S. Reich, & S. Evans (Eds.), *Community psychology: In pursuit of well-being and liberation* (3rd ed., Chapter 21). Macmillan.

Kloos, B., & Moore, T. (2000). The prospect and purpose of locating community research and action in religious settings. *Journal of Community Psychology*, *28*(2), 119–138. https://doi.org/bcqxnp

Kloos, B., & Shah, S. (2009). A social ecological approach to investigating relationships between housing and adaptive functioning for persons with serious mental illness. *Journal of Community Psychology*, *44*(3–4), 316–326. https://doi.org/10.1007/s10464-009-9277-1

Knapp, S. J., & VandeCreek, L. D. (2012). *Practical ethics for psychologists: A positive approach* (2nd ed.). American Psychological Association.

Kohn-Wood, L. P., & Wilson, M. N. (2005). The context of caretaking in rural areas: Family factors influencing the level of functioning of serious mentally ill patients living at home. *American Journal of Community Psychology*, *36*(1–2), 1–13. https://doi.org/c7z5rp

Kornbluh, M., Neal, J. W., & Ozer, E. J. (2016). Scaling-up youth-led social justice efforts through an online school-based social network. *American Journal of Community Psychology, 57*(3–4), 266–279. https://doi.org/10.1002/ajcp.12042

Kosciw, J., Palmer, N., & Kull, R. (2015). Reflecting resiliency: Openness about sexual orientation and/or gender identity and its relationship to well-being and educational outcomes for LGBT students. *American Journal of Community Psychology, 55*(1–2), 167–178. https://doi.org/10.1007/s10464-014-9642-6

Kral, G. (2006). Online communities for mutual help: Fears, fiction, and facts. In M. Murero & R. E. Rice (Eds.), *The Internet and health care: Theory, research, and practice* (pp. 215–232). Lawrence Erlbaum Associates.

Kral, M. J., García, J. I. R., Aber, M. S., Masood, N., Dutta, U., & Todd, N. R. (2011). Culture and community psychology: Toward a renewed and reimagined vision. *American Journal of Community Psychology, 47*(1–2), 46–57. https://doi.org/10.1007/s10464-010-9367-0

Kral, M. J., & Idlout, L. (2008). Community wellness and social action in the Canadian Arctic: Collective agency as subjective well-being. In L. J. Kirmayer & G. G. Valaskakis (Eds.), *Healing traditions: The mental health of Aboriginal peoples in Canada* (pp. 315–336). UBC Press.

Kress, J. S., & Elias, M. J. (2000). Infusing community psychology and religion: Themes from an Action-Research project in Jewish identity development. *Journal of Community Psychology, 28*(2), 187–198. https://doi.org/dr37xm

Kretzmann, J. P., & McKnight, J. L. (1993). *Building communities from the inside out: A path toward finding and mobilizing a community's assets.* ACTA Publications.

Kriegel, L. S., Townley, G., Brusilovskiy, E., & Salzer, M. S. (2020). Neighbors as distal support for individuals with serious mental illnesses. *American Journal of Orthopsychiatry, 90*(1), 98–105. https://doi.org/10.1037/ort0000403

Kulis, S., Nieri, T., Yabiku, S., Stromwall, L. K., & Marsiglia, F. F. (2007). Promoting reduced and discontinued substance use among adolescent substance users: Effectiveness of a universal prevention program. *Prevention Science, 8*(1), 35–49. https://doi.org/10.1007/s11121-006-0052-3

Kumpfer, K. L., & Alvarado, R. (2003). Family-strengthening approaches for the prevention of youth problem behaviors. *American Psychologist, 58*(6–7), 457–465. https://doi.org/ckmnj2

Kuo, F. E., & Sullivan, W. C. (2001). Environment and crime in the inner city: Does vegetation reduce crime? *Environment and Behavior, 33*(3), 343–367. https://doi.org/10.1177/00139160121973025

Kuo, F. E., Sullivan, W. C., Coley, R. L., & Brunson, L. (1998). Fertile ground for community: Inner-city neighborhood common spaces. *American Journal of Community Psychology, 26*(6), 823–851. https://doi.org/10.1023/A:1022294028903

Kuperminc, G., Emshoff, J. G., Reiner, M. N., Secrest, L. A., Niolon, P., & Foster, J. D. (2005). Integration of mentoring with other programs and services. In D. L. DuBois & M. J. Karcher (Eds.), *Handbook of youth mentoring* (pp. 314–333). Sage. https://doi.org/10.4135/9781412976664.n21

Kwon, S. (2019). Perceived neighborhood disorder and psychological distress among Latino adults in the United States: Considering spousal/partner relationship. *Journal of Community Psychology.* Advance online publication. https://doi.org/10.1002/jcop.22288

Kyrouz, E. M., Humphreys, K., & Loomis, C. (2002). A review of research on the effectiveness of self-help mutual aid groups. In B. J. White & E. J. Madera (Eds.), *The self-help group sourcebook* (7th ed., pp. 71–85). American Self-Help Group Clearinghouse.

LaFromboise, T., Coleman, H. L. K., & Gerton, J. (1993). Psychological impact of biculturalism: Evidence and theory. *Psychological Bulletin, 114*(3), 395–412. https://doi.org/c6cvkq

Laing, C. M., & Moules, N. J. (2014). Children's cancer camps: A sense of community, a sense of family. *Journal of Family Nursing, 20*(2), 185–203. https://doi.org/10.1177/1074840714520717

Langhout, R. D. (2003). Reconceptualizing quantitative and qualitative methods: A case study dealing with place as an exemplar. *American Journal of Community Psychology*, *32*(3–4), 229–244. https://doi.org/10.1023/B:AJCP.0000004744.09295.9b

Langhout, R. D. (2015). Considering community psychology competencies: A love letter to budding scholar-activists who wonder if they have what it takes. *American Journal of Community Psychology*, *55*(3–4), 266–278. https://doi.org/10.1007/s10464-015-9711-5

Langhout, R. D. (2016). This is not a history lesson; this is agitation: A call for a methodology of diffraction in US-based community psychology. *American Journal of Community Psychology*, *58*(3–4), 322–328. https://doi.org/10.1002/ajcp.12039

Langhout, R. D., Buckingham, S., Oberoi, A., Chávez, N., Rusch, D., Esposito, S., & Suarez-Balcazar, Y. (2018). Statement on the effects of deportation and forced separation on immigrants, their families, and communities. *American Journal of Community Psychology*, *62*(1–2), 3–12. https://doi.org/10.1002/ajcp.12256

Langhout, R. D., Collins, C., & Ellison, E. (2014). Examining relational empowerment for elementary school students in a yPAR program. *American Journal of Community Psychology*, *53*(3–4), 369–381. https://doi.org/10.1007/s10464-013-9617-z

Langhout, R. D., & Fernández, J. S. (2014). Empowerment evaluation conducted by 4th and 5th grade students. In D. Fetterman, S. Kaftarian, & A. Wandersman (Eds.), *Empowerment evaluation: Knowledge and tools for self-assessment, evaluation capacity building, and accountability* (pp. 193–232). Sage.

Langhout, R. D., & Thomas, E. (2010a). Children as protagonists: Participatory action research in collaboration with children [Special issue]. *American Journal of Community Psychology*. *46*(1–2).

Langhout, R. D., & Thomas, E. (2010b). Imagining participatory action research in collaboration with children: An introduction. *American Journal of Community Psychology*, *46*(1–2), 60–66. https://doi.org/10.1007/s10464-010-9321-1

Lappe, F. M., & DuBois, P. M. (1994). *The quickening of America: Rebuilding our nation, remaking our lives*. Jossey-Bass.

Lave, J., & Wenger, E. (1991). *Situated learning: Legitimate peripheral participation*. Cambridge University Press. https://doi.org/10.1017/CBO9780511815355

Lazarus, R. S., & Folkman, S. (1984). *Stress, appraisal, and coping*. Springer.

Lee, E., & Chan, K. (2009). Religious/spiritual and other adaptive coping strategies among Chinese American older immigrants. *Journal of Gerontological Social Work*, *52*(5), 517–533. https://doi.org/10.1080/01634370902983203

Lehavot, K., Balsam, K., & Ibrahim-Wells, G. (2009). Redefining the American quilt: Definitions and experiences of community among ethnically diverse lesbian and bisexual women. *Journal of Community Psychology*, *37*(4), 439–458. https://doi.org/10.1002/jcop.20305

Lehrner, A., & Allen, N. (2008). Social change movements and the struggle over meaning-making: A case study of domestic violence narratives. *American Journal of Community Psychology*, *42*(3–4), 220–234. https://doi.org/10.1007/s10464-008-9199-3

Leijten, P., Gardner, F., Melendez-Torres, G. J., van Aar, J., Hutchings, J., Schulz, S., Knerr, W., & Overbeek, G. (2019). Meta-analyses: Key parenting program components for disruptive child behavior. *Journal of the American Academy of Child & Adolescent Psychiatry*, *58*(2), 180–190. https://doi.org/10.1016/j.jaac.2018.07.900

Lenzi, M., Sharkey, J., Furlong, M. J., Mayworm, A., Hunnicutt, K., & Vieno, A. (2017). School sense of community, teacher support, and students' school safety perceptions. *American Journal of Community Psychology*, *60*(3–4), 527–537. https://doi.org/10.1002/ajcp.12174

Lerner, R. M. (1995). *America's youth in crisis: Challenges and options for programs and policies*. Sage. https://doi.org/10.4135/9781483327167

Leventhal, T., Fauth, R. C., & Brooks-Gunn, J. (2005). Neighborhood poverty and public policy: A 5-year follow-up of children's educational outcomes in New York City moving to opportunity demonstration. *Developmental Psychology, 41*(6), 933–952. https://doi.org/c3hw5t

Levine, A. (1982). *Love Canal: Science, politics, and people.* Heath.

Levine, M. (1981). *The history and politics of community mental health.* Oxford University Press.

Levine, M., & Levine, A. (1970). *A social history of helping services.* Oxford University Press.

Levine, M., & Levine, A. (1992). *Helping children: A social history.* Oxford University Press.

Levine, M., Perkins, D. D., & Perkins, D. V. (2005). *Principles of community psychology: Perspectives and applications* (3rd ed.). Oxford University Press.

Levine, M., & Perkins, D. V. (1987). *Principles of community psychology: Perspectives and applications.* Oxford University Press.

Lewin, K. (1935). *A dynamic theory of personality.* McGraw-Hill.

Lewis, J. (1998). *Walking with the wind: A memoir of the movement.* Simon & Schuster.

Lewis, J. A., Gee, P. M., Ho, C. L. L., & Miller, L. M. S. (2018). Understanding why older adults with type 2 diabetes join diabetes online communities: Semantic network analyses. *JMIR Aging, 1*(1), e10649.

Liegghio, M., Nelson, G., & Evans, S. (2010). Partnering with children diagnosed with mental health issues: Contributions of a sociology of childhood perspective to participatory action research. *American Journal of Community Psychology, 46*(1–2), 84–99. https://doi.org/10.1007/s10464-010-9323-z

Lilienfeld, S. O. (2007). Psychological treatments that cause harm. *Perspectives on Psychological Science, 2*(1), 53–70. https://doi.org/d8fdfn

Lim, Y. (2009). Can "refundable" state Earned Income Tax Credits explain child poverty in the American states? *Journal of Children & Poverty, 15*(1), 39–53. https://doi.org/10.1080/10796120802685415

Limber, S. P., Olweus, D., Wang, W., Masiello, M., & Breivik, K. (2018). Evaluation of the Olweus Bullying Prevention Program: A large scale study of U.S. students in grades 3–11. *Journal of School Psychology, 69,* 56–72. https://doi.org/10.1016/j.jsp.2018.04.004

Lin, Y., & Israel, T. (2012). Development and validation of a Psychological Sense of LGBT Community Scale. *Journal of Community Psychology, 40*(5), 573–587. https://doi.org/10.1002/jcop.21483

Lincoln, Y., & Guba, E. (1985). *Naturalistic inquiry.* Sage. https://doi.org/10.1016/0147-1767(85)90062-8

Linney, J. A. (1986). Court-ordered school desegregation: Shuffling the deck or playing a different game. In E. Seidman & J. Rappaport (Eds.), *Redefining social problems* (pp. 259–274). Plenum. https://doi.org/10.1007/978-1-4899-2236-6_15

Linney, J. A. (1989). Optimizing research strategies in the schools. In L. A. Bond & B. E. Compas (Eds.), *Primary prevention in the schools* (pp. 50–76). Sage.

Linney, J. A. (1990). Community psychology into the 1990s: Capitalizing opportunity and promoting innovation. *American Journal of Community Psychology, 18*(1), 1–17. https://doi.org/10.1007/BF00922686

Linney, J. A. (2000). Assessing ecological constructs and community context. In J. Rappaport & E. Seidman (Eds.), *Handbook of community psychology* (pp. 647–668). Kluwer/Plenum. https://doi.org/10.1007/978-1-4615-4193-6_27

Linney, J. A., & Reppucci, N. D. (1982). Research design and methods in community psychology. In P. Kendall & J. Butcher (Eds.), *Handbook of research methods in clinical psychology* (pp. 535–566). Wiley.

Linney, J. A., & Wandersman, A. (1991). *Prevention plus III: Assessing alcohol and other drug prevention programs at the school and community level: A four-step guide to useful program assessment.* U.S. Department of Health and Human Services, Office for Substance Abuse Prevention.

Lisker, J. (2016, May 8). Stonewall Inn raid enrages the homosexual community in 1969. *New York Daily News.* https://www.nydailynews.com/new-york/manhattan/stonewall-raid-enrages-homosexual-community-1969-article-1.2627685 (Original work published 1969)

Loeb, P. (1999). *Soul of a citizen: Living with conviction in a cynical time.* St. Martin's Press.

Lohmann, A., & McMurran, G. (2009). Resident-defined neighborhood mapping: Using GIS to analyze phenomenological neighborhoods. *Journal of Prevention & Intervention in the Community*, *37*(1), 66–81. https://doi.org/10.1080/10852350802498714

Long, D., & Perkins, D. D. (2003). Confirmatory factor analysis of the Sense of Community Index and development of a Brief SCI. *Journal of Community Psychology*, *31*(3), 279–296. https://doi.org/10.1002/jcop.10046

Lonner, W. (1994). Culture and human diversity. In E. J. Trickett, R. J. Watts, & D. Birman (Eds.), *Human diversity: Perspectives on people in context* (pp. 230–243). Jossey-Bass.

Loomis, C., & Wright, C. (2018). How many factors does the Sense of Community Index assess? *Journal of Community Psychology*, *46*(3), 383–396. https://doi.org/10.1002/jcop.21946

Lott, B. (2001). Low-income parents and the public schools. *Journal of Social Issues*, *57*(2), 247–259. https://doi.org/10.1111/0022-4537.00211

Lott, B., & Bullock, H. (2001). Who are the poor? *Journal of Social Issues*, *57*(2), 189–206. https://doi.org/10.1111/0022-4537.00208

Lounsbury, D. W., & Mitchell, S. G. (2009). Introduction to special issue on social ecological approaches to community health research and action. *American Journal of Community Psychology*, *44*(3–4), 213–220. https://doi.org/10.1007/s10464-009-9266-4

Luke, D. (2005). Getting the big picture in community science: Methods that capture context. *American Journal of Community Psychology*, *35*(3–4), 185–200. https://doi.org/10.1007/s10464-005-3397-z

Luke, D., Rappaport, J., & Seidman, E. (1991). Setting phenotypes in a mutual help organization: Expanding behavior setting theory. *American Journal of Community Psychology*, *19*(1), 147–168. https://doi.org/10.1007/bf00942263

Lukes, S. (2005). *Power: A radical view* (2nd ed.). Palgrave Macmillan. https://doi.org/10.1007/978-0-230-80257-5

Lurie, S. & Goldbloom, D.S. (2015). *More for the mind* and its legacy. *Canadian Journal of Community Mental Health*, 2015, *34*(4), 7–30. https://doi.org/10.7870/cjcmh-2015-007

Luthar, S. S., Cicchetti, D., & Becker, B. (2000). The construct of resilience: A critical evaluation and guidelines for future work. *Child Development*, *71*(3), 543–562. https://doi.org/10.1111/1467-8624.00164

Lykes, M. B. (2017). Community-based and participatory action research: Community psychology collaborations within and across borders. In M. A. Bond, I. Serrano-García, & C. B. Keys, (Eds.), *APA handbook of community psychology: Vol. 2. Methods for community research and action for diverse groups and issues* (pp. 43–58). American Psychological Association. https://doi.org/10.1037/14954-003

Lykes, M. B., Terre Blanche, M. T., & Hamber, B. (2003). Narrating survival and change in Guatemala and South Africa: The politics of representation and a liberatory community psychology. *American Journal of Community Psychology*, *31*(1–2), 79–90. https://doi.org/bf7rgd

Lyons, M. D., McQuillin, S. D., & Henderson, L. J. (2019). Finding the sweet spot: Investigating the effects of relationship closeness and instrumental activities in school-based mentoring. *American Journal of Community Psychology*, *63*(1–2), 88–98. https://doi.org/10.1002/ajcp.12283

Maldonado-Torres, N. (2007). On the coloniality of being: Contributions to the development of a concept. *Cultural Studies*, *21*(2–3), 240–270. https://doi.org/cf5z3c

Mammana-Lupo, V., Todd, N. R., & Houston, J. D. (2014). The role of sense of community and conflict in predicting congregational belonging. *Journal of Community Psychology*, *42*(1), 99–118. https://doi.org/10.1002/jcop.21596

Mankowski, E. S., & Maton, K. I. (2010). A community psychology of men and masculinity: Historical and conceptual review. *American Journal of Community Psychology*, *45*(1–2), 73–86. https://doi.org/10.1007/s10464-009-9288-y

Mann, J. M. (1989). AIDS: A worldwide pandemic. In M. Gottlieb, D. Jeffries, D. Mildvan, A. Pinching, & T. Quinn (Eds.), *Current topics in AIDS* (Vol. 2, pp. 1–10). John Wiley & Sons.

Mannarini, T., Rochira, A., & Talò, C. (2014). Negative psychological sense of community: Development of a measure and theoretical implications. *Journal of Community Psychology, 42*(6), 673–688. https://doi.org/10.1002/jcop.21645

Manning, M., Homel, R., & Smith, C. (2010). A meta-analysis of the effects of early developmental prevention programs in at-risk populations on non-health outcomes in adolescence. *Children and Youth Services Review, 32*(4), 506–519. https://doi.org/fqcvnj

Marecek, J., Fine, M., & Kidder, L. (1997). Working between worlds: Qualitative methods and social psychology. *Journal of Social Issues, 53*(4), 631–644. https://doi.org/drkbtb

Marrow, A. J. (1969). *The practical theorist.* Basic Books.

Marsella, A. J. (1998). Toward a "global-community psychology": Meeting the needs of a changing world. *American Psychologist, 53*(12), 1282–1291. https://doi.org/10.1037/0003-066X.53.12.1282

Martín-Baró, I. (1986). Hacia una psicología de la liberación [Toward a psychology of liberation]. *Boletin de Psicologia* (El Salvador), 5(22), 219–231.

Martín-Baró, I. (1994). *Writings for a liberation psychology* (A. Aron & S. Corne, Eds.). Harvard University Press.

Marx, R., & Kettrey, H. (2016). Gay-straight alliances are associated with lower levels of school-based victimization of LGBTQ+ youth: A systematic review and meta-analysis. *Journal of Youth and Adolescence, 45*(7), 1269–1282. https://doi.org/10.1007/s10964-016-0501-7

Mason, C., Chapman, D., & Scott, K. (1999). The identification of early risk factors for severe emotional disturbances and emotional handicaps: An epidemiological approach. *American Journal of Community Psychology, 27*(3), 357–381. https://doi.org/10.1023/A:1022281910190

Masten, A. S. (2001). Ordinary magic: Resilience processes in development. *American Psychologist, 56*(3), 227–238. https://doi.org/10.1037/0003-066X.56.3.227

Masten, A. S., & Powell, J. (2003). A resilience framework for research, policy, and practice. In S. Luthar (Ed.), *Resilience and vulnerability: Adaptation in the context of childhood adversities* (pp. 1–26). Cambridge University Press. https://doi.org/10.1017/CBO9780511615788.003

Maton, K. I. (1987). Patterns and psychological correlates of material support within a religious setting: The bidirectional support hypothesis. *American Journal of Community Psychology, 15*(2), 185–207. https://doi.org/10.1007/BF00919278

Maton, K. I. (1988). Social support, organizational characteristics, psychological well-being, and group appraisal in three self-help group populations. *American Journal of Community Psychology, 16*(1), 53–77. https://doi.org/10.1007/BF00906072

Maton, K. I. (2000). Making a difference: The social ecology of social transformation. *American Journal of Community Psychology, 28*(1), 25–57. https://doi.org/10.1023/A:1005190312887

Maton, K. I. (2001). Spirituality, religion, and community psychology: Historical perspective, positive potential, and challenges. *Journal of Community Psychology, 29*(5), 605–613. https://doi.org/10.1002/jcop.1039

Maton, K. I. (2008). Empowering community settings: Agents of individual development, community betterment, and positive social change. *American Journal of Community Psychology, 41*(1–2), 4–21. https://doi.org/10.1007/s10464-007-9148-6

Maton, K. I. (2016). *Influencing social policy: Applied psychology serving the public interest.* Oxford University Press. https://doi.org/10.1093/acprof:oso/9780199989973.001.0001

Maton, K. I., Humphreys, K., Jason, L. A., & Shinn, M. (2017). Community psychology in the policy arena. In M. A. Bond, I. Serrano-García, & C. B. Keys (Eds.), *APA handbook of community psychology:*

*Vol. 2. Methods for community research and action for diverse groups and issues* (pp. 275–295). American Psychological Association. https://doi.org/10.1037/14954-016

Maton, K. I., & Salem, D. A. (1995). Organizational characteristics of empowering community settings: A multiple case study approach. *American Journal of Community Psychology*, *23*(5), 631–656. https://doi.org/10.1007/BF02506985

Maton, K. I., Schellenbach, C., Leadbeater, B., & Solarz, A. (Eds.). (2004). *Investing in children, youth, families, and communities: Strengths-based research and policy*. American Psychological Association. https://doi.org/10.1037/10660-000

Mattis, J., & Jagers, R. (2001). A relational framework for the study of religiosity and spirituality in the lives of African Americans. *Journal of Community Psychology*, *29*(5), 519–539. https://doi.org/10.1002/jcop.1034

Maya Jariego, I. (2016). Ecological settings and theory of community action: "There is nothing more practical than a good theory" in community psychology. *Global Journal of Community Psychology Practice*, *7*(2), 1–6. https://doi.org/10.7728/0702201605

Mayer, J., & Davidson, W. S. (2000). Dissemination of innovation as social change. In J. Rappaport & E. Seidman (Eds.), *Handbook of community psychology* (pp. 421–438). Kluwer Academic/Plenum. https://doi.org/10.1007/978-1-4615-4193-6_18

McChesney, K. Y. (1990). Family homelessness: A systemic problem. *Journal of Social Issues*, *46*(4), 191–205. https://doi.org/10.1111/j.1540-4560.1990.tb01806.x

McConnell, E. A., Odahl-Ruan, C. A., Kozlowski, C., Shattell, M., & Todd, N. R. (2016). Trans women and Michfest: An ethnophenomenology of attendees' experiences. *Journal of Lesbian Studies*, *20*(1), 8–28. https://doi.org/10.1080/10894160.2015.1076234

McConnell, E. A., Todd, N. R., Odahl-Ruan, C., & Shattell, M. (2016). Complicating counterspaces: Intersectionality and the Michigan Womyn's Music Festival. *American Journal of Community Psychology*, *57*(3–4), 473–488. https://doi.org/10.1002/ajcp.12051

McDonald, K. E., & Keys, C. B. (2008). How the powerful decide: Access to research participation by those at the margins. *American Journal of Community Psychology*, *42*(1–2), 79–93. https://doi.org/10.1007/s10464-008-9192-x

McDonald, K. E., Keys, C. B., & Balcazar, F. E. (2007). Disability, race/ethnicity and gender: Themes of cultural oppression, acts of individual resistance. *American Journal of Community Psychology*, *39*(1–2), 145–161. https://doi.org/10.1007/s10464-007-9094-3

McDonald, K. E., Raymaker, D., & Gibbons, C. (2017). A call to consciousness: Community psychology and disability. In M. A. Bond, I. Serrano-García, C. B. Keys, & M. Shinn (Eds.), *APA handbook of community psychology: Vol. 1. Theoretical foundations, core concepts, and emerging challenges* (pp. 403–419). American Psychological Association. https://doi.org/10.1037/14953-020

McIntosh, P. (1998). White privilege and male privilege: A personal account of coming to see correspondences through work in women's studies. In M. L. Andersen & P. H. Collins (Eds.), *Race, class, and gender: An anthology* (3rd ed., pp. 94–105). Wadsworth.

McLaughlin, M., & Mitra, D. (2001). Theory-based change and change-based theory: Going deeper, going broader. *Journal of Educational Change*, *2*(4), 301–323. https://doi.org/10.1023/A:1014616908334

McLoyd, V. C. (1998). Socioeconomic disadvantage and child development. *American Psychologist*, *53*(2), 185–204. https://doi.org/10.1037/0003-066X.53.2.185

McMahon, S. D., & Wolfe, S. M. (2017). Career opportunities for community psychologists. In M. A. Bond, I. Serrano-García, and C. B. Keys (Eds.), *APA handbook of community psychology: Vol. 2. Methods for community research and action for diverse groups and issues* (pp. 645–659). American Psychological Association. https://doi.org/10.1037/14954-038

McMillan, B., Florin, P., Stevenson, J., Kerman, B., & Mitchell, R. E. (1995). Empowerment praxis in community coalitions. *American Journal of Community Psychology*, *23*(5), 699–727. https://doi.org/10.1007/BF02506988

McMillan, D. (1996). Sense of community. *Journal of Community Psychology*, *24*(4), 315–325. https://doi.org/b35qjg

McMillan, D., & Chavis, D. (1986). Sense of community: Definition and theory. *Journal of Community Psychology*, *14*(1), 6–23. https://doi.org/fvxz24

McNally, R., Bryant, R., & Ehlers, A. (2003). Does early psychological intervention promote recovery from posttraumatic stress? *Psychological Science in the Public Interest*, *4*(2), 45–79. https://doi.org/10.1111/1529-1006.01421

McPherson, M., Smith-Lovin, L., & Cook, J. M. (2001). Birds of a feather: Homophily in social networks. *Annual Review of Sociology*, *27*, 415–444. https://doi.org/10.1146/annurev.soc.27.1.415

Meissen, G., Hazel, K., Berkowitz, B., & Wolff, T. (2008). The story of the first ever Summit on Community Psychology Practice. *Community Psychologist*, *41*(1), 40–41.

Melton, G. B. (1995). Bringing psychology to Capitol Hill: Briefings on child and family policy. *American Psychologist*, *50*(9), 766–770. https://doi.org/10.1037/0003-066X.50.9.766

Melton, G. B. (2000). Community change, community stasis, and the law. In J. Rappaport & E. Seidman (Eds.), *Handbook of community psychology* (pp. 523–540). Kluwer Academic/Plenum. https://doi.org/10.1007/978-1-4615-4193-6_22

Mennis, J., Mason, M., & Ambrus, A. (2018). Urban greenspace is associated with reduced psychological stress among adolescents: A Geographic Ecological Momentary Assessment (GEMA) analysis of activity space. *Landscape and Urban Planning*, *174*, 1–9. https://doi.org/10.1016/j.landurbplan.2018.02.008

Merrell, K. W., Gueldner, B. A., Ross, S. W., & Isava, D. M. (2008). How effective are school bullying intervention programs? A meta-analysis of intervention research. *School Psychology Quarterly*, *23*(1), 26–42. https://doi.org/10.1037/1045-3830.23.1.26

Merrill, J., Pinsky, I., Killeya-Jones, L., Sloboda, Z., & Dilascio, T. (2006). Substance abuse prevention infrastructure: A survey-based study of the organizational structure and function of the D.A.R.E. program. *Substance Abuse Treatment, Prevention, and Policy*, *1*, Article 25. https://doi.org/10.1186/1747-597X-1-25

Meyers, J. (2000). A community psychologist in the public policy arena. In J. Rappaport & E. Seidman (Eds.), *Handbook of community psychology* (pp. 761–764). Kluwer/Plenum.

Michalopoulos, C., Faucetta, K., Warren, A., & Mitchell, R. (2017). *Evidence on the long-term effects of home visiting programs: Laying the groundwork for long-term follow-up in the mother and infant home visiting program evaluation* (OPRE Report No. 2017-73). Office of Planning, Research and Evaluation, Administration for Children and Families, U.S. Department of Health and Human Services.

Michalopoulos, C., Lee, H., Duggan, A., Lundquist, E., Tso, A., Crowne, S., Burrell, L., Somers, J., Filene, J., & Knox, V. (2015). *The mother and infant home visiting program evaluation: Early findings on the Maternal, Infant, and Early Childhood Home Visiting Program* (OPRE Report No. 2015-11). Office of Planning, Research and Evaluation, Administration for Children and Families, U.S. Department of Health and Human Services.

Milkman, R. (2017). A new political generation: Millennials and the post-2008 wave of protest. *American Sociological Review*, *82*(1), 1–31. https://doi.org/10.1177/0003122416681031

Miller, J. B. (1976). *Toward a new psychology of women*. Beacon Press.

Miller, R., & Shinn, M. (2005). Learning from communities: Overcoming difficulties in dissemination of prevention and promotion efforts. *American Journal of Community Psychology*, *35*(3–4), 169–183. https://doi.org/10.1007/s10464-005-3395-1

Mirowsky, J., & Ross, C. (1989). *Social causes of psychological distress*. Aldine de Gruyter.

Mishel, L., Bernstein, J., & Shierholz, H. (2009). *The state of working America 2008/2009*. Economic Policy Institute.

Mishel, L., & Schieder, J. (2017). *CEO pay remains high relative to the pay of typical workers and high-wage earners*. Economic Policy Institute. https://www.epi.org/publication/ceo-pay-remains-high-relative-to-the-pay-of-typical-workers-and-high-wage-earners/

Moane, G. (2003). Bridging the personal and the political: Practices for a liberation psychology. *American Journal of Community Psychology*, *31*(1–2), 91–101. https://doi.org/10.1023/A:1023026704576

Mock, M. (1999). Cultural competency: Acts of justice in community mental health. *Community Psychologist*, *32*(1), 38–41.

Mohatt, G., Hazel, K., Allen, J., Stachelrodt, M., Hensel, C., & Fath, R. (2004). Unheard Alaska: Culturally anchored participatory action research on sobriety with Alaska Natives. *American Journal of Community Psychology*, *33*(3–4), 263–273. https://doi.org/10.1023/B:AJCP.0000027011.12346.70

Montero, M. (1996). Parallel lives: Community psychology in Latin America and the United States. *American Journal of Community Psychology*, *24*(5), 589–605. https://doi.org/10.1007/BF02509715

Montero, M. (Ed.). (2002). Conceptual and epistemological aspects in community social psychology [Special issue]. *American Journal of Community Psychology*, *30*(4).

Montero, M. (2007). The political psychology of liberation: From politics to ethics and back. *Political Psychology*, *28*(5), 517–533. https://doi.org/10.1111/j.1467-9221.2007.00588.x

Montero, M., Sonn, C. C., & Burton, M. (2017). Community psychology and liberation psychology: A creative synergy for an ethical and transformative praxis. In M. A. Bond, I. Serrano-García, C. B. Keys, & M. Shinn (Eds.), *APA handbook of community psychology: Vol. 1. Theoretical foundations, core concepts, and emerging challenges* (pp. 149–168). American Psychological Association. https://doi.org/10.1037/14953-007

Montero, M., & Varas-Díaz, N. (2007). Latin American community psychology: Development, implications, and challenges within a social change agenda. In S. M. Reich, M. Riemer, I. Prilleltensky, & M. Montero (Eds.), *International community psychology: History and theories* (pp. 63–98). Springer.

Moore, G. F., Audrey, S., Barker, M., Bond, L., Bonell, C., Hardeman, W., Moore, L., O'Cathain, A., Tinati, T., Wight, D., & Baird, J. (2015). Process evaluation of complex interventions: Medical Research Council guidance. *British Medical Journal*, *350*, h1258. https://doi.org/10.1136/bmj.h1258

Moore, T. (1977). Social change and community psychology. In I. Iscoe, B. Bloom, & C. D. Spielberger (Eds.), *Community psychology in transition* (pp. 257–266). Hemisphere.

Moore, T., Kloos, B., & Rasmussen, R. (2001). A reunion of ideas: Complementary inquiry and collaborative interventions of spirituality, religion, and psychology. *Journal of Community Psychology*, *29*(5), 487–495. https://doi.org/10.1002/jcop.1032

Moos, R. (1973). Conceptualizations of human environments. *American Psychologist*, *28*(8), 652–665. https://doi.org/10.1037/h0035722

Moos, R. (1974). *Evaluating treatment environments: A social ecological approach*. Wiley.

Moos, R. (1984). Context and coping: Toward a unifying conceptual framework. *American Journal of Community Psychology*, *12*(1), 5–36. https://doi.org/10.1007/BF00896933

Moos, R. (1994). *The social climate scales: A user's guide* (2nd ed.). Consulting Psychologists Press.

Moos, R. (2002). The mystery of human context and coping: An unraveling of clues. *American Journal of Community Psychology*, *30*(1), 67–88. https://doi.org/10.1023/A:1014372101550

Moos, R. (2003). Social contexts: Transcending their power and their fragility. *American Journal of Community Psychology*, *31*(1–2), 1–13. https://doi.org/10.1023/A:1023041101850

Moos, R., & Holahan, C. J. (2003). Dispositional and contextual perspectives on coping: Toward an integrative framework. *Journal of Clinical Psychology*, *59*(12), 1387–1403. https://doi.org/10.1002/jclp.10229

Moos, R., & Trickett, E. J. (1987). *Classroom Environment Scale manual* (2nd ed.). Consulting Psychologists Press.

Morgan, D. (2019). After triangulation, what next? [Editorial]. *Journal of Mixed Methods Research*, *13*(1), 6–11. https://doi.org/10.1177/1558689818780596

Morris, M. (2015). Professional judgment and ethics. In V. C. Scott & S. M. Wolfe (Eds.), *Community psychology: Foundations for practice* (pp. 132–156). Sage. https://doi.org/10.4135/9781483398150.n5

Mozur, P. (2018, October 15). A genocide incited on Facebook, with posts from Myanmar's military. *New York Times*. https://nyti.ms/2QToYQA

Mrazek, P., & Haggerty, R. (1994). *Reducing risks for mental disorders: Frontiers for preventive intervention research*. National Academy Press.

Muehrer, P. (Ed.). (1997). Prevention research in rural settings [Special issue]. *American Journal of Community Psychology*, *25*(4).

Mulder, P. L., Shellenberger, S., Streigel, R., Jumper-Thurman, P., Danda, C. E., Kenkel, M. B., Constantine, M. G., Sears, S.F., Jr., Kalodner, M., & Hager, A. (1999). *The behavioral healthcare needs of rural women*. Rural Women's Work Group of the Rural Task Force of the American Psychological Association and the American Psychological Association's Committee on Rural Health. http://www.apa.org/pubs/info/reports/rural-women.pdf

Mulvey, A. (1988). Community psychology and feminism: Tensions and commonalities. *Journal of Community Psychology*, *16*(1), 70–83. https://doi.org/fhrq3p

Mulvey, A. (2002). Gender, economic context, perceptions of safety, and quality of life: A case study of Lowell, Massachusetts (U.S.A.), 1982–96. *American Journal of Community Psychology*, *30*(5), 655–679. https://doi.org/10.1023/A:1016321231618

Munn-Giddings, C., & Borkman, T. (2017). Self-help / mutual aid as a psychosocial phenomenon. In S. Ramon & J. E. Williams (Eds.), *Mental health at the crossroads: The promise of the psychosocial approach* (pp. 153–170). Routledge.

Murray, C. D., & Fox, J. (2006). Do internet self-harm discussion groups alleviate or exacerbate self-harming behaviour? *Australian e-Journal for the Advancement of Mental Health*, *5*(3), 225–233. https://doi.org/10.5172/jamh.5.3.225

Murray, H. (1938). *Explorations in personality*. Oxford University Press.

Myers, J. K., & Bean, L. L. (1968). *A decade later: A follow-up of social class and mental illness*. Wiley.

Nagler, M. (2001). *Is there no other way? The search for a nonviolent future*. Berkeley Hills Books.

Nation, M., Crusto, C., Wandersman, A., Kumpfer, K. L., Seybolt, D., Morrissey-Kane, E., & Davino, K. (2003). What works in prevention: Principles of effective prevention programs. *American Psychologist*, *58*(6–7), 449–456. https://doi.org/10.1037/0003-066X.58.6-7.449

National Conference of State Legislatures. (2019). *Tax credits for working families: Earned Income Tax Credit (EITC)*. http://www.ncsl.org/research/labor-and-employment/earned-income-tax-credits-for-working-families.aspx

Neal, J. (2014). Exploring empowerment in settings: Mapping distributions of network power. *American Journal of Community Psychology*, *53*, 394–406. https://doi.org/10.1007/s10464-013-9609-z

Neal, J., & Neal, Z. (2011). Power as a structural phenomenon. *American Journal of Community Psychology*, *48*(3–4), 157–167. https://doi.org/10.1007/s10464-010-9356-3

Neal, Z. (2017). Taking stock of the diversity and sense of community debate. *American Journal of Community Psychology*, *59*(3–4), 255–260. https://doi.org/10.1002/ajcp.12132

Neal, Z., & Neal, J. (2014). The (in)compatibility of diversity and sense of community. *American Journal of Community Psychology*, *53*(1–2), 1–12. https://doi.org/10.1007/s10464-013-9608-0

Neigher, W., & Fishman, D. (2004). Case studies in community practice. *Community Psychologist*, *37*(2), 30–34. https://www.scra27.org/files/4913/9015/9175/tcp04.spring.pdf#page=30

Nelson, D. L., & Simmons, B. L. (2003). Health psychology and work stress: A more positive approach. In J. C. Quick & L. E. Tetrick (Eds.), *Handbook of occupational health psychology* (pp. 97–119). American Psychological Association. https://doi.org/10.1037/10474-005

Nelson, G., Kloos, B., & Ornelas, J. (Eds.). (2014). *Community psychology and community mental health: Towards transformative change.* Oxford University Press.

Nelson, G., Lavoie, F., & Mitchell, T. (2007). The history and theories of community psychology in Canada. In S. M. Reich, M. Reimer, I. Prilleltensky, & M. Montero (Eds.), *The history and theories of community psychology: An international perspective* (pp. 13–36). Springer.

Nelson, G., & Prilleltensky, I. (Eds.). (2010). *Community psychology: In pursuit of liberation and well-being* (2nd ed.). Palgrave Macmillan.

Nelson, G., Prilleltensky, I., & MacGillivary, H. (2001). Building value-based partnerships: Toward solidarity with oppressed groups. *American Journal of Community Psychology, 29*(5), 649–677. https://doi.org/10.1023/A:1010406400101

Nevid, J. S., & Rathus, S. A. (2016). *Psychology and the challenges of life* (13th ed.). Wiley.

New Freedom Commission on Mental Health. (2003). *Achieving the promise: Transforming mental health care in America* (Final report, DHHS Publication No. SMA-03-3832).

Newbrough, J. R. (1995). Toward community: A third position. *American Journal of Community Psychology, 23*(1), 9–37. https://doi.org/10.1007/BF02506921

Newbrough, J. R. (Ed.). (1996). Sense of community [Special issue]. *Journal of Community Psychology, 24*(4).

Newton, L., Rosen, A., Tennant, C., Hobbs, C., Lapsley, H. M., & Tribe, K. (2000). Deinstitutionalisation for long-term mental illness: An ethnographic study. *Australian and New Zealand Journal of Psychiatry, 34*(3), 484–490. https://doi.org/10.1080/j.1440-1614.2000.00733.x

Nicotera, N. (2007). Measuring neighborhood: A conundrum for human service researchers and practitioners. *American Journal of Community Psychology, 40*(1–2), 26–51. https://doi.org/10.1007/s10464-007-9124-1

Norris, F., Friedman, M., Watson, P., Byrne, C., Diaz, E., & Kaniasty, K. (2002). 60,000 disaster victims speak: Part I. An empirical review of the empirical literature, 1981–2001. *Psychiatry, 65*(3), 207–239. https://doi.org/10.1521/psyc.65.3.207.20173

Norris, F., Stevens, S., Pfefferbaum, B., Wyche, K., & Pfefferbaum, R. (2008). Community resilience as a metaphor, theory, set of capacities, and strategy for disaster readiness. *American Journal of Community Psychology, 41*(1–2), 127–150. https://doi.org/10.1007/s10464-007-9156-6

Northwest Regional Educational Laboratory. (1999). *Making the case: Measuring the impact of your mentoring program.* http://www.nwrel.org/mentoring/pdf/makingcase.pdf

Nowell, B., & Boyd, N. (2010). Viewing community as responsibility as well as resource: Deconstructing the theoretical roots of psychological sense of community. *Journal of Community Psychology, 38*(7), 828–841. https://doi.org/10.1002/jcop.20398

Nowell, B., & Boyd, N. (2014). Sense of community responsibility in community collaboratives: Advancing a theory of community as resource and responsibility. *American Journal of Community Psychology, 54*(3–4), 229–242. https://doi.org/10.1007/s10464-014-9667-x

Nowell, B., Izod, A., Ngaruiya, K., & Boyd, N. (2016). Public service motivation and sense of community responsibility: Comparing two motivational constructs in understanding leadership within community collaboratives. *Journal of Public Administration Research and Theory, 26*(4), 663–676. https://doi.org/10.1093/jopart/muv048

Nussbaum, M. C. (2000). *Women and human development: The capabilities approach.* Cambridge University Press. https://doi.org/10.1017/CBO9780511841286

Nussbaum, M. C. (2011). *Creating capabilities: The human development approach.* Harvard University Press. https://doi.org/10.4159/harvard.9780674061200

Oakford, P., Brumfield, C., Goldvale, C., Tatum, L., diZerega, M., & Patrick, F. (2019). *Investing in futures: Economic and fiscal benefits of postsecondary education in prison.* Vera Institute for Justice. https://storage.googleapis.com/vera-web-assets/downloads/Publications/investing-in-futures-education-in-prison/legacy_downloads/investing-in-futures.pdf

Obst, P., & Stafurik, J. (2010). Online we are all able bodied: Online psychological sense of community and social support found through membership of disability-specific websites promotes well-being for people living with a physical disability. *Journal of Community & Applied Social Psychology, 20*(6), 525–531. https://doi.org/10.1002/casp.1067

Obst, P., & White, K. (2004). Revisiting the Sense of Community Index: A confirmatory factor analysis. *Journal of Community Psychology, 32*(6), 691–705. https://doi.org/10.1002/jcop.20027

O'Connor, E. L., Longman, U., White, K. M., & Obst, P. L. (2015). Sense of community, social identity and social support among players of massively multiplayer online games (MMOGs): A qualitative analysis. *Journal of Community & Applied Social Psychology, 25*(6), 459–473. https://doi.org/10.1002/casp.2224

O'Donnell, C. R. (2005, June 9–10). *Beyond diversity: Toward a cultural community psychology* [Presidential address]. Biennial Meeting of the Society for Community Research and Action, Champaign-Urbana, IL.

O'Donnell, C. R., & Tharp, R. G. (2012). Integrating cultural community psychology: Activity settings and the shared meanings of intersubjectivity. *American Journal of Community Psychology, 49*(1–2), 22–30. https://doi.org/10.1007/s10464-011-9434-1

O'Donnell, C. R., Tharp, R. G., & Wilson, K. (1993). Activity settings as the unit of analysis: A theoretical basis for community intervention and development. *American Journal of Community Psychology, 21*(4), 501–520. https://doi.org/10.1007/BF00942157

O'Donnell, C. R., & Yamauchi, L. (Eds.). (2005). *Culture and context in human behavior change: Theory, research, and applications.* Peter Lang.

Oesterle, S., Kullinski, M., Hawkins, D., Skinner, M., Guttmannova, K., & Rhew, I. (2018). Long-term effects of the Communities That Care trial on substance use, antisocial behavior, and violence through age 21 years. *American Journal of Public Health, 108*(5), 659–665. https://doi.org/10.2105/AJPH.2018.304320

Office of the Surgeon General. (2016). *Facing addiction in America: The surgeon general's report on alcohol, drugs, and health.* U.S. Department of Health and Human Services.

Ohlemacher, S. (2010, April 17). *Nearly half of US households escape fed income tax.* Associated Press. http://finance.yahoo.com/news/Nearly-half-of-US-households-apf-1105567323.html?x=0&.v=1

Ohmer, M. L. (2007). Citizen participation in neighborhood organizations and its relationship to volunteers' self- and collective efficacy and sense of community. *Social Work Research, 31*(2), 109–120. https://doi.org/10.1093/swr/31.2.109

Olweus, D. (1997). Bully/victim problems in school: Facts and intervention. *European Journal of Psychology of Education, 12*, 495–510. https://doi.org/10.1007/BF03172807

Olweus, D., & Limber, S. P. (2010). Bullying in school: Evaluation and dissemination of the Olweus Bullying Prevention Program. *American Journal of Orthopsychiatry, 80*(1), 124–134. https://doi.org/10.1002/fqbc47

Olweus, D., Limber, S., & Mihalic, S. (1999). *Blueprints for violence prevention: Vol. 10. The Bullying Prevention Program.* Center for the Study and Prevention of Violence.

Olson, B. (2004, Fall). Thoughts on attending SCRA at the APA convention this year. *The Community Psychologist, 37*, 48-49.

O'Neil, J. (2014). *Men's gender role conflict: Psychological costs, consequences, and an agenda for change.* American Psychological Association.

O'Neill, P. (2005). The ethics of problem definition. *Canadian Psychology, 46*(1), 13–20. https://doi.org/10.1037/h0085819

Ortiz-Torres, B., Serrano-García, I., & Torres-Burgos, N. (2000). Subverting culture: Promoting HIV/AIDS prevention among Puerto Rican and Dominican women. *American Journal of Community Psychology*, *28*(6), 859–881. https://doi.org/10.1023/A:1005167917916

Ostrove, J., & Cole, E. (2003). Privileging class: Toward a critical psychology of social class in the context of education. *Journal of Social Issues*, *59*(4), 677–692. https://doi.org/10.1046/j.0022-4537.2003.00084.x

Ott, D. (2005, July 19). Revitalization efforts gets failing grade, survey says. *Philadelphia Inquirer*, B1, B6.

Oxley, D., & Barrera, M., Jr. (1984). Undermanning theory and the workplace: Implications of setting size for job satisfaction and social support. *Environment and Behavior*, *16*(2), 211–234. https://doi.org/10.1177/0013916584162004

Ozer, E., & Russo, I. (2017). Development and context across the lifespan: A community psychology synthesis. In M. A. Bond, I. Serrano-García, C. B. Keys, & M. Shinn (Eds.), *APA handbook of community psychology: Vol. 1. Theoretical foundations, core concepts, and emerging challenges* (pp. 421–436). American Psychological Association. https://doi.org/10.1037/14953-021

Ozer, E., & Wright, D. (2012). Beyond school spirit: The effects of youth-led participatory action research in two urban high schools. *Journal of Research on Adolescence*, *22*(2), 267–283. https://doi.org/10.1111/j.1532-7795.2012.00780.x

Padgett, D., Henwood, B. F., & Tsemberis, S. J. (2016). *Housing First: Ending homelessness, transforming systems, and changing lives*. Oxford University Press.

Pager, D. (2003). The mark of a criminal record. *American Journal of Sociology*, *108*(5), 937–975. https://doi.org/10.1086/374403

Pargament, K. I. (1997). *The psychology of religion and coping: Theory, research, practice*. Guilford Press.

Pargament, K. I. (2008). The sacred character of community life. *American Journal of Community Psychology*, *41*(1–2), 22–34. https://doi.org/10.1007/s10464-007-9150-z

Park, R. (1952). *Human communities: The city and human ecology*. Free Press.

Parrott, S., & Parrott, C. T. (2015). U.S. television's "mean world" for White women: The portrayal of gender and race on fictional crime dramas. *Sex Roles*, *73*(1–2), 70–82. https://doi.org/10.1007/s11199-015-0505-x

Pascoe, E. A., & Smart Richman, L. (2009). Perceived discrimination and health: A meta-analytic review. *Psychological Bulletin*, *135*(4), 531–554. https://doi.org/10.1037/a0016059

Patton, M. Q. (2006). Evaluation for the way we work. *Nonprofit Quarterly*, *13*(1), 28–33. https://nonprofitquarterly.org/evaluation-for-the-way-we-work/

Patton, M. Q. (2008). *Utilization-focused evaluation* (4th ed.). Sage Publications.

Paxton, P. (2002). Social capital and democracy: An interdependent relationship. *American Sociological Review*, *67*(2), 254–277. https://doi.org/10.2307/3088895

Paxton, P. (2007). Association membership and generalized trust: A multilevel model across 32 countries. *Social Forces*, *86*(1), 47–76. https://doi.org/10.1353/sof.2007.0107

Payne, B. K., Vuletich, H. A., & Lundberg, K. B. (2017). The bias of crowds: How implicit bias bridges personal and systemic prejudice. *Psychological Inquiry*, *28*(4), 233–248. https://doi.org/10.1080/1047840X.2017.1335568

Peasant, C., Parra, G. R., & Okwumabua, T. M. (2015). Condom negotiation: Findings and future directions. *Journal of Sex Research*, *52*(4), 470–483. https://doi.org/dr2b

Pepler, D., & Slaby, R. (1994). Theoretical and developmental perspectives on youth and violence. In L. Eron, J. Gentry, & P. Schlegel (Eds.), *Reason to hope: A psychosocial perspective on violence and youth* (pp. 27–58). American Psychological Association. https://doi.org/10.1037/10164-001

Perisho Eccleston, S. M., & Perkins, D. D. (2019). The role of community psychology in Christian community development. *Journal of Community Psychology*, *47*(2), 291–310. https://doi.org/10.1002/jcop.22121

Perkins, D. D., Brown, B. B., & Taylor, R. B. (1996). The ecology of empowerment: Predicting participation in community organizations. *Journal of Social Issues*, *52*(1), 85–110. https://doi.org/fpfjth

Perkins, D. D., Crim, B., Silberman, P., & Brown, B. (2004). Community development as a response to community-level adversity: Ecological theory and strengths-based policy. In K. I. Maton, C. J. Schellenbach, B. J. Leadbeater, & A. L. Solarz (Eds.), *Investing in children, youth, families, and communities: Strengths-based research and policy* (pp. 321–340). American Psychological Association. https://doi.org/10.1037/10660-018

Perkins, D. D., Florin, P., Rich, R., Wandersman, A., & Chavis, D. M. (1990). Participation and the social and physical environment of residential blocks: Crime and community contexts. *American Journal of Community Psychology, 18*(1), 83–115. https://doi.org/10.1007/BF00922690

Perkins, D. D., Hughey, J., & Speer, P. (2002). Community psychology perspectives on social capital theory and community development practice. *Journal of the Community Development Society, 33*(1), 33–52. https://doi.org/10.1080/15575330209490141

Perkins, D. D., & Long, D. A. (2002). Neighborhood sense of community and social capital: A multi-level analysis. In A. Fisher, C. Sonn, & B. Bishop (Eds.), *Psychological sense of community: Research, applications and implications* (pp. 291–318). Kluwer/Plenum. https://doi.org/10.1007/978-1-4615-0719-2_15

Perkins, D. D., & Schensul, J. J. (2017). Interdisciplinary contributions to community psychology and transdisciplinary promise. In M. A. Bond, I. Serrano-García, C. B. Keys, & M. Shinn (Eds.), *APA handbook of community psychology: Vol. 1. Theoretical foundations, core concepts, and emerging challenges* (pp. 189–209). American Psychological Association. https://doi.org/10.1037/14953-009

Perkins, D. D., & Taylor, R. (1996). Ecological assessments of community disorder: Their relationship to fear of crime and theoretical implications. *American Journal of Community Psychology, 24*(1), 63–107. https://doi.org/10.1007/bf02511883

Perkins, D. D., & Zimmerman, M. A. (1995). Empowerment theory, research and application. *American Journal of Community Psychology, 23*(5), 569–579. https://doi.org/10.1007/BF02506982

Perkins, D. V., Burns, T. F., Perry, J. C, & Nielsen, K. P. (1988). Behavior setting theory and community psychology: An analysis and critique. *Journal of Community Psychology, 16*(4), 355–372. https://doi.org/dfd4t4

Peterson, N. A., & Reid, R. J. (2003). Paths to psychological empowerment in an urban community: Sense of community and citizen participation in substance abuse prevention activities. *Journal of Community Psychology, 31*(1), 25–38. https://doi.org/10.1002/jcop.10034

Peterson, N. A., Speer, P. W., & McMillan, D. (2008). Validation of a Brief Sense of Community Scale: Confirmation of the principal theory of sense of community. *Journal of Community Psychology, 36*(1), 61–73. https://doi.org/10.1002/jcop.20217

Peterson, N. A., & Zimmerman, M. (2004). Beyond the individual: Toward a nomological network of organizational empowerment. *American Journal of Community Psychology, 34*(1–2), 129–145. https://doi.org/dmdm3j

Peterson, R. B. (2018). Taking it to the city: Urban-placed pedagogies in Detroit and Roxbury. *Journal of Environmental Studies and Sciences, 8*(3), 326–342. https://doi.org/10.1007/s13412-017-0455-4

Petrosino, A., Buehler, J., & Turpin-Petrosino, C. (2003). *"Scared Straight" and other juvenile awareness programs for preventing juvenile delinquency.* Campbell Collaboration. https://campbellcollaboration.org/better-evidence/juvenile-delinquency-scared-straight-etc-programmes.html

Phillips, D. (2000). Social policy and community psychology. In J. Rappaport & E. Seidman (Eds.), *Handbook of community psychology* (pp. 397–419). Kluwer/Plenum. https://doi.org/10.1007/978-1-4615-4193-6_17

Phinney, J. (1990). Ethnic identity in adolescents and adults: Review of research. *Psychological Bulletin, 108*(3), 499–514. https://doi.org/10.1037/0033-2909.108.3.499

Phinney, J. (2003). Ethnic identity and acculturation. In K. Chun, P. Organista, & G. Marin (Eds.), *Acculturation: Advances in theory, measurement, and applied research* (pp. 63–81). American Psychological Association. https://doi.org/10.1037/10472-006

Phinney, J. S. (1993). A three-stage model of ethnic identity development in adolescence. In M. Bernal & G. Knight (Eds.), *Ethnic identity: Formation and transmission among Hispanics and other minorities* (pp. 61–79). State University of New York Press

Pianta, R., & Ansari, A. (2018). Does attendance in private schools predict outcomes at age 15? Evidence from a longitudinal study. *Educational Researcher, 47*(7), 419–434. https://doi.org/10.3102/0013189X18785632

Pickren, W., & Tomes, H. (2002). The legacy of Kenneth B. Clark to the APA: The Board of Social and Ethical Responsibility. *American Psychologist, 57*(1), 51–59. https://doi.org/10.1037/0003-066X.57.1.51

Pieterse, A. L., Todd, N. R., Neville, H. A., & Carter, R. T. (2012). Perceived racism and mental health among Black American adults: A meta-analytic review. *Journal of Counseling Psychology, 59*(1), 1–9. https://doi.org/10.1037/a0026208

Pistrang, N., Barker, C., & Humphreys, K. (2008). Mutual help groups for mental health problems: A review of effectiveness studies. *American Journal of Community Psychology, 42*(1–2), 110–121. https://doi.org/10.1007/s10464-008-9181-0

Plas, J. M., & Lewis, S. E. (1996). Environmental factors and sense of community in a planned town. *American Journal of Community Psychology, 24*(1), 109–143. https://doi.org/10.1007/BF02511884

Pokorny, S., Baptiste, D., Tolan, P., Hirsch, B., Talbot, B., Ji, P., Paikoff, R., & Madison-Boyd, S. (2004). Prevention science: Participatory approaches and community case studies. In L. A. Jason, C. Keys, Y. Suarez-Balcazar, R. Taylor, & M. Davis (Eds.), *Participatory community research: Theories and methods in action* (pp. 87–104). American Psychological Association. https://doi.org/10.1037/10726-005

Ponce, A. N., & Rowe, M. (2018). Citizenship and community mental health care. *American Journal of Community Psychology, 61*(1–2), 22–31. https://doi.org/10.1002/ajcp.12218

Pool, B. (2009, October 16). Woman, 97, has a front seat to homelessness. *Los Angeles Times.* http://articles.latimes.com/2009/oct/16/local/me-bessie16

Portillo, N. (2012). The life of Ignacio Martín-Baró: A narrative account of a personal biographical journey. *Peace and Conflict: Journal of Peace Psychology, 18*(1), 77–87. https://doi-org.pallas2.tcl.sc.edu/10.1037/a0027066

Potts, R. G. (2003). Emancipatory education versus school-based prevention in African-American communities. *American Journal of Community Psychology, 31*(1–2), 173–183. https://doi.org/10.1023/A:1023039007302

Prelow, H. M., Danoff-Burg, S., Swenson, R. R., & Pulgiano, D. (2004). The impact of ecological risk and perceived discrimination on psychological adjustment of African American and European American youth. *Journal of Community Psychology, 32*(4), 375–389. https://doi.org/10.1002/jcop.20007

Prestby, J. E., Wandersman, A., Florin, P., Rich, R., & Chavis, D. (1990). Benefits, costs, incentive management and participation in voluntary organizations: A means to understanding and promoting empowerment. *American Journal of Community Psychology, 18*(1), 117–149. https://doi.org/10.1007/BF00922691

Pretty, G. M. H. (2002). Young people's development of the community-minded self: Considering community identity, community attachment, and sense of community. In A. Fisher, C. Sonn, & B. Bishop (Eds.), *Psychological sense of community: Research, applications, and implications* (pp. 183–203). Kluwer/Plenum.

Prezza, M., Amici, M., Roberti, T., & Tedeschi, G. (2001). Sense of community referred to the whole town: Its relations with neighboring, loneliness, life satisfaction, and area of residence. *Journal of Community Psychology, 29*(1), 29–52. https://doi.org/cxswrf

Price, R. (1989). Bearing witness. *American Journal of Community Psychology, 17*(2), 151–167. https://doi.org/10.1007/BF00931004

Price, R., & Lorion, R. (1989). Prevention programming as organizational reinvention: From research to implementation. In D. Shaffer, I. Phillips, & N. Enzer (Eds.), *Prevention of mental disorders, alcohol and other drug use in children and adolescents* (pp. 97–123). Department of Health and Human Services Publication No. ADM 89-1646.

Prilleltensky, I. (1997). Values, assumptions, and practices: Assessing the moral implications of psychological discourse and action. *American Psychologist, 52*(5), 517–535. https://doi.org/10.1037/0003-066X.52.5.517

Prilleltensky, I. (1999). Critical psychology foundations for the promotion of mental health. *Annual Review of Critical Psychology, 1*, 95–112. https://discourseunit.com/annual-review/1-1999/

Prilleltensky, I. (2001). Value-based praxis in community psychology: Moving toward social justice and social action. *American Journal of Community Psychology, 29*(5), 747–778. https://doi.org/10.1023/A:1010417201918

Prilleltensky, I. (2003). Understanding, resisting, and overcoming oppression: Toward psychopolitical validity. *American Journal of Community Psychology, 31*(1–2), 195–201. https://doi.org/10.1023/A:1023043108210

Prilleltensky, I. (2008). The role of power in wellness, oppression, and liberation: The promise of psychopolitical validity. *Journal of Community Psychology, 36*(2), 116–136. https://doi.org/10.1002/jcop.20225

Prilleltensky, I. (2012). Wellness as fairness. *American Journal of Community Psychology, 49*(1–2), 1–21. https://doi.org/10.1007/s10464-011-9448-8

Prilleltensky, I., & Gonick, L. (1994). The discourse of oppression in the social sciences: Past, present, and future. In E. J. Trickett, R. J. Watts, & D. Birman (Eds.), *Human diversity: Perspectives on people in context* (pp. 145–177). Jossey-Bass.

Prilleltensky, I., & Nelson, G. (2002). *Doing psychology critically: Making a difference in diverse settings.* Palgrave Macmillan. https://doi.org/10.1007/978-1-4039-1462-0

Prilleltensky, I., & Nelson, G. (2009). Community psychology: Advancing social justice. In D. Fox, I. Prilleltensky, & S. Austin (Eds.), *Critical psychology: An introduction* (2nd ed., pp. 126–143). Sage Publications Ltd.

Primavera, J. (2004). You can't get there from here: Identifying process routes to replication. *American Journal of Community Psychology, 33*(3–4), 181–191. https://doi.org/10.1023/B:AJCP.0000027004.75119.f0

Primavera, J., & Brodsky, A. (Eds.). (2004). Process of community research and action [Special issue]. *American Journal of Community Psychology, 33*(3–4).

Prinz, R., Sanders, M., Shapiro, C., Whitaker, D., & Lutzker, J. (2009). Population-based prevention of child maltreatment: The U.S. Triple P System Population Trial. *Prevention Science, 10*(1), 1–12. https://doi.org/10.1007/s11121-009-0123-3

Proescholdbell, R. J., Roosa, M. W., & Nemeroff, C. J. (2006). Component measures of psychological sense of community among gay men. *Journal of Community Psychology, 34*(1), 9–24. https://doi.org/10.1002/jcop.20080

Pruitt, A., Barile, J., Ogawa, T., Peralta, N., Bugg, R., Lau, J., Lamberton, T., Hall, C., & Mori, V. (2018). Housing First and photovoice: Transforming lives, communities, and systems. *American Journal of Community Psychology, 61*(1–2), 104–117. https://doi.org/10.1002/ajcp.12226

Putnam, R. (1996). The strange disappearance of civic America. *American Prospect, 24*, 34–43.

Putnam, R. (2000). *Bowling alone: The collapse and revival of American community.* Simon & Schuster.

Putnam, R., & Feldstein, L. (with Cohen, D.). (2003). *Better together: Restoring the American community.* Simon & Schuster.

Quillian, L., Pager, D., Hexel, O., & Midtbøen, A. H. (2017). Meta-analysis of field experiments shows no change in racial discrimination in hiring over time. *Proceedings of the National Academy of Sciences, 114*(41), 10870–10875. https://doi.org/10.1073/pnas.1706255114

Rahm, J. (2002). Emergent learning opportunities in an inner-city youth gardening program. *Journal of Research in Science Teaching, 39*(2), 164–184. https://doi.org/10.1002/tea.10015

Ramirez, J., Heredia, A., Cardoso, E., & Nolan, J. (n.d.). *Salinas: CHAMACOS youth council.* http://yparhub.berkeley.edu/in-action/salinas-chamacos-youth-council/

Rania, N., Migliorini, L., Zunino, A., & Lena, C. (2019). Psychological well-being and healthy communities: Women as makers of relational well-being by social street strategies. *Journal of Prevention & Intervention in the Community*. Advance online publication. https://doi.org/10.1080/10852352.2019.1624355

Rapkin, B. D., Weiss, E., Lounsbury, D., Michel, T., Gordon, A., Erb-Downward, J., Sabino-Laughlin, E., Carpenter, A., Schwartz, C. E., Bulone, L., & Kemeny, M. (2017). Reducing disparities in cancer screening and prevention through community-based participatory research partnerships with local libraries: A comprehensive dynamic trial. *American Journal of Community Psychology*, 60(1–2), 145–159. https://doi.org/10.1002/ajcp.12161

Raposa, E. B., Rhodes, J., Stams, G. J. J. M., Card, N., Burton, S., Schwartz, S., Sykes, L. A. Y., Kanchewa, S., Kupersmidt, J., & Hassain, S. (2019). The effects of youth mentoring programs: A meta-analysis of outcome studies. *Journal of Youth and Adolescence*, 48(3), 423–443. https://doi.org/10.1007/s10964-019-00982-8

Rappaport, J. (1977a). *Community psychology: Values, research, and action.* Holt, Rinehart, and Winston.

Rappaport, J. (1977b). From Noah to Babel: Relationships between conceptions, values, analysis levels, and social intervention strategies. In I. Iscoe, B. L. Bloom, & C. D. Spielberger (Eds.), *Community psychology in transition: Proceedings from the national conference on training in community psychology.* John Wiley & Sons.

Rappaport, J. (1981). In praise of paradox: A social policy of empowerment over prevention. *American Journal of Community Psychology*, 9(1), 1–25. https://doi.org/10.1007/BF00896357

Rappaport, J. (1987). Terms of empowerment/exemplars of prevention: Toward a theory for community psychology. *American Journal of Community Psychology*, 15(2), 121–148. https://doi.org/10.1007/BF00919275

Rappaport, J. (1993). Narrative studies, personal stories, and identity transformation in the mutual help context. *Journal of Applied Behavioral Science*, 29(2), 239–256. https://doi.org/10.1177/0021886393292007

Rappaport, J. (1995). Empowerment meets narrative: Listening to stories and creating settings. *American Journal of Community Psychology*, 23(5), 795–807. https://doi.org/10.1007/BF02506992

Rappaport, J. (2000). Community narratives: Tales of terror and joy. *American Journal of Community Psychology*, 28(1), 1–24. https://doi.org/10.1023/A:1005161528817

Rappaport, J., Davidson, W. S., Wilson, M. N., & Mitchell, A. (1975). Alternatives to blaming the victim or the environment: Our places to stand have not moved the earth. *American Psychologist*, 30(4), 525–528. https://doi.org/10.1037/h0078449

Rapping, E. (1997). There's self-help and then there's self-help: Women and the recovery movement. *Social Policy*, 27(3), 56–61.

Rasmussen, A., Aber, M., & Bhana, A. (2004). Adolescent coping and neighborhood violence: Perceptions, exposure, and urban youths' efforts to deal with danger. *American Journal of Community Psychology*, 33(1–2), 61–75. https://doi.org/c332ps

Ravitch, D. (2010). *The death and life of the great American school system: How testing and choice are undermining education.* Basic Books.

Reason, P., & Bradbury, H. (Eds.). (2001). *Handbook of action research: Participative inquiry and practice.* Sage.

Reich, S. M., Bishop, B. J., Carolissen, R., Dzidic, P., Portillo, N., Sasao, T., & Stark, W. (2017). Catalysts and connections: The (brief) history of community psychology throughout the world. In M. A. Bond, I. Serrano-García, & C. Keys (Eds.), *APA handbook of community psychology: Vol. 1. Theoretical foundations, core concepts, and emerging challenges* (pp. 21–66). American Psychological Association. https://doi.org/10.1037/14953-002

Reinharz, S. (1984). Alternative settings and social change. In K. Heller, R. Price, S. Reinharz, S. Riger, & A. Wandersman (Eds.), *Psychology and community change* (2nd ed., pp. 286–336). Dorsey.

Reinharz, S. (1994). Toward an ethnography of "voice" and "silence." In E. J. Trickett, R. J. Watts, & D. Birman (Eds.), *Human diversity: Perspectives on people in context* (pp. 178–200). Jossey-Bass.

Resnicow, K., Braithwaite, R., Ahluwalia, J., & Baranowski, T. (1999). Cultural sensitivity in public health: Defined and demystified. *Ethnicity & Disease, 9*(1), 10–21.

Rheingold, H. (1993). *The virtual community: Homesteading on the electronic frontier.* MIT Press.

Rhodes, J. E. (2002). *Stand by me: The risks and rewards of mentoring today's youth.* Harvard University Press.

Rhodes, J. E., & DuBois, D. L. (2008). Mentoring relationships and programs for youth. *Current Directions in Psychological Science, 17*(4), 254–258. https://doi.org/10.1111/j.1467-8721.2008.00585.x

Rhodes, J. E., Spencer, R., Keller, T. E., Liang, B., & Noam, G. (2006). A model for the influence of mentoring relationships on youth development. *Journal of Community Psychology, 34*(6), 691–707. https://doi.org/10.1002/jcop.20124

Rhodes, J. E., & Woods, M. (1995). Comfort and conflict in the relationships of pregnant, minority adolescents: Social support as moderator of social strain. *Journal of Community Psychology, 23*(1), 74–84. https://doi.org/fbrjvs

Rich, R. C., Edelstein, M., Hallman, W., & Wandersman, A. (1995). Citizen participation and empowerment: The case of local environmental hazards. *American Journal of Community Psychology, 23*(5), 657–676. https://doi.org/10.1007/BF02506986

Rickard, K. M. (1990). The effect of feminist identity level on gender prejudice toward artists' illustrations. *Journal of Research in Personality, 24*(2), 145–162. https://doi.org/10.1016/0092-6566(90)90013-V

Ridgeway, C. L. (2001). Gender, status, and leadership. *Journal of Social Issues, 57*(4), 637–655. https://doi.org/10.1111/0022-4537.00233

Riessman, F. (1990). Restructuring help: A human services paradigm for the 1990s. *American Journal of Community Psychology, 18*(2), 221–230. https://doi.org/10.1007/BF00931302

Riessman, F., & Banks, E. C. (2001). A marriage of opposites: Self-help and the health care system. *American Psychologist, 56*(2), 173–174. https://doi.org/dfshdw

Riger, S. (1989). The politics of community intervention. *American Journal of Community Psychology, 17*(3), 379–383. https://doi.org/10.1007/BF00931046

Riger, S. (1990). Ways of knowing and organizational approaches to community research. In P. Tolan, C. Keys, F. Chertok, & L. Jason (Eds.), *Researching community psychology* (pp. 42–50). American Psychological Association. https://doi.org/10.1037/10073-004

Riger, S. (1992). Epistemological debates, feminist voices: Science, social values, and the study of women. *American Psychologist, 47*(6), 730–740. https://doi.org/10.1037/0003-066X.47.6.730

Riger, S. (1993). What's wrong with empowerment? *American Journal of Community Psychology, 21*(3), 279–292. https://doi.org/10.1007/BF00941504

Riger, S. (2001). Transforming community psychology. *American Journal of Community Psychology, 29*(1), 69–81. https://doi.org/10.1023/A:1005293228252

Riger, S. (2017). Feminism and community psychology: Compelling convergences. In M. A. Bond, I. Serrano-García, C. B. Keys, & M. Shinn (Eds.), *APA handbook of community psychology: Vol. 1. Theoretical foundations, core concepts, and emerging challenges* (pp. 129–148). American Psychological Association. https://psycnet.apa.org/doi/10.1037/14953-006

Rivers, I., & D'Augelli, A. R. (2001). The victimization of lesbian, gay, and bisexual youths. In A. R. D'Augelli & C. J. Patterson (Eds.), *Lesbian, gay, and bisexual identities and youth: Psychological perspectives* (pp. 199–223). Oxford.

RMC Research Corporation. (1995). *National Diffusion Network schoolwide promising practices: Report of a pilot effort.*

Robbins, B. (2014). *Modjeska Monteith Simkins: A South Carolina revolutionary.* South Carolina Progressive Network.

Robertson, N., & Masters-Awatere, B. (2007). Community Psychology in Aotearoa/New Zealand: Me tiro whakamuri a- kia- hangai whakamua. In S. M. Reich, M. Riemer, I. Prilleltensky, & M. Montero

(Eds.), *International community psychology: History and theories* (pp. 140–163). Springer. https://doi.org/10.1007/978-0-387-49500-2_7

Robinson, W. L. (1990). Data feedback and communication to the host setting. In P. Tolan, C. Keys, F. Chertok, & L. Jason (Eds.), *Researching community psychology: Issues of theory and methods* (pp. 193–195). American Psychological Association.

Rosanbalm, K. D., & Murray, D. W. (2017). *Promoting self-regulation in the first five years: A practice brief* (Office of Planning, Research, and Evaluation Brief No. 2017-79). Office of Planning, Research, and Evaluation, Administration for Children and Families, U.S. Department of Health and Human Services.

Rosario, M., Hunter, J., Maguen, S., Gwadz, M., & Smith, R. (2001). The coming-out process and its adaptational and health-related associations among gay, lesbian, and bisexual youths: Stipulation and exploration of a model. *American Journal of Community Psychology*, *29*(1), 133–160. https://doi.org/10.1023/A:1005205630978

Rosmarin, D., Pargament, K., Krumrei, E., & Flannelly, K. (2009). Religious coping among Jews: Development and initial validation of the JCOPE. *Journal of Clinical Psychology*, *65*(7), 670–683. https://doi.org/10.1002/jclp.20574

Ross, L. (1977). The intuitive psychologist and his shortcomings. In L. Berkowitz (Ed.), *Advances in experimental social psychology* (Vol. 10, pp. 173–220). Academic Press.

Rossi, P. H., Lipsey, M. W., & Henry, G. T. (2018). *Evaluation: A systematic approach* (8th ed.). Sage Publications.

Rotheram-Borus, M. J. (1988). Assertiveness training with children. In R. Price, E. Cowen, R. Lorion, & J. Ramos-McKay (Eds.), *Fourteen ounces of prevention* (pp. 83–97). American Psychological Association. https://doi.org/10.1037/10064-007

Rotter, J. B. (1954). *Social learning and clinical psychology*. Prentice-Hall. https://doi.org/10.1037/10788-000

Rotter, J. B. (1990). Internal versus external control of reinforcement: A case history of a variable. *American Psychologist*, *45*(4), 489–493. https://doi.org/10.1037/0003-066x.45.4.489

Rowe, M., Kloos, B., Chinman, M., Davidson, L., & Cross, A. B. (2001). Homelessness, mental illness, and citizenship. *Social Policy and Administration*, *35*(1), 14–31. https://doi.org/10.1111/1467-9515.00217

Rudkin, J. K. (2003). *Community psychology: Guiding principles and orienting concepts*. Prentice Hall.

Rudman, L. A., & Glick, P. (2001). Prescriptive gender stereotypes and backlash toward agentic women. *Journal of Social Issues*, *57*(4), 743–762. https://doi.org/10.1111/0022-4537.00239

Ruiz, L., McMahon, S., & Jason, L. (2018). The role of neighborhood context and school climate in school-level academic achievement. *American Journal of Community Psychology*, *61*(3–4), 296–309. https://doi.org/10.1002/ajcp.12234

Rutter, M. (1979). Protective factors in children's responses to stress and disadvantage. In M. W. Kent & J. E. Rolf (Eds.), *Primary prevention of psychopathology: Social competence in children: Vol. 3. Social competence in children* (pp. 49–74). University Press of New England.

Rutter, M., & Sroufe, L. A. (2000). Developmental psychopathology: Concepts and challenges. *Development and Psychopathology*, *12*(3), 265–296. https://doi.org/br82p8

Ryan, W. (1971). *Blaming the victim*. Random House.

Ryan, W. (1981). *Equality*. Pantheon.

Ryan, W. (1994). Many cooks, brave men, apples, and oranges: How people think about equality. *American Journal of Community Psychology*, *22*(1), 25–35. https://doi.org/10.1007/bf02506815

Sabina, C., Cuevas, C. A., & Schally, J. L. (2012). The cultural influences on help-seeking among a national sample of victimized Latino women. *American Journal of Community Psychology*, *49*(3–4), 347–363. https://doi.org/10.1007/s10464-011-9462-x

Saegert, S. (1989). Unlikely leaders, extreme circumstances: Older Black women building community households. *American Journal of Community Psychology, 17*(3), 295–316. https://doi.org/10.1007/BF00931038

Saegert, S., & Carpiano, R. M. (2017). Social support and social capital: A theoretical synthesis using community psychology and community sociology approaches. In M. A. Bond, I. Serrano-García, C. B. Keys, & M. Shinn (Eds.), *APA handbook of community psychology: Vol. 1. Theoretical foundations, core concepts, and emerging challenges* (pp. 295–314). American Psychological Association. https://doi.org/10.1037/14953-014

Saegert, S., & Winkel, G. (1990). Environmental psychology. *Annual Review of Psychology, 41*, 441–477. https://doi.org/10.1146/annurev.ps.41.020190.002301

Saegert, S., & Winkel, G. (1996). Paths to community empowerment: Organizing at home. *American Journal of Community Psychology, 24*(4), 517–550. https://doi.org/10.1007/BF02506795

Saegert, S., & Winkel, G. (2004). Crime, social capital, and community participation. *American Journal of Community Psychology, 34*(3–4), 219–233. https://doi.org/10.1007/s10464-004-7416-2

Salem, D., Reischl, T., Gallacher, F., & Randall, K. (2000). The role of referent and expert power in mutual help. *American Journal of Community Psychology, 28*(3), 303–324. https://doi.org/10.1023/A:1005101320639

Salem, D., Reischl, T., & Randall, K. (2008). The effect of professional partnership on the development of a mutual-help organization. *American Journal of Community Psychology, 42*(1–2), 179–191. https://doi.org/10.1007/s10464-008-9193-9

Salina, D., Hill, J., Solarz, A., Lesondak, L., Razzano, L., & Dixon, D. (2004). Feminist perspectives: Empowerment behind bars. In L. A. Jason, C. Keys, Y. Suarez-Balcazar, R. Taylor, & M. Davis (Eds.), *Participatory community research: Theories and methods in action* (pp. 159–175). American Psychological Association. https://doi.org/10.1037/10726-009

Salo, C. D., & Birman, D. (2015). Acculturation and psychological adjustment of Vietnamese refugees: An ecological acculturation framework. *American Journal of Community Psychology, 56*(3–4), 395–407. https://doi.org/10.1007/s10464-015-9760-9

Salzer, M. S., McFadden, L., & Rappaport, J. (1994). Professional views of self-help groups. *Administration and Policy in Mental Health, 22*(2), 85–95. https://doi.org/10.1007/BF02106543

Sampaio, F., Barendregt, J., Feldman, I., Lee, Y., Sawyer, M., Dadds, M., Scott, J., & Mihalopoulos, C. (2018). Population cost-effectiveness of the Triple-P parenting programme for the treatment of conduct disorder: An economic modelling study. *European Child & Adolescent Psychiatry, 27*, 933–944. https://doi.org/10.1007/s00787-017-1100-1

Sánchez, B., Esparza, P., & Colón, Y. (2008). Natural mentoring under the microscope: An investigation of mentoring relationships and Latino adolescents' academic performance. *Journal of Community Psychology, 36*(4), 468–482. https://doi.org/10.1002/jcop.20250

Sánchez, B., Rivera, C., Liao, C. L., & Mroczkowski, A. L. (2017). Community psychology interventions and U.S. Latinos and Latinas. In M. A. Bond, I. Serrano-García, & C. B. Keys (Eds.), *APA handbook of community psychology: Vol. 2. Methods for community research and action for diverse groups and issues* (pp. 491–506). American Psychological Association. https://doi.org/10.1037/14954-029

Sanders, M. (1999). Triple P—Positive Parenting Program: Towards an empirically validated multilevel parenting and family support strategy for the prevention of behavior and emotional problems in children. *Clinical Child and Family Psychology Review, 2*(2), 71–90. https://doi.org/10.1023/A:1021843613840

Sandler, I. N., Gensheimer, L., & Braver, S. (2000). Stress: Theory, research and action. In J. Rappaport & E. Seidman (Eds.), *Handbook of community psychology* (pp. 187–213). Kluwer/Plenum. https://doi.org/10.1007/978-1-4615-4193-6_9

Sarason, S. B. (1972). *The creation of settings and the future societies.* Jossey-Bass.

Sarason, S. B. (1974). *The psychological sense of community: Prospects for a community psychology.* Jossey-Bass.

Sarason, S. B. (1978). The nature of problem-solving in social action. *American Psychologist, 33*(4), 370–380. https://doi.org/10.1037/0003-066X.33.4.370

Sarason, S. B. (1982). *The culture of the school and the problem of change* (2nd ed.). Allyn & Bacon.

Sarason, S. B. (1988). *The making of an American psychologist: An autobiography.* Jossey-Bass.

Sarason, S. B. (1990). *The challenge of art to psychology.* Yale University Press.

Sarason, S. B. (1993). American psychology, and the needs for the transcendence and community. *American Journal of Community Psychology, 21*(2), 185–202. https://doi.org/10.1007/BF00941621

Sarason, S. B. (1994). The American worldview. In S. B. Sarason (Ed.), *Psychoanalysis, General Custer, and the verdicts of history, and other essays on psychology in the social scene* (pp. 100–118). Jossey-Bass.

Sarason, S. B. (1995a). *Parental involvement and the political principle: Why the existing governance structure of schools should be abolished.* Jossey-Bass.

Sarason, S. B. (1995b). [Untitled videotape interview]. In J. G. Kelly (Ed.), *The history of community psychology: A video presentation of context and exemplars.* Society for Community Research and Action. https://vimeo.com/69635912

Sarason, S. B. (2003a). American psychology and the schools: A critique. *American Journal of Community Psychology, 32*(1–2), 99–106. https://doi.org/10.1023/A:1025603125213

Sarason, S. B. (2003b). The obligations of the moral-scientific stance. *American Journal of Community Psychology, 31*(3–4), 209–211. https://doi.org/10.1023/A:1023946301430

Sasao, T. (1999). Cultural competence promotion as a general prevention strategy in urban settings: Some lessons learned from working with Asian American adolescents. *Community Psychologist, 32*(1), 41–43.

Sasao, T., & Sue, S. (1993). Toward a culturally anchored ecological framework of research in ethnic-cultural communities. *American Journal of Community Psychology, 21*(6), 705–727. https://doi.org/10.1007/BF00942244

Sasao, T., & Yasuda, T. (2007). Historical and theoretical orientations of community psychology practice and research in Japan. In S. M. Reich, M. Riemer, I. Prilleltensky, & M. Montero (Eds.), *International community psychology: History and theories* (pp. 164– 179). Springer. https://doi.org/10.1007/978-0-387-49500-2_8

Satcher, D. (2001). *Youth violence: A report of the surgeon general.* http://www.surgeongeneral.gov/library/youthviolence/chapter5/sec4.html

Saul, J., Wandersman, A., Flaspohler, P., Duffy, J., Lubell, K., & Noonan, R. (Eds.). (2008). Research and action for bridging science and practice in prevention [Special Issue]. *American Journal of Community Psychology, 41*(3–4).

Scaccia, J. P., Cook, B. S., Lamont, A., Wandersman, A., Castellow, J., Katz, J., & Beidas, R. S. (2015). A practical implementation science heuristic for organizational readiness: R = MC$^2$. *Journal of Community Psychology, 43*(2), 484–501. https://doi.org/10.1002/jcop.21698

Scales, P., Leffert, N., & Lerner, R. (2004). *Developmental assets: A synthesis of the scientific research on adolescent development.* Search Institute Press.

Scally, C., Batko, S., Popkin, S., & DuBois, N. (2018). *The case for more, not less: Shortfalls in federal housing assistance and gaps in evidence for proposed policy changes.* The Urban Institute. https://www.urban.org/sites/default/files/publication/95616/case_for_more_not_less.pdf

Scheier, M. F., Carver, C. S., & Bridges, M. W. (2001). Optimism, pessimism, and psychological well-being. In E. C. Chang (Ed.), *Optimism and pessimism: Implications for theory, research, and practice* (pp. 189–216). American Psychological Association. https://doi.org/10.1037/10385-009

Schembri, A. J. (2009). *Scared Straight programs: Jail and detention tours* [Booklet]. Florida Department of Juvenile Justice.

Schensul, J. J., & Trickett, E. (2009). Introduction to multi-level community based culturally situated interventions. *American Journal of Community Psychology, 43*(3–4), 232–240.

Schoggen, P. (1989). *Behavior settings.* Stanford University Press.

Schorr, L. (1997). *Common purpose: Strengthening families and neighborhoods to rebuild America.* Anchor Books.

Schultz, D. A., Shacht, R. L., Shanty, L. M., Dahlquist, L. M., Barry, R. A., Wiprovnick, A. E., Groth, E. C., Gaultney, W. M., Hunter, B. A., & DiClemente, C. C. (2019). The development and evaluation of a statewide training center for home visitors and supervisors. *American Journal of Community Psychology, 63*(3–4), 418–429. https://doi.org/10.1002/ajcp.12320

Schwartz, S., Syed, M., Yip, T., Knight, G., Umaña-Taylor, A., Rivas-Drake, D., Lee, R., & Ethnic and Racial Identity in the 21st Century Study Group. (2014). Methodological issues in ethnic and racial identity research with ethnic minority populations: Theoretical precision, measurement issues, and research designs. *Child Development, 85*(1), 58–76. https://doi.org/10.1111/cdev.12201

Schweinhart, L. J., Montie, J., Xiang, Z., Barnett, W. S., Belfield, C. R., & Nores, M. (2005). *Lifetime effects: The High/Scope Perry Preschool study through age 40.* High/Scope Press.

Scott, J. T., Kilmer, R. P., Wang, C., Cook, J. R., & Haber, M. G. (2018). Natural environments near schools: Potential benefits for socio-emotional and behavioral development in early childhood. *American Journal of Community Psychology, 62*(3–4), 419–432. https://doi.org/10.1002/ajcp.12272

Scott, V. C., Alia, K., Scaccia, J., Ramaswamy, R., Stout, S., Leviton, L., Wandersman, A. (2020). Formative evaluation and complex health improvement initiatives: A learning system to improve theory, implementation, support, and evaluation. *American Journal of Evaluation, 41*(1), 89–106. https://doi.org/10.1177/1098214019868022

Scott, V. C., Kenworthy, T., Godly-Reynolds, E., Bastien, G., Scaccia, J., McMickens, C., Rachel, S., Cooper, S., Wrenn, G., & Wandersman, A. (2017). The Readiness for Integrated Care Questionnaire (RICQ): An instrument to assess readiness to integrate behavioral health and primary care. *American Journal of Orthopsychiatry, 87*(5), 520–530. https://doi.org/10.1037/ort0000270

Scott, V. C., & Wolfe, S. M. (Eds.). (2014). *Community psychology: Foundations for practice.* Sage Publications.

Scottham, K. M., Cooke, D. Y., Sellers, R. M., & Ford, K. (2010). Integrating process with content in understanding African American racial identity development. *Self and Identity, 9*(1), 19–40. https://doi.org/10.1080/15298860802505384

Search Institute. (2004). *40 developmental assets.* https://page.search-institute.org/40-developmental-assets

Seaton, E. K., Scottham, K. M., & Sellers, R. M. (2006). The status model of racial identity development in African American adolescents: Evidence of structure, trajectories, and well-being. *Child Development, 77*(5), 1416–1426. https://doi.org/d4xc7f

Seaton, E. K., Yip, T., & Sellers, R. M. (2009). A longitudinal examination of racial identity and racial discrimination among African American adolescents. *Child Development, 80*(2), 406–417. https://doi.org/fdrm34

Seedat, M., & Suffla, S. (2017). Community psychology and its (dis)contents, archival legacies and decolonisation. *South African Journal of Psychology, 47*(4), 421–431. https://doi.org/10.1177/0081246317741423

Seely Brown, J., & Duguid, P. (1993). Stolen knowledge. *Educational Technology, 33*(3), 10–15.

Segal, S. P. (2018). Self help organized through mutual assistance in helping communities. In R. A. Cnaan & C. Milofsky (Eds.), *Handbook of community movements and local organizations in the 21st century* (pp. 309–322). Springer. https://doi.org/dvfn

Seidman, E. (1988). Back to the future, community psychology: Unfolding a theory of social intervention. *American Journal of Community Psychology, 16*(1), 3–24. https://doi.org/10.1007/BF00906069

Seidman, E., Aber, J. L., Allen, L., & French, S. E. (1996). The impact of the transition to high school on the self-system and perceived social context of poor urban youth. *American Journal of Community Psychology, 24*(4), 489–515. https://doi.org/10.1007/BF02506794

Seidman, E., Aber, J. L., & French, S. E. (2004). The organization of schooling and adolescent development. In K. Maton, C. Schellenbach, B. Leadbeater, & A. Solarz (Eds.), *Investing in children, youth, families, and communities* (pp. 233–250). American Psychological Association. https://doi.org/10.1037/10660-013

Seidman, E., Allen, L., Aber, J. L., Mitchell, C., & Feinman, J. (1994). The impact of school transitions in early adolescence on the self-system and perceived social context of poor urban youth. *Child Development*, *65*(2), 507–522. https://doi.org/10.2307/1131399

Seidman, E., & Cappella, E. (2017). Social settings as loci of intervention. In M. A. Bond, I. Serrano-García, & C. B. Keys (Eds.), *APA handbook of community psychology: Vol. 2. Methods for community research and action for diverse groups and issues* (pp. 235–254). American Psychological Association.

Seidman, E., & Rappaport, J. (1974). The educational pyramid: A paradigm for training, research, and manpower utilization in community. *American Journal of Community Psychology*, *2*(2), 119–130. https://doi.org/10.1007/BF00878039

Seidman, E., & Rappaport, J. (Eds.). (1986). *Redefining social problems*. Plenum. https://doi.org/10.1007/978-1-4899-2236-6

Seidman, I. (2006). *Interviewing as qualitative research: A guide for researchers in education and the social sciences* (3rd ed.). Teachers College Press.

Sellers, R. M., Caldwell, C. H., Schmeelk-Cone, K. H., & Zimmerman, M. A. (2003). Racial identity, racial discrimination, perceived stress, and psychological distress among African American young adults. *Journal of Health and Social Behavior*, *44*(3), 302–317. https://doi.org/10.2307/1519781

Sellers, R. M., Copeland-Linder, N., Martin, P. P., & Lewis, R. L. (2006). Racial identity matters: The relationship between racial discrimination and psychological functioning in African American adolescents. *Journal of Research on Adolescence*, *16*(2), 187–216. https://doi.org/b478d7

Sellers, R. M., Rowley, S. A. J., Chavous, T. M., Shelton, J. N., & Smith, M. A. (1997). Multidimensional Inventory of Black Identity: A preliminary investigation of reliability and construct validity. *Journal of Personality and Social Psychology*, *73*(4), 805–815. https://doi.org/10.1037/0022-3514.73.4.805

Sellers, R. M., & Shelton, J. N. (2003). The role of racial identity in perceived racial discrimination. *Journal of Personality and Social Psychology*, *84*(5), 1079–1092. https://doi.org/10.1037/0022-3514.84.5.1079

Sellers, R. M., Smith, M., Shelton, J. N., Rowley, S., & Chavous, T. (1998). Multidimensional model of racial identity: A reconceptualization of African American racial identity. *Personality and Social Psychology Review*, *2*(1), 18–39. https://doi.org/10.1207/s15327957pspr0201_2

Serrano-García, I. (1994). The ethics of the powerful and the power of ethics. *American Journal of Community Psychology*, *22*(1), 1–20. https://doi.org/10.1007/BF02506813

Serrano-García, I. (2020). Resilience, coloniality, and sovereign acts: The role of community activism. *American Journal of Community Psychology*, *65*(1–2), 3–12. https://doi.org/10.1002/ajcp.12415

Shapiro, A. (Director). (1978). *Scared straight!* [Documentary]. Golden West Television.

Shapiro, D. H., Jr., Schwartz, C. E., & Astin, J. A. (1996). Controlling ourselves, controlling our world: Psychology's role in understanding positive and negative consequences of seeking and gaining control. *American Psychologist*, *51*(12), 1213–1230. https://doi.org/bx2gsz

Shapiro, V., Oesterle, S., & Hawkins, J. D. (2015). Relating coalition capacity to the adoption of science-based prevention in communities: Evidence from a randomized trial of Communities That Care. *American Journal of Community Psychology*, *55*(1–2), 1–12. https://doi.org/10.1007/s10464-014-9684-9

Shaw, C., & McKay, H. (1969). *Juvenile delinquency and urban areas*. University of Chicago Press.

Shaw, J., Campbell, R., Cain, D., & Feeney, H. (2017). Beyond surveys and scales: How rape myths manifest in sexual assault police records. *Psychology of Violence*, *7*(4), 602–614. https://doi.org/10.1037/vio0000072

Sherman, L. W., Gottfredson, D. C., MacKennzie, D. L., Eck, J., Reuter, P., & Bushway, S. D. (1998). *Preventing crime: What works, what doesn't, what's promising*. U.S. Department of Justice, National Institute of Justice.

Sherriff, N., Hamilton, W., Wigmore, S., & Giambrone, B. (2011). "What do you say to them?": Investigating and supporting the needs of lesbian, gay, bisexual, trans, and questioning (LGBTQ) young people. *Journal of Community Psychology, 39*(8), 939–955. https://doi.org/10.1002/jcop.20479

Shiell, A., & Riley, T. (2017). Methods and methodology of systems analysis. In M. A. Bond, I. Serrano-García, & C. B. Keys, (Eds.), *APA handbook of community psychology: Vol. 2. Methods for community research and action for diverse groups and issues* (pp. 155–169). American Psychological Association. https://doi.org/10.1037/14954-010

Shin, J. H. (2014). Living independently as an ethnic minority elder: A relational perspective on the issues of aging and ethnic minorities. *American Journal of Community Psychology, 53*(3–4), 433–446. https://doi.org/10.1007/s10464-014-9650-6

Shinn, M. (1990). Mixing and matching: Levels of conceptualization, measurement, and statistical analysis in community research. In P. Tolan, C. Keys, F. Chertok, & L. Jason (Eds.), *Researching community psychology* (pp. 111–126). American Psychological Association. https://doi.org/10.1037/10073-010

Shinn, M. (1992). Homelessness: What is a psychologist to do? *American Journal of Community Psychology, 20*(1), 1–24. https://doi.org/10.1007/BF00942179

Shinn, M. (Ed.). (1996). Ecological assessment [Special issue]. *American Journal of Community Psychology, 24*(1).

Shinn, M. (2009). *Ending homeless for families: The evidence for affordable housing.* National Alliance to End Homelessness. http://www.endhomelessness.org/content/article/detail/2436

Shinn, M. (2015). Community psychology and the capabilities approach. *American Journal of Community Psychology, 55*(3–4), 243–252. https://doi.org/10.1007/s10464-015-9713-3

Shinn, M. (2016). Methods for influencing social policy: The role of social experiments. *American Journal of Community Psychology, 58*(3–4), 239–244. https://doi.org/10.1002/ajcp.12072

Shinn, M., Baumohl, J., & Hopper, K. (2001). The prevention of homelessness revisited. *Analyses of Social Issues and Public Policy, 1*(1), 95–127. https://doi.org/10.1111/1530-2415.00006

Shinn, M., & McCormack, M. M. (2017). Understanding and alleviating economic hardship: Contributions from community psychology. In M. A. Bond, I. Serrano-García, and C. B. Keys (Eds.), *APA handbook of community psychology: Vol. 2. Methods for community research and action for diverse groups and issues* (pp. 345–359). American Psychological Association. https://doi.org/10.1037/14954-020

Shinn, M., & Perkins, D. N. T. (2000). Contributions from organizational psychology. In J. Rappaport & E. Seidman (Eds.), *Handbook of community psychology* (pp. 615–641). Kluwer Academic/Plenum. https://doi.org/10.1007/978-1-4615-4193-6_26

Shinn, M., & Rapkin, B. (2000). Cross-level research without cross-ups in community psychology. In J. Rappaport & E. Seidman (Eds.), *Handbook of community psychology* (pp. 669–695). Kluwer/Plenum. https://doi.org/10.1007/978-1-4615-4193-6_28

Shinn, M., & Toohey, S. (2003). Community contexts of human welfare. *Annual Review of Psychology, 54*, 427–459. https://doi.org/10.1146/annurev.psych.54.101601.145052

Shinn, M., & Yoshikawa, H. (Eds.). (2008). *Toward positive youth development: Transforming schools and community programs.* Oxford University Press. https://doi.org/bgphj2

Shriver, T. (1992). [Untitled video segment]. In T. Levine (Producer), *The world of abnormal psychology: An ounce of prevention.* A. H. Perlmutter.

Silva, J. M., & The Students for Diversity Now. (2018). #WEWANTSPACE: Developing student activism through a decolonial pedagogy. *American Journal of Community Psychology, 62*(3–4), 374–384. https://doi.org/10.1002/ajcp.12284

Silva, J. M., & The Students for Diversity Now. (n.d.). *Demystifying decolonialization: A practical example from the classroom.* https://www.communitypsychology.com/demystifying-decolonialization/

Silva, W. (1994). A brief history of prison higher education in the United States. In M. Williford (Ed.), *Higher education in prison: A contradiction in terms?* (pp. 17–31). Oryx Press.

Simons, R., Johnson, C., Beaman, J., Conger, R., & Whitbeck, L. (1996). Parents and peer group as mediators of the effect of community structure on adolescent problem behavior. *American Journal of Community Psychology*, *24*(1), 145–171. https://doi.org/10.1007/BF02511885

Singh, S., Granski, M., Victoria, M., & Javdani, S. (2018). The praxis of decoloniality in researcher training and community-based data collection. *American Journal of Community Psychology*, *62*(3–4), 385–395. https://doi.org/10.1002/ajcp.12294

Sloan, T. (2002). *Psicologia de la liberacion*: Ignacio Martín-Baró. *Interamerican Journal of Psychology*, *36*(1–2), 353–357.

Smedley, A., & Smedley, B. (2005). Race as biology is fiction, racism as social problem is real: Anthropological and historical perspectives on the social construction of race. *American Psychologist*, *60*(1), 16–26. https://doi.org/10.1037/0003-066X.60.1.16

Smeeding, T., & Thevenot, C. (2016). Addressing child poverty: How does the United States compare with other nations? *Academic Pediatrics*, *16*(3)(Suppl.), S67–S75. https://doi.org/10.1016/j.acap.2016.01.011

Smith, D. (2012). The American melting pot: A national myth in public and popular discourse. *National Identities*, *14*(4), 387–402. https://doi.org/10.1080/14608944.2012.732054

Smith, J. (2006). At a crossroad: Standing still and moving forward. *American Journal of Community Psychology*, *38*(1–2), 27–29. https://doi.org/10.1007/s10464-006-9058-z

Smith, R. S. (2008). The case of a city where 1 in 6 residents is a refugee: Ecological factors and host community adaptation in successful resettlement. *American Journal of Community Psychology*, *42*(3–4), 328–342. https://doi.org/10.1007/s10464-008-9208-6

SmithBattle, L., Chantamit-o-pas, C., & Schneider, J. (2018). A meta-analysis of interventions to reduce repeat pregnancy and birth among teenagers. *Journal of Adolescent and Family Health*, *9*(1), Article 4. https://scholar.utc.edu/jafh/vol9/iss1/4

Snowden, L. R. (1987). The peculiar successes of community psychology: Service delivery to ethnic minorities and the poor. *American Journal of Community Psychology*, *15*(5), 575–586. https://doi.org/10.1007/BF00929910

Snowden, L. R. (2005). Racial, cultural and ethnic disparities in health and mental health: Toward theory and research at community levels. *American Journal of Community Psychology*, *35*(1–2), 1–8. https://doi.org/10.1007/s10464-005-1882-z

Social Security Administration. (2017). *Wage statistics for 2017*. https://www.ssa.gov/cgi-bin/netcomp.cgi?year=2017

Solarz, A. L. (2001). Investing in children, families, and communities: Challenges for an interdivisional public policy collaboration. *American Journal of Community Psychology*, *29*(1), 1–14. https://doi.org/10.1023/A:1005285425527

Solnit, R. (2012, August 20). Men explain things to me. *Guernica*. https://www.guernicamag.com/rebecca-solnit-men-explain-things-to-me/ (Original work published 2008)

Solórzano, D., Ceja, M., & Yosso, T. (2000). Critical race theory, racial microaggressions, and campus racial climate: The experiences of African American college students. *Journal of Negro Education*, *2000*(1–2), 60–73.

Somerfield, M. R., & McCrea, R. R. (2000). Stress and coping research: Methodological challenges, theoretical advances, and clinical applications. *American Psychologist*, *55*(6), 620–625. https://doi.org/brhdt2

Sonn, C. (2016). Swampscott in international context: Expanding our ecology of knowledge. *American Journal of Community Psychology*, *58*(3–4), 309–313. https://doi.org/10.1002/ajcp.12038

Sonn, C. (2018). Mobilising decolonial approaches for community-engaged research for racial justice. *Australian Community Psychologist*, *29*(1), 8–21.

Sonn, C., Arcidiacono, C., Dutta, U., Kiguwa, P., Kloos, B., & Maldonado, N. (2017). Beyond Disciplinary Boundaries: Speaking Back to Critical Knowledges, Liberation and Community. *South African Journal of Psychology*, *47*(4), 448–458. https://doi.org/10.1177/0081246317737930

Sonn, C., & Fisher, A. (1996). Psychological sense of community in a politically constructed group. *Journal of Community Psychology*, *24*(4), 417–430. https://doi.org/dnj3w9

Sonn, C., & Fisher, A. (1998). Sense of community: Community resilient responses to oppression and change. *Journal of Community Psychology*, *26*(5), 457–472. https://doi.org/bscffc

Sonn, C., & Fisher, A. (2003). Identity and oppression: Differential responses to an in-between status. *American Journal of Community Psychology*, *31*(1–2), 117–128. https://doi.org/10.1023/A:1023030805485

Sonn, C., & Fisher, A. (2010). Immigration and settlement: Confronting the challenges of cultural diversity. In G. Nelson & I. Prilleltensky (Eds.), *Community psychology: In pursuit of liberation and well-being* (2nd ed., pp. 371–388). Palgrave Macmillan.

Sonn, C., Stevens, G., & Duncan, N. (2013). Decolonization, critical methodologies, and why stories matter. In G. Stevens, N. Duncan, & D. Hook (Eds.), *Race, memory, and the apartheid archive: Studies in the psychosocial* (pp. 295–314). Palgrave Macmillan. https://doi.org/10.1057/9781137263902_15

Soriano, F. (1995). *Conducting needs assessments: A multidisciplinary approach*. Sage.

Spanierman, L. B., & Soble, J. R. (2010). Understanding whiteness: Previous approaches and possible directions in the study of white racial attitudes and identity. In J. G. Ponterotto, J. M. Casas, L. A. Suzuki, & C. M. Alexander (Eds.), *Handbook of multicultural counseling* (3rd ed., pp. 283–299). Sage.

Spanierman, L. B., Todd, N. R., & Anderson, C. J. (2009). Psychosocial costs of racism to Whites: Understanding patterns among university students. *Journal of Counseling Psychology*, *56*(2), 239–252. https://doi.org/10.1037/a0015432

Spaulding, J., & Balch, P. (1983). A brief history of primary prevention in the twentieth century: 1908 to 1980. *American Journal of Community Psychology*, *11*(1), 59–80. https://doi.org/10.1007/BF00898419

Speer, P. (2000). Intrapersonal and interactional empowerment: Implications for theory. *Journal of Community Psychology*, *28*(1), 51–61. https://doi.org/bnt3mx

Speer, P. (2008). Altering patterns of relationship and participation: Youth organizing as a setting-level intervention. In M. Shinn & H. Yoshikawa (Eds.), *Toward positive youth development: Transforming schools and community programs* (pp. 213–228). Oxford University Press. https://doi.org/djnt65

Speer, P., & Hughey, J. (1995). Community organizing: An ecological route to empowerment and power. *American Journal of Community Psychology*, *23*(5), 729–748. https://doi.org/10.1007/BF02506989

Speer, P., Hughey, J., Gensheimer, L., & Adams-Leavitt, W. (1995). Organizing for power: A comparative case study. *Journal of Community Psychology*, *23*(1), 57–73. https://doi.org/cxmmwf

Spencer, R. (2006). Understanding the mentoring process between adolescents and adults. *Youth & Society*, *37*(3), 287–315. https://doi.org/10.1177/0743558405278263

Sperry, D., Sperry, L., & Miller, P. (2019). Reexamining the verbal environments of children from different socioeconomic backgrounds. *Child Development*, *90*(4), 1303–1318. https://doi.org/10.1111/cdev.13072

Stack, C. (1974). *All our kin: Strategies for survival in a Black community*. Harper. https://doi.org/10.1037/10073-008

Stake, R. (2003). Case studies. In N. Denzin & Y. Lincoln (Eds.), *Strategies of qualitative inquiry* (2nd ed., pp. 134–164). Sage.

Stanley, J. (2003). An applied collaborative training program for graduate students in community psychology: A case study of a community project working with lesbian, gay, bisexual, transgender, and questioning youth. *American Journal of Community Psychology*, *31*(3–4), 253–265. https://doi.org/10.1023/A:1023958604156

Stark, W. (2012). Community psychology as a linking science: Potentials and challenges for transdisciplinary competencies. *Global Journal of Community Psychology Practice, 3*(1), 42–49. https://www.gjcpp.org/en/resource.php?issue=10&resource=45

Steele, C. M. (1997). A threat in the air: How stereotypes shape intellectual identity and performance. *American Psychologist, 52*(6), 613–629. https://doi.org/10.1037/0003-066X.52.6.613

Stein, C. H., & Mankowski, E. S. (2004). Asking, witnessing, interpreting, knowing: Conducting qualitative research in community psychology. *American Journal of Community Psychology, 33*(1–2), 21–35. https://doi.org/10.1023/B:AJCP.0000014316.27091.e8

Sternberg, R. J., Grigorenko, E. L., & Kidd, K. K. (2005). Intelligence, race, and genetics. *American Psychologist, 60*(1), 46–59. https://doi.org/10.1037/0003-066X.60.1.46

Stetler, C. B., Legro, M. W., Wallace, C. M., Bowman, C., Guihan, M., Hagedorn, H., Kimmel, B., Sharp, N. D., & Smith, J. L. (2006). The role of formative evaluation in implementation research and the QUERI experience. *Journal of General Internal Medicine, 21*(2)(Suppl.), S1–S8. https://doi.org/10.1007/s11606-006-0267-9

Stice, E., Shaw, H., Bohon, C., Marti, C. N., & Rohde, P. (2009). A meta-analytic review of depression prevention programs for children and adolescents: Factors that predict magnitude of intervention effects. *Journal of Consulting and Clinical Psychology, 77*(3), 486–503. https://doi.org/10.1037/a0015168

Stivala, A., Robins, G., Kashima, Y., & Kirley, M. (2016). Diversity and community can coexist. *American Journal of Community Psychology, 57*(1–2), 243–254. https://doi.org/10.1002/ajcp.12021

Stone, C., Trisi, D., Sherman, A., & Taylor, R. (2018). *A guide to statistics on historical trends in income inequality.* Center for Budget and Policy Priorities. https://www.cbpp.org/sites/default/files/atoms/files/11-28-11pov_0.pdf

Stone, R. A., & Levine, A. G. (1985). Reactions to collective stress: Correlates of active citizen participation at Love Canal. *Prevention in Human Services, 4*(1–2), 153–177. https://doi.org/10.1080/10852358509511166

Stovall, A. J. (2005). The philosophical bases for Black cultural centers. In F. L. Hood (Ed.), *Black culture centers: Politics of survival and identity* (pp. 102–112). Third World Press.

Straub, R. O. (2019). *Health psychology* (6th ed.). Worth Publishers.

Suarez-Balcazar, Y. (1998, July). Are we addressing the racial divide? *Community Psychologist, 31*(3), 12–13.

Suarez-Balcazar, Y., Davis, M., Ferrari, J., Nyden, P., Olson, B., Alvarez, J., Molloy, P., & Toro, P. (2004). University-community partnerships: A framework and an exemplar. In L. Jason, C. Keys, Y. Suarez-Balcazar, R. Taylor, & M. Davis (Eds.), *Participatory community research: Theories and methods in action* (pp. 105–120). American Psychological Association. https://doi.org/10.1037/10726-006

Substance Abuse and Mental Health Services Administration. (2014, January 28). *Intervention summary: Keepin' it REAL.* U.S. Department of Health and Human Services. https://web.archive.org/web/20150913055046/http://www.nrepp.samhsa.gov:80/ViewIntervention.aspx?id=133

Sue, D. W. (2004). Whiteness and ethnocentric monoculturalism: Making the "invisible" visible. *American Psychologist, 59*(8), 761–769. https://doi.org/10.1037/0003-066X.59.8.761

Sue, D. W. (2010). *Microaggressions in everyday life: Race, gender, and sexual orientation.* John Wiley & Sons.

Sue, D. W., Alsaidi, S., Awad, M. N., Glaeser, E., Calle, C. Z., & Mendez, N. (2019). Disarming racial microaggressions: Microintervention strategies for targets, White allies, and bystanders. *American Psychologist, 74*(1), 128–142. https://doi.org/10.1037/amp0000296

Sue, D. W., Capodilupo, C. M., Torino, G. C., Bucceri, J. M., Holder, A., Nadal, K. L., & Esquilin, M. (2007). Racial microaggressions in everyday life: Implications for clinical practice. *American Psychologist, 62*(4), 271–286. https://doi.org/dkmjk3

Suffla, S., & Seedat, M. (2015). Reflexivity, positionality, contexts and representation in African and Arab enactments of community psychology [Editorial]. *Journal of Community Psychology, 43*(1), 4–8. https://doi.org/10.1002/jcop.21716

Suffla, S., Seedat, M., & Bawa, U. (2015). Reflexivity as enactment of critical community psychologies: Dilemmas of voice and positionality in a multi-country photovoice study. *Journal of Community Psychology*, *43*(1), 9–21. https://doi.org/10.1002/jcop.21691

Suiter, S. V. (2017). Navigating community development conflicts: Contested visions of poverty & poverty alleviation. *American Journal of Community Psychology*, *60*(3–4), 459–466. https://doi.org/10.1002/ajcp.12194

Sullivan, C. (2003). Using the ESID model to reduce intimate male violence against women. *American Journal of Community Psychology*, *32*(3–4), 295–303. https://doi.org/10.1023/B:AJCP.0000004749.87629.a3

Sundquist, E. J. (Ed.). (1996). *The Oxford W. E. B. Du Bois reader*. Oxford University Press.

Sykes, C. (1992). *A nation of victims: The decay of the American character*. St. Martin's Press.

Talò, C., Mannarini, T., & Rochira, A. (2014). Sense of community and community participation: A meta-analytic review. *Social Indicators Research*, *117*, 1–28. https://doi.org/10.1007/s11205-013-0347-2

Tandon, S. D., Azelton, L. S., Kelly, J. G., & Strickland, D. A. (1998). Constructing a tree for community leaders: Contexts and processes in collaborative inquiry. *American Journal of Community Psychology*, *26*(4), 669–696. https://doi.org/10.1023/A:1022149123739

Tarakeshwar, N., Pargament, K. I., & Mahoney, A. (2003). Initial development of a measure of religious coping among Hindus. *Journal of Community Psychology*, *31*(6), 607–628. https://doi.org/10.1002/jcop.10071

Tashea, J. (2015, November 5). Why a campaign against coal was all about olives. *Mob Lab*. https://mobilisationlab.org/stories/why-a-campaign-against-coal-was-all-about-olives/

Tatum, B. (1997). *Why are all the Black kids sitting together in the cafeteria?* Basic Books.

Tax Policy Center. (2018). T18-0128 - Tax units with zero or negative income tax under current law, 2011-2028. https://www.taxpolicycenter.org/model-estimates/tax-units-zero-or-negative-income-tax-liability-september-2018/t18-0128-tax-units

Taylor, A., Wiley, A., Kuo, F., & Sullivan, W. (1998). Growing up in the inner city: Green spaces as places to grow. *Environment and Behavior*, *30*(1), 3–27. https://doi.org/10.1177/0013916598301001

Taylor, R., Oberle, E., Durlak, J. A., & Weissberg, R. P. (2017). Promoting positive youth development through school-based social and emotional learning interventions. A meta-analysis of follow-up effects. *Child Development*, *88*(4), 1156–1171. https://doi.org/10.1111/cdev.12864

Taylor-Ritzler, T., Balcazar, F., Dimpfl, S., Suarez-Balcazar, Y., Willis, C., & Schiff, R. (2008). Cultural competence training with organizations serving people with disabilities from diverse cultural backgrounds. *Journal of Vocational Rehabilitation*, *29*(2), 77–91. https://content.iospress.com/articles/journal-of-vocational-rehabilitation/jvr00435

Tebes, J. K. (2005). Community science, philosophy of science, and the practice of research. *American Journal of Community Psychology*, *35*(3–4), 213–230. https://doi.org/10.1007/s10464-005-3399-x

Tebes, J. K. (2017). Foundations for a philosophy of science of community psychology: Perspectivism, pragmatism, feminism, and critical theory. In M. A. Bond, I. Serrano-García, & C. B. Keys, (Eds.), *APA handbook of community psychology: Vol. 2. Methods for community research and action for diverse groups and issues* (pp. 21–40). American Psychological Association. https://doi.org/10.1037/14954-002

Tebes, J. K. (2018). Team science, justice, and the co-production of knowledge. *American Journal of Community Psychology*, *62*(1–2), 13–22. https://doi.org/10.1002/ajcp.12252

Tebes, J. K., Thai, N. D., & Matlin, S. L. (2014). Twenty-first century science as a relational process: From Eureka! to team science and a place for community psychology. *American Journal of Community Psychology*, *53*(3–4), 475–490. https://doi.org/10.1007/s10464-014-9625-7

Tedeschi, R. G., & Calhoun, L. G. (2004). Posttraumatic growth: Conceptual foundations and empirical evidence. *Psychological Inquiry*, *15*(1), 1–18. https://doi.org/ff94pz

Terry, R., & Townley, G. (2019). Exploring the role of social support in promoting community integration: An integrated literature review. *American Journal of Community Psychology*, *64*(3–4), 509–527. https://doi.org/10.1002/ajcp.12336

Thapar, A., & Rutter, M. (2019). Do natural experiments have an important future in the study of mental disorders? *Psychological Medicine*, *49*(7), 1079–1088. https://doi.org/10.1017/S0033291718003896

Thoits, P. A. (1983). Multiple identities and psychological well-being: A reformulation and test of the social hypothesis. *American Sociological Review*, *48*(2), 174–187. https://doi.org/10.2307/2095103

Thomas, D. (2018). *Black scholars matter: Development and validation of a campus racial climate measure for African American college students* [Dissertation, Georgia State University]. https://doi.org/dw7k

Thomas, E., Pate, S., & Ranson, A. (2015). The crosstown initiative: Art, community, and placemaking in Memphis. *American Journal of Community Psychology*, *55*(1–2), 74–88. https://doi.org/10.1007/s10464-014-9691-x

Thomas, E., & Rappaport, J. (1996). Art as community narrative: A resource for social change. In M. B. Lykes, A. Banuazizi, R. Liem, & M. Morris (Eds.), *Myths about the powerless: Contesting social inequalities* (pp. 317–336). Temple University Press.

Thorn, B. E., & Dixon, K. E. (2007). Coping with chronic pain: A stress-appraisal coping model. In E. Martz & H. Livneh (Eds.), *Coping with chronic illness and disability: Theoretical, empirical, and clinical aspects* (pp. 313–335). Springer Science. https://doi.org/fssqh7

Tobler, N. S., Roona, M. R., Ochshorn, P., Marshall, D., Streke, A., & Stackpole, K. (2000). School-based adolescent drug prevention programs: 1998 meta-analysis. *Journal of Primary Prevention*, *20*(4), 275–336. https://doi.org/c6tzs7

Todd, N. R. (2012). Religious networking organizations and social justice: An ethnographic case study. *American Journal of Community Psychology*, *50*(1–2), 229–245. https://doi.org/10.1007/s10464-012-9493-y

Todd, N. R. (2017). A community psychology perspective on religion and religious settings. In M. A. Bond, I. Serrano-García, C. B. Keys, & M. Shinn (Eds.), *APA handbook of community psychology: Vol. 1. Theoretical foundations, core concepts, and emerging challenges* (pp. 437–452). American Psychological Association. https://doi.org/10.1037/14953-022

Todd, N. R., Boeh, B. A., Houston-Kolnik, J. D., & Suffrin, R. L. (2017). Interfaith groups as mediating structures for political action: A multilevel analysis. *American Journal of Community Psychology*, *59*(1–2), 106–119. https://doi.org/10.1002/ajcp.12121

Todd, N. R., Spanierman, L. B., & Aber, M. S. (2010). White students reflecting on whiteness: Understanding emotional responses. *Journal of Diversity in Higher Education*, *3*(2), 97–110. https://doi.org/10.1037/a0019299

Tolman, D., & Brydon-Miller, M. (Eds.). (2001). *From subjects to subjectivities: A handbook of interpretative and participatory methods*. NYU Press.

Tönnies, F. (1957). *Community and society* (C. P. Loomis, Trans.). Michigan State University Press. (Original work published 1887)

Tornatzky, L., & Fleischer, M. (1986, October). *Dissemination and/or implementation: The problem of complex socio-technical systems* [Paper presentation]. Meeting of the American Evaluation Association, Kansas City, MO.

Toro, P. (1998). A community psychologist's role in policy on homelessness in two cities. *Community Psychologist*, *31*(1), 25–26. http://scra27.org/files/5313/9017/8537/tcp98.Number_1.pdf

Townley, G. (2017). Interdependent diversities: Reflections on the community-diversity dialectic. *American Journal of Community Psychology*, *59*(3–4), 265–268. https://doi.org/10.1002/ajcp.12133

Townley, G., Brusilovskiy, E., Snethen, G., & Salzer, M. S. (2018). Using geospatial research methods to examine resource accessibility and availability as it relates to community participation of individuals with serious mental illnesses. *American Journal of Community Psychology, 61*(1–2), 47–61. https://doi.org/10.1002/ajcp.12216

Townley, G., & Kloos, B. (2009). Development of a measure of sense of community for individuals with serious mental illness residing in community settings. *Journal of Community Psychology, 37*(3), 362–380. https://doi.org/10.1002/jcop.20301

Townley, G., & Kloos, B. (2014). Mind over matter? The role of individual perceptions in understanding the social ecology of housing environments for individuals with psychiatric disabilities. *American Journal of Community Psychology, 54*(3–4), 205–218. https://doi.org/10.1007/s10464-014-9664-0

Townley, G., Kloos, B., Green, E. P., & Franco, M. (2011). Reconcilable differences? Human diversity, cultural relativity, and sense of community. *American Journal of Community Psychology, 47*(1–2), 69–85. https://doi.org/10.1007/s10464-010-9379-9

Townley, G., Pearson, L., Lehrwyn, J., Prophet, N., & Trauernicht, M. (2016). Utilizing participatory mapping and GIS to examine the activity spaces of homeless youth. *American Journal of Community Psychology, 57*(3–4), 404–414. https://doi.org/10.1002/ajcp.12060

Tran, N., & Chan, W. Y. (2017). A contemporary perspective on working with Asian and Asian American communities in the United States. In M. A. Bond, I. Serrano-García, & C. B. Keys, (Eds.), *APA handbook of community psychology: Vol. 2. Methods for community research and action for diverse groups and issues* (pp. 475–490). American Psychological Association. https://doi.org/10.1037/14954-028

Treitler, P., Petereson, N. A., Howell, T. H., & Powell, K. G. (2018). Measuring sense of community responsibility in community-based prevention coalition: An item response theory analysis. *American Journal of Community Psychology, 62*(1–2), 110–120. https://doi.org/10.1002/ajcp.12269

Trickett, E. J. (1984). Toward a distinctive community psychology: An ecological metaphor for the conduct of community research and the nature of training. *American Journal of Community Psychology, 12*(3), 261–279. https://doi.org/10.1007/BF00896748

Trickett, E. J. (1996). A future for community psychology: The contexts of diversity and the diversity of contexts. *American Journal of Community Psychology, 24*(2), 209–234. https://doi.org/10.1007/BF02510399

Trickett, E. J. (1997). Ecology and primary prevention: Reflections on a meta-analysis. *American Journal of Community Psychology, 25*(2), 197–205. https://doi.org/bcrdbp

Trickett, E. J. (2009). Community psychology: Individuals and interventions in community context. *Annual Review of Psychology, 60*, 395–419. https://doi.org/10.1146/annurev.psych.60.110707.163517

Trickett, E. J., Barone, C., & Watts, R. (2000). Contextual influences in mental health consultation: Toward an ecological perspective on radiating change. In J. Rappaport & E. Seidman (Eds.), *Handbook of community psychology* (pp. 303–330). Kluwer/Plenum. https://doi.org/10.1007/978-1-4615-4193-6_13

Trickett, E. J., & Espino, S. L. R. (2004). Collaboration and social inquiry: Multiple meanings of a construct and its role in creating useful and valid knowledge. *American Journal of Community Psychology, 34*(1–2), 1–69. https://doi.org/bdjw9j

Trickett, E. J., Kelly, J. G., & Todd, D. M. (1972). The social environment of the school: Guidelines for individual change and organizational redevelopment. In S. Golann & C. Eisdorfer (Eds.), *Handbook of community mental health* (pp. 331–406). Appleton-Century-Crofts.

Trickett, E. J., Trickett, P., Castro, J., & Schaffner, P. (1982). The independent school experience: Aspects of the normative environments of single-sex and coed secondary schools. *Journal of Educational Psychology, 74*(3), 374–381. https://doi.org/10.1037/0022-0663.74.3.374

Trickett, E. J., Watts, R. J., & Birman, D. (Eds.). (1994). *Human diversity: Perspectives on people in context.* Jossey-Bass.

Trimble, J., Helms, J., & Root, M. (2003). Social and psychological perspectives on ethnic and racial identity. In G. Bernal, J. Trimble, K. Burlew, & F. Leong (Eds.), *Handbook of racial and ethnic minority psychology* (pp. 239–275). Sage. https://doi.org/10.4135/9781412976008.n13

Trotter, J., & Allen, N. (2009). The good, the bad, and the ugly: Domestic violence survivors' experiences with their informal social networks. *American Journal of Community Psychology*, *43*(3–4), 221–231. https://doi.org/10.1007/s10464-009-9232-1

Trout, L., McEachern, D., Mullany, A., White, L., & Wexler, L. (2018). Decoloniality as a framework for Indigenous youth suicide prevention pedagogy: Promoting community conversations about research to end suicide. *American Journal of Community Psychology*, *62*(3–4), 396–405. https://doi.org/10.1002/ajcp.12293

Tsemberis, S. (2010). *Housing first: The pathways model to end homelessness for people with mental illness and addiction*. Hazelden.

Tsemberis, S., Gulcur, L., & Nakae, M. (2004). Housing first, consumer choice, and harm reduction for homeless individuals with a dual diagnosis. *American Journal of Public Health*, *94*(4), 651–656. https://doi.org/10.2105/AJPH.94.4.651

Tseng, V., Chesir-Teran, D., Becker-Klein, R., Chan, M. L., Duran, V., Roberts, A., & Bardoliwalla, N. (2002). Promotion of social change: A conceptual framework. *American Journal of Community Psychology*, *30*(3), 401–427. https://doi.org/10.1023/A:1015341220749

Tseng, V., & Seidman, E. (2007). A systems framework for understanding social settings. *American Journal of Community Psychology*, *39*(3–4), 217–228. https://doi.org/10.1007/s10464-007-9101-8

Tseng, V., & Yoshikawa, H. (2008). Reconceptualizing acculturation: Ecological processes, historical contexts, and power inequities. *American Journal of Community Psychology*, *42*(3–4), 355–358. https://doi.org/10.1007/s10464-008-9211-y

Ttofi, M., Farrington, D., & Baldry, A. (2008). *Effectiveness of programmes to reduce school bullying*. Swedish National Council for Crime Prevention. https://www.bra.se/download/18.cba82f7130f475a2f1800023387/1371914733490/2008_programs_reduce_school_bullying.pdf

Turner, H. (2007). The significance of employment for chronic stress and psychological distress among rural single mothers. *American Journal of Community Psychology*, *40*(3–4), 181–193. https://doi.org/10.1007/s10464-007-9141-0

Turner, S., & Bound, J. (2003). Closing the gap or widening the divide: The effects of the G.I. Bill and World War II on the educational outcomes of black Americans. *Journal of Economic History*, *63*(1), 145–177. https://doi.org/10.1017/S0022050703001761

Ullman, S. E., & Townsend, S. M. (2008). What is an empowerment approach to working with sexual assault survivors? *Journal of Community Psychology*, *36*(3), 299–312. https://doi.org/10.1002/jcop.20198

Unger, D., & Wandersman, A. (1983). Neighboring and its role in block organizations: An exploratory report. *American Journal of Community Psychology*, *11*(3), 291–300. https://doi.org/10.1007/BF00893369

Unger, D., & Wandersman, A. (1985). The importance of neighbors: The social, cognitive, and affective components of neighboring. *American Journal of Community Psychology*, *13*(2), 139–169. https://doi.org/10.1007/BF00905726

Unger, R. (2001). Marie Jahoda [obituary]. *American Psychologist*, *56*(11), 1040–1041. https://doi.org/10.1037/0003-066x.56.11.1040

United Nations Educational, Scientific and Cultural Organization. (2017). *School violence and bullying: global status report*. https://unesdoc.unesco.org/ark:/48223/pf0000246970

Utsey, S. O., & Ponterotto, J. G. (1996). Development and validation of the Index of Race-Related Stress (IRRS). *Journal of Counseling Psychology*, *43*(4), 490–501. https://doi.org/bgsdmd

Van Egeren, L., Huber, M., & Cantillon, D. (2003, June 4–7). *Mapping change: Using geographic information systems for research and action* [Poster presentation]. Biennial Meeting of the Society for Community Research and Action, Las Vegas, NM.

van Uchelen, C. (2000). Individualism, collectivism and community psychology. In J. Rappaport & E. Seidman (Eds.), *Handbook of community psychology* (pp. 65–78). Kluwer/Plenum. https://doi.org/10.1007/978-1-4615-4193-6_3

Vanden-Kiernan, M., D'Elio, M. A., O'Brien, R., Banks Tarullo, L., Zill, N., & Hubbell-McKey, R. (2010). Neighborhoods as a developmental context: A multilevel analysis of neighborhood effects on Head Start families and children. *American Journal of Community Psychology*, *45*(1–2), 68–72. https://doi.org/10.1007/s10464-009-9279-z

Varas-Díaz, N., & Serrano-García, I. (2003). The challenge of a positive self-image in a colonial context: A psychology of liberation for the Puerto Rican experience. *American Journal of Community Psychology*, *31*(1–2), 103–115. https://doi.org/10.1023/A:1023078721414

Velázquez, T., Rivera-Holguin, M., & Morote, R. (2017). Disasters and postdisasters: Lessons and challenges for community psychology. In M. A. Bond, I. Serrano-García, & C. B. Keys (Eds.), *APA handbook of community psychology: Vol. 2. Methods for community research and action for diverse groups and issues* (pp. 425–439). American Psychological Association. https://doi.org/10.1037/14954-025

Venkatesh, S. (2002). *American project: The rise and fall of a modern ghetto*. Harvard University Press.

Vinokur, A. D., & Selzer, M. L. (1975). Desirable versus undesirable life events: Their relationship to stress and mental distress. *Journal of Personality and Social Psychology*, *32*(2), 329–337. https://doi.org/ctshqs

Viola, J. J., & Glantsman, O. (Eds.). (2017). *Diverse careers in community psychology*. Oxford University Press. https://doi.org/dw3h

Vivero, V. N., & Jenkins, S. R. (1999). Existential hazards of the multicultural individual: Defining and understanding "cultural homelessness." *Cultural Diversity and Ethnic Minority Psychology*, *5*(1), 6–26. https://doi.org/10.1037/1099-9809.5.1.6

Vogel, L. (2015, April 21). Dear sisters, amazon, festival family [Status update]. Facebook. https://www.facebook.com/michfest/posts/10153186431364831

Vora, R. S., & Kinney, M. N. (2014). Connectedness, sense of community, and academic satisfaction in a novel community campus medical education model. *Academic Medicine*, *89*(1), 182–187. https://doi.org/f5n9rf

Wagner, P., & Rabuy, B. (2017). *Following the money of mass incarceration*. Prison Policy Initiative. https://www.prisonpolicy.org/reports/money.html

Walker, K., & Saito, R. (2011). You are here: Promoting youth spaces through community mapping. *Afterschool Matters*, *14*, 30–39. https://www.niost.org/2011-Fall/youare-here-promoting-youth-spaces-through-community-mapping

Walsh, J. P., & O'Connor, C. (2019). Social media and policing: A review of recent research. *Sociology Compass*, *13*(1), e12648. https://doi.org/10.1111/soc4.12648

Walsh, R. (1987). A social historical note on the formal emergence of community psychology. *American Journal of Community Psychology*, *15*(5), 523–529.

Wandersman, A. (1984). Citizen participation. In K. Heller, R. Price, S. Reinharz, S. Riger, & A. Wandersman (Eds.), *Psychology and community change* (2nd ed., pp. 337–379). Dorsey.

Wandersman, A. (1990). Prevention is a broad field: Toward a broad conceptual framework of prevention. In P. Mueherer (Ed.), *Conceptual research models for preventing mental disorders*. National Institute of Mental Health.

Wandersman, A. (2003). Community science: Bridging the gap between science and practice with community-centered models. *American Journal of Community Psychology*, *31*(3–4), 227–242. https://doi.org/10.1023/A:1023954503247

Wandersman, A. (2009). Four keys to success (theory, implementation, evaluation, and resource/system support): High hopes and challenges in participation. *American Journal of Community Psychology*, *43*(1–2), 3–21. https://doi.org/10.1007/s10464-008-9212-x

Wandersman, A., Alia, K., Cook, B., Hsu, L., & Ramaswamy, R. (2016). Evidence-based interventions are necessary but not sufficient for achieving outcomes in each setting in a complex world: Empowerment Evaluation, Getting To Outcomes, and demonstrating accountability. *American Journal of Evaluation*, *37*(4), 544–561. https://doi.org/f9cd93

Wandersman, A., Coyne, S., Herndon, E., McKnight, K., & Morsbach, S. (2002). Clinical and community psychology: Case studies using integrative models. *Community Psychologist, 35*(3), 22–25. http://www.scra27.org/files/9213/9016/1506/tpc02.Number3.pdf

Wandersman, A., Duffy, J., Flaspohler, P., Noonan, R., Lubell, K., Stillman, L., Blachman, M., Dunville, R., & Saul, J. (2008). Bridging the gap between prevention research and practice: The interactive systems framework for dissemination and implementation. *American Journal of Community Psychology, 41*(3–4), 171–181. https://doi.org/10.1007/s10464-008-9174-z

Wandersman, A., & Florin, P. (2000). Citizen participation and community organizations. In J. Rappaport & E. Seidman (Eds.), *Handbook of community psychology* (pp. 247–272). Plenum. https://doi.org/10.1007/978-1-4615-4193-6_11

Wandersman, A., & Hallman, W. (1993). Are people acting irrationally? Understanding public concerns about environmental threats. *American Psychologist, 48*(6), 681–686. https://doi.org/10.1037/0003-066X.48.6.681

Wandersman, A., Imm, P., Chinman, M., & Kaftarian, S. (1999). *Getting To Outcomes: Methods and tools for planning, evaluation, and accountability.* Center for Substance Abuse Prevention.

Wandersman, A., Imm, P., Chinman, M., & Kaftarian, S. (2000). Getting To Outcomes: A results-based approach to accountability. *Evaluation and Program Planning, 23*(3), 389–395. https://doi.org/10.1016/S0149-7189(00)00028-8

Wandersman, A., Keener, D., Snell-Johns, J., Miller, R., Flaspohler, P., Livet-Dye, M., Mendez, J., Behrens, T., Bolson, B., & Robinson, L. (2004). Empowerment evaluation: Principles and action. In L. Jason, C. Keys, Y. Suarez-Balcazar, R. Taylor, & M. Davis (Eds.), *Participatory community research: Theories and methods in action* (pp. 139–156). American Psychological Association. https://doi.org/10.1037/10726-008

Wandersman, A., Kloos, B., Linney, J. A., & Shinn, M. (2005). Science and community psychology: Enhancing the vitality of community research and action. *American Journal of Community Psychology, 35*(3–4), 105–106. https://doi.org/10.1007/s10464-005-3387-1

Wandersman, A., Morsbach, S. K., McKnight, K., Herndon, E., & Coyne, S. M. (2002). Clinical and community psychology: Complementarities and combinations. *Community Psychologist, 35*(3), 4–7. http://www.scra27.org/files/9213/9016/1506/tpc02.Number3.pdf

Wandersman, A., Snell-Johns, J., Lentz, B., Fetterman, D., Keener, D., Livet, M., Imm, P., & Flaspohler, P. (2005). The principles of empowerment evaluation. In D. Fetterman & A. Wandersman (Eds.), *Empowerment evaluation principles in practice* (pp. 27–41). Guilford Press.

Washington State Institute for Public Policy. (2018a). *Triple-P Positive Parenting Program (System).* https://www.wsipp.wa.gov/BenefitCost/Program/79

Washington State Institute for Public Policy. (2018b). *Communities That Care.* https://www.wsipp.wa.gov/BenefitCost/Program/115

Washington State Institute for Public Policy. (2018c). *Juvenile justice.* https://www.wsipp.wa.gov/BenefitCost?topicId=1

Washington State Institute for Public Policy. (2018d). *Adult criminal justice.* https://www.wsipp.wa.gov/BenefitCost?topicId=2

Wasserman, M. (2006). *Implementation of home visitation programs: Stories from the states.* Issue Brief No. 109. Chapin Hall Center for Children.

Waters, M. (1999). *Black identities: West Indian immigrant dreams and American realities.* Harvard University Press.

Watson, N. N., & Hunter, C. D. (2016). "I had to be strong": Tensions in the strong Black woman schema. *Journal of Black Psychology, 42*(5), 424–452. https://doi.org/10.1177/0095798415597093

Watson-Thompson, J., Fawcett, S., & Schultz, J. (2008). Differential effects of strategic planning on community changes in two urban neighborhood coalitions. *American Journal of Community Psychology, 42*(1–2), 25–38. https://doi.org/10.1007/s10464-008-9188-6

Watts, R. J. (1994). Paradigms of diversity. In E. J. Trickett, R. J. Watts, & D. Birman (Eds.), *Human diversity: Perspectives on people in context* (pp. 49–79). Jossey-Bass.

Watts, R. J. (2010). Advancing a community psychology of men. *American Journal of Community Psychology, 45*(1–2), 201–211. https://doi.org/10.1007/s10464-009-9281-5

Watts, R. J., & Serrano-García, I. (Eds.). (2003). The psychology of liberation: Responses to oppression [Special issue]. *American Journal of Community Psychology, 31*(1–2).

Watts, R. J., Williams, N. C., & Jagers, R. (2003). Sociopolitical development. *American Journal of Community Psychology, 31*(1–2), 185–194. https://doi.org/10.1023/A:1023091024140

Watzlawick, P., Weakland, J., & Fisch, R. (1974). *Change: Principles of problem formation and problem resolution.* Norton.

Weber, L. (2010). *Understanding race, class, gender, and sexuality: A conceptual framework.* Oxford University Press.

Weick, K. (1984). Small wins: Redefining the scale of social issues. *American Psychologist, 39*(1), 40–49. https://doi.org/dp8zw9

Weinstein, R. (2002a). Overcoming inequality in schooling: A call to action for community psychology. *American Journal of Community Psychology, 30*(1), 21–42. https://doi.org/10.1023/A:1014311816571

Weinstein, R. (2002b). *Reaching higher: The power of expectations in schooling.* Harvard University Press.

Weinstein, R. (2005, June). *Reaching higher in community psychology* [Seymour Sarason Award address]. Biennial Meeting of the Society for Community Research and Action, Champaign-Urbana, IL.

Weinstein, R., Soulé, C., Collins, F., Cone, J., Mehlhorn, M., & Simontacchi, K. (1991). Expectations and high school change: Teacher-researcher collaboration to prevent school failure. *American Journal of Community Psychology, 19*(3), 333–364.

Weissberg, R. P. (2019). Promoting the social and emotional learning of millions of children. *Perspectives on Psychological Science, 14*(1), 65–69. https://doi.org/10.1177/1745691618817756

Weissberg, R. P., & Durlak, J. (2006). *Meta-analysis of the effect of social-emotional learning and positive youth development programs on academic achievement and problem behaviors.* Collaborative for Academic, Social, and Emotional Learning.

Weissberg, R. P., Durlak, J. A., Domitrovich, C. E., & Gullotta, T. P. (2015). Social and emotional learning: Past, present, and future. In J. A. Durlak, C. E. Domitrovich, R. P. Weissberg, & T. P. Gullotta (Eds.), *Handbook of social and emotional learning: Research and practice* (pp. 3–19). Guilford Press.

Weissberg, R. P., Kumpfer, K. L., & Seligman, M. E. P. (2003). Prevention that works for children and youth: An introduction. *American Psychologist, 58*(6–7), 425–432. https://doi.org/10.1037/0003-066X.58.6-7.425

Weisstein, N. (1993). Psychology constructs the female; Or the fantasy life of the male psychologist (with some attention to the fantasies of his friends, the male biologist and the male anthropologist). *Feminism and Psychology, 3*(2), 194–210. https://doi.org/10.1177/0959353593032005 (Reprinted from *Psychology constructs the female*, by N. Weisstein, 1971, New England Free Press)

Werner, E. E. (1993). Risk, resilience, and recovery: Perspectives from the Kauai Longitudinal Study. *Development and Psychopathology, 5*(4), 503–515. https://doi.org/10.1017/S095457940000612X

Werner, E. E. (1996). Vulnerable but invincible: High risk children from birth to adulthood. *European Journal of Child and Adolescent Psychiatry, 5*(1)(Suppl.), 47–51. https://doi.org/10.1007/BF00538544

Werner, E. E. (2005). Resilience and recovery: Findings from the Kauai Longitudinal Study. *Research, Policy, and Practice in Children's Mental Health, 19*(1), 11–14. https://www.pathwaysrtc.pdx.edu/pdf/fpS0504.pdf

Wernick, L. J., Kulick, A., & Woodford, M. R. (2014). How theater with a transformative organizing framework cultivates individual and collective empowerment among LGBTQQ Youth. *Journal of Community Psychology, 42*(7), 838–853. https://doi.org/10.1002/jcop.21656

Wexler, L., Moses, J., Hopper, K., Joule, L., & Garoutte, J. (2013). Central role of relatedness in Alaska Native youth resilience: Preliminary themes from one site of the Circumpolar Indigenous Pathways to Adulthood

(CIPA) study. *American Journal of Community Psychology, 52*(3–4), 393–405. https://doi.org/10.1007/s10464-013-9605-3

White, G. (2010). Ableism. In G. Nelson & I. Prilleltensky (Eds.), *Community psychology: In pursuit of liberation and well-being* (pp. 431–452). Palgrave Macmillan.

Wicker, A. (1973). Undermanning theory and research: Implications for the study of psychological and behavioral effects of excess populations. *Representative Research in Social Psychology, 4*, 185–206.

Wicker, A. (1979). Ecological psychology: Some recent and prospective developments. *American Psychologist, 34*(9), 755–765. https://doi.org/10.1037/0003-066X.34.9.755

Wicker, A. (1987). Behavior settings reconsidered: Temporal stages, resources, internal dynamics, and context. In D. Stokols & I. Altman (Eds.), *Handbook of environmental psychology* (Vol. 1, pp. 613–653). Wiley.

Wicker, A., & Sommer, R. (1993). The resident researcher: An alternative career model centered on community. *American Journal of Community Psychology, 21*(4), 469–482. https://doi.org/10.1007/BF00942153

Wickes, R., Hipp, J. R., Sargeant, E., & Homel, R. (2013). Collective efficacy as a task specific process: Examining the relationship between social ties, neighborhood cohesion and the capacity to respond to violence, delinquency and civic problems. *American Journal of Community Psychology, 52*(1–2), 115–127. https://doi.org/10.1007/s10464-013-9582-6

Wiesenfeld, E. (1996). The concept of "we": A community social psychology myth? *Journal of Community Psychology, 24*(4), 337–346. https://doi.org/d9p8kq

Wilcox, B. L. (1981). Social support in adjusting to marital disruption: A network analysis. In B. Gottlieb (Ed.), *Social networks and social support* (pp. 97–116). Sage.

Wiley, A., & Rappaport, J. (2000). Empowerment, wellness, and the politics of development. In D. Cicchetti, J. Rappaport, I. Sandler, & R. Weissberg (Eds.), *The promotion of wellness in children and adolescents* (pp. 59–99). CWLA Press.

Williams, A. (2007). Support, expectations, awareness & influence: Reflections on youth & democracy articles. *Journal of Community Psychology, 35*(6), 811–814. https://doi.org/10.1002/jcop.20181

Williams, D. R., & Williams-Morris, R. (2000). Racism and mental health: The African American experience. *Ethnicity & Health, 5*(3–4), 243–268. https://doi.org/10.1080/713667453

Williams, M., & Husk, K. (2013). Can we, should we, measure ethnicity? *International Journal of Social Research Methodology, 16*(4), 285–300. https://doi.org/10.1080/13645579.2012.682794

Wilson, B. D. M., Harper, G. W., Hidalgo, M. A., Jamil, O. B., Torres, R. S., Fernandez, I., & Adolescent Medicine Trials Network for HIV/AIDS Interventions. (2010). Negotiating dominant masculinity ideology: Strategies used by gay, bisexual, and questioning male adolescents. *American Journal of Community Psychology, 45*(1–2), 169–185. https://doi.org/10.1007/s10464-009-9291-3

Wilson, B. D. M., Hayes, E., Greene, G. J., Kelly, J. G., & Iscoe, I. (2003). Community psychology. In D. Freedheim (Ed.), *Handbook of psychology: Vol. 1. History of psychology* (pp. 431–449). John Wiley. https://doi.org/10.1002/0471264385.wei0121

Wingood, G. M., DiClemente, R. J., Villamizar, K., Er, D. L., DeVarona, M., Taveras, J., Painter, T. M., Lang, D. L., Hardin, J. W., Ullah, E., Stallworth, J., Purcell, D. W., & Jean, R. (2011). Efficacy of a health educator-delivered HIV prevention intervention for Latina women: A randomized controlled trial. *American Journal of Public Health, 101*(12), 2245–2252. https://doi.org/10.2105/AJPH.2011.300340

Wise, N. (2015). Placing sense of community. *Journal of Community Psychology, 43*(7), 920–929. https://doi.org/10.1002/jcop.21722

Wolff, T. (Ed.). (2001). Community coalition building: Contemporary practice and research [Special section]. *American Journal of Community Psychology, 29*(2), 165–329. https://doi.org/10.1023/A:1010314326787

Wolff, T. (2004). Collaborative solutions: Six key components. *Collaborative Solutions.* https://www.tomwolff.com/collaborative-solutions-fall04.html#components

Wolff, T. (2010). *The power of collaborative solutions: Six principles and effective tools for building healthy communities.* Jossey-Bass.

Wolff, T. (2014). Community psychology practice: Expanding the impact of psychology's work. *American Psychologist, 69*(8), 803–813. https://doi.org/10.1037/a0037426

Wolff, T., & Lee, P. (1997, June). *The Healthy Communities movement: An exciting new area for research and action by community psychologists* [Workshop]. Biennial Meeting of the Society for Community Research and Action, Columbia, SC.

Wolitski, R. J. (2003). What do we do when the crisis does not end? *Community Psychologist, 36*(4), 14–15. http://www.scra27.org/files/1513/9016/0105/tcp03.Number4.pdf

Wong, P. T. P., Wong, L. C. J., & Scott, C. (2006). Beyond stress and coping: The positive psychology of transformation. In P. T. P. Wong & L. C. J. Wong (Eds.), *Handbook of multicultural perspectives on stress and coping* (pp. 1–26). Springer. https://doi.org/10.1007/0-387-26238-5_1

Wright, P., & Kloos, B. (2007). Housing environment and mental health outcomes: A levels of analysis perspective. *Journal of Environmental Psychology, 27*(1), 79–89. https://doi.org/10.1016/j.jenvp.2006.12.001

Wright, R. (1996). The missing or misperceived effects of punishment: The coverage of deterrence in criminology textbooks, 1956 to 1965 and 1984 to 1993. *Journal of Criminal Justice Education, 7*(1), 1–22. https://doi.org/10.1080/10511259600083551

Wuthnow, R. (1994). *Sharing the journey: Support groups and America's new quest for community.* Free Press.

Xu, Q., Perkins, D. D., & Chow, J. C.-C. (2010). Sense of community, neighboring, and social capital as predictors of local political participation in China. *American Journal of Community Psychology, 45*(3–4), 259–271. https://doi.org/10.1007/s10464-010-9312-2

Ybarra, M. L., & Eaton, W. W. (2005). Internet-based mental health interventions. *Mental Health Services Research, 7*(2), 75–87. https://doi.org/dj2msj

Yip, T., Seaton, E. K., & Sellers, R. M. (2006). African American racial identity across the lifespan: Identity status, identity content, and depressive symptoms. *Child Development, 77*(5), 1504–1517. https://doi.org/fjfkmz

Yoshikawa, H., & Shinn, M. (2002). Facilitating change: Where and how should community psychology intervene? In T. A. Revenson, A. R. D'Augelli, S. E. French, D. L. Hughes, D. Livert, E. Seidman, M. Shinn, & H. Yoshikawa (Eds.), *A quarter century of community psychology: Readings from the American Journal of Community Psychology* (pp. 33–49). Plenum Publishers. https://doi.org/10.1007/978-1-4419-8646-7_2

Yoshikawa, H., Wilson, P., Hseuh, J., Rosman, E., Chin, J., & Kim, J. (2003). What front-line CBO staff can tell us about culturally anchored theories of behavior change in HIV prevention for Asian/Pacific Islanders. *American Journal of Community Psychology, 32*(1–2), 143–158. https://doi.org/10.1023/A:1025611327030

Zander, A. (1995). [Untitled videotape interview]. In J. G. Kelly (Ed.), *The history of community psychology: A video presentation of context and exemplars.* Society for Community Research and Action. https://vimeo.com/69635912

Zautra, A., & Bachrach, K. M. (2000). Psychological dysfunction and well-being: Public health and social indicator approaches. In J. Rappaport & E. Seidman (Eds.), *Handbook of community psychology* (pp. 165–185). Kluwer/Plenum. https://doi.org/10.1007/978-1-4615-4193-6_8

Zeldin, S., Krauss, S. E., Collura, J., Lucchesi, M., & Sulaiman, A. H. (2014). Conceptualizing and measuring youth–adult partnerships in community programs: A cross national study. *American Journal of Community Psychology, 54*(3–4), 337–347. https://doi.org/10.1007/s10464-014-9676-9

Zero Hour. (n.d.). *People's platform.* http://thisiszerohour.org/files/zh-peoples-platform-web.pdf

Zhang, Z., & Zhang, J. (2017). Perceived residential environment of neighborhood and subjective well-being among the elderly in China: A mediating role of sense of community. *Journal of Environmental Psychology, 51*, 82–94. https://doi.org/10.1016/j.jenvp.2017.03.004

Ziliak, J. (Ed.). (2009). *Welfare reform and its long-term consequences for America's poor*. Cambridge University Press. https://doi.org/10.1017/CBO9780511605383

Zimmerman, M. A. (2000). Empowerment theory: Psychological, organizational, and community levels of analysis. In J. Rappaport & E. Seidman (Eds.), *Handbook of community psychology* (pp. 43–63). Kluwer/Plenum. https://doi.org/10.1007/978-1-4615-4193-6_2

Zimmerman, M. A., Bingenheimer, J. B., & Notaro, P. C. (2002). Natural mentors and adolescent resiliency: A study with urban youth. *American Journal of Community Psychology*, *30*(2), 221–243. https://doi.org/10.1023/A:1014632911622

Zins, J., Elias, M. J., & Maher, C. A. (Eds.). (2007). *Bullying, victimization, and peer harassment: A handbook of prevention and intervention*. Haworth Press.

Zins, J., Weissberg, R., Wang, M., & Walberg, H. J. (Eds.). (2004). *Building academic success on social and emotional learning: What does the research say?* Teachers College Press.

Zuckerman, M. (1990). Some dubious premises in research and theory on racial differences: Scientific, social, and ethical issues. *American Psychologist*, *45*(12), 1297–1303. https://doi.org/10.1037/0003-066X.45.12.1297

Zych, I., Ortega-Ruiz, R., & Del Rey, R. (2015). Systematic review of theoretical studies on bullying and cyberbullying: Facts, knowledge, prevention, and intervention. *Aggression and Violent Behavior*, *23*, 1–21. https://doi.org/10.1016/j.avb.2015.10.001

# INDEX

# ABOUT THE AUTHORS

**Bret Kloos, PhD,** is Professor of Psychology and Director of the Clinical-Community Psychology Doctoral Program at the University of South Carolina. He uses community psychology approaches to conceptualize, investigate, and intervene with human problems typically overlooked in clinical settings. Along with students and community partners, his work has focused on social inclusion for persons with psychiatric disabilities, housing and homelessness, mutual help, and social change approaches to promoting mental health. Several federal agencies have funded this work, including the National Institute of Mental Health, National Institute on Disability and Rehabilitation Research, Substance Abuse and Mental Health Services Administration, and Housing and Urban Development. He teaches courses in community psychology, including service learning, and has served as the president of the Society for Community Research and Action.

**Jean Hill, PhD,** is Professor Emeritus of Psychology at New Mexico Highlands University and has served as the Executive Director and President of the Society for Community Research and Action. She has worked on school-based prevention and promotion programs and helped lead a community-wide initiative based on the Communities That Care model. She has written on sense of community, the role of spirituality in the field of community psychology, and the intersection of feminism and community psychology.

**Elizabeth Thomas, PhD,** is Professor of Psychology and Plough Chair of Urban Studies at Rhodes College in Memphis, Tennessee. She teaches undergraduate courses in community psychology, research methods, and urban studies, and she supervises students in engaged learning and research from introductory courses to senior capstones. Her research with undergraduate students and community partners focuses on learning and civic engagement, the role of arts in community building, and participatory strategies for research and action with youth. She has served as editor of *The Community Psychologist* and secretary of the Society for Community Research and Action.

**Andrew D. Case, PhD,** is Assistant Professor of Psychological Science, core faculty in the Community Psychology graduate program, and an affiliate faculty in the Public Health Sciences graduate program at the University of North Carolina at Charlotte. He teaches courses in community psychology, health psychology, and diversity. He helps inform community efforts to reduce racial inequities in health, economic mobility, and the justice system. His scholarship also spans areas including counterspaces and social determinants of health. He has served on the Research Council of the Society of Community Research and Action and the editorial board of the *American Journal of Community Psychology*.

**Victoria C. Scott, PhD, MBA,** is Assistant Professor of Psychological Science at the University of North Carolina at Charlotte and core faculty of her department's graduate Community Psychology program. Drawing on interdisciplinary approaches, Dr. Scott works in community settings to promote health equity and collective wellness through systems-level (organizational and community) improvement and capacity building efforts. She cofounded the *Global Journal of Community Psychology Practice;* coedited, with Susan M. Wolfe, *Community Psychology: Foundations for Practice* (2015) to expand the availability of literature for community practitioners; and has served as administrative director of the Society of Community Research and Action.

**Abraham Wandersman, PhD,** is President and CEO of the Wandersman Center and a Distinguished Professor Emeritus at the University of South Carolina. He retired from the university in 2017. He continues work in program evaluation, and community psychology and transdisciplinary research and action with treasured colleagues at the Wandersman Center, many of whom graduated from the University of South Carolina. His first involvement with a community psychology text was with Ken Heller, Rick Price, Stephanie Riger, and Shula Reinharz in 1984. Dr. Wandersman was a president of the Society for Community Research and Action.